The
INTERPRETATION
of the
NEW TESTAMENT
in GRECO-ROMAN
PAGANISM

The
INTERPRETATION
of the
NEW TESTAMENT
in GRECO-ROMAN
PAGANISM

JOHN GRANGER COOK

HENDRICKSON
PUBLISHERS

Hendrickson Publishers, Inc.
P. O. Box 3473
Peabody, Massachusetts 01961-3473

First printing — March 2002

Printed in the United States of America

The cover image, from a woodcut titled "Porphire Sophiste," is reprinted from http://www.phil-fak.uni-duesseldorf.de/philo/galerie/antike/porphyr.html courtesy of Dr. Lutz Geldsetzer and Dr. Larry Steindler, Philosophisches Institut, Universität Düsseldorf.

Library of Congress Cataloging-in-Publication Data

Cook, John Granger.
    The intepretation of the New Testament in Greco-Roman paganism / by John Granger Cook.
      p. cm.
    Originally published: Tübingen: Mohr Siebeck, 2000.
    Includes bibliographical references and index.
    ISBN 1-56563-658-9 (pbk. : alk. paper)
    1. Bible. N.T.—Criticism, interpretation, etc.—History and criticism.
    2. Christianity—Controversial literature—History and criticism.
    3. Christianity and other religions—Roman. I. Title.
    BS2350 .C64 2002
    225.6'0937—dc21
                            2002000827

For my parents

Acknowledgements

For the initial idea of doing this project and for continual encouragement I thank Prof. Martin Hengel. For accepting this work in his series Studien und Texte zu Antike und Christentum and for his patient and energetic work on the manuscript I thank Prof. Christoph Markschies. Working with him has been a pleasure. I am grateful to Mr. Georg Siebeck for providing the series with a fine home. Many have read parts of the manuscript and offered me helpful and critical comments. Those include Prof. Timothy Barnes, Prof. John Finamore, Dr. Richard Goulet, Prof. William Schoedel, and Prof. Steven Strange. Their remarks and suggestions have been invaluable. I thank Prof. Strange for our many hours of conversation on the topic. Dr. Goulet made his forthcoming translation (Sources chrétiennes) of Macarius Magnes' *Apocriticus* available to me along with his extensive introduction to that text. I owe him a debt of gratitude. Prof. Robert Berchman kindly provided me with his forthcoming translation of many fragments of Porphyry. I thank Prof. Vernon Robbins for his extensive bibliographical help – without which this book would not have been possible. I thank LaGrange College and Dean Frank James for providing me with a Summer Research Grant in 1996. I am grateful to President Stuart Gulley and Dean Jay Simmons (LaGrange College) for providing me with the opportunity to do this work. Two longsuffering librarians at the college have been invaluable in procuring sources for me: Steve Weaver and Dr. Arthur Robinson. My students at the college who have proofread the manuscript and made suggestions for change have been immensely helpful: April Purcell, Stephanie Thornton, Antipas Harris, Rex Campbell, Will Coil, and Jessica Pridgen. I thank my colleague Prof. Sam Hornsby for reading parts of the manuscript with his inimitable patience.

Reprinted by permission of the publishers and the trustees of the Loeb Classical Library ® are selections from:
Libanius, Selected Works. The Julianic Orations, Volume I, translated by A. F. Norman, Cambridge, Mass.: Harvard University Press, 1987;
Julian, The Works of the Emperor Julian, Volumes I–III, translated by W. C. Wright, Cambridge, Mass.: Harvard University Press, 1913–23.
The Loeb Classical Library ® is a registered trademark of the President and Fellows of Harvard College.

Acknowledgements

Reprinted by kind permission of the Catholic University of America Press are selections from:
Lactantius, The Divine Institutes Books I–VII, Trans. Mary F. McDonald, O.P., FC 49, Washington: Catholic University of America Press, 1964.

I thank the Guild of St. Raphael for permission to quote from T. W. Crafer, The Apocriticus of Macarius Magnes, New York / London: MacMillan / S.P.C.K., 1919.

The Greek font I used (Graeca) is from Linguist's Software, P. O. Box 580, Edmonds, WA 98020, USA. 206-775-1130.

Table of Contents

Introduction

The genesis of this monograph on the interpretation of the New Testament in Greco-Roman paganism is a long interest in religion and philosophy. My dissertation on Mark accepted by Emory University in 1985 (and later extensively revised into *The Structure and Persuasive Power of Mark*[1]) prompted me to ask questions about the function of the text — its actual effect on ancient readers. During a period of post doctoral studies with Vernon K. Robbins on the topic of the relationship of early Christianity with Greco-Roman culture I had the opportunity to search for responses of ancient readers to the New Testament. Two articles emerged from those studies: "Some Hellenistic Responses to the Gospels and Gospel Traditions" and "The Protreptic Power of Early Christian Language: From John to Augustine"[2]. The first article summarized the pagans' readings of parts of the New Testament. The second article summarized the positive responses of some figures in Christian antiquity who were persuaded by early Christian language. The idea for the article on the pagans was suggested to me by Elaine Pagels' books on Gnosticism's exegesis of the New Testament[3]. I am grateful to Prof. Martin Hengel for asking me to expand my article into a monograph. His suggestion and encouragement have prompted this work.

Two scholars that have been most helpful in producing the book are Pierre de Labriolle and Robert Wilken[4]. De Labriolle's magisterial survey of the pagan authors who reacted to Christianity is still unsurpassed in its scope and erudition. Wilken's work is one of the most recent to comprehensively address the themes that were important to pagan authors in their attack on Christianity. Late in the project I discovered Giancarlo Rinaldi's extensive collection of

---

[1] J. G. COOK, The Structure and Persuasive Power of Mark, Semeia Studies, Atlanta 1995.

[2] J. G. COOK, Some Hellenistic Responses to the Gospels and Gospel Traditions, ZNW 84, 1993, 233-54 / The Protreptic Power of Early Christian Language: From John to Augustine, VigChr 48, 1994, 105-134.

[3] E. PAGELS, The Gnostic Gospels, New York 1979 / The Gnostic Paul. Gnostic Exegesis of the Pauline Letters, Philadelphia 1975.

[4] P. DE LABRIOLLE, La réaction païenne. Étude sur la polémique antichrétienne du Ier au VIe Siècle, Paris 1948 / R. WILKEN, The Christians as the Romans Saw Them, New Haven/London 1984.

pagan comments on biblical passages. It will be indispensable in future research on this topic[5]. What remains to be done is a work that analyzes the pagan interpretation of the New Testament in particular. Below I intend to examine the response to the New Testament in the writings of Celsus, Porphyry, Hierocles, the anonymous pagan philosopher in Macarius Magnes' *Apocriticus*, and the emperor Julian[6].

Apologetics in Judaism and Christianity

The encounter between paganism and Christianity that produced the literature to be surveyed in this book continued an exchange that had already begun between paganism and Judaism[7]. The first Hellenistic Jewish author (other than the translators of the LXX) was Demetrius the chronographer who was active toward the end of the third century B.C.E.[8]. While not an apologist in the sense of an author who directs his comments towards people outside the faith, Demetrius does take up issues about the LXX using the method of questions and solutions (*aporiai* and *luseis*),[9] and he demonstrates the extreme antiquity of the patriarchs. Questions he answers include problems such as the

---

[5] G. RINALDI, Biblia Gentium: primo contributo per un indice delle citazioni, dei riferimenti e delle allusioni alla bibbia negli autori pagani, greci e latini, di età imperiale, Rome 1989.

[6] For a recent review of these authors (with bibliography) see RINALDI, Biblia Gentium, 103-66.

[7] See M. HENGEL, for example, on the Jewish and Christian apologetic view that Greek philosophers borrowed their wisdom from the patriarchs and Moses in Judaism and Hellenism. Studies in Their Encounter in Palestine in the Hellenistic Period, Vols. 1-2, Philadelphia 1974, I, 90. I thank Prof. HENGEL for suggestions on the relationship between Jewish and Christian apologetic. On the whole issue see M. FRIEDLÄNDER, Geschichte der jüdischen Apologetik als Vorgeschichte des Christentums, Zürich 1903 and G. BARDY, Art. Apologetik, RAC I, 1950, 533-43. K. THRAEDE discusses the issue of cultural dependence as a topos in ancient Jewish apologetic in Art. Erfinder II (geistesgeschichtlich), RAC V, 1962, (1191-1278) 1241-46.

[8] On Demetrius see C. R. HOLLADAY, Fragments from Hellenistic Jewish Authors. Volume I. Historians, SBLTT 20, Pseudepigrapha Series 10, Chico, CA 1983, 51-92 (the text, translation, comments and bibliography) / J. HANSON, Demetrius the Chronographer, in: OTP, ed. J. H. CHARLESWORTH, II, 843-54 / HENGEL, Judaism and Hellenism, I, 69 / P. DALBERT, Die Theologie der hellenistisch-jüdischen Missionsliteratur unter Ausschluss von Philo und Josephus, Hamburg-Volksdorff 1954, 27-34 / J. FREUDENTHAL, Alexander Polyhistor und die von ihm erhaltenen Reste judäischer and samaritanischer Geschichtswerke, Hellenistische Studien 1-2, Breslau, 1875, 35-82, 205-207.

[9] On this method see H. DÖRRIE/H. DÖRRIES, Erotapokriseis, RAC VI, 1966, 342-70 / DE LABRIOLLE, La réaction, 487-89 / G. BARDY, La littérature des Quaestiones et Responsiones sur l'Écriture Sainte, RB 41, 1932, 210-36, 341-69, 515-37; 42, 1933, 14-30, 211-229, 328-53. On chronology see F. 2, Eus. P.E. 9.21.18 (I, 72,5-12 HOLLADAY).

following: why did Joseph give Benjamin a five-fold portion at the banquet even though he could not consume it all; why scripture does not contradict itself (ἀντιπίπτει) in saying that Moses and Zipporah lived at the same time; and how Israel obtained weapons since they left Egypt unarmed[10]. Whether Demetrius should be described as an apologist, exegete, or historian, he does deal with the kind of questions apologists were later forced to answer[11]. The apologetic literature that began in Jewish writers such as Aristobulus reached a highly developed stage in Josephus' *Contra Apionem*. The Christian apologetic writers such as Quadratus, Aristides, Justin, Athenagoras, and Minucius Felix continued this tradition begun by writers such as Aristobulus, Philo, and Josephus[12]. Pagan writers such as Fronto and Celsus who attacked Christianity emerged in the second century and used the same kind of rhetorical and polemical apologetic that the Christian and Jewish writers used. Celsus may even have known the works of Justin.

Aristobulus the Alexandrian Jewish philosopher wrote an apologetic work that he addressed to Ptolemy VI Philometor (181-145 BC)[13]. Some issues that were important to Aristobulus continued to be important in the debate between Judaism, Christianity, and paganism. These include the allegorical interpretation of Old Testament texts and the relation of Greek philosophy to Old Testament (and later NT) teaching. To understand the biblical description of God's hands, Aristobulus explains the hand as the power of God. He notes with reference to allegory: "And I wish to exhort you to receive the

---

[10] F. 2, Eusebius, P.E. 9.21.14; F. 3, P.E. 9.29.1-3; F. 5, P.E. 9.29.16 (I, 70,6-9; 74,10-76,2; 76,17-18 HOLLADAY).

[11] On this question see HOLLADAY, Fragments, I, 53 with reference to J. FREUDENTHAL, Alexander Polyhistor, 67 who describes Demetrius as engaging in Hellenistic midrash. DALBERT, Theologie, 29 describes his method as exegesis in the interest of apologetics.

[12] V. TCHERIKOVER argues that most Hellenistic Jewish literature was internal and not directed to outsiders in: Jewish Apologetic Literature Reconsidered, Eos 48, 1956, (169-93) 182. In the Roman period he is willing to concede that Philo's *Apologia pro Iudaeis, In Flaccum*, and *De legatione ad Gaium* are directed to Gentiles (Roman authorities) and that the writings of Josephus are for the Gentiles (Jewish Apologetic, 182, 183 n. 32). L. FELDMAN argues that *De vita contemplativa* and *Quod omnis probus liber sit* are addressed to Gentiles. He finds statements in Philo that are also addressed to a non-Jewish audience. See Jew and Gentile in the Ancient World. Attitudes and Interactions from Alexander to Justinian, Princeton 1993, 318-19.

[13] On Aristobulus see: HENGEL, Judaism and Hellenism, I, 163-69 / C. R. HOLLADAY, Fragments from Hellenistic Jewish Authors. Volume III. Aristobulus, SBLTT 39, Pseudepigrapha Series 13, Atlanta 1995 (the text, comments and bibliography) / A. YARBRO COLLINS, Aristobulus, in: OTP, ed. J. H. CHARLESWORTH, II, 831-42 (her translations are used here) / N. WALTER, Der Thoraausleger Aristobulos. Untersuchungen zu seinen Fragmenten und zu pseudepigraphischen Resten der jüdisch-hellenistischen Literatur, TU 86, Berlin 1964, 35-40 (his relation to Ptolemy).

interpretations according to the laws of nature and grasp the fitting conception of God and not to fall into the mythical (τὸ μυθῶδες) and human way of thinking about God."[14] He also, in his view of Greek philosophy, claims that Plato followed Old Testament legislation and that Pythagoras "transferred many of our doctrines and integrated them into his own system of beliefs"[15].

Josephus added to this apologetic tradition with his *Contra Apionem*[16]. He refuted Apion's charges that Jews worship an ass's head in the temple (C. Ap. 2.80-81)[17] and that they annually fatten up a Greek to later sacrifice him and eat him (C. Ap. 2.91-96). Josephus attacks the Greek conceptions of the gods (C. Ap. 2.242-249; e. g. their quarrels and sexual passions) and rejects the attempt of Greek allegorists to defend the poets' conceptions of the gods (C. Ap. 2.255-57). He notes Plato's polite dismissal of Homer from his republic (C. Ap. 2.256) and continues Aristobulus' line of argument by claiming that the Greek philosophers were disciples of Moses in conduct and philosophy (C. Ap. 2.168, 257, 281). Arthur Droge argues that Josephus never actually claims that the Greek philosophers "read" Moses[18]. This position is similar to Philo's claim that Heraclitus got his doctrine of opposites from Moses[19]. Josephus defends Judaism's rejection of image worship (C. Ap. 2.73-75;

---

[14] Fragment 2, Eusebius, P.E. 8.10.2, 8 (III, 136,20-23; 138,43-53 HOLLADAY). TCHERIKOVER argues that "Such explanations of passages which had been subject to false interpretations could only be meant for people accustomed to read the Bible, i.e. for Jews and not for the King" (Jewish Apologetic, 173 n. 20). On the other hand the pagan critique of the NT (and OT) shows that some Gentiles were aware of biblical texts. See also HOLLADAY, Fragments, III, 71.

[15] F. 3, Eus. P.E. 13.12.1 (III, 152,17-22; 154,39-43 HOLLADAY). See also F. 4, Eus. P.E. 13.12.4 (III, 162,7-17 HOLLADAY) where Pythagoras, Socrates, and Plato follow Moses. On this issue see HOLLADAY, Fragments, III, 68, 207 n. 36. Philo attributes Heraclitus' doctrine of opposites to Moses (Quaest. in Gen. 3.5, 4.152). On these texts and on the relationship of Greek philosophy to Judaism see: FELDMAN, Jew and Gentile, 318 / H. A. WOLFSON, Philo. Foundations of Religious Philosophy in Judaism, Christianity, and Islam, Vol. 1, Cambridge 1947, 141-42 / J. GEFFCKEN, Zwei griechische Apologeten, (1st ed. 1907) Hildesheim 1970, 31.

[16] M. FRIEDLÄNDER reviews this work in his Geschichte der jüdischen Apologetik, 346-437. He draws many connections between Josephus' text against Apion and early Christian apologetics. See also GEFFCKEN, Zwei griechische Apologeten, xxix-xxxii who reviews the *C. Apionem* and then notes that in a certain sense Christian apologetics is the inheritor of Jewish apologetics.

[17] On this charge that was later used against the Christians see S. BENKO, Pagan Rome and the Early Christians, Bloomington/Indianapolis 1986, 58, 74 n. 8 with reference to Minucius Felix, Octavius 9.3 (7,18-19 KYTZLER) and other texts. W. SCHÄFKE reviews the breadth of this tradition in Frühchristlicher Widerstand, ANRW II.23.1, 1979, (460-723) 596-99.

[18] A. DROGE, Homer or Moses? Early Christian Interpretations of the History of Culture, HUTh 26, Tübingen 1989, 46 n. 107.

[19] Quaest. in Gen. 3.5, 4.152.

including statues of emperors) and its refusal to worship the Alexandrian gods (C. Ap. 2.66). He rejects Apion's charges that the Jews cause sedition (C. Ap. 2.68-70) and that Jewish laws and ceremonies are in error because the Jews are not masters of an empire (C. Ap. 2.125-26). Apion called the Jews atheists (C. Ap. 2.148). Celsus, the second century critic of Christianity, later used some of the same charges against Christianity that had been used against Judaism in Josephus' time[20].

The sharp attack on Christianity in the second century helped prompt Christian apologists to respond in the same fashion as Josephus had earlier. Quadratus, the earliest apologist, responded to the attacks of some "wicked men," according to Eusebius, who were troubling the Christians. During the reign of Hadrian, Quadratus answered with a defense of Christ's miracles and wrote that some of the individuals who had been healed and raised survived to "our own time"[21]. Aristides, the Athenian philosopher, is the next apologist whose work has survived. He wrote an apology that included attacks on Hellenistic polytheism and the allegorical defense of the gods' lawless acts[22]. Aristides does mention accusations of Christians' practicing homosexual and incestuous acts[23]. He also obviously knew of the pagans' defense of their own traditions.

M. Cornelius Fronto (ca. 100-166) composed an oration against Christianity during the reign of Marcus Aurelius[24]. Celsus probably wrote soon after Fronto. Minucius Felix created a pagan character named Caecilius in his *Octavius* who quoted Fronto's charges of sexual promiscuity during Christian

---

[20] Concerning the relationship of Celsus with Josephus see L. H. FELDMAN who notes that Celsus did not take over Apion's more scurrilous charges (such as the worship of an ass's head), Origen's *Contra Celsum* and Josephus' *Contra Apionem*: The Issue of Jewish Origins, VigChr 44, 1990, (105-35) 106. See also FELDMAN, Jew and Gentile, 217 for a number of topics common to both texts.

[21] Eus., H.E. 4.3.1-2. This is the only extant fragment of his apology. See J. QUASTEN, Patrology. Volume 1. The Beginnings of Patristic Literature, Westminster, Md 1992, 190-91.

[22] Apol. 13.7 (20,24-21,10 GEFFCKEN, Zwei Griechische Apologeten). Aristides addressed his work to Hadrian or Antoninus Pius. GEFFCKEN argues for the latter (Zwei Griechische Apologeten, 29-31) on the basis of the title in the Syriac translation. C. VONA has published a translation of the Syriac text and included the Greek fragments in: L'apologia de Aristide. Introduzione versione dal siriaco e commento, Lateranum, N.S. 16, Rome 1950. VONA argues that the text was addressed to Hadrian (L'apologia, 19-24). R. GRANT, Greek Apologists of the Second Century, Philadelphia 1988, 36-39 suggests that the shorter Greek version might have been addressed to Hadrian.

[23] Apol. 17. 2 and compare 8.2 for similar practices among the gods (27,8-12; 11,18-20 GEFF.).

[24] On Fronto see S. BENKO, Pagan Rome, 54-58 / idem, Pagan Criticism of Christianity During the First Two Centuries A.D, ANRW II.23.2, 1980, 1081-90 with bibliography / DE LABRIOLLE, La réaction, 87-94.

banquets[25]. Caecilius included a charge of cannibalism immediately before his reference to Fronto[26]. Werner Schäfke notes that the charges of Thyestean feasts and Oedipodean intercourse were a topos of the pagans' polemic against Christianity[27]. It is unclear how much of Caecilius' arguments in the rest of the *Octavius* are due to Fronto's oration. Caecilius believes that Christians rashly yield to any sort of opinion and that they are unskilled in letters, but yet make categorical statements about the nature of the universe (Oct. 5.3-4 [3,20-26 Kytzler]). This is similar to Celsus' statement that Christians regularly make arrogant statements about matters which they know nothing about (C. Cels. 5.65 [GCS Origenes I, 68,26 Koetschau]). If Fronto is Caecilius' source here, then Fronto and Celsus hold similar opinions in this case[28]. Celsus, however, did not make the charges of cannibalism and incest[29]. Caecilius (Fronto?) and Celsus share other similarities in their attacks on Christianity including the following: shock at the Christian belief in the destruction of the universe[30]; skepticism concerning the resurrection[31]; comments on the fact that God (or his Son) is not protecting Christians from persecution[32]; revulsion at the low classes and credulous women who are attracted to Christianity[33]; references to Christian refusal to take part in the processions, temple worship, and worship around altars and images[34]; and the charge that Christians are guilty of

---

[25] Oct. 9.6-7 (8,1-10 KYT.). Concerning the relationship with Celsus see J.-M. VERMANDER, Celse, source et adversaire de Minucius Felix, REAug 17, 1971, 13-25. See also GRANT, Greek Apologists, 132-35 who is somewhat skeptical of VERMANDER's claims with regard to Theophilus' use of Celsus (J.-M. VERMANDER, Théophile d'Antioche contre Celsus: A Autolycos III, REAug 17, 1971, 203-25). See also ibid., La parution de l'ouvrage de Celse et la datation de quelques apologies, REAug 18, 1972, 27-42 and De quelques répliques à Celse dans l'Apologeticum de Tertullien, REAug 16, 1970, 205-25.

[26] Oct. 9.5 (7,26-32 KYT.).

[27] W. SCHÄFKE, Frühchristlicher Widerstand, 579-96. See also BENKO, Pagan Rome, 54-74. Justin, Apol. 1.26.7 (71,29-32 MARCOVICH) concedes that Gnostic Christians may do such things although he does not know. In Apol. 1.29.2 (75,5 MARC.) Justin denies that Christians do such things. See also MARCOVICH's notes ad loc.

[28] BENKO, Pagan Rome, 58.

[29] BENKO, Pagan Rome, 157. See, however, Origen, C. Cels. 5.63 [GCS Origenes II, 66,9-11 KOETSCHAU] for evidence that Celsus was aware of iniquitous practices of some Christian groups.

[30] Oct. 11.1 (8,31 KYT.), C. Cels. 4.11, 4.79 (281,22-23; 349,12 KOET.).

[31] Oct. 11.7 (9,21-24 KYT.), C. Cels. 5.14 (15,1-25 KOET.).

[32] Oct. 12.4-5 (10,8-15 KYT.) and compare 10.4 (8,20-23 KYT.) on the miserable situation of the Jews; C. Cels. 8.39 (253,24-29 KOET.).

[33] Oct. 8.4 (6,32 KYT.), C. Cels. 3.55 (250,16-20 KOET.).

[34] Oct. 8.4, 10.2, 12.5 (7,3; 8,14; 10,13-15 KYT.), C. Cels. 7.62, 8.24 (211,17-19; 240,28 KOET.).

conspiracy[35]. It seems quite possible that Fronto may have helped justify the persecutions of the church under Marcus Aurelius.[36] Celsus and Justin share a number of common interests and are both middle Platonists.[37] Justin, for example, argues that Greek philosophy was dependent on Moses — while Celsus argues that Christ was dependent on Greek philosophy[38]. They both discuss the possibility of resurrection, the way to know God, the incarnation, and Greek parallels to the story of Christ (such as the birth of Perseus). Celsus, however, does not seem to answer Justin's specific arguments[39]. Quintino Cataudella argued that they are independent[40]. It seems more likely that Celsus was aware of Justin, but simply regarded his specific arguments as unworthy of refutation. Celsus is familiar with basic Christian beliefs, and he must have known more of Christianity than just what he could learn from the NT (e.g. his attack on Christian allegory). Robert Grant notes:

> The significance of Celsus' work lies in the fact that he has investigated second-century Christianity and knows a good deal about it, perhaps more than Origen admits. He attacks it not on the basis of slander and scandal but from the standpoint of an enlightened, philosophically minded, pro-Roman Greek of the late second century, intolerant of

---

[35] Oct. 8.4 (6,33 KYT.), C. Cels. 8.14 (231,8 KOET.).

[36] Compare BENKO, Pagan Rome, 52 n. 44. DE LABRIOLLE, La réaction, 94, however, urges caution with regard to the question of Fronto's influence on Marcus.

[37] This relationship is richly explored in C. ANDRESEN's Logos und Nomos. Die Polemik des Kelsos wider das Christentum, AKG 30, Berlin 1955, 357-63 and passim. See § 1.1 below.

[38] Justin, Apol. 1.59.1-60.11 (115,1-117,30 MARC.). Origen, C. Cels. 7.58 (207,13-15 KOET.).

[39] CATAUDELLA notes that Celsus does not answer Justin's arguments in reference to these topics (Celso e gli Apologeti Cristiani, NDid 1, 1947, 29-33): resurrection (Justin, Apol. 1.18.1-19.8 [59,1-61,30 MARC.], C. Cels. 5.14 [15,1-25 KOET.]); the knowledge of God (Dial. 3.7 [76,56-60 MARC.], C. Cels. 7.36 [186,13-27 KOET.]); the incarnation (Dial. 127.2 [290,6-12 MARC.], C. Cels. 4.5 [277,18; 278,8-9 KOET.]); Greek parallels (Apol. 1.22.5-6, 1.54.1-10 [65,15-19; 108,1-109,39 MARC.], Dial. 67.2, 69.1-3, 70 [185,5-9; 189,1-190,16 MARC.], C. Cels. 1.67, 3.24, 7.53 [121,6; 220,13; 203,10-15 KOET.]). They also discuss the fate of those before Christ came (Apol. 1.46.1-6, 2.10.1-7, 2.13.1-6 [97,1-23; 151,1-152,27; 157,1-19 MARC.], C. Cels. 4.7 [279,11 KOET.]). H. CHADWICK argues that Celsus was aware of Justin and that he shuts his eyes to the existence of a "rational Christian theology" in: Early Christian Thought and the Classical Tradition, Oxford 1984, 22-24. GRANT (Greek Apologists, 138) makes the important point that "... Celsus makes no special effort to reply to the apologists, who in turn paid little if any attention to his arguments." GRANT does not deny that Celsus may have read Justin's Apology.

[40] Celso e gli Apologeti, 33. See also RINALDI, Biblia Gentium, 126 n. 56. Others such as A. DROGE argue that Celsus was aware of Justin either directly or through intermediaries (Homer or Moses, 76-78). CHADWICK mentions many common topics in Celsus and Justin in: Early Christian Thought, 132 n. 59.

innovation especially in religious affairs. The work is not directly relevant to the second-century apologists, however. Both Christians and pagans failed to communicate before Origen replied to Celsus about seventy years later[41].

Athenagoras (writing during the reign of Marcus Aurelius) replies to some of the same kinds of criticism Fronto and Celsus raised. He defends Christians against the charges of atheism, Thyestean feasts, and Oedipodean intercourse[42]. Although sharing some of Celsus' interests, he writes from the other side of the debate[43]. He describes the Hellenistic defense of image worship which refers to the gods in whose honor the statues are made and to whom the sacrifices are actually offered[44]. The apologist attacks the immorality of the gods while Celsus attacks the character and actions of Jesus[45]. Athenagoras rejects the allegorical explanations of the gods, and Celsus attacks Christian allegory of the Old Testament[46]. He defends the Christian refusal to sacrifice to the gods, and Celsus attacks the Christian refusal to take part in the Hellenistic cult[47]. Athenagoras also responded to criticism of the resurrection that was based on the various destinies of corpses — a pagan objection that became a topos[48].

Another kind of response the pagans used was a sort of deathly silence with regard to Christianity. De Labriolle notes that Julian was aware of the long silence of the ancient historians who simply ignored Christianity[49]. Dio Cassius[50], for example, does not mention the Christians unless Flavius

---

[41] Greek Apologists, 138-39.

[42] Legatio 3.1-2, 4.1-2, 31.1 (8, 76 SCHOEDEL).

[43] It is doubtful that Athenagoras used Celsus given his appeal to the omnipotence of God to defend the doctrine of the resurrection (De res. 9.2 [108 SCH.]). Celsus had argued against such an appeal (C. Cels. 5.14, 23 [15,13; 24,11 KOET.]). On this issue see B. POUDERON, Athénagore d'Athènes. Philosophe Chrétien, ThH 82, Paris 1989, 99 in criticism of J. M. VERMANDER, Celse et l'attribution à Athénagore d'un ouvrage sur la résurrection des morts, MSR 85, 1978, 125-35. L. W. BARNARD argues that Athenagoras did not know Celsus' work given the evidence of his Legatio in Athenagoras. A Study in Second Century Christian Apologetic, ThH 18, Paris 1972, 66.

[44] Legatio 18.1 (36 SCH.). For Celsus' views on images see § 1.7.1 below.

[45] Legatio 20.3 (42 SCH.). See § 1.2.12 below for Celsus.

[46] Legatio 22.1-12 (48-52 SCH.). See § 1.4.1 below.

[47] Legatio 13.1-4 (26-28 SCH.). See § 1.6.6 and 1.7.1 below.

[48] De res. 4.1-4 (96-98 SCH.). See § 3.51 below.

[49] La réaction, 1 with reference to Julian, C. Galilaeos 206a,b (142,10-14 MASARACCHIA). The text is discussed in § 5.2.1 below.

[50] Historia Romana 67.14.1-3 in M. STERN, ed., Greek and Latin Authors on Jews and Judaism. Volume II. From Tacitus to Simplicius, Jerusalem 1980, II, F. 435. STERN argues that they were probably Jewish (II, 380-84). Although he shared many interests with the apologists, Maximus of Tyre was also silent about Christianity (M. B. TRAPP, Maximus of Tyre. The Philosophical Orations, Oxford 1997, xlix).

Crescens and Flavia Domitilla, victims of Domitian's wrath, were not Jews but actually Christians. In another text Dio composes a speech put in Maecenas' mouth (before Augustus) in which he discourages the tolerance of atheists[51]. Christians may be the intended reference[52]. The Jewish apologetic writers paved the way for the Christian response to the pagan critique. This brief survey of the second century debate between pagans and Christians indicates that both groups made use of similar apologetic techniques. Ancient rhetoric and literary criticism provide some categories useful for understanding those various techniques that appear in the Hellenistic authors' attack on the NT. Below I will sketch some of the concepts that will aid the analysis carried out in the following chapters.

Rhetorical and Literary Tools in Polemic and Apologetic

The Christians and pagans were each attempting to persuade the other. One of Gorgias' definitions of rhetoric in Plato's dialogue is "the creator of persuasion" (πειθοῦς δημιουργός)[53]. Aristotle defines rhetoric as the "... faculty of discovering the possible means of persuasion in reference to any subject whatever"[54]. In epideictic rhetoric the hearer is a spectator. In forensic rhetoric the hearer judges about things past, and in deliberative rhetoric the hearer judges about things to come. Deliberative rhetoric is either hortatory (protreptic - προτροπή) or dissuasive (apotreptic - ἀποτροπή)[55] and could include questions of the rites of religion[56]. Epideictic rhetoric either praises or blames, and forensic rhetoric either accuses or defends. The moral character of the speaker (ethos ἦθος), the speech (logos λόγος) itself with its proofs, and

---

[51] H. R. 52.35-36 quoted in § 1.6.5 below.

[52] WILKEN, Christians, 62-63 notes that the text may be a commentary on Pliny's (Ep. 10.96) persecution of the Christians in Bithynia. W. ENSSLIN, The Senate and the Army, CAH XII, 60 believes that the speech could contain allusions to Severus Alexander's policies. Compare SCHÄFKE, Frühchristlicher Widerstand, 608-09.

[53] Plato, Gorgias 453a. Plato disapproves of this amoral understanding of rhetoric and gives a definition more ethically oriented in 503a.

[54] Rhet. 1.2.1 δύναμις περὶ ἕκαστον τοῦ θεωρῆσαι τὸ ἐνδεχόμενον πιθανόν. Compare Cic., Brutus 15.59 where the orator's function is to bring about persuasion — πειθώ, *suadam*. H. LAUSBERG, (Handbuch der Literarischen Rhetorik. Eine Grundlegung der Literaturwissenschaft, Stuttgart ³1990, § 33) gives other similar definitions of rhetoric.

[55] Rhet 1.3.2,3. LAUSBERG discusses the three kinds extensively (Handbuch, § 59ff.).

[56] Rhet. ad Alex. 1423a and compare Rhet. ad Her. 1.4.7 where the author includes the worship of the gods as a possible topic in the introduction of a judicial speech.

the rousing of the hearers to emotion (pathos πάθος) produce persuasion[57]. The Hellenistic texts to be considered below are apotreptic because they attempt to persuade the hearer to reject the Christian faith[58]. They also make liberal use of the techniques of epideictic rhetoric — specifically of the rhetoric of vituperation or blame. The charges that Jesus is a magician or a god who died in delusions, for example, exhibit features of vituperative rhetoric. Occasionally forensic rhetoric is involved because the authors sometimes use arguments to justify persecutions of the Christians.

Besides ancient rhetoric, Hellenistic historical and literary criticism are also a source of concepts important for understanding the critique of the NT in Greco-Roman paganism[59]. In summarizing the various criticisms of poetry (and Homer in particular), Aristotle wrote, "The censures they bring are of five kinds: that things are either impossible or irrational or harmful or inconsistent (ὑπεναντία) or contrary to artistic correctness."[60]   These problems (προβλημάτων Poet. 25.1) assume that the poet represents reality. An impossibility appears in *Iliad* 22.205 where Hector is pursued, and the Greeks do not shoot at him on Achilles' orders[61]. Homer has "taught the others the proper way of telling lies" according to Aristotle[62]. Plutarch is impressed by the presence of mutual contradictions in the poets (ὑπεναντιώσεις πρὸς αὐτούς). He asserts that when "comparison of passages makes their contradictions (τὰς ἀντιλογίας) evident, we must advocate the better side"[63]. Plutarch believes that the solutions (λύσεις) to these problems are obvious if one directs the young to the better side. He offers an example in which a poet asks why sacrifice when we must die and then says the worship of the gods is not toil[64]. Both Porphyry and Macarius' anonymous philosopher made extensive use of this principle of contradiction to attack the NT.

Aristotle includes the criterion of whether something is morally good or bad[65]. In this context he mentions Xenophanes who argued that stories about the gods were untrue because immoral[66]. Rudolf Pfeiffer refers to one of Xenophanes' statements in which he attacked Homer and Hesiod: "Homer and

---

[57] Rhet. 1.2.3-6. LAUSBERG, Handbuch, § 257 (the three forms of persuasion: *docere, delectare* and *movere* which correspond to logos, ethos, and pathos), 355 (gives examples of this trilogy in ancient rhetorical theory).

[58] This paragraph is largely from COOK, Some Hellenistic Responses, 233-34.

[59] I am indebted for this suggestion to Prof. W. SCHOEDEL.

[60] Poet. 25.32. ET from Aristotle, The Poetics, ed. and trans. W. H. FYFE, LCL, Cambridge/London 1965.

[61] Poet. 24.16-17 and 25.8.

[62] Poet. 24.18.

[63] Quomodo adolescens poetas audire debeat 20c.

[64] Quomodo 20d.

[65] Poet. 25.15.

[66] Poet. 25.13

Hesiod have imputed to the gods all that is shame and blame (ψόγος) for people: stealing, adultery, and deceiving each other."[67] According to Diogenes Laertius, Xenophanes wrote iambics against Homer and Hesiod[68]. He also criticized the conception of the gods in different nations using a philosophical argument: "Ethiopians say their gods are snub-nosed and black, Thracians believe they are blue-eyed and red-haired."[69] Pagans used arguments based on morality in their critique of the NT. Macarius' anonymous pagan, for example, found it immoral that Jesus would send demons into the swine[70].

Plato's critique of Homer in his *Republic* is similar to that of Xenophanes[71]. Homer and Hesiod told "false stories" (or "lying myths" μύθους ... ψευδεῖς)[72]. The wars of the gods in the poets are objectionable: "...the battles of the gods in Homer's verse are things that we must not admit into our city either wrought in allegory (ἐν ὑπονοίαις ... ἄνευ ὑπονοιῶν) or without allegory"[73]. Homer errs by making the gods cause of good and evil[74]. Homer's verse, "The gods, in the likeness of strangers, many disguises assume as they visit the cities of mortals," is unacceptable because the gods do not deceive in word or in deed[75]. For Plato "there is no lying poet in God"[76]. The gods do not lament (as often in Homer), nor do they lack self control (as Zeus does when he is overcome by sexual passions)[77]. Plato was also concerned with the depiction of heroes: "Neither, then, said I, must we believe this, or suffer it to be said, that Theseus, the son of Poseidon, and Pirithous, the son of Zeus, attempted such dreadful rapes, nor that any other child of a god or hero would have brought himself to accomplish the terrible and impious (ἀσεβῆ) deeds that they now falsely relate of them."[78] For the poets to depict the gods

---

[67] R. PFEIFFER, History of Classical Scholarship. From the Beginnings to the End of the Hellenistic Age, Oxford 1968, 9 with reference to F. 21.B.11 (= Sext., Adv. math 9.193), H. DIELS/W. KRANZ, Die Fragmente der Vorsokratiker, Vol. I, Berlin 1954. Fragment 21.B.12 is similar where Xenophanes claims that Homer and Hesiod ascribe unlawful works to the gods (ἀθεμίστια ἔργα).

[68] Diog. Laert. 9.18 = DIELS, Fragmente, 21.A.1.

[69] DIELS, Fragmente, 21.B.16. On Xenophanes see P. DECHARME, La critique des traditions religieuses chez les Grecs, Paris 1904, 44-50 and F. BUFFIÈRE, Les mythes d'Homère et la pensée grecque, Paris 1956, 14.

[70] See § 3.3 below.

[71] On Plato's attack see BUFFIÈRE, Les mythes, 9-20.

[72] Resp. 377d; ET of P. SHOREY in: The Collected Dialogues of Plato, ed. by E. HAMILTON and H. CAIRNES, BollS 71, Princeton 1961. On the criticism of Homer see DECHARME, La critique.

[73] Resp. 378d.

[74] Resp. 379c,d.

[75] Od. 17.485ff in Resp. 381d.

[76] Resp. 382d.

[77] Resp. 388b, 389b,c

[78] Resp. 391c,d.

as causes of evil or to depict heroes as no better than humans is both impious and false[79]. Cyril, in his response to Julian's attacks on the Galilaeans, found these Platonic criticisms of Homer to be useful[80]. Epicurus also attacked poetry, and according to Heraclitus the allegorist (ca. I C.E.), he saw it to be a destructive pit of myths (ὀλέθριον μύθων δέλεαρ)[81]. Plato and Epicurus both cast Homer out of the cities[82]. Epicurus attacked the "silly tales" (μωρολογημάτων) in Homer[83]. Proclus, in a defense of Homer, argues that Homer supports Platonic doctrines. This is his answer to one of the Epicureans' attempts to attack such myths (as the one about Hades)[84].

Allegory was one response to the criticisms of Homer. One of the oldest figures who engaged in that kind of interpretation was Theagenes of Rhegium (VI B.C.E.) who interpreted, for example, the Homeric Apollo to be fire and Poseidon to be water[85]. Metrodorus of Lampsachus (V B.C.E.) allegorized everything according to Tatian and investigated Homer's physical doctrines according to Diogenes Laertius[86]. Metrodorus also heaped abuse onto the poet according to Plutarch[87]. Heraclitus in his *Homeric Problems. The Allegories of Homer Concerning the Gods* began his work with: "A great and harsh trial is proclaimed against Homer concerning his irreverence towards the divinity. He was impious in all things if he allegorized nothing (πάντα γὰρ ἠσέβησεν, εἰ μηδὲν ἠλληγόρησεν). Sacrilegious myths full of god-opposed madness rage through both poems — if indeed one should think that it all was said according to poetic tradition without any philosophical vision or any underlying allegorical

---

[79] Resp. 391d,e.

[80] Contra Julianum 2.40 (PG 76, 561b). See § 5.2.1.

[81] Heraclitus, Quaest. Hom. 4.2 (CUFr, 4 BUFFIÈRE) = USENER, Epicurea, Leipzig 1887, F. 229.

[82] USENER, Epicurea, F. 228 from Athenaeus 5.12.

[83] USENER, Epicurea, F. 228 from Plutarch, Moralia 1086.

[84] USENER, Epicurea, F. 229 from Proclus, in Platonis rem publicam (382 BAS).

[85] DECHARME, La Critique 273, DIELS, Fragmente 8.2. See BUFFIÈRE, Les mythes, 103-105. J. TATE argues that Pherecydes of Syros (born around 600 B.C.) interpreted Homer allegorically before Theagenes in The Beginnings of Greek Allegory, CIR 41, 1927, 214-15. See also his other articles: Plato and Allegorical Interpretation, CQ 23, 1929, 142-54, continued in CQ 24, 1930, 1-10; and On the History of Allegorism, CQ 28, 1934, 105-14. See also H.-J. KLAUCK, Allegorie und Allegorese in synoptischen Gleichnistexten, NTA 13, München ²1986, 37-39.

[86] Tatian, Oratio 21.6 (43,24-26 MARCOVICH), Diogenes Laert. 2.11 (who remarks that he was a friend of Anaxagoras). See DECHARME, La Critique, 283, BUFFIÈRE, Les mythes, 82, 125, and A. A. LONG, Stoic Readings of Homer, in: Homer's Ancient Readers. The Hermeneutics of Greek Epic's Earliest Exegetes, ed. by R. LAMBERTON/J. J. KEANEY, Princeton 1992, 44.

[87] Non posse suaviter vivi secundum Epicurum 1087a.

meaning."[88] Heraclitus denies that there are any immoral stories in Homer or that Homer is impious in any way[89]. After a set of allegorical interpretations of Homer, Heraclitus finishes his work with a critique of Plato's and Epicurus' attacks on Homer. He finds Homeric moral values to be superior to those of either philosopher[90]. Allegory played an important role in the argument between Hellenism and Christianity. Pagans attacked the Christians' use of allegory, and the Christians in turn could attack the pagans' use of allegory[91]. Critique of historical traditions by Hellenistic writers is also a useful point of comparison in analyzing the pagans' attack on Christian texts.

Decharme investigated texts of Herodotus in which the early (and often credulous) historian disputed various traditions[92]. Faced with two traditions about the source of oracles in Greece (two doves or two women who were enslaved in Thebes and sold respectively in Libya and Greece), Herodotus chooses the non-miraculous account[93]. With reference to the Homeric gods Plutarch finds that some statements "are sound opinions (δόξαι) about gods, and true, but those other accounts have been fabricated (πέπλασται) to excite the astonishment of people"[94]. He distinguishes the moral teaching of philosophers from that of poets: "Philosophers, at any rate, for admonition and instruction, use examples from known facts (παραδείγμασι ... ἐξ ὑποκειμένων); but the poets accomplish the same thing by inventing actions of their own imagination, and by recounting mythical tales" (πλάττοντες αὐτοὶ πράγματα καὶ μυθολογοῦντες)[95]. Lucian's discourse on *How to Write History* contains a distinction in literary or historical criticism that is crucial for the writings of the pagans about Christianity: the distinction between myth and history. The historian should know: "So it is a great deal — all too great a fault

---

[88] Quaest. Hom. 1.1-3 (1 BUFF.).

[89] Quaest. Hom. 2.1 and 3.1 (2; 3 BUFF.).

[90] Quaest. Hom. 4.1-4, 76.1-79.11 (3-4; 82-88 BUFF.). On Stoic allegorical interpretation see DECHARME, La Critique, 305-53 and BUFFIÈRE, Les mythes, 137-54. A. A. LONG denies that Heraclitus was an orthodox Stoic and argues that the Stoics did not attempt to make Homer a "strong allegorist" who intended his work to be understood allegorically — Stoic Readings, 43, 46-8. See also § 2.3.6 in the present work for a discussion of Dio Chrysostom's reference to contradictions in Homer (53.5) and Zeno's attempt to remove those inconsistencies.

[91] See Celsus (§ 1.4.1), Porphyry (§ 2.3.3) and Macarius' philosopher (§ 3.27). For the Christian attack on the pagan use see § 2.3.3. Eusebius attacks pagan allegory of their own myths in P.E. 15.1.1-3 (GCS Eusebius VIII/2, 343,11-344,1 MRAS).

[92] DECHARME, La Critique, 69-74.

[93] Herodotus 2.54-57. It is at least interesting that the gods do not appear in the work of Thucydides. His attitude to religious traditions is not clear, according to DECHARME, La Critique, 83-90. He does appear to approve an oracle of Apollo (Thuc. 2.17.1-3).

[94] Quomodo 20f.

[95] Quomodo 20b,c.

14   *Introduction*

— not to know how to keep the attributes of history and poetry separate, and to bring poetry's embellishments into history (ἱστορίᾳ) — myth and eulogy (τὸν μῦθον καὶ τὸ ἐγκώμιον) and exaggeration of both ..."[96]. History is to publish truth[97]. Lucian notes that "Homer indeed in general tended towards the mythical (μυθῶδες) in his account of Achilles, yet some nowadays are inclined to believe him; they cite as important evidence of his truthfulness the single fact that he did not write about him during his lifetime: they cannot find any motive for lying."[98] That some found Homer to write lies is apparent, and Lucian tends to believe that Homer wrote some mythical accounts.

The distinction between myth (or fiction) and history became important in the debate between Hellenism and Christianity. Celsus describes the gospels as fictions (πλάσματα) and viewed them as largely unhistorical[99]. Macarius' anonymous philosopher takes the story of the demoniac in Mk 5:1-20 to be a fiction (πλάσμα)[100]. The incongruities (τὸ ... ἀσύστατον) of the *Vita Apollonii* prompt "Eusebius"[101] to argue for its mythical and miracle-mongering character (μυθῶδές τε καὶ τερατῶδες)[102]. Problems in the story of Apollonius' averting a plague from Ephesus convince Eusebius that the story is a fiction (πλάσμα) and full of magic (γοητείας)[103]. Stories such as tripods walking expose the mythical character of all of Philostratus' narrative (διήλεγξεν τὴν μυθολογίαν)[104].

For those miracles that Eusebius does accept as historical he uses the concept of magic (or the demonic) to explain Apollonius' extraordinary abilities. The charge of magic was a familiar one in the Greco-Roman world[105]. The texts of Apuleius and Philostratus are two examples in which pagans defend themselves

---

[96] Lucian, Hist. Conscr. 8.
[97] Hist. Conscr. 9, 40.
[98] Hist. Conscr. 40.
[99] See § 1.2 in this work.
[100] Apocriticus 3.4 (discussed in § 3.3. of this work).
[101] For the identity of this individual as Eusebius the sophist (instead of Eusebius of Caesarea) see § 4.3.
[102] Contra Hieroclem 36 (SC 333, 180 FORRAT/DES PLACES). This text will be abbreviated "C.H." The chapter numbers are different from those of F. C. CONYBEARE's edition in the LCL. For a succint and superb overview of Eusebius' arguments see M. T. FÖGEN, Die Enteignung der Wahrsager. Studien zum kaiserlichen Wissensmonopol in der Spätantike, Frankfurt am Main 1993, 212-215. Eusebius also claims some of Apollonius' miracles may have been done with the help of demons (C.H. 35.28-29 [SC 333,178 F./DES P.]).
[103] C.H. 27.15 (SC 333, 156 F./DES P.) with reference to Philostratus, Vita Ap. 4.4 and 4.10.
[104] C.H. 24.1-7 (SC 333, 150, F./DES P.) with reference to Vita Ap. 3.27.
[105] On laws related to magic see COOK, In Defense of Ambiguity: Is There a Hidden Demon in Mark 1.29–31?, NTS 43, 1997, (184-208) 200.

or are defended from the charge of magic[106]. Hierocles, for example, viewed Apollonius' thaumaturgic feats as due to a certain divine and indescribable wisdom (θείᾳ τινὶ καὶ ἀρρήτῳ σοφίᾳ) and not magic[107]. Some of the thaumaturgic feats Eusebius found simply incredible, but others he attributed to demonic powers and therefore concluded that Apollonius was clearly a magician[108]. Celsus and Hierocles both adopted this tactic with regard to the miracles of Jesus. They did not contest the historicity of at least some of the miracles, but they did attribute them to Jesus' practice of magic[109].

The pagans who were responsible for the critique of Christianity used the same tools used by the Christian apologists. The techniques of rhetoric and literary criticism were adopted by both. Praise and vituperation, apology, and deliberation were tools to be used. The apologies for Hellenism in the works of Celsus and the others are designed to encourage their audience to convert to Hellenism or to remain Hellenes (i.e. pagans).

Tertullian's statement that "no one turns to our literature who is not already Christian" is a mournful recognition of reality — at least as Tertullian saw it[110]. Arnobius describes some pagans who believed that "the writings, by which the Christian religion is confirmed (*comprobetur*) and the authority of ancient times [tradition] is overthrown (*uetustatis opprimatur auctoritas*), should be destroyed"[111]. Responding to those who attacked the narrative truth of the gospels (*eis ueracis narrationis derogent fidem*)[112] Augustine wrote: "Through these texts the Christian religion has been disseminated through the whole world (*per quos christiana religio disseminata per mundum*)." By Augustine's time even the Roman aristocracy was finding it

---

[106] Apologia 26, 103 (32-33; 122-123 VALLETTE); Philostratus, Vita Ap. 1.2, 8.7.2.

[107] C.H. 2.1-2 (100 F./DES P.).

[108] C.H. 29.8-13, 30.3-6, 31.20-23, 35.1-5, 37.1, 39.1-3 (160; 162; 166; 176; 180; 184 F./DES P.). From chapter 35 on Eusebius drops the historical critique of Apollonius' miracles and concentrates on his charge that they were done by magic (cf. M. FORRAT in SC 333, 223). Philostratus is puzzled that people took Apollonius to be a magician (C.H. 44.5-6 [198 F./DES P.]), but Eusebius is not (C.H. 44.15-16 [198 F./DES P.]).

[109] Origen, Contra Celsum 1.28 and 1.68 ([79,29; 122,5 KOET.] discussed in § 1.2.5 and 1.2.8 in this work). On Hierocles see Lactantius, Div. Inst. 5.3.9, 19 (SC 204, 142; 144 MONAT) discussed in § 4.8.

[110] ... *ad quas nemo venit nisi iam Christianus*, Tert., Test. Animae 1 (CChr.SL 1, 175,31 WILLEMS); quoted by R. MACMULLEN, Two Types of Conversion to Early Christianity, Vig Chr 34, 1983, (174-192) 177.

[111] See P. COURCELLE, Anti-Christian Arguments and Christian Platonism: from Arnobius to St. Ambrose, in: The Conflict Between Paganism and Christianity in the Fourth Century, ed. A. MOMIGLIANO, Oxford 1963, 155-56 quoting Arn., Adv. nat. 3.7 (165,6-9 MARCHESI). Adv. nat. 4.36 (244,20-21 MARCH.) shows that Arnobius may have also included Christian writings along with his reference to those of Cicero in 3.7.

[112] Aug., De cons. evang. 1.7.10 (CSEL 43, 10,17-19 WEIHRICH).

politic to become Christian[113]. These authors (Tertullian, Arnobius, and Augustine) indicate that Christian teaching and the NT in particular became gradually more influential in the Greco-Roman world. This book will hopefully contribute to an understanding of the debate between Hellenism and Christianity that resulted from the Christians' efforts at recruitment.

---

[113] For a reassessment of the issue of the conversion of the Roman aristocracy see T. D. BARNES, Statistics and the Conversion of the Roman Aristocracy, JRS 85, 1995, 135-147. BARNES argues that the process had begun in earnest even by Constantine's time.

1. Celsus

Celsus' Critique of the New Testament and Early Christian Discourse

Tertullian, the second century rhetor, lamented that "no one turns to our literature who is not already Christian"[1]. One exception to that general observation was the second century philosopher, Celsus. Celsus was a passionate critic of the Christian faith although he did not exhibit the exegetical skill of a Porphyry. The *Contra Christianos* of Porphyry ultimately scared the church far more than Celsus' broad-stroked attack on Christianity. Celsus was something of a social conservative who viewed Christianity as a departure from everything that was ancient and true in Hellenistic tradition. He has the distinction of being the first pagan to mount an extensive critique of the "new" faith — at least his is the earliest attack that has survived. It seems likely that if Origen had known of an earlier attack of the same scope as that of Celsus, he would have mentioned it. But arguments from silence are notoriously unreliable!

Below I will concentrate on Celsus' attitude toward NT traditions by reconstructing his work into a sort of pagan's commentary on the gospels with a few scattered references to traditions from other parts of the NT. After reviewing his explicit references to NT traditions, I have chosen to review a number of issues that emerge from Celsus' response to NT traditions. These include: Celsus' attack on the christology of the Christians; his attack on the Christian use of the Hebrew Scriptures to support their faith (including their "argument from prophecy"); his comparison of Christian and Hellenistic prophets; his sociological views on Christians and their recruitment techniques; and his sketch of a religious philosophy in response to the Christians' use of an "argument from hell" and their critique of Hellenistic image worship and polytheism.

1.1 Introductory Issues

One great embarrassment in the study of Celsus is that he is virtually an anonymous figure. Origen himself seems unsure of the identity of his pagan

---

[1] Tert., Test. Animae 1.4 (CChr.SL 1, 175,30-31 WILLEMS).

antagonist. Although Celsus' thought is Platonist, Origen accuses him of being a closet Epicurean[2]. Origen admits that it is in his other writings that one recognizes Celsus as an Epicurean (Contra Celsum 1.8 [60,24-25 Koet.]). Marcel Borret notes that Origen has his doubts about whether Celsus is an Epicurean or not (1.68; 3.49, 80; 4.36, 54 [122,17-18; 246,5-6; 271,2-4; 307,16-19; 326,28-30 Koet.]). In 4.36 [307,16-19 Koet.] Origen questions whether Celsus is the same as the Celsus who composed two books against the Christians. He wrote several works against magic (1.68 [122,17-18 Koet.]) and could have been one of two Epicurean philosophers named Celsus who were contemporaries of Nero[3] and Hadrian (1.8 [61,1-8 Koet.]). Lucian had dedicated his *Alexander the False Prophet* to the latter Celsus, and as Henry Chadwick notes, that Celsus was an Epicurean (Alex. 25, 43, 61 [100,23-102,12; 117,10-11; 130,12-15 Victor]) who wrote against magic (Alex. 21 [98,21-23 Victor])[4]. Chadwick argues against identifying Origen's Celsus

---

[2] C. Cels. 1.8, 10, 3.22, 35, 80, 5.3 [60,25; 63,13; 218,19; 231,19; 271,3; 3,22 KOETSCHAU]. See H. CHADWICK, Origen: Contra Celsum. Translated with an Introduction & Notes, Cambridge 1953, xxv-xxvi (referred to below as "CHADWICK, Origen"). Another ET may be found in R. J. HOFFMANN, Celsus. On the True Doctrine. A Discourse Against the Christians, New York/Oxford 1987. The original text used is from Origenes Werke, Vols. I-II, ed. P. KOETSCHAU, GCS 2, 3, Leipzig 1899. Vol. I contains books I to IV, and Vol. II contains books V to VIII of the *Contra Celsum*. Below I will include the page and line numbers from KOETSCHAU and indicate the book and chapter with Arabic numerals. Celsus' remarks are edited by R. BADER, Der ΑΛΗΘΗΣ ΛΟΓΟΣ des Kelsos, TBAW 33, Stuttgart/Berlin 1940; referred to below as "BADER"). The papyrus finds from Toura are incorporated into the edition of M. BORRET s.j., Origène Contre Celse. Introduction, Texte Critique, Traduction et Notes, Vols. I-V, SC 132, 136, 147, 150, 227, Paris 1967-1976; referred to below as "BORRET" with volume and page). BORRET discusses the issue of Celsus' Epicureanism in V.130-133 and concludes that Origen perhaps did not finally choose any one of the three possibilities that he mentions in 4.54 (326,28-30 KOET.). For a recent and comprehensive survey of scholarship on Celsus see K. PICHLER, Streit um das Christentum. Der Angriff des Kelsos und die Antwort des Origenes, Regensburger Studien zur Theologie 23, Frankfurt am Main/Bern 1980, 5-101. The translations below are my own and were done with reference to those of CHADWICK and BORRET.

[3] M. FREDE notes that this Celsus is ruled out because Origen's Celsus knew of Marcion in: Celsus Philosophus Platonicus, ANRW II.36.7, 1994, 5186 (with reference to C.Cels. 5.62 [66,6 KOET.]).

[4] CHADWICK, Origen, xxiv. Galen corresponded with this Celsus, De libris propriis 16 (II, 124 MÜLLER = XIX, 48 KÜHN). The scholiast on Lucian identified this Celsus with the author of the True Doctrine (180,14 RABE). Celsus the Epicurean is summarized in Prosopographia Imperii Romani .. Pars II , ed. E. GROAG/A. STEIN; Berlin 1936, (P.I.R.) 642 (p. 146). U. VICTOR notes that the question of the identity of Lucian's friend Celsus and the opponent of Origen cannot be answered without new arguments. He does concede that Origen's Celsus is not an Epicurean but a Platonist (Lukian von Samosata. Alexandros oder der Lügenprophet, Religions in the Graeco-Roman World 132, Leiden/New York/Köln 1997, 132). See the summary in HOFFMANN, Celsus. On the True Doctrine, 29-33. C. MARKSCHIES argues that Origen's identification of Celsus as an Epicurean is false; for

with Lucian's since Origen's Celsus leaves no trace of Epicurean philosophy in the fragments that have survived[5]. Michael Frede's summary of Celsus' Platonist philosophy finds no traces of Epicureanism in his thought (with reference to Celsus' belief in providence, eschatology and demons)[6]. Frede does find points of contact with the philosophy of Numenius[7]. Whether Celsus has a developed philosophy of history is an open question. It is at least clear that he believes the ancient teaching of Greece is true teaching. Carl Andresen argues that Celsus subsumed the practices (nomos) and doctrine (logos) of Hellenistic tradition in his word "logos"[8]. Andresen believes that Celsus found a philosophy of history in Justin and is responding to that.[9] Borret is critical of

---

Origen, Epicureanism is an evil spirit that one must drive out of the halls of philosophy (Epikureismus bei Origenes und in der origenistischen Tradition, in: Epikureismus in der frühen Kaiserzeit, ed. W. ERLER, Stuttgart 1999 [forthcoming]).

[5] CHADWICK, Origen, xxv.

[6] See FREDE, Celsus, 5191-92 and Celsus' Attack on the Christians, in: Philosophia Togata II. Plato and Aristotle at Rome, ed. J. BARNES/M. GRIFFIN, Oxford 1997, 223-28. FREDE does not make use of Q. CATAUDELLA's important study on Celsus' "Epicureanism" (Celso e l'Epicureismo, ASNSP 12, 1943, 1-23) which has not been surpassed in its survey of the relationship of Epicurean sources and Celsus' thought. CATAUDELLA attempts to answer such arguments by claiming that "providence" for Celsus refers to immutable physical laws (Celso, 17 with reference to C. Cels. 4.99 [372,10-20 KOET.]). Epicurus seems to have been open to some action of the gods to help the good and hurt the evil (Diog. Laert. 10.124). Celsus is skeptical about Christian hopes for the future (3.78 [269,10-11 KOET.]), but also accepts the doctrine of future punishments (8.48, 49 [262,29; 264,13 KOET.]). CATAUDELLA suggests that Celsus may see an educational use in such doctrines (Celso, 21). Lucretius saw no such value (1.102-11 on terrifying statements of prophets and fears of eternal punishments; and see 3.976-1021 versus a literal hell). Of Celsus' demonology CATAUDELLA (Celso, 12) questions its sincerity and refers to Cic., De nat. deor. 1.30.85 in which the Academic Cotta notes that some people believe: "...Epicurus really abolished the gods, but nominally retained them in order not to offend the people of Athens" (*Epicurum ne in attentionem Atheniensium caderet, verbis reliquisse deos, re sustilisse*). Epicurus did not counsel the abandonment of the cult, and Celsus uses demonology to justify the polytheism of Hellenistic tradition. The dissertation by K. SCHMIDT is unfortunately difficult to obtain: De Celsi libro qui inscribitur Alethes Logos, quaestiones ad philosophiam pertinentes, Diss. Göttingen 1921. C. ANDRESEN (Logos und Nomos. Die Polemik des Kelsos wider das Christentum, AKG 30, Berlin 1955, 44) summarizes some of his results and in particular his important use of the Platonist Albinos (now usually identified as Alcinous; ca 150 C.E.) to illuminate Celsus' thought. Cf. J. WHITTAKER, Art. Alcinoos, Dictionnaire des Philosophes Antiques, Vol. I, ed. R. GOULET, Paris 1989, 112-13. For Celsus' affinities with Stoicism see H. CHADWICK, Origen, Celsus, and the Stoa, JThS 48, 1947, 34-49.

[7] FREDE, Celsus, 5193, 5194 ("Who is Plato but Moses speaking Attic?" from Eus. P.E. 11.10.14), 5208 (on the Platonic trinity in Eus. P.E. 11.18), 5211.

[8] ANDRESEN depends on 1.14 (67,15-17 KOET.) in particular to come to this conception (Logos, 9, 10, 189, 190), 1.16 (68,7-9.21 KOET. in Logos, 203-05), and 5.41 (44,19-22 KOET. in Logos, 194). For ANDRESEN the historical logos as the principle of intellectual and religious history is identical with logos and nomos (Logos, 190).

Andresen's systematization of Celsus' philosophy which occasionally led Andresen to make translations that are based more on his view of Celsus' view of history than on Greek usage[10]. Borret is more open to Epicurean influence in Celsus' thought as his index indicates. Most of the references in his index, however, are to claims Origen makes about Celsus' secret Epicurean philosophy, and there are no formal quotations of Epicurus[11]. The only citation of Epicurus in Celsus' text that Borret identifies is not a verbal citation, but a close parallel in thought. In 1.8 Celsus writes: "And I do not mean that a person who embraces a good doctrine, if he is about to run into danger from people because of it, ought to renounce the doctrine, or pretend that he had renounced it, or come to deny it."[12] This is somewhat similar to one of Epicurus' statements in Diogenes Laertius 10.117: "Moreover, he who has once become wise nevermore assumes the opposite habit, not even in semblance, if he can help it" (ἀλλὰ καὶ τὸν ἅπαξ γενόμενον σοφὸν μηκέτι τὴν ἐναντίαν λαμβάνειν διάθεσιν μηδὲ πλάττειν ἑκόντα δοκεῖ 'Επικούρῳ)[13]. Origen[14] sees traces of Epicureanism in expressed or unexpressed presuppositions of Celsus' including: an attack on providence (1.8, 10 [61,5; 63,11-13 Koet.]), the pursuit of pleasure (2.42, 3.75 [165,23-25; 266,24 Koet.]), reduction of

---

9 ANDRESEN, Logos, 308-400. ANDRESEN does not find evidence for a philosophy of history in middle Platonism (239-307). ANDRESEN's successors have occasionally been supportive of the claim that Celsus knew Justin or at least shared common traditions with Justin that were current among Christian apologetics of the time. See A. DARBY NOCK, JThS 7, 1956, 314-317, and BORRET V.185-92. DROGE, Homer, 76-78 argues for Celsus' knowledge of Justin — whether he knew his arguments at first hand or through intermediaries. Q. CATAUDELLA argues that Celsus could not have known Justin directly given his ignorance of Justin's counter-arguments to his positions (Celso e gli Apologeti Cristiani, NDid 1, 1947, 28-34). G. T. BURKE, Celsus and Justin. Carl Andresen Revisited, ZNW 76, 1985, 107-116 regards the connection between Justin and Celsus as undemonstrated. See also RINALDI, Biblia Gentium, 126. Celsus may simply have ignored Justin's arguments. On this issue see also the introduction.

10 BORRET V. 153-82; the references to translation problems are 167-70 (e.g. ἀλόγως in 1.23 [73,12 KOET.] is translated by ANDRESEN as "in their non-historical thought," Logos 210). ANDRESEN's reviewers were critical of the view that Celsus has a philosophy of history. J. DANIÉLOU, RSR 44, 1956, 580-85 / NOCK, JThS 7, 1956, 314-317 / J. H. WASZINK, VigChr 12, 1958, 166-77. WASZINK would replace ANDRESEN's "philosophy of history" with "recognition of tradition" (177).

11 BORRET V.288

12Καὶ οὐ τοῦτο λέγω, ὡς χρὴ τὸν ἀγαθοῦ δόγματος περιεχόμενον, εἰ μέλλει δι' αὐτὸ κινδυνεύειν παρ' ἀνθρώποις, ἀποστῆναι τοῦ δόγματος ἢ πλάσασθαι ὡς ἀφέστηκεν ἢ ἔξαρνον γενέσθαι (60,17-20 KOET.). Discussed in BORRET V.129-130, 532. The index to Epicurus is on V.288.

13 The fragment is numbered 222a in H. USENER, Epicurea, Leipzig, 1887. ET from the LCL edition of HICKS.

14 BORRET V.130.

Jesus' miracles to sorcery (1.68 [122,17-20 Koet.]), deceitfulness of visions and dreams (2.60 [182,27-29 Koet.]),[15] the absence of divine presence in cultic sights (3.35 [231,19 Koet.]), the attribution of natural phenomena to chance (4.75 [344,16-17 Koet.]),[16] insolent comparison of the healing power of birds and the power of magic (4.86 [357,10-12 Koet.]), complete refusal of any descent of God or God's son (5.3 [3,21-23 Koet.]), and a defense of the cult of images to accommodate oneself to popular opinion (7.66 [215,18-22 Koet.])[17]. It must be conceded that only the questions of visions and chance are explicit ties between Celsus' thought and that of the Epicureans. The other examples are Origen's own accusations about the presuppositions that lie hidden behind Celsus' texts. Celsus is also inconsistent with Epicureanism in his esteem for providence (Origen's point in 4.4 [277,3-5 Koet.]). However, Celsus' denial that the world was made for humans could be Epicurean (4.74 [343,14-15 Koet.])[18]. He also respects the pagan oracles (7.3 [154,18-25 Koet.]), and believes that they have helped cities (8.45 [259,29 Koet.])[19].

---

[15] Here BORRET is able to find a comparative text that shows Celsus' thought is similar to that of Lucretius 1.132-35 where dreams give us the idea of encountering dead people. In 5.1167-80 Lucretius traces belief in the gods to such visions and dreams. Epicurus established the distinction between the phantasms of sick people and those who dream (Diog. Laert. 10.32 — BORRET I.415 n. 57). See CATAUDELLA (Celso e l'Epicureismo, 22). The other examples BORRET appeals to are comparisons made by Origen who alleges that such thoughts are hidden presuppositions of Celsus' thought.

[16] Compare Lactantius, Div. inst. 3.17 (= USENER, Epicurea, 370 fin) where Epicurus denies that natural phenomena are produced by providence (BORRET II.370 n.1). See also CATAUDELLA (Celso e l'Epicureismo, 14) who discusses this point of view extensively. Cp. Diog. Laert. 10.76-82 for Epicurus' non-theistic explanations for meteorological phenomena. Lucretius adopts the same point of view in Book VI.

[17] BORRET IV.166 n.4 refers to USENER, Epicurea, 390, 391 on pretending to pray to statues. See Sextus Empiricus, Adv. Math. 9.49 where the skeptic conforms to ancestral customs and laws, declares that the gods exist, and does all the acts required for their adoration and veneration, but refuses to undertake a philosophical examination of the question. Origen remarks that some philosophers, despite their high idea of God, also take part in superstitious rites (C. Cels. 5.43; 7.44 [47,1-3; 195,22-26 KOET.]).

[18] CATAUDELLA (Celso e l'epicureismo, 14-17). Lucretius 5.195-99: "the universe was not created for us by divine power" (*nequaquam nobis divinitus esse paratam naturam rerum*). Compare 5.156-65. CHADWICK remarks that Plato had a similar belief (Origen, Celsus, and the Stoa, 36 with reference to Laws 903c).

[19] BORRET V.131. CATAUDELLA, however, notes that Epicurus did not withdraw from civic religious activities (Celso, 12) even though his concept of the gods was radically different from that of Hellenism. In Diog. Laert. 10.135, Epicurus is said to have rejected divination (and compare Lucretius' skepticism towards Delphi in 1.737-39). He did, however, believe in attending state festivals (θεωρίαις) and in setting up votive images according to Diog. Laert. (εἰκόνας 10.120).

22   *1. Celsus*

Cataudella, however, notes that Caecilius, the pagan in the *Octavius* of
Minucius Felix, was an "Epicurean" who accepted oracles[20].
He occasionally quotes Plato admiringly (6.9, 6.18 [79,6-15; 89,2-8
Koet.])[21]. The fact that Celsus' thought is so close to Platonism throws the
charge of Epicureanism into question. Origen finally concludes that three
hypotheses are possible: " ... he is either pretending not to hold his Epicurean
belief, or as one might say, he later changed to better doctrines, or as someone
else might say, he only shares a name with the Epicurean" (4.54 [326,28-30
Koet.]). Origen does not mention the Epicurean connection after 5.3 (3,22
Koet.). The charge of Epicureanism was probably convenient to Origen, and
the word could serve as a general term of abuse in Greek and Hebrew
literature[22]. Cataudella suggests that Celsus may have been a Platonizing
Epicurean (or an Epicureanizing Platonist)[23]. He compares such eclecticism to
the Socrates of Ps. Plato's *Axiochos*. However the evidence for Celsus'
Epicureanism is so slender that creating such an obscure figure (an
Epicureanizing Platonist) is unnecessary. As Frede points out, Celsus' belief in
the reality of magic is a clear refutation of the thesis that he was an Epicurean[24].
Eusebius provides the only external evidence for the date of Origen's work:
"At that time also he composed the treatises, eight in number, in answer to the
work against us, entitled *True Discourse of Celsus the Epicurean* "[25]. Origen
was over sixty years of age when he wrote during the reign of Philip the
Arab[26]. He was anxious (3.15 [214,5-8 Koet.]) about an impending
persecution of the church given the revolt taking place in his time (νῦν

---

[20] Celso e l'epicureismo, 7, with reference to Octavius 7. Even if one cannot call the
pagan an "Epicurean," he at least is an eclectic who accepted Epicurus' atomic theory, Oct.
5.7.

[21] I count 29 citations of Plato by Celsus in BORRET's index (V.292-295).

[22] CHADWICK, Origen, xxvi and compare M. JASTROW's lexicon, s.v. אפּיקורוס (A
Dictionary of the Targumim, the Talmud Babli and Yerushalmi, and the Midrashic Literature,
Vol. I, Brooklyn 1967, 104). Maximus of Tyre, for example, has not one good word to say
about Epicurus who appears often in his discourses and only as the subject of the
philosophical rhetorician's scorn (e.g. in Diss. 4.4 Epicurus is neither poet nor philosopher;
compare 4.8 and 33.3 [BiTeu, 31,63-64; 35,143-44; 266,39-40 TRAPP]).

[23] Celso e l'epicureismo, 22.

[24] Celsus' Attack, 224 with reference to C. Cels. 1.68 and 4.86 [122,5-16; 357,2
KOET.]. Cp. VICTOR, Lukian, 132.

[25] Eus, H.E. 6.36.2.

[26] Philip ruled 244-249 and Origen would have been 60 after 245 according to
CHADWICK (Origen, xiv). Eusebius (H.E. 6.2.2) dates Origen's passion for martyrdom to
the tenth year of the reign of Severus who was acclaimed emperor in 193. S. N. MILLER,
Art. The Army and the Imperial House, CAH XII, 1939, 3. Eus. then narrates the death of
his father when Origen was not quite seventeen (6.2.12) and, in Origen's eighteenth year he
came to preside over the catechetical school in Alexandria (H.E. 6.3.3) which must have been
in 204 or later. Origen may have been born in 186 leaving a *terminus ab quo* of 245/246 for
the C. Cels.

στάσεως). W. Ensslin mentions three pretenders to the throne in the first year after Rome's millennium (247): the Danubians set up Pacatianus as emperor; in the east between Cappadocia and Syria, Jotapianus assumed the purple; and in Syria a usurper named Antoninus appeared[27]. These blows brought Philip to the point that he offered to abdicate. Decius accepted the military command of Moesia and Pannonia, and in 249 his troops compelled him to become emperor[28]. Decius instituted his persecution of the church in 249[29]. Origen himself was tortured repeatedly with the stocks and fire[30]. Consequently the book would have been written between 246 and 248.

The date of the *True Discourse* ('Αληθὴς Λόγος) of Celsus is much harder to pin down. A text of Celsus (8.71 [288,6 Koet.]) that describes "those who rule" convinced some that the document should be dated to a time of joint rule when Marcus Aurelius came to power and shared it with Lucius Verus (161-169)[31]. From 177 to 180 he shared power with Commodus[32]. The reference may be merely to the fact that the Romans rule the empire[33]. Celsus' indication that persecution of the Christians is underway (8.69 [286,6-8 Koet.]) has encouraged many scholars to date the text to the persecution under Marcus

---

[27] W. ENSSLIN, Art. The Senate and the Army, CAH XII, 1939, 92.

[28] ENSSLIN, Ibid. 93.

[29] H. LIETZMANN, Art. The Church in the West, CAH XII, 1939, 520-21.

[30] Eus. H.E. 6.39.5.

[31] J. SCHWARTZ opts for a date in the first years of Marcus Aurelius' reign in Celsus Redivivus, RHPhR 53, 1973, 399-405. His original investigation was Du Testament de Lévi au Discours véritable de Celse, RHPhR 40, 1960, 126-45. Lucian uses ἀνασκολοπίζειν in the passive to describe Jesus' crucifixion in *De morte Peregr.* 11, 13, for example, as does Celsus (C. Cels. 2.36 [161,26 KOET.], and see its use for persecuted Christians in 7.40 [191,9 KOET.]). Cp. M. FÉDOU, Christianisme et religions païennes dans le Contre Celse d'Origène, ThH 81, Paris 1988, 40 and BORRET V.194. BORRET (V.192-96) discusses SCHWARTZ's argument that Celsus was Lucian's friend, and that Celsus influenced the work of Lucian. BORRET argues that the linguistic evidence does not necessarily establish a dependence between Lucian and Celsus, and even if there is a dependence it is not clear who borrowed from whom.

[32] CHADWICK, Origen, xxvi.

[33] FREDE, Celsus, 5188-89. FREDE mentions a similar usage in Athenaeus, Deipn. 3.53, 98c (I, 226,5 KAIBEL) and compare 3.94, 121f (I, 278,13-14 KAIBEL): Rome is the βασιλεύουσα πόλις. He refers to H.-U. ROSENBAUM, Zur Datierung von Celsus' ΑΛΗΘΗΣ ΛΟΓΟΣ, VigChr 26, 1972, (102-11) 104ff who argues that οἱ νῦν βασιλεύοντες ἡμῶν may only refer to the Romans as rulers of the world. ROSENBAUM gives two usages in Hippolytus' commentary on Daniel in which the Persians and Babylonians rule: οἱ Πέρσαι διεκράτησαν βασιλεύοντες 4.24.7 (GCS I, 248,8 BONWETSCH); and ἐβασίλευσαν τότε Βαβυλώνιοι 2.12.3 (66,22 BONWETSCH). Other texts of Celsus seem to imply a monarchy (8.68, 73 [284,13-16; 290,16 KOET.]). ROSENBAUM speculates that J. SCHWARTZ may be correct who dates Celsus' writing to the period shortly after 160 because of his contention that Lucian used Celsus (Du Testament de Lévi au Discours véritable de Celse, RHPhR 40, 1960, 126-45). Julian has a similar usage in which he describes the Imperial city in Or. 11.3, 131d (II/2, 102 ROCHEFORT; ἡ βασιλεύουσα πόλις).

Aurelius in 177[34]. Celsus could have written between 177-180[35]. The date is conjectural and open to skeptical attack[36]. Celsus' title has, as Chadwick comments, a strongly Platonic ring[37]. Arthur Droge, following Wifstrand, interprets the title as a reference to a *theologia perennis* — an ancient logos (1.14, 3.16 [67,15; 215,6 Koet.]) — which is a "qualitative" monotheism in which one God coexists with many subordinate divinities[38].

Celsus did not find anything to praise in the new religion. Origen complains about (4.47 [319,29-30 Koet.]) "... the one who wrote *The True Discourse* which does not set forth doctrines, but accuses Christians and Jews" (ὁ ἀληθῆ λόγον ἐπιγράψας τὸν οὐ δόγματα ἐκτιθέμενον ἀλλὰ Χριστιανῶν καὶ Ἰουδαίων κατηγορήσαντα). Celsus' own loyalties are to the ancient traditions of Hellenistic culture, and they provide the ground for his refutation of Christianity[39]. His love for the traditions of the past is evident in his quotations of Plato (29), Herodotus (24), Homer (6), Heraclitus (5), Hesiod (3), Aristotle (2), Pherecydes (2), Empedocles (1), Euripides (1), and Pindar (1)[40]. Celsus appears to share Maximus of Tyre's belief that poets and philosophers share the same conception of god and that "poetry is philosophy"[41]. Origen probably did not include all of Celsus' material, and

---

[34] CHADWICK, Origen, xxviii. FREDE notes that once one gives up the assumption of a joint imperium, that Celsus' reference to persecution could refer to any of the waves of persecution under Marcus (Celsus, 5189) e.g. in 170. He refers to Marcus' apparent anger toward Christians in Med. 11.3.

[35] W. H. C. FREND dates the persecutions under Marcus to 164-168 and 176-178 in Martyrdom and Persecution in the Early Church, New York 1967, 196. P. KERESZTES notes the difficulty of dating the persecutions and places them between 161-168 and dates the outbreak of the intense second wave to 177. He dates Celsus' book between 176 and 180 (Rome and the Christian Church I. From Nero to the Severi, ANRW, II.23.1, 1979, 297-304).

[36] Compare BORRET with bibliography on the question (V.128-129).

[37] Compare Plato, Ep. 7.342a quoted by Celsus in 6.9 [79,6-15 KOET.], Meno 81a, Laws 757a, 783a, Tim. 20d, Epin. 992c, Phaedr. 270c, and Epin. 977d. ANDRESEN (Logos, 370-71) also refers to the use of the phrase in Justin (e.g. Apol. 1.43.6 [93,20 MARC.] and Dial. 92.6 [230,37 MARC.]).

[38] DROGE, Homer 80. A. WIFSTRAND, Die wahre Lehre des Kelsos, Bulletin de la Société royale des Lettres de Lund, 1941-42, 5, 1942, (391-431) 396-404. He also refers to ANDRESEN's critique of WIFSTRAND (Logos, 38, 113-14). ANDRESEN relates the title to the entire principle of Hellenistic historical tradition. NOCK makes the important point, however, that Celsus does not make a plain equation of "old" and "true" (review of ANDRESEN in JThS 7, 1956, 315).

[39] ANDRESEN, Logos, 38 and passim; DROGE, Homer, 78.

[40] See BORRET's index in V.284-99. The list comprises all the pagan authors that Celsus cites. On techniques of quotation in antiquity see A. VAN DEN HOEK, Techniques of Quotation in Clement of Alexandria. A View of Ancient Literary Working Methods, VigChr 50, 1996, 223-43.

[41] Diss. 4.1 (29,5-30,17 TR.).

may have rearranged some of it[42]. In particular, Origen probably left out some of the historical material that Celsus used[43].

His attack on the Christians occasionally mentions OT traditions that come from the following texts identified by Borret: Genesis (16); Exodus (2); Numbers (1); Deuteronomy (8); Daniel (1); and Jonah (1)[44]. Most of the references are quite vague and there are few verbal citations. He does quote "Let there be" in 6.60 (130,15 Koet.) from Gen. 1. He mentions Moses, the prophets (6.50 [121,21 Koet.]), and Jonah and Daniel by name (7.53 [203,29 Koet.]).

His discussion of NT texts will be treated below, but one can say at the outset that Celsus does not bother to give verbal quotations from OT or NT texts with some rare exceptions. He quotes Jesus' words without identifying Matthew (2.24 [154,9 Koet.] is close to Mt 26:39): Ὦ πάτερ, εἰ δύναται τὸ ποτήριον τοῦτο παρελθεῖν. In 6.16 (86,13-14 Koet.) he quotes Mt 19:24 par. He also quotes a Gnostic Christian who knows Gal 6:14 without mentioning Galatians (5.65 [68,10-11 Koet.]): Ἐμοὶ κόσμος ἐσταύρωται, κἀγὼ κόσμῳ. He approaches Paul's words in 1 Cor 3:19 in 6.12 (82,12 Koet.) when he states: φαμὲν τὴν ἐν ἀνθρώποις σοφίαν μωρίαν εἶναι παρὰ θεῷ. Hebrews' word for Jesus, ἀρχηγόν (founder), may be reflected in Celsus' question (5.33 [35,1 Koet.]) about who is the author of the Christians' traditional laws (ἀρχηγέτην πατρίων νόμων). In his next sentence he remarks that they can name no other source for their teacher and chorus leader than the Jews. He does not call Jesus ἀρχηγέτην. He knows of Gnostic Christians whose self designation is Paul's infamous word from Phil 3:8: σκυβάλων (excrement; 6.53 [124,12 Koet.]). Borret identifies twenty one references to texts from Matthew by Celsus, no references to Mark, eight references to Luke (most of which are parallel to Mt), four references to John, one to 1 Cor 10:20, and one to Col 2:18[45]. Jesus is one of the few NT figures Celsus is willing to call by name. He mentions the following figures: John the Baptist (1.41 [92,1 Koet.]); Herod the tetrarch (1.58 [109,18-19 Koet.] — meaning Herod the Great); a poor adulterous woman (Mary in 1.28 [79,24-26 Koet.]); the carpenter who was not Jesus' physical father (1.28 [79,25 Koet.]); the Chaldeans (Magi, 1.58 [109,16 Koet.]); Panthera, Jesus' physical father and Mary's lover (1.32 [83,19 Koet.]); ten or eleven miserable tax collectors and sailors who were Jesus' followers (1.62 [113,8 Koet.]); the

---

[42] ANDRESEN, *Logos*, 22-43.

[43] For instance, Empedocles, whom Origen said was frequently mentioned by Celsus (1.32 [84,20-21 KOET.]), is only quoted in 8.53 [268,13 KOET.]. The diagram of the Ophites was also omitted (6.26 [96,18-27 KOET.]). In 3.32 (228,22-23 KOET.) Origen admits that he has not included all the story of the Clazomenian.

[44] BORRET V.251-59.

[45] BORRET V.260-72.

judge who had Jesus put to death (2.63 [185,2 Koet.]); those who mocked
Jesus with a purple robe and crown of thorns (2.34,35 [161,5-7.18 Koet.]);
the voice from heaven (2.72 [194,2 Koet.]); Satan (2.49 [171,20 Koet.]); a
hysterical woman who had a hallucination of the risen Jesus along with an
unnamed disciple and Jesus' confraternity (2.55, 70, 3.22 [178,25-26; 192,20;
218,16 Koet.]); and the one or two angels at Jesus' tomb along with the angel
who came to the carpenter and the angel who told them to go the Egypt (5.52
[56,10-16 Koet.]). Glaring absences are Pilate (anonymous in 2.63 [185,2
Koet.]?) and his soldiers and any names for disciples or NT authors. He
mentions different Christian texts that differ on the number of angels at the
tomb (5.52 [56,10 Koet.]) and once calls a gospel a drama or tragedy with a
catastrophe (καταστροφὴν τοῦ δράματος 2.55 [178,20 Koet.]). Some
Christians alter the texts of the gospel (τὸ εὐαγγέλιον 2.27 [156,3 Koet.]).
Celsus does know a tradition from Enoch (5.52 [56,7 Koet.]). A Christian text
that contains an argument between a Jew and Christian over Christ was known
to Celsus (4.52 [325,5-6 Koet.]) as was a Gnostic text called the *Heavenly
Dialogue* (8.15 [232,11 Koet.]). Celsus' knowledge of the scripture (in
Origen's presentation) is thus very limited, but he does have a good feel for the
major points of Christian proclamation including Jesus' birth, the incarnation,
the arguments from prophecy concerning Jesus, the miracles of Jesus, and
Jesus' passion and resurrection[46].

1.2 Celsus on the Gospels

Celsus (and his Jew's) attitude to the gospels is that they are unhistorical (2.13
[141,19-22 Koet.]): "Even though I have many true things to say concerning
what happened to Jesus — and not at all like what was written by the disciples
of Jesus — those I willingly leave aside." Origen notes that Celsus believed the
disciples composed fictions about Jesus (πλάσματα). Celsus' Jew accused the
disciples of pure invention (2.26 [155,21 Koet.]): "Even though you were
lying you were unable to persuasively conceal your fictions (πλάσματα)"[47].
Celsus charges that (2.27 [156,1-5 Koet.]): "Some of the believers, as though
coming off a drunk, stand against themselves and reshape (μεταχαράττειν)
the original text of the gospel three or four or more times and counterfeit

---

[46] S. BENKO, Pagan Criticism of Christianity During the First Two Centuries A.D.,
ANRW II.23.2, 1980, 1102 summarizes Celsus' criticisms of the NT. See also BENKO,
Pagan Rome and the Early Christians, Bloomington/Indianapolis 1986, 151.

[47] Origen's complains (5.57 [60,15-19 KOET.]) that Greek stories are not thought to be
"fictions and myths" (πλάσματα καὶ μῦθοι) while Christians willing to die for their faith, if
they claim to have seen angels, are deemed unworthy of belief. The phrase "fictions and
myths" may be one of Celsus' charges or that of other pagans. See § 2.3.5, § 4.6 and
§ 5.2.1 below.

(μεταπλάττειν)[48] it so that they are able to deny criticisms." Origen takes Celsus to mean Marcion's alteration of the gospel, although Chadwick points out that Celsus could have the canonical or apocryphal gospels in mind[49].

1.2.1 Celsus' Jewish Antagonist of Gospel Traditions

In the discussion below I will recast Celsus' objections in the narrative order of Matthew, which Celsus seems to have known best. Origen conjectures in 1.40 [90,22-23 Koet.], for example, that he took his narrative of the baptism from Matthew, and perhaps the other gospels. In the first two books Celsus introduces an imaginary Jew to bring objections against the gospel narratives about Jesus. The rhetoricians called this prosopopoeia (προσωποποιεῖ 1.28 [79,15 Koet.]). Origen likens Celsus' activity to the progymnastic exercises of children and is always quick to point out when Celsus says something that a Jew probably would not say. Aphthonius defines characterization (ethopoeia) as "an imitation of the character of a proposed person ... ethopoeia, having [for its subject] a known person, is invented as to character only... for example, the words which Hercules might say, when Eurytheus was commanding him ... It is prosopopoeia whenever all things are invented, both character and person (ἦθος ... πρόσωπον), just as when Menander made up Confutation (ἔλεγχον)."[50] Celsus represents the Jew as having a conversation with Jesus and with Jewish Christians. Though his exact source is unclear, Celsus must have had some kind of access to Jewish tradition — written or oral[51]. The Jew of Celsus is sort of a counter-foil to the Jew (Papiscus) in the *Dialogue of Jason and Papiscus* who finally converts to Christianity.[52] Celsus' Jew is quite happy to remain a determined critic of the Christian faith who also knows

---

[48] On Christians' counterfeiting doctrines see DROGE, Homer, 77.

[49] CHADWICK, Origen, 90 n.2 ("more" would then refer to the apocryphal gospels with "three or four" referring to the canonical texts).

[50] Progymn. 11 (44,20-45,3 L. SPENGEL, Rhetores Graeci II, Leipzig). ET from R. NADEAU, The Progymnasmata of Aphthonius, Speech Monographs 19, 1952, (264-285) 278. Theon conflates the two varieties (Theon, Progymnasmata 10 [115,12-19 SPENGEL]). Hermogenes makes the distinction in Progymn. 9 (20,7-14 H. RABE, Rhetores Graeci VI, Leipzig 1913). See also LAUSBERG, Handbuch, § 826-829.

[51] BORRET (V.191) draws attention to the possibility that Celsus might have been aware of Justin's Dialogue with Trypho in which a more conciliatory Jew dialogues with Justin with reference to A. D. NOCK's review (JThS 7, 1956, 316) of C. ANDRESEN's Logos and Nomos. D. ROKEAH is skeptical of Celsus' use of written Jewish sources, but provides no alternative hypothesis (Jews, Pagans and Christians in Conflict, StPB 33, Jerusalem-Leiden 1982, 58). M. LODS, Étude sur les sources juives de la polémique de Celse contre les chrétiens, RHPhR 21, 1941, (1-33) 31 is more open to Celsus' use of Jewish traditions and to Justin's Dialogue. M. FÉDOU also believes Celsus used written Jewish sources (Christianisme, 42 n. 29). See also L. FELDMAN, Jew and Gentile in the Ancient World. Attitudes and Interactions from Alexander to Justinian, Princeton 1993, 197, 199.

[52] See 1.3.1 below.

Hellenistic tradition and is willing to use it against Christianity. In book three, Celsus drops his Jewish antagonist of Christianity, and attacks both Judaism and Christianity with the same passion, although he does have some grudging respect for the ancient past of Judaism (5.25 [26,3 Koet.]). He also criticizes Judaism and especially those who abandon their own traditions and accept the Jewish faith (5.41 [44,21 Koet.])[53].

1.2.2 The Genealogy of Jesus

The genealogy of Jesus is traced through Mary in Celsus' perception of the gospels' traditions (2.32 [159,13-16 Koet.]). Celsus writes that "the genealogists boldly described Jesus as descending from the first born person and from the kings of the Jews." He argues against the genealogy's historicity by claiming that "the carpenter's wife would not have been unaware of such a family." Celsus was aware of Matthew and Luke's traditions, since only Luke (3:23-38) traces Jesus back to Adam and since only Mt 1:1-17 mentions the kings of Judah in Jesus' family tree. Origen notes that Celsus does not mention the problem of the discrepancies between the genealogies[54]. He is not impressed by Celsus' apparent assumption that poor people must be descended entirely from poor parents and kings descended from kings. Origen does not mention the fact that the genealogies trace Jesus' descent through Joseph in the first place. Augustine had to tangle with that issue[55]. Justin traces Mary to Jacob and consequently to Judah[56]. This example is typical for Celsus who knows the broad outline of certain gospel traditions, but is not the careful philologist Porphyry was. If Celsus knew Justin, he must have also known the gospels first hand as the other texts in this chapter will show. But his reading of the gospels was not close and accurate in a Porphyrian sense.

1.2.3 The Virgin Birth

The claims about Jesus' virgin birth were simply incredible to Celsus. Celsus' Jew speaks with Jesus himself, and Celsus summarizes the charges: "He made up (πλασαμένου) the story of the virgin birth ... he was from a Jewish village

---

[53] See Tac. Hist. 5.2 (they abandon ancestral religion) and Iuv. 14.100-106.

[54] 2.32 (159,10-11.20-21 KOET.). See § 2.3.8 for Porphyry's comment on this problem and see Julian in § 5.2.2.

[55] De cons. ev. 2.1.2-3 (CSEL 43, 82-84 WEIH.).

[56] See Apol. 1.32.12-14 and Dial. 100.3 (79,40-49; 241,18-242,21 MARC.) where Justin identifies Mary as belonging to the family of David, Jacob, Isaac, and Abraham. Discussed briefly in BORRET V.185 n. 3 with reference to É. PELAGAUD, Un conservateur au second siècle. Étude sur Celse et la première escarmouche entre la philosophie et le christianisme naissant, Lyon et al. 1878, 413ff. Ambrosiaster has an anonymous question about the Davidic descent of Mary in Quaestiones Vet. et N. Test. 86 (CSEL 50, 147 SOUTER = RINALDI, Biblia Gentium F. 438).

and from a rustic, poor woman who spun for hire (χερνήτιδος)[57] ... she was put away by her husband whose skill was carpentry because she was proved to have committed adultery ... after being cast out by her husband and wandering dishonorably she gave birth to Jesus in secret" (1.28 [79,21-28 Koet.]). Celsus adds to this revised birth narrative: "Jesus' mother was put away by the carpenter betrothed to her after being convicted of adultery and becoming pregnant[58] by a soldier named Panthera" (1.32 [83,17-20 Koet.]). The name's similarity to *parthenos* (virgin) has been noticed[59]. Celsus emphasizes the social status of Jesus and Mary who are outsiders[60].

In addition to his hypothesis about Jesus' real father, Celsus' Jew indicates his conceptual problems with the gospel tradition about Jesus' birth: "A god would not have had such a body as yours ... the body of a god would not have been begotten the way you, Jesus, were begotten" (ἐσπάρης; 1.69 [123,10-21 Koet.]). Origen notes that Celsus is thinking of the illegitimate birth (1.69 [124,1 Koet.]). Justin's Trypho has similar problems with the birth story[61]. Celsus is probably also objecting to the idea of God's son coming to earth as a baby (6.73 [142,18-23 Koet.]): "If he wanted to send a spirit from himself down, why was it necessary to breathe into the womb of a woman? Since he already knew how to create people he could have created a body for this spirit and not cast his spirit into such defilement (μίασμα). He would not thus have been doubted (ἠπιστεῖτο), had he been begotten immediately from above." Celsus may have been aware of John 3:3, but if he is, he has no use for John's conception. Celsus can see no merit in believing that God would send his spirit

---

[57] LSJ s.v. note that the word means spinning for daily hire.
[58] The papyrus reads κύουσα instead of τίκτουσα. See BORRET I.162 n. 3.
[59] Extensive bibliography can be found in BORRET I.163 n. 4 and CHADWICK, Origen, 31 n. 3. One could add R. T. HERFORD, Christianity in Talmud & Midrash, (rep. of 1903 ed.) New York 1975, 35, 103-104. T. Hul. 2.22, 27 mentions פנדירא בן. J. Z. LAUTERBACH argues that the word may have been a family name of Joseph (Jesus in the Talmud, in: Rabbinic Essays, Cincinnati 1951, 532-37). LAUTERBACH's attempt to deny that the texts imply Jesus' illegitimate birth is unlikely given the other evidence (such as that of Celsus and the patristic figures cited by CHADWICK and BORRET). b. Shabb. 104b also mentions the name. LAUTERBACH, Jesus, 529 also finds the identification of ben Stada and Jesus to be questionable. The important fact that some Jews claimed Jesus to have been illegitimate (at least in Celsus' time) is the best argument against LAUTERBACH's unwillingness to interpret Talmudic texts in the same light. ROKEAH, Jews, 62 refers to his article Ben Stara is Ben Pantera — Towards the Clarification of a Philological-Historical Problem, Tarb. 39, 1969, 9-18 (Hebrew). LODS (Les Sources, 5) draws attention to similar accusations in the NT Apocrypha such as Acta Pilati A.II.3-5, IX.1, B.II.2-3 and Gesta Pilati II.3-6, IX.1 (224-225; 240; 291-92; 344-47; 358 TISCHENDORF).
[60] E. GALLAGHER, Divine Man or Magician? Celsus and Origen on Jesus, SBLDS 64, Chico, Calif. 1982, 53-54.
[61] Dial. 68.1 (187,1-2 MARC.), referred to by BORRET I. 271 n.1.

into a woman's body[62]. Based on that philosophical position, he finds the story about Panthera attractive. Origen responds that even if a body had been formed for Jesus without birth, those who saw it would not have believed it was birthless (6.73 [143,3-5 Koet.]).

Celsus' Jew was not convinced by the Greek narratives of divine births: "The ancient myths (μῦθοι) that attributed a divine begetting (σποράν) to Perseus, Amphion, Aeacus, and Minos (we do not believe these) nevertheless truly showed their great and marvelous works for humankind so that they would not seem unpersuasive (ἀπίθανοι). But you, what beautiful or marvelous thing have you done in word or deed? You showed us nothing even though they summoned you in the temple to present a clear sign (ἐναργὲς γνώρισμα) that you were the child of God" (1.67 [121,5-12 Koet.])[63]. Celsus' Jew may be referring to an episode such as John 10:23-4 conflated with Mt 16:1-4. The plausible birth stories of the Greeks and their wonderful works are more impressive to Celsus' Jew than Jesus' refusal to perform a sign for those who wanted proof that he was "Child of God." Origen counters (1.67 [121,12-16 Koet.]) Celsus here by challenging the Greeks to show, for one of the figures listed, "a shining deed, useful for life, and extending to later generations of such a sort as to make persuasive (πιθανότητα) the myth which holds them to have been begotten divinely"[64]. Of course Origen can find nothing done by them that is comparable to Jesus' deeds. Origen also calls the story of Plato's birth from Amphictione and Apollo a "myth" in 1.37 (89,10-12 Koet.). According to the story Ariston could not have sexual intercourse with her until she gave birth. Origen notes that Celsus also quotes myths about

[62] Compare Macarius' pagan's problems with God in a woman's body in § 3.49 below. See GALLAGHER, Divine Man, 94-95. On Celsus' Platonic dualism see ANDRESEN, Logos, 74-5.

[63] These figures were sons of Zeus and women according to the entries in the 2OCD. LODS (Les Sources, 31) refers to a similar text in Justin, Dial. 67.2 (185,5-8 MARC.) in which Trypho recounts the narrative of Danae and Perseus.

[64] GALLAGHER discusses this method of evaluation of the birth stories in Hellenism and Christianity (Divine Man, 62).

Danae,[65] Melanippe,[66] Auge,[67] and Antiope[68] (1.37 [89,19-20 Koet.]) presumably not believing any of them[69].

Celsus indulges in some characteristic invective when he discourses on the beauty of Mary: "Was Jesus' mother beautiful, and did God have sex with her due to her beauty although according to nature God does not love a perishable body? It is not reasonable that God lusted for her — she being neither rich nor royal — since nobody, not even her neighbors, knew her ... when she was hated by the carpenter and cast out, no divine power or persuasive word saved her. These things, therefore, have nothing to do with God's kingdom" (1.39 [90,12-19 Koet.])[70]. Celsus' retelling of the story depends on Greek mythology and is aimed at showing the absurdity of the virgin birth narrative. His admiration of Greek tales breaks the fictional character's identity as a good Jew.

1.2.4 The Magi

Origen remarks that Celsus commented on the narrative about the star by mentioning "the star that arose at the birth of Jesus and other miracles" in Matthew (1.34 [85,31-32 Koet.]). Celsus omits the prophecy from Isaiah 7:10-14 in Mt 1:23. Celsus' Jew does comment on the "Chaldeans"[71] (astrologers): "It is said by Jesus that they were moved by his birth to come and worship him — still a baby — as God, and they made this known to Herod the tetrarch. He sent people to kill those who had been born in that time thinking that he could kill him (Jesus) along with them — lest after surviving for the necessary time he might reign" (1.58 [109,16-22 Koet.]). Origen reflects on Celsus' omission of the star in this text, and compares the star with

---

[65] Perseus was the son of Danae and Zeus (^{2}OCD). Tertullian refers to the narrative with scorn in Apol. 21.8 (124,36-39 DEKKERS). See Apollod., Bibl. 2.4.1.

[66] BADER refers to Hyginus, Fab. 186 (BiTeu 155,1-156,12 MARSHALL). See also the review of source material in T. GANTZ, Early Greek Myth. A Guide to Literary and Artistic Sources, Baltimore/London 1993, 734-35. One reconstruction of the story has Melanippe raped by Poseidon. The two children she bears are Aiolos and Boitos. A krater pictures Melanippe and her children.

[67] Telephus was her son by Heracles (Art. Telephus, ^{2}OCD). See Apollod., Bibl. 3.9.1.

[68] Amphion and Zethus were the sons of Antiope and Zeus (Art. Amphion, ^{2}OCD). Apollod., Bibl. 3.5.5.

[69] See ROKEAH, Jews, 99 who argues that one can reasonably assume that "Jews of the Hellenistic Diaspora did not refrain from using Greek mythology in order to inveigh against the Christians who, as former pagans, had once accepted such myths and now appeared to be dissociating themselves from them."

[70] CHADWICK, Origen, 41 n. 2 refers to Celsus' use of this phrase in 3.59, 6.17 and 8.11 (253,32; 87,18-19; 228,21 KOET.).

[71] In 6.80 [151,22 KOET.] Celsus says (including the Magi in this group), "the most inspired peoples from the beginning were the Chaldeans (ἐνθεώτατα)." He apparently is slightly confused about the identity of the magi.

comets (1.58-59 [109,26; 110,10-14 Koet.]) and further guesses that the demons of the Magi lost strength at Jesus' birth. Consequently they went to find Jesus (1.60 [111,3-10 Koet.]). He also points out that Celsus' Jew did not believe the story about Herod's plot against the child (1.61 [111,29-30 Koet.])[72]. He does not comment on Celsus' confusion of Herod the Great with Herod the tetrarch. Celsus' Jew asks if Herod actually did this, why did Jesus not act like a king when he grew up, but instead wandered begging (1.61 [112,25-28 Koet.]; to be discussed further below)? The whole narrative about the magi and Herod is unconvincing to Celsus who sees no evidence that Jesus acted like a "king."

1.2.5 Jesus' Sojourn in Egypt

Celsus accepts the narrative of Jesus' sojourn in Egypt, but gives it a characteristic twist: "This one (Jesus) because of poverty worked for pay in Egypt and there became experienced with certain powers for which the Egyptians are distinguished. He returned thinking great things and in possession of the powers, and because of them he proclaimed himself god" (1.28 [79,28-31 Koet.]). Origen later gives a similar version, but begins with "He was raised in secret and worked for pay in Egypt ..." (1.38 [89,30-31 Koet.]). The Egyptian sojourn turned Jesus into a magician, according to Celsus' Jew. This tradition is also reflected in rabbinic tales about Jesus' study of magic in Egypt[73]. In b. San. 107b Jesus returns from a stay in Egypt, practices magic, leads astray and deceives Israel (כישף והסית והדיח). Celsus continues this line of attack with this summary: "These are acts of one hated by God and of an evil magician" (1.71 [124,24-25 Koet.]). Later anonymous pagans used the same charge of an Egyptian source of Jesus' magical powers[74].

---

[72] GALLAGHER summarizes Origen's response to Celsus in Divine Man, 65-67.

[73] b. Shabb. 104b, b. San. 67a. See HERFORD, Christianity, 35, 50 and LAUTERBACH, Jesus 481, 490-94, 526. A modern exponent (and proponent) of this whole tradition is M. SMITH, Jesus the Magician, New York 1978. GALLAGHER reviews the material from Jesus' life in Divine Man, 75-135. On the motif of Jesus as magician in Jewish and pagan polemic see ROKEAH, Jews, 76 n. 92 with reference to Eus, Dem. Evang. 3.5.110 (GCS Eusebius VI, 131,22-26 HEIKEL). Celsus also argued that Moses was a sorcerer (C. Cels. 5.41 [45,15-16 KOET.] and see ROKEAH, Jews, 170, 173, 177). Apollonius Molon and Lysimachus claimed Moses was a "sorcerer and deceiver" (Jos. C. Ap. 2.145). Compare Philo's similar comment in Eus. P.E. 8.6.2. BADER, 48 (with reference to C. Cels. 1.21 [72,3-5 KOET.]) refers to other such traditions about Moses in paganism such as Plin., N.H. 30.2.11 (= STERN, Greek and Latin Authors, I, F. 221).

[74] Compare Arnobius, Adv. nat. 1.43 (37,25-39,3 MARCHESI): magus fuit, clandestinis artibus omnia illa perfecit, Aegyptiorum ex adytis angelorum potentium nomina et remotas furatus est disciplinas. Augustine mentions the charge that Jesus composed magical books and performed his deeds by using magical arts De cons. ev. 1.9.14, 1.11.17 (CSEL 43, 14,

Besides his charge that Jesus learned magic in Egypt, Celsus' Jew criticizes the narrative with this diatribe: "Why, when still a baby, was it necessary that you be carried out to Egypt lest you be slaughtered? It is not reasonable for a god to have feared death. But an angel came from heaven commanding you and your family to flee lest being abandoned you should all die. Was the great God, who had already sent two angels because of you, unable to protect his own son there?" (1.66 [119,6-12 Koet.])[75]. Origen (1.66 [120,12-18 Koet.]) finds it better that Jesus depart for Egypt than a case in which providence should hinder Herod's free will by striking those who came to kill the child (as in the Sodom story). Celsus' Jew is reading the story of the flight to Egypt from Greek eyes — the gods of the Homeric epics, for example, would not fear death and flee earthly kings, nor would Bacchus in Euripides' *Bacchae* (to which Celsus actually refers in 2.34 [160,12 Koet.]) fear such kings. Here the Jew becomes the Greek or at least a thoroughly Hellenized Jew.

1.2.6 The Baptism of Jesus (Mt 3:13-17 par)

The story of Jesus' baptism also lacks credibility in the eyes of Celsus' Jew: "While bathing next to John you say that an apparition of a bird of the air flew to you ... what credible witness (ἀξιόχρεως μάρτυς) saw this apparition (φάσμα), or who heard a voice from heaven adopting you as son of God? Except that you assert it and bring forward some one of those who were punished with you" (1.41 [92,1-5 Koet.]). The evaluation of witnesses in conjectural *stasis* is discussed in another chapter[76]. Celsus' point is that the witnesses have no credibility and are not worthy of belief. Origen's response is an interesting discussion of the difficulty of establishing a historical fact as certain. In cases such as the Trojan war in which stories of the gods are interwoven with historical facts the task is very difficult. He pleads for an open mind (εὐγνωμοσυνῆς) and not a simple irrational faith (1.42 [92,6-10; 93,4-6 Koet.])[77]. On Jewish presuppositions about the nature of God, such things could happen (1.43 [93,21.29 Koet.] with reference to Ezekiel 1 and Isaiah 6). On the other hand, an Epicurean or peripatetic philosopher will reject such stories. Origen also argues that the miracles of Jesus and the apostles were

---

20-22; 16,17-23 WEIHRICH) and Contra Faustum 12.45 (CSEL 25.1, 374 ZYCHA). On the issue see Courcelle, Anti-Christian Arguments, 153.

[75] LODS (Les Sources, 31) calls attention to Justin, Dial. 102.3 (245,16-17 MARC.) as a possible source of this objection.

[76] See § 3.23 and § 3.30 below.

[77] GALLAGHER (Divine Man, 76) refers to a possible context of Origen's remarks in 1.42: In his eleventh oration, Dio argues against the historical accuracy of the Homeric poems. The reference is by R. M. GRANT, The Earliest Lives of Jesus, New York 1961, 71. Was Dio serious about doubting the existence of the Trojan war?

instrumental in attracting hearers to the Christian movement[78]. In a treatment of
the christianization of the Roman empire, Ramsay MacMullen comments on
claims similar to those which Origen makes that "So-and-so believed such-and-
such, because he saw":

> ...our testimonies adduced are all reasonably close to contemporary. It might, of course,
> all be discounted on the grounds that the laws of nature could never have been really
> suspended, first, and, second, that no sane or candid person could ever have thought so.
> Therefore the true explanations remain to be sought among probabilities as they are seen
> in better-known situations. But, even if that first objection is sustained, the second still
> confronts overwhelming difficulties: for, beyond dispute, inhabitants of the empire by and
> large took it for granted that the laws of nature had always been and always would be
> continually suspended.[79]

Origen's answer to a philosopher who would not accept the possibility of
miracle is quite simple (1.46 [96,13-15 Koet.]): "If we should ourselves write
of them although having been present and having seen them (παρατυχόντες
καὶ ἰδόντες), we will incur a great deal of laughter among the unbelievers
who think that we have made them up like the others who as they suppose have
already fabricated stories (πλάσσειν)." Even the account of an eyewitness to
an "actual" miracle would be unpersuasive to a person unwilling to consider the
possibility of miracle on philosophical presuppositions.

Celsus attacks the narrative (baptism or transfiguration, Mt. 3:17, 17:5) from
another point of view by constructing the following dilemma: "If he wanted to
escape notice why was the voice from heaven heard proclaiming him to be son
of God? If, however, he did not want to escape notice why was he punished,
or why did he die?" (2.72 [194,1-3 Koet.]). Origen responds by remarking
that the texts do not say that the crowds heard the voice from heaven at the
baptism, and only three heard the voice in the transfiguration story. Origen has
a version of a messianic secret : "he did not want everything about himself to
be known by all who were present by chance, nor did he want all things
concerning himself to escape notice" (2.72 [194,4-9 Koet.]). Celsus' dilemma
is a favorite technique of Porphyry[80]. Origen chooses to slip between the
horns of the dilemma.

---

[78] 1.43, 46 (93,11; 96,1-4 KOET.). The author's Protreptic Power, 128 n. 35 includes
the following note: "RAMSEY MACMULLEN reviews testimonies of people believing
because they had seen miraculous events (Christianizing the Roman Empire (A.D. 100—
400), New Haven 1984, 62-63). He gives many instances of Christian persuasion through
exorcism, healing, and other strange deeds with reference to figures such as Gregory the
Wonderworker (MACMULLEN, Christianizing, 22, 26-29, 59ff). MACMULLEN also gives
instances of conversion in paganism through wondrous deeds (Christianizing, 123 n. 10).
Compare idem, Two Types of Conversion to Early Christianity, VigChr 37, 1983, 187 where
MACMULLEN remarks that the church grew in historically significant numbers through
demonstrations of miraculous power."

[79] MACMULLEN, Christianizing, 62-3.

[80] See § 2.3.26 and § 2.3.32 below.

1.2.7 Jesus' Ministry and Disciples

Celsus accepts the designation of Jesus as a person from Nazareth (7.18 [169,18 Koet.] Ναζωραῖος) and gives a bare minimum of comments on the narrative about Jesus' ministry in the gospels. He assumes that Jesus was a carpenter (6.34 [103,22 Koet.]) as does Justin (Dial. 88.8 [224,40-42 Marc.])[81]. Jesus was "small and ugly and ignoble (μικρὸν καὶ δυσειδὲς καὶ ἀγεννές)" (6.75 [144,21-22 Koet.])[82]. He reserves his greatest scorn for the passion, resurrection, and incarnation. Celsus (in his Jewish persona) sums up Jesus' ministry with the following withering critique in reference to Herod's slaughter of the innocents which he carried out, "lest you should reign instead of him after you were grown. Why then when you were grown did you not reign? But you, child (παῖς) of God, ignobly beg in this manner, poking about in fear and wandering up and down in ruin" (1.61 [112,25-30 Koet.]). This comment indicates that Celsus was aware of some of the social characteristics of the portrayal of Jesus and his disciples in the gospels (e.g. carrying no food or money as in Mt 10:9-11). "Evangelical poverty" was unimpressive to Celsus. The title "king" for such an impoverished individual is ridiculous to Celsus. Jesus never became a "king" in the sense of the word that Celsus takes for granted.

Jesus the fearful wanderer did more than beg: "Jesus, choosing ten or eleven infamous people for himself, the most evil tax collectors and sailors, ran away here and there shamefully and with difficulty collecting food" (1.62 [113,7-10 Koet.])[83]. Later Celsus repeats the same charge: "While present he caught only ten ruined sailors and tax collectors and not even all of them" (2.46 [168,14-15 Koet.]). There are at least ten wicked examples of tax collectors and sailors in the Greco-Roman world, according to Celsus. Origen comments that Celsus does not appear to have read the gospels, since he gets the number of disciples wrong (1.62 [113,11-13 Koet.]). Celsus may have excluded Judas and Peter from the "ten" since they betrayed or denied Jesus. The sailors, according to Origen, probably include James and John — he prefers to call Peter and Andrew fishermen as in Mt 4:18-22. Unless the tradition was mediated to Celsus through a Jewish informant, his reading of Matthew was cursory at best — not like Porphyry's careful and scholarly reading. Carl Andresen makes the point that sailors were occasionally maligned in the ancient world[84]. Celsus has no respect for them. Origen notes that Celsus did believe

---

[81] Compare BORRET V.185.

[82] In Justin, Dial. 88.8 (224,39-41 MARC.) Jesus is without form (ἀειδής) and made ploughs and yokes. Clem. Al., Paed. 3.1.3.3 (SC 158, 17 MONDÉSERT/MATRAY) states that the "Lord was uncomely in aspect" although he had true beauty.

[83] Compare 1.63 (115,14-15 KOET.). This may explain Celsus' reference to Jesus' life as the service of a slave (7.17 [168,13 KOET.]).

[84] ANDRESEN, Logos, 233 n.19 with reference to the figure (Hierocles) in Lact., Div. inst. 5.2.17 who scorns the occupation of fishermen and with reference to Plutarch, De tuenda

the gospels were correct in their portrayal of the disciples as lacking even a primary education (τὰ πρῶτα γράμματα) and as lacking learning (ἰδιωτείας)[85]. He censures Celsus for not trying to discover the gospels' persuasive power (δύναμις πειστική). He quotes 1 Cor 2:4-5 and Ps 67:12-13 LXX "The Lord will give the word to those who proclaim the gospel with great power" (Κύριος δώσει ῥῆμα τοῖς εὐαγγελιζομένοις δυνάμει πολλῇ). If Jesus had chosen people who were wise in the crowds' eyes and skilled in rhetorical arts (ῥητορικὰς τέχνας) as a means of spreading his teaching, then he would have been suspected of using a method similar to those philosophers who were leaders of a school (αἱρέσεως)[86]. The (wandering?) philosophers of the Greco-Roman world were at least not uneducated in Origen's eyes. Origen (1.65 [118,12-17 Koet.]) compares Jesus' wandering with Aristotle's decision to leave Athens when he was about to be charged with impiety: "Let us leave Athens lest we give the Athenians a pretext to bear guilt a second time (like they bore because of Socrates) and less they act impiously against philosophy a second time."[87] He can find no portrayal of Jesus begging in the gospels, but does point out Susanna's support of Jesus (1.65 [118,22-25 Koet.], Lk 8:2-5). A philosopher, according to Origen, gets money for his needs from his pupils.

1.2.8 The Miracles of Jesus

Celsus recounts few narratives from the gospels. As mentioned above (§ 1.2.5), he portrays Jesus as an adept of Egyptian magic. He accepts the reality of some of the miracle stories, but gives them an alternative explanation (1.68 [121,31-122,16 Koet.] with Origen's words in brackets):

> [they have written about] healings, resurrection [Mt 9:23-26 par], a few loaves [Mt 14:13-21 par, Mt 15:32-39 par] feeding many (from which many pieces remained), and whatever other things the miracle-mongering (τερατευσαμένους) [he thinks] disciples have told. [And he adds:] Come, let us believe that these things were done by you. [And he straightaway sees things in common with] the works of magicians who promise to do even more marvelous things (θαυμασιώτερα) and with the things done by those who have studied with the Egyptians — in the middle of the agoras for a few obols they divulge solemn doctrines, drive out demons from people, blow off illnesses, call up the souls of

---

sanit. 25 (Moralia 136c) on harbor stays of sailors (see Hierocles in § 4.7 below). On tax collectors, ANDRESEN refers to Lucian, Nekyomant. 11. See O. MICHEL, τελώνης, TDNT VIII, 1972, 8-105.

[85] See ANDRESEN, Logos, 12.

[86] 1.62 (114,10-24 KOET.) On schools of philosophy see J. HAHN, Der Philosoph und die Gesellschaft: Selbstverständnis, öffentliches Auftreten und populäre Erwartungen in der hohen Kaiserzeit, Heidelberger althistorische Beiträge und epigraphische Studien Bd. 7, Stuttgart 1989.

[87] CHADWICK, Origen, 60 n.3 refers to Aelian, Var. Hist. 3.36, Vita Arist. 19 (I. DÜRING, Aristotle in the Ancient Biographical Tradition, Studia Graeca et Latina Gothoborgensia 5, Göteborg 1957, 134); Diog. Laert. 5.5, and Seneca, De otio 8.1.

heroes, and exhibit expensive meals, tables, pastries, dishes that do not exist, and make objects move like living things that are not alive, but which seem so as far as appearance goes. [And he says] since they do these things, is it necessary that we think them to be sons of God or should one say that they are practices of evil people possessed by evil spirits?[88]

His unfavorable comparison with the magicians Celsus has seen at work in the marketplaces empowers his conclusion: Since these people do such things, is it necessary that we consider them to be sons of God? Celsus' Jew adopts the tradition of Jesus as a magician that also appears in the later rabbinic literature. J. Lauterbach conjectures that it may go back to the Pharisees' charge that Jesus casts out demons by Beelzebul (Mt 12:24 and 9:34)[89]. Celsus himself was more open to the miracles of Hellenistic tradition as in the case of Asclepius[90].

Celsus also comments on the miracles of Jesus in one of his characteristic attacks on the belief in Jesus as son of God (2.48 [169,16-19 Koet.]): "[we] believed him to be son of God for this reason — since he healed the lame[91] and the blind[92]. [He adds this:] As you say he raised the dead." Origen responds by quoting Is 35:5-6 and affirms that Jesus did raise the dead mentioning Lk 7:11-17, 8:52 and John 11:38-44. He admits that Christians do regard the miracles as a reason for viewing Jesus as Christ and son of God. People with an open mind (εὐγνωμονεστέροις) and particularly Jews who are aware of the miracles of Elijah and Elisha will be open to the reality of Jesus' miracles (2.48 [169,21-170,8 Koet.]).

Celsus regards the argument as foolish, given his theory that Jesus was a wicked magician — any magician on the street could claim to be son of God given what he considers to be the Christians' miserable argument (i.e. Jesus' miracles prove that he is son of God):

Light and Truth! He expressly declares with his voice, as also you have written, that others will come to you using similar powers, bad people and magicians, and he names a certain Satan as contriving these things. Therefore not even he denies that these works are not in the least divine, but are the works of evil people. Being forced by the truth he both revealed the works of others and exposed his own. How, therefore, is it not a wretched

---

[88] See PGM I.96, 105-106, 120-23 (I, 8 PREISENDANZ) on familiar spirits, magical preparation of meals, and travel over air and sea.

[89] J. Z. LAUTERBACH, Jesus, 526. See the § 1.2.5 above on Jesus' magical activities in Egypt according to rabbinic tradition. FÉDOU, Christianisme, 396-419 examines the issue of magic and miracle in the Contra Celsum. LODS (Les Sources, 13) calls attention to similar Jewish charges in Justin, Dial. 69.7 (191,40-41 MARC.), Ps. Clement, Recog. 1.58.1 (GCS Die Pseudoklementinen II, 41,11 REHM/PASCHKE), and Ev. Nicod. (Descensus Christi ad Inf.) 12, 13 (410; 414 TISCHENDORF).

[90] 3.24 [220,13-17 KOET.]. Compare ANDRESEN, Logos, 47 who refers to the texts in 3.22-33 [218-229 KOET.]. Such openness on Celsus' part to Hellenistic miracles is in accord with ANDRESEN's view that anything in Greek tradition is better than Christian tradition.

[91] Mt 11:5 par.

[92] Mt 20:29-34 par, Mt 11:5 par.

inference (σχέτλιον) to conclude from the same works that one is a god and the others are magicians? Why must one think on the basis of the same deeds that the others are evil rather than this person — using Jesus himself as witness (μάρτυρι)? As he himself confessed, these are works not of a divine nature but are signs (γνωρίσματα) of certain deceivers and depraved individuals (2.49 [171,17-29 Koet.]).

Origen mentions Mt 24:23-27 and Mt 7:22-23 in his introduction to this fragment and notes that Celsus misrepresents the texts because he does not say that Christ is warning his disciples against those who claim to be Christ (Mt 24:23-27) and do miracles in the name of Jesus (Mt 7:22-23). The divine power in those texts comes from Christ, according to Origen (2.49 [171,4-15; 172,10-15 Koet.]). He may be setting up a straw man to argue against, however, because in 2.50 (172,16-173,4 Koet.) he quotes 2 Th 2:1-12 where it is actually a question of an Antichrist figure doing signs and lying wonders by the power of Satan and not the power of Christ. Origen correctly notes that Jesus does not say in the gospels that "others will come to you using similar powers, bad people and magicians." He affirms that the antichrist's miracles are "lying" and different in character than the wonders of Christ and the disciples that bear fruit not in deceit ("by all deceit of unrighteousness" 2 Th 2:10), but in the salvation of souls (2.50 [173,8-18 Koet.]). Origen considers that Jesus did say "one Satan will devise this", but charges that Celsus begs the question (συναρπάζει τὸν λόγον) because he combines miracles done by God and those done by sorcery. If Celsus believes in evil miracles, then he should believe in the existence of good miracles (2.51 [173,20-174,5 Koet.])[93]. As a matter of fact, the "real" Celsus (not Celsus the "Jewish impersonator") did believe in good miracles if Asclepius (and not Christ) was the god in question. Celsus claims that many people have seen Asclepius who heals and does good and predicts the future (3.24 [220,13-17 Koet.]). One philosopher who claimed to have seen Asclepius was Maximus of Tyre: "I have seen Asclepius, not in a dream (ὄναρ); I have also seen Hercules — in a real appearance (ὕπαρ)."[94] Finally Origen argues (2.51 [174,14-17 Koet.]) that if one agrees to the existence of magic done by the power of demons, one should consider the magicians' "life and character (ἤθους) and those things that follow in consequence of their works of power (τῶν ἀπακολουθούντων ταῖς δυνάμεσιν) — whether they result in harm to people or improvement of their characters (ἠθῶν ἐπανόρθωσιν)." Origen's argument is a version of the

---

[93] CHADWICK points to a Stoic commonplace in which opposites imply one another (Origen, 106 n.1) with reference to SVF 2.1169, 1181 and Philo, De aetern. mundi 104.

[94] Diss. 9.7 (76,178-79 TR.). LSJ s.v. ὕπαρ list a number of examples of this opposition including Homer, Od. 19.547. Maximus uses the same pair to describe other appearances of the gods (8.6 [66,129-30 TR.]). Demons appear to mortals and heal them, reveal unseen things, and are responsible for many other activities (8.8 [69,196-205 TR.]).

argument from consequence defined by Aristotle that became very important in the arguments of Christians and pagans[95].

1.2.9 The Miracles of Christians

Celsus uses the same argument against the miracles of later Christians. He charges (1.6 [59,8-10 Koet.]) that "Christians are powerful because of the names and invocations of certain demons." Christians (6.14 [84,25-28 Koet.]) are magicians who "urgently avoid people of taste (χαριεστέρους) because they are not ready to be deceived, and we entrap countrified individuals (ἀγροικοτέρους)." Celsus claims to have a first hand knowledge of Christian magicians (6.40 [109,14-18 Koet.]), because he "has seen books in the possession of certain priests (πρεσβυτέρους) of our belief that contain the barbarian names of demons and miracle recipes (τερατείας)." A certain Dionysus (6.41 [109,24-29 Koet.]) told him that magical arts were only effective with uneducated and depraved people, and not effective on those who had studied philosophy. He claims that Christians know this magical technique (8.37 [252,14-16 Koet.]): "If they name them in a foreign language, they will have power, but if in Greek or Latin, they will have none." Origen simply denies the charges (6.40 [109,13-22 Koet.]). However, as the sources of nearly illiterate Christian people show, there were individuals in late antiquity who practiced Christianity and magic with equal verve[96]. Celsus' charges were on the mark in their case.

1.2.10 Satan and Jesus

Celsus' Jew accepts the reality of Satan. The "pagan" Celsus despises the concept. It is impious to divide the "kingdom of God" between a good and an evil power (8.11 [228,19-22 Koet.])[97]. He charges the Christians with blasphemy with regard to their concept of a "Satan" (6.42 [110,20-111,8 Koet.]):

> They are wrong in the most impious ways — also in respect to this great piece of ignorance which in a like manner is mistakenly derived from the divine enigmas (αἰνιγμάτων), when they make an opponent to God, calling him "slanderer" (διάβολον) and in the Hebrew language "Satan." Above all, these are utterly mortal ideas, and it is not holy to say that the greatest God, wanting to help human beings in some way, has one who acts against him and is powerless. The child (παῖς) of God, overcome by the slanderer and punished by him, teaches us to scorn the punishments that he (Satan) inflicts. He declares beforehand that Satan himself will likewise appear and show great and amazing deeds making God's glory his own. We should not be nourished by them and

---

[95] See Julian in § 5.2.26 and COOK, Protreptic Power, 111-13.

[96] See COOK, In Defense of Ambiguity: Is There a Hidden Demon in Mark 1:29?, NTS 43, 1997, 198-203.

[97] FREDE, Celsus, 5205 discusses Celsus' rejection of metaphysical dualism. See E. PAGELS' discussion in: The Origin of Satan, New York 1995, 138-46.

turn away to that being, but believe in him only. These are outright statements of an individual who is a magician, who is making a profit and guarding himself against those of contrary opinion and against those who are his competitors in begging.

Celsus is more open to a sort of "divine war" in heaven when the source is Greek mythology and philosophy (Heraclitus, Pherecydes, Zeus versus Vulcan)[98]. His alternative picture of the universe and a heavenly struggle anticipate Porphyry's objection to the picture of Christ versus Satan using his alternative of Achilles versus Hector[99]. Celsus' long fragment on the meaning of the Greek mysteries of a divine conflict concludes with this attack on Christ (6.42 [113,7-11 Koet.]): "The son of God's punishment by the slanderer teaches us that when we are punished by him we ought to persevere. All these things are laughable. I think he should have punished the slanderer (διάβολον) and not threaten the people who had been slandered by him (τοῖς ὑπ' αὐτοῦ διαβεβλημένοις ἀνθρώποις ἀπειλεῖν)." Celsus may have been thinking about Jesus' attacks on the scribes and Pharisees (Mt 23:13-29) whom he had "slandered" or attacked[100]. Celsus apparently conceives of Jesus' death as a punishment by Satan. In any case the entire character of Satan is useless and blasphemous in Celsus' eyes. Celsus' Jew does find it useful, however, in creating a logical problem for Christians who believe that Satan and Jesus perform miracles.

1.2.11 Jesus' Body

Celsus' Jew is offended by the entire quality of Jesus' life and ministry (1.69, 70 [123,10.20; 124,5.14 Koet.]): "... the body of a God would not be of such a kind as yours ... The body of a God would not have been begotten as you Jesus were begotten ... the body of a god does not eat such things ... the body of a god does not use such a voice or such a form of persuasion (πειθοῖ)." In 7.13 (165,1-2 Koet.) Celsus accuses Jesus of eating dung (σκατοφαγεῖν) because he ate sheep and drank vinegar and gall[101]. Jesus' body, food, voice,

---

[98] 6.42 (111,8-113,5 KOET.). Celsus also believes in fallen demons; see ANDRESEN, Logos, 62. On Celsus' view of "Satan" as a Christian error see ANDRESEN, Logos, 163.

[99] See Didymus' fragment in § 2.3.42.

[100] Compare the play on the word "devil" (slanderer) in Macarius' pagan (§ 3.28 below). Celsus' Jew is scandalized by Jesus' threats and woe sayings in 2.76 [196,26-29 KOET.]: "he threatens and reviles with ease whenever he says, 'woe to you' (Mt 23:13-29; Οὐαὶ ὑμῖν) and 'I tell you beforehand' (προλέγω ὑμῖν). For with these words he openly avows that he is unable to persuade (πεῖσαι ἀδυνατεῖ) — which would not happen to a god or prudent person." Celsus may be thinking of Jesus' "amen" sayings such as Mt 21:21. In 4.73 [342,26-28 KOET.] Celsus is also offended that God, furious and angry and with threats (ἀπειλῶν), sends his son to earth.

[101] The scatological imagery could get worse as in b. Gittin 56b, 57a when Onkelos the nephew of Titus raises Jesus [according to the Munich MS; changed to the "sinners of Israel" by the censors] who is being punished in boiling excrement because he mocked (מלעיג) the words of the sages. The text is discussed (but not the punishment) in LAUTERBACH, Jesus,

and method of persuasion were all objectionable. Celsus is really arguing from
Hellenistic presuppositions as the section below on his comparison of Jesus
with Greco-Roman figures will make clear. Origen responds that it was
important that Jesus assume a human body capable of dying (1.69 [123,11-13
Koet.]). Celsus' objections to the virgin birth have been discussed above
(§ 1.2.3). His objections to any sort of incarnation will be discussed below
(§ 1.3.1). Origen also argues that Jesus ate precisely because he had a body.
He even ate in his resurrection body (John 21:13). As to Jesus' voice, Origen
notes that the Pythian and Didymean Apollo used the voices of the Pythian
priestess and the prophetess at Miletus. Origen of course views the power of
Christian discourse as superior to that of the oracles: "It was much better than
this for God to use a voice that created an indescribable kind of persuasion
(ἄφατόν τινα πειθώ) in the hearers because it was expressed with power"
(1.69 [124,12-22 Koet.]). The word Celsus and Origen use for persuasion is
the fundamental goal of the rhetoricians[102]. Presumably Celsus would be more
open to the persuasion effected by the inspired oracles[103].

1.2.12 Jesus' Teaching

Jesus' teaching contradicted that of Moses and was also a corruption of
Plato's teaching according to Celsus. This is an ironic reversal of Justin's
argument that Greek wisdom was dependent on Hebrew tradition (Apol. 1.59,
60 [115,1-116,14 Marc.])[104]. In a discussion of prophecy Celsus makes his
point (7.18 [169,10-27 Koet.]):

> Will they not think deeply about that again? If the prophets of the God of the Jews
> predicted this person to be the child of God, how is it that God through Moses ordains by
> law that they should be rich and have dominion [Deut. 15:6, 28:11-12] and fill the earth
> and slaughter their enemies from the youth up and kill the entire race — which he does
> before the eyes of the Jews, as Moses says. In addition to these, if they do not obey he
> explicitly threatens to do to them what he does to the enemies. But his son, the person
> from Nazareth, ordains contradictory laws saying that one may not come to God who is

---

501-02; he dates the Munich MS to 1343 (p. 481). Justin, Dial. 88.2 (223,9-10 MARC.)
also comments on Jesus' varied nourishment.

[102] Compare Gorgias' definition of rhetoric as the creator of persuasion: πειθοῦς
δημιουργός (Plato, Gorgias 453a). Cicero has a similar definition in De or. 1.31.138
primum oratoris officium esse dicere ad persuadendum accomodate (quoted in LAUSBERG,
Handbuch, § 33). Compare Cic., Brutus 15.59 where the orator's function is to bring about
persuasion — πειθώ, suadam.

[103] See his views on oracles below in § 1.5.2.

[104] Described in general terms by BORRET V.186 n. 3 who summarizes the work of
PÉLAGAUD. BADER, commenting on C. Cels. 6.19 [89,13 KOET.], also refers to Clem. Al.,
Protr. 6.70.1, Paed. 2.1.18 (GCS Clemens Alex. I, 53,10 and 166,23 STÄHLIN/TREU), and
Strom 1.1.10 and 1.22.150 (GCS Clemens Alex. II, 8,5; 93,10 STÄHLIN/FRÜCHTEL). Jos.,
C. Ap. 2.257 claims Plato followed Mosaic legislation.

wealthy [Mt 19:24 par] or likes to rule or seek after wisdom [Mt 11:25 par] (σοφίας)[105] or glory [Mt 20:25-27 par] (δόξης), and one must not be more anxious about food and storehouse than the ravens and should be even less anxious about clothing than the lilies [Mt 6:26-9 par], and to a person who hits one must submit oneself again to be hit [Mt 5:39].[106] Which of the two is lying, Moses or Jesus? Or did the father when he sent this one forget what he had commanded Moses? Or condemning his own laws, did he change his mind and send his messenger (ἄγγελος) with a contrary design?

Andresen notes Celsus' attempt to find an inner contradiction in the God of his opponents[107]. Origen attempts to respond to Celsus by arguing that the OT teaching about God's promise of material blessing for Israel (as in Deut 15:6, 28:12) cannot be taken literally since the righteous did occasionally live in extreme poverty (Heb 11:37-8; 7.18 [170,1-13 Koet.]). Celsus' attempt to find contradictions between the Mosaic laws and those of Jesus anticipates Julian's attack on the Galilaeans[108]. More importantly, Celsus finds that Jesus' teachings have already been enunciated earlier by Plato:

> They have this command: not to defend oneself (ἀμύνεσθαι) against one who mistreats you. If one strikes you on the cheek, he says, offer the other also [Luke 6:28, Mt 5:39]. This is ancient and has been better said before. They have recalled it in a more countrified (ἀγροικότερον) form. For Socrates is made by Plato to say these things in the *Crito* ...

Celsus goes on to quote Plato's text in *Crito* 49b-e in which Socrates counsels Crito to "do no damage in return (ἀντικακουργεῖν) even when one suffers (πάσχοντα) grievously." Celsus concludes that "...these things were taught even earlier by inspired men (θείοις ἀνδράσι δεδογμένα). But on this point, like the other teachings that they corrupt, what has been said is enough. Whoever wants to find more of these examples will know how" (7.58 [207,10-

---

[105] This issue is also reflected in Celsus' objection that Jesus taught (7.23 [175,8-9 KOET.]) that a wise person cannot "come to the Father." In 6.12 [82,12-29 KOET.] Celsus argues that the principle that the wisdom of people is foolishness with God (1 Cor 3:19) is actually a Greek idea. He quotes Heraclitus: "Human character does not have thoughts, but the divine has"; and "Childish one! A man hears that from a genius (δαίμονος) just as a child hears it from a man" (F. 78, 79 DIELS). Plato's Apol. 20d also has a similar thought according to Celsus: "For me, Athenians, it is due to nothing other than wisdom that I have this name. Of what kind is this wisdom? It is probably a human wisdom. For, really, there is a chance that I am wise with this wisdom."

[106] CHADWICK hypothesizes that Celsus is drawing upon Marcionite sources, as Origen seems to imply in 7.25 with regard to the person who strikes one on the cheek (Origen, 409 n. 7).

[107] ANDRESEN, Logos, 101.

[108] For Julian see § 5.2.9, 5.2.30.1 and § 5.2.17 and see the anonymous pagan of Macarius on the teaching about wealth in § 3.15 below. Ambrosiaster records an anonymous objection to the fact that God takes an oath in Gen 22:16 while Jesus prohibits oaths in Mt 5:34-36 in Ambrosiaster, Quaestiones de Vet. Test. 47 (CSEL 50, 427,1-4 SOUTER) = RINALDI, Biblia Gentium, F. 99.

208,8 Koet.]). Celsus is unimpressed by Christian ethics[109]. Maximus also believed that one should not repay evil with evil in a lecture devoted to the topic (Εἰ τὸν ἀδικήσαντα ἀνταδικητέον). He also used as an example Socrates' refusal to take revenge[110]. Origen responds simply that the Jews were earlier than the Greeks. And the poorer style and simpler language of the Jews and Christians, though not equal to the beauty of Greek style, is of more benefit to the majority of people (7.59 [208,17-209,15 Koet.])[111].

Celsus also attacked the teaching on wealth using a similar argument (6.16 [86,12-18 Koet.]):[112]

> Jesus' exclusion of the rich, "It is easier for a camel to go through the eye of a needle than for a rich person to enter the kingdom of God," [Mt 19:24, Mark 10:25, Luke 18:25] [he says] was openly taken from Plato. Jesus corrupted the Platonic teaching, where Plato said "For one who is exceptionally good, it is impossible to be exceptionally rich."[113]

Origen finds it incredible that Jesus (who had not read Greek or Hebrew writings [John 7:15]) could have read Plato. He also argues that if Celsus had read the gospels without "hatred and enmity" he could have considered that the camel, a naturally crooked animal, is like a rich person (6.16 [86,22-87,4 Koet.]).

The next fragment that Origen summarizes is an attack on Jesus' teaching of the kingdom of God that apparently used the same line of argument (6.17 [87,17-23 Koet.]): "[Since he wanted next to cheapen things written among us about] the kingdom of God [he presented none of these as if not worthy of his record and perhaps since he didn't know them. He sets forth] words of Plato from the Epistles and the Phaedrus [as] inspired sayings" (ἐνθέως εἰρημένων)[114]. Origen responds (6.17 [87,26-28 Koet.]) by noting that Plato polluted his religion by what the Christians called "idolatry" or in popular language "superstition" (δεισιδαιμονία). It is difficult to know exactly what Celsus meant by "kingdom of God," but it is clear that he thought the story of Mary being turned out by her husband because of adultery had nothing to do with God's kingdom (1.39 [90,19 Koet.]). The Christian desire to split God's kingdom between a good and an evil power was blasphemous in Celsus' eyes (8.11 [228,20 Koet.]). The Christian proclivity for inviting all kinds of wretches with these words was repellent to Celsus: "Whoever is a sinner, whoever is witless, whoever is a little child, and to say it simply, whoever is

---

[109] Christian humility (6.15 [85,9-15 KOET.]) and the ideal of poverty (6.16 [86,12-18 KOET.]) are both misunderstandings of Platonic philosophy (see ANDRESEN, Logos, 70, 156, 300).

[110] 12.8 (100, app. crit.; 106,143-47 TR.).

[111] On simple style in Christian *elocutio* see COOK, Protreptic Power, 121.

[112] See ANDRESEN, Logos, 355.

[113] Plato, Laws 743a.

[114] On Celsus' view that Christian teaching (such as the kingdom of God) is a degeneration of similar themes in Hellenistic culture see ANDRESEN, Logos, 160.

ill-starred (κακοδαίμων), the kingdom of God will receive that person."[115] It is apparent Celsus believed that those who are pure should be invited into God's kingdom and that those who summoned people into the Hellenistic mysteries did exactly that (3.59 [253,24-32 Koet.]). Whatever Celsus meant by the expression "kingdom of God" he found nothing meaningful in the NT discussion of the category.

Celsus does make one comment on Jesus' predilection for inviting sinners (2.71 [193,13-28 Koet.]): "[Jesus taught us] who it was who sent him ... But the reasons for which the Father sent him are [in the thousands] ... and he will lead those who live reverently to the light, and those who sin or who change their mind he will have mercy on (τοὺς δὲ ἁμαρτάνοντας ἢ μεταγνόντας ἐλεήσων)." Origen responds that Jesus enlightens the pious, but punishes sinners (2.71 [193,25-26 Koet.]). It is not clear what gospel traditions Celsus is thinking of. They could include parables such as Mt 20:1-16 or stories about Jesus' meal partners such as Mt 9:9-13. Celsus' scandalized response to the wretches that the Christians invited into the kingdom indicates that his problem with Jesus' proclamation of grace was probably along the same lines.

To summarize the teaching of Jesus, Celsus (1.26 [77,28-78,1 Koet.]) mentions him as "the leader [in the creation of our identity as Christians, and he says] that a very few years ago[116] he established this teaching and is believed by the Christians to be the son of God." Origen then describes the changes for the better in the lives of converts to the message (προσερχομένων αὐτοῦ τῷ λόγῳ) of Jesus. He compares this change with Celsus' analysis: "[As Celsus and those who think the same things he does say] they were led astray and have accepted a teaching (λόγον) that damages [as they say] human life" (1.26 [78,19-24 Koet.]). Origen's and Celsus' response to Jesus' teaching in this instance is to engage in an argument from consequence: what are the practical results in people's lives of adopting the teaching of Jesus. For Celsus the results are clear: they are harmful to human life. An example of a harmful doctrine adopted by Christians who accept the teaching that a person cannot serve two masters is the condemnation of polytheism which Celsus defends passionately arguing that if divine (and earthly authorities) are not properly respected they can become harmful to human beings. While he does not identify the principle that one cannot serve two masters as coming from the teaching of Jesus, he was probably aware of it as a gospel tradition (Mt 6:24,

---

[115] Celsus' response to early Christian proclamation will be discussed below in § 1.6.2, 1.6.3.

[116] Celsus also emphasizes the recent (and not ancient) nature of Jesus' appearance when his Jew states that "It is yesterday or the day before when we punished the one who led you like a flock, that you abandoned your ancestral law (2.4 [130,21-23 KOET.])." BADER, 51 refers to other texts that emphasized the newness and corruption of Christianity such as Suet., Nero 16.

Lk 16:13)[117]. Celsus summarizes Jesus' teaching as "false pretension" and claims "Jesus lied about great things." Celsus' Jew, in the same text, speaks of Jesus' "unholy" (τὰ ἀνόσια) actions (2.7 [132,32; 133,8.11 Koet.]). It is not clear which actions or teachings in particular are in question. One can assume it is the entire ministry. Origen (2.7 [133,13 Koet.]) assumes Celsus meant Jesus' abandoning literal Sabbaths, and feasts, and new moons, but in another text (2.6 [132,18-20 Koet.]) Celsus' Jew affirms: "Jesus observed all the Jewish customs including their sacrifices. [Why does he conclude this:] one should not have faith in him as the son of God?" Probably Celsus was thinking of stories such as Mt 12:1-8 where Jesus did not keep the Sabbath as his critics believed he should. In another text Celsus' Jew summarized Jesus' life by saying "he did not prove himself to be pure from all evil deeds" (2.41 [164,24 Koet.]). What evils in particular he is thinking about are unclear. He also asserts (2.42 [165,7 Koet.]) that "Jesus was also not blameless (ἀνεπίλεπτον)." He may be thinking of the teaching of Jesus with its harmful results or Jesus' miserable life of begging and his miserable death. Origen describes this judgment of Celsus on Jesus' impiety and wicked doctrines (μοχθηρὰ δόγματα): "These are the acts of one hated by God and of an evil magician" (1.71 [124,23-25 Koet.]). Jesus' life and teaching earn him a blanket condemnation at the hands of his critic Celsus.

1.2.13 Jesus' Foreknowledge of his Passion

Of all the narratives in the gospels, Jesus' passion and resurrection come under Celsus' closest scrutiny. As a prelude to that critique Celsus' Jew attacks the notion that Jesus had foreknowledge (Mt 16:21, 17:12, 22, 20:18) of his destiny (2.13 [141,19-29 Koet.]): "Even though I have many true things to say concerning what happened to Jesus and not at all like what was written by the disciples of Jesus — those I willingly leave aside ... [He accuses] the disciples of having fabricated (πλασαμένοις) the tale that he knew all that was going to happen to him beforehand and predicted it (προῄδει καὶ προειρήκει)." Origen responds with other examples of Jesus' prophecies that came true in later generations such as Mt 10:18 (2.13 [141,34 Koet.]). Celsus continues the attack (2.15 [144,7-9 Koet.]): "Since even the disciples of Jesus had nothing to cover the notorious fact with, they contrived the notion of saying that he knew all things beforehand." Presumably Celsus is referring to Jesus' very public death. Origen counters that if, as Celsus believes, the disciples were composing fictions (πλάσματα), they would not "have mentioned the denial of Peter or the desertion of Jesus' disciples [Mt 26:31]" (2.15 [144,15-17 Koet.]).

---

[117] Celsus discusses the Christians' use of the principle to condemn polytheism in 7.68 and 8.15 (217,3-11; 232,22 KOET.). His defense of polytheism will be discussed below in § 1.7.2. He notes (8.35 [250,20-21 KOET.]) that divine and earthly authorities who are slighted can become harmful. See ANDRESEN, Logos, 221.

Celsus engages in his characteristic invective in the attack on Jesus' foreknowledge. He classifies Jesus together with unrighteous people and murderers (2.16 [144,24-29; 145,10-12; 146,7-8 Koet.]):

> the disciples wrote such things in apology for what happened to Jesus. [He says] it is like someone who says that somebody is just and then shows the person to be unjust, and while saying someone is holy shows the person to be a killer, and while saying someone is immortal shows him to be dead, adding to all these things that the person happened to have foretold them ... For you did not say that he appeared to impious people to suffer these things, but did not suffer. Rather, you openly confess that he suffered ... Why then is it credible (πιστόν) that he foretold all. How can a dead person be immortal?

Celsus' problems with foreknowledge are bound up with his rejection of the entire concept of "resurrection." Origen (2.16 [145,16-20 Koet.]) responds with some of the Greek stories about the revival of dead people such as Er and Heraclides' story about a lifeless woman who was revived[118]. Celsus' critique at this point is focused on the lack of credible evidence that Jesus made any such predictions.

The entire narrative of Jesus' foreknowledge is incredible to Celsus (2.17 [146,16-29 Koet.]): "What god, or demon, or prudent person who knew beforehand that such things would happen to him, would not (if he could) have avoided them, but instead encountered what he foreknew?" Origen gives several counterexamples including Socrates who knew his future destiny and yet refused to escape and Leonidas the Spartan general who fought at Thermopylae even though he knew he would die in battle: "Let us eat breakfast, for we shall eat supper in Hades" (2.17 [146,19-26 Koet.]).

Celsus attempts to refute the narrative by his knowledge of psychology (2.18 [147,6-8.21 Koet.]): "How, if he foretold both the one who would betray him and the one who would deny him, did they not fear him as God so that the one not betray him (Mt 26:14-16) and the other not deny him (Mt 26:69-75)? ... They betrayed and denied him with no concern for him." Origen counters that if, as God, Jesus foreknew the future they could not have acted otherwise. He also argues that the betrayer and denier acted with concern (2.18 [147,9-12 Koet.]). Celsus continues this attack (2.19 [147,26-34 Koet.]):

> Surely if a person is plotted against and is aware of it, if he should speak of it beforehand to the ones plotting, they will desist and be on guard ... It is not therefore the case that because these things were foretold, they happened — for that is impossible. But since they did take place, the foretelling is shown to be a lie. It is in every way impossible (πάντῃ γὰρ ἀμήχανον) that those who heard beforehand would still betray and deny.

---

[118] Er's story is told by Plato, Resp. 614-21. CHADWICK, Origen, 82 n.2 refers to texts such as Diog. Laert. 8.60, 61, 67 and Pliny N.H. 7.52.175 for Heraclides' story about Empedocles' preservation of a woman who did not breathe for many days.

Origen denies Celsus' sense of historical possibility, and affirms that people have conspired against those who perceived that there was a plot against them. Origen's answer is that since the events happened, it is true that Jesus foretold them (2.19 [147,27-28; 148,2-4 Koet.]).

Celsus indulges in a little philosophy (2.20 [148,9-18 Koet.]):[119]

> Being a god [he says] he foretold these things, and it was certainly necessary that what was foretold came to pass. A god, therefore, led his disciples and prophets — with whom he ate and drank — round and around with the result that they became impious and unholy. Above all he ought to have been a benefactor to all people and especially to those who lived with him. One who shared table with a person would not continue to conspire against him. Would one who feasted with a god have conspired against him? And what is even more absurd (ἀτοπώτερον), God himself conspired against those who were at table with him making them betrayers and ungodly (δυσσεβεῖς) people.

Celsus is willing, for the sake of argument, to assume that it is possible that Jesus foretold the events that came to pass. But the results are patently immoral since Jesus would have been the cause of his disciples' becoming unholy and impious. Origen denies that an event takes place because it was predicted, and argues that the future event is the cause of the prediction. He also assumed, for the sake of example, the oracle to Laius warning him not to beget any children, one of whom will kill him (Euripides, Phoenissae 18-20)[120]. Laius was free to have or not have children, but once he chose to have children, he suffered in consequence (2.20 [148,20-150,9 Koet.]).

Returning to the rhetoric of vituperation (2.44 [166,13-17.24-27 Koet.])[121] Celsus counters the claim that Jesus' foreknew the passion:

> If while inventing absurd (ἀτόπους) defenses, for things by which you have been laughably deceived, you think that you defend yourselves truly, what prevents others who have been condemned and finished with an even unhappier end (κακοδαιμονέστερον) from thinking themselves greater and more divine messengers (than Jesus) ... Any person of the shameless bunch could likewise claim concerning a robber or killer who had been punished that this one was not a robber but a god. For he announced to his fellow robbers that he would suffer these things — which indeed he did suffer.

---

[119] Parts of this fragment are repeated in 2.21, 22 [151,18; 152,6 KOET.]. GALLAGHER summarizes the issue in Divine Man, 120-21.

[120] CHADWICK notes that this was a stock argument in antiquity (Origen, Celsus, and the Stoa, 46 n.2). Arguments about fate and possibility among the Stoics are contained in SVF 2.959-64. Alexander of Aphrodisias examined the statement: "there will be a sea battle tomorrow" with regard to the problem of fate and possibility (SVF 2.961). See also Aristotle's original discussion of the sea battle tomorrow in De int. 9 (18b, 19a). Origen and Celsus are into an old argument over foreknowledge and free will. As will be seen below in § 1.5.2, Celsus did not deny the reality of Greek prophecy.

[121] PICHLER, Streit, 124-25 finds the categories of epideictic rhetoric (praise and blame) to be useful in the evaluation of Celsus' attack on Jesus. He refers to Theon, Progymn. 8 (102-112 SPENGEL) and Hermogenes, Progymn. 7 (14-18 RABE) as examples of encomiastic rhetoric. See the use of this kind of rhetoric in by Porphyry (§ 2.2.3.1, § 2.2.3.3, and § 2.3.38).

Celsus is willing to classify Jesus with any kind of murderer or robber. Eugene Gallagher writes: "Crucifixion does not put Jesus in exclusive company; for Celsus it confirms, as did the facts of his lowly birth, his base origins and his unworthy character."[122] Death by crucifixion obviously held those connotations for an intelligent pagan such as Celsus. Origen is of course scandalized by the comparison, and argued that Jesus did not deserve to be put to death, nor did those genuine disciples who followed him to death for the sake of their faith (2.44 [167,10-14 Koet.]).

1.2.14 The Betrayal by the Disciples

Celsus asserts that the passion of Jesus was the result of his disciples' betrayal and of Jewish activity. According to Celsus, Jesus "was handed over by those whom he named to be disciples." Celsus called Judas "many disciples" according to Origen (2.11 [138,26 Koet.]). Origen, in Chadwick's words, denies the "total depravity of Judas" with reference to Mt 27:3-5 and other texts[123]. Origen also sees the event prophesied in Ps 108 (2.11 [140,1-5 Koet.]). Celsus finds it incredible that Jesus could have been betrayed by his disciples (2.12 [140,17-23 Koet.]):

> A good commander who led tens of thousands was never betrayed (προυδόθη), nor was an evil robber-leader and ruler of utterly evil individuals — while he seemed useful to his companions. But he was betrayed by those under him and did not lead like a good commander, nor after he had deceived his disciples did he create among those whom he deceived the kind of good will (εὔνοιαν) — as I may call it — that a robber-leader does.

Origen (2.12 [140,29-141,2 Koet.]) responds by pointing to Plato whose student Aristotle deserted him after twenty years of listening, criticized "the doctrine of the immortality of the soul, and called the Platonic Ideas 'twitterings' (τερετίσματα)"[124].

1.2.15 The Denial (Mt 26:69-75 par)

The fact that Jesus' disciples were unwilling to die with him was objectionable to Celsus who contrasted their attitude with those of contemporary Christians in Celsus' own time (2.45 [167,16-21 Koet.]): "Then those who were with him while he was alive, who heard his voice and had him as teacher, when they saw him punished and dying, they did not die with him or for him nor were they persuaded to look down on punishments. But they denied being his disciples. Now, however, you die with him." Origen notes that Celsus is silent about the disciples' reformation when in the end they finally died for Jesus' teaching. He

---

[122] Divine Man, 122.

[123] Origen, 76 n. 4 with reference to Comm. ser. in Mat. 117 (GCS Origenes XI, 245-46 KLOSTERMANN).

[124] Atticus was also unimpressed with Aristotle's critique of Plato (Fr. 9 DES PLACES = Eus. P.E. 15.13.1-6)

quotes texts such as John 21:18-19 to support this response (2.45 [167,21-168,1 Koet.]).

1.2.16 Gethsemane and Jesus' Passion

Celsus does not mention any role for the Romans in Jesus' destiny: "as an offender he was punished by the Jews" (2.5 [132,1-2 Koet.])[125]. Celsus' reading of the Gethsemane narrative is in the words of his Jew (2.9 [135,4-14 Koet.]):

> How could we consider him to be God who, among other things (as people heard), did not make a display of any of the things he promised, and when we had proved him guilty, passed sentence on him, and decided he should be punished (Mt 26:57-66), he was taken while hiding and shamefully running away (Mt 26:47-56) — delivered up by those whom he called disciples Mt 26:48-50)? However it was not possible if he were a god either to escape or to be led away bound, and even least of all if he was considered to be a savior, son, and messenger of the greatest God to be abandoned and betrayed by his companions who had intimately shared everything with him and regarded him as teacher.[126]

Origen responds by discussing the Christian charge that the Jews do not believe in Jesus as God (mentioned by Celsus in 2.8 [133,27 Koet.])[127]. He argues that the prophets bear witness to "a God under the God and Father of the Universe" and claims that texts such as Gen 1:3, 6, and 26 are addressed to the Logos (word; 2.9 [135,29-136,6 Koet.]). The entire episode, from the trial to Gethsemane and the crucifixion, is disreputable in Celsus' eyes. In 2.10 (137,28-138,6 Koet.) Origen denies that Jesus was caught against his will and quotes John 18:4-8 to illustrate his argument. Celsus' Jew reverses the narrative (trial before arrest) and emphasizes Jesus' shameful hiding. He again claims that "Jesus hid himself" in 2.70 (192,11-13 Koet.) and continues: "What messenger (ἄγγελος) who has been sent on a mission ever hid himself instead of announcing the things he was commanded to announce?" Origen simply denies that Jesus hid himself given Jesus' response to those who came to arrest him in Mt 26:55 (2.70 [192,14-15 Koet.]).

Celsus attacks the episode from the point of view of philosophy (2.23 [152,11-14 Koet.]): "If these things had been resolved on by him, and if obeying God he was punished, it is evident that because he was a god and willed it, the things done to him according to his wishes were neither painful nor sorrowful to him." Celsus finds this self-evident principle to be contradicted by Jesus' pain (2.24 [153,7-10 Koet.]): "Why does he implore loudly (ποτνιᾶται), and wail (ὀδύραται), and pray to escape the fear of death saying something like, 'Father if this cup could pass by' (Mt 26:39)?" Origen

---

[125] Compare 2.4 (130,22-23 KOET., "it was yesterday or the day before when we had punished him").

[126] Elements of this fragment are repeated in 2.10 [137,17 KOET.].

[127] GALLAGHER discusses Origen's treatment of the composite nature of Jesus (Divine Man, 117-18).

(2.23 [152,14-18 Koet.]) accuses Celsus of contradicting himself (ἐναντία εἰπών) since Celsus granted that Jesus really was punished, and since it is "not possible that the things done by those who punished him should not be painful, for pain is not a matter of free choice." Celsus and Origen are reading the story from different presuppositions. Celsus views Jesus as a Greek god who does not experience pain. Origen views Jesus as capable of all the human feelings. He also asserts (2.24 [153,16-17 Koet.]) that Jesus did not "wail" in the gospels and also that Celsus does not accurately quote the statement in Mt 26:39. Celsus does not finish quoting the text which shows that Jesus was ready to face his own suffering.

Celsus seems to think that it would have been better for the Christians to claim that Jesus only appeared to suffer (2.16 [145,10-12 Koet.]): "For you did not say that he appeared to impious people to suffer these things, but did not suffer; instead you openly confess that he suffered." Celsus' Jew rejects the Christians' theology of the cross (2.38 [163,1-4 Koet.]): "Do you reproach us, you most credulous people (πιστότατοι), because we do not think that this person is god and because we do not agree with you that he endured these things to help humankind, so that we too may scorn punishments?" Interestingly Origen does not attempt to develop a theology of the cross at this point, but he argues that Christians criticize Jewish unbelief because they did not believe the one who showed divine power among the human race, but used Beelzebul to explain Jesus' power (Mt 9:34, 12:24)[128]. Celsus' Jew continues his attack on the passion (2.39 [163,26-27 Koet.]): "During his lifetime he persuaded nobody — not even his disciples — and he was punished and endured such things?" Origen notes that it is incorrect to claim that Jesus did not convince his disciples and gives Peter's tears as an example (Mt 26:75; 2.39 [164,2-7 Koet.]). The bottom line for Celsus' Jew is that Jesus "ought not to have died" (2.40 [164,14 Koet.]). The entire passion is objectionable to Celsus' Jew's concept of the son of God. That concept will be discussed below in his critique of the Christians' use of the argument from prophecy (§ 1.4.2).

1.2.17 The Cross

Celsus does not doubt the narrative of the cross. In a later text in which he discusses the doctrines of Gnostic Christians including their imagery of the tree of life and the resurrection of the flesh by means of the tree, he states that (6.34 [103,21-104,4 Koet.]):

> their teacher was nailed to the cross and by craft was a carpenter. So that if by chance he had been thrown from a cliff, or thrust into an abyss, or strangled by hanging, or if he had been a shoemaker or stonecutter or ironworker, there would have been above the heavens a

---

[128] 2.38 (163,16-19 KOET.). He does develop such a theology in 1.54 and 55 (105,3-106,31 KOET.).

cliff of life, an abyss of resurrection, a rope of immortality, a stone of blessing, an iron of love, or a holy leather. What drunk[129] old woman lulling a child to sleep by singing a fable (μῦθον) would not be ashamed to whisper such stories?[130]

Celsus shows some appreciation for the power of the Christian symbolism surrounding the death of Christ, but he finds it completely worthless.

Celsus also finds the narrative about Jesus' thirst on the cross to be blameworthy. Origen writes that he makes this reproach: "Jesus hastened greedily to drink the vinegar (Mt 27:34, 48) and the gall (χολήν), and could not endure his thirst, as even an ordinary person often endures it." Origen refers to Ps 68:22 and its fulfillment in the narrative (2.37 [162,17-19.22-25 Koet.]). Celsus viewed the consumption of such things as disgusting (7.13 [165,1-2 Koet.]) and is unimpressed by the Christians' use of the story to argue that the Jews are under the wrath of God : "And the Christians add certain reasons to those held by the Jews and say that because of the sins of the Jews, the son of God has already been sent and because the Jews punished Jesus and had him drink gall (χολήν), they brought on themselves the wrath (χόλον) of God." Origen argues that the destruction of the Jewish nation less than one generation after the crucifixion of Jesus is an argument for the Christian interpretation of the Jewish experience of suffering (4.22 [291,18-22.23-25 Koet.]).

In the context of an attempt to discount the resurrection of Jesus, Celsus' Jew includes the following remarks on the passion with reference to several Greek heroes who reappeared after death:

> Or do you think that the accounts of the others both really are myths and appear to be, but that you have invented a noble and persuasive denouement of your tragedy (καταστροφὴν τοῦ δράματος εὐσχημόνως ἢ πιθανῶς) with his cry from the cross when he breathed his last and the earthquake and the darkness (Mt 27:50, 51, 45)? Because when he was alive he didn't help himself (Mt 27:42) ... (2.55 [178,19-23 Koet.).

J. H. Waszink argues that Celsus may be responding to the apology of Aristides (13.7 [21,9-10 Geffcken]) who claimed that if the narratives about the gods were allegories, then they were myths (μῦθοι) and nothing else[131]. The fact that Jesus did not help himself during the crucifixion made a strong impression on Celsus: "[Because Celsus who proclaims that he knows everything about the word, reviles the savior because of his passion since] he was not helped by his Father nor could he help himself ..." Origen argues that Jesus' passion was prophesied by Is 52:13-53:8 (1.54 [105,3-5; 105,7-106,2 Koet.]). It is apparent, however, that Celsus does not doubt some of the extraordinary events that accompanied the death of Jesus. The stories were,

---

[129] KOETSCHAU refers to 6.37 (106,22 KOET.) for this addition.

[130] CHADWICK, Origen, 350 n.1 and 3 gives parallels from Gnostic and patristic texts.

[131] Review of ANDRESEN, VigChr 12, 1958, 176 with reference to Logos und Nomos, 50-51.

however, neither noble or convincing. That is, they did not convince Celsus that Jesus was the son of God.

Celsus mocks Jesus' blood, because it is not like the blood of the gods: "What does he say while his body is being fixed to the cross? Was it (his blood; John 19:34) like 'Ichor such as flows in the blessed gods'?" Celsus may be thinking of the story of the wounded Alexander the Great who remarked that his blood was not ichor[132]. Origen remarks that the narrative in John 19:34-35 that mentions blood from the side of Jesus does not describe the mythical ichor of the Homeric gods (2.36 [161,26-28; 162,2-5 Koet.])[133]. Celsus, in another text, narrates a number of stories of Greek figures who died violent and noble deaths (Heracles, Asclepius, Orpheus) and who said heroic things while suffering violence such as Anaxarchus[134] and Epictetus. He goes on to ask (7.53 [203,23-30 Koet.]):

> What did your god say that was similar while being punished? If you should have proposed the Sibyl,[135] whom some of you use, as the child of God, it would have been more reasonable. But you can only interpolate at random in her verses many blasphemous things, and you present as god he who experienced an infamous life and miserable death. Jonah under the gourd, or Daniel delivered from the beasts, or others with even more amazing actions (τερατωδέστεροι) would have been more suitable for you than Jesus.

Origen (7.54 and 55 [204,1-205,2 Koet.]) responds that Heracles was not always morally upstanding. He also argues that Jesus' silence under the scourge was a manifestation of great courage and patience.

Celsus clarifies what he thought Jesus should have said during his passion (2.33): "What noble action worthy of a god did Jesus do? Did he despise people, or did he laugh and jest about what was happening to him?" Origen notes that Celsus did not accept the reality of texts such as Mt 27:51 that recounted miracles at the death of Jesus. He goes on to quote Phlegon as support for the eclipse in the time of Tiberius Caesar and the earthquake at that time (2.33 [159,26-28; 159,30-160,10 Koet.]).

What Celsus would like to see is the courage and power shown by Bacchus in Euripides' *Bacchae* 498: "'The demon himself will free me when I wish' ... But the one who condemned him suffered nothing like Pentheus who was driven mad and torn apart." Celsus goes on to mention "those who mocked him and clothed him in a purple robe, a crown of thorns, and put a reed in his

---

[132] From Homer, Il. 5.340 (also quoted in 1.66). CHADWICK, Origen, 96 n.1 gives the evidence for the story about Alexander (e.g. Athenaeus 6.57, 251a [II, 60, 15-17 KAIBEL] and Plutarch, Alex. 28.3).

[133] This narrative in John earned the scorn of Macarius' anonymous pagan (§ 3.30 below).

[134] BADER, 189 gives many references to this narrative such as Tert., Apol. 50.6 (170,27-30 DEK.).

[135] CHADWICK, Origen, 440 n.2, refers to similar pagan complaints about Christian forgeries of the oracle.

hand" (2.34 [160,12.25-26; 161,5-7 Koet.]). What he wants to see is clear (2.35 [161,16-18 Koet.]): "Why therefore, if he hadn't done it before, at least then did he not exhibit something divine, save himself from this shame, and avenge himself on those who outraged both him and his Father?" In Euripides' play Pentheus was punished for not honoring Dionysus as a god[136]. Celsus, reading the text of the gospels from this point of view, wants Jesus to at least show some of Dionysus' threatening power. Origen (2.35 [161,19-25 Koet.]) responds that God does not always punish people who insult the deity, and he repeats his reference to the divine sign of the eclipse of the sun. Celsus' Jew wants Jesus to act decisively (2.68 [189,20-22 Koet.]): "If then he was under such an obligation to show his divinity (εἰς ἐπίδειξιν θεότητος), he should have disappeared suddenly far from the cross"[137]. Origen notes that, even though Celsus would have regarded it as fictitious, Jesus did later vanish in one of the gospels' episodes (Lk 24.30-31; 2.68 [189,30-190,3 Koet.]). Jesus would have appeared more like an acceptable Hellenistic hero in Celsus' eyes if he had immediately punished his punishers and had then disappeared.

Celsus' summary of Jesus' passion as being an example of an infamous life and a miserable death is based on his entire experience of Hellenistic culture. The Jesus of the gospels simply does not measure up to the standards for a Greco-Roman hero. His destiny was unworthy of God in the first place. Celsus draws an analogy with the Babylonian king who was angry with the Jews and burned Jerusalem: a man who was angry with the Jews [Nebuchadnezzar] could destroy them all and burn down their city, but "when the greatest God, as they say, is enraged, angry, and threatens, he sends his son, and he (Jesus) suffers such things" (4.73 [342,24-28 Koet.]). The passion narrative is pointless in Celsus' eyes.

1.2.18 The Passion and Jesus' Identity as Son of God

In a discussion of the reasons Christians give for believing in Jesus as son of God, Celsus depicts the Christian argument in this way (6.10 [80,27-31 Koet.]): "'Believe that the one whom I am describing to you is the son of God even though he was most dishonorably bound, most shamefully punished, and even though yesterday and the day before he roamed about disgracefully before all eyes. [Nor do we say] even more reason to believe (πίστευσον).'" Celsus' concept of "son of God" (to be discussed below in § 1.3.1) is incompatible with Jesus' poverty, arrest and death. Origen denies that Christians use this argument in the first place (6.10 [80,31 Koet.]). But is it impossible that none

---

[136] CHADWICK, Origen, 95 n.1. In 8.42 Celsus again emphasizes that those who punished Jesus were not punished (in the context of an argument about whether people who blaspheme the gods [such as Christians] are punished or not).

[137] This anticipated Macarius' pagan who asks why Jesus did not vanish like Apollonius before Domitian (HARNACK, Porphyrius, F. 63) and see § 3.21 below.

of Celsus' conversation partners would have used such a paradoxical form of reasoning? The rhetorical context of the conversation is clear. Celsus makes use of a rhetorically vituperative set of words for dishonorable actions, and the Christian emphasizes his or her desire to persuade the pagan. For Celsus it is impossible to believe that God's son could suffer (7.15 [166,9-10 Koet.]).

Celsus makes a similar point in 2.31 (158,21-25; 159,3 Koet.) when he "[accuses Christians] of using sophistries when they say the son of God is the Logos [word; reason] itself ... although we announce that the Logos is the son of God we present instead of a pure and holy Logos a person who was most dishonorably led away and crucified[138] ... If indeed the Logos is for you the son of God, we also agree ." Celsus is apparently aware of Hellenistic Judaism's belief in the Logos as son of God (Philo, de Agric. 51, de Conf. Ling. 146)[139]. What he cannot accept is a crucified Logos.

1.2.19 The Empty Tomb

Celsus finds it strange that Jesus could not open the tomb (5.52 [56,12-13 Koet.]): "For the child of God, as it appears, could not open the tomb, but needed another to move the rock (Mt 28:2)." Origen responds that it was dignified for the inferior servant to roll away the stone for the one who rose, so that the Logos could convince those that conspired against him that he was not dead but alive. Celsus is aware of the empty tomb in his comparison of Jesus' tomb with that of Zeus on Crete (3.43 [238,21-24 Koet.]): "we mock those who worship Zeus since his tomb is exhibited in Crete, — not knowing how and why they do it — and we nonetheless worship the one who left the tomb"[140]. Origen is happy to use Callimachus' poem against Celsus in which the poet writes: "The Cretans, always liars. For you, O Lord, a tomb they have made. But you didn't die, you exist forever."[141] Origen then complains that Celsus believes the gospels when they state that Jesus died and was buried, but believes that it is a fiction (πλάσμα) when they claim that he rose from the dead (3.43 [239,6-7.20-22 Koet.]).

1.2.20 Jesus in Hades

Celsus may know a tradition (1 Pet 3:19, 4:6) about Jesus preaching in Hades after his death: "You will, doubtless, not say concerning him that having persuaded (πείσας) no one here, he set out for Hades to persuade (πείσων)

---

[138] BORRET translates ἀποτυμπανισθέντα as "beaten with rods" (I.363). See Celsus' other use of the word in 8.54 (271,5-6 KOET.) where it is used in the context of torture. In Jos, C. Ap. 1.149 and Aristot., Rhet. 2.5.14 (1383a) it is an action that leads to death.

[139] CHADWICK, Origen, 93 n. 3. BORRET I.363 n.7 gives further bibliography on the issue. See Justin Apol. 1.63.4-10 (121,9-122,22 MARC.).

[140] See Cic., De nat. deor. 3.21.53 and apologists such as Tert, Apol. 25.7 (136,29-32 DEK.). Many references are in CHADWICK, Origen, 157 n.2, and BADER, 94.

[141] Hymn to Zeus 8-9.

people there." Origen argues that while in the body Jesus "...persuaded so many that the multitude of those persuaded (πειθομένων) by him plotted against him. And his soul, naked without body, talked with souls that were naked without body, and he converted to himself (ἐπιστρέφων) the souls of those who wanted to or whom he saw to be more disposed to do so for reasons that he himself knew" (2.43 [166,4-6.7-11 Koet.])[142]. The words for persuasion and conversion indicate that the discussion between Celsus and the Christians is concerned with joining or not joining the Christian movement.

1.2.21 The Resurrection Narratives

The resurrection is no more convincing to Celsus or Celsus' Jew. He attacks the resurrection based on what he considers to be the inadequate evidence and then, as a Hellenistic philosopher, attacks it conceptually as an impossible event. Celsus' Jew says that the Christian doctrines of resurrection and last judgment are "nothing new." Origen (2.5 [132,6.11-12 Koet.]) responds quoting Mt 21:43 and engages in some virulent rhetoric by claiming that all contemporary Jewish teachings are myths and futile statements (μύθους καὶ λήρους).

Celsus' Jew merges into Celsus the Hellenist in an attempt to completely devalue the resurrection narratives. He asks of his fellow Jews who had become believers: "What reason led you unless it was because he foretold that after he died he would rise?" Origen responds that Moses also foretold his own death (Dt 34:5-6; 2.54 [177,27-28.29-32 Koet.]). But the resurrection itself is inherently doubtful for Celsus (2.55 [178,8-179,4 Koet.]):

> Well, let us believe (you) that he said that. How many others tell amazing stories for the sake of persuading naive hearers and making a profit by their deceit. They say that Zamolxis the slave of Pythagoras is an example of this (among the Scythians) along with Pythagoras himself in Italy and Rhampsinitus in Egypt. This last one played dice in Hades with Demeter and obtained from her a napkin spangled with gold that he brought back as a gift. So also Orpheus among the Odrysians, Protesilaus in Thessaly, Heracles in Taenarum, and Theseus.[143] But one must examine this: whether anyone who truly died ever rose in the same body. Or do you think that the accounts of the others both really are myths (μύθους) and appear to be, but that you have invented a noble and persuasive denouement of your tragedy (καταστροφὴν τοῦ δράματος) with his cry from the cross when he breathed his last and the earthquake and the darkness? Because when he was alive he didn't help himself; dead, he arose, and he showed the signs of his punishment, how his hands had been pierced (John 20:20, 25). Who saw that? A frantic woman (Mt 28:9, John 20:16), as you say, and perhaps another victim of the same bewitchment who either as a consequence of a certain disposition had a dream and according to his desire had an image in his mind due to his mistaken belief, something that has happened to tens of thousands, or, what is more likely, he wanted to amaze others

---

142 Clem Al., Strom. 6.8.64.4 (464,4 S./F.).

143 CHADWICK, Origen, 109 gives references for these stories as do BORRET I.414-15 and BADER, 79.

by this amazing story (τερατείᾳ), and by such a lie to give other beggars an opportunity.[144]

Here Celsus' Jew forgets his identity and become a Hellenist. The figures mentioned mostly had experiences in the land of the dead and lived to tell the tale. Celsus' point is that these apparent myths do not establish a person ever rose again from death with the same body. His psychology of religion provides an acceptable explanation for the Christian belief in the Risen Lord: It was all a hallucination or, what is more probable to Celsus, an intentional lie. Origen quotes a narrative in Ex 20:21 which he takes to be similar to the Greek tales of heroes in the land of the dead (2.55 [179,14-19 Koet.]). He also argues (2.56 [180,5-12 Koet.]) that Jesus' story is not like that of the Greek heroes since Jesus was crucified and publicly put to death. He also notes (2.57 [181,8-11 Koet.]) that Jews would not doubt resurrection stories given the stories in 1 Kings 17:21-22 and 2 Kings 4:34-35. Jesus underwent what he did of his own free will (2.59 [182,18-19 Koet.]) and so did not help himself in the Hellenistic sense (e.g. like Bacchus). Origen calls Celsus' attack on the resurrection appearances Epicurean,[145] and he argues that the Greeks who believe in the immortality of the soul can accept the "shadowy phantoms" (Phaedo 81d, σκιοειδῆ φαντάσματα) of dead people around their tombs[146]. The Christian visions of Jesus did not occur by night but during the daytime. Origen believes that Celsus' view of the visions (as hallucinations) would be more convincing if they had occurred at night (2.60 [182,29; 183,4-8.12-14 Koet.]).

With regard to the story of Thomas (John 20:25), Celsus thinks according to Origen's summary: (2.61 [183,17-19 Koet.]) "After his death ... Jesus emitted an image (φαντασίαν) of his wounds received on the cross, although he didn't truly exist with the wounds"[147]. Origen responds that the narrative was to prove that Jesus had been raised in a body like that which he had before (2.61 [183,24-25 Koet.]), but Origen also thinks (2.62 [184,12-16 Koet.]) that Jesus' risen body was in an intermediate state (μεθορίῳ) between the solidity of his body before the passion and a disembodied soul. This is the case because Jesus came into a secured room (John 20:26-27). Origen believes that the appearances of Jesus were more miraculous than the Hellenistic stories of appearances and visions that Celsus is aware of.

Celsus' Jew is highly critical of the set of people who witnessed Jesus' appearances (2.63 [184,30-185,2 Koet.]): "If Jesus wanted to really manifest

---

[144] LSJ note that this was a word (ἀγύρταις) for the begging priests of Cybele.

[145] See the above discussion of Celsus' alleged Epicureanism in § 1.1.

[146] According to Maximus (Diss. 9.7 [76,174-75 TR.]), for example, Hector appears (φαντάζεται) in the region of Ileum. On the issue of seeing the gods see FOX, Pagans and Christians, 102-67.

[147] Compare Porphyry's problem with the narrative of Jesus' wounds (§ 2.3.32 below).

his divine power, he should have appeared to those who abused him, to the one who condemned him, and in short to everyone." This is one of the only cases in which Celsus makes a possible reference to Pilate, but even here it is not clear. Macarius' pagan was also scandalized that Jesus did not appear to his judges and the Roman Senate[148]. Origen responds (2.67 [188,28-31 Koet.]) that it would not have been right for Jesus to have appeared to those who condemned him because they would have been struck with blindness as the people of Sodom were (Gen 19:10-11). Celsus (2.67 [189,10-12 Koet.]) further argues: "For he assuredly no longer feared anyone because he had died, and as you say, he was a god; and he was not sent principally to remain hidden." Origen answers with a version of the messianic secret (2.67 [189,12-17 Koet.]): "For he was sent not only to be known but also to remain hidden. For everything that he was was not known even by those who knew him, but something about him was hidden from them. To some he was completely unknown. But he opened the gates of light to those who were sons of darkness and night and who consecrated themselves to become sons of the day and the light."[149]

Celsus' Jew finds it very paradoxical that Jesus would preach to all while alive and only appear to a few after death (2.70 [192,18-21; 193,7-8 Koet.]): "When he was in the body he was disbelieved, and he preached freely to all. When he wanted to produce strong faith after he rose from the dead he only appeared in secret to one little woman and to the members of his association (θιασώταις) ... While being punished he was seen by all, but after rising by only one; the opposite should have happened." Celsus' number of those seeing the Risen Jesus varies (from one to all his "association"), but the point is clear. No enemies of Jesus saw him after death. Origen thinks it is impossible and irrational that Jesus would have been seen by one person while being punished and by all after rising (2.70 [193,10-12 Koet.]). This would not answer the force of Celsus' objection. If Jesus had wanted to prove his resurrection, he should have appeared to many. This line of thought is continued by Macarius' anonymous pagan who extends it to the Roman Senate.

Celsus' Jew carries the argument to its obvious conclusion: "he wanted, through the punishments that he suffered, to teach us to scorn death [does not imply that] after he rose from the dead he should have openly called all to the light and taught the reason for which he descended." Jesus had already called all people clearly to the light, according to Origen who appeals to Mt 11:28. The reason he came down is recorded in his parables and the sermon on the mount (2.73 [194,24-27; 194,27-195,1 Koet.]).

---

[148] See § 3.23 below.
[149] CHADWICK, Origen, 118 n. 1 compares these texts to Origen's view of the incarnation concealing and revealing God in 2.72 (194,5-6 KOET.).

No longer in the persona of a Jew, Celsus attacks the notion of Jesus' resurrection as a Hellene in 3.22 (218,10-17 Koet.): He mentions "the Dioscuri, Heracles, Asclepius, and Dionysus, [these people are believed by the Greeks to have become gods. He says that] we cannot bear to consider these to be gods, because they were people, despite the many and noble deeds they have provided humanity with; but we say that Jesus, after his death, appeared to his association (or "religious guild" θιασωτῶν). [He adds to the accusation:] We say he appeared, yes, his shadow (σκίαν)."[150] In 3.42 (238,8-10 Koet.), Celsus also argues concerning Jesus: "But after he put off this body, perhaps he will have become a god? And why not rather Asclepius, Dionysus, and Heracles?"[151] Origen (3.22 [219,5-12 Koet.]) argues that Heracles, Asclepius and the Dioscuri cannot sensibly be regarded as gods given Heracles' licentiousness, Asclepius' death by Zeus' thunderbolt, and the fact that the Dioscuri were gods on alternate days (Homer, Od. 11.303-4). Origen also denies (3.23 [220,3-4 Koet.]) that Jesus appeared as a phantom/shadow.

1.2.22 Appearances by Greek Divinities

Celsus is convinced that Asclepius is a better object of belief (3.24 [220,14-17 Koet.]): "of Asclepius it is said that a great crowd of people, both Greeks and barbarians, agree (ὁμολογεῖ) that it has often seen and still sees him, not as a phantom (φάσμα), but healing and acting beneficently and predicting the things to come." Maximus of Tyre (9.7 [76,178-79 Trapp]) states, for example, that "I saw Asclepius himself, it was not a dream."[152] Asclepius was acceptable in Celsus' eyes because he belonged to the Greco-Roman pantheon. Origen denies that Celsus can show that a great multitude of people believe in

---

[150] ANDRESEN, Logos, 363-64 finds a close parallel in Justin, Apol. 1.21.1-2 (63,1-11 MARC.) who mentions, in this order, Asclepius, Dionysus, Heracles and the Dioscuri. In Apol. 1.21.3 (64,28-30 MARC.) Justin refers to witnesses on oath who saw the ascent of the deified emperors (ἑωρακέναι). Tertullian argues that the gods were originally people (Apol. 10.3 [106,15-16 DEK.]). Compare Min. Fel., Oct. 21.1 (18,30-32 KYT.) who refers to Euhemerus on people accepted as gods.

[151] Earlier in the same text Celsus compared Jesus' flesh to gold, silver, and rock and claimed it was more corruptible than these (3.42 [237,19-21 KOET.]). Celsus in 3.3 and 3.26 (205,11-12; 222,9 KOET.) also mentions Aristeas the Proconnesian, a certain Clazomenian, and Cleomedes the Astypalean as figures who appeared and then disappeared, followed by a miraculous reappearance. Origen recounts the stories of Cleomedes and Aristeas in 3.25 and 26 (221,15; 222,15-224,4 KOET.). Celsus tells the story of Cleomedes in 3.33 (229,20-24 KOET.). Hermotimus, the Clazomenian, left his body and wandered in a bodiless state even though people did not think him a god (3.32 [228,22-26 KOET.]) according to Celsus. CHADWICK, Origen, 149 n. 1 gives references to the Clazomenian's story. Maximus refers to his own vision of the Dioscuri (as bright stars) in Diss. 9.7 (76,176-79 TR.). He also personally claims to have seen Asclepius and Heracles whom he elsewhere calls a child (παῖδα) of Zeus (14.1 [118,9 TR.]).

[152] CHADWICK, Origen, 142 n.3.

Asclepius (3.24 [220,22-23 Koet.]). Origen (3.25 [221,1-10 Koet.]) is willing to concede that a demon called Asclepius [153] has the power to heal. He does doubt that those who perform the healings are good[154]. Those who are good and evil have the gift of healing, so that there is nothing intrinsically divine about the healing of Asclepius.

Celsus is also more impressed by the manifestations of gods in human form at the shrines of the oracles (7.35 [185,18-21.27-29 Koet.]):

> [We do not then need, as if we were searching for God in this way] to go [where Celsus sends us] to the temples of Trophonius and Amphiaraus and Mopsus where [he says] the gods are seen in human forms and [as Celsus adds] without fraud but rather in full clarity (οὐ ψευδομένους ἀλλὰ καὶ ἐναργεῖς) ... one will see them not stealthily slipping in just one time like the one who deceived these people, but always consorting with those who want to.[155]

Origen affirms again that these figures are demons who feed on burnt offerings and are held down in prisons made by their lusts. He also develops an argument from consequence: how could a phantom who appeared secretly have such a great effect after the vision and persuade so many souls (ἐπιστρέφειν τὰς τῶν τοσούτων ψυχὰς καὶ πειθὼ ἐμποιεῖν αὐταῖς περὶ τοῦ πάντα δεῖν ἀρεσκόντως πράττειν θεῷ) that they should please God in every way. And he asks how the phantom could expel demons, and bring about other events of great significance (7.35 [185,21-24; 186,2-8 Koet.]). Presumably Celsus would counter that his Hellenistic divine figures produced similar results.

1.2.23 The Possibility of Resurrection

Celsus is enthusiastic about the disembodied appearances of the Greek gods and heroes. But the concept of a bodily resurrection is repugnant to him (5.14 [15,1-25 Koet.]):

> Another stupidity on their part is to think that when God (like a cook[156]) brings on the fire, every other race will be grilled, but they only will remain — and not only the living but also those who died once upon a time will come up out of the earth with those same bodies — absolutely the hope of worms (1 Th 4:15)! For what kind of human soul would regret a putrefied body? Since this teaching is not shared by some of you (Jews) and some of the Christians, its extreme impurity, its abominable character, and its impossibility (ἀδύνατον) are apparent. Which body after its complete decay could return to its original nature and to that same first composition from which it was dissolved? Having nothing to

---

[153] See E. J. EDELSTEIN/L. EDELSTEIN, Asclepius. A Collection and Interpretation of the Testimonies, Vols. I, II, New York 1975 (rep. of 1945 ed). For Origen's and Celsus' comments regarding Asclepius see EDELSTEIN I. Texts 261, 292-93 and the comment in II.135.

[154] Celsus' other comparisons with Jesus will be discussed below (§ 1.3.2).

[155] Celsus also refers to oracles in 3.34 (230,25-28 KOET.).

[156] Celsus also compares the God of Christian judgment to a torturer applying fire in 4.11 (281,22-23 KOET.).

answer, they have recourse to a most absurd retreat: "All is possible to God" (ἀτοπωτάτην ἀναχώρησιν, ὅτι πᾶν δυνατὸν τῷ θεῷ). But God can do no shameful things, nor does he will anything contrary to nature (παρὰ φύσιν). If you were to desire something disgusting in accord with your depravity, God could not do this, and it is not necessary to believe that it will immediately happen. For God is not the originator of wrongful desire or wandering excess but of right and just nature. He could grant everlasting life (αἰώνιον βιοτήν), but as Heraclitus says, "Corpses should be cast out even more than dung."[157] Therefore a body, full of things it is not pretty to describe, God would not against reason (παραλόγως) either will or be able (δυνήσεται) to make everlasting. For he is himself the reason (λόγος) of all things that exist; therefore he can do nothing against reason (παράλογον) or against himself.

Both Porphyry and Macarius' anonymous Hellene were offended by the Christians' appeal to the principle that "all things are possible to God"[158]. The Hellene in particular was critical of Christian eschatology. Origen (5.15 [16,1-3 Koet.]) responds that Celsus is also ridiculing the Stoic idea of world conflagration (ἐκπύρωσις)[159]. Celsus is not far from the Stoic view of history when he affirms that there is no net increase of good or evil in the universe and that everything repeats itself in cycles (4.67 [337,3-9 Koet.])[160]. Origen concedes (5.16 [17,12-27 Koet.]) that some ignorant (1 Cor 1:27-28) Christians believe all the others will be "grilled, and they only will remain." Such words are useful to exhort such Christians to lead pure lives. Origen (5.18 [Koet.]) does not think that the resurrection bodies will be identical with those that have been long dead (1 Cor 15:35-38) and affirms that "it is sown a psychic body and raised a spiritual body" (5.19 [19,12-23 Koet.]). Consequently, Christians are not worms that desire rotted bodies. Origen's point about the Stoic belief in world conflagration is that they are the ones who believe that dead people will return to the condition that they had before death since each world period is indistinguishable. Socrates will, for example, wear the same clothes that he had before (5.20 [21,23-22,10 Koet.]. The Christians

---

[157] Frag. 86 DIELS.

[158] See § 2.3.21 and § 3.51 below. Celsus' Jew also appeals to the principle in C.Cels. 2.77 (199,15 KOET.). BADER, 128 draws attention to Athenag., Resurr. 9 who confronts a similar pagan argument. See also Justin, Apol. 1.19.5-6 (61,16-24 MARC.) and 1 Clem. 27.2 and CHADWICK, Origen, Celsus, and the Resurrection of the Body, HThR 41, 1948, 83-102.

[159] SVF 4.48 gives a variety of references to this Stoic belief. CHADWICK, Origen, 279 n. 6 briefly discusses the doctrine. BADER, 47 refers to H. DIELS, Doxog. gr. 430a.7, 469.22, 23, 291a.25, 292a.7 (including the view that the world is uncreated). Compare Clem. Al., Strom. 5.1.9 (332,4 S./F.). FREDE notes that Celsus accepted a universe with partial conflagrations and floods but not a total conflagration (C. Celsum 4.79 [349,11-14 KOET.]; Celsus, 5206). Even Platonists such as Atticus who believed in a creation in time of the world could not accept the concept that the world was destructible (Fr. 4 and 25, DES PLACES).

[160] According to Tatian (Adv. Graec. 3 = SVF 1.109), Zeno believed Anytus and Meletus would again accuse (Socrates). Compare Chrysippus' identical view in SVF 2.623-31.

are willing to concede some limits to divine omnipotence, Origen claims, and he writes, "For we know to understand 'all' to not include things that do not exist or that are not conceivable" (5.23 [24,12-16 Koet.])[161]. Origen also argues that the "reason" which Celsus equates with God is God's son (5.24 [25,23-28 Koet.]) and quotes John 1:1. It is apparent that Celsus' objection to the resurrection of Jesus and to that envisioned in Christian eschatology is based on fundamental values in Greco-Roman philosophy — values that affirmed the importance of the immortal soul, but had no use for any kind of risen body.

Celsus' philosophically based objections to the resurrection are perhaps clearest in 6.72 (141,30-142,14 Koet.) where he creates doctrines for the Christians that are more in line with his own:

> Since the son is a spirit from God born in a human body, the son of God himself would not be immortal. [Then he confuses the doctrine for himself pretending that some of us do not confess that] God is spirit but only his son. [And he thinks he can refute this by saying:] It is not the nature of spirit to always remain ... [Then again of his own accord he takes up something not said by us:] It is necessary that God breathes in (ἀναπεπνευκέναι) his spirit. From that follows the impossibility of Jesus rising with his body, for God would not have taken the spirit back that he gave when it was soiled by the nature of body.

Origen refuses to respond to the objection on the grounds that the Christians would not assert such statements (6.72 [142,14-15 Koet.]). The later response in paganism to the Christian doctrine of resurrection makes it clear, however, that the philosophical objections were most important. The fact that Jesus only appeared to "a frantic woman" and other members of his "religious guild" is a historical critique that is motivated by the fact that Hellenistic philosophy had no room for a resurrection. God's spirit could not rise with any body — whether Jesus' or Dionysus' or Asclepius' or Heracles' — because it would be a spirit defiled by the body[162]. Origen admits as much in 1.7 (60,5-6 Koet.) where he writes, "But since the mystery of the resurrection is not understood, it is laughed about in common talk (θρυλεῖται)[163] by the unbelievers." Things had not changed much since Mars Hill (Acts 17:32).

---

[161] Macarius also took this response to the anonymous Hellene (§ 3.51 below), as did Didymus the blind before him (§ 2.3.21 below). CHADWICK, Origen, 281 n. 5 refers to other texts in Origen where he holds the same view.

[162] In § 3.51 the manifold pagan objections to the resurrection referred to by the Christian writers are canvassed.

[163] Macarius' pagan uses this word to deride the resurrection of Christ that Christians "babble" about everywhere (Apocriticus 2.14 [23,2 BLONDEL] = HARNACK, Porphyrius F. 64).

1.3 Celsus' Attack on the Christology of the Christians and his Alternative Christology

As part of his critique of the Gospels' traditions about Jesus, Celsus mounted a sustained attack on the Christian belief in Jesus as the incarnation of the supreme God. He found such a claim to be incredible from a Hellenistic point of view. His comparison of Jesus with lesser gods of the pantheon buttressed his argument that Jesus cannot be understood to be the son of the supreme God. He occasionally sketches an "alternative Christology" that is extremely critical of the character and identity of Jesus of Nazareth.

1.3.1 Celsus on the Incarnation

The incarnation was offensive to Celsus' philosophical sensibilities. Michel Fédou describes this attack: Celsus' objections to the incarnation "summarize Celsus' difficulties with the Christian message"[164]. In an attack on Jews and Christians alike he writes (4.2 [274,11-14 Koet.]): "With regard to this fact about some of the Christians and the Jews: some say that a certain god or son of God has come down, or (as others say) will come down to earth as a judge of all here — this is a shameful claim, and the refutation does not require a long argument." Other pagans had trouble believing in the incarnation. Arnobius (Adv. Nat. 1.42 [37,3.10-11.15-16 March.]) depicts an objector who claims that Jesus was born a human being and who doubts that Christ is a god. He asks for proof that God sent him to us. Celsus starts books five and six with similar assertions. In 5.2 (2,20-3,1 Koet.) he remarks: "Jews and Christians, no god or child (παῖς) of God has descended or would descend. If you speak about some angels, say what these are, god or another species. Probably another one — the demons." In book six where Celsus discussed Plato's understanding of philosophy and of ultimate reality he continues (6.8 [77,22-78,3 Koet.]):

> The Good is knowable by a "small number," since the many with an "unjust disdain are filled with a high and conceited hope as if they had learned some holy things,"[165] when they say certain things are true. [He adds:] Plato said this before and yet does not tell an amazing story, nor does he stop the tongue of one who wants to inquire about what he can possibly be promising, nor does he immediately urge people to first believe that God is such, and that he has such a son, and that the latter came down to speak with me.

Despite Celsus' apparent skepticism about any kind of "descent" of a god to earth, Origen (6.8 [78,3-6 Koet.]) points out that Aristander wrote that Plato was not the son of Ariston but "of an apparition that came to Amphictione in the

---

[164] M. FÉDOU, Christianisme, 537. Compare 536-43. ANDRESEN, Logos, 89-91 also treats the issue.
[165] Plat., Ep. 7.341e.

form of Apollo"¹⁶⁶. Celsus' opinion in 5.2 (3,9-15 Koet.), according to Origen, contradicts the opinions of people he had mentioned earlier who believed in manifestations of God. In 3.22 and 24 (218,10-11; 220,13 Koet.), for example, Celsus had mentioned Heracles, Asclepius, and Dionysus in approving terms and seems to have supported contemporary appearances of Asclepius (3.24 [220,15 Koet.]). It is apparent that Celsus was more comfortable with the idea of a hero becoming a god (3.22 [218,12 Koet.]) than with the idea of God coming to earth.

The characteristics of Jesus' appearance that have already been surveyed above were not consistent with what a son of God would do. He attacks Christians, because (3.41 [237,1-3 Koet.]) "Even though Jesus was formed from a mortal body we think that he is a god, and in this we believe we are doing pious deeds." Celsus' objections to the birth narrative have been treated above (§ 1.2.3). Christians regard Jesus to be the son of God because he healed people (2.48 [169,16-18 Koet.]), and Celsus (as described above in § 1.2.8) thought such an argument to be miserable because magicians (and Satan) could also perform miracles (2.49 [171,24-25 Koet.]). The fact that Jesus was not believed by all is also offensive (2.75 [195,33-196,3 Koet.]): "What god coming to people is disbelieved — indeed when he appears to those who hope for such?" For Celsus, a god would command a great deal more assent than Jesus apparently did. Jesus' death was also inconsistent with Celsus' concept of a god. Any robber or murderer that was punished could claim to be a god (2.44 [166,24-26 Koet.]). Celsus is particularly offended by Christians who encourage belief in Jesus as God's son despite his passion. Origen (6.10 [80,27-30 Koet.]) affirms, "[We do not say to everyone who comes, 'First believe that the one whom I am describing to you is the son of God' ... We do not say as Celsus claims mockingly:] 'Believe that the one whom I am describing to you is the son of God even though he was most dishonorably bound and most shamefully punished and even though yesterday and the day before he roamed about disgracefully before all eyes.' [Nor do we say,] 'Even more reason to believe.'" The discussion of the passion above (§ 1.2.16) illustrates Celsus' disgust towards the concept of Jesus' death. Celsus was also critical of the fact that "The child of God, apparently, was not able to open the tomb, but needed another to move the rock" (5.58 [61.23 Koet.]).

The reasons for Celsus' critique of the gospels' picture of Jesus as God's son are predominantly philosophical in nature. He writes (4.5 [277,18-20; 278,8-9 Koet.]) that Christians believe: "God himself will descend to people. [And he thinks this entails that] God abandons his throne ... For if you should change (μεταβαλοῖς) the least of things here below, all things would be

---

¹⁶⁶ CHADWICK, Origen, 321 n. 12 with reference to texts such as Plutarch, Mor. 717e-718b and Diog. Laert. 3.2.

overturned and ruined by you." Origen rejects that argument and claims that God's power changes certain things including souls who receive the "coming of the Word of God."

Celsus' attack stems from a conception of God that will admit no incarnation (4.14 [284,2-12 Koet.]):

> Still [he says] let us take up the argument anew with more proofs. I am not saying anything new but things that have long been established opinions. God is good, beautiful, happy, and in the highest degree of beauty and excellence.[167] Therefore, if he comes down to people, he must submit to change (μεταβολῆς), a change from good to bad, from beauty to ugliness, from happiness to misfortune, and from what is most excellent to what is most evil. Who would choose such a change? It is true that for a mortal, its nature is to change and to be transformed, but for an immortal it is to remain in the same state in the same way.[168] God would not accept such a change.

Celsus might be willing to accept the after death appearances of heroes like Aristeas or Asclepius (3.24, 26 [220,13; 222,10 Koet.]), but the idea of God incarnate as Jesus was utterly impossible in his frame of reference. Origen argues that the gods of Epicurus and of the Stoics are corporeal (4.14 [284,21-24 Koet.]). The divine Word did not change from good to bad (4.15 [285,1-3 Koet.]), was sinless, and was like a healer of wounds[169].

Celsus uses his position "God does not change" to construct a dilemma for the Christians (4.18 [287,4-12 Koet.]):

> Either God truly changes, as these say, into a human body, and it has already been said that this is impossible. Or, he does not change himself, but makes those who see think (that he does), and he misleads them and lies. Trickery and lies are generally evil, except when someone uses them in place of medicine to heal in the case of friends who are sick and out of their minds or in the case of enemies when one is intending to avoid a danger. But no one who is ill or out of their mind is God's friend, nor does God fear anyone to the point of trickery to escape danger.

Origen grasps the first horn of Celsus' dilemma (4.18 [288,1-4.12-17 Koet.]) and denies that a change of essence occurred when Jesus' soul entered his body. He refers to Phil 2:5-9 to describe the descent of Jesus' soul.

Celsus ridicules a work (Aristo of Pella's *Controversy between one Papiscus and Jason*) that describes an argument between a Christian and a Jew over the prophecies about the Messiah used by Christians to describe Jesus (4.52 [325,10-15 Koet.])[170]. Celsus continues with one of his fundamental objections to incarnational thinking:

---

[167] Compare Plat., Resp. 381b and Phaedr. 246d.

[168] Plat., Phaedo 78c.

[169] Compare Macarius in § 3.49 below.

[170] On Aristo see J. QUASTEN, Patrology. Volume 1. The Beginnings of Patristic Literature, Westminster, Md 1992, 195-96 / and Hermiae Philosophi Irrisio..., Corpus Apologetarum Christianorum IX, ed. J. C. T. OTTO, Wiesbaden 1969 (rep. of 1872 ed.), 349-63. See A. V. HARNACK, Geschichte der altchristlichen Litteratur bis Eusebius, 1. Teil Die

But I rather choose to teach this according to nature (φύσιν): God has made nothing mortal. But all the immortals are the works of God, while mortals are their works. The soul is the work of God, but the nature of the body is distinct. And indeed with regard to this there will be no difference between the body of a bat, maggot, frog, or person: the matter is the same, and the principle of corruption is also similar.

This position of Celsus explains why he is unwilling to contemplate the Logos of God having mortal flesh (compare 2.31). God did not create mortal bodies in the first place[171].

One final conceptual objection Celsus has to the incarnation is the fact that for Celsus the sum total of evil and good in the universe cannot increase of decrease. This fact vitiates any need for God or the son of God to come down and deal with human sin: "There would never be an increase or decrease of evils in the world in the past, present, or in the future: for the nature of all things (ἡ τῶν ὅλων φύσις) is one and the same, and the generation of evils is always the same." Origen writes that Celsus is probably paraphrasing *Theaetetus* 176a where Socrates says "It is not possible for evils to perish from among people or for them to be established among the gods." Origen denies that Celsus has understood Plato correctly (4.62 [333,21-23.24-27 Koet.]). Celsus again refers to Plato's text in 8.55 (271,26-272.1 Koet.) where he asserts that "For this is nature (φύσις): that all people should experience evils. For evils are necessary and have no other place to exist (than this life)." Plato's text has: "It is not possible for evil to be abolished ... for there must always be something opposed to the good; nor is it established among the gods, but of necessity it wanders about mortal nature and this earth."

Celsus' view of history and evil is cyclical (4.65 [335,16-22 Koet.]). Given the fact that evil is not going to disappear, Celsus apparently argues that there is no need for an incarnation: "The generation of evils is not easy to know for one who has not philosophized (φιλοσοφήσαντι); but it is not enough to tell the multitude that evils are not from God, that they are inherent in matter and are citizens among the mortals. The period of mortals is similar from the beginning to the end, and according to the determined cycles (ἀνακυκλήσεις) the same things have always been, are, and always will be." With such a view of history, there could be no purpose in the descent of God's son. Origen denies

---

Überlieferung und der Bestand der altchristlichen Litteratur bis Eusebius, bearb. unter Mitwirkung v. E. PREUSCHEN, Leipzig 1893 = 1958; 2. Teil Die Chronologie der altchristlichen Litteratur, Leipzig 1896 = 1958, I, 92-95; II, 391. B. R. VOSS has a very able discussion of the document and its function of converting the Jewish Papiscus using Messianic prophecies in: Der Dialog in der frühchristlichen Literatur, Studia et testimonia antiqua 9, München 1970, 317-21.

[171] For Ps. Sallustius the "mundane" gods create the universe in De diis 6 (10,28-29 NOCK); for parallels to these "mundane gods" see NOCK's edition (Sallustius, lvii n.83; e.g. Max. Tyr. 11.12 (100,289-97 TR.) who speaks of a hierarchy of gods). See also Plato's Timaeus 42d on the "younger gods" who made mortal bodies and Alcin., Didask. 16 171,38-42 (CUFr, Alcinoos, 36 WHITTAKER/LOUIS).

that it is easy for anyone to know the origin of evils (4.65 [335,27-336,19 Koet.]). Anyone who knows the origin of evil needs to know the truth about the devil and his angels, demons, God and so forth. Celsus does not spell out the consequences of his point of view, but its presence within a set of fragments arguing against the descent of the son of God to earth explains his inclusion of the above conceptual difficulties he has with the incarnation.

Besides his conceptual objections to incarnational thinking, Celsus attacks it from the point of view of teleology. What would be the purpose in the first place of God or a son of God coming to earth? Celsus asks (2.47 [168,33-169,3 Koet.]): "By what reasoning were you led to believe this person to be son of God? ... we were led by this reasoning because we know that his punishment happened in order to destroy the father of evil." Celsus' criticisms of the concept of Satan, covered above (§ 1.2.10), illustrate how weak he found that argument. Again (4.3 [275,18-26 Koet.]) Celsus asks: "What was God's thought in such a descent ... was it that he might learn what is happening among people ... for does he not know all things? ... is it that he knows and does not reform and cannot reform by his divine power?" Origen (4.3 [276,5-10 Koet.]) argues that because of the element of free will in human nature, God did not take away evil altogether and implant virtue in people.

Celsus compares the behavior of the Christian's God to a person who has become one of the newly wealthy: "But perhaps if God were unknown among people and because of this thought himself to be diminished, would he want to be recognized and to put both believers and unbelievers to the test (διαπειράσαι), like the newly rich among humans who wish to show themselves off? That is to bear witness against God of a great and excessively mortal love of honor (φιλοτιμίαν)." Origen replies that God wanted to make himself known to bad people because such knowledge delivers such people from misfortune (4.6 [278,16-21.22-24 Koet.]).

Then Celsus begins an argument that anticipates later positions of Porphyry and the anonymous Hellene of Macarius[172]. He wonders why God waited so long to make himself known (4.7 [279,6-12 Koet.]):

God does not want to be known for the sake of himself, but for the sake of our salvation he desires to give us knowledge of himself — so that those who receive it, becoming good, may be saved and those who refuse it, shown to be evil, might be punished. [Having said that he raises a new question.] Is it now after such a long age that God remembered to pass sentence on the life of people while he had no care about it before?

Porphyry and the Hellene were as equally troubled by this issue as Celsus was. Origen argues (4.8-9 [280,1-15 Koet.]) that after many prophets who were reformers of Israel, Christ came as reformer of the entire world. Origen is convinced that God set the boundaries of all nations according to the number of

---

[172] See § 2.3.30 and § 3.52 (Book I, Index 5 [a lost objection]).

the angels of God. Despite the fact that God chose Israel, he also had a place for the other nations (Ps. 2:8).

Eternal life is no more convincing to Celsus as a reason for the advent of Christ (4.23 [292,20-293,5 Koet.]). He likens the arguments between Jews and Christians to those of bats, ants, frogs or worms:

> ... holding an assembly in a muddy corner arguing with each other about which of them are most sinful and saying: God reveals and predicts all things beforehand to us and neglects the whole universe, the heavenly movement, and overlooking the vast earth he governs for us alone and to us alone he communicates by heralds — not ceasing to send them and to seek that we might be united with him forever. [He continues his fiction describing us to be] similar to worms who say that God exists and immediately after him we who have been created by him entirely like God, and he has subordinated all things to us: the earth, water, and stars; all things exist for our sake and have been ordained to serve us. [And the worms that he describes, certainly us, say] Now, since some of us sin, God will come or will send his son to burn the unrighteous, and the rest of us will have everlasting life with him. [And he adds to all this:] These things would be more honorable coming from worms and frogs than from Jews and Christians arguing with each other.

Celsus has little use for the creation narratives in Genesis (or for any other narratives in Genesis)[173]. Plotinus agreed that humans have an insignificant place in the universe[174]. Origen denies that God cares only for "us alone" (4.28 [297,7-14 Koet.]) because God's mercy is upon all and he sends his rain upon the just and unjust (Mt 5:45). Jesus came on behalf "of sinners in all places, that they may forsake their sin and entrust themselves to God."

That God would sent his spirit into a corner of the world as incarnational thinking envisions is incredible to Celsus (6.78 [149,22-31 Koet.]):

> There is more. If God like the Zeus of comedy, woke up from a long sleep and wanted to deliver the human race from its evils, why ever did he send this spirit that you speak of into one corner? He should have breathed in a like manner into a great number of bodies and sent them over the whole earth. The comic poet, provoking laughter in the theater, wrote that when Zeus woke up he sent Hermes to the Athenians and Lacedaemonians.[175] And you, do you not think that it is even more laughable to make the son of God be sent to the Jews?

---

[173] Book IV of the *Contra Celsum* contains many fragments against Genesis (e.g. 4.33, 36, 37, 40, 41, 43, 45, 46, 78, 79 [303,17; 306,25; 307,20; 313,9; 314,3; 315,26; 317,25; 319,7; 347,26; 348,27 KOET.]). See also Books V, VI, and VII: 5.59; 6.49, 50, 60, 61; 7.62 and 66 [63,6; 120,32; 121,18; 130,11; 131,15; 212,17; 216,7 KOET.].

[174] Plotinus, Ennead. 3.2.8 (OCT, Plotini Opera, I, 256,4-257,16 HENRY/SCHWYZER) and compare Marcus Aurel. 4.3.3. Plotinus believed that all things were for each other (Ennead. 6.7.3 [III, 187,19 H./S.]).

[175] CHADWICK, Origen, 391 n.5 refers to T. KOCK, Comicorum Atticorum Fragmenta, 3.406, F. 43 [apparently not included in J. M. EDMONDS, Fragments of Attic Comedy]. Celsus also makes comparisons with comedy in 6.49 (121,8 KOET.). Macarius' Hellene also uses the imagery of the theater to ridicule Christian teaching (§ 3.3 below).

Origen (6.78 [150,1-12 Koet.] defends the incarnation (ἐνσωμάτωσιν) as the completion of a work that had long been happening among human beings when God's Logos visited their souls. Jesus came to one corner, "since it was necessary that the one who was prophesied came to those who had learned of the one God, who had read his prophets, and who had learned of the Christ that was proclaimed, and that he came at the time when the word (teaching) was going to poured out from one corner to the whole world."

Celsus' objections to the incarnation are fundamentally philosophical. Although his universe is populated with all kinds of demons, heroes, gods, goddesses, oracles, and the Supreme Good, there is an order of nature that would be violated by the incarnation of Christian teaching. The characteristics of Jesus' life that seem so ludicrous to Celsus are simply an offshoot of his basic position: God cannot change or appropriate a human body.

Celsus' objections to viewing Jesus as the incarnation of the Supreme God on earth explain his willingness to compare Jesus to the heroes and lesser gods of the Greco-Roman pantheon. These comparisons are not intended to "glorify" Jesus, but to denigrate him. They serve effectively as tools of vituperative rhetoric (as opposed to the rhetoric of praise). Celsus' "alternative Christology," to be described below, is an example of this rhetoric of blame.

1.3.2 Comparisons with Jesus from the Pantheon

The pantheon provides Celsus with many rich sources of comparison with Jesus. Those who condemned Jesus did not suffer as Pentheus[176] did after he disbelieved Bacchus who remarked that "the god himself will free me when I wish"[177] (2.34 [160,13.26 Koet.]). The honor given to Jesus is no different from that given to Hadrian's boy-love (Antinous 3.36 [232,3-6 Koet.]). With reference to the profound mysteries (αἰνίγματα) that the Egyptian worship of animals comprises, Celsus charges that Christians "are foolish because we do not introduce into our explications (διηγήσεσι) concerning Jesus anything more holy than the goats and dogs of the Egyptians" (3.19 [216,21-23 Koet.]). So the worship of Jesus is worth no more than the worship of the Egyptians' goats and dogs. Celsus compares the worship of the one who was arrested and died to the reverence for Zamolxis,[178] Mopsus, Amphilochus,[179] Amphiaraus,[180] and Trophonius (3.34, 7.35 [230,26-28; 185,17-20 Koet.])[181]. The gods are seen in human form at those oracles. People who died noble and/or violent deaths and who have become "the object of divine

---

[176] BADER 73 refers to Apollod., Bibl. 3.5.2 and Ovid, Met. 3.513-731.

[177] Eur., Bacchae 498.

[178] On Zamolxis see H.-D. BETZ, Art. Gottmensch II (Griechisch-römische Antike und Urchristentum), RAC XII, 1982, 247.

[179] Mentioned by Maximus of Tyre in Diss. 9.7 (76,161-62 TR.).

[180] On Amphiaraus see BETZ, Gottmensch, 242.

[181] See BETZ, Gottmensch, 247.

myths" include Heracles, Asclepius, and Orpheus (7.53 [203,12-13 Koet.]). In
addition Anaxarchus and Epictetus said inspired things while being violently
treated (7.53 [203,18-20 Koet.]) — unlike Jesus. Christians are upset if a
Greek compares (παραβάλης) Jesus with Apollo or Zeus (3.37 [233,14
Koet.]). Figures who disappeared (or died and disappeared) and then
miraculously reappeared (or traveled without their body) include: Aristeas,
Cleomedes, and the Clazomenian, (3.3, 26, 32, 33 [205,11-12; 222,10;
228,22; 229,21 Koet.])[182]. Celsus notes that people do not think these figures
are gods (3.29, 32). Another unfavorable comparison is Abaris (3.31 [228,8-
10 Koet.]): "No one considers Abaris the Hyperborean to be a god who had so
much power that he could be carried about on an arrow."[183] He is more
positive if the Christians would say that Jesus put off his flesh and perhaps
became a god. In that case Asclepius, Dionysus and Heracles would be the
same (3.42 [238,9-11 Koet.]). Many have seen Asclepius alive after his death
(3.24 [220,13-16 Koet.]), and he continues to heal and do good. Even Jesus'
wisdom is not impressive to Celsus who finds Zeno the Stoic to be wiser (5.20
[22,19 Koet.])[184]. Celsus' activity of comparison is not as systematic as the
treatise that Hierocles later undertook in which he compared Jesus and
Apollonius — with Jesus appearing in an unfavorable light[185].

1.3.3 Celsus' "Alternative Christology"

These comparisons indicate that Celsus entertained what one might entitle an
"alternative Christology." Jesus (2.29 [157,14 Koet.]) was a pestilent (or
ruinous) fellow (ὄλεθρον) and not the great prince predicted by the prophets.
He was hated by god and a wicked magician (1.71 [124,24-25 Koet.]). He was
a boaster (ἀλαζών) and a sorcerer (2.32 [159,6 Koet.]). Jesus' life was not
free from evil or blame (2.41, 42 [164,24; 165,7 Koet.]). Celsus' Jew
concludes his description of Jesus: "That individual was therefore a person of
such a kind as the truth itself shows and reason (ὁ λόγος) proves" (2.79
[201,8-9 Koet.])[186]. Jesus is the teacher and chorus-leader of the Christians
(5.33, 6.34 [35,2-3; 103,21 Koet.]). Jesus was an angel for the Jews who

[182] See BETZ, Gottmensch, 244.
[183] From Herodotus 4.36, and see Porphyry, Vita Pyth. 28-29 (CUFr 49,5-8.23-25 DES
PLACES). CHADWICK, Origen, 148. n.1 gives bibliography.
[184] ANDRESEN conjectures a connection between this fragment and 6.73 (142,27 KOET.)
where Origen discusses the Stoic concept of the "indifferent." This concept would then be the
term of comparison between Zeno and Jesus (ANDRESEN, Logos, 26-27).
[185] § 4.9 and 4.12 below.
[186] Is Celsus playing on the title of his book? This christology was adopted by
Porphyry, Hierocles, Julian, and pagans in general (§ 2.2.3, 2.2.5, 4.10, 5.2.23). LODS (Les
Sources, 37) refers to similar traditions in Justin, Dial. 8.3, 10.3 (85,20; 87,18-19 MARC.),
Tertullian, Apol. 21.17 (125,84-85 DEK.), Ep. Barnabas 12.10-11, Acta Io. 3, Acta Philippi
15 (BONNET) and so forth.

were doing something wrong, but there are many more angels (5.52 [56,3.19 Koet.]). The risen Jesus is only a shadow according to the Christians (3.22 [218,17 Koet.]). Jesus' single and stealthy resurrection appearance deceived the Christians (7.35 [185,28 Koet.]). However, Jesus is worse than a phantom, because he is dead (7.36, [186,26 Koet.])[187]. As a corpse Jesus is not a god or even a demon (7.68 [217,1 Koet.]). Jesus lived an infamous life and died a miserable death (7.53 [203,27-28 Koet.]). Celsus, near the end of his work, taunts the Christians that "anyone who stands before your demon" and blasphemes him and banishes him from land and sea suffers no vengeance (8.39 [253,24-25 Koet.]). He is rarely willing to even call Jesus a "demon." Nothing has happened since the death of Christ that would encourage Celsus to believe that Jesus was not a sorcerer, but God's son (8.41 [255,9-11 Koet.]).

1.4 Celsus' Attack on the Christian Use of the Hebrew Scriptures to Support their Faith

Given his attitude toward Jesus it is not surprising that Celsus would find the early Christians' use of the Old Testament to buttress their faith in Jesus to be unconvincing. In fact he views the Hebrew Scriptures with distaste and categorizes them as mythical. Since they are "stupid myths," there is no need to attempt allegory. Consequently his attack on the Christian use of the OT is twofold: first, the Hebrew scriptures are not worthy of allegorical interpretation because of their stupidly mythical nature; second, even if one were to concede that the OT was a worthy text, it provides no grounds for believing that Jesus fulfilled OT prophecies. It should be remarked that Celsus here is somewhat inconsistent with his charge that Christians never offer any reasons for their faith (see § 1.6.1 below). In Celsus' defense one should note that his attack on the "argument from prophecy " is made in Celsus' persona as a Jew who would naturally accept the validity of the Hebrew Scriptures. The Christians' reasoning is faulty when they appeal to the OT to support their faith in Christ.

1.4.1 Against the Christians' Allegorical Interpretation of the Jewish Scriptures

Celsus objects to allegorical interpretations of the Hebrew scriptures because of his belief that they are "empty myths (μῦθοι) that do not allow allegory (1.20 [72,27-72,1 Koet.] and see 1.17 [69,21 Koet.]). In this text he is defending the Hellenistic beliefs in many floods and conflagrations from all eternity (1.19, 20 [70,21-24; 71,12 Koet.])[188]. Celsus, on the other hand (1.27 [79,10.13-14 Koet.]), seems to admire those who interpret allegorically in contrast to the vast

---

[187] This was Julian's term for Jesus ("a corpse"). See § 5.2.30 below.

[188] In 4.79 (349,13-14 KOET.) Celsus makes it clear that he does not believe in a total conflagration.

number of uneducated Christians who are attracted by the simplicity (τò ἰδιωτικόν) of the word: among them are some moderate, reasonable, and intelligent people (μετρίους καὶ ἐπιεικεῖς καὶ συνετούς) who are ready to understand allegory." Christians (3.19 [216,18-23 Koet.]) laugh at the Egyptians' worship of animals even though they "offer many enigmas (αἰνίγματα) that are not ordinary (φαῦλα) because they teach that these are worship of eternal ideas, and not as many think, the worship of ephemeral animals. They are foolish because they do not introduce into the narrative about Jesus anything more holy than the goats and dogs of the Egyptians." Celsus does not find the Christians' interpretations of their faith in Jesus to be any better than the Egyptians' allegorical interpretation of their worship[189]. The narratives (4.21 [290,7-11 Koet.]) of the flood and tower of Babel are obvious (σαφής) and have no hidden truth (μηδὲν αἰνίσσηται)[190]. Reasonable Jews and Christians are ashamed of OT narratives such as the creation of Adam by God's hands and so try to allegorize the stories (4.38 [308,26-29 Koet.]). Origen (4.38 [308,26 Koet.]) notes that Celsus did not believe that such stories were allegories. After mentioning stories such as those of Joseph sold into slavery and the flight of the Jews from Egypt (4.47 [320,7-15 Koet.]), Celsus (4.48 [320,23-24 Koet.]) claims that because more reasonable Jews and Christians are ashamed of those things they take refuge in allegory[191]. Celsus' view in Origen's description is that the Christians' writings "are not susceptible to allegory" (4.49 [321,24 Koet.]). This is the case because they are "stupid myths" (4.50 [323,27-29 Koet.] εὐηθέστατα μεμυθολόγηται). The conclusion Celsus draws (4.51 [324,8-11 Koet.]) is: "At least the allegories apparently written concerning them are much more shameful and absurd (ἀτοπώτεραι) than the myths, because they connect, by an amazing and altogether obtuse foolishness, things that cannot in any way be made to fit together (ἁρμοσθῆναι)." The vocabulary of Celsus' attack is similar to Porphyry's later critique of Christian exegesis of the Hebrew scriptures[192].

---

[189] CHADWICK, Origen, 139 n.3 refers to mockery of Egyptian animal-worship by Jews and Christians (Jos. C. Ap. 2.7.81 and Aristeas 138). The skeptics were also critical of such worship (Sextus Emp., P.H. 3.219).

[190] Celsus believes the story is a corruption of the story of Aloeus. Atticus also found the story of the Aloeids impressive (Fr. 2, DES PLACES). Julian critiqued the story of Babel in C. Gal. 134d-135d (116,4-117,37 MASARACCHIA).

[191] FÉDOU, Christianisme, 125-27 surveys Celsus' attack on Christian allegory and his own use of allegory in reference to Hellenistic texts. He also surveys (128-39) Origen's use and defense of allegory.

[192] HARNACK, Porphyrius F. 39 in § 2.3.3 below. Celsus also despises the Gnostic Christian exegesis of the Jewish scriptures, and in particular their proclivity for finding another God instead of the God of the OT (6.29 [99,5-18 KOET.]). ROKEAH (Jews, 94, 97) refers to Velleius' (an Epicurean) rejection of Zeno's allegorical interpretation of Hesiod's *Theogonia* in Cicero, De nat. deorum 1.14.36. Josephus (C. Ap. 2.255) also rejected allegory of Greek myths. Compare FREDE, Celsus, 5195. LONG, Stoic Readings, 48, 59-63 argues

Despite Celsus' obvious scorn for the "stupid myths" of the OT, he is willing to consider the possibility that oracles in the OT could apply to the future. In this belief he is simply adopting the Hellenistic faith in the reality of oracles. Possibly Celsus finds the prophetic writings of the OT to be more attractive than books such as Genesis.

1.4.2 The Argument from Prophecy

The issue of Jewish and Christian prophecy troubled Celsus deeply. His respect for the oracles and inspired people of Greco-Roman culture was not abated by the Christians' attempt to use Hebrew prophecy to defend their new religion and their faith in the figure who "recently" appeared, Jesus of Nazareth. He was aware of the Jewish belief that God had inspired the prophets (6.29 [99,14 Koet.]). Celsus (6.74 [143,28-30 Koet.]) challenges the Christians with the following question: "How can the one who endured such punishments be proved (ἀποδειχθήσεται) to be the child (παῖς) of God, if this was not predicted?" None of the Christians' arguments are successful to Celsus : "Let us see how they will invent an excuse. Those who introduce another god give none, and those who keep the same God will say the same thing again — that evidently very subtle statement — that 'it was necessary (ἐχρῆν) for it to be this way, and the proof (τεκμήριον) is that these things were predicted long ago'." Origen responds that even those Christians who teach the existence of another God could answer Celsus' weak arguments (7.2 [154,5-8.9-12 Koet.]). Both Origen and Celsus accept the fundamental basis of the argument: the testimony of ancient people is worthy of acceptance. "Supernatural witness" included the statements made by oracles from the past[193].

Celsus' Jew attacks the notion that Jesus fulfilled ancient prophecies (1.57 [108,3-5.12-15 Koet.]): "If you say that every person born according to divine providence is son of God[194], what is the difference between you and another person? ... Others by the millions (μυρίοι) ... will refute Jesus claiming that these things which were prophesied concerning him were said about

---

that Zeno did not actually allegorize Homer — based on the textual evidence of Zeno's literary criticism of Homer (e.g. SVF 1.274). He denies that Heraclitus (Quaestiones Homericae, ed. BUFFIÈRE) was an orthodox Stoic. Heraclitus did allegorize Homer (Stoic Reading, 47). Cicero's Stoic, Balbus, does indicate (De nat. deorum 2.24.63-28.72) that the Stoics found physical meanings in unworthy tales of the gods. As LONG notes, the Stoic does not attempt to salvage the veracity of the poets (Stoic Readings, 52).

[193] See COOK, Proptreptic Power, 113-15 on the use of ancient testimonies in rhetoric. Celsus attacks Gnostic Christians in Book V (5.61, 62, 63, 64 [64,9; 65,26; 66,8; 67,16; KOET.]) and Book VI (6.24, 27, 28, 29, 30, 34, 36, 38, 39, 40, 51, 74 [94,15; 97,1; 98,5; 99,3.31; 103,13; 105,8; 107,3; 108,1; 109,14; 122,19; 143,22 KOET.]), 7.40 (190,22 KOET.), and 8.15, 16 (232,11; 233,26 KOET.).

[194] CHADWICK, Origen, 52 translates "every man has become a son of God by divine providence."

themselves." Origen argued that Jesus is far superior to every one who because of virtue is called a son of God (with reference to Rom 8:14-15). He also wonders whether Celsus knew of people who gave themselves the title of sons of God or power of God (Acts 8:10) and mentions Theudas, Judas of Galilee, Dositheus the Samaritan, and Simon the magician (1.57 [108,8-109,6 Koet.]). Celsus' Jew is quite sure that others could claim to be the fulfillment of the Messianic prophecies. He claims (2.28 [156,14-15.21-23 Koet.]): "Christians cite the prophets who predicted the things concerning Jesus ... the prophecies can be applied to millions (μυρίοις ἐφαρμοσθῆναι) of others more persuasively (πιθανώτερον) than to Jesus." Origen (2.28 [157,1-5 Koet.]) argues that a Jew would not agree that the prophecies could be applied to millions far more plausibly than to Jesus, but would rather explain each prophecy and reply to the Christian interpretation.

Celsus' Jew, for example, argues for a vision of a different Messiah in the ancient prophecies. In 1.49 (100,21-22 Koet.) he states: "My prophet said in Jerusalem once that the son of God will come — a judge of the holy and punisher of the unrighteous." He asks: (1.50 [101,13-14.17-18.27-28 Koet.]) "Why would it be you, rather than millions of others who were born after the prophecy, of whom those prophecies were made? ... the prophecies that are referred to the events of his life can be fit to other realities." Origen knows (1.49 [100,23; 101,5-12 Koet.]) many other prophets than "one" who prophesied such things about the Messiah, and he also knows that a Jew would not say that a certain "prophet said that God's son would come" because they speak in terms of the "Christ of God" and do not approve of the title "son of God" because that title is not mentioned in the prophets. Origen does not concede that the "son of God" is not mentioned in prophecy. Celsus' Jew is skeptical about that title (2.4 [131,18-20 Koet.]): "If anyone predicted to you that indeed the child of God would come to people it was our prophet, our God's prophet." In that context (2.4 [130,21-23.25-27 Koet.]), Celsus' Jew uses the argument to criticize Jewish Christians for abandoning the law of their fathers: "It was yesterday or the day before when we had punished him who led you like a flock that you deserted your ancestral law ... How, when you started from our holy writings, and then progressed, could you dishonor them when you can give no other origin for your doctrine than our law?" The argument about prophecy in this context is useful for calling the Christians back to their Jewish roots.

Celsus' Jew expects a Messiah who will punish the unrighteous (2.8 [133,20-21.26-28; 133,30-134,1; 134,24-25 Koet.]):

> Many others like Jesus could have appeared to those who wanted to be deceived ... those who believe in Jesus make the accusation against the Jews that they did not believe in Jesus as in God ... But how, after we have made known to all people that from God will come one to punish the unrighteous, would we have dishonored him when he came? ...

Why would we have dishonored the one we publicly predicted (προεκηρύσσομεν)? In order to be punished more than the others?

Origen (2.8 [134,18-22 Koet.]) indulges in some anti-Judaism when he claims that after Jesus' advent "the Jews are entirely abandoned not possessing any of the things that of old were thought to be sacred — not even a sign of the presence of the divine among them. For they no longer have prophets or miracles; while there are traces (of miracles) that are found of a certain importance among the Christians — and even greater ones (John 14:12)." Origen seems unable to enter into the spirit of the argument with Celsus' Jew whose different conception of the advent of the Messiah escapes Origen completely.

Celsus' Jew is quite clear about his conception (2.29 [157,9-11 Koet.]): "It is a great ruler (δυνάστην), lord (κύριον) of all the earth and of all nations and armies whom the prophets say will come (τὸν ἐπιδημήσοντα) ... But they have not announced this plague (ὄλεθρον)." Origen (2.29 [157,7 Koet.]) responds to the argument by claiming that two advents of Christ were prophesied. In 1.56 (107,2-108,2 Koet.) Origen outlines these two advents: in the first Christ is subject to human passions and a deeper humiliation, and in the second he comes in glory and divinity. Origen used Ps 44:3-9 LXX to describe the reign of the Messiah, but he admits that a Jew with whom he had discussed the passage applied the words "thy throne, O God, is for ever and ever" to the God of the universe (and not the Messiah). Origen does not explain how he finds two advents in any particular Hebrew prophecy. His interpretation of Is 52-53, mentioned above (§ 1.2.17), is presumably an example of his view of the first advent. Origen (2.29 [157,14-17 Koet.]) also uses an argument from consequence to answer Celsus' reviling of Jesus as a "plague": "Indeed, neither the Jews nor Celsus nor any other person could establish with proof (ἀποδείξεως) that a plague could convert (ἐπιστρέφει) so many people from a flood of evils to a life conforming to nature with temperance and all the other virtues." Celsus' Jew believes in the resurrection (2.77 [199,12-15 Koet.]): "Doubtless we hope to rise in our body and have everlasting life and that the one who is sent to us will be the model and initiator (ἀρχηγέτην) of that, showing it is not impossible (ἀδύνατον) for God to raise someone with the body."

Celsus' conclusion is that none of the prophetic proofs are worthy. Neither are any of the other kinds of proofs that Christians use (2.30 [157,18-158,1 Koet.]): "No one proves a god or a son of god by such tokens and false reports (συμβόλων καὶ παρακουσμάτων), nor by such ignoble arguments (ἀγεννῶν τεκμηρίων) ... For [he says] as the sun that illuminates all other things first shows itself, so the son of God should have done." Celsus' Jew is expecting a Messiah who will illuminate the entire earth. Origen argues that Jesus did actually illuminate the entire earth:

For the words "in his days justice rose and an abundance of peace" (Ps 71:7) began to come to pass with his birth. God was preparing the nations for his teaching that all might be under the one king of the Romans and so that due to the large number of kingdoms the isolation of the nations might not make it harder for the apostles of Jesus to carry out what he had commanded them saying, "Go forth and make disciples of all the nations" (Mt 28:19). It is clear that Jesus was born during the reign of Augustus who, so to speak, made uniform by his one reign the majority of people on the earth. The existence of many kingdoms would have been an obstacle to the diffusion of the teaching of Jesus ...[195]

Origen again does not seem to be aware of the extreme difficulty that Celsus' Jew has with conceiving a Messiah that dies on a cross instead of ruling the world.

1.4.3 The Content of the Prophecies about Jesus: Against the Possibility that Jesus' Passion could have been Prophesied

Besides having problems with the issue of the application of Jewish prophecies to Jesus, Celsus has objections to the fundamental content of the prophecies about Christ that the Christians use. He charges (7.12 [163,17-20 Koet.]) that "those who defend the material about Christ using the prophets have nothing to the purpose to say if something evil, or shameful, or impure (ἀκάθαρτον), or defiled (μιαρόν) appears to have been said about the divine." Origen's answer (7.12 [164,1-9 Koet.]) assumes that there may be some Christians who may not know how to understand the divine scriptures. He says that Celsus gave no examples of such disgraceful sayings. Without examples, one is hard pressed to identify Celsus' problematic passages. The next fragment makes it likely that Celsus was concerned with the suffering of Christ (7.13 [164,16-19 Koet.]): "[And if he should say,] it was predicted that God serves evil and suffers very shameful things (αἴσχιστα)," he should have, according to Origen, have cited the texts from the prophets. Celsus' remarks on the passion that have been discussed above (§ 1.2.16) give his attitude toward the Christian proclamation of Jesus' death. Origen (7.13 [164,21-22 Koet.]) simply responds that the prophets did predict what the Christ was to suffer. The fundamental disagreement between Celsus and the Christians is over the issue of God's son suffering.

He makes this clear (7.14 [165,12-22 Koet.]):

Well! If the prophets predicted that the great God (not to say something even more coarse) would be a slave, or be sick, or die, would it be necessary that God die or be a slave, or be sick because it was predicted — in order that by his death it be believed that he was God? But the prophets would not have predicted this because it is evil and unholy (ἀνόσιον). Therefore one does not need to examine if they predicted or did not predict it, but whether

---

[195] 2.30 (158,2-13 KOET.). CHADWICK, *Origen*, 92 n.2 makes other references to the Christians' view on the *pax Romana* and the spread of the gospel (Eus, H.E. 4.26.7 and Hippolytus, Comm. in Dan. 4.9).

the deed is worthy of God and beautiful (καλόν). If the deed is shameful (αἰσχρῷ) and evil, and even if all people should seem to predict it while in a trance (μαινόμενοι), it should not be believed. How then could these things done to Jesus (as if done to God) be holy?

Origen (7.14 [165,23-24.26-30 Koet.]) responds that "He appears from these words to have suspected the strength for persuading the hearers (πρὸς πειθὼ τῶν ἀκουόντων) of the argument that Jesus was prophesied." This comment exemplifies the rhetorical context of the debate. These arguments are concerned with the persuasion of people to leave or join the Christian movement. Origen also notes that instead of showing no regard for whether the prophets predicted these things or not, he should have shown that they did not predict what the Christians claim they did or that what they did predict was not fulfilled in Christ. What Origen has difficulty with is Celsus' Hellenistic perspective from which he cannot envision God's son suffering. Celsus (7.15 [166,7-10 Koet.]) simply thinks it impossible that God should do and suffer the things that the Christians proclaim about Jesus. Origen also uses an argument of the following form to deny Celsus' premise: "If *1* is true, then *2* is true also; if *1* is true, then *2* is not true; then *1* is not true." If the same premise yields contradictory conclusions then the premise is denied. Celsus' premise is: "If the prophets of the supreme God were to say that God will serve as a slave or will be sick or even that He will die, then these things will happen to God." Origen also notes that if the same premise is true (i.e. the prophets say such things), then because such things are impossible, what the prophets say will not happen. In this case "1" results in two contradictory conclusions: "these things will happen to God" and "these things will not happen to God"[196]. Origen's conclusion is that, therefore, the prophets did not foretell that God would be sick and die (7.15 [166,11-26 Koet.]). The one that suffered the sorrows of Is 53:2-3 (7.16 [167,12-28 Koet.]) was a human. After mentioning several of Jesus' titles of majesty such as "only son of God" and "Firstborn," Origen says: "The reasoning about this being and his essence is quite different from that concerning the discerned human aspect of Jesus." One can easily imagine that Celsus would have found that argument opaque.

---

[196] CHADWICK, Origen, 407 n.1 refers to the use of the principle (syllogism of the two propositions) in Sextus Emp. P.H. 2.3 and Galen, De Hippocr. et Plat. placit. 2.3.18 (DE LACY, in SVF 2. 248). J. M. RIST analyzes the argument at length and remarks that Origen provides the only formalization of the argument (Stoic Logic in the Contra Celsum, in: Neoplatonism and Early Christian Thought. Essays in Honour of A. H. Armstrong, ed. H. J. BLUMENTHAL/R. A. MARKUS, London 1981, 73-75).

1.5 Celsus' Comparison of Christian and Hellenistic Prophets

In addition to his attack on the Christians' argument from prophecy, Celsus also attacked contemporary Christian prophets of whom he claimed to have personal knowledge. He found them to be frauds and liars. They admitted as much to him, according to his own testimony. These fraudulent prophets paled, in Celsus' eyes, in comparisons with the great oracles of the Greco-Roman tradition[197].

1.5.1 Contemporary Christian Prophets

Celsus is aware of the existence of contemporary Christians who prophesy. Origen (2.8 [134,21-22 Koet.]) also claims the contemporary existence of prophecy and wonders among the Christians[198]. Celsus is not impressed by these people, but he is aware of them (1.50 [101,20-22 Koet.]): "Some inspired individuals (ἐνθυσιῶντες) and others who are beggars say they have come from on high as son of God." Celsus is probably aware of Christian prophets speaking in the name of Jesus. He claims to have done some ethnographic research in the history of religions (7.9 [160,30-161,19 Koet.]):

[Since Celsus promises to speak about] the manner of prophecies (τὸν τρόπον τῶν ... μαντειῶν) in Phoenicia and Palestine [as something] which he has heard and examined very closely, [let us consider these matters]. He says first] that there are many forms of prophecies (προφητειῶν), [without indicating them]. He had none to give, but was bragging falsely. Let us see what he describes as the] most accomplished kind among the men of this region. There are [he says] many anonymous individuals who readily and for any chance cause in the temples and outside the temples and others who beg and go about cities and encampments who are apparently moved as if giving an oracle. It is common and customary for each to say, I am God or a child (παῖς) of God, or a divine Spirit. And I have come (ἥκω).[199] For the world is perishing and you, people, will perish because of

---

[197] On prophecy in the period in question see: J. L. ASH, The Decline of Ecstatic Prophecy in the Early Church, ThS 37, 1976, 227-252 / D. E. AUNE, Prophecy in the Early Christianity and the Ancient Mediterranean World, Grand Rapids 1983 / G. DAUTZENBERG, Urchristliche Prophetie: Ihre Prophetie, ihre Voraussetzungen im Judentum und ihre Struktur im ersten Korintherbrief, BWANT 104, Stuttgart 1975 / J. FONTENROSE, Didyma. Apollo's Oracle, Cult, and Companions, Berkeley, Los Angeles, London 1988, 77-105 / Ibid., The Delphic Oracle: Its Responses and Operations, Berkely/Los Angeles 1978.

[198] Compare 1.2 and 2.33 (57,17; 160,5-6 KOET.). See Origen, In Jer. h. 4.3 (GCS III, 25,15 KLOSTERMANN), Eus., H.E. 5.7, and Iren., Adv. haer. 2.31.2 (resurrections still happen, and false teachers do not prove their proclamation by miracles; SC 294, 328,8-20 ROUSSEAU et al.) and 5.6.1 (Christian prophets, SC 153, 74,13-20 ROUSS.), and Chrysostom, Hom. in Matt. 32.7 (PG 57, 386-7).

[199] BORRET IV.35 n. 3 and CHADWICK, Origen, 402 n.5 give references to literature on this formula. See Corp. Herm. 1.30 (CUF I, 17,14-22 NOCK-FESTUGIÈRE; and see the comment on 27 n. 78) and the pneumatic Marcosians ap. Iren., Adv. Haer. 1.21.5 (SC 264, 304,96-98 ROUSS.). Compare John 8:42 and 10:10. O. WEINREICH, De dis ignotis

your unrighteous deeds. But I want to save you. And you will see me coming again with heavenly power. Blessed is the one who worships me now. On all others I will cast everlasting fire — both in cities and in fields. And the people who do not know the punishments waiting for them will repent and groan in vain. But those who have been persuaded (πεισθέντας) by me I will keep forever. [Then he continues:] After brandishing these threats they add unknown, frantic, and completely obscure words (ἄγνωστα καὶ πάροιστρα καὶ πάντη ἄδηλα) whose signification (γνῶμα) no one with a mind could discover, for they are unclear (ἀσαφῆ), have no meaning, and furnish for any occasion a pretext for any senseless person or charlatan to appropriate what is said in any sense (σφετερίζεσθαι) he/she wishes.

Chadwick refers to the existence of the *Didache* and Syrian characters such as Alexander of Abonuteichos and Peregrinus Proteus to illustrate the probable existence of wandering prophets in Syria, and concludes: "But the content of their proclamation is Celsus' parody of perfectly good ante-Nicene Christian preaching of a rather enthusiastic type."[200] The nonsensical words with which the prophets end may be a form of glossolalia[201]. Origen (7.10 [161,20-24; 162,1-9 Koet.]) responds by taking the prophecy to be an example of a person believing himself to be a son of God or the Holy Spirit. For him the prophets spoke without any obscurity for the moral reformation of their hearers and put the more mysterious and esoteric truths in parables or proverbs — dark sayings that Celsus takes to be meaningless utterances. Origen notes that (7.11 [163,10-13 Koet.]) Celsus claims to have examined these alleged prophets: "[The lie of Celsus seems to me to be altogether obvious:] The apparent prophets which he heard himself, when exposed (ἐλεγχθέντες) by him, confessed to him why they begged and that they fabricated deceitful words (ὡμολόγησαν αὐτῷ οὗ τινος ἐδέοντο, καὶ ὅτι ἐπλάσσοντο λέγοντες ἀλλοπρόσαλλα)[202]. Origen's word ἐδέοντο probably implies that the prophets

---

quaestiones selectae ARW 18, 1915, (1-52) 38 refers to an epigram of Artemiodorus that begins with ἥκω Πρίαπος. See ibid, 34-45 for similar texts.

[200] CHADWICK, Origen, 402 n. 6 with reference to E. FASCHER, Προφήτης. Eine sprach- u. religionsgeschichtliche Untersuchung, Giessen 1927, 190-209 (who discusses various pagan prophets such as Peregrinus Proteus) and W. L. KNOX, Hellenistic Elements in Primitive Christianity, London 1944, 83 n. 2. On the passage in Origen see AUNE, Prophecy in Early Christianity, 41, 72, 239.

[201] M. KELSEY, Tongue Speaking. The History and Meaning of Charismatic Experience, New York 1981, 39 calls Celsus' reporting "part fact, part healthy pagan imagination"! On contemporary glossolalia cf. Iren., Adv. haer. 5.6.1 (SC 153, 74.13-20 ROUSS.). See also T. W. GILLESPIE, "A Pattern of Prophetic Speech in First Corinthians," JBL 97, 1978, 74-95 for a pattern (in Corinth) of comprehensible prophetic speech followed by ecstatic speech (glossolalia). Cp. AUNE, Prophecy in Early Christianity, 365 n. 133.

[202] BORRET V.41 translates this last phrase as "lui ont avoué leur imposture et qu'ils forgeaient des discours sans suite." Compare ἀλλοπρόσαλλον and πολύμορφον in Eunapius 496 (522 WRIGHT) on the multiform (all things to all people) nature of Libanius. The words can be appropriated in any way according to the above text from C. Celsum 7.9. See also

confessed to Celsus why they were begging[203]. Origen cannot believe that Celsus would have the experience he claims to have had. Perhaps, however, Celsus like his possible friend Lucian, was able to expose some kind of Christian prophet who was involved in fraudulent activity. The texts in *Didache* on greedy prophets are not without a certain amount of irony concerning the difficulty of distinguishing true and false prophets[204]. This is particularly apropos if Celsus encountered a prophet feigning glossolalia who was hungrier than he was inspired.

1.5.2 Prophecy in Hellenism

Despite his problems with Christian prophets, Celsus (like the rhetoricians) took prophecy seriously. He found Hellenistic prophecy to be vastly superior to the fraudulent activities of the Christian prophets. His view of inspired utterances in Hellenism was respectful (7.3 [154,18-25 Koet.]):[205]

> The things predicted by the Pythian oracle, or by the priestess of Dodona, or the god of Claros, or the Branchide oracles, or by the temple of Ammon and by thousands of other prophets, by whom probably the whole world was colonized, are held to be of no value. But the things predicted by the inhabitants of Judea, made in their manner — whether really said or not and following the usage still in force in Phoenicia and Palestine — these are considered to be amazing and unalterable (θαυμαστὰ καὶ ἀπαράλλακτα).

Much from the peripatetic school could be used against the oracles, according to Origen (7.3 [154,25-29; 155,13-18 Koet.])[206]. Origen does not apparently find it to be a problem that the philosophical objections to the oracles could also be used against the Hebrew prophets. Origen also seeks to discount the Pythian prophetess by asserting that an evil demon enters her via her genitalia[207]. He discounts her ecstatic trance, but does not discuss prophetic

---

ASH, Decline of Prophecy, 247-48 for Origen's views on the absence of prophets like those of ancient times in the church of Celsus' time.

[203] See LSJ s.v. δέω II.2.

[204] Compare Didache 11, 13.

[205] See § 1.2.22 above for a reference to Celsus' remarks (7.35 [185,17-20 KOET.]) that the gods appear in human form at the oracles of Mopsus, Amphiaraus, and Trophonius. Compare 3.34 (230,26-28 KOET.). See the discussion of Celsus' views on Hellenistic prophecy in FÉDOU, Christianisme, 426-32. FASCHER, Προφήτης, 217-219 discusses Origen's argument against pagan prophecy. Maximus describes Trophonius' cave and oracular practice in Diss. 8.2 (62,20-25 TR). On the Branchidai see FONTENROSE, Didyma, 45.

[206] CHADWICK (Origen, 396 n. 4) refers to Eus., P.E. 4.2.13 and 4.3.14 and to the naturalistic explanation of oracles in Ps. Arist. De mundo 4, 395b,26-30 (CUFr, 71-72 LORIMER). Cicero devotes the entire second book of De div. to an attack on divination and oracles.

[207] Compare 3.25 (221,29-222,1 KOET.). BORRET 4.18 n. 3 refers to Chrysostom, In Cor. h. 29.1 who shares the same view of the Pythian's experience. FONTENROSE regards the remarks of Chrysostom and Origen as worthless evidence (The Delphic Oracle, 199, 210-11). CHADWICK, Origen, 396 n.6 also provides bibliography. P. AMANDRY, La mantique

ecstasy in Hebrew prophecy. Origen is also offended that the Delphic Apollo prophesies through a woman, and uses that argument to show that the Delphic spirit is not a god (7.5 [157,14-17 Koet.]). Origen again uses an argument from consequence in 7.6 (157,27; 158,10-11 Koet.) and asks Celsus why the god does not use his foreknowledge as an incentive "if I may dare to say for the conversion, healing, and moral reformation of people" (πρὸς τὴν ἐπιστροφὴν καὶ θεραπείαν καὶ ἠθικὴν κατόρθωσιν τῶν ἀνθρώπων). The oracles answer people's petitions positively when the correct sacrifices (as bribes) are given to the evil demons.

Celsus would respond to Origen's argument with a text that Origen himself includes (8.45 [259,22-260,11 Koet.]):

> Is it necessary to reckon up all that came from the oracle-seats (χρηστηρίων) — all the things that prophets and prophetesses and other possessed individuals, both men and women, predicted in an inspired voice (ἐνθέῳ φώνῃ); all the marvels that have been heard in the innermost sanctuaries; all that has been revealed from victims and sacrifices to the inquirers; all that has been revealed from marvelous signs (τεραστίων συμβόλων)? Palpable appearances (ἐνάργη παρέστη φάσματα)[208] have come to some. All of life is full of these facts. How many cities have been built due to oracles and have put off epidemics and famine, and how many have been destroyed for not caring about or for forgetting them? How many were sent to colonize and following what was commanded have prospered? How many rulers and how many private individuals for the same reason have ended up better or worse? How many distressed by childlessness have received what they asked for and escaped the anger of demons? How many bodily infirmities have been healed? How many after outraging sanctuaries have been immediately caught? Some captured there on the spot lost their minds. Others confessed what they had done. Others killed themselves. Others were seized by incurable diseases. A deep voice from the innermost sanctuaries themselves has even destroyed some.

Celsus is obviously proud of the many good things that have been the result of oracles. Origen does his best to critique the oracles by appealing to the schools of Democritus, Epicurus, and Aristotle. Again he misses the fact that such a critique would also attack Hebrew prophecy. Origen also notes that Celsus regards the Greek appearances as "distinct" and the Christian stories as "myths" (τεράστια). Origen argues that the philosophical skeptics such as Democritus did not believe in the Greek stories. He wonders why Celsus' stories should not be mythical fictions (ἀναπλάσματα μυθικά). But the skeptics like Democritus would have believed in the Christian miracles had they met Moses or one of the prophets or even Jesus (8.45 [260,11-19 Koet.]). He also (8.46 [261,1-2 Koet.]) recounts Greek stories in which the Pythian prophetess was

---

apollinienne à Delphes, Paris 1950, 21-23 is skeptical of Origen's theory but does not categorically deny it. AMANDRY's index provides material on the oracles quoted by Celsus. Dodona and Ammon were Zeus' oracles and Delphi and Branchidae were oracles of Apollo.

[208] For such appearances see 3.24 (220,13-17 KOET.) and 7.35 (185,17-20 KOET.). The same verb appears in Acts 27:23.

bribed[209]. It is obvious that both figures, Origen and Celsus, are convinced that the oracles and prophecies of their own culture are superior. Both claim good results in the lives of humankind and both claim miraculous events associated with the prophets.

Celsus was not above a little constructive criticism of Greek oracles. After narrating the story of Aristeas the Proconnesian who vanished so miraculously and then so clearly appeared, he records that Apollo commanded the Metapontines to regard Aristeas as a god (ἐν θεῶν μοίρᾳ), even though nobody still thinks him to be a god (3.26, [222,14-15; Koet.])[210]. Origen gleefully notes (3.29 [226,19-25 Koet.]) that the Metapontines knew Aristeas was a human, and perhaps not a very good one, and were willing to discount the oracle that pronounced him to be a god — even if they were disobeying Apollo. It is clear that Celsus did not consider the oracles to be infallible.

Celsus (7.29 [178,23 Koet.]) believes in all kinds of "divinely inspired men" (θείοις ἀνδράσι). He argues (7.45 [197,5-8 Koet.]):[211] "And if you believe that a spirit comes down from God to announce divine (θεῖα) things, it may be this spirit which proclaims (κηρύττον) these things; in truth it was because the men of old were filled with it that they announced many fine truths." Origen notes that Celsus did not see the difference between his ancients and the truths that the Christians speak of (7.51 [201,27 Koet.]). The inspired individuals include "inspired poets (ἐνθέους) ... wise people and philosophers" (7.41 [191,24-25 Koet.])[212]. Hesiod was an example of an inspired poet, for Celsus (4.36, 38 [306,20-23; 308,29 Koet.]): "The Jews, cowering in a corner of Palestine, completely uneducated (ἀπαίδευτοι),[213] had not heard that Hesiod and millions of other inspired men (μυρίοις ἀνδράσιν ἐνθέοις) had sung these things." The Sibyl (7.53 [203,15-26 Koet.]), although her teachings have been corrupted by the Christians, and Anaxarchus (who spoke by a divine spirit while being beaten) are examples of other inspired people. In Celsus' eyes whole races such as the Chaldeans, Egyptians, Indians, and Persians are inspired (6.80 [151,20-33 Koet.]; ἐνθεωτάτοις). Celsus' philosopher *par excellence* is Plato whose teaching about not returning violence (discussed above in § 1.2.12 with reference to "turn the other cheek") is far superior to that of Jesus (7.58 [207,13 Koet.]). This is the case even

---

[209] CHADWICK, Origen, 485 n. 4 refers to Herodotus 6.66 and Cicero, De div. 2.57.118 and Minucius Felix, Oct. 26.6.

[210] Maximus also discusses these traditions of Aristeas (Diss. 10. 2, 3; 38.3 [78,39-79,51; 305,47-306,65 TR.]) although he does not identify Aristeas as a god. On Aristeas see BETZ, Gottmensch, 242-44.

[211] Celsus explains his philosophical underpinnings for this belief in 7.45 (196,19-197,13 KOET.). 7.45 contains a Platonist theory of knowledge.

[212] See the rhetoricians' use of this kind of ancient testimony in COOK, Protreptic Power, 113. Celsus regards Zeno the Stoic as wiser than Jesus (5.20).

[213] BADER, 112 refers to Jos. C. Ap. 2.135.

though Plato does not claim that the son of God "talked with me" (6.8 [78,13-3 Koet.])[214]. Celsus identifies the spirit that gave these teachings as divine (7.45 [197,5-8 Koet.]). It is apparent that the argument between Celsus and Origen over prophecy is an example of the fundamental differences between Hellenistic and the emerging Christian culture. Celsus is quite satisfied with the oracles of his own culture and dismisses the idea that Hebrew prophets could have prophesied the death and suffering of a divine being. He is repulsed by what he sees as the miserable example of contemporary Christian prophecy.

1.6 Celsus on Christianity and Society

The vagabonds whom Celsus knows to be Christian prophets are not much different from the despised people who found Christianity attractive — according to Celsus' observations. Celsus' distaste for Jesus is matched by his distaste for the character of the people who were attracted to the Christian religion. At times Celsus seems to become something like a modern sociologist of religion. He offers explanations for the attractiveness of Christian belief to those of a certain social class (low). Gender (specifically female) and age (children) also plays a role in his sociological analysis of early Christian recruits. His "conservative" social philosophy provides him grounds for defending persecution of Christians. Christians who refuse to serve the lords of creation should cease to exist from the earth. He finally encourages them to take their place in Greco-Roman society. They should take part in public festivals and in the sacrifices. Their place in society could include serving as officers or soldiers in the emperor's legions.

1.6.1 Blind Faith and the Simpletons who Accept It

Christianity is irrational for Celsus[215]. The Christian people that he had encountered were unwilling to give any reasons for their faith. Origen writes that Celsus urges us to (1.9 [61,9-21 Koet.]):

> accept doctrines by following reason and a rational guide. Error certainly comes to one who assents to certain doctrines without doing so. [And he compares them to] those who believe, with no reason, the beggar priests of Cybele, and the diviners, and the devotees of

---

[214] The Greeks in general do not claim that their ideas had been announced by a god or the son of a god (6.1 [70,6-8 KOET.]) according to Celsus. Origen notes that Celsus quoted from Plato's Epistles and Phaedrus as if they were ἐνθέως εἰρημένων (inspired utterances; 6.17 [87,22 KOET.])

[215] Plutarch recommends philosophy to guard against the errors of superstition and atheism in De Is. et Os. 67-68 (377f-378d). Compare Galen's (COOK, Some Hellenistic Responses, 239-40) and Porphyry's complaints about the irrationality of Christian belief (§ 2.3.4). See FREDE, Celsus, 5197 and ANDRESEN, Logos, 168. For bibliography on the text see RINALDI, Biblia Gentium, F. 646.

Mithras and Sabazius and whatever else one might encounter, apparitions of Hecate, or of another demon or demons. For as often among them perverse people use the ignorance (ἰδιωτείᾳ) of easily deceived individuals (εὐεξαπατήτων) and lead them where they will, so it happens [he says] among the Christians. [He says] that some do not want to give or receive a reason for what they believe and use sayings such as "do not examine (ἐξέταζε) but believe," and "your faith will save you." [And he says that they claim:] "The wisdom of the world is bad, and foolishness is good" (1 Cor 3:19).

Origen shares Celsus' enthusiasm for philosophy, but regrets that few people in the world are enthusiastic about rational thought (1.9 [61,27-62,3 Koet.]). He distinguishes the multitude of believers from those who advance in the study of rational arguments. Celsus thinks (3.18 [216,14-16 Koet.]) that Christians "drive away every wise person (σόφον) from the doctrine (or reason) of their faith (τοῦ λόγου τῆς πίστεως), and call only those who are ignorant and servile people." For Celsus, consequently, faith is not something that is laudable but blind (3.39 [235,15-16 Koet.]): "our faith, overpowering our souls, creates such an assent to Jesus." Christians in Celsus' experience (6.7 [77,4-5 Koet.]) demand immediate faith. This contrasts to Plato's use of dialectic (questions and answers) to illuminate those who follow his philosophy[216]. Plato also speaks of friendly proofs (or refutations εὐμενεῖς ... ἔλεγχοι) in *Ep.* 7.344b — something Celsus does not find among the Christians. Plato is not arrogant nor does he tell lies, "saying that he himself has found a new thing or has come from heaven to announce it, but he avows the source of these teachings" (6.10 [80,7-9 Koet.]). Celsus admires Plato for not putting any matter beyond discussion (ἀνεξέλεγκτον 6.10 [79,22-23 Koet.]). Celsus again comments on the irrationality of the Christian demand for blind faith (6.11 [80,33-81,4 Koet.]): "If some [he means the Christians] propose this one, others propose another, and all have a common and ready saying: believe if you want to be saved or leave! What should those who truly want to be saved do? Should they divine by a throw of the dice where they should turn and with whom they should associate?" Origen denies that many have claimed to visit human life as sons of God. Competitors like Simon the Samaritan and Dositheus have no significance according to Origen (6.11 [81,5-20 Koet.]). Origen misses Celsus' point that philosophy provides a superior alternative to any faith in a savior. What Celsus' philosophy is will be briefly viewed at the end of this chapter. It includes belief in a supreme God, the gods, the demons who do things such as control the human body, the worship of images, civic service of the emperor and state, reincarnation for as many as 30,000 ages, and an ultimate destiny in heaven for some immortal souls.

---

[216] *Ep.* 7. 344b. BORRET 3.195 also refers to Prot. 312d, Crat. 390c, and Resp. 534d, e. PICHLER, Streit, 115, refers to Albinus, Eisagoge 1 (147,15-19 HERMANN) and Alcin., Didask. 4-6 154,10-160,41 (4-16 W./L.) for a Middle Platonist's discussion of dialectic.

1.6.2 The Effectiveness of Christian Recruitment of the Socially Objectionable Classes

Celsus is highly critical of Christian proclamation, of the Christians' ability to persuade people to join their movement, and of the kinds of people who join the movement. For Celsus and his Jew, Jesus either convinced no one while on earth (2.43 [166,5 Koet.]), or he convinced only ten sailors and tax collectors (2.46 [168,14-15 Koet.]). Sometimes Celsus denies that Jesus convinced anyone at all — even his own disciples (2.39 [164,3 Koet.]). He doubts that a god among people would be disbelieved as Jesus was (2.74, 75 [195,14; 196,1 Koet.]). Even Jesus (2.76 [196,26-29 Koet.]) with his woes and threats was unable to effect persuasion (πεῖσαι ἀδυνατεῖ). At one point Celsus' Jew mentions the Jewish hope in the resurrection that the messianic leader will inaugurate. He poses this skeptical question: "Where then is he that we might see and believe (2.77 [199,30-31 Koet.])?" His argument is that it is (and was) quite easy to disbelieve in Jesus[217]. Celsus' problem is that even though Jesus convinced nobody, those who wish (the Christians) persuade (πείθουσιν) multitudes (2.46 [168,25-26 Koet.]). Celsus is offended that the Christians are able to persuade (πείθειν) only the foolish (ἠλιθίους), dishonorable (ἀγεννεῖς), stupid (ἀναισθήτους), slaves, women, and little children (3.44 [240,3-5 Koet.])[218]. He notes, "we say these things to exhort (προτροπήν) sinners being unable to attract (προσάγεσθαι) any truly worthy and just man, and because of this we open the doors to the most unholy and ruined (ἐξωλεστάτους) people" (3.65 [258,22-25 Koet.]). The wise are uninterested in Christianity: "no sensible (φρόνιμον) person is persuaded by this teaching (πείθεσθαι τῷ λόγῳ), being alienated by the crowd of those who surrender (προσερχομένων) to it" (3.73 [264,15-17 Koet.]). Christians even stoop to using music to draw in converts: "we stupefy people beforehand by flute playing and sounds like those who make booming sounds around those who are being initiated into the rites of the Corybantes (οἱ τοὺς κορυβαντιζομένους περιβομβοῦντες)" (3.16 [215,5-8 Koet.]). Near the conclusion of his work Celsus recounts an utterly intolerable Christian fantasy of persuading the rulers of the empire (8.71 [287,23-288,4 Koet.]):

> It is true that this proposal of yours is not tolerable: If those who rule over us after being persuaded (πεισθέντες) by you are captured, you will persuade those who rule afterward, and then others if these are captured; and others upon others, until after all those who are

---

[217] The Jew also asks if the purpose of Jesus' coming down was that "we might disbelieve" (2.78 [200,8-9 KOET.]). Origen answers that the "sin" of the Jews results in the call of the Gentiles into God's kingdom.

[218] This theme continues in 3.48, 49, 50, 52 and the famous passage in 3.55 about proselytizing women and children (244,15; 245,18; 246,7; 248,9; 250,16 KOET.). Caecilius the pagan makes similar charges about uneducated people and credulous women who are attracted to Christianity in Minucius Felix, Oct. 5.4, 8.4 (3,23; 6,32-33 KYT.).

persuaded by you are captured, when a prudent ruler who foresees what is happening will utterly destroy you with your whole race before he is destroyed first.

One can feel Celsus' *frisson* of horror at the possibility that the leaders of the empire could be overcome by the Christians' proclamation.

Origen, in response to Celsus' question about whether God is able to persuade (6.57 [128,5-11 Koet.]) quotes the definition of rhetoric in Plato's *Gorgias* 453a in which rhetoricians are called "creators of persuasion" (πειθοῦς δημιουργῶν). He notes that even the person trained to the highest degree in rhetoric may be unable to persuade a person. Likewise God can use persuasive language and still not persuade a person, because God does not cause the act of assent. There is an element of human freedom in the issue of persuasion, according to Origen.

1.6.3 The Content of Christian Propaganda: the Appeal to the Unhappy and Sinful

The content of the Christians' preaching is responsible for their ability to persuade in Celsus' understanding. The Christian preachers (3.55 [250,16-251,8 Koet.]) are shameless:

> We indeed see in private homes wool-workers, leather-workers, fullers, and the most uneducated and countrified people (ἀπαιδευτοτάτους τε καὶ ἀγροικοτάτους). Before their older and wiser masters they would not dare to speak anything. But if they take their children in private and with them some silly women, they expound some amazing beliefs: they should not heed father and teachers but should believe (πείθεσθαι) them. The others talk nonsense and are senseless, and nothing that is truly good do they know, nor can they do — being preoccupied with empty nonsense. But they only know how one should live, and if the children believe them, they will be happy (μακαρίους) and produce a home that is happy (τὸν οἶκον ἀποφανεῖν εὐδαίμονα). And if while speaking they see one of the teachers of the youth coming, or one of the more prudent individuals, or even the father himself, the more discreet of them run trembling away, and the bolder ones stir the children up to rebel, whispering that if the father is present or one of their teachers they do not wish nor can they explain anything good to the children, because they are repelled by the stupidity and awkwardness of these completely corrupted individuals who have advanced far in vice and who punish them. If they wish, they have only to leave their father and teachers and go with the women and little children whom they play with into the weaver's workshop[219], the leather-worker's shop, or the fuller's shop that they may attain perfection (τὸ τέλειον). And by saying these things they persuade (πείθουσι).

The content of the Christian preaching that Celsus is aware of is quite simple: a promise that happiness will illumine the household of the children and that they themselves will be happy and that they will learn perfection. The content of the proclamation in relation to the narrative of Jesus is equally simple according to Origen (1.7 [60,1-5 Koet.]) who summarized the preaching (κήρυγμα) of the Christians as including Jesus' birth from a virgin, his crucifixion, his

---

[219] For this translation of γυναικωνῖτιν see W. DEN BOER, Gynaeconitis, a centre of christiana propaganda, VigChr 4, 1950, 61-64.

resurrection, and the proclamation of judgment which punishes sinners and pronounces the righteous worthy of reward. It is probably no accident that Celsus (and his Jew) spend the first two books (of Origen's work) attacking precisely the elements of Christian proclamation that surround the life of Jesus. Celsus had already expressed his indignation at the willingness of Jesus to have mercy on sinners (2.71 [193,28 Koet.]) whether they repent or not.

Celsus is unable to accept the Christians' desire to call sinners into the kingdom of God. He writes:

> That I am not accusing them any more bitterly than the truth forces me, let one judge by this. Those who call to other initiations (τελετάς) proclaim publicly: "Whoever is pure in hand and wise in voice." Again others say: "Whoever is pure from every defilement and whose heart is conscious of no evil, and who has lived well and justly." These things are what the ones who promise the purification from sins publicly proclaim. Let us hear whom they (Christians) call: "Whoever, they say, is a sinner, whoever is witless, whoever is a little child, and in brief, whoever is miserable (κακοδαίμων), the kingdom of God will welcome this individual." Now by "sinner" do you not mean the unjust, the thief, the housebreaker, the poisoner, the temple-robber, and the grave-robber? What others would a robber call in his public proclamation (3.59 [253,22-254,3 Koet.]?

Origen responds (3.59 [254,4-15 Koet.]) by conceding that Christians do encourage sinners and unwise to come. When, however, they have done all in their power to live better lives, then "we call them to our initiations (τελετάς). 'For we speak wisdom among the perfect' (1 Cor 2:6)." Celsus finds the fact that Christians invite bad people into their community to be scandalous. The proclaimers of the mysteries only invite those who are pure to begin with.

Celsus also believes that if God has been sent to sinners, he should also have been sent to those without sin[220]. "God will welcome the unjust, if he humbles himself from his wickedness, but the righteous person, if he from the beginning looks up to him, God will not welcome." Origen in turn denies that anyone is without sin (3.62 [256,20-22.23-26 Koet.]). Celsus does appear (3.63 [257,22-26 Koet.]) to accept that "This is probably true: It is natural for the human race to sin ... He should have, therefore, simply called everyone if all in fact are sinners." He then asks (3.64 [258,1-2 Koet.]), "Why then this honoring of sinners over others?" Christians are unable to convert good people, and this explains their preference for sinners (3.65 [258,22-25; 259,8-12 Koet.]): "We say such things to exhort sinners, being unable to attract anyone really good and just, and for this reason we open the doors to the most unholy and ruined people (ἐξωλεστάτους) ... Certainly it is quite clear that no one could completely change, even by punishment or by pity, those who are naturally inclined to sin and who have the habit of sinning. It is extraordinarily difficult to radically change nature. Those who are without sin participate in a

---

[220] Macarius' pagan objected to baptismal teaching from this point of view (§ 3.38 below).

better life"[221]. Celsus finds the Christians' desire to use the principle that "God will be able to do all things"[222] to be inadequate against his argument that: "He will not will anything unjust [admitting that he could do what is unjust, but does not wish to do so] (3.70 [262,19-20.27-28 Koet.])." What Celsus finds to be unrighteous in the Christians' image of God is God's desire to accept sinners and not accept the righteous (3.71 [263,5-8 Koet.]): "Similar to those who are slaves by pity, enslaved by pity for those who lament, God relieves the evil and rejects the good who do nothing like that — which is most unjust."[223] Celsus' problems with Christian proclamation are probably based on the sociological model of the convert that he sketched above (3.55 [250,15 Koet.]). Those who are wise want nothing to do with the church, and consequently Celsus assumes that the proclamation encourages sinners and turns away good, wise, and intelligent people. He remarks that Christians explain this by claiming (3.72 [263,23-25 Koet.]): "The wise (σόφοι) repulse the things we say, misled and fettered by wisdom." Christian teachers seek the stupid (3.74 [265,14 Koet.]) and are like people who promise to restore bodies to health, but turn their patients away from expert physicians (3.75 [266,7-11 Koet.]). Their teachers are like "a drunken person coming among drunkards who slanders the sober individuals by saying they are drunk" (3.76 [268,5-7 Koet.])[224]. Or the teacher is like a person with ophthalmia who accuses sharp eyed people of having defective vision (3.77 [268,21-24 Koet.]). Celsus' view of Christian proselytizing is that it takes people away from what could really help them (i.e. Hellenistic tradition): "I make these accusations and others similar (that I may not have to enumerate them all). I say that they sin against God and speak disparagingly of him so that they may lead evil people on with empty hopes and beguile them to despise superior goods (κρειττόνων)[225], as if abstaining from them they will be better off" (3.78 [269,8-12 Koet.]).

---

[221] NOCK remarks that Celsus may have been provoked by Justin, Apol. 1.14.1-3 (52,1-53,18 MARC.) who argues that since becoming Christians people have changed their lives for the better (review of ANDRESEN VigChr 12, 1958, 317). BADER, 99 refers to Plut., Mor. 551d-f and 555d-f.

[222] Compare § 2.3.21 and § 3.51 below for attacks on omnipotence.

[223] Celsus also likens the Christian God to a judge who is influenced by flattery and not like good judges who stop people from wailing that their judgment not be affected by feelings of mercy, but be based on truth (3.63 [257,7-11 KOET.]).

[224] Macarius' pagan also makes liberal use of the image of drunkenness when attacking the NT (Apocriticus 3.19 (99,19 BLONDEL) = HARNACK, Porphyrius F. 23 with reference to Jesus; Apocriticus 3.33 [128,6 BLONDEL] = HARNACK, Porphyrius F. 30 with reference to Paul).

[225] CHADWICK, Origen, 180 translates with "good men." See 3.81 (271,20-21 KOET.) where Origen interprets it is a neuter.

1.6.4 What Christian Recruits are Like

Celsus' opinions about the Christians' intelligence is clear from his thoughts about the characteristics of those whom they are able to persuade, and the character of those whom they invite. Christians only call stupid and slavish people (ἀνοήτους καὶ τοὺς ἀνδραποδώδεις 3.18 [216,16 Koet.]). The Christians are clear about who they want in their movement (3.44 [239,26-240,5 Koet.]):

> They command such things: Let no educated, wise, or prudent person come forward. For such characteristics are thought to be evil by us. But if anyone is unlearned (ἀμαθής), unintelligent, uneducated (ἀπαίδευτος), or a little child, let him come with confidence. By obviously admitting that only such people are worthy of their God, they are conspicuous because they wish and are able to persuade only silly, ignoble, insensate, and slavish people, women, and little children.

Celsus cannot understand why the Christians believe education in Hellenistic philosophy to be an evil (3.49 [245,18-22 Koet.]): "Above all what evil is there in being educated, in cultivating the best traditions (πεπαιδεῦσθαι λόγων τῶν ἀρίστων), and in both being and appearing prudent (φρόνιμον)?²²⁶ Why does this prevent knowing God? Why is it not instead useful and a better means by which one could attain the truth?" Because Christians say the wisdom of people is foolishness with God they aim to convert only the uneducated and stupid (6.12 [82,12.15-16 Koet.]). They summon only miserable people (3.59 [253,31 Koet.]) and lead away the wicked (3.78 [269,10 Koet.]) hoping to persuade them to become good. Christians (3.75 [267,20-21 Koet.] and compare 6.1 [70,12-13 Koet.]) take refuge with childish and silly rustics (νηπίους καὶ ἠλιθίους ἀγροίκους). Christian magic is effective only with the uneducated and depraved (6.40, 41 [109,14-16.26-28 Koet.]). Christians are a fearful (δειλόν) and carnal race (7.39 [189,13-14 Koet.]) and are maimed in their souls (7.45 [197,11 Koet.]) because they are bound to the flesh. To sum up (8.49 [264,4-5 Koet.]), they are countrified (ἄγροικοι), unclean, without reason and are diseased with rebellion (ἀκάθαρτοι καὶ χωρὶς λόγου τῇ στάσει συννοσοῦντες). Origen, of course, objects at every point, but Celsus' critique is more social than conceptual. The Christians he knew (or claimed to know about) were utter boors. Celsus has no problems justifying persecution of these unattractive recruits to the Christian faith.

---

²²⁶ In 4.10 (280,30-281,4 KOET.) Celsus charges that the Christians arouse the amazement of the uneducated (ἰδιώτων) using terrors and phantoms like those in Bacchic mysteries (the argument from hell). See COOK, Protretpic Power, 118-19.

1.6.5 Celsus on Persecution

Celsus was a social conservative who believed that people should revere their ancestral traditions[227]. He viewed Christians as rebels (3.5 [στασίασαντες πρὸς τὸ κοινόν], 14; 5.33; 8.49 [στάσει] [206,18; 213,16; 35,4-5; 264,5 Koet.]) against Jewish and Hellenistic tradition who were guilty of forming a secret society (1.1 [συνθηκῶν], 1.3; 8.20 [ἀφανοῦς καὶ ἀπορρήτου κοινωνίας] [56,9; 57,20; 238,4-5 Koet.]). Christians, if one was found still wandering about in secret, were "searched out to be condemned to die" (8.69 [286,7-8 Koet.]). Celsus frequently mentions the fact of persecution of Christians (1.3 [death penalty decreed for Christians]), 2.45, 8.39, 8.65 [57,22-23; 167,21; 253,27; 281,5-6 Koet.]). He (8.39 [253,24-29 Koet.]) charges that those who bind and crucify Christians (and ridicule Jesus) do not suffer revenge at the hand of the Christians' demon (or son of God)[228]. His rationale for persecutions is twofold. Christians dishonor the gods and the emperor. If Christians refuse to worship the lords (ἐπιστατάς) who are in charge of activities such as marriage and the procreation of children, and other things in life, then they ought not to do those things and in fact should cease to exist on earth (8.55 [271,19-23 Koet.]). In political terms Christians are "mad" (μεμήναμεν) and "we rush headlong to excite the anger of the emperor or a governor against ourselves which brings assaults, tortures, and even death on us" (8.65 [281,4-6 Koet.]). Christians refuse[229] to swear by the fortune (genius [τυχήν]) of the emperor (8.65 [281,19-20 Koet.]). Describing the ruling powers, Celsus says, "it is not without demonic power that they have been deemed worthy (to rule)" (8.63 [279,23-24 Koet.]). Arnaldo Momigliano notes, however, that Roman authors did not attempt to compare the structure of Olympus with the structure of the Roman empire[230].

---

[227] R. WILKEN, The Christians as the Romans Saw Them, New Haven/London 1984, 94. On Christians as enemies of tradition see also SCHÄFKE, Frühchristlicher Widerstand, 630-48 who also discusses charges that Christianity was a conspiracy (611-15).

[228] This is similar to an anonymous pagan in Arnobius, Adv. nat. 2.76 (155,17 MARCHESI): "Why, if you are the servants of the almighty God and if, according to your own belief, he watches over your safety and salvation, why then does he allow you to suffer so much persecution, so many trials and torments?" Cf. COURCELLE, Anti-Christian Arguments, 155.

[229] CHADWICK, Origen, 502 n.2 gives references to this refusal. Compare BORRET IV.325 n. 4.

[230] A. MOMIGLIANO, The Disadvantages of Monotheism for a Universal State, in: On Pagans, Jews, and Christians, Hanover, NH 1987, (142-58) 148. Without mentioning specific primary sources CHADWICK refers to Roman "imperial theology" with reference to 8.67, 68 (Origen, 503, n.5).

Momigliano[231] does quote a very interesting text from Dio Cassius (Histories 52.35-36), in which Maecenas discourages Augustus from having gold or silver images of himself and temples made for himself. He argues that virtue raises people to the level of gods:

> ... worship the divine power everywhere and in every way in accordance with the traditions of our fathers (κατὰ τὰ πάτρια) and compel all others to honor it. Those who attempt to distort our religion with strange rites, you should abhor and punish not merely for the sake of gods ... but because such men, by bringing new divinities in place of old, persuade many to adopt foreign practices from which spring up conspiracies, factions (συστάσεις) and cabals which are far from profitable to monarchy. Do not, therefore, permit anybody to be an atheist or sorcerer... For such men, by speaking the truth sometimes, but generally falsehood, often encourage a great many to attempt revolutions. The same thing is done also by many who pretend to be philosophers, hence I advise you to be on your guard against them too (trans. E. Cary, LCL).

Dio's speech (from the early third century) displays attitudes that are similar to those of Celsus with regard to Christianity. Christians, for Celsus, are seditious and the adoption of Christian teaching would result in social anarchy. Celsus has very specific prescriptions for Christians.

1.6.6 Celsus on the Civic Duties of a Christian

Christians should take part in public festivals (πανθοινίας) and should sacrifice to the demons (8.24 [240,28-30 Koet.]). They should propitiate demonic powers and the emperors who hold their position by the power of demons (8.63 [279,21-24 Koet.])[232]. They should take oaths by the emperor (8.65, 67 [281,19; 284,1-2 Koet.]). If all refuse to do this, as the Christians do, then the emperor would be abandoned and anarchy would ensue (8.68 [284,15-20 Koet.]). Not only anarchy would follow, but a Christianized Roman empire would be defenseless, because the Christian God would surely not fight for it (8.69 [285,24-286,2 Koet.]): "You will certainly not say that if the Romans were persuaded (πεισθέντες) by you, were to neglect their customary practices towards gods and people, and should call on your Highest or whomever you wish, he would descend and fight for them, and there would be no necessity for any other force." Celsus notes that even though God promised to defend the Jews, they have been left with no land or home, and that Christians are searched out and condemned to death (8.69 [286,2-8 Koet.]). Celsus apparently thinks the goal of Christian evangelism is political and completely absurd (8.72 [288,14-18 Koet.]): "If only it were possible for the inhabitants of Asia, Europe, Libya, both Greeks and barbarians all the way to the ends of the earth, to agree on one law ... the one who thinks this knows

---

[231] *Disadvantages*, 146. SCHÄFKE argues that the text obviously refers to Christians in: *Frühchristlicher Widerstand*, 608-09.

[232] Compare Celsus' quotation of Homer (Il. 2.205) in 8.68 (284,14 KOET.): "Let there be one king, him to whom the son of crafty Kronos gave the power."

nothing." This comment is preceded by Celsus' horrified comment about the Christians' belief that eventually they will persuade "those who now reign over us" to become Christians (8.71 [287,24-25 Koet.])[233]. Instead Christians should "aid the emperor with all our strength, take part in his just actions, fight for him, go on campaign with him if he urges, and be fellow-generals with him" (8.73 [290,15-18 Koet.])[234]. They should also "take part in governing the country, if it is necessary to do so for the defense of the laws and of piety" (8.75 [292,1-2 Koet.]).

1.7 Celsus' Sketch of a Religious Philosophy: His Defense of Images, Reincarnation/Eternal Life, and a Hellenistic View of God

Although Origen does not gives any sustained texts of Celsus in which Celsus describes his own philosophy, there are many intimations of Celsus' own views in the context of his critique of Christianity. In particular his discussion of the Christians' attack on images and polytheism reveals some of Celsus' own beliefs. In addition his attack on the Christian use of the fear of hell to recruit people also illustrates his own eschatology. He believes in reincarnation and eternal life. His God is the supreme God of the Greco-Roman pantheon.

1.7.1 Celsus on the Christian Critique of Image Worship

Celsus was quite offended at the Christians' refusal to worship statues of the gods. He, with the Christians, did not believe that statues themselves were gods (1.5 [58,22-29 Koet.]):

> For this reason they do not think things made by hands are gods, since it is not reasonable that the things made by the most ordinary artisans of evil character are gods — often fabricated by unjust people. [In what follows he wants to regards this as a common belief — one not invented by the Christians — and cites the passage of Heraclitus:] "Those who approach inanimate objects as if they were gods do things similar to a person who chatters with houses."[235]

---

[233] ANDRESEN, Logos, 362, in a very perceptive comment, hypothesizes that Celsus may be responding to Justin's attempt to do just that in his first apology.

[234] Maximus devoted an oration to praising the virtues of those who will fight for the state (Diss. 23 [194,1-201,172 TR.]). Compare Plotinus' discussion of civic virtues in Ennead. 1.2.1 (I, 55,16-46,23 H./S.)

[235] Heraclitus, F. B5 Diels quoted in 7.62 (212,3 KOET.). Compare Clem Al., Protr. 4.50.4 (39,9 S./T.), and an attack on the character of image-makes in Protr. 4.53.4-6 (41,16-29 S./T.). ANDRESEN, Logos, 248 refers to Plutarch, De Iside 17 (379 c-d) where the moralist asserts that some Greeks looked on images as gods. J. GEFFCKEN's article is still of fundamental importance — Der Bilderstreit des heidnischen Altertums, ARW 19, 1916-19, 286-315.

Origen notes that Celsus claims that "the Persians also think this [citing] Heraclitus who puts it on record"[236]. Origen goes on the quote the *Republic* of Zeno of Citium: "To build temples will not be necessary; for one should believe that no work of architects and artisans is sacred, worth much, or holy" (1.5 [59,1-6 Koet.])[237].

Again in 7.62 (211,18-212,22 Koet.) Celsus writes that "They cannot tolerate the view of temples, altars, and statues (ἀγάλματα)."[238] He continues with references to the Scythians, Libyan nomads, Seres, and Persians who have similar beliefs and again refers to Heraclitus:

> He covertly intimates that it is stupid to pray to statues if one does not know gods and heroes — who they are. Such is the thought of Heraclitus. They openly dishonor statues. If it is because an object of stone, wood, copper, or gold — which one artisan or another made — cannot be a god, then their wisdom is laughable. For who other than a very little child thinks that these things are gods and not votive offerings and images (ἀγάλματα) of the gods? If it is that one should regard no images (εἰκόνας) as divine because God has a different form (μορφήν), as the Persians think, then they have forgotten as they refute themselves when they say "God made the human in his own image" (Gen 1:26-27) and of a form (εἶδος) similar to this own. They will agree that the statues are in honor of certain beings, of like or unlike form (εἶδος), but that the beings to whom the statues are dedicated are not gods but demons, and whoever worships God should not serve demons.

Celsus is not willing to argue that objects of wood and gold are gods, but he does defend the worship of such images which honor the divine beings that they resemble[239]. Maximus of Tyre was also an energetic defender of the use of images of the gods. All the peoples of the world use images of some sort[240]. Origen (7.64 [215,1-23 Koet.]) responds to Celsus that the Scythians, Libyan nomads, and Seres believe in no gods and so are led to their rejection of image worship by a different doctrine than are the Christians. Jews and Christians reject temples, altars and images because of the commandments in Exodus 20:3-5 and Deut. 6:13. The Persians worship the sun (7.65 [214,24-26 Koet.]). Origen (7.65 [215,13-17 Koet.]) also concedes that is "is possible to know God, his only-begotten son, and those who are honored by God with the title of God and who take part in his divinity and who are different from all the gods of the nations that are demons. But it is not possible to known God

---

[236] Herodotus 1.131.

[237] SVF 1.265. Compare Clem. Al., Strom. 5.11.76 (377,1 S./F.) and Plutarch, Mor. 1034b.

[238] Caecilius also notes the Christians' rejection of altars, temples, and images in Min. Fel. 10.2 (8,15 KYT.).

[239] FÉDOU, Christianisme, 305-10 has an excellent summary of Celsus' defense of images.

[240] Diss. 2 Εἰ θεοῖς ἀγάλματα ἱδρυτέον (13, app. crit. TR.) and in particular 2.2 (15,34-37.40-42 TR.). Maximus also defends the practice of clothing statues (4.5 [33,91-94 TR.]) to glorify the gods. Maximus observes that God is above all language and human conception, and that images help human weakness (2.10 [20,183-21,192 TR.]).

and to pray to statues." Origen, in 3.37 (234,2-4 Koet.), explains that angels participate in the divine nature. This reply is similar to Macarius' answer to the Hellene who is also offended at the Christians' refusal to take part in the worship of images[241].

To respond to the Christians' claim that the images are dedicated to demons, Celsus replies (7.68 [216,31-217,2 Koet.]): "They themselves are clearly convicted of worshipping not a god, nor a demon, but a corpse (νεκρόν)." Celsus then argues that people should worship demons (his argument is quoted below in the section on polytheism).

Celsus continues this line of attack in 8.17 (234,15-17 Koet.) when he charges that "we shrink from establishing altars, statues, and temples [since he thinks it is] the unmistakable password (πιστόν ... σύνθημα) of our secret and mysterious association (κοινωνίας)"[242]. Origen argues that images and votive offerings appropriate to God are formed in us by the divine Logos and include the virtues "which are imitations of the Firstborn of every creature in whom are the models (μιμήματα) of justice, temperance, courage, wisdom, piety, and the other virtues" (8.17 [234,24-235,1 Koet.]). This ethical imagery is based on Col 1:15 and John 1:18.

Celsus knows or claims to know of Christians who behave in shocking ways with regard to images of the gods (8.41 [255,4-21 Koet.]):

You revile (λοιδορῶν) and laugh at their statues (ἀγάλματα),[243] but if you reviled Dionysus himself or Heracles in his presence, you would perhaps not get away unpunished. But when your God was present, those who tortured and punished him had to suffer nothing for doing these things and not even afterwards during their life. And since that time what new thing has come to pass by which one might believe that he was not a human magician but the child of God. And the one who sent his son for the sake of certain messages allowed him to be punished so cruelly that the message perished with him, and after so much time has passed he has paid no attention. What father is so unholy (ἀνόσιος)? He may have possibly, as you say, willed it, therefore he suffered such outrages. But the gods whom you blaspheme can also say that they themselves will it, and therefore they endure blasphemy. For it is best to compare equal things to each other. But these gods severely requite the one who blasphemes them who either must consequently escape and hide, or being captured is put to death.

---

[241] § 3.48 below.

[242] Celsus also calls Christianity a secret society (or people with secret doctrines) in 1.1, 1.3 and 8.20 (56,2; 57,20; 238,4 KOET.).

[243] In 8.38 (253,2-5 KOET.) Celsus charges similarly: "Christians say, See, standing by the statue (ἀγάλματι) of Zeus, or Apollo, or any other god, I blaspheme it and hit it; but it does not retaliate against me." Apollo's priests affirm that "The mills of the gods grind slowly on the children's children and those who are born later" (8.40 [254,13-15 KOET.]). On this issue see also Julian's Letter to a Priest, Ep. 89b, 295a-c (I/2, 162,16-163,9 BIDEZ) where Julian compares the profanation of temples to the destruction of the Jewish temple. Consequently one cannot count profanation as a reproach against divine providence.

Origen denies this form of Christian behavior (8.41 [256,1-14 Koet.]), and argues that even if certain demons are established in certain images (Dionysus and Heracles), Christians would not revile even them. He also believes that the suffering of the Jews (8.42 [257,2-10 Koet.]) including the destruction of Jerusalem was punishment for the crucifixion. The "new thing" includes the birth the race of Christians (8.43 [257,19-22 Koet.]), and the punishment of Jesus did not destroy God's message. Origen also believes that the demons take vengeance on Christians, because Christians drive them out of the statues and bodies and souls of human beings (8.43 [258,19-22 Koet.]). This issue naturally leads into Celsus' defense of polytheism.

1.7.2 Celsus on the Christian Critique of Polytheism

Celsus' argument for image worship (7.68 [216,31 Koet.]), mentions angels and demons who each have authority from the "great God." In Celsus' conception each nation of the earth (5.25 [26,8-13 Koet.]) has its own law and customs and worship (which should be followed) — including the Jews:

> .... but it is also probable that the different regions of the earth from the beginning have been assigned to different tutelary powers (ἐπόπταις), and have been divided into so many dominions, and in this way are administered. Indeed the things done in each dominion are done correctly if accomplished in a manner pleasing to those powers. But to break laws (νενομισμένα)[244] that have been established in every region since the beginning is not holy.[245]

Origen points out (5.27 [27,23-28,12 Koet.]) that such a position leads to all kinds of ethical problems given the Scythians' laws that allow parricide and the Persians' laws that allow incest, the Taurians' customs where victims are offered to Artemis, and the Libyans' practice of child sacrifice to Kronos[246].

In his defense of image worship Celsus develops a theory of the community of divine beings in which each has his or her place in God's providential care for reality (7.68 [217,3-11 Koet.]):

> First I will ask, why should demons not be served? Nevertheless, are not all things governed according to the will of God and is not all providence from him? That which exists in the universe, whether work of god, angels, other demons, or heroes, all these things have a law from the greatest God. And over every (work) has there not been appointed a being who has been deemed worthy to receive power? Would not the one who worships God justly serve this being who has obtained authority from him? Indeed, it is not possible, he says, for the same person to serve several lords (Mt 6:24, Lk 16:13).

---

[244] On the translation of this term see BORRET III.74 n.3.

[245] ANDRESEN, Logos, 198 discusses the relationship of Celsus' demonology to his view of law.

[246] CHADWICK, Origen, 284 n. 3 notes that these are stock example about the relativity of moral codes and religious practices with reference to idem, Origen, Celsus, and the Stoa, 35. Lucian, Jupp. Trag. 42.

Origen takes issue with Celsus' claim that all things keep God's law (7.68 [218,6-9 Koet.]). The evil demons, in his view, transgress God's law. Those who invoke demons for love-philtres and for spells that produce hatred and so forth worship demons and not God. The worship of the gods of the gentiles is the worship of demons (Ps 95:5 LXX). "Therefore we have resolved to flee the service of demons like a plague. And we say that all the reputed worship of the gods among the Greeks at altars, statues, and temples is the service of demons" (7.69 [218,22-219,4 Koet.]).

Celsus continues his critique of the Christian desire to avoid polytheism by an attack on the statement "It is impossible for the same person to serve several lords" (Mt 6:24, Lk 16:13) (8.2 [222,2-20 Koet.]):

This is [as he thinks] a cry of revolt of those who [he calls it] separate themselves and make a break with the rest of the human race[247]. [He thinks that] those who say this, in as much as it depends on them, model their own feeling onto God. Among humans [he thinks] the one who is slave to a certain individual cannot rationally be slave to another, because the first would be harmed by the service of the other, nor can a person who has sworn an oath with one swear an oath with another because he would harm the first. And it is rational not to serve at the same time different heroes and demons. But in the case of God, to whom neither harm nor sorrow comes, [he thinks] it is irrational to avoid serving several gods as if it were a case of humans or heroes or demons of this kind. [He says] that to serve several gods is to serve one of those who belong to the great God and in this respect is to do something agreeable to him. [He adds that] it is not permitted to honor one whom God has not given such a privilege. Therefore, [he says,] anyone who worships all that belong to him does not bring sorrow to God, to whom they all belong.

Celsus is willing to serve several gods but not several heroes or demons at the same time. He sees this as no affront the God, but as a lawful honor given to certain other beings by God[248]. They have the right to be worshipped — which Celsus would understand to include altar, temple, and image. Origen interprets Ps 81:1 LXX "God stood in the meeting of the gods, in their midst he judges gods" to not mean the gods of the gentiles (Ps 95:5 LXX). They are gods to whom God gives work, and "the prophetic word knows a kind of assembly of them" (8.3 [222,26-223,4 Koet.]). He also claims that Christians (8.5 [224,16-19 Koet.]) ascend above those who are worshipped as gods by the nations of the earth and that Christians do no action loved by demons. He draws an analogy (8.6 [225,15-18 Koet.]) from Herodotus 7.136 with the Spartan ambassadors who did not worship the emperor of the Persians despite considerable pressure from the bodyguard because they feared their own lord, the law of Lycurgus.

Celsus believes (8.12 [229,13-15 Koet.]) that the Christians are not being consistent with monotheism because they worship "to excess this one who

---

[247] BADER 195 refers to Min. Fel. 8.4 *latebrosa at lucifugax natio* (7,2 KYT.) and Eus. H.E. 6.40.
[248] See ANDRESEN, Logos 222 on Celsus' defense of polytheism.

recently appeared" whom Celsus calls God's servant (ὑπηρέτης). Origen responds with a Trinitarian formulation using the concept of two hypostases (ὑποστάσεις) of Father and son (8.12 [229,21-24 Koet.]). Celsus knows that Christians will not give up Jesus (8.14 [231,5-10 Koet.]):

> If you would teach them that Jesus is not his child (παῖς), but that God is the father of all, whom only one ought to truly worship, they would refuse unless you included him who is the chief of their revolt (στάσεως ἀρχηγέτης). And they have actually named him son (υἱόν) of God, not because they offer God supreme worship, but because they supremely exalt Jesus.

In the course of his defense of polytheism, Celsus attempts to show that the Christians are not monotheists themselves.

For Celsus "whenever they eat bread, drink wine, taste fruits, drink water itself, and take a breath of the air itself, do they not receive each one of these things from certain demons to whom has been allotted in detail the care of each of these things?" (8.28 [243,30-244,2 Koet.]). Celsus uses this argument to show that Christians should follow Pythagoras and be vegetarian, so that they could avoid feasting with demons (1 Cor 10:20). Origen only denies that Christians can be partakers of the table of demons (8.30 [245,3-4 Koet.]). He denies that any food implies associating with demons (8.31, 32 [246,23-247,2.31-33 Koet.]), because the ones who administer nature are angels and not demons. A related claim of Celsus is that thirty-six demons (decans) have charge of the entire human body and can cause good and ill health (8.58 [274,23-24 Koet.])[249].

Celsus believes (8.33 [248,15-19 Koet.]): "Hence one should either renounce living and coming here in any place and in any way, or one who enters life in these conditions should give thanks to the demons who have received by share the things on earth, and one should offer them first fruits and prayers as long as we live so that we may obtain their benevolence." His reasoning for this position is that they can do harm if slighted (8.35 [250,16-21 Koet.]): "The satrap, prefect, general, or procurator of the king of Persia or emperor of Rome, those indeed who have inferior offices, charges, and services would have the power to do great harm if they are neglected, whereas the satraps and ministers of the air and earth would only cause slight harms if they were treated despitefully?" This argument is similar to that of Macarius' Hellene who also introduces the concept of monarch (Apocr. 4.20 [199,1-9 Blondel]) and subjects to defend polytheism[250]. Maximus of Tyre also used

---

[249] On Celsus' demonology see ROKEAH, Jews, 150-55. See also FREDE, Celsus, 5208-5209. Compare the demonology of the Middle Platonist Alcin., Didask. 15, 171,15-37 (35-36 W./L. and the comment on 119 n. 299).

[250] DROGE, Homer, 79 refers to similar discussions in Ps. Aristotle, De mundo 6, 398a,1-398b,10 (82-85 LORIMER) where the author compares God to the kings of Persia who ruled by means of "generals and satraps and Kings, slaves of the Great King" (ET of E. S. FORSTER). God rules the universe by means of his power through which he moves the

the image of a king with his kingdom of loyal subjects to illustrate the relationship of God and the gods[251]. These views of Celsus on demonology are a conclusive piece of evidence that Celsus was a Platonist and not an Epicurean (see § 1.1 above). Origen believes that the angels, the true satraps of God, (8.36 [251,13-28 Koet.]) do no harm to those who slight them. If demons do so, then it is because they are evil and harm those who are under their power. If people renounce demons, then they are no longer under their power.

1.7.3 Celsus Against the Christians' Argument from Hell

The Christian use of fear did not impress Celsus. The use of fear was an element in rhetorical arguments that manipulated emotions (pathos) as opposed to proofs using reason primarily (logos) or that emphasized the moral character of the speaker (ethos)[252]. Origen describes Celsus' attack on one of these arguments (3.16 [214,22-24; 215,5-6 Koet.]): "[Let anyone who wishes prove, as Celsus writes without proof what] kind of miscellaneous things we draw in and what objects of terror we fabricate" (συμπλάσσομεν δείματα). Celsus describes such fabrications as "deformations of the ancient tradition" (παλαιοῦ λόγου). Celsus then notes the Christians' use of music and flutes to excite people like priests of Cybele do (3.16 [215,6-8 Koet.]). On the other hand Celsus accepts the doctrine of final punishments (8.49 [264,11-15 Koet.]):[253] "At least they correctly think this, that those who have lived well will be happy, but the unrighteous will be afflicted forever with everlasting evils. And may they and any other person never abandon this doctrine." He did not scoff at the idea of hell the way some of Arnobius' anonymous pagans

---

heavenly bodies. Ps. Aristotle does not use the image of "satraps" to defend polytheism, however, as Celsus does. He argues, instead, that "he needs no contrivance or the service of others, as our earthly rulers, owing to their feebleness, need many hands to do their work" (398b; ET, FORSTER). Maximus of Tyre affirms that "there is one uniform custom and doctrine (νόμος καὶ λόγος) in all the earth, that there is one God, the king and father of all, and many gods, sons of god, who rule together with him. This is believed by both the Greek and barbarian" (Diss. 11.5 [91,76-79 TR.], ET by DROGE, Homer, 79). For Maximus, God has more than 30,000 "children and friends" (παῖδες καὶ φίλοι; 11.12 [99,277-78 TR.]). Compare Plotinus, Ennead. 2.9.9 (I, 216,30-217,59 H./S.). See DROGE, Homer, 79 and R. M. GRANT, Gods and the One God, Library of Early Christianity 1, Philadelphia 1986, 75-83. Like Celsus, Ps. Arist. uses the argument that God has many names including Zen and Zeus (401a; compare Celsus in C.C. 5.41 [45,2-4 KOET.]).

[251] Diss. 11.12 (100,289-97 TR.).

[252] See the introduction for a brief development of these concepts.

[253] Celsus' word for Christian babbling (θρυλοῦσιν) about God and the doctrine of final punishments in 4.10 (280,30 KOET.) is shared by Macarius' pagan in *Apocriticus* 2.14 (23,2 BLONDEL) = HARNACK, Porphyrius F. 64. In the text from Macarius the babbling is about the resurrection of Jesus.

did[254]. Christians, Celsus claims, "do not say true things about the punishments [necessary] for those who have sinned. [Wherefore he compares us] to those in the Bacchic initiations who evoke apparitions and terrors" (φάσματα καὶ τὰ δείματα 4.10 [281,1-3 Koet.]). Origen defends the use of such threats by using an argument from consequence:

> As for us, we defend our doctrines saying that our goal is to reform the human race either through warnings of punishments which we are persuaded to be necessary for everyone and which probably are not useless to those who will suffer them, or through promises for those who have lived virtuously including the happy life in the kingdom of God for those who merit to be ruled by it (4.10 [281,6-12 Koet.]).

The threat of punishments produced beneficial results, according to Origen, and so was justified by the consequences. He attempts to put the argument in the larger context of promises of eternal life.

In response to Christian eschatology, Celsus affirms that there is a cycle of floods and conflagrations which the Christians did not understand (4.11 [281,17-21 Koet.]): "These teachings have made them, in their erroneous opinion, say that God will descend bringing fire in the manner of a torturer." His belief in these world-cycles shows that he was not an Epicurean. Origen denies that Moses and the prophets (4.12 [282,8-14 Koet.]) got the idea of world conflagration from others, and he denies that there is an endless cycle of repeated occurrences[255]. Celsus also attacks the eschatology when he charges that (5.14 [15,1-3 Koet.]) "It is a stupidity of theirs to think that when God like a cook brings on the fire every other race will be grilled, and they alone will remain ..." His view of God as a torturer or cook is an attempt to discount Christian conceptions using the resources of vituperative rhetoric. Celsus found this eschatology proclaimed by the wandering prophets of whom he claimed to have first hand knowledge (7.9 [161,7-9.10-13 Koet.]): "For the world is perishing and you, people, will perish because of your unrighteous deeds ... Blessed is the one who worships me now. On all others I will cast everlasting fire — both in cities and in the fields. And the people who do not know the punishments waiting for them will repent and groan in vain." This kind of hellfire preaching was close to that of the preachers of the mystery religions according to the experience of Celsus who also claimed first hand knowledge of their proclamation (8.48 [262,27-263,8 Koet.]):

> Most of all, my dear friend, as you believe in everlasting punishments, so also the interpreters of the sacred mysteries believe, both initiators and mystagogues. The threats you make to others, they make to you. It is permissible to examine which of the two is

---

[254] Adv. nat. 2.14 (81,14-16 MARCH.). Arnobius calls his opponent's attention to Plato's doctrine of eschatological punishment. See also Plotinus, Ennead. 1.1.12 (I, 52,1-5 H./S.).

[255] See also 4.62, 67, 68 and 5.20 (334,1; 337,16; 338,3; 21,23 KOET.) for discussion of this issue.

truer and more powerful. For in discourse each of them maintain with equal strength their own doctrines. But if proofs (τεκμηρίων) are necessary, these can show many distinct things (ἐναργῆ δεικνύουσιν)²⁵⁶ and present works of certain powerful demons and oracles, resulting from all kinds of prophecies.

Celsus' belief in final punishments has its parallels in Platonic texts²⁵⁷. His objection is to the Christians' attempt to persuade people to join their movement by the inventions of the terrors of hellfire and damnation. He also could not believe that the entire universe could perish in a fire, since the universe was uncreated and indestructible²⁵⁸. As the defender of the cultural consensus of Hellenism, Celsus is far more attracted to the mysteries and the philosophical pearls he may find in them than he is to Christianity.

1.7.4 Celsus on Eternal Life

Celsus' alternative to Christian eschatology is a belief in reincarnation and an ultimate ascent of some souls to God. Christians believe in resurrection because they misunderstand the doctrine of reincarnation (7.32 [182,30 Koet.])²⁵⁹. For Celsus "the road for souls to the earth and away from the earth goes through the planets" (6.21 [91,19-21 Koet.]). Celsus approves of the Mithraic cosmology in which the soul passes through seven gates (the planets) on its way to the sphere of the stars (6.22 [92,2-13 Koet.])²⁶⁰. He included some kind of diagram comparing Christian and Persian (Mithraic) cosmologies (6.24, 25 [94,14-21; 95,3-4 Koet.])²⁶¹. The image of the happy life in the Elysian fields for happy souls (εὐδαίμων βίος ψυχαῖς εὐδαίμοσιν) is

---

²⁵⁶ On "distinct" appearances see 3.26 and 8.45 (222,11; 259,28 KOET.).

²⁵⁷ See Porphyry (§ 2.3.25) for another perspective. His remarks on punishment may be a response to Justin (Apol. 1.45.6 [96,17-20 MARC.]) who spoke of the danger in which even the emperor stood. Compare Celsus' statements in 3.16 and 4.10 (215,2; 281,1 KOET.) about punishment. See NOCK's review of ANDRESEN in VigChr 12, 1958, 317. Clement of Alexandria argues that the Greeks took their doctrine of final punishment from "barbarian" (Hebrew) philosophy in Strom. 5.14.4 (385,24 S./F.). See also Ps. Sallustius, De diis 19 (34,13-25 NOCK) on punishments for souls after bodily death. Cr. G. MAY, Kelsos und Origenes über die ewigen Strafen, in: Mousopolos Stephanos. Festschrift für Herwig Görgemanns, ed. M. BAUMBACH/H. KÖHLER/A. M. RITTER, Bibliothek der Klassischen Altertumswissenschaften. Reihe 2. Neue Folge 102, Heidelberg 1998, 346-51.

²⁵⁸ C. Cels. 4.79 (349,11-14 KOET.). Compare § 3.39 below. Caecilius also defends the eternal order of the universe against Christian eschatology in Min. Fel., Oct. 11.1.

²⁵⁹ Maximus also accepted the doctrine of reincarnation by approving of the accounts of Pythagoras' former lives (Diss. 10.2 [78,26-39 TR.]). Compare Alcinous, Didask. 16 171,38-172,19 (36-37 W./L.). See § 2.2.4 below.

²⁶⁰ CHADWICK, Origen 334 n. 2 gives much bibliography on the seven gates of Mithraism. ANDRESEN, Logos, 366 remarks that Celsus' comparison of Mithraism and Christianity is similar to that which Justin makes in Apol. 1.66.4 (128,17-20 MARC.) and Dial. 70.1, 78.6 (191,1-5; 205,26-32 MARC.).

²⁶¹ He is interested in Gnostic cosmology (6.30, 34 [99,31; 103,12 KOET.]), but casts a highly critical gaze upon it.

attractive to Celsus who attributed the belief to divinely inspired men (θείοις ἀνδράσι) in the ancient times (7.28 [178,23-25 Koet.]). Quoting Homer (Od. 4.563-5) and Plato (Phaedo 109a,b), he is happy to accept the doctrine of the immortal soul (7.28 [178,25-179,11 Koet.])[262], a true heaven (7.31 [182,2-3 Koet.]), and an eternal dwelling of the soul or mind with God (8.49 [264,5-11 Koet.]). Those who live good lives will be happy and the wicked will suffer eternal evils (8.49 [264,11-13 Koet.]). Before souls can reach heaven, they must pay the penalty for their sin (8.53 [268,11-16 Koet.]): "Because it is necessary, according to Empedocles[263], for 'the soul to roam about for 30,000 seasons away from the happy ones, becoming through time every kind of mortal being.' One must believe that they are committed to the guard of certain jailers of this prison." This belief helps to explain Celsus' refusal to countenance the possibility of resurrection.

1.7.5 Celsus on God

Many of Celsus' positions on Christianity can be clarified by the fact that his understanding of God is at variance with that of the ancient Christians. God is king of all (6.18 [89,2-5 Koet.], from Plato Ep. 2.312e) and there exists a second and a third being[264]. This concept is the forerunner of the Neoplatonic trinity of supreme God, mind, and world soul[265]. Celsus critiqued the Christians' understanding of God existing above the heavens (6.19 [89,18-20; 90,7-12 Koet.]) and affirms, using Plato's Phaedrus 247c: "This place above heaven, no poet of those here has ever celebrated in hymn or will celebrate it as it merits ... Being which is really without color, without shape, impalpable, the object of contemplation for the pilot of the soul (our mind alone), and the object of true knowledge, occupies this place."

Celsus' God is the cause of being (οὐσίας) which is the cause of intelligible (νοητόν) reality (7.45 [196,19-197,3 Koet.]). Knowledge (ἐπιστήμη) is of intelligible reality. God transcends (πάντων ἐπέκεινα) all things and is intelligible by a "certain indescribable power" (ἀρρήτῳ τινὶ δυνάμει νοητός). This God cannot make evil or be incapable of persuading humans (6.54 [125,11-12 Koet.]). He cannot repent when humans become wicked and threaten to destroy his offspring (6.53 [124,18-21 Koet.]). Celsus' God has neither mouth nor voice (6.62 [132,15.22 Koet.]) nor any other characteristics

---

[262] This teaching found a home in Middle Platonism (e.g. Atticus, Fr. 7, DES PLACES; Alcin., Didask. 25 177,16-178,45 [48-51 W./L.]).

[263] F. 115 Diels. Origen discusses the Pythagorean belief in metempsychosis and that of Empedocles in 5.49 (54,1-5 KOET.). See Porphyry's approval of this doctrine in § 2.2.4.

[264] FÉDOU, Christianisme. 235-41 discusses Celsus' concept of God as does ANDRESEN, Logos, 93-96. FREDE, discusses Celsus' philosophy (Celsus, 5203-12).

[265] See FREDE, Celsus, 5207-08 with reference to Numenius in Eus. P.E. 11.18 who took Plato to refer to a divine Trinity.

which we know[266]. God did not make humans in his image (6.63 [133,16-17 Koet.]) because God does not resemble any form. God does not participate in being (οὐσίας) and does not participate (μετέχει) in shape, color, or motion (6.64 [134,15-16 Koet.])[267]. God is not attainable by reason and cannot be named (6.65 [135,24-26 Koet.]). Christians and Stoics both believe that God is spirit (6.71 [141,7-9 Koet.]) that permeates all things[268]. Celsus (7.27 [178,4-6 Koet.]) claims that Christians believe God is corporeal and has a body with human form (ἀνθρωποειδοῦς). Only the eye of the soul can see God (7.39 [189,19-21 Koet.]). God can be known by synthesis, analysis, and analogy (7.42 [192,29-32 Koet.])[269].

1.8 Concluding Remarks

From these views it is clear why Celsus would have problems with Christian belief in incarnation and so forth. Celsus' God would never be angry with people, for example (4.99 [372,15-18 Koet.]), because God takes care of the universe which is complete and perfect and never becomes more evil[270]. Celsus cannot accept a God who is angry with people and sends his son with threats (4.73 [342,26-28 Koet.]). The discussion of gospel traditions above shows that Celsus' God would not countenance an incarnation and a passion. Probably Celsus viewed his work and philosophy as a definitive refutation of Christianity and its basis (the OT and NT).

As will be seen in the next chapter, Celsus does not approach NT texts with the critically honed razor of a Porphyry. He rejects allegory of Christian texts, as did Porphyry, but (unlike Porphyry) does not spend time looking for internal contradictions. His approach is more impressionistic and global than Porphyry's. He is willing to make comparisons between Jesus and figures

---

[266]Compare Alcin., Didask. 10 165,10-15 (24 W./L.) for a description of God that includes the denial that God has or does not have qualities. Cp. Maximus' negative theology in Diss. 11.9 (96,200-213 TRAPP).

[267] BADER 170 compares this with Plat. Phaedr. 247c, Justin. Dial. 4.1 (76,1-77,10 MARC.), Orig. De princ. 1.1.6 (SC 252, 100,149 CROUZEL/SIMONETTI).

[268] CHADWICK, Origen, 385 n. 5 refers to SVF 2.416, 473. Other references in BADER 172.

[269] CHADWICK, Origen, 429 n. 4 refers to Albinus (Alcinous), Didask. 10.5-6 (23,5-26,2 W./L.). Compare Plato, Symp. 210d,e, Ep. 7.341c,d, and Clement of Alex., Strom. 5.11.71 (373,25-374,23 S./F.) on these logical processes.

[270] Cicero's Epicurean philosopher is also scandalized by the poets' descriptions of the gods as inflamed by anger or lust (De nat. deorum 1.16.42). Compare Epicurus, Ep. 1.76-77 quoted by BORRET II.433. Porphyry also denies that the gods experience wrath (Ad Marcellam 18 [24,2-4 PÖTSCHER]).

from the Hellenistic pantheon using broad brush strokes, for example, while Porphyry seemed to have a finer sense for detail[271].

Origen does not explain (and surely did not know) how Celsus got his hands on a set of Christian scriptures[272]. The source could have been a Christian acquaintance or possibly a magistrate who had confiscated the texts. In any case it is difficult to imagine Celsus pouring through the texts with Porphyry's sense for exegetical details. Celsus thinks with narrative scenes in mind: Jesus gathering a small band of sailors and tax collectors (including a traitor); Jesus leading a miserable life and suffering a miserable death; Jesus drinking gall; Jesus practicing magic in Egypt; and Jesus' life being in no way the fulfillment of the glorious hopes for a future ruler expressed by the prophets of Israel. Using his Platonistic philosophy as armor and weapons, Celsus carried out his attack.

---

[271] See § 1.3.2.

[272] Tert. Apol. 31.1 (142,5-6 DEK.) says that Christians do not hide their books which "many occasions transfer to outsiders." A. VON HARNACK describes the sale of Bibles in the fourth century (Über den privaten Gebrauch der heiligen Schriften in der alten Kirche, Beiträge zur Einleitung in das Neue Testament, Leipzig 1912, 68-69). He argues that Celsus had no trouble obtaining a copy of the gospels (Über den privaten Gebrauch, 31).

2. Porphyry

Porphyry's Attack on the New Testament

Porphyry was probably the most acute and philologically skilled critic of Christianity. While Celsus attacked in broad strokes, Porphyry delighted in finding contradictions in the Christian scriptures using his formidable historical and philological knowledge. The fact that the church chose to burn Porphyry's work (*Against the Christians*) twice indicates the power of his attack and the fear that Porphyry's critique inspired in Christian political leaders.

This chapter will briefly describe Porphyry's life and then investigate his two works that analyze Christianity: *On Philosophy Drawn from Oracles* and the *Contra Christianos* (*Against the Christians*). The oracles' opinions of Christ and the Christians are somewhat different so they will be treated separately. The *Contra Christianos* will be surveyed using the Synoptic Gospels, John, and Paul as a structuring mechanism — so that the work can appear as a sort of pagan's commentary on the NT. Several more general fragments appear at the end of the treatment including Porphyry's view of the role of women in the church.

2.1 Porphyry's Life

Basileus, as Amelius referred to him, was originally named "Malchus" in the native language of Tyre (Phoenecian) and was probably born in 234[1].

---

[1] Porphyry, Vita Plot. 4.1-3, 5.1-3, 17.6-15, 21.14-16 (I, 5; 7; 20; 28 H./S.). Porphyry had some kind of connection to the region Batanaea or to a Palestinian village of that name near Caesarea according to several texts (A. SMITH, Porphyrii philosophi fragmenta, Bibliotheca Teubneriana, Stuttgart/Leipzig 1993, 8aT, 8bT). See also J. BIDEZ, Vie de Porphyre, le philosophe néo-platonicien, lst ed. 1913, Hildesheim 1964, 5. J. BOUFFARTIGUE/M. PATILLON, Porphyre. De l'abstinence, Vol. I, CUF, Paris 1977, XI refer to a horoscope in Hephaestio, Apotelesmatica II.10 (I, 112,16-20 PINGREE) that has been identified as part of Porphyry's horoscope with a date of birth of October 5, 234. See O. NEUGEBAUER, A History of Ancient Mathematical Astronomy, Vol. 2, Berlin 1975, 944. Hephaestio does not identify the date as that of Porphyry's birth. SMITH, Porphyrius 489F does not identify it as Porphyry's birth date (nor does NEUGEBAUER). In a private communication, Prof. T. BARNES notes that "the child with this horoscope survived birth but died before its first birthday" and that Porphyry "was thirty (i.e., 29) in 10 Gallienus" (Vita

Longinus named him "Porphyry," the color of imperial clothing[2]. He became a master of Greek and Hellenistic tradition — whether he knew any Semitic languages or not[3]. At an early age he visited Caesarea, according to a Christian tradition and was beaten up by Christians. The same tradition claimed Porphyry had been a Christian to begin with and abandoned it after his beating[4]. Wolfram Kinzig argues that given the symbiotic development of philosophy and theology in the liberal religious atmosphere of the first half of the third century that a Christian background for Porphyry is certainly conceivable[5]. Robert Grant is willing to say that at one time "he was fairly

---

Plotini 4.1-3, 5.1-3; cf. T. D. BARNES, The Chronology of Plotinus' Life, GRBS 17, 1976, 65-70). "Both statements appear to exclude Porphyry pretty conclusively!" The article cited argues that Porphyry used Egyptian regnal years (beginning 29 Aug. or 1 Sept.); with the result that 10 Gallienus runs from 29 Aug. 262 to 28 Aug. 263. On the life of Porphyry see further BARNES, Constantine and Eusebius, Cambridge 1981, 175. R. GOULET also argues that the horoscope belongs to a child who was one of the ἄτροφοι — children who did not survive in Le système chronologique de la Vie de Plotin, in: Porphyre. La vie de Plotin, Vols. I, II, ed. L. BRISSON/M.-O. GOULET-CAZÉ/R. GOULET/D. O'BRIEN et al., Histoire des doctrines de l'antiquité classique 6, Paris 1982/1992, I, (189-227) 211.

[2] Eunapius, Vitae Sophistarum 456 (LCL Philostratus and Eunapius, 354-55 WRIGHT). In Vita Plot. 21.14 (I, 28 H./S.), Porphyry notes that Longinus called him "Basileus of Tyre." WOLFF refers to other occurrences of the name "Malchus" (Porphyrii de philosophia ex oraculis haurienda. librorum reliquiae, 1st ed. 1856, Hildesheim 1962, 7 n. 2). Aeneas of Gaza, a scholiast on Theophrastus, notes that the name "Porphyry" could also refer to the purple goods industry in Tyre (SMITH, Porphyrii, 5aT).

[3] On the issue of Porphyry's language see F. MILLAR, Porphyry: Ethnicity, Language, and Alien Wisdom, in: Philosophia Togata II. Plato and Aristotle at Rome, ed. J. BARNES/M. GRIFFIN, Oxford 1997, (241-262) 248-50. MILLAR argues that Syriac was spoken along the Euphrates and to the East in Mesopotamia, and that there is no proof for the third century and the preceding period that Phoenecian was still spoken in Tyre or used in written documents. He agrees that it is conceivable that an educated person from Tyre could have spoken Syriac.

[4] Socrates, H. E. 3.23.37-39 (222,25-223,2 HANSEN = SMITH, Porphyrii, 9T) and a theosophical text in SMITH, Porphyrii, 10T. BIDEZ is doubtful of the tradition. Socrates indicates that he is taking his tradition from Eusebius (Vie de Porphyre, 7, 8). Compare R. BEUTLER's skepticism. BEUTLER believes the tradition was invented to explain Porphyry's hostility against the Christians (Art. Porphyrios 21, PRE, XXII 1954, 276). DROGE believes the tradition should not be doubted (Homer or Moses? Early Christian Interpretations of the History of Culture, HUTh 26, Tübingen 1989, 172 n. 17). Recently W. KINZIG has ably defended the view that Porphyry had a Christian background and was sympathetic to it in some form, although he had not necessarily been baptized (War der Neuplatoniker Porphyrios ursprünglich Christ?, in: Mousopolos Stephanos. Festschrift für Herwig Görgemanns, ed. M. BAUMBACH/H. KÖHLER/A. M. RITTER, BKA Reihe 2. Neue Folge 102, Heidelberg 1998, 320-32).

[5] War der Neuplatoniker, 324-25. KINZIG also argues that the setting of the story in Caesarea of Palestine is a sign of authenticity since no other stories describe a stay of Porphyry in that place. The story is from Eusebius' treatise against Porphyry which Socrates and the theosophical text both used independently (War der Neuplatoniker, 326).

favorable toward Christianity; at least he admired Jesus as a teacher, as he indicates in his book *On the philosophy from oracles*"[6]. He heard Origen when he was young, presumably at Caesarea, and was incensed by Origen's attempt to combine Greek philosophy with Jewish tradition — using the allegorical method. J. Bidez assumes that Porphyry was a student of Origen, from whom he learned his Bible[7].

Porphyry studied with Longinus in Athens (and other teachers such as Demetrius the geometer and Apollonius the grammarian) where he developed his philological skills. He studied grammar and rhetoric[8]. Eusebius recounts their celebration of Plato's birthday during which they discussed plagiarism in a philological *tour de force* [9]. When he was thirty (i.e. 29 in modern reckoning) he came to Rome (July or August 263) and studied with Plotinus for six years[10]. In a fit of melancholy he contemplated suicide, but Plotinus persuaded him to go to Sicily in 268. At Lilybaeum in Sicily he attended the lectures of one Probus[11]. He made a side trip to Carthage[12]. According to Eusebius, Porphyry wrote his powerful work against the Christians (the Κατὰ Χριστιανῶν) in Sicily[13]. After Plotinus' death he returned to Rome[14]. At the

---

[6] R. M. GRANT, Porphyry among the Early Christians, in: Romanitas et Christianitas. Studia J. H. Waszinck, ed. W. DEN BOER et al., Amsterdam/London 1973, (181-87) 181. GRANT also notes that Porphyry did not write until many years after the "beating" which he conjectures may have been a verbal argument.

[7] Eus., H.E. 6.19.5-8. On the probable sojourn in Caesarea see P. SELLEW, Achilles or Christ. Porphyry and Didymus in Debate Over Allegorical Interpretation, HThR 82, 1989, 88. BIDEZ, Vie de Porphyre, 12.

[8] Eunapius, Vitae Soph. 456 (352-55 WR.) and Porphyry, Vita Plot. 20.90-92 (I, 27 H./S.). On Porphyry's teachers see also SMITH, Porphyrii, 13T, 14T and BEUTLER, Porphyrios, 276.

[9] P. E. 10.3.1-15; SMITH, Porphyrii, 408F.

[10] Vita Plot. 4.1-10, 5.1-6 (I, 5; 7 H./S.; in Gallienus' tenth year and shortly before his tenth anniversary). Gallienus reigned in 253 (Art. Gallienus, A. H. M. JONES/J. R. MARTINDALE/J. MORRIS, The Prosopography of the Later Roman Empire, Vol I, Cambridge 1971, 383; henceforth cited as PLRE). See BARNES, Chronology, 67 n. 15, 69: Gallienus reigned "not long after 29 Aug. 253"; Porphyry stayed with Plotinus from 10 Gallienus until a period near the end of 15 Gallienus (Vita 5.1ff, 5.59ff).

[11] Vita Plot. 6.1-3 (15th year of Gallienus), 11.16-18 (= SMITH, 25T, 26T). SMITH includes other texts mentioning Porphyry's interest in the fires of Mt. Etna (28T, 29T, 29aT). See also BIDEZ, Vie de Porphyre, 59.

[12] De abst. 3.4.7 (CUFr, Porphyre. De l'abstinence, Vol. 2, 157 BOUFFARTIGUE/PATILLON).

[13] Eus., H. E. 6.19.2 = SMITH, Porphyrii, 30T.

[14] De vita Plot. 2.11-34 (I, 2-3 H./S.) / BIDEZ, Vie de Porphyre 105ff / Eunapius, Vitae Soph. 456 (356 WR.). Plotinus died in Claudius' second year. That would be 270 (or possibly 269) according to PLRE 209. BARNES (Chronology, 68) reckons 2 Claudius from 29 Aug. 269 — Aug. 270 with the result that the end of 2 Claudius would be July or August 270. BARNES notes that the publication of P. Oxy. XL.2892-2940 (1972) has put the

time of his composition of his life of Plotinus he was 68 years old (i.e. 67)[15]. When he was an old man he married a woman named Marcella, whom Christian tradition later claimed to have been Jewish[16]. He died[17] in Rome during the reign of Diocletian according to the Suda (by 305, the year of Diocletian's abdication).

2.2 De philosophia ex oraculis haurienda

Porphyry's first attack on the Christian tradition is his *De philosophia ex oraculis haurienda* (*On Philosophy Derived from Oracles*). Eunapius seems to refer to this as a work of Porphyry's youth when he writes: "He [Porphyry] himself says (but perhaps as seems likely he wrote this while he was still young), that he was granted an oracle different from the vulgar sort; and in the same book he wrote it down, and then went on to expound at considerable length how men ought to pay attention to these oracles."[18] The work contained a heavy dose of theurgy. Eusebius, for example, quotes a passage in which a prophet who hopes to see the divine is told that such a thing is impossible

---

chronology of Claudius on a firm basis (Chronology, 66). Claudius reigned circa Sept. 268 and died circa August 270. On the school of Plotinus see M.-O. GOULET-CAZÉ, L'école de Plotin, in BRISSON et al., Porphyre La Vie de Plotin, II.201. Porphyry had to stay long enough in Sicily to receive the letter from Longinus (De vita Plot. 19) who was at Zenobia's court. The letter would have to be written before 272. BRISSON et al., Porphyre La Vie de Plotin, I.94. Either during this stay or during a later stay Porphyry composed the *Isagoge* and also probably composed *De abst.* and the *Contra Christianos* (BIDEZ, Vie de Porphyre, 57).

[15] De vita Plot. 23.12-14 (I, 31 H./S.).

[16] Porphyry, Ad Marcellam 1 (7,9-10 PÖTSCHER) and the theosophical text (SMITH, Porphyrii, 10T, 31T).

[17] Suda (SMITH, Porphyrii, 2T); accepted by BIDEZ, Vie de Porphyre, 127. Eunapius refers to Porphyry as being at the height of his powers from the reign of Gallienus to that of Probus, Vitae Soph. 457 (360-63 WR.). T. D. BARNES has his doubts about the Suda's date (Porphyry Against the Christians: Date and the Attribution of Fragments, JThS 24, 1973, 432). This is due to BARNES' theory about the late date of the text in question.

[18] Eun., Vitae Soph. 457 (358-59 WR.). On the text and its date see BIDEZ, Vie de Porphyre, 14-16. P. F. BEATRICE identifies the *Philosophy from Oracles* with the *Contra Christianos* based on a text from Eus., Dem. Ev. 3.6.39 (GCS Eusebius VI, 139,34-140,2 HEIKEL): τίς δ' ἂν γένοιτό σοι τούτων ἀξιόπιστος ὁμολογία [μᾶλλον] τῆς τοῦ καθ' ἡμῶν πολεμίου γραφῆς, ἣν ἐν οἷς ἐπέγραψεν Περὶ τῆς ἐκ λογίων φιλοσοφίας ἐν τρίτῳ συγγράμματι τέθειται. This text does not establish the identity of the two works. BEATRICE has to reject the explicit and external evidence in Eunapius for the dating of the *De philosophia ex oraculis haurienda*. (P. F. BEATRICE, Towards a New Edition of Porphyry's Fragments Against the Christians, in: ΣΟΦΙΗΣ ΜΑΙΗΤΟΡΕΣ «Chercheurs e sagesse» Hommage à Jean Pépin, ed. M.-O. GOULET-CAZÉ/G. MADEC/D. O'BRIEN, Collection des Études Augustiniennes 131, Paris 1992, 349).

before one sacrifices to what Eusebius calls the evil demon[19]. Bidez notes that Porphyry seemed to have some sympathy for Jesus in this work, but charged the Christians with grievous error. Porphyry attempted to fit Jesus into the pantheon of Greek heroes and pious souls. He may have been attempting to persuade Christians to adopt an acceptable Hellenistic approach to Jesus. Book III of the work on oracles has a section that G. Wolff entitled "Who are the heroes" immediately before the section in which Porphyry treated Christianity. A commentator (on Theophrastus) remarked that Porphyry believed Dionysus and Heracles were originally mortal[20]. Porphyry includes an oracle of Apollo at Miletus which describes the ascent of the soul to heaven in response to a question concerning whether the soul survives death or is dissolved[21]. Using these views on heroes and souls, Porphyry could make sense of Jesus.

2.2.1 The Oracles' Views of Christ

At the risk of a little repetition, I will first discuss the oracles' views of Christ, and then discuss the oracles' views of Christians. The oracles of Apollo give varying evaluations of Christ.

2.2.1.1 The Crucifixion

In reference to a Christian wife, Apollo says that she laments "... for a god dead in his illusions, who was destroyed by right-minded judges, and in specious circumstances the worst death — bound with iron — killed him"[22]. Lactantius preserves a similar oracle of the Milesian Apollo (not necessarily from Porphyry) in which the god is asked if Christ is a god or a human. Apollo answered: "he was mortal according to the flesh, a wise man with marvelous works, but he was seized by the Chaldean [Hebrew] judges and

---

[19] Eusebius, Praep. Ev. 4.20.1 (SC 262, 206,1-6 ZINK/DES PLACES). G. WOLFF, Porphyrii, 2.174-181, p. 152-154 (= SMITH, Porphyrii, 329F).

[20] WOLFF, Porphyrii, 177 (= SMITH, Porphyrii, 469F, from an unknown work).

[21] WOLFF, Porphyrii, 3.310-15 (177-178; not included in SMITH). R. WILKEN (The Christians as the Romans Saw Them, New Haven/London 1984, 148-156) comments on the following texts as does R. L. FOX (Pagans and Christians, Cambridge et al. 1988, 258). See also J. J. O'MEARA, Porphyry's Philosophy from Oracles in Augustine, Paris 1959, 49-61, and on the relationship between Arnobius and Porphyry cf. M. B. SIMMONS, The Function of Oracles in the Pagan-Christian Conflict during the Age of Diocletian: The Case of Arnobius and Porphyry, StPatr XXXI, ed. E. A. LIVINGSTONE, Leuven 1997, 349-56.

[22] Augustine, De civ. D. 19.23 (CChr.SL 48, 690,10-13 DOMBART/KALB = SMITH, Porphyrii, 343F). The ET in this chapter of Porphyry's text is a revision of M. DODS' translation in *St. Augustin's City of God and Christian Doctrine*, NPNF Series 1, Vol. 2, Buffalo 1887. Occasionally I consulted H. BETTENSON's ET in: Augustine, City of God, trans. H. BETTENSON, Great Britain 1972, 884-885. BETTENSON is very close to DODS' translation in many cases.

being fastened with spikes he accomplished a bitter death"[23]. Both Porphyry's version of the oracle and Lactantius' agree on the historicity of the crucifixion or bitter death. Celsus' Jew also claims that the Jews "punished" Christ[24]. The first oracle describes Christ as a deluded god condemned by right-thinking judges while the second oracle chooses to describe him as a wise mortal. Both versions of the oracle say nothing about Christ being one of the heroes that made the transition from mortal to heavenly life. The Milesian Apollo in Lactantius' text asserts Christ's wonderful works (τερατώδεσιν ἔργοις) — works of a wise (σοφός) and mortal man. Porphyry's Apollo calls Christ neither wise nor a worker of wonders. The oracles may be "twins" as Wolff remarks, but each has a different slant.[25] Apollo's use of the word "god" in "a god who died in his illusions" was surely ironic. The ironic contrast can be compared with Celsus' statement that Christians "... present instead of a pure and holy Logos a person who was most dishonorably led away and crucified"[26]. Arnobius records a tradition in which the pagans claim: "The gods are hostile to you not because you worship the all-powerful god, but because you allege that a being who was born a human and who died on the cross (a death which would bring shame on the vilest of people) was god, that he still survives to this day, and you address your daily prayers to him."[27] Interestingly enough Porphyry's gods do not take the position that some of Arnobius' pagans do: namely that Christ was a magician who learned his secret arts and the names of powerful angels in Egypt and who was merely a human being[28]. Crucified heroes could be called "son of God," however, as in the case of Cleomenes on the cross with a snake wrapped around his head.

---

[23] WOLFF, Porphyrii, 184-85: (from Lactantius, Inst. 4.13.11): *Propterea Milesius Apollo consultus, utrumne (i.e. Christus) deus an homo fuerit, hoc modo respondit:* θνητὸς ἔην κατὰ σάρκα, σοφός· τερατώδεσιν ἔργοις, ἀλλ' ὑπο Χαλδαίοισι δικασπολίαισιν ἀλώσας [ἀλωκώς conj. WOLFF] γομφωθεὶς σκολόπεσσι πικρὴν ἀνέπλησε τελευτήν (= SMITH, Porphyrii, note to 343 F).

[24] C. Cels. 2.4, 5, 9 (130,22-23; 132,1-2; 135,5-7 KOET.).

[25] WOLFF, Porphyrii, 184.

[26] Origen, Contra Cels. 2.31 (158,24-25 KOET.).

[27] ET based on COURCELLE, Anti-Christian Arguments, 153 from Adv. nat. 1.36 (30,1-6 MARCHESI): *Sed non, inquit, idcirco dii uobis infesti sunt, quod omnipotentem colatis deum, sed quod hominem natum et, quod personis infame est uilibus, crucis supplicio interemptum et deum fuisse contenditis et superesse adhuc creditis et cotidianis supplicationibus adoratis.*

[28] Adv. nat. 1.43, 45 (37,25-38,3; 39,6 MARCH.). See COURCELLE, Anti-Christian Arguments, 153. Arnobius challenges his opponent to produce magicians such as Zoroaster, an unnamed Bactrian, an unnamed Armenian who was grandson of Hosthanes, Pamphilus friend of Cyrus, Apollonius, Damigero, Dardanus, Velus, Julianus, and Baebulus. The most unlearned of Christians can accomplish with a word what the magicians accomplish with their spells, herbs, and gods (Adv. nat. 1.52 [48,1-8.19-21 MARCH.]).

Onlookers called him a "son of the gods"[29]. They were perhaps influenced by the mysterious appearance of the snake. Other anonymous pagans were willing to call Jesus a wise man, but deny that he is a son of God[30]. Porphyry's use of the oracle to discourage adherence to the Christian faith will be discussed below. De Labriolle makes the important point that such texts in Porphyry's oracles show that he had no unreserved admiration for Christ in this work[31].

2.2.1.2 Christ as Faithful

In another oracle from the same work, Porphyry notes that what he is about to say will appear to be a paradox (παράδοξον) to some: "The gods have proclaimed that Christ was most faithful [piissimum, εὐσεβέστατον], and has been made immortal; they remember him with a good public proclamation [cum bona praedicatione, εὐφήμως τε αὐτοῦ μνημονεύουσι]."[32] The gods in this summary of oracular Christology identify Christ with one of the immortals like Greek heroes such as Dionysus and Hercules. It is Christ's soul that became immortal — like that of Apollonius of Tyana (Philostratus, Vita Ap. 8.31)[33]. There is, of course, no question of a resurrection.

2.2.1.3 Hecate's View of Christ

As an example of a goddess who calls Christ "faithful," Porphyry quotes an oracle of Hecate: "But to some who asked Hecate whether Christ was a god, she replied, 'Indeed you have learned that the immortal soul advances after the body [dies], but when it is cut off from wisdom it always errs. That soul [of Christ] belongs to a man pre-eminent in faithfulness (viri pietate praestantissimi)...'"[34]. Porphyry's interpretation is:

---

[29] Plutarch, Cleom. 39. 823e.
[30] Aug., De cons. ev. 1.7.11 (CSEL 43, 11,20-21 WEIHRICH: eique tribuunt excellentissimam sapientiam). The same opponents argue that the disciples claim more for Jesus than he was when they call him Son of God or Word of God.
[31] La réaction, 233 correcting positions held by HARNACK (Kritik des Neuen Testaments von einem griechischen Philosophen des 3. Jahrhunderts [Die im Apocriticus des Macarius Magnes enthaltene Streitschrift], TU 37.4, Leipzig 1911, 141) and GEFFCKEN (Zwei Griechische Apologeten, 298, 303).
[32] Aug., De civ. D. 19.23 (691,47-51 D./K. = SMITH, Porphyrii, 345aF). The Greek fragments are from Eus., Dem. Ev. 3.7 and can be found in WOLFF, Porphyrii, 180 and in SMITH.
[33] WOLFF, Porphyrii, 178.
[34] Aug., De civ. D. 19.23 (691,55-58 D./K. = SMITH, Porphyrii, 345aF). WOLFF, Porphyrii, 180: Περὶ γοῦν τοῦ Χριστοῦ ἐρωτησάντων, εἰ ἐστὶ θεός, φησὶν [ἡ Ἑκάτη]· Ὅττι μὲν ἀθανάτη ψυχὴ μετὰ σῶμα προβαίνει, γιγνώσκεις· σοφίης δὲ τετμημένη αἰὲν ἀλᾶται. ἀνέρος εὐσεβίη προφερεστάτου ἐστὶν ἐκείνη ψυχή. J. HECKENBACH finds few other examples of oracles from Hecate (all from Porphyry) in Euseb. P.E. 4.23.6, 5.8.4-6, and 12.13.4 in Art. Hekate, PRE VII, 1912, (2769-82) 2781.

She said, then, that "he was a very faithful (*piissimum*) man, and that his soul, like that of other faithful people was considered worthy of immortality after death" ... And to those who asked why he was condemned (*damnatus*), the goddess responded with an oracle: "The body, indeed, is always subject to debilitating torments, but the soul of the faithful ones abides in a heavenly habitation ..."

Hecate charges "that soul" with giving a fatal gift of entanglement in error. The error is not believing in the gods. She concludes: "He himself, however, was faithful and departed into heaven as other faithful people. So you are not to blaspheme him, but should have mercy on human folly ..."[35] Hecate's oracles are interwoven with condemnation of the Christians. The condemnation will be discussed below. Due to his faithfulness, Christ is added to the group of outstanding souls in heaven. If Wolff is correct in calling Book Three "On Heroes," Hecate may be associating Christ with the set of Greek heroes and faithful/pious ones (εὐσεβεῖς). In no way is he different from any other devout individual except possibly in the superior quality or quantity of his faithfulness (*piissimum virum*). In rhetorical terms Hecate uses epideictic oratory for Christ and vituperative rhetoric for the Christians (to be discussed below)[36]. Francine Culdaut notes that Hecate is associated with the purification of souls. If that is the case in Porphyry's work, then Hecate is particularly qualified to comment on the impure souls of the Christians who worship a deified soul and not the gods[37]. Wealthy Romans were attracted to

---

[35] Aug., De civ. D. 19.23 (691,59-692,72 D./K. = SMITH, Porphyrii, 345aF). WOLFF, Porphyrii, 182: Αὐτὸς οὖν εὐσεβὴς καὶ εἰς οὐρανούς, ὥσπερ οἱ εὐσεβεῖς, χωρήσας. ὥστε τοῦτον μὲν οὐ βλασφημήσεις, ἐλεήσεις δὲ τῶν ἀνθρώπων τὴν ἄνοιαν.

[36] Cicero defines piety/faithfulness as justice in reference to the gods (De nat. deor. 1.41.115: *est enim pietas justitia adversus deos*). On piety/faithfulness in rhetoric see LAUSBERG, Handbuch § 176 (with ref. to Quint. 7.4.6 on *pietas*). See also Rhet. ad Her. 2.13.19. For Plutarch each break with religious tradition is impiety/unfaithfulness (de superstit. 3 παρανομεῖν τὸ θεῖον καὶ πάτριον ἀξίωμα τῆς εὐσεβείας). See ANDRESEN, Logos, 263 for a discussion of piety in relation to law. On the oracle from Hecate see F. CULDAUT, Un oracle d'Hécate dans la Cité de Dieu de Saint Augustin: «Les dieux ont proclamé que le Christ fut un homme très pieux» (XIX, 23, 2), REAug 39, 1992, 271-289.

[37] CULDAUT, Un oracle d'Hécate, 278-80. Unfortunately the texts CULDAUT quotes from the *Oracula Chaldaica* are quite cryptic. See the oracles in F. 6, 26, 50, 51, 52, 97 (DES PLACES). Compare H. LEWY, Chaldaean Oracles and Theurgy. Mysticism, Magic and Platonism in the Later Roman Empire, reedited by M. TARDIEU, Paris 1978, 47. For a discussion of Hecate as a liminal goddess (of birth and death) and as "keyholder" of Hades see S. I. JOHNSON, HEKATE SOTEIRA. A study of Hekate's Roles in the Chaldean Oracles and Related Literature, Atlanta 1990, 29-48. JOHNSON also includes evidence for the identification of Hecate with Plato's cosmic soul in the thought of the Chaldean oracles (153-63).

Hecate and were still being initiated into her cult during the time of Augustine[38].

Porphyry specifically mentions heroes in other writings. There are demigods and heroes who surpass others in birth and virtue: ἐπεὶ καὶ οἱ ἡμίθεοι καὶ οἱ ἥρωες πάντες καὶ γένει καὶ ἀρετῇ ἡμῶν προύχοντες ... Two examples are Heracles and Pythagoras[39]. In his *Vita Pythagorae*, Porphyry approves the conception of Pythagoras as a god. Some consider him the son of Apollo[40]. The Crotonians considered him a god (Vita Pyth. 20 [45,12 des Places]). He showed a priest his golden thigh to prove he was Hyperborean Apollo (Vita Pyth. 28 [49,5-8 des Places]) and taught people to speak well of the race of gods, demons, and heroes[41]. He uses the same term of commendation for heroes (εὔφημον) that he uses to describe the gods' speech about Christ (εὐφήμως τε αὐτοῦ μνημονεύουσι)[42]. Porphyry admires the worship of heroes in *De antro nympharum* 6 (8,23-24 Seminar Classics 609) in which he notes that people build temples and altars for the Olympian gods and sacrificial hearths for the heroes. Porphyry probably distinguishes Christ and the devout souls from the group of heroes — although the distinction is a little hazy. In his *Epistula ad Anebonem*, Porphyry lists three kinds of "greater races" that accompany the gods: demons, heroes and "undefiled souls" (ψυχῶν ἀχράντων)[43]. Consequently, since neither the oracles nor Porphyry calls Christ a "hero," one should probably assume that Porphyry classified Christ in this third set of superior beings. Porphyry (in *De regressu animae*) accepts a theory of reincarnation (into human bodies alone). However, the souls of the wise (*sapientium animas*) are liberated from the body and return to the Father forever. They are purified in eternal happiness without any return to former miseries[44]. It seems that Porphyry's oracles assign to

---

[38] CULDAUT, Un oracle d'Hécate, 285-86. Among many CULDAUT mentions Sextilius Agesilaus Aedesius as *hierofanta Haecatarum* on August 13, 376 (CIL VI.510).

[39] De abst. 1.22.2-23.1 (58 B./P.).

[40] Vita Pyth. 2 (CUFr 37,6-7 DES PLACES).

[41] παρῄνει δὲ περὶ μὲν τοῦ θείου καὶ δαιμονίου καὶ ἡρῴου γένους εὔφημον εἶναι... (Vita Pyth. 38 [36,22-24 DES PLACES]).

[42] WOLFF, Porphyrii, 180, Eus., Dem. Ev. 3.7.1 (140,3-5 HEIKEL), Aug., De civ. D. 19.23 (691,50 D./K. = SMITH, Porphyrii, 345aF).

[43] Epistula ad Anebonem 1.1b (3,2-3; ed. A. R. SODANO, Porfirio. Lettera ad Anebo, Naples 1958).

[44] *et non solum ab animis humanis removisse corpora bestiarum, verum etiam sapientium animas ita voluisse de corporeis nexibus liberari, ut corpus omne fugientes beatae apud Patrem sine fine teneantur* (Aug., De civ. D. 13.19. = De regressu animae 11.5 [BIDEZ, Vie de Porphyre 41*] = SMITH, Porphyrii, 300bF, 301aF). O'MEARA conjectures that this treatise is identical with the *Philosophy from Oracles* (O'MEARA, Porphyry's Philosophy, 7-13). The theory has not found widespread acceptance (SMITH, Porphyrii, 351 note to P.43). Compare Porphyry's discussion of the relationship to god enjoyed by the wise soul during its

Jesus' soul a destiny similar to that which Apollo assigns to the soul of Plotinus whose "pure soul" becomes a "demon" and goes to the place where Plato and Pythagoras are[45].

2.2.2 Christ as one of the Wise People of the Hebrews

Porphyry, in his work on oracles, must have included an oracle of Apollo that spoke in better terms of Christ than the one above that identified him with a god who died in illusions. To warn people away from the worship of small earthly spirits, Porphyry refers to the "wise ones of the Hebrews (of whom even that Jesus was one as you have heard from the oracles of Apollo cited above)..."[46]. The oracle of Milesian Apollo from Lactantius, while not specifically identified as Porphyrian, resembles the one to which Porphyry here refers. Wisdom, besides being a topic of praise for rhetoricians, was an attribute of people Porphyry admired such as Pythagoras (Vita Pyth. 15 [42,20.26 des Places]) and Thales[47].

2.2.3 The Oracles' Views of Christians

The oracles are more positive about Christ than they are about Christians. They identify Christ with a class of beings (the wise, the faithful) who enter heaven like the Greek heroes. Dionysus and Heracles, Porphyry tells us, were once mortal (θνητούς) and were good[48]. Most of the oracles praise Christ, but do not identify him as a god. The oracles do agree, however, that Christians are wrong to worship him. Porphyry's oracles about Christ appear in a context designed to discourage people from the Christian faith.

---

earthly existence (ψυχὴ σόφου) in the letter to Marcella (Ad Marcellam 16 [22,8-9 PÖT.]). Ps. Sallustius continues the Neo-Platonist belief in μετεμψυχώσεις (transmigrations) of souls in De diis 20 (34,26-36,10 NOCK). Compare Plotinus, Ennead. 1.1.12, 2.9.4, 3.2.13, 3.4.2 (I, 52,4; 207,19-22; 262,1-13; 284,11-285,30 H./S.).

[45] Porphyry Vita Plot. 22,8-63 (I, 28-31 H./S.). My thanks to Prof. S. STRANGE for this suggestion.

[46] Aug., De civ. D. 19.23 (693,115-117 D./K.), WOLFF, Porphyrii, 185 (= SMITH, Porphyrii, 346F).

[47] Hist. philos. frag. 1.4 (6,14 NAUCK). For a discussion of wisdom in rhetoric see Aristotle, Rhet. 1.9.6 and COOK, Some Hellenistic Responses, 250 n. 80. Compare Plotinus, Ennead. 1.2.6 (I, 62,12 H./S.).

[48] WOLFF, Porphyrii, 177. Although this text is not specifically identified as being from the De philosophia ex oraculis haurienda, WOLFF assumes that it might belong to Book III. Wherever it comes from, it illuminates Porphyry's discussion of heroes (= SMITH, Porphyrii, 469F).

2.2.3.1 The Faith of a Christian Woman

Augustine refers to a Porphyrian text, in which Apollo speaks to a pagan husband:[49]

> "To one who inquired what god he should propitiate in order to recall his wife from Christianity, Apollo said these words in verses." Then those words are given as words of Apollo: "You will probably find it easier to write imprinted letters on water or to fill light wings with air and fly like a bird than to recall a polluted unfaithful (*pollutae ... impiae*) woman to sense. Let her go on as she pleases persevering in her foolish illusions (*fallaciis*) and lament singing to the god dead in his illusions who was destroyed by right-minded judges, and in specious circumstances the worst death — bound by iron — killed him." Then after these verses of Apollo (which we have given in a Latin version that does not preserve the metrical form), he goes on to say: "In these verses Apollo exposed the incurability of their thinking (*inremediabile sententiae eorum*), saying that the Jews embrace God rather than the Christians."

The incurability of Christian thinking is illustrated by the case of the wife whom no god can induce (or persuade, *reuocari*) to abandon her faith. Celsus, like Porphyry's oracle, described the Christians as unclean or polluted (ἀκάθαρτοι) and irrational. He chose this description because of their devotion to the body and other Christian beliefs[50]. Apollo's description of the woman as polluted and unfaithful (*pollutae impiae*) and persisting in vain illusions (*inanibus fallaciis perseuerans*) is similar to the description of the Christians in the other oracular texts. Perhaps the oracle (or Porphyry himself) was aware of the persistent belief of the Christian women who were martyred because of their refusal to swear by images (Blandina), their refusal to swear by the genius of the emperor (Scillitans), their refusal to sacrifice for the emperor (Perpetua), and their refusal to eat sacrificial meat (Irene). Vibia Perpetua, Blandina, Scillitan martyrs such as Donata and Secunda, martyrs under Diocletian such as Irene, and a host of other names could be remembered[51]. The proconsul accuses the Scillitan martyrs of obstinately persevering in the Christian rite (*ritu*

---

[49] Text in Augustine, De civ. D. 19.23 (690,5-17 D./K.). WOLFF, Porphyrii, 183-84 (= SMITH, Porphyrii, 343F).

[50] Contra Cels. 8.49 (264,5 KOET.). He emphasizes the Christians' stupidity (3.44, 73, 74, 6.12 [240,3; 264,15; 265,14; 82,16 KOET.]) and foolishness (5.14 [15,1 KOET.]) and see § 1.6.4 above. Celsus mentions the impurity and impiety of Christians (and their beliefs) often (4.10, 40, 6.42, 7.14, 8.11 [280,31; 313,8; 110,20; 165,18; 228,20 KOET.]). For other charges against credulous Christian women (*mulieribus credulis*) see Min. Fel. 8.4 (6,32 KYTZLER).

[51] For Perpetua, the Scillitan martyrs, and the martyrs under Diocletian including Irene, see H. MUSURILLO, Acts of the Christian Martyrs, Oxford 1972, 106-31, 86-89, 280-93. Eusebius describes Blandina's resistance in H.E. 5.1.17-56. Collections include M. R. LEFKOWITZ/M. B. FANT, Women's Life in Greece & Rome, Baltimore 1992, § 445, 446 and R. S. KRAEMER, Maenads, Martyrs, Matrons, Monastics. A Sourcebook on Women's Religions in the Greco-Roman World, Philadelphia 1988, § 122, 123.

Christiano ... obstinanter perseuerauerunt)[52]. In contrast to the pollution and error of the Christian wife in Porphyry's oracle, one can compare several texts from the Porphyrian treatise that Augustine entitled *De regressu animae*. In one passage the purified soul returns to the Father and is no longer subject to the "polluting touch of evil things"[53]. The words for the woman's error, illusions, and incurable opinions can be compared to Augustine's description of Porphyry's views concerning the errors of the theurgists: "What helps since you cannot deny that people err because of the practice of theurgy and that a very great number are deceived *(fallere)* through its blind and foolish thinking *(sententiam)*, and that it is a most certain error *(errorem)* to run to principalities and angels with sacrifices and prayer."[54] The apotreptic rhetoric in Apollo's text is obviously designed to discourage rational people from becoming Christian believers. In the rhetoric of praise (epideictic), a person's faithfulness or piety was one of the topics, so by inference impiety could function as a topic in the rhetoric of blame or vituperation[55]. The "dominant" society identified Christianity with impiety. Maximin Daia in a rescript in response to the citizens of Tyre wrote: "Let as many as have been rescued from that blind folly and error and returned to a right and goodly frame of mind rejoice indeed the more, as if they were delivered from an unexpected hurricane or severe illness ..." He states that if they persist in their accursed folly that they should be driven from the city so that "your city may be separated from all pollution and unfaithfulness (μιάσματος καὶ ἀσεβείας), and, following its natural desire, may respond with due reverence to the worship of the immortal gods"[56].

---

[52] Acts of the Scillitan Martyrs 14 (MUSURILLO).

[53] *purgatamque animam ob hoc reverti dixit ad Patrem, ne aliquando iam malorum polluta contagione teneatur* 11.1, BIDEZ, Vie de Porphyre 40* = Aug., De civ. D. 10.30 (CChr.SL 47, 308,51-53 DOMBART/KALB = SMITH, Porphyrii, 298F). Plotinus discusses the purification (κάθαρσις) of the soul in Ennead. 3.6.5 and 4.7.10 (I, 313,13-15; II, 160,40 H./S.). Compare Porphyry's conception of the purified (καθαρά) soul in Sententiae 32 (34,11 LAMBERZ) where he does not express any doctrine of metempsychosis. BIDEZ, Vie de Porphyre, 106-107 locates the text during Porphyry's stay in Rome after his return from Sicily. He regards it as a vulgarization of Plotinus' philosophy — a sort of practical handbook for the soul.

[54] *negare non potuisti "errare homines theurgica disciplina et quam plurimos fallere" per caecam insipientemque sententiam atque esse certissimum errorem agendo et supplicando ad principes angelosque decurrere*, De regressu 7, BIDEZ, Vie de Porphyre 34-35* = Aug., De civ. D. 10.27 (303,67-70 D./K. = SMITH, Porphyrii, 289bF). SMITH only includes the words I have put in quotations as Porphyry's words.

[55] On vituperation see LAUSBERG, Handbuch § 61.3 and the ad Herennium 3.6.10.

[56] Eus., H.E. 9.7.11-12 commented on in DROGE, Homer, 179.

2.2.3.2 Polluted Christians

Porphyry embodies other oracles (already mentioned above) in a context of the slanders (*blasphemiis*) that the gods used against the Christians:

> "What we are going to say will truly appear to some to be contrary to opinion. The gods have proclaimed that Christ was most faithful and has been made immortal; they remember him with a good public proclamation. The Christians, however, he says, are polluted, contaminated, and hemmed in by error. And many other such blasphemies [*blasphemiis*] are used against them." Then he appends alleged oracles of the gods slandering the Christians...[57].

Augustine has not included these particular slanders. The gods admire Christ, but charge the Christians with being polluted, contaminated and hemmed in by error (*pollutos ... contaminatos et errore implicatos*). This charge is illustrated by the description of the "polluted and unfaithful/impious" Christian wife who perseveres in her delusions. Culdaut comments that Christians, in worshipping the man, turn away from the realities on high and fall into the world of matter and sensation. Hence they become "polluted"[58]. "Error" could function in the rhetoric of defense (apologetic)[59]. Quintilian claims that perverse deeds originate in false opinions. These opinions result in errors (*errores*) and bad passions. Ignorance (*ignorantia*) accompanies these errors and bad affections[60]. The oracles accuse, however, more than they excuse.

2.2.3.3 Hecate's View of Christians

To further illustrate the error of the Christians, Porphyry quotes an oracle of Hecate, and Augustine includes Porphyry's interpretation of the oracle:

> But to some who asked Hecate whether Christ were a god, she replied: "Indeed you have learned that the immortal soul advances after the body [dies], but when it is cut off from wisdom it always errs. That soul [of Christ] belongs to a man pre-eminent in faithfulness; this they worship, truth being alien from them." To this so-called oracular response he adds the following words of his own: "She said, then that he was a very faithful man, and that his soul, like that of other faithful people was considered worthy of immortality after death and that ignorant Christians (*Christianos ignorantes*) worship it ...[61].

---

[57] Aug., De civ. D. 19.23 (691,48-53 D./K. = WOLFF, Porphyrii, 180 = SMITH, Porphyrii, 345aF).

[58] CULDAUT, Un oracle d'Hécate, 281-82.

[59] LAUSBERG, Handbuch, § 188.

[60] Quintilian 5.10.33-34 in LAUSBERG, Handbuch, § 379.

[61] Aug., De civ. D. 19.23 (691,55-62 D./K. = WOLFF, Porphyrii, 181 = SMITH, Porphyrii, 345aF).

The ignorant Christians worship the soul of a faithful man[62]. Porphyry's obvious presupposition is that one should not worship the souls of faithful people. One wonders why he spoke so approvingly of the worship of the Hellenistic heroes[63]. He may view the souls of the devout as being of a genus different from that of heroes (as in Vita Pyth. 38 [53,11 des Places]). Hecate and Porphyry seem unwilling to include Christ in the class of heroes. His point may be that Christians are wrong to worship Christ's soul as God.

To explain the crucifixion, Hecate claims that Christ's soul gave other souls the fatal gift of entanglement in error:

> And to those who asked "why, therefore, was he condemned?" the goddess responded with an oracle: "The body indeed is always subject to debilitating torments, but the soul of the faithful ones abides in a heavenly habitation. And the soul you inquire about has fatally caused other souls to be wrapped in error (*errore implicare*) — souls which the fates did not grant to obtain gifts from the gods nor to have perception of immortal Jove." [Therefore such souls are hated by the gods; for they were not fated to know God or to acquire gifts from the gods. He was the fatal cause of these being wrapped in error. He himself, however, was faithful and departed into heaven as other faithful people. So you are not to blaspheme him, but should have mercy on human folly — from him comes an easy and headlong danger to them.][64]

The words in brackets are probably the commentary of Porphyry since they correspond with the part of the text that Eusebius gives in Greek in prose. The oracle's words (in Eusebius) are in verse[65]. Augustine consequently assimilated Hecate's words to those of Porphyry. Augustine places these words in a context of epideictic rhetoric in which the orator uses praise (*laudare*) or vituperation (*vituperare*)[66]. He claims:

> Who is so stupid as not to see that these oracles were either composed by a clever man with a strong animus against the Christians, or were uttered as responses (*responsa*) with a similar design — that is to say, in order that their praises (*laudant*) of Christ may win credence for their vituperation (*vituperare*) of the Christians; and that thus they may if possible close the way of eternal salvation, the way by which one is made a Christian? For they believe that is not contrary to their harmful and thousand-formed cunning if it is believed that they praise (*laudantibus*) Christ, on condition that their vituperation

---

[62] Maximin Daia described Christianity with words similar to those of Porphyry's oracles. He charged them with "error" (πλάνη) and "ignorance" (ἀγνοία) in the rescript to the Tyrians contained in Eus., H.E. 9.7.3. Maximin Daia's response to Christianity is discussed in WILKEN, Christians, 156-59, and DROGE, Homer, 178.

[63] De antro nymph. 6 (9,24 Seminar Classics 609, State University of New York at Buffalo, Porphyry. The Cave of the Nymphs in the Odyssey, Buffalo 1969).

[64] Aug., De civ. D. 19.23 (691,62-692,73 D./K. = WOLFF, Porphyrii, 181-82 = SMITH, Porphyrii, 345aF).

[65] CULDAUT, Un oracle d'Hécate, 276 n. 17. Compare Eus., D.E. 3.7.1-2 (140,3-19 HEIKEL) printed in SMITH, Porphyrii, 345F. Eusebius notes: "he [Porphyry] adds after the oracle" and then includes some of the text of Augustine that appears between the brackets.

[66] LAUSBERG, Handbuch, § 62.3; Quintilian 3.4.15.

(*vituperantibus*) of the Christians is also believed; so that whether or not one believed that they were making such praise of Christ, he would not wish to become a Christian, and so that however much Christ is praised by those demons he might not liberate him from that domination ...[67].

To persuade people not to become Christians is a concern of the apotreptic branch of deliberative rhetoric — persuading people not to follow a course of action[68]. The vituperative words used in describing Christian belief would be persuasive to individuals with a culturally based respect for the oracles. Porphyry himself seemed untroubled by the gods' disagreement about Christ (as a deluded god or a wise man). Apollo seems to have disagreed with himself in his evaluation of Christ. Consequently Augustine's remarks about the oracles' contradictory christologies might not have affected pagans much.

2.2.3.4 Christians Reverence Forbidden Demons

Porphyry's final remarks on the oracles gloss over the contradictions of Apollo's own view of Christ in order to establish that Christians revere demons and do not worship God.

"There are", he says, "in a certain place very small earthly spirits subject to the power of evil demons. The wise ones of the Hebrews (*sapientes Hebraeorum*), among whom was this Jesus, as you have heard from the oracles of Apollo cited above, turned religious persons (*religiosos*) from these very wicked demons and minor spirits, and prohibited them from giving time (*uacare*) to them; but rather taught them to more properly venerate the celestial gods and to a greater degree to venerate God the father." "This," he said, "the gods enjoin; and we have already shown how they admonish the soul to turn to God and command it to worship him everywhere. But uneducated and unfaithful natures (*indocti et impiae naturae*) to whom fate (*fatum*) has not granted the reception of gifts from the gods nor a concept of immortal Jove, not listening to the gods or to inspired men (*deos et diuinos uiros*), have opposed all gods and have not hated, but have revered prohibited demons. Pretending to worship God, they do not do those things by which alone God is worshipped. Indeed God, being the Father of all is in need of nothing; but for us it is well when we adore him through justice, chastity, and the other virtues and thus make life itself a prayer to him through imitation and investigation of him ..."[69]

It is not clear why Porphyry thinks Christians reverence demons. Perhaps by pretending to worship God and not practicing virtue, Christians in Porphyry's view are actually worshipping demons. By not practicing justice and philosophical contemplation, as a good Neo-Platonist in Plotinus' school would, Christians miss God and find the demons. Such views of ritual also pervade Porphyry's *De abstinentia* in which he claims people offer sacrifice to

---

[67] Aug., De civ. D. 19.23 (692,77-84 D./K.).

[68] LAUSBERG, Handbuch, § 61.2.b. Apotreptic rhetoric can take place in public or in private according to Aristotle, Rhetoric 1.3.3 (1558b).

[69] Aug., De civ. D. 19.23 (693,113-127 D./K. = SMITH, Porphyrii, 346F).

demons[70]. While discussing a passage from the *Letter to Anebo*, Augustine notes that Porphyry believes some forms of divination and certain magical deeds (such as closing doors) are due to a kind of being. He writes, "... some suppose that there is a race of beings whose property it is to listen to people — beings of deceitful nature, taking all forms, with many ways of acting (*multimodum*), simulating gods, demons, and the souls of the dead — and that it is this race which brings about all these things which have the appearance of good or evil ..."[71]. Porphyry may be charging that the Christians revere deceitful demons who can take all kinds of forms — as gods or as departed spirits. If this is the case, he may view Christian worship of Christ as being instead the worship of a deceitful demon that pretends to be the departed spirit of Christ[72]. He would then reverse Paul's charge against pagan worship in which Paul identifies the gods with demons (1 Cor 10:20). Augustine also claims that the oracles are the responses of impure demons. Porphyry and Augustine are playing a mirror game in which each accuses the other of confusing the real and the apparent according to Culdaut[73]. Wilken summarizes Porphyry's entire argument succinctly by noting that Jesus, like other pious people, worshipped God and taught others to worship him. Christians, however, fell into error and taught people to worship Jesus[74].

---

[70] See for example De abst. 2.37.5 (104 B./P.).

[71] Aug., De civ. D. 10.11 (284,23-26 D./K.) summarizing Epistula ad Anebonem 2.3a, 2.6a, 2.7 (11,5-11; 15,3-9; 16,1-17,8 SODANO). The last text includes the following statement: Οἱ δὲ εἶναι μὲν ἔξωθεν τίθενται τὸ ὑπήκοον γένος ἀπατηλῆς φύσεως, παντόμορφόν τε καὶ πολύτροπον, ὑποκρινόμενον καὶ θεοὺς καὶ δαίμονας καὶ ψυχὰς τεθνηκότων· καὶ διὰ τούτων πάντα δύνασθαι τῶν δοκούντων ἀγαθῶν ἢ κακῶν εἶναι.

[72] CULDAUT does not identify the demon with the departed spirit of Christ, but rather with the demons who govern nature (Un oracle d'Hécate, 283).

[73] De civ. Dei 19.23 (692,76 D./K.). See CULDAUT, Un oracle d'Hécate, 286, 288.

[74] WILKEN, Christians, 153. Some parallel passages from Augustine's *De consensu evang.* (CSEL 43) illuminate the background of Porphyry's alternative christology. 1.7.11 (11,20-21 WEIH.: the pagans believe that Christ is to be honored as the wisest of people (*sapientissimum uirum*), but not worshipped as God); 1.15.23 (22,1-6 WEIH.: Porphyry concedes that the gods' oracles are compelled to praise (*laudare*) Christ when asked about him = SMITH, Porphyrii, 345cF); 1.16.24 (22,15-19 WEIH.: the destruction of temples and the condemnation of sacrifices is not what Christ taught, but is the teaching of the apostles according to the pagans). See also 1.34.52 (57,20-58,3 WEIH.) for similar opinions about Jesus among pagans. They want to establish that Christ worshipped their gods in a magical rite and that the disciples lied saying he was a god when he was only a human of extraordinary wisdom (*excellentissimae sapientiae*).

2.3 Contra Christianos

The dating of Porphyry's treatise *Against the Christians* in fifteen books depends on a disputed text in Eusebius[75]. After commenting that some philosophers dedicated their books to Origen and submitted them to him for his judgment, Eusebius wrote: "But why need one say this, when even Porphyry, who settled in our day in Sicily, issued treatises against us, attempting in them to slander the sacred Scriptures, and mentioned those who had given their interpretations of them? (τί δεῖ ταῦτα λέγειν, ὅτε καὶ ὁ καθ' ἡμᾶς ἐν Σικελίᾳ καταστὰς Πορφύριος συγγράμματα καθ' ἡμῶν ἐνστησάμενος)" The text is usually taken to mean that Porphyry wrote the *Contra Christianos* (*C. Chr.*) in Sicily — sometime after 270[76]. Timothy D. Barnes, however, has recently attempted to disassociate the composition of the *C. Chr.* from Porphyry's stay in Sicily[77]. Barnes argues that the phrase in Eusebius' text, ὁ καθ' ἡμᾶς ἐν Σικελίᾳ καταστάς (who settled in our day in Sicily), is "not in direct syntactical connection" with the phrase that follows ("issued treatises against us"). Barnes interprets Eusebius' remark to be an insult of Porphyry for settling in the "intellectual backwater of Sicily"[78]. There is no direct syntactical relationship between the remark about Sicily and the composition of the texts against the Christians. Barnes takes the participle καταστάς (settled) in a characterizing and not temporal sense[79]. Barnes'

---

[75] Eus., H. E. 6.19.2; SMITH, Porphyrii, 30T. ET is J. E. L. OULTON's in the LCL edition. A. VON HARNACK, Porphyrius "Gegen die Christen," 15 Bücher. Zeugnisse, Fragmente und Referate, APAW.PH 1, Berlin 1916, T. 3 is the Suda's statement that the work was in fifteen books (= SMITH, Porphyrii, 2T).

[76] The Suda (II, 472,24-25 ADLER) interprets Eusebius with its phrase τότε συγγράφοντος ἐν Σικελίᾳ (See SMITH, Porphyrius 30T). Compare BIDEZ, Vie de Porphyre, 67 / DE LABRIOLLE, La réaction, 242. See A. CAMERON, The Date of Porphyry's ΚΑΤΑ ΧΡΙΣΤΙΑΝΩΝ, CQ 17, 1967, 382-384 and B. CROKE, The Era of Porphyry's Anti-Christian Polemic, JRH 14, 1983, (1-14) 2. 270 plays a role in the dating since Porphyry used Callinicus Sutorius of Petra in his interpretation of Daniel (Jerome, In Dan. prol. (CChr.SL 75a, 775,86-95 GLORIE). Callinicus dedicated his history of Alexandria to Zenobia of Palmyra who controlled Egypt between 270 (after 28 August) until 272 (BARNES, Scholarship or Propaganda? Porphyry Against the Christians and its Historical Setting, BICS 39, 1994, 58-59). Consequently Callinicus would not have had time to write a history until 271.

[77] Scholarship or Propaganda, 61-62.

[78] BARNES, Scholarship or Propaganda, 61 with reference to Augustine's *Porfyrius Siculus* in Retractationes 2.25 [57].1. He finds a parallel insult in Chrysostom, Jerome, and Anastasius' name for Porphyry as the "man from Bataneae" (HARNACK, Porphyrius, Zeugnis XVI, F. 21a, 65).

[79] The other usages of the participle καταστάς in Eus. that BARNES adduces do not bear the same conceptual meaning "dwell". The usages do show that the word does not necessarily have a temporal component.

argument does show that a translation such as that of Gustave Bardy ("Porphyre s'est établi en Sicile, y a composé des écrits contre nous") reads too much geography ("y") into the text of Eusebius[80]. But it is still an undeniable fact that Eusebius chooses to relate (by proximity) Porphyry's stay in Sicily with the composition of his work against the Christians. Eusebius does not just write that Porphyry the Sicilian wrote against us, but that Porphyry the Sicilian settler wrote against us — leaving the reader with a *prima facie* impression that the text is connected to Sicily. It is also apparent that Eusebius believes Porphyry spent a long period in Sicily. Eusebius' text ("... Porphyry who settled in our day in Sicily, issued [ἐνστησάμενος] treatises against us") may indicate that Porphyry completed the work elsewhere. The fact that LSJ's entry on ἐνστησάμενος includes the frequent meaning "begin" could lead to the interpretation that Porphyry began his work in Sicily and finished elsewhere (Rome as Barnes hypothesizes?)[81].

The *Sitz im Leben* for which Barnes argues is circa 300, immediately before the Great Persecution of February 303[82]. His central argument for such a date is that Eusebius did not criticize Porphyry in the first edition of the *Chronicle* (290s), but did in the second (around 325-26)[83]. The preface to the first edition of the *Chronicle* in the *Preparation for the Gospel* (10.9.1-10, 16-25) when compared to the preface of the second edition of the *Chronicle* in Jerome's translation "implies that the first edition lacked the polemic against

---

[80] G. BARDY, Eusèbe de Césarée Histoire Ecclésiastique, Livres V-VII, SC 41, Paris 1955, 113.

[81] Scholarship or Propaganda, 62.

[82] Scholarship or Propaganda, 58-59. P. PIRIONI connects the work to the purge of Christians from the army, which she dates to 297 (Il soggiorno siciliano di Porfirio e la composizione del Κατὰ Χριστιανῶν, RSCI 39, 1985, 502-508). She also identifies Lactantius' anonymous hedonistic philosopher with Porphyry (Div. inst. 5.2.3). H. CHADWICK asks whether Porphyry might have written the first three books in Sicily and the others for Diocletian's propaganda [The Sentences of Sextus, TaS 5, Cambridge 1959, 142-43]. CHADWICK refers to Porphyry, Ad Marcellam 4 (in which Porphyry writes that he was called for the need of the Greeks) and Lactantius, Div. inst. 5.2.3-11 who mentions an anonymous philosopher who wrote three books, but his hedonistic tendencies do not well accord with what we know about Porphyry's ascetic disposition. PÖTSCHER also associates Porphyry with the figure in Lactantius (Porphyrios, 66-67). B. CROKE lists several scholars who followed BARNES' earlier arguments (The Era of Porphyry's Anti-Christian Polemic, Journal of Religious History 14, 1983, 2 n. 12) including A. MEREDITH, Porphyry and Julian Against the Christians, ANRW II.23.2, 1980, 1126. MEREDITH actually is guarded in his acceptance of the later date writing "perhaps it ought to be" accepted. BARNES' earlier article was Porphyry Against the Christians: Date and the Attribution of Fragments, JThS 24, 1973, 424-442. Those arguments have been superseded by the ones in Scholarship or Propaganda.

[83] Scholarship or Propaganda, 59, 64.

Porphyry which occurs near the beginning of the second"[84]. After Eusebius quotes from his *Chronicle* (P.E. 10.9.1-10) he identifies the quotation as coming from the *Chronicle*, then refers to a text from Porphyry concerning the chronology of Moses that Eusebius notes is from Book IV of the *C. Chr.*[85]. In Jerome's translation the text from Porphyry's *C. Chr.* is incorporated into Eusebius' preface to the second edition *Chronicle*[86]. Barnes draws this conclusion: "Eusebius' habits of quotation in the *Preparation* indicate that if the preface to the *Canons* had existed in its present form at the time of writing he would have contented himself with a single long quotation."[87] Barnes' argument that Eusebius did not include his quotation and criticism of the text from the *C. Chr.* in the first edition's preface seems successful. The preface as it stands in Jerome's translation is a complete revision of the material from the preface in *P.E.* 10.9.1-10 and 16-25[88]. The issue is further complicated by the fact that texts that used to be attributed to Porphyry's own *Chronicle* must now be attributed to the *Contra Christianos* given the strong arguments by Brian Croke that Porphyry never wrote a *Chronicle* [89]. Eusebius' *Chronicle* includes several texts from Porphyry that used to be identified as from the *Chronicle*, and now must probably be identified as from the *C. Chr.*[90]. In addition, the

---

[84] Scholarship or Propaganda, 64. The text of Jerome's translation is R. HELM's edition of Eusebius' Chronicle (GCS Eusebius XVII).

[85] P.E. 10.9.11; SC 369.416-17. The text is in HARNACK, Porphyrius, F. 41. On this text see R. GOULET, Porphyre et la datation de Moïse, RHR 4, 1977, 137-164.

[86] Jerome, Chronicle, praef. (8,1-7 HELM).

[87] Scholarship or Propaganda, 64 quoting his Constantine and Eusebius, 341 n. 70. He refers to K. MRAS' stylistic note in his introduction to the P.E. in GCS Eusebius VIII/1, lv-lviii.

[88] There is, incidentally, no explicit note in P.E. 10.9.16 that he is again resuming a quotation from his Chronicle. Eus. (P.E. 10.9.11-15) quotes (and comments on) a passage from Porphyry, and Jerome's Chronicle summarizes Eusebius' quoted passage (8.1-7 HELM). The revisions are apparent: P.E. 10.9.4 corresponds to Jerome, (10,14 HELM); P.E. 10.9.9 corresponds to Jerome, (11,8 HELM); P.E. 10.9.9 also corresponds to Jerome, (12,18ff. HELM); then the order of correspondence breaks down; P.E. 10.9.11-17 corresponds (roughly) to Jerome, (8,1ff. HELM); P.E. 10.9.18 corresponds to Jerome, (15 HELM); P.E. 10.9.20 corresponds to Jerome, (27b HELM); P.E. 10.9.22 corresponds to Jerome, (12,11-13,3 HELM); and a little of P.E. 10.9.24, 25 corresponds to Jerome, (14 HELM). CROKE's doubts about the existence of Porphyry's Chronicle (see the note below) also throw BARNES' argument into question (as he admits in Scholarship or Propaganda, 64), since the fragments of Eus., Chronicle in JACOBY FGrH 260 F 2,3 (from Porphyry's alleged Chron.) now have to be attributed to the Contra Christianos.

[89] CROKE presents arguments against the existence of a Porphyrian Chronicle (Porphyry's Anti-Christian Chronology, JThS 34, 1983, 168-185). The one Arabic author (of the Fihrist) who explicitly mentions the Chronicle quotes a text otherwise attributed to Porphyry's history of philosophy. BARNES (Scholarship or Propaganda, 55-57) proves that the Fihrist was erroneously translated to support the existence of a Chronicle.

fact that Eusebius and Porphyry both use Semiramis for a historical anchor (for Abraham in Eusebius' case or Moses in Porphyry's case) may imply that Eusebius was aware of Porphyry's work when he wrote the preface to his first edition of the *Chronicle*[91]. As Barnes notes two possibilities exist: either Eusebius quoted Porphyry's *C. Chr.* in his first edition of the *Chronicle* but did not criticize him, or the second edition was heavily revised[92]. The revision of the preface, therefore, does not appear to be enough evidence to prove that Porphyry's *Contra Christianos* did not exist during the 290's.

A less complex but equally interesting argument that Barnes presents is from Harnack's fragment one of the *Contra Christianos* which although anonymous was identified by U. Wilamowitz-Moellendorf as Porphyrian[93]. In that text an anonymous pagan asks "how people who leave their ancestral traditions and who become zealots for foreign Jewish mythologies (that are universally criticized) should not be justly subject to any kind of punishments" (Ποίαις δ' οὐκ ἂν ἐνδίκως ὑποβληθεῖεν τιμωρίαις οἱ τῶν μὲν πατρίων φυγάδες ...)[94]. This text coheres well with Porphyry's statement that Origen's way of life was Christian and illegal (Χριστιανῶς ζῶν καὶ παρανόμως)[95]. Barnes' conclusion is that since illegality should be punished "Porphyry argued, it was right to arrest, imprison and execute Christians for their religion. It is (I submit) more probable *a priori* and on general grounds that he argued this thesis c. 300 rather than c. 270."[96] These arguments are certainly plausible. On the other hand, if the *C. Chr.* was written during the reign of Aurelian, the Christians' belief that Aurelian was on the verge of a persecution shortly before he died provides a meaningful context for the work[97]. Lactantius does not state

---

[90] JACOBY, FGrH 260 F 2,3 from the Armenian version of Eusebius' Chronicle (74,20-79,20, 109,7-113,32 KARST); see BARNES, Scholarship or Propaganda, 59. BARNES gives a superb overview of the problems of Eusebius' Chronicle in Constantine and Eusebius, 106-120.

[91] HARNACK, Porphyrius, F. 40 = Eus., Chron. (8 HELM) and Eusebius' preface to his first edition in P.E. 10.9.10 (SC 369, 416). I am indebted to R. GOULET for pointing this possibility out to me. See further his discussion of these texts in Porphyre et la datation, 146-150.

[92] Scholarship or Propaganda, 64.

[93] Scholarship or Propaganda, 65. See § 2.3.4 below.

[94] HARNACK, Porphyrius, F. 1; Eus., P.E. 1.2.1-4 (SC 206, 104,1-106,7 SIRINELLI/DES PLACES).

[95] Eus., H.E. 6.19.7; HARNACK, Porphyrius, F. 39. See § 2.3.3 below.

[96] Scholarship or Propaganda, 65.

[97] W. H. C. FREND, Martyrdom and Persecution in the Early Church, New York 1967, 328 / CAMERON, Date, 384 / P. KERESZTES, Rome and the Christian Church II. From Gallienus to the Great Persecution, ANRW II.23.1, 1979, 380-84. A. ALFÖLDI, (The Crisis of the Empire (A.D. 249-270), in: Studien zur Geschichte der Weltkrise des 3. Jahrhunderts nach Christus, Darmstadt 1967, 307) notes that Aurelian once recognized the competence of church authorities in an ecclesiastical matter (see Eus., Hist. Eccles. 7.30.19 in reference to Paul of Samosata).

that Aurelian openly persecuted the church, but he charges that Aurelian was planning a persecution when he died[98]. Augustine notes that Porphyry was active during a time in which Christians were being persecuted, although Augustine does not identify the persecutions he had in mind[99]. In the somewhat tantalizing reference to the necessity that caused him to leave Marcella, the elderly Porphyry,[100] wrote: "the need of the Greeks called and the gods urged on with them..." Édouard des Places conjectures that the letter may have been written around 303 and that Porphyry was assisting in the persecution. If this speculation is correct, then Porphyry's work against the Christians may have qualified him, in the eyes of the magistrates, to take part in the deliberations. Barnes' dating is plausible, although Eusebius' note about Sicily probably cannot be dismissed in deciding where the book was written and when.

2.3.1 Date of the C. Chr.: Third Century Crisis (F. 80 on the Disease in the City) or Diocletian's Persecution?

Andreas Alföldi uses the term "world crisis" to describe the middle of the third century. The pressures of the barbarian hordes on the empire's boundaries and the army's proclivity for choosing new emperors are two examples[101]. Lukas De Blois writes: "it was not only the countless wars and other forms of violence that made the third century a period of darkness and misery. The whole century was a sequence of economic crises, social upheavals, natural disasters and religious changes and a time of cultural decadence."[102] There were twenty six emperors between 253-285, only one of whom died a natural death[103]. Such conditions may provide the general context for Porphyry's work against the Christians. In the *Contra Christianos*, Porphyry reflects these changes with his mention that "a disease" has not left the city (Rome?) that had formerly been protected by the gods[104]. The philosopher traces the existence of

---

[98] Lact. De mort. pers. 6. Eus., H. E. 7.30.20-21.

[99] De civ. d. 10.32 (310,52-311,57 D./K.).

[100] Ad Marcell. 1, 4 (7,9-10; 8,22-23 PÖT.). PÖTSCHER, Porphyrios, 66-67, in his comment on the text, agrees that it may refer to Porphyry assisting in the great persecution. See also É. DES PLACES, S.J., Porphyre. Vie de Pythagore. Lettre a Marcella, CUF, Paris 1982, 89, 157. Compare BIDEZ, Vie de Porphyre, 112, 116.

[101] A. ALFÖLDI, Crisis, 342-74 (= CAH XII.165-231). L. DE BLOIS, The Policy of the Emperor Gallienus, Studies of the Dutch Archaeological and Historical Society 7, Leiden 1976, 1-22

[102] DE BLOIS, Policy, 9.

[103] M. ROSTOVTZEFF, Rome, ed. E. BICKERMANN, London et al. 1960, 269.

[104] Porphyry's text is in HARNACK, Porphyrius, F. 80 (= Eus, P.E. 5.1.9-10 [244,1-5 Z./DES P.]). Tertullian (Apol. 40.1-2 [153,1-9 DEK.]) mentions famine and plague as reasons for the Christians to be thrown to the lions. See SCHÄFKE, Frühchristlicher Widerstand, 648-57. CHADWICK comments on this common pagan attitude. Origen remarks that pagans

the disease to the fact that Asclepius and the other gods no longer reside in the city. No one, he claims, has seen public evidence of the gods' help since Jesus has been honored[105]. The plague could have been the same one that Porphyry mentions in the *Vita Plot.* 2.7 which took place before the death of Plotinus. It may be the plague that killed Claudius II in 270[106].

The merit of such a setting for Porphyry's work is that it is close to the usual interpretation of the text of Eusebius. But Barnes' arguments cannot be ignored. A plausibility argument could conclude as does Arthur Droge that:

> ... it is entirely possible that Porphyry's treatise was written shortly before or during the persecution of Diocletian (303-13). Indeed, Henry Chadwick has suggested that Porphyry was called upon by the emperor to compose a defense of traditional religion which might be used in suppressing Christianity. Support for Chadwick's attractive hypothesis can be

---

blamed Christians for the "rebellion" (Contra Cels. 3.15 [214,5-9 KOET.]; Origen: Contra Celsum, xv, 137). Compare Maximin's charge that the Christians were responsible for many terrible evils befalling the empire (Eus., H.E. 9.7.8-9). Origen also notes that pagans ascribed wars, famines, pestilences, and earthquakes to the multitude of Christians and the dereliction of the cult of the gods (In Matt. 24:9 Comment. Ser. 39 [GCS Origenes XI, 74,32-75,6 KLOSTERMANN]; discussed by ALFÖLDI, Crisis, 289). Arnobius also records similar charges in which the gods bring epidemics, droughts, wars, famines, locusts, mice, hail and other things on people because of unlawful acts and offences (*iniuriis .. offensionibus*) of the Christians (Adv. nat. 1.3 [4,13 MARCH.] — discussed by COURCELLE, Anti-Christian Arguments, 152). Although the disease mentioned by Porphyry cannot be precisely identified, DE BLOIS notes the existence of pestilence and plague during the period from 253 to 268 (Policy, 12, 56).

105 Νυνὶ δὲ θαυμάζουσιν εἰ τοσοῦτον ἐτῶν κατείληφεν ἡ νόσος τὴν πόλιν, Ἀσκληπιοῦ μὲν ἐπιδημίας καὶ τῶν ἄλλων θεῶν μηκέτι οὔσης. Ἰησοῦ γάρ τιμωμένου οὐδεμιᾶς δημοσίας τις θεῶν ὠφελείας ἤσθετο. Eus, P.E. 5.1.9-10 (244 Z./DES P.) = HARNACK, Porphyrius, F. 80. The text is repeated in Theodoret, Graecarum Affectionum Curatio 212.96-97 (= EDELSTEIN, Asclepius, I.506). Celsus mentioned the healings of Asclepius (C. Cels. 3.3, 3.24 [205,8; 220,13-16 KOET.]) immediately after discussing the Christian and Jewish belief in a savior who will come to dwell (ἐπιδημήσων) among humankind (3.1, 3 [203,15-17; 205,27 KOET.]). Celsus mentions many other Hellenistic rivals to Christ (C. Cels. 2.55, 3.26, 31, 32, 34, 42 [178,9-19; 222,10-15; 228,8; 230,25-28; 238,9-10 KOET.]). Arnobius recounts the objections of pagans who preferred the healings of Asclepius to those of Christ. After claiming that Christ healed many more than Asclepius, Arnobius considers the possibility that pagans would respond that the gods only healed those (the good) who deserved to be healed! Adv. nat. 1.49 (44,6 MARCH.). Compare Justin, Apol. 1.54.10 (109,37-38 MARC.) who notes that pagans compared Jesus' healings and resurrections of the dead with those of Asclepius (in EDELSTEIN, Asclepius, I.332). Justin carries out the reverse comparison in Dial. 69.3 (190,14-16 MARC.) in response to pagans who admire Asclepius.

106 See the notes on this plague in BRISSON et al., Porphyre la Vie de Plotin, 2.199-200, 337. BRISSON refers to Zosimus, Hist. Nova 1.46.2 (CUFr, 42 PASCHOUD) for the plague that killed Claudius in 270 "if one believes Zosimus."

found in the similarity, already noted, between the attitude and language of several official documents from the time of the persecution and Porphyry's *Against the Christians*.[107] Is it not more intrinsically probable that Porphyry wrote his work shortly before a period of severe persecution (as did Hierocles), than that he wrote it during the relatively quiet (for the Christians at least) reign of Aurelian? What seems plausible to us may not be historically correct. If one is not convinced by this appeal to "plausibility," then Eusebius' text implies a date closer to 270. Whether the *Contra Christianos* is dated to the period shortly after 270 or to the period before the Great Persecution in 303, it is probably the case that persecutions loom in the background. This is true because of the fact that some Christians feared a persecution under Aurelian and that the proem of the *C. Chr.* refers to justified persecutions[108].

2.3.2 The Fate of the Contra Christianos

The *Contra Christianos* created such vexation in the Christian church that it was condemned to be destroyed several times[109]. Constantine condemned it at the Council of Nicaea. In the time of Severian of Gabala (ca 400) the work was still troublesome. Severian claims that Porphyry drew many people away from the divine doctrine (καὶ τοῦ θείου δόγματος πολλοὺς ἀποστήσαντι)[110]. Theodosius II and Valentinian continued the job on Feb. 17, 448 when they condemned the work of Porphyry and others to be burned[111]. An act of the Council of Chalcedon (451?) prohibits possessing or even speaking about Porphyry's work[112]. Justinian, also given to book burning in the case of other heretics, remembered his predecessor's decisions concerning Porphyry

---

[107] DROGE, Homer, 179-10; with reference to CHADWICK, The Sentences of Sextus, 66, 143-43. DROGE draws attention to documents such as ILCV 1b (= CIL III.12132,9-27) and Eusebius, H.E. 9.7.11-12 in which Maximin Daia refers to the error and ignorance of the Christians.

[108] Augustine also claims Porphyry did not become a Christian because of his fear of persecution (De civ. D. 10.32 [310,52-311,57 D./K.]). Of course Augustine may be referring to earlier persecutions under Decius and Valerian.

[109] Socrates, Hist. Eccl. 1.9.30 (33,19-34,10 HANSEN = SMITH, Porphyrii, 38T). Compare Athanasius, De decret. Nic. synod. 39.1-2 (37,33-38,10 OPITZ). Athanasius records Constantine's comparison of Porphyry with Arius. It became a capital crime to possess one of Arius' works. Latin and Syriac versions of this decree can be found in H. G. OPITZ, Athanasius Werke: Urkunden zur Geschichte des arianischen Streites 318-328, Urkunde 33, III.1, Berlin 1935, 66-68. Athanasius' document states that those in possession of Arian documents who do not turn them over will be put to death. Since Constantine calls them "Porphyrians" can it be inferred that those possessing Porphyry's work were also subject to the death penalty?

[110] HARNACK, Porphyrius, F. 42 (from De mundi creatione orat. 6).

[111] Cod. Just. 1.1.3 = SMITH, Porphyrii, 40T.

[112] SMITH, Porphyrii, 42T.

(536)[113]. Methodius (10,000 lines), Apollinarius (30 books), and Eusebius (25 books) devoted works to combat Porphyry's composition[114]. The only Latin father to write against Porphyry is a "Pacatus" whose identity is disputed[115]. Due to the ferocity of the condemnation little has survived of Porphyry's work[116]. Many of the fragments in Adolf von Harnack's edition come from a dialogue between a Christian and an anonymous pagan philosopher written by Macarius Magnes[117]. These fragments have become

---

[113] Const. Just. Corpus Novellarum 42 = SMITH, Porphyrii, 43T.

[114] Jerome, Ep. 48 (ad Pammach.) 13 in HARNACK, Porphyrius XVII. GRANT, Porphyry, 183-186 surveys the Christian use of Porphyry's writings. See also RINALDI, Biblia Gentium, 132-40.

[115] See CPL § 1152a. A. VON HARNACK, Neue Fragmente des Werks des Porphyrius gegen die Christen. Die Pseudo-Polycarpiana und die Schrift des Rhetors Pacatus gegen Porphyrius, SDAW.PH 1921, 266-284 and Nachträge zur Abhandlung 'Neue Fragmente des Werks des Porphyrius gegen die Christen', ibid. 834-5. BARNES, Porphyry, 425-26 argues against attributing the text to the rhetor L. Pacatus Drepanius (see PLRE 272). W. A. BAEHRENS presents philological arguments against the identification (Pacatus, Hermes 56, 1921, 443-45). E. GALLETIER asserts that it is impossible to identify the orator with the Pacatus who intended to write a life of Paulinus of Nola after the latter's death in 431 (Panégyriques Latins, III, CUF, Paris 1955, 45 n. 4). The transmission of the text of Pacatus is quite convoluted. Pacatus was excerpted by Victor of Capua (died 554). Several different catenae preserve texts from Victor. The catenae themselves are elusive. Five fragments of Pacatus (from a Verdun catena on the four gospels now lost) were excerpted by F. FEUARDENTIUS (who attributed the fragments to Polycarp) in his 1596 edition of Irenaeus. One edition is: Sancti Irenaei Lugdunensis ..., ed. F. FEUARDENTIUS, Paris 1639) with references to Victor's texts in the Praefatio and to the lost Catena on 240, 242; the texts appear on 241. J. B. PITRA printed other fragments from Pacatus drawn from a catena of John the Deacon (6th century) on the Hexateuch (Paris MS 838 Sangerm. 60, X C.E.) and Pacatus fragments from a catena to which he obscurely alludes (Spicilegium Solesmense..., I, Paris 1852, LIII, LVIII; cf. CPL 951). HARNACK surveys the problem (Neue Fragmente, 266-75).

[116] Fragments discussed below come from HARNACK, Porphyrius / HARNACK, Neue Fragmente / G. BINDER, Eine Polemik des Porphyrios gegen die allegorische Auslegung des alten Testaments durch die Christen, ZPE 3, 1968, 81-95 / M. GRONEWALD, Porphyrios Kritik an den Gleichnissen des Evangeliums, ZPE 3, 1968, 96 / F. ALTHEIM/R. STIEHL, Neue Bruchstücke aus Porphyrios' κατὰ Χριστιανούς [sic], in: Gedenkschrift für Georg Rohde, ΑΠΑΡΧΑΙ: Untersuchungen zur klassischen Philologie und Geschichte des Altertums 4, 1961, 23-38 / D. HAGEDORN/R. MERKELBACH, Ein neues Fragment aus Porphyrios 'Gegen die Christen', VigChr 20, 1966, 86-90 / COOK, A Possible Fragment of Porphyry's Contra Christianos from Michael the Syrian, ZAC 2, 1998, 113-22. On the whole issue see BEATRICE, Towards a New Edition, 347-55. BEATRICE has also written an extensive history of the question: LE TRAITÉ DE PORPHYRE CONTRE LES CHRÉTIENS. L'ÉTAT DE LA QUESTION, Kronos 4, 1991, 119-138. URSULA PETERS (of the Berlin-Brandenburgische Akademie der Wissenschaften) is preparing a critical edition of the Contra Christianos for the GCS series.

[117] A. VON HARNACK, Kritik des Neuen Testaments.

controversial in recent years due to their anonymous nature. They probably preserve some of Porphyry's arguments, but will be discussed in a later chapter[118]. Richard Goulet argues, for example, that the objections of the *Apocriticus* are not textual quotations from Porphyry due to so many shared expressions between the pagan and the Christian. Macarius may have used a treatise against Porphyry such as the one of Apollinarius[119]. This alters the picture of Porphyry's book that appears in de Labriolle's superb review since de Labriolle believed that the fragments from Macarius could be attributed to Porphyry[120].

The following discussion of Porphyry's fragments from the *Contra Christianos* will unfold in the order of his comments on the synoptic gospels, John, Acts and Paul[121]. To introduce Porphyry's stance toward Christianity I will first examine the fragment concerning Origen along with the alleged proem to the *Contra Christianos*. I will emphasize Porphyry's comments about the NT and Christian tradition, although some mention will be made concerning his opinions about the Christian use of the OT.

---

[118] HARNACK remarks that it would be hypercritical pedantry to omit Macarius' 52 fragments from the collection of Porphyry's work and only to include the other fragments that are certainly Porphyrian (Porphyrius, 9). BARNES has reopened the question of attribution and argues that Macarius may be preserving the main force of Porphyry's arguments, but only indirectly through later writers (Porphyry, 428-430). R. WILKEN argues that the fragments cannot with confidence be used to reconstruct Porphyry's lost work against the Christians (Christians, 136). Compare A. MEREDITH, Porphyry and Julian, 1127. A. BENOIT has a table of the fragments of Porphyry and agrees with R. GOULET's conclusions regarding the Apocriticus (Le «Contra Christianos» de Porphyre: Où en est la collecte des fragments?, in: Paganisme, Judaïsme, Christianisme. Mélanges offerts à Marcel Simon. Influences et affrontements dans le monde antique, Paris 1978, 262-275).

[119] R. GOULET, Porphyre et Macaire de Magnésie, in: StPatr XV, ed. E. LIVINGSTONE, TU 128, Berlin 1984, 448-52.

[120] La réaction, 242-296.

[121] The actual order of Porphyry's work is unknown with the exception of several fragments that are identified as coming from specific books in the fifteen-book text. A. B. HULEN summarizes the known content: I. The origins of Christianity, and its separation from Judaism (Peter and Paul — HARNACK, Porphyrius F. 21a); II. The Jewish records, from which Christianity came (this is a conjecture by HULEN with no explicit textual basis); III. The impossibility of allegorizing the records (Origen — HARNACK, Porphyrius F. 39); IV. The inferiority of the Hebrew records to other accounts (Sanchuniathon — HARNACK, Porphyrius F. 40-41); XII. The attack on Daniel's Prophecy — HARNACK, Porphyrius F. 43; XIII. An attack either on the Christian eschatology or upon the Christian abuse of the Old Testament (the abomination of desolation — HARNACK, Porphyrius F. 44); XIV. Mark's misquotation from the Old Testament— HARNACK, Porphyrius F. 9; HULEN, Porphyry's Work Against the Christians. An Interpretation, YSR 1, Scottdale 1933, 48, 49. Compare BARNES' similar reconstruction in Scholarship or Propaganda, 62-63. He adds the hypothesis that some of the lost books might have contained the material from Didymus the Blind in which Porphyry allegorizes Homeric passages. See § 2.3.42 below.

2.3.3 F. 39: Christian Interpretation of the Hebrew Scriptures

Eusebius has preserved one of the longest Greek fragments of Porphyry's work that explicitly mentions the author[122]. In the text Porphyry opposes the interpretation of Moses' writings by allegorists including especially Origen[123]. Eusebius summarized Porphyry's comments by noting that Porphyry attempted to slander (διαβάλλειν) the sacred scriptures. The historian also mentions the interpreters whom Porphyry also "slandered." Eusebius wrote that Porphyry accused Origen of Christianity and mentioned his devotion to philosophical studies (καὶ τότε μὲν ὡς Χριστιανοῦ κατηγορῶν, τοτὲ δὲ τὴν περὶ τὰ φιλόσοφα μαθήματα ἐπίδοσιν αὐτοῦ διαγράφων). Origen the Platonist (who was a true Hellene) may have been confused with Origen the Christian by Porphyry according to a protracted and convincing argument by Richard Goulet[124]. Whether Porphyry is correct or not he pictured Origen as an apostate from paganism. The opposition Porphyry saw was between Christianity and philosophy[125]. A fragment from Barhebraeus, probably from the same Porphyrian text as that of Eusebius, reads: "He said, when he (Origen) left to teach pagans in a village that they said to him, 'Worship with us and we will yield to you in all things and be baptized.' And as he prayed, the pagans laughed at him and did not become believers [הימנו]."[126] The fragment

---

[122] H. E. 6.19.9 identifies the fragment as an excerpt from book III of the *C. Chr.* The Suda repeats part of this fragment, Suda s.v. Ὠριγένης entry 182 (ADLER). For bibliography on this text see RINALDI, Biblia Gentium, F. 14.

[123] HARNACK, Porphyrius, F. 39. Eus., Hist. Eccl. 6.19.4-8. SELLEW, "Achilles" has an extensive discussion of allegorical method in Porphyry's fragment in Didymus the Blind's commentary on Ecclesiastes, to be discussed below. He includes bibliography on allegory (idem, 86). The most extended discussion of the fragment (questioning Porphyry's knowledge of Origen the Christian and his possible confusion of Origen with Origen the Platonist) is R. GOULET, Porphyre, Ammonius, les deux Origène et les Autres, RHPhR 57, 1977, 471-96.

[124] GOULET, Porphyre, Ammonius, 471-96. The likelihood that Origen the Christian was actually of pagan upbringing is slim. The Platonist is found in texts such as Porphyry, Vita Plot. 3.24, 14.20, 20.37 (I, 4; 18; 25 H./S.); and Porph., *In Platonis Timaeum commentaria* Book 1, fragments 8, 10, and 21 (SODANO); and SMITH, Porphyrii, 427F, 468F.

[125] Eus., Hist. Eccl. 6.19.2-3. Compare his Vita Plot. 16 where he makes Gnostics a sub-group of Christians who (i. e. the Gnostics) had abandoned the old philosophy. See J. IGAL, The Gnostics and 'The Ancient Philosophy' in Porphyry and Plotinus, in: Neoplatonism and Early Christian Thought. Essays in Honour of A. H. Armstrong, ed. H. J. BLUMENTHAL/R. A. MARKUS, London 1981, 138-39.

[126] ALTHEIM/STIEHL, Neue Bruchstücke, Barhebraeus, Chron. Eccl. 1.15.11 (ed. and trans. into Latin by J. B. ABBELOOS and T. J. LAMY, Gregorii Barhebraei Chronicon Ecclesiasticum, I, Louvain 1872, col. 51-52). BARNES, Porphyry, 427 urges caution in relation to Barhebraeus' error in another report concerning Porphyry. Epiphanius, Panarion 64.1.4 (GCS Epiphanius II, 403,12-20 HOLL) describes the young Origen being forced to

is also found in a slightly variant form in Michael the Syrian[127]. The brief fragment shows that one of Porphyry's goals, if not his main goal, was to persuade people not to adopt the Christian faith.

Porphyry had a low view of the Jewish scriptures. He uses the words "wickedness" and "foreign myths" (μοχθηρία[128] ... ὀθνείοις ... μύθοις) to describe them. Instead of giving them up, interpreters such as Origen engage in an absurd form of interpretation (τρόπος τῆς ἀτοπίας)[129]. The absurdity is not allegory in itself, but the using of allegory on writings that are plain (τὰ φανερῶς παρὰ Μωυσεῖ λεγόμενα) to create enigmas full of hidden mysteries (αἰνίγματα). Celsus made similar points about Christian allegories of the OT[130]. Celsus' and Porphyry's interest in this issue indicate the existence of a protracted conflict between Jews, pagans, and Christians over allegory. Josephus argued against the allegories of Greek tales[131]. Arnobius of Sicca quoted a pagan opponent: "You are mistaken ... for all these stories, which seem disgraceful to you and leading to the dishonor of the divine, contain holy mysteries [*mysteria ... sancta*], wonderful and elevated thoughts ... that which is written is not made known nor said, rather, all of these things are understood in their allegorical senses..."[132]. Arnobius has a long argument against the allegorical interpretation of pagan myths[133]. The Christian interpretations, according to Porphyry, do not cohere with or harmonize with what is written (ἀσυγκλώστους καὶ ἀναρμόστους τοῖς

---

give worshippers palm branches in a Serapeum. In 64.2.2-6 (404,4-16 HOLL) he is forced to offer incense on a pagan altar (I am indebted to R. GOULET for this reference).

[127] Chronique de Michel le Syrien. Patriarche jacobite d'Antioche (1166-1199) Éditée pour la première fois et traduite en français, ed. J.- B. CHABOT, Vol. 1, Paris 1899-1924, § 112, 188-89; (Syriac Text is on page 112, column 1, of Vol. 1). See COOK, A Possible Fragment of Porphyry's Contra Christianos from Michael the Syrian, ZAC 2 1998, 113-22.

[128] Celsus uses this word in different contexts in Contra Cels. 3.62 and 5.14 (256,27; 15,16 KOET.). Eusebius uses it to describe Philostratus' contradictory flattery and praise of Domitian in C.H. 43.51 (SC 333, 196 F./DES P.).

[129] Ps. Sallustius, in De diis 3 (4,18 NOCK), believes the "strangeness" (ἀτοπία) of myths encourages philosophically minded people to seek hidden meaning. He lists adulteries and thefts and binding of fathers as examples.

[130] Celsus uses a similar word (μηδὲν αἰνίσσηται) in his denial (Contra Cels. 4.21 [290,9-11 KOET.]) that there are mysteries in the narratives about the tower of Babel. The story is clear (σαφής). The allegories are more absurd (ἀτοπώτεραι) than the myths (4.51 [324,8-11 KOET.]). They do not harmonize (ἁρμοσθῆναι) with anything. Compare C. Cels. 1.17 (69,23 KOET.) and see § 1.4.1 above. Porphyry may also be objecting, like Celsus before him (C. Cels. 2.28 [156,21-23 KOET.]) to Christians' application of OT prophecies to Christ.

[131] C. Ap. 2.255-56. See ROKEAH, Jews, 97-107.

[132] Adv. nat. 5.32 (290,1-10 MARCH.), ET in ROKEAH, Jews, 104.

[133] Adv. nat. 5.38-45 (297,8-305,6 MARCH.).

γεγραμμένοις)[134]. Such interpretations bewitch the mind's critical faculty (τὸ κριτικὸν τῆς ψυχῆς καταγοητεύσαντες).

Porphyry mentions that Origen had learned his "figurative" interpretation (μεταληπτικὸν ... τρόπον)[135] from Stoics such as Chaeremon and Cornutus. He had learned philosophy from Plato and others including Cronius[136]. He "introduced Greek ideas into foreign myths"[137]. Porphyry (in another text) approved of Cronius' allegorical interpretations of Homer who communicated things about the gods and demons by means of enigmas (αἰνιγμῶν)[138].

---

[134] Compare Porphyry's use of the word ἀσυγκλώστον to describe the incompatibility between plants and reason (De abst. 3.18.2 [172 B./P.]). J. PÉPIN interprets the reference to mean interpretations that are not "internally coherent" Mythe et Allégorie. Les Origines Grecques et les Contestations Judéo-Chrétiennes, Aubier 1958, 463. PÉPIN has an extended discussion of Porphyry's allegorical techniques of interpreting Homer in Porphyre, exégète d'Homère, Entretiens sur l'Antiquité Classique 12, Vandoeuvres-Geneva 1965, 231-72.

[135] LAUSBERG, Handbuch, § 571 discusses metalepsis — the use of synonyms that are inappropriate to the context. He refers to Tryphon's discussion of the term in his περὶ τρόπων II (195,10 SPENGEL). This is close to Porphyry's use of the word for the replacement of one concept by another. W. BERNARD believes the "metaleptic" method is a Stoic form of allegory by replacement (with references to natural realities) that contrasts with a Platonic form of allegory that appeals to reason and refers the deeper meaning of texts to "true being." He calls the Platonic method "diairetic." The two kinds of allegory are, however, intertwined in antiquity (Spätantike Dichtungstheorien. Untersuchungen zu Proklos, Herakleitos und Plutarch, Beiträge zur Altertumskunde 3, Stuttgart 1990, 65, 267). Whether such a distinction can be carried out with reference to Porphyry is at least questionable given Porphyry's proclivities toward interpreting certain theological matters with reference to natural realities as in e.g. De cultu simulacrorum (from Eus., P.E. 1.11.1; BIDEZ, Vie de Porphyre Fr. 4 = SMITH, Porphyrii, 355F). BIDEZ comments on Porphyry's Stoic and "physical allegories" in this work (Vie de Porphyre 152). DE LABRIOLLE approves of BIDEZ' thesis that Porphyry may have Jews and Christians in mind in his work on images in which he attacks the "unlearned" who only see wood and stone in images and instead of books see woven papyrus (SMITH, Porphyrii, 351F from Eus., P.E. 3.7.1 [= BIDEZ, Vie de Porphyre, F. 1, 1*]).

[136] SMITH's index (SMITH, Porphyrii) refers to Porphyry's discussions of these figures in the fragments: Apollophanes (408F.50 = Eus., P.E. 10.3.1-15); Moderatus (276F.3,13; 435F.5); Chaeremon (353F.10). For Chaeremon see also De abst. 4.6.1 (CUFr III, PATILLON/SEGONDS/BRISSON). Numenius and Cronius (Vita Plot. 14.11-12, 21.7 [I, 17; 27 H./S.]; SMITH, Porphyrii, 433F, 444F).

[137] Eus., H.E. 6.12.7. Celsus relentlessly critiqued the Christians' (and Jews') use of Greek ideas (On the Jews see C. Cels. 1.21, 4.11, 21 (72,3-5; 281,17-23; 290,16-20 KOET.) and for Christians misuse of Greek tradition and Platonic doctrine see 3.16, 5.65, 6.1, 7, 15, 16 (215,4-6; 68,23-27; 70,6-8; 76,29; 85,6-9; 86,12-18 KOET.).

[138] SMITH, Porphyrii, 372F from Porphyry's περὶ Στυγός. The text is translated and discussed in R. LAMBERTON, Homer the Theologian: Neoplatonist Allegorical Reading and the Growth of the Epic Tradition, Berkeley et al. 1989, 113. On his use of the word "enigma" see also SMITH, Porphyrii, 305F (the gods speak through enigmas) and 382F (some lines from Homer, Od. 10.239-40, are a μῦθος that is an αἴνιγμα concerning the things of the

Cronius, the Pythagorean, finds deeper meaning (ὑπονοίας) in the poet although "he fits (ἐφαρμόζει) extraneous material to the texts in question since he is unable to apply Homer's own, and he has not endeavored to accommodate his ideas to the poet's words but rather to accommodate the poet to his own ideas." Porphyry also refers to Cronius' opinions in his allegorical exposition of Homer's cave of the Nymphs[139]. In that writing Porphyry carries out a sustained allegory of Homer's text in which he depends on the work of interpreters such as Cronius. At the end of his text he argues:

> However, it must not be thought that an interpretation of this sort is forced, that it is the type of thing dreamers of ingenious arguments know how to make plausible. When the wisdom of antiquity, all the intelligence of Homer, and his perfection in every virtue are taken into account, one should not reject the possibility that in the form of a fairy-tale [μυθαρίου] the poet was intimating images of higher things [εἰκόνας τῶν θειοτέρων].[140]

The critic of Christianity believes that Moses' writings hold no such hidden meanings. Porphyry nevertheless indulged in some allegorical interpretation of his own with regard to the Hebrew Scriptures. Given Porphyry's antipathy toward the Christian doctrine of the resurrection (see below § 2.3.32), it is easy to see why he would choose to allegorize Daniel 12:1-3[141]. The texts that metaphorically (μεταφορικῶς) describe the resurrection of the dead actually refer to Maccabean fighters who fled Antiochus Epiphanes and hid in caves and caverns, and after the victory they emerged (like those raised from the dead). The resurrected ones in Daniel are those who defended the law under Antiochus' oppression of the Jews.

After attacking Origen's exegetical method, Porphyry describes Origen's study of philosophy under Ammonius Saccas. Origen, however, did not choose the right life (ὀρθὴν τοῦ βίου προαίρεσιν). Ammonius, being a Christian and being raised a Christian, when he undertook thinking and philosophy became a Greek and changed to lawful behavior. Origen, "raised a

---

soul). Maximus of Tyre also believed that Homer could make enigmatic references (αἰνίττεσθαι) to deeper realities (Diss. 22.2 [186,29-30 TR.]). What the poets describe as Jupiter is mind; Athena is prudence (φρόνησιν); Apollo is the sun (Diss. 4.8 [36,168-70 TR.]). Homeric thought is communicated in myth (Diss. 26.5 [220,115-18 TR.]). Plotinus also allegorized Platonic myths (Ennead. 3.5.9 [I, 303,24-305,57 H./S.]).

[139] De antro 21 (22,2-5 Sem.Cl. 609). Cronius sees the cave as a symbol for the cosmos in motion. DE LABRIOLLE notes the great irony of the passage against Christian allegory, due to the fact that Porphyry indulged in the method so often himself (La réaction, 264-65).

[140] De antro 36 (34,8-12 Sem.Cl. 609; ET from ed. Seminar Classics 609, 36).

[141] HARNACK, Porphyrius, F. 43w = Jer., Comm. in Dan. 12:1-3 (936,497-937,523 GLORIE). This text is conveniently found in M. STERN, Greek and Latin Authors on Jews and Judaism. From Tacitus to Simplicius, Vol. 2, Jerusalem 1980, § 464t (472-74).

Greek and educated in Greek learning," drifted into barbarian recklessness[142] and lived a Christian life contrary to law[143]. Celsus also believed that Christians lived a rebellious and lawless life[144]. Porphyry apparently believed that changing from Christianity to philosophy or from philosophy to Christianity was a choice (ἐφ' ἡμῖν)[145]. This position contrasts with his mention of the influence fate has on Christian belief in the fragments from the philosophy from oracles discussed above. Not only does Porphyry oppose philosophy to Christianity, but he identifies it with an illegal way of life.

This text (and others) prompted Robert M. Grant to sketch out a position in which he argues that Origen's lost *Stromateis* induced Porphyry to write the *C. Chr.* Jerome writes that "in imitation of Clement, Origen wrote ten *Stromateis*, comparing the views of Christians and philosophers with one another and confirming all the doctrines of our religion out of Plato and Aristotle, Numenius and Cornutus"[146]. Grant's survey of the fragments of the *Stromateis* (and other texts in Origen) shows that Porphyry (or Macarius' pagan) attacked many of the same texts that Origen allegorized. Whether it is this lost text of Origen that Porphyry attacked in the *C. Chr.* he clearly found Origen's work to be an impetus to create his own. Robert M. Berchman approves of Grant's thesis and builds upon it to argue that Porphyry's straightforward interpretation of Plato (as opposed to his exegesis of Homer) is the same kind of exegesis he viewed as correct for Biblical literature[147].

---

[142] Celsus described the origin (Jewish) of Christianity as barbarian in C. Cels. 1.2 (57,1-2 KOET.) and apparently described magical Christian language as barbarian in 8.37 (252,14-16 KOET.).

[143] Plato, Pol. 302e describes obedience and contravention of laws using the same terms in a different context (παρανόμως ... κατὰ νόμους). ALFÖLDI believes Plotinus uses similar language to refer to Christianity (Crisis, 253). DU BLOIS rightfully doubts the validity of this view of Plotinus (Policy, 188) and doubts that Gallienus enlisted Plotinus in an intellectual fight against the Christians.

[144] C. Cels. 1.1, 3.5, 14, 8.2, 14 (56,2; 206,22-23; 213,16; 222,4; 231,8 KOET.).

[145] Porphyry discusses the choosing of lives by transmigrating souls (αἱρέσεως τῶν βίων) in a treatment of Plato's myth of Er (Resp. 617e, 620-21; SMITH, Porphyrii, 268F from Porphyry's περὶ τοῦ ἐφ' ἡμῖν). Porphyry uses προαίρεσις several times in the same treatise to discuss ethical choices (SMITH, Porphyrii, 268F.74, 91) and compare Aristotle, Poet 15.2, LAUSBERG, Handbuch § 1226. Aristotle defines it so: ἡ προαίρεσις ἂν εἴη βουλευτικὴ ὄρεξις τῶν ἐφ' ἡμῖν (in EN 1113a.10). See also Porphyry, Ad Marcell. 23 (28,2 PÖT.) where he uses the word for human free choice.

[146] Jerome Ep. 70.3 (CSEL 54, 705,19-706,3 HILBERG) quoted in GRANT, The Stromateis of Origen, in: Epektasis. Mélanges patristiques offerts au Cardinal Jean Daniélou, ed. J. FONTAINE/C. KANNENGIESSER, Paris 1972, 286.

[147] R. M. BERCHMAN, In the Shadow of Origen: Porphyry and the Patristic Origins of New Testament Criticism, in: Origeniana Sexta. Origène et la Bible / Origen and the Bible, ed. G. DORIVAL/A. BOULLUEC et al.. BEThL 118, Leuven 1995, 657-673. BERCHMAN has also made a translation of many of the fragments of the Contra Christianos (Porphyry

Berchman argues that Augustine adopted non-allegorical straightforward exegesis in *De consensu evangelistarum* to interpret the NT in response to Porphyry's attack. The work of these two scholars locates Porphyry clearly in the tradition of patristic exegesis.

2.3.4 F. 1: The Proem?

It is possible that Eusebius has preserved a fragment of the work against the Christians in an introductory passage in the *Praeparatio Evangelica* (1.2.1-4). Harnack conjectured that the passage could have been part of the proem of the *Contra Christianos*. Ulrich von Wilamowitz-Moellendorff argued that the text came from an opponent of Christianity important enough to be answered by Eusebius — namely, Porphyry. The passage also contains some shared vocabulary with the Porphyrian text discussed above that concerns Origen's choice of life[148]. Therefore, Eusebius' anonymous Hellene (P.E. 1.2.5) was perhaps created from the objections of Porphyry. Christians who leave their ancestral traditions (τῶν ... πατρίων)[149] and who become zealots for foreign Jewish mythologies (ὀθνείων ... μυθολογημάτων) are justly subject to any sort of punishments[150]. Barnes argues that this statement is best understood in a context of the years around 300 — shortly before the Great Persecution[151]. One rhetorician remarked that not to destroy ancestral traditions (πάτρια) is the true mark of piety towards the gods[152]. Besides the echoes with *Hist. Eccl.* 6.19.4-8, the text from Eusebius is related to Porphyry's comments to his

---

Against the Christians. Introduction, Fragments, Translation, Notes, [forthcoming from U. of Pennsylvania Press]).

[148] HARNACK, Porphyrius F. 1. Vocabulary shared by the two texts includes: προαίρεσιν τοῦ βίου, ὀθνείων, μοχθηρίας, οἰκείοις. U. VON WILAMOWITZ-MOELLENDORFF, Ein Bruchstück aus der Schrift des Porphyrius gegen die Christen, ZNW 1, 1900, 104. J. SIRINELLI appears to accept WILAMOWITZ' arguments (SC 206, 224-229) but notes that the identification is uncertain (SC 206, 31 n. 3).

[149] Celsus is concerned with this concept (C. Cels. 5.25 [26,3-5 KOET.]); see ANDRESEN, Logos, 192 n. 7. Compare Origen's summary of this charge in 5.35 (38,9-39,13 KOET.). Galerius complains that Christians have not followed the "usages of the ancients" (*veterum instituta*) in the edict of April 30, 311 in Lact., De mort. pers. 34.2 (52 CREED). G. LOESCHE refers to Porphyry's veneration of ancestral tradition in his definition of piety: καρπὸς εὐσεβείας τιμᾶν τὸ θεῖον κατὰ τὰ πάτρια in Ad Marcellam 18 (22,25 PÖT.) in: Haben die späteren Neuplatonischen Polemiker gegen das Christenthum das Werk des Celsus benutzt?, ZWTh 27, 1884, (257-302) 269. Julian also uses the concept to distinguish Christianity from Hellenism C. Gal. 238d (153,22 MASARACCHIA). Whatever its historical value, 3 Macc 1:3 describes a Jew who had apostatized from "ancestral traditions" (πατρίων δογμάτων) to Hellenism.

[150] Eus., P.E. 1.2.1-4 (104,1-106,17 S./DES P.).

[151] Scholarship or Propaganda, 65.

[152] Rhet. ad Alex. 2, 1423b-1424a: ἕξει δὲ πρὸς μὲν τοὺς θεοὺς ὁσίως ἐὰν τὰ πάτρια μὴ καταλύηται. Compare Isocrates' concept of piety (Areopagiticus 29-30) in which one does not add to or subtract from τὰ πάτρια.

134   2. Porphyry

lapsed vegetarian friend, Castricius, in *De abst.* There he tells Castricius that
he (C.) does not scorn his ancestral traditions (vegetarianism — πατρίων ...
νόμων) because of greed. He also does not have a nature inferior to people
(ἰδιωτῶν) who accept laws contrary to those by which they once lived (νόμους
ἐναντίους) and endure the amputation of their body parts and refuse to eat the
flesh of certain animals[153]. The anonymous Hellene in Eusebius' text
continues by claiming that "... it is the final degree of wickedness and
recklessness (μοχθηρίας ... εὐχερείας) to carelessly abandon one's native
traditions (οἰκείων) and accept with an irrational and unexamined faith (ἀλόγῳ
δὲ καὶ ἀνεξετάστῳ πίστει) the impious traditions of those (the Jews) who
oppose all nations. Christians do not even devote themselves to the God of the
Jews according to Jewish customs (νόμιμα), but hew out a new and deserted
road-that-is-no-road (ἐρήμην ἀνοδίαν). They neither keep Hellenistic nor
Jewish traditions." They are atheists because they have abandoned their
ancestral gods[154]. These objections are very similar to those Porphyry raised
against Origen[155]. The complaint that Christians do not argue for their faith
continues a tradition begun by Celsus and Galen[156]. The text (presumably from
Porphyry) probably inspires the entire *Preparation of the Gospel* of Eusebius,
which can be viewed as an answer to Porphyry[157].

2.3.5 F. 2: The Falsehood of the Evangelists

Most of the fragments of the *Contra Christianos* that mention Porphyry by
name come from Jerome, who seems to have known the text through one (or
more) of the Christian treatises that responded to Porphyry[158]. Summarizing
the work of the "impious" commentators (Celsus, Porphyry, and Julian)

---

[153] De abst. 1.2.3 (43 B./P.). N. LARDNER believed Porphyry is referring to Christians
in this text (The Works of Nathaniel Lardner ... The Credibility of the Gospel History...,
Vol. 7.2, 1st ed. 1788, London 1837, 443).

[154] Compare Ad Marcellam 21 (26,4-11 PÖT.) and Julian, C. Gal. 43a (89,9-10 MAS.).
See W. SCHÄFKE, Früchristlicher Widerstand, ANRW II.23.1, 1979, 624-27 and § 3.47,
5.2.9 below. They are atheists and have chosen impious and atheistic traditions (ἀσεβῆ καὶ
ἄθεα τῶν ἐν ἀνθρώποις) in Eus., P.E. 1.2.2, 3 (104,9; 106,6 S./DES P.)

[155] Plotinus uses a similar argument against the Gnostics: the teachings of the ancients
(παλαιοῖς) is superior to that of the Gnostic innovators (Ennead. 2.9.6 [I, 211,52-55 H./S.]).

[156] See COOK, Some Hellenistic Responses, 239-40 for Galen and see § 1.6.1 above for
Celsus. HARNACK compares this text to several in Eusebius in which pagans object to
Christianity because of Christians' lack of argumentation (Porphyrius F. 73; D.E. 1.1.12 and
P.E. 1.3.1). See also C. Cels. 1.9 (61,9-21 KOET. discussed in § 1.6.1 above) and DE
LABRIOLLE, La réaction, 272 n. 1.

[157] BARNES argues that the entire P.E. may be a response to Porphyry's critique
(Constantine and Eusebius, 178-82).

[158] HARNACK, Porphyrius, 7 n. 4. Jerome hardly ever gives verbal quotations from
Porphyry, and often mentions those who wrote against Porphyry in the immediate context of
his summaries of Porphyry's objections to Christianity.

Jerome remarks that they charged the evangelists with "falsehood" (*falsitatis*)[159]. In a letter, Jerome discussed problems concerning the accuracy of Mt 1:22-23 in relation to Is 7:4, Mark's conflation of two prophets (Malachi 3:1 and Isaiah 40:3) in Mk 1:1-13, and Mark's mention of Abiathar in Mk 2:25-26 instead of Ahimelech (1 Sam 21:16)[160]. Jerome's response is that the evangelists are more concerned with the sense than with the letter, and in reference to the problem of Malachi he solicits indulgence for an "error"[161].

2.3.6 A Pacatus Fragment: The Beginnings of the Gospels

One of Pacatus' responses to Porphyry (contained in Victor of Capua's work) treats the different beginnings of all four gospels[162]. Although the text does not preserve Porphyry's objection, one can assume that it was concerned with inconsistencies between the gospels' beginnings. Pacatus concludes that nothing "contrary" (*contrarium*) is found. Finding "contraries" was one of Porphyry's best loved methods of attacking the New Testament. Porphyry discussed Aristotle's logic of contraries and contradictory propositions[163]. From a literary standpoint, Porphyry could have found the technique of looking for inconsistencies in an author among the Homeric critics. Dio Chrysostom, for example, finds contradictory lies in the Homeric poems (τὰ ψευδῆ ἀλλήλοις μάχεται)[164]. Dio also referred to Zeno's attempt "to save Homer from appearing to be at war with himself in certain matters which are held to be inconsistent with each other as narrated by Homer (αὐτὸς αὐτῷ μαχόμενος ἐν τισι δοκοῦσιν ἐναντίως εἰρῆσθαι)"[165].

---

[159] G. J. M. BARTELINK refers to many texts in Jerome in which the scholar refers to the opponents of Christianity; Hieronymus liber de optimo genere interpretandi (epistula 57), Leiden 1980, 93. Celsus called Christian miracles tall tales (C. Cels. 8.45 [260,11-12 KOET.]) and found many points in the gospels that could be refuted (2.27 and see 2.13 [156,1-5; 141,19-22 KOET.]).

[160] HARNACK, Porphyrius, F. 2 from Jerome, Ep. 57.8.1-9.5 (16-18 BARTELINK = CSEL 54.1, 519 HILBERG).

[161] Ep. 57.9 (519,4; 520,10-11 HILB.).

[162] HARNACK, Neue Fragmente, 270. On this text cf. J. M. BOVER, Un fragmento atribuído a S. Policarpo sobre los principios de los Evangelios, EE 14, 1935, 5-19 (he attempts to show it is a text of Polycarp).

[163] SMITH, Porphyrii, 97aF in reference to Aristotle, De int. 7 (17b.8). "He is sick" and "He is well" are examples of contraries given by Porphyry in the fragment from Boethius' commentary on Aristotle.

[164] 11.56 (The Eleventh Discourse Maintaining that Troy was not Captured).

[165] 53.5 (On Homer). A. A. LONG notes that Dio does not reveal what apparent inconsistencies Zeno sought to remove — Stoic Readings of Homer, Homer's Ancient Readers. The Hermeneutics of Greek Epic's Earliest Exegetes, ed. R. LAMBERTON/J. J. KEANEY, Princeton 1992, (41-66) 59. Plutarch has a distinction between theological truth and fabrication in his On How to Study Poetry 20f. This is similar to Zeno's distinction between "opinion" (δόξα) and "truth" in Dio 53.5 (LONG, Stoic Reading, 61).

2.3.7 F. 9: Mark's Conflation of Malachi and Isaiah

In another text, Jerome remarks that Porphyry's objection to Mark's conflation of Malachi 3:1 and Isaiah 40:3 appears in the fourteenth book of the *C. Chr.* (one of the few verbal quotations): "The evangelists were inexperienced [or ignorant] people, not only in secular matters but even in the divine scriptures, so that they attributed a testimony [or proof] written in one place to another prophet."[166] Jerome responds that the solution can be found in "your speeches" where presumably authors are quoted without explicit reference. Mark uses the Malachi text to explain Isaiah's reference to the voice in the wilderness[167]. Ambrosiaster (ca 370-74) preserves an almost identical question concerning the problem in Mark[168].

2.3.8 F. 11: The Genealogies

Porphyry found the genealogies of Jesus to contain errors, although Jerome does not mention the specific objection[169]. Porphyry must have claimed that Matthew skipped a generation between 1:11 and 1:12 because Jerome argues that 1:11 ends with Jehoiakim and 1:12 begins with Jehoiakin[170]. Julian also commented on problems in Matthew's genealogy with regard to Mt 1:16[171]. Ambrose preserves an objection to the women of ill-repute in Matthew's genealogy: namely Tamar, Ruth and Bathsheba[172].

---

[166] *Euangelistae tam inperiti fuerunt homines, non solum in saecularibus, sed etiam in scripturis diuinis, ut testimonium quod alibi scriptum est, de alio ponerent propheta*; Tract. in Marci Evan. I, 1-12 (CChr.SL 78, 452,33-36 MORIN = HARNACK, Porphyrius, F. 9). Arnobius (Adv. nat. 1.58 [53,7 MARCH.]) has an anonymous pagan who charges that the Christian writings were "written by unlearned an ignorant people and therefore should not be readily believed" (*Sed ab indoctis hominibus et rudibus scripta sunt ed idcirco non sunt facili auditione credenda*).

[167] CChr.SL 78, 452,37-48 MORIN. Eusebius claimed there was a scribal error; Supplementa minora ad quaestiones ad Marinum (PG 22, 1008).

[168] Quaestiones Vet. et N. Test. 57 (CSEL 50, 103,19 SOUTER) discussed in DE LABRIOLLE, La réaction, 493, 497 / RINALDI, Biblia Gentium, F. 291).

[169] HARNACK, Porphyrius, F. 11; Jerome, In Dan. I 1.1 (777,14-20 GLORIE). See also RINALDI, Biblia Gentium, F. 318 for bibliography.

[170] Ambrosiaster preserves several anonymous objections to the number of generations in Matthew's genealogy in Quaestiones de N. Test. 6, 7 (432,1-2 and 21-24 SOUTER = RINALDI, Biblia Gentium, F. 321-22).

[171] Comm. in Matth. 1:16 (SC 242, 74,46-76,49 BONNARD). See § 5.2.2 for a reference to a text from Ish'odad of Merv who notes an objection about the genealogies from Julian and Porphyry (A. GUIDA, ed., Teodoro di Mopsuestia, Replica a Giuliano Imperatore. Adversus criminationes in Christianos Iuliani Imperatoris, Biblioteca Patristica, Florence 1994, 200).

[172] COURCELLE, Anti-Christian Arguments, 160 referring to Ambrose, In Lucam 3.17 (CSEL 32.4, 110,17 C. and H. SCHENKL).

2.3.9 A Fragment from Pacatus on the Genealogies

The treatise by Pacatus against Porphyry written in Latin contains an answer to the genealogical problem which claims that two kings (Jehoiakim and Jehoiakin) are in Mt 1:11-12 and uses Levirate marriage to explain the discrepancy[173]. The problem of the divergent genealogies of Jesus was a sensitive one for ancient Christians who devoted a great deal of energy toward its solution. Eusebius mentions the letter of Africanus to Aristides on "The Supposed Discord between the Genealogies of Christ in Matthew and Luke" (H.E. 1.7.1-1.7.17; 6.31.3). Augustine also treated the problem (De cons. ev. 2.3.5—2.4.10). He notes that king "Jechonias" is mentioned twice (2.4.10).

2.3.10 F. 12: Inconsistencies in the Gospels: the Birth Stories

Epiphanius writes that several Hellenistic philosophers (Porphyry, Celsus and Philosabbatios) "examine the gospel material for the sake of its refutation and accuse the holy evangelists..." ([εἰς] τὴν κατὰ τῆς εὐαγγελικῆς πραγματείας διεξιόντες ἀνατροπὴν τῶν ἁγίων εὐαγγελιστῶν κατηγοροῦσι)[174]. The philosophers ask how the events recounted by Luke on and following the day of Jesus' birth (birth, circumcision eight days later, journey to Jerusalem forty days later, things done by Simeon and Anna) can happen at the same time as the events of the night of Jesus' birth in which an angel appeared after the magi left (Mt 2:13) and told "him" to go to Egypt. If, on the night he was born, he was taken to Egypt until Herod died, how can he remain and be circumcised eight days later or after forty days ...? Luke "is found to be lying ... when he says 'On the fortieth day they brought him to Jerusalem and returned to Nazareth'" (Lk 2:21, 39). Origen (Contra Celsum 1.66) mentions Celsus' objections to the flight to Egypt because a god would not be afraid of death. The objection to the birth stories that Epiphanius recounts could come from Porphyry, Celsus, or the Jewish philosopher Philosabbatios. The method of looking for contradictions in Biblical narrative is very consistent with Porphyry's scholarly technique. One cannot claim that Epiphanius preserves an explicit Porphyrian quotation. He may well, however, have preserved the sense of one of Porphyry's objections[175].

---

[173] HARNACK, Neue Fragmente, 276. The text comes from PITRA's unidentified catena mentioned above (Spicilegium Solesmense, LVIII-LIX). ALTHEIM and STIEHL believe that a text from Al-bîrûnî (p. 20, lines 12ff. SACHAU) that preserves a long discussion of the divergent genealogies may be a Porphryian fragment, although Al-bîrûnî does not identify his source (Neue Bruchstücke, 30-31, 33-34). BARNES, Porphyry, 427 doubts the attribution to Porphyry and notes the ET of Al-bîrûnî by C. E. SACHAU, The Chronology of Ancient Nations: An English Version of the Arabic Text of the Athâr-ul-bâkiya of Albîrûnî, 1879, 24ff.

[174] HARNACK, Porphyrius F. 12 from Panarion 51.8 (258,6-259,6 HOLL).

[175] F. 92 (§ 2.3.32) has a brief comment of Porphyry on the virgin birth.

138   2. Porphyry

Epiphanius responds to the objections by nothing that Matthew and Luke have different time frames since the magi came two years after the birth[176]. Augustine was also aware of the chronological difficulties, but in his attempted harmonization of the narratives he places the visit of the magi after the circumcision and before the presentation in the temple. The angel's warning to Joseph then comes after the presentation in the temple (De cons. ev. 2.5.17; 2.11.24).

2.3.11 F.49: Demonic Miracles

Jerome makes a brief reference to Porphyry (and the Arian bishop Eunomius) in his work against Vigilantius. Vigilantius argued against the miracles which occur in the basilicas of the martyrs and claimed that they were signs for unbelievers and not believers. Jerome responds: "Unless perhaps in accord with the opinions of the Gentiles and the impious Porphyry and Eunomius, these are illusions fabricated by demons, and the demons do not really cry out, but simulate being in torment."[177] Harnack thinks the reference is to Mk 5:7 (or Mt 8:29). Lardner also mentions Mk 1:23-24 as a possibility[178]. Celsus was quite willing to countenance the possibility that Christians do powerful deeds by using demonic assistance (C. Cels. 1.6 [59,8-10 Koet.]). Macarius' anonymous philosopher treats the passage in Mk 5:1-20 that will be discussed in a later chapter (§ 3.3). Porphyry believed in the ability of demons to work wonders as he makes clear in his letter to Anebo[179]. In the demonology of De abst. (2.42.1 [109 B./P.]), bad demons can deceive through the working of wonders (ἀπατῆσαι ἱκανοὶ διὰ τῆς τερατουργίας). According to Porphyry either God or evil demons dwell in the human soul — a person who does evil is possessed by an evil demon (πονηροῦ δὲ δαίμονος)[180].

2.3.12 F. 6: The Call of the Disciples

The call of the disciples was no more persuasive to Porphyry than the birth stories and genealogies. Jerome reports Porphyry's (and Julian's) arguments concerning Mt 9:9: "Porphyry and Julian Augustus asserted in this text either the ignorance of a lying historian or the stupidity of those who immediately

---

[176] Panarion 51.8 (259,7-260,1 HOLL).
[177] HARNACK, Porphyrius, F. 49, Contra Vigilant. 10 (PL 23, 363-64): *Nisi forte in more gentilium impiorumque Porphyrii et Eunomii has praestigias daemonum esse confingas, et non vere clamare daemones, sed sua simulare tormenta.*
[178] HARNACK, Porphyrius, 78. LARDNER, Works, 427.
[179] The text from Macarius is also given in HARNACK's Porphyrius, F. 49. Epistula ad Anebonem 2.3a, 2.6a, 2.7 (summarized above in § 2.2.3.4 on Porphyry's Philosophy from Oracles).
[180] Ad Marcellam 21 (24,27-26,4 PÖT.).

followed the savior, as if they would have irrationally followed anyone who called them" (*Arguit in hoc loco Porphyrius et Julianus Augustus uel imperitiam historici mentientis uel stultitiam eorum qui statim secuti sunt saluatorem, quasi irrationabiliter quemlibet uocantem hominem sint secuti...*)[181]. Julian believed Jesus and Paul deluded maidservants and slaves and through them people like Cornelius and Sergius[182]. He also viewed the gospels as a "fabrication" (σκευωρίας) even though they might happen to mention some historical events such as minor healings and exorcisms[183]. The charges of stupidity and irrationality levelled against the disciples correspond to the charges Porphyry made against Christian belief in his earlier work on the *Philosophy from Oracles* and with Eusebius' anonymous Hellene who believed the Christian faith was irrational and unexamined[184]. Macarius' anonymous pagan also questioned the choosing of the disciples and had problems with the statement, "will make you fishers of people." The content of the objection is not preserved[185]. Porphyry was more impressed with the ability of Pythagoras to draw followers to himself: "Thus he turned (ἐπέστρεψεν) all to himself so that in only one lecture, as Nicomachus says, which he gave after arriving in Italy he captured (ἑλεῖν) more than two thousand people with his words with the result that no one departed for home ..."[186]. Presumably Porphyry would claim that Pythagoras captured people by the art of reason — in contrast to Jesus' command to follow him. Jerome responded that the apostles' call had been preceded by miracles and signs (*uirtutes ... signa*) so that they saw before they followed.

2.3.13 A Fragment from Didymus on the Parables

Didymus the Blind has preserved an apparent comment by Porphyry concerning Mt 13:9, 43 par (or 11:15). In a discussion of Ps 43:2 LXX, Didymus quotes Is 50:4-5 to distinguish between physical hearing and an "epistemic" kind of ear that hears in a godly way (ὠτίον, τὸ ἐπιστημονικόν, τὸ θεοπρεπῶς ἀκοῦον)[187]. Didymus claims that this is what the "...savior means when he said 'Let the one who has ears to hear hear.' Not all had ears that heard the hidden words of Jesus that were proclaimed in parables. Therefore Porphyry was driven mad concerning this" (ταῦτα ἐν [νῷ ὁ

---

[181] HARNACK, Porphyrius, F. 6, Comm. in Matth. 9:9 (170,51-55 BONN.).

[182] Julian, C. Gal. 206a (142,7-12 MAS.).

[183] C. Gal. 218a (145,4 MAS.); 191e (136,9-10 MAS.).

[184] HARNACK, Porphyrius, F. 1.

[185] See § 3.52 below for the indexes to some of the lost texts of the Apocriticus.

[186] Vita Pyth. 20 (45,3-6 DES PLACES).

[187] Comm in Ps 43:2 (ed. M. GRONEWALD, Didymus der Blinde. Psalmenkommentar, pt. 5, PTA 12, Bonn 1970, Codex p. 308). See also M. GRONEWALD, Porphyrios Kritik an den Gleichnissen des Evangeliums, ZPE 3, 1968, 96.

σω]τὴρ ἔχων [ἔλεγεν]· "ὁ ἔχων ὦτα ἀκούειν ἀκουέτω". οὐ πάντες δὲ εἶχον τὰ ἀκούοντα τῶν Ἰησοῦ ἐπικε[καλυμμ]ένων λόγω[ν, τῶν] ἐν παραβολαῖς ἀπαγγελλομένων λόγων. ὅθεν ἐμάνη Πορφύριος καὶ ἐν τούτω)[188]. M. Gronewald refers to two texts from the *Apocriticus* of Macarius in which the anonymous pagan (whom Gronewald identifies as Porphyry) takes offense at Mt 11:25 and at the parables in Mt 13:31, 33, 45[189]. One who teaches divine things should use clear examples and not incomprehensible ones. They should be clear especially because they were written, not for the use of the wise and understanding, but for infants. Porphyry seems to have objected to the fact that not every one had ears to hear the parables. The texts in the *Apocriticus* reinforce this possibility. Didymus does not say if Porphyry took offense at allegorical interpretation of the parables. Porphyry's objection appears to be that the parables are incomprehensible, or at least incomprehensible to some people.

2.3.14 F. 10: On Mt 13:35

A simpler objection to the parables is contained in Jerome's comment on Ps 77. Jerome notes that Porphyry critiqued Mt 13:35 in which the text from Psalm 78:2 (LXX 77:2) is attributed to Isaiah: "Your evangelist Matthew was ignorant (*inperitus*) when he said 'What was written in Isaiah the prophet...'"[190]. Jerome responds that an ignorant scribe (one of the *inperitis ... gentibus*) erred who replaced "Asaph," whom he had never heard of, with "Isaiah." Here Porphyry's objection is similar to his critique of Mark's conflation of Malachi with Isaiah. The charge of ignorance was traded back and forth between pagans and Christians. In Augustine's letter to Paulinus of Nola, he calls the pagans ignorant and arrogant (*inperitissimos et superbissimos qui de Platonis libris Dominum profecisse contendunt*) who think that Jesus learned from the books of Plato. Ambrose had written a book (*De philosophia*) against them[191].

2.3.15 F. 55: On Galilee

Porphyry took offense at the narrative of Jesus walking on the waters of Galilee (Mt 14:22-33; Mk 6:45-52). Jerome wrote: "In vain therefore does Porphyry accuse the evangelists of manufacturing a miracle for the ignorant,

---

[188] Porphyry was also "driven mad" during his inspired reading of a poem (Vita Plot. 15.3-4 [I, 18 H./S.]).
[189] GRONEWALD, Porphyrios, 96. The texts are in HARNACK, Porphyrius, F. 52, 54 from Apocr. 4.9 and 4.8 (167,1-11; 166,1-10 BLONDEL). See § 3.7 and 3.9 below.
[190] HARNACK, Porphyrius, F. 10, Tract. de Psalmo 77 (66,75-77 MORIN). Jerome's solution is on 67,85-87.
[191] Aug., Ep. 31.8 (CSEL 34.2, 8,2-4 GOLDBACHER) and see COURCELLE, Anti-Christian Arguments, 158 on Ambrose's lost *Philosophia*.

because the Lord had walked on the 'sea'; instead of 'lake of Gennesaret' they called it a 'sea' ..." (*frustra igitur Porphyrius euangelistas ad faciendum ignorantibus miraculum eo, quod dominus super mare ambulauerit, pro lacu Genesareth mare appellasse...*)[192]. Jerome's response is that in Hebrew any body of salt water or fresh water is called a "sea." The response that Macarius Magnes makes to the objection is the same as Jerome's[193]. Goulet believes that the very close relationship between the responses of Jerome and Macarius (to a similar objection) indicates that Macarius might have taken the pagan's objection from the same text against Porphyry that Jerome used such as that of Apollinarius of Laodicea[194]. Porphyry's critique of the miracle is not only an objection to calling a "lake" a "sea." He charges the evangelists with "creating a miracle." This claim is similar to the general approach toward the gospels that Jerome finds in Celsus, Porphyry, and Julian who accuse the evangelists of "falsehood"[195]. Origen summarizes Celsus' approach to the gospels as "myths and fictions" (μύθοι, πλάσματα)[196]. Celsus has his Jewish narrator say that he could write a true account of Jesus' life that would not be anything like the disciples' writings (C. Cels. 2.13 [141,19-22 Koet.]). It is apparent that Porphyry exerted his critical faculties more on the gospels than he did on the life of his beloved Pythagoras of whom many more wondrous and divine things (θαυματότερα καὶ θειότερα) could be told than those that Porphyry included[197]. The miraculous stories about Pythagoras are told uniformly and harmoniously (ὁμαλῶς καὶ συμφώνως) — a quality Porphyry does not find in the Gospels.

2.3.16 F. 56: Mt 15:17

An anonymous fragment in Jerome notes that many places in the gospels are a scandal among "heretics and perverse people," and some bring charges against Mt 15:17 par because the Lord, ignorant of reasoning about nature, believes that all food goes into the stomach and in the privy is then carried away[198]. Porphyry's charge that the gospel writers were ignorant in secular and spiritual

---

192 HARNACK, Porphyrius, F. 55; Quaest. in Gen 1.10 (CChr.SL 72, 3,20-4,23 DE LAGARDE).

193 Apocriticus 3.13 (84,8-16 BLONDEL); see § 3.10 below.

194 Porphyre et Macaire de Magnésie, in: StPatr XV, TU 128, Berlin 1984, 452.

195 HARNACK, Porphyrius, F. 2.

196 C.Cels. 2.15; 3.27; 5.57 (144,15; 224,14.16; 60,15.26 KOET.).

197 Vita Pyth. 28 (49,12-13 DES PLACES).

198 HARNACK, Porphyrius, F. 56 (Comm. in Matth 15:17 (328,108-112 BONN.). *Secessum* for "privy" is also found in Jer. Ep. 64.2 (CSEL 54, 589,15 HILB.).

matters is consistent with the anonymous critic's opinion about Jesus' knowledge of physical matters[199].

2.3.17 A Pacatus Fragment on Lk 14:12-13

In reference to the saying in Lk 14:12-13, Pacatus has preserved a fragment of one of Porphyry's typical objections:

> He commanded that not friends but the sick should be invited to a meal; but if a lame person or one of the infirm happens to be a friend, without a doubt such a person should by no means be asked because of the friendship. Therefore the commandments themselves are seen to oppose (*impugnare*) each other; for if not friends but the lame and the blind should be invited, if it happens that those are also friends, we must not invite them at all.[200]

Porphyry's method is often to look for contradictions between verses of the NT. His presupposition is the Aristotelian principle that two statements that contradict each other cannot both be true as in the case of "Socrates is white" and "Socrates is not white"[201]. Porphyry was aware of this principle of Aristotelean logic because he had commented on this section of *De int.* including the line in which Aristotle discussed contradictory (ἀντικεῖσθαι ... ἀντιφατικῶς) opposites[202]. Although Aristotle's logic is for propositions and not commands, Porphyry uses it to show that the command is incoherent — on his reading. Pacatus responded that "friends" means "those whom we value because of earthly considerations and not for insight into divine contemplation. He (Jesus) gave the weak as an example because we can desire them for the sake of nothing we need — except for an eternal reward."[203]

2.3.18 A Pacatus Fragment on Mt 19:5

Porphyry objected to Matthew's attribution (19:5) of the statement in Genesis (2:24) to the Lord because Moses wrote (Gen 2:23) that Adam said, "This now is bone from my bones ...." Pacatus' response is that Adam prophesied the words by divine inspiration so that the words themselves are correctly held to have been said by the Lord[204]. Again, the method Porphyry uses is to identify contradictions between statements in the Christian scriptures. In interpreting Homer, Porphyry wrote: "Since I believe that it is right to clarify Homer with

---

[199] HARNACK, Porphyrius, F. 9 = Tract. in Marci Evan. I, 1-12 (CChr.SL 78, 452,33-36 MORIN).

[200] HARNACK, Neue Fragmente, 270.

[201] Aristotle, De interpretatione 7 (17b). See also Metaphysica 1011b and Analytica posteriora 72a.12.

[202] De int. 7 (17b.17) discussed by Porphyry in a fragment (SMITH, Porphyrii, 98F). Compare Porphyry's discussion of *contradictio* in SMITH, Porphyrii, 95F.

[203] HARNACK, Neue Fragmente, 270-71.

[204] HARNACK, Neue Fragmente, 269.

Homer, I used to point out that he explains himself" ('Αξιῶν δὲ ἐγὼ "Ομηρον ἐξ 'Ομήρου σαφηνίζειν αὐτὸν ἐξηγούμενον ἑαυτὸν ὑπεδείκνυον ...)[205]. Porphyry wrote to the Neoplatonic philosopher Anatolius that Homer often provides his own explanation[206]. Porphyry, instead of using his "Homer-by-Homer" principle of exegesis transforms it into the principle: "Scripture refutes scripture."

2.3.19 A Pacatus Fragment on Mt 20:23

Only Pacatus' response to Porphyry's critique of Mt 20:23 par survives. Pacatus argues that James suffered martyrdom and that John had the mind of a martyr. John was immersed in a jar of boiling oil[207]. Consequently Porphyry must have argued that Jesus' prophecy was unfulfilled in the case of John. Porphyry the historian emerges here — not just Porphyry the logician and philosopher[208].

2.3.20 F. 3: Faith Moves Mountains?

While commenting on Mt 21:21, Jerome remarks that the "gentile dogs bark against us in their books which they left in memory of their own impiety, asserting that the apostles did not have faith, because they could not move mountains"[209]. The pagan "dogs" probably include Porphyry since Jerome alludes to him several times in his commentary on the gospel[210]. The anonymous pagan in Macarius' *Apocriticus* also attacked a verse that combined elements from Mt 17:20, Lk 17:6 and Mt 21:21. The pagan critic concludes that neither do Christians belong to the faithful (πιστοῖς) because they cannot move mountains, nor are bishops or priests worthy of the name ("faithful")[211]. Porphyry (or the anonymous pagan "dog") attempts a *reductio ad absurdum* of

---

[205] Ed. and trans. R. R. SCHLUNK, Porphyry. The Homeric Questions, Lang Classical Studies 2, New York et al. 1993, 46-7. SCHLUNK translated the SODANO edition of the text. R. PFEIFFER attributes the invention of this principle to Porphyry and not Aristarchus in History of Classical Scholarship. From the Beginnings to the End of the Hellenistic Age, Oxford 1968, 225-26. For an extensive discussion of the principle see B. NEUSCHÄFER, Origenes als Philologe, Schweizerische Beiträge zur Altertumswissenschaft 18/1, 2 Vols., Basel 1987, I, 276-85.

[206] SCHLUNK, Porphyry, 2.

[207] HARNACK, Neue Fragmente, 269. HARNACK (269 n. 10) gives examples of the legend in texts from Latin-speaking authors of the Christian west.

[208] W. DEN BOER emphasizes the historical nature of many of Porphyry's objections (A Pagan Historian and his Enemies: Porphyry Against the Christians, CP 69, 1974, 198-208).

[209] HARNACK, Porphyrius, F. 3 = Comm. in Matth. 21:21 (SC 259, 122,305-309 BONNARD).

[210] HARNACK, Porphyrius, F. 6, 9, 44. Anonymous fragments that may be from Porphyry include numbers 14 and 56.

[211] HARNACK, Porphyrius, F. 95, from Apocriticus 3.17 (97,1-7 BLONDEL).

the verse. Jerome counters that given the world's incredulity with regard to the miracles of scripture, it would also be skeptical (*incredulis*) about even greater miracles [of the apostles that have not been written]. He also allegorizes the mountain to mean the devil, who when he possessed a soul, is cast into the sea by the apostles[212].

2.3.21 A Didymus Fragment: All Things are Possible for God?

That Jerome was referring to Porphyry in his comment on Mt 21:21 is also confirmed by one of the fragments of Porphyry found in the works of Didymus the Blind. While commenting on Job 10:13, Didymus argues that there are active (according to which we act) and passive powers (according to which we become). God does not have passive powers. He writes:

> It is not possible to say that God becomes something else. God does not have powers that dispose him for certain things. One may not say that God lies or changes or denies himself. He [Job] therefore says that what suits God is possible for God. Some teach sophistically, including Porphyry and those like him, that "if all things are possible to God," then also lying [is possible]. And if "all things are possible to a believer," he or she can make a bed or a human being.
>
> (οὐ γὰρ οἶόν τε εἰπεῖν αὐτὸν γενέσθαι ἄλλο τι ‑ οὐ γὰρ ὑπάρχουσιν αὐτῶι αἱ κατ᾽ ἐπιτηδειότητα δυνάμε[ι]ς ‑ οὐδὲ λεκτέον, ὅτι δύναται ψεύδεσθαι ἢ μετ[α]βάλλεσθαι ἢ ἀρνήσασθαι ἑαυτόν. ἃ ἁρμόζει οὖν θ(ε)ῷ, δυνατὰ αὐτῷ λέγω. σοφίζονται γάρ τινες, ὧν ἐστι καὶ Πορφύριος καὶ ὅμοιοι, ὅτι εἰ πάντα δυνατὰ τῷ θ(ε)ῷ, καὶ τὸ ψεύσασθαι, καὶ εἰ πάντα δυνατὰ τῷ πιστῷ, δύναται καὶ κλίνην ποιῆσαι καὶ ἄνθρωπον ποιῆσαι)[213].

Porphyry refers to several phrases from the NT. "If all things are possible to God" is an echo of Mt 19:26 par and Mk 14:36. "All things are possible to the believer" is reminiscent of Mt 17:20 and Mk 9:23. This topic is similar to that of Jerome's fragment of pagan objections to Mt 21:21. Jerome's statement (on Mt 17:20) that there exist people who accuse the apostles and believers of not having faith because they cannot move mountains indicates that the pagans attacked such verses frequently[214].

Porphyry found it absurd to claim that God can do everything. Dieter Hagedorn and Reinhold Merkelbach refer to similar discussions of the limits of divine power in Pliny, *Hist. nat.* 2.27 (God can't bring the dead to life or commit suicide) and Macarius' *Apocriticus* 4.24 where the anonymous pagan objects to the resurrection by attacking the belief that all things are possible to

---

212 Comm. in Matth. on 21:21 (122,305-124,328 BONN.).

213 Commentarii in Job 10:13 (ed. U. HAGEDORN/D. HAGEDORN/K. KOENEN, Didymus der Blinde. Kommentar zu Hiob, pt. 3, PTA 3, Bonn 1968, codex 280.15-28). See also HAGEDORN/MERKELBACH, Ein neues Fragment, 86-90 and RINALDI, Biblia Gentium, F. 382.

214 Comm. in Matth. 17:20 (40,191-94 BONN.).

God. God, for example, cannot make two plus two to equal five[215]. God only does what accords with his being. This is similar to Didymus' position. Didymus refers to 2 Tim 2:12 and Heb 6:18 to defend his view that all things are possible to God that suit God (ἁρμόζει ... θεῷ). Porphyry's attack on the principle that all things are possible to the believer is a little different from the one contained in Jerome's fragment that itself probably comes from Porphyry[216]. In that text, the apostles do not have faith because they cannot move mountains. Here Porphyry argues that the consequences of the principle are absurd. A person of faith should be able to make a human or a bed. Porphyry's method is to attempt to create a *reductio ad absurdum* argument against both principles: the consequences of accepting "all things are possible to God" and "all things are possible to the believer" are absurd.

2.3.22 F. 44: Mt 24:15 and the Antichrist

In the thirteenth book of his *Contra Christianos*, Porphyry attacked Mt 24:15. Jerome merely notes that Porphyry "blasphemed many things against us" in reference to the text. Eusebius responded to this charge in his work against Porphyry, and Apollinarius responded most fully. Jerome does not wish to discuss in one small chapter that which had been disputed in thousands of lines[217]. He sees possible references of the figure of the abomination in Matthew 24:15 to be the statue of "Caesar" that Pilate put in the temple, the equestrian statue of Hadrian that is "now" where the Holy of Holies was, or

---

[215] HAGEDORN/MERKELBACH, Ein neues Fragment, 88-9. The text from Macarius is HARNACK, Porphyrius F. 94 (204,1-205,9 BLONDEL). Compare Apocriticus 4.2 (159,1-160,8 BLONDEL; an objection to 1 Th 4:15-17 with its people on clouds). The response of Macarius in 4.30 (to 4.24) contains a text with a statement that God can do all, but only acts in accordance with the natural order of things (SCHALKHAUßER, Zu den Schriften des Makarios, 71-72). This fact prompted GOULET to state that Macarius probably placed this objection in the pagan's mouth (Porphyre et Macaire, 451). Patristic authors discussed the concept of what God could and could not do. See S. DOWD, Prayer, Power, and the Problem of Suffering: Mark 11:22-25 in the Context of Markan Theology, SBLDS 105, Atlanta 1988, 69-94.

[216] HARNACK, Porphyrius, F. 3; compared above (§ 2.3.20) to HARNACK, Porphyrius, F. 95 from the Apocriticus 3.17 (97,1-7 BLONDEL).

[217] HARNACK, Porphyrius, F. 44 from the Comm. in Matth. 24:16-18 (192,105-194,109 BONNARD). Apollinarius responded to Porphyry's critique of Daniel in his 26th book against Porphyry, and Eusebius responded in his 18th, 19th and 20th books (Jerome, In Dan. Prologue [771,8-772,10 GLORIE] = HARNACK, Porphyrius F. 43a). P. M. CASEY argues that Porphyry appropriated a tradition of interpretation of Daniel represented in the Christian east by Syriac speaking authors (Porphyry and the Origin of the Book of Daniel, JThS 27, 1976, 15-33). A. J. FERCH has responded to Casey by arguing that the interpretation of Daniel in the Christian east was not in conformity to most of Porphyry's opinions (Porphyry: An Heir to Christian Exegesis?, ZNW 73, 1983, 141-47).

simply the Antichrist.[218] It is not difficult to reconstruct some of Porphyry's objection to the text given his view of the relation of Daniel to Maccabean history. Jerome makes it quite clear that the things in Daniel which were believed by the Christians to refer to the Antichrist at the end of the world were believed by Porphyry to have been fulfilled by Antiochus Epiphanes[219]. Jerome concedes that a statue of Jove Olympus and statues of Antiochus were placed in the temple — the abomination of the desolation. Jerome responded that they are a type of the Antichrist[220]. Porphyry identified the aggressor in Daniel 11:25-26 with Antiochus Epiphanes, but Jerome argued that in a "deeper sense" (*superiorem sensum*) it referred to the Antichrist[221]. In his comment on 11:36, Jerome noted that Porphyry (and those who follow him) interpret the text to mean Antiochus Epiphanes — who put his statue in the temple of Jerusalem[222]. Porphyry's objection to Matthew was probably the same as his objection to the Christian interpretation of Daniel: Matthew (or Jesus) uses Daniel to refer to a figure in the future. But the text from Daniel, for Porphyry, had already been fulfilled by the appearance and activity of Antiochus Epiphanes.

2.3.23   F. 14: Mt 27:45 and the Darkness

Porphyry may have objected to the account of the darkness (Mt 27:45 par) during the crucifixion of Jesus. Jerome, commenting on this passage, summarized: "Those who wrote against the gospels suspect that an eclipse of the sun (which normally happens in certain established times) was interpreted by the disciples of Christ because of ignorance in reference to the resurrection of the Lord" (*Qui scripserunt contra evangelia suspicantur deliquium solis, quod certis statutisque temporibus accidere solet, discipulos Christi ob imperitiam super resurrectione domini interpretatos*)[223]. Jerome clarifies this somewhat cryptic comment by arguing that an eclipse of the sun only happens at a new moon and not at the full moon of the passover feast. Consequently the critics are wrong to identify the three hours of darkness with an eclipse. The charge of ignorance concerning earthly matters is one of Porphyry's criticism of the gospels mentioned by Jerome elsewhere[224]. Probably Porphyry (and

---

[218] Comm. in Matth. 24:15 (192,83-87 BONN.).

[219] In Dan. Prologus (772,19-24 GLORIE) = HARNACK, Porphyrius, F. 43a.

[220] In Dan. 11:31 (921,170-922,178 GLORIE).

[221] In Dan. 11:25-26 (918,93-101 GLORIE) = HARNACK, Porphyrius, F. 43r.

[222] In Dan. 11:36 (925,253-57 GLORIE) = HARNACK, Porphyrius, F. 43u.

[223] HARNACK, Porphyrius, F. 14 = Comm. in Matth. 27:45 (294,307-296,312 BONN.). É. BONNARD (SC 259, 294 n.96) conjectures that Jerome refers to Porphyry and Celsus (C. Cels. 2.33 [159,6-25 KOET.]). See also C. Cels. 2.55 (178,22-23 KOET.).

[224] HARNACK, Porphyrius, F. 9 = Tract. in Marci Evan. I, 1-12 (452,33-36 MORIN) and compare Julian and Porphyry on the ignorance (*imperitiam*) of Matthew in F. 6.

possibly Julian) found Mt 27:45 to be objectionable because the evangelists "mistook" an eclipse for miraculous darkness. Other critics charged that the alleged phenomena that accompanied the death of Christ (earthquake, the sea drawing back, the darkness of the day) were a physical impossibility and so throw into question the veracity of the narratives about Jesus[225].

2.3.24 Fragments from Jerome and Pacatus: The Hour of Crucifixion

The time of the crucifixion also apparently posed a problem for Porphyry. Immediately after giving Porphyry's criticism of Mt 13:35, Jerome refers to another question: "How is it written in Matthew (sic) and John (19:14) that the Lord was crucified on the sixth hour, but in Mark it is written that he was crucified on the third hour (Mk 15:25)?"[226] That Porphyry was the source of this objection is confirmed by its presence in the work of Victor of Capua who is the source of Pacatus' response to Porphyry (*Contra Porphyrium*): "How does he assert the crucifixion on the third hour while John bears witness to the sixth hour?"[227] The objections' proximity to Porphyry's name in Jerome and its presence in Victor's work make it probable that Porphyry is the source. The method of finding contradictions in Christian scriptures is certainly Porphyry's. Jerome responds that there is nothing conflicting (*diversum*) because there was a scribal error. A scribe changed the stigma ("sixth") to gamma ("third")[228]. Eusebius had earlier claimed the reverse: a scribe of John changed the gamma into a stigma, since the two signs are so similar[229]. Victor harmonizes the two texts by claiming that John's sixth hour is reckoned from the time Jesus taken into the house of Annas. One can detect the discomfort of the church fathers in response to Porphyry's (or someone else's) objection[230].

2.3.25   F. 91: Eternal Punishment

Augustine's letter to his "fellow presbyter" Deogratias contains six questions that a pagan friend of Deogratias posed to him (Ep. 102.1). The questions are

---

[225] COURCELLE, Anti-Christian Arguments, 153-54 referring to Arn., Adv. nat. 1.53 (49,15-21 MARCH.). Compare Adv. nat. 1.55 (50,12 MARCH.).

[226] Tract. de Psalmo 77 (CChr.SL 78, 66,77-67,81 MORIN). HARNACK overlooked it in his edition of Porphyry (Neue Fragmente, 277 n. 3). Jerome is surely thinking of Mt 27:45.

[227] HARNACK, Neue Fragmente, 276 n. 2 (PITRA, Spicilegium Solesmense, LXIV). Victor's text comes from PITRA's "old catena" that he does not identify, but which is very similar to that of John the Deacon (Paris nr. 838).

[228] CChr.SL 78, 67,82-85 MORIN.

[229] Supplementa minora ad quaestiones ad Marinum (PG 22, 1009).

[230] Augustine also struggled with the issue in De consensu evang. 3.13.40-50. A similar question appears in Ambrosiaster, Quaestiones Vet. et N. Test. 65 (CSEL 50, 114,7 SOUTER discussed in DE LABRIOLLE, La réaction, 497). See also RINALDI, Biblia Gentium, F. 433 and GUIDA, Teodoro di Mopsuestia, 205.

a selection of some of the "more weighty arguments of Porphyry against the Christians" (Ep. 102.8, 28)[231]. The fourth question is about the proportion between sin and punishment:

> "Christ threatens eternal punishment to those who do not believe in him" and yet He says in another place "With the measure you measure it will be measured to you again." "Here," he remarks "is something sufficiently absurd and contradictory (*ridicule ... contrarie*); for if He is to award punishment according to measure, and all measure is limited by the end of time, what mean the threats of eternal punishment?"[232]

It is not certain if these are the words of Porphyry, or Porphyry's words in the paraphrase of Deogratias' friend. In any case, Porphyry's usual method of finding apparent contradictions is at work. Porphyry alludes to NT texts such as Mk 16:16, John 3:18, Mt 7:2, and Mk 4:24. Eternal punishment for sins was absurd in Porphyry's view. Not all followers of Plato were opposed to the doctrine of eschatological punishment. Plato himself believed in eschatological punishments for evil people. According to Celsus, the priests and interpreters of the mystery religions believed in eternal punishments[233]. Augustine responds that not all measurements are temporal and defends the concept of eternal punishment — a concept that Celsus could also defend, but apparently not Porphyry[234]. Porphyry's belief in the transmigration of souls may have predisposed him against ideas of eternal punishment, although in *De regressu animae* he makes it clear that he believes the wise soul can escape the cycle of transmigration and go back to God[235].

2.3.26   F. 86: The Logos of John (1:1-18)

Porphyry also found the Gospel of John to be full of contradictions and incoherence. Theophylact refers to a sophism (σόφισμα) of Porphyry who tried to refute (ἀνατρέπειν) the gospel by using the following distinctions: "If the Son of God is the word (logos, λόγος), he is either the uttered (προφορικός) logos or the logos that resides in the mind (ἐνδιάθετος). But he is neither the latter nor the former, therefore he is not the logos."[236]

---

[231] ET based on that of NPNF 1. Text from CSEL 34.2, 544-578 GOLDBACHER.

[232] Ep. 102.22 (563,24-564,6 GOLD.) = HARNACK, Porphyrius, F. 91 .

[233] C. Cels. 8.48 (263,1 KOET.). Compare 3.16 and 4.10 (215,1-8; 281,1-3 KOET.). CHADWICK refers to Plato's remarks about penalties the soul pays after death as in Ep. 7.335a (Origen, 138 n. 2). Plato believed in a form of final judgment in Laws 959b. See also Resp. 10.615-16a where the punishments are temporally limited. Arguments based on the fear of hell were current in early Christianity (COOK, Protreptic Power, 118-19).

[234] Aug., Ep. 102.23-27 (564,7-568,25 GOLD.).

[235] See the discussion of this text above in reference to Porphyry's philosophy from oracles (§ 2.2.4).

[236] HARNACK, Porphyrius, F. 86; Enarr. in Joh. PG 123, 1141.

Porphyry constructs the dilemma[237] by relying on a Stoic distinction that he made use of in *De abst.* 3.2.1-3.3.2 (153-54 B./P.) in his discussion of the presence of reason (or language) in animals. The distinction was also current in middle Platonism[238]. Plotinus used a similar concept to explain the relationship of soul and Intellect: "... just as thought in its utterance [λόγος ὁ ἐν προφορᾷ] is an image of the thought in soul, so soul itself is the expressed thought of Intellect..."[239]. Porphyry may be thinking of this application of the Stoic distinction to the divine hypostases. Anthony Meredith notes that early patristic writers used the distinction to describe different stages in the life of the word[240]. As Amos B. Hulen notes, Theophylact denied that the distinction applied to the logos. Instead it only applies to created beings[241]. Celsus earlier attacked the Christian concept of Christ as logos because of the fact that Christ had been arrested and crucified (C. Cels. 2.31 [158,22-25 Koet.]). His approach is in contrast to Porphyry's use of Stoic logic.

Plotinus' student Amelius, however, was attracted to the concept of logos and, according to Eusebius, wrote the following words:

> And this then was the Word, on whom as being eternal depended the existence of the things that were made, as Heracleitus also would maintain, and the same forsooth of whom, as set in the rank and dignity of *the beginning*, the Barbarian maintains that He *was with God and was God*: through whom absolutely *all things were made*; in whom the living creature, and life, and being had their birth: and that He came down into bodies, and clothed Himself in flesh, and appeared (φαντάζεσθαι) as man, yet showing withal even then the majesty of his nature; aye, indeed, even after dissolution He was restored to deity (ἀποθεοῦσθαι), and is a God, such as He was before He came down to dwell in the body, and the flesh, and Man.[242]

---

[237] See LAUSBERG, Handbuch, § 343 for the use of dilemma as a powerful tool in rhetoric.

[238] M. PATILLON refers to Philo, De animal. 12 and S.V.F. II. 135, 223 = Sex. Emp. Adv. Math. 8.275 (Adv. logicos II) and other texts (BOUFFARTIGUE/PATILLON, Porphyre. De l'abstinence, II, 231-232). LSJ (s.v. προφορικός) refer to Plutarch, Moralia 777c, 973a.

[239] Ennead. 5.1.3 (II, 189,7-8 H./S.). My thanks to Prof. S. STRANGE for this reference.

[240] MEREDITH, Porphyry, 1135 n. 22. For uses of the distinction to describe the logos (Christ) see LAMPE, PGL s.v. λόγος II.B.2. Theophilus, Ad Autolycum 2.22 (62 GRANT) uses it.

[241] HULEN, Porphyry's Work, 54. E. MASARACCHIA, Giuliano, 238 quotes a statement of Alexander Alexandrinus, Ep. ad omnes episc. 6 that is relevant: ἴσμεν γὰρ αὐτὸν ἡμεῖς οὐχ ἁπλῶς λόγον προφορικὸν ἢ ἐνδιάθετον τοῦ θεοῦ, ἀλλὰ ζῶντα θεὸν λόγον καθ' ἑαυτὸν ὑπάρχοντα, καὶ υἱὸν θεοῦ καὶ Χριστόν.

[242] Eus., Praep. Ev., 11.18.26-11.19.1 (44,17-45,10 MRAS). ET in Eusebius, Preparation for the Gospel Part 2. Books 10-15, trans. E. HAMILTON GIFFORD, rep. of 1903 ed., Grand Rapids, 1981, 583. For bibliography on the text see RINALDI, Biblia Gentium, F. 479.

Amelius was far more willing to accept the Christian understanding of logos than was Porphyry. He probably found the text in John to be philosophically appealing. Porphyry simply found it to be unintelligible from the standpoint of Stoic logic.

2.3.27 A Pacatus Fragment on John 2:20

Victor of Capua has preserved a response that may also be from Pacatus' work against Porphyry. In it he explains that the forty six years of temple construction did not hold true for Solomon's temple but for the second temple restored by Zerubbabel[243]. Consequently Porphyry may have attacked John 2:20. The nature of his attack is unclear, but it probably centered on the chronological issue. This is consistent with Porphyry's interest in chronology that is shown by the fragments concerning the temporal relationship between the time Moses and that of the Trojan war[244].

2.3.28 F. 70: The Inconsistency of John 7:8 and 10

Porphyry objected to the change in Jesus' plans between John 7:8 and 7:10 according to Jerome: "He denied that he would go, and did what he had early denied. Porphyry barks and accuses him of inconstancy and change (inconstantiae ac mutationis), not knowing that all scandals should be related to the flesh."[245] The inconsistency between the two texts provided material for Porphyry's favorite kind of attack. Ambrosiaster preserved a similar objection to Jesus' change of intention[246].

2.3.29 F. 81: Christ the only Way of Salvation?

Porphyry found the Christian claim that Jesus was the unique way of salvation to be incredible. Augustine summarizes Porphyry's charge quoted by pagan detractors of Christianity: "If Christ," they say, "declares Himself to be the Way of salvation, the Grace and the Truth, and affirms that in Him alone, and only to souls believing in Him, is the way of return to God, what has become of men who lived in the many centuries before Christ came?"[247] Here

---

[243] HARNACK, Neue Fragmente, 276 n.1. PITRA, Spicilegium Solesmense, LXII.

[244] HARNACK, Porphyrius F 40, 41 / discussed by R. GOULET, Porphyre et la datation de Moïse, RHR 4, 1977, 137-164 / P. NAUTIN, Sanchuniathon chez Philon de Byblos et chez Porphyre, RB 56, 1949, 259-73. NAUTIN's proposed new fragments from Porphyry have not been generally accepted (Trois autres fragments du livre de Porphyre «Contre les Chretiens», RB 57, 1950, 409-416). See GOULET, Porphyre et la datation, 151, n. 29 and BARNES, Porphyry, 426.

[245] HARNACK, Porphyrius F. 70 from Jerome, Adv. Pelag. 2.17. (PL 23, 578-579).

[246] Quaestiones Vet. et N. Test. 74 (126,13 SOUTER / discussed in DE LABRIOLLE, La réaction, 497 and RINALDI, Biblia Gentium, F. 508.

[247] HARNACK, Porphyrius, F. 81 from Aug., Ep. 102.8 (551,5-552,5 GOLD.). ET in NPNF 1.416.

Porphyry combines phrases from John 14:6 and 1:17. People in ancient Latium worshipped god for many centuries without "Christian law" (*Christiana lege*). "What then, has become of such an innumerable multitude of souls, who were in no wise blameworthy, seeing that He in whom alone saving faith can be exercised (*is, cui credi posset*) had not yet favoured men with His advent?" Porphyry, or his followers, argued that Judaism was also no provision for the human race because it did not come to Rome until the time of Gaius[248]. His argument is a form of *reductio ad absurdum*. The Christian teaching of Christ as the unique way of salvation ignores the vast numbers of people who lived before his advent. Celsus asks if God did not care about the people who existed before he decided to "judge the life of people" (by sending Christ; C. Cels. 4.7 [279,11-12 Koet.]). Macarius' pagan also questioned why Christ did not come at the beginning of time, but at the end[249]. Ambrosiaster also preserves a question concerning why Christ did not come earlier to save those in ignorance[250].

For Porphyry the way of salvation was philosophical. His own view was that the purified souls of the wise could return to God[251]. In his *De regressu* he states that philosophy has not yet offered "a universal way for the liberation of the soul" (*universalem ... viam animae liberandae*)[252]. According to Augustine, Porphyry did not doubt that such a way existed[253]. Of course Augustine identifies Christianity with such a way. In his *Philosophy from Oracles*, Porphyry gives his own concept of the "salvation of the soul" (τῆς ψυχῆς σωτηρίαν)[254]. The salvation of the soul, for Porphyry, is an immense labor that is identical with the lofty and rugged way to the gods (ἡ πρὸς θεοὺς ὁδὸς αἰπεινή τε καὶ τραχεία)[255]. For Plotinus also, the practice of virtue was an integral part of the soul's purification[256].

---

[248] HARNACK doubts that Porphyry would have confused Judaism and Christianity like this (Porphyrius 95). DEN BOER (A Pagan Historian, 202) believes that it was a common practice in Porphyry's time to lump together the two religions.

[249] See § 3.4 and the index in § 3.52.1. The content of the objection is lost.

[250] Quaestiones Vet. et N. Test. 83 (140,1 SOUTER; DE LABRIOLLE, La réaction, 498).

[251] From Aug., De civ. D. 13.19.39-49 = De regressu animae 11.5 (BIDEZ, Vie de Porphyre 41* = SMITH, Porphyrii, 300bF, 301aF).

[252] From Aug., De civ. D. 10.32 (309,5-8 D./K. = De regressu animae 12 (BIDEZ, Vie de Porphyre 42* = SMITH, Porphyrii, 302F). Compare Symmachus quoted below in 2.3.30.

[253] SMITH, Porphyrii, 302F from Aug., De civ. D. 10.32 (310,11 D./K.).

[254] SMITH, Porphyrii, 304F from Eus., P.E. 4.8.1.

[255] SMITH, Porphyrii, 324F from Eus., P.E. 14.10.5.

[256] Plotinus, Ennead. 2.9.15 (I, 225,27-32 H./S.). For his conception of "pure souls" see 6.4.14 (III, 133,19-20 H./S.).

2.3.30 F. 82: The Generations before Christ

In his letter to Ctesiphon, Jerome has preserved a fragment of Porphyry that is very similar to Augustine's concerning the generations before Christ:

> And — as your comrade Porphyry used to object — by what reason did the compassionate and merciful God allow all the generations (from Adam to Moses and from Moses to the coming of Christ) to perish by ignorance of the law and commandments of God? And not even Britain, the fertile province of tyrants, or the Scottish peoples, or all the barbarian nations along the way to the Ocean knew Moses and the prophets. Why was it necessary that he came in the last time and not before an innumerable multitude of people perished?[257]

The reference to the tyrants of Britain may be from Jerome, and so is not much use in determining the date of the *C. Chr.* [258]. The text seems to preserve the same objection alluded to in Augustine's letter to Deogratias. For Porphyry, the principle that people are saved in Christ leads to an absurd consequence — namely, that all the people before Christ in the "barbarian nations" perished. Arnobius records a similar objection: "if Christ was sent by God to save unhappy souls from a destructive end, what of the fate of previous generations, which before his coming were destroyed in their mortal condition"[259]? Augustine's answer to the problem is that from the beginning of humanity whosoever believed in the Word and lived a pious and just life was saved — including people who partook in the mystery (*sacramenti*) who did not belong the nation of Israel[260].

Neither Porphyry nor Augustine is willing to countenance the syncretistic possibility affirmed by Symmachus in 384 in his *Relatio* in which he attempted to argue for the restoration of the altar and statue of *Victoria* to the Roman Senate which had been removed by Constantius[261]. Symmachus argues: "we look at the same stars, the heaven is common to all, the same world surrounds

---

[257] HARNACK, Porphyrius, F. 82; from Jerome, Ep. 133.9 (CSEL 56, 255,15-23 HILBERG).

[258] BARNES, Porphyry Against the Christians, 436-37 notes that the phrase could be from Jerome. BARNES gives a list of usurpers in Britain.

[259] ET slightly modified from COURCELLE, Anti-Christian Arguments, 155, from Arn., Adv. nat. 2.63 (139,11-14 MARCH.): *Sed si, inquiunt, Christus in hoc missus a Deo est, ut infelices animas ab interitionis exitio liberaret, quid saecula comeruerunt priora, quae ante ipsius adventum mortalitatis condicione consumpta sunt?* Compare Celsus' question (C. Cels. 4.8 [270,30-31 KOET.]): "Is it only now after such a long age that God has remembered to judge the human race? Did He not care before?"

[260] Augustine, Ep. 102.12, 15 (554,11-555,6; 557,12-558,8 GOLD.).

[261] Symmachus, Relatio 6. See the text, notes, and bibliography in M. LAVARENNE, Prudence, 85-113. The senators burned grains of incense on the altar of the god of the temple in which the meetings were held (Suet, Aug. 35), and the altar guarantied the fidelity (*fidem*) of the senators (Relatio 5). A profane place (without the altar) would give free reign to perjurors (Relatio 5).

us, what difference does the understanding (*prudentia*) make by which each seeks the truth (*uerum requirat*)? It is not possible to reach so great a mystery (*tam grande secretum*) by one path (*uno itinere*)[262].

2.3.31 A Pacatus Fragment on John 17:4

In one of the fragments that probably came from Pacatus' work against Porphyry, Victor of Capua quoted this critique of the gospel: "Why did he mention that he had fulfilled the work of human salvation when he had not yet ascended the banner of the cross (*crucis vexillum*)?" The question referred to John 17:4 according to Feuardentius[263]. The method is Porphyry's usual attempt to find contradictions between verses of the Christian scriptures. Pacatus' answer was that "because of the decision of Jesus' will, by which he decreed that all the signs of the venerable passion approached, he correctly signified that he had finished the work."

2.3.32   F. 92: The Resurrection of Christ and of Lazarus

The Gospel of John provided Porphyry with a focus for his attack on the resurrection. The pagan detractors of Christianity, who summarized some of Porphyry's work, ask whether Christ's resurrection or that of Lazarus corresponds to the promised resurrection.

> If the resurrection of Christ corresponds, how can the resurrection of those born of seed correspond with that of Christ who was not born in consequence of seed? If it is asserted that the resurrection of Lazarus corresponds, this (resurrection) does not appear to be suited, if indeed Lazarus' resurrection was made of a body that had not yet decomposed and of the same body by which Lazarus was named — whereas our body will be dug out of a confused mass (*ex confuso eruetur*)? Then, if the post-resurrection state is blessed (*beatus*) with no injuries to the body and no need to hunger, what does it mean to say that Christ ate and showed his wounds? But if he did it for the sake of doubt he deceived. If, on the other hand, he showed something true, then in the resurrection wounds received will also be there in the future.[264]

Porphyry's two dilemmas (at the beginning and end of the fragment) exhibit his love for that form of argument. The raising of Lazarus in John 11 and the resurrection narratives in John 20:27, 21:5-12 are both incompatible with the Christian hope in a future resurrection. Macarius' anonymous Hellene also asked a question about the resurrection of Lazarus, but unfortunately the content of the objection has been lost[265]. Augustine grasps one of the horns of the first dilemma, and denies that the resurrection of Lazarus is suitable, since Lazarus died after his resurrection. God is powerful enough to raise dissolved

---

[262] Relatio 10. Compare COURCELLE, Anti-Christian Arguments, 158.

[263] HARNACK, Neue Fragmente, 271. FEUARDENTIUS quoted 17:4 in his superscript.

[264] HARNACK, Porphyrius, F. 92 (from Aug., Ep. 102.2 [545,17-546,12 GOLD.]).

[265] See § 3.52.2 below.

bodies. Christ ate food to show that he was not a ghost, but did not have to eat. The scars of the wounds could have been willed away, but Christ chose to keep them to show that it was really his body that had been raised[266]. Here Porphyry does not attack the concept of resurrection itself, but attempts to show that the concept of a future resurrection cannot be identical with either that of Christ or that of Lazarus. The anonymous pagan of Macarius mounts an attack on the concept of resurrection — any resurrection[267]. Porphyry could, of course, have continued his argument in this direction. According to a tradition of Isho'dad of Merv, Porphyry may have also attacked the divergences in the hour of the discovery of the resurrection of Christ.[268] However, the objection is probably that of Julian and not Porphyry.

2.3.33 F. 64: The Pentecost and Christ's Public Descent

Only two fragments explicitly show that Porphyry directed his criticism toward the Acts of the Apostles[269]. He does comment several times on the actions of the apostles, however, and these actions correspond to the kinds of narratives contained in Acts. Anastasius Sinaita, the seventh century abbot of St. Catherine's Monastery on Mt. Sinai, called Julian of Halicarnassus, the monophysite, by one of the names given Porphyry by the Christians —"Bataneotes"[270]. He wrote: "But if, as the new Bataneotes says, Jesus wanted to be believed to be a human and greater than human, why did he not rather gather Jews and Greeks from all the nations in Zion, as he did at Pentecost, and with all looking, descend as a human from heaven, as he will descend at his second coming?"[271] The reference to Acts 2:1 is clear, but what is not clear is how much material comes from Julian of Halicarnassus and how much from Porphyry. That Porphyry demanded more witnesses to establish Jesus' identity is very possible. Macarius' anonymous pagan also made such a

---

[266] Aug., Ep. 102.3-7 (546,13-551,3 GOLD.).

[267] See § 3.51 below. J. PÉPIN argues that Porphyry is the source of an objection to the heavenly existence of resurrected bodies in Aug, De civ. D. 22.11 (829,1-830,46 D./K.) in Théologie cosmique et théologie chrétienne [Ambroise Exam. I. 1, 1-4], Paris 1964, 453 n. 2, 457. The objection is based on the fact that the earthly element cannot exist in the heavenly element. On this topos see § 3.44.

[268] He writes: "Julianus and Porphyrius, the wicked, here accuse the Evangelists of disagreement, that is to say, about the times forsooth and the hours in regard to the Resurrection of our Lord." Mt 28:1, Mc 16:2, Luke 24:1, John 20:1 are mentioned. The text is his Comm. in John 20 (278-279 GIBSON; quoted in A. GUIDA, Teodoro di Mopsuestia, 207).

[269] HARNACK, Porphyrius, F. 8, 25.

[270] On the name, see SMITH, Porphyrii, 8aT, 8bT and HARNACK, Porphyrius T. 3.

[271] HARNACK, Porphyrius, F. 65; Hodegos c. 13 (PG 89, 233).

demand for Jesus' resurrection: he wanted to Roman Senate to have witnessed the event[272].

2.3.34 F. 25: Ananias and Sapphira

A "philosopher" (possibly Porphyry) was troubled by the narrative of Ananias and Sapphira (Acts 5:1ff.). Jerome writes: The apostle Peter never calls down (*imprecatur*) death on Ananias and Sapphira — as the stupid (*stultus philosophus*) philosopher falsely accuses (*calumniatur*)[273]. In I. Hilberg's edition, he notes that earlier editions read *"Porphyrius"* instead of *"philosophus"*[274]. Since Celsus, Porphyry, and Julian are the philosophers Jerome likes to attack it is probably one of these three here. He also refers to Porphyry in *Ep.* 133.9. Harnack notes that in another letter Jerome did admit that the severity of Peter destroyed the unfortunate pair (*Petri seueritatem Ananiam et Sapphiram trucidantis*)[275]. The pagan in the *Apocriticus* charges that Peter "killed those who had done nothing wrong"[276]. The philosophers found the story to be morally repellent.

2.3.35 F. 8: Acts 15:20

A scholion to Acts 15:20 in a tenth century minuscule mentions a text in Eusebius' sixth and seventh books against Porphyry, in which Porphyry "slandered the oracle" (ἐπὶ διαβολῇ μεμνημένον τῆς χρήσεως)[277]. The text in the minuscule includes the negative form of the golden rule between two text critical symbols (καὶ ὅσα ἂν μὴ θέλωσιν αὐτοῖς γενέσθαι ἑτέροις μὴ ποιεῖν). The scholiast does not mention what Porphyry's objection to the verse was. Harnack speculates that Porphyry might have accused Luke of plagiarism. Eusebius mentioned that Porphyry slandered (διαβάλλειν) the Jewish scriptures in another context in which Porphyry objected to their allegorical interpretation by the Christians[278]. Porphyry did write about Hellenistic plagiarism in his *Philological Lecture* (Φιλόλογος ἀκρόασις)[279]. It is also possible that Porphyry derived some kind of contradiction from the golden rule or found Christian behavior to be inconsistent with it.

---

[272] HARNACK, Porphyrius, F. 64, from Apocriticus 2.14 (23,3-6 BLONDEL).

[273] HARNACK, Porphyrius, F. 25, from Jerome, Ep. 130.14 (CSEL 56, 194,15-16 HILB.). HARNACK adopts an editor's version which replaces *philosophus* in the MS tradition with *Porphyrius*.

[274] CSEL 56, 194,16 HILB. and see the apparatus.

[275] Ep. 109.3 in HARNACK, Porphyrius, F. 25 (CSEL 55, 354,14-15 HILB.).

[276] HARNACK, Porphyrius, F. 25 from Apocriticus 3.21 (101,4 BLONDEL).

[277] HARNACK, Porphyrius, F. 8, from MS 1739 (Gregory), Codex Athos B' 64 (Lavra).

[278] HARNACK, Porphyrius, F. 39 from Eus., H.E. 6.19.2.

[279] Eus., P. E. 10.3.1-15; SMITH, Porphyrii, 408F.

2.3.36   F. 5: The Apostles' Use of Ancient Testimonies

The apostles in Acts use Jewish scriptures as evidence in their orations. Porphyry may be thinking of such uses of ancient scriptures in another fragment from Jerome. In his commentary on Joel 2:28, Jerome wrote: "They [the apostles] used to discern what was useful for their audience — not to repel those present — and they strengthened [their orations] with testimonies (*testimoniis*) from another time not that they might abuse the simplicity and ignorance (*simplicitate et imperitia*) of the audience, as the impious Porphyry falsely charges."[280] Celsus and Julian both objected to the Christian use of the OT scriptures[281]. Porphyry's point here is probably that the apostles misuse the ancient testimonies — in solidarity with Celsus' and Julian's similar critiques[282]. The use of ancient oracles was an accepted practice in rhetoric. The evidence was considered "divine"[283]. Porphyry had no problem with the use of ancient oracles in itself as the *De philosophia ex oraculis haurienda* shows, but he objected to the use of Jewish scriptures by Christians as "proof." Cicero attacked augury and oracles, however, and passes on an interesting critique of augury that Porphyry could have used in his attack on Christianity: some augurs "used to say that it [augury] was a superstitious practice shrewdly invented to gull the ignorant" (*ad opinionem imperitorum esse fictas religiones*)[284].

2.3.37   F. 4: Apostolic Miracles

The apostles' claims to have done miracles (Rom 15:19, Acts passim) troubled Porphyry. Jerome also preserved this objection in the midst of a discussion of Peter and Paul:

> [Paul] subdued the whole world from the Ocean to the Red Sea. Let someone say, "They did all this for the sake of wealth." Porphyry said this, "Rustic[285] and poor people, since they had nothing, did certain signs (*signa*) by magic arts. To do signs, however, is

---

[280] HARNACK, Porphyrius F. 5, Comm in Joel 2:28 (CChr.SL 76, 194,663-67 ADRIAEN).

[281] COOK, Protreptic, 115 with reference to C.Cels. 7.18 (169,10-27 KOET.) and Julian, C. Gal. 253c,d (157,16-29 MAS.), C. Gal. F. 101 (189,1-6 MAS.), and 290d,e (162,17-163,25 MAS.).

[282] Compare Porphyry's critique of Mark's use of ancient testimonies (HARNACK, Porphyrius, F. 9) and see § 5.2.4 below.

[283] See LAUSBERG, Handbuch, § 354 on *testimonia*. COOK, Protreptic, 113, 120, 121 has a discussion of "divine speech" drawn from Quintilian 5.7.35-36 and Aristotle, Rhet. 1.15.14.

[284] Cic., De div. 1.47.105.

[285] Julian also accused the Christians of irrationality and rusticity (ἀλογία ... ἀγροικία) in contrast to "us" who have letters and Hellenism (Greg. Naz., Or. 4.102 [SC 309, 250 BERNARDI]).

nothing great, because the magicians also did signs in Egypt against Moses.[286] Apollonius also did signs as did Apuleius, and they did innumerable signs." I concede to you, Porphyry, that they did signs by magic arts so that "they accepted riches from rich little women (*divitibus mulierculis*) whom they persuaded" — this also you say. Why then did they die? Why were they crucified?[287]

And Jerome continues his argument against Porphyry in this manner. Signs were part of the rhetoricians' basic arsenal[288]. Although the magicians' "signs" are not in themselves rhetorical tools, Christians could use miracles in recruiting people to the faith. Here Porphyry is attacking not the fact of miracles, but their use as evidence in arguments by Christians. It would be interesting to know how Porphyry explained his own power to exorcize demons, if Eunapius' story is true! Eunapius writes that Porphyry says that he cast out a demon from a bath. The locals called the demon "Kausatha"[289]. It is doubtful that Porphyry looked upon himself as a sorcerer. His teacher Plotinus was also interested in understanding the phenomena of magic[290].

Celsus was quite willing to concede that sorcerers did miracles (C.Cels. 1.6, 1.38, 1.68 [59,9.21-29; 89,25-29; 122,1-16 Koet.]) and identified Jesus as a sorcerer[291]. Celsus notes that others, as even the Christians admit, can do miracles with the help of "Satan" (C.Cels. 2.49, 53 [171,17-29; 176,11-14 Koet.]). He also says that "Christians get the power which they seem to possess by pronouncing the names of certain demons and incantations" (C.Cels. 1.6, and compare 6.40 and 8.37 [59,8-10; 109,14-16; 252,14-16 Koet.]). Porphyry does not compare Apollonius and Apuleius with Jesus but with Christian miracle workers. Some pagans did compare Apollonius and Apuleius' miracles to those of Jesus[292]. Macarius Magnes also notes that some accused Peter and Paul of doing their miracles by magic[293]. By showing that

---

[286] Other pagan philosophers were interested in the case of the Egyptian magicians. See Numenius, ed. and trans. É. DES PLACES, Numénius Fragments, CUF, Paris 1973, F. 9 (51).
[287] HARNACK, Porphyrius F. 4, Tract. de Psalmo 81 (89,224-34 MORIN).
[288] COOK, Protreptic, 109. LAUSBERG, Handbuch § 358-75 summarizes the rhetoricians' use of signs in argumentation. Aristotle, for example, distinguishes between "necessary" signs and "non-necessary" signs (Rhet. 1.2.14-18). "Breathing hard" is a non-necessary sign of having a fever, because one might not really have a fever even though the sign was present.
[289] Eunapius, Vitae Soph. 457 (358 WRIGHT).
[290] Plotinus, Ennead. 2.9.14, 4.4.26, 40, 43 (I, 223,1-240,45; II, 84,3-4; 106,1; 110,1 H./S.).
[291] S. BENKO discusses pagan charges that Christians were magicians (Pagan Rome and the Early Christians, Bloomington/Indianapolis 1986, 114).
[292] Aug., Ep. 136.1, 137.13, 138.18 (CSEL 34, 94,10-14; 115,1-3; 145,5-8 GOLDBACHER). And see Lactantius, Div. inst. 5.3.7 and 21. Hierocles omits the comparison with Apuleius. See § 4.9.
[293] Apocriticus 4.14 (182,22 BLONDEL).

magicians could do "signs," Porphyry undermined the usefulness of signs in Christian arguments. Despite criticisms such as Porphyry's, Christians found narratives of miracles to be effective means of recruitment in antiquity[294].

2.3.38 Fragments 20-21: Galatians' Portrayal of Peter and Paul's Argument

Porphyry found problems in Paul's letter to the Galatians. In reference to 1:16 he seems to have attacked the apostles. Jerome, in his commentary on that verse, writes that "Many believe that this was said of the apostles. For Porphyry also objects that after the revelation of Christ, Paul did not deign to go (*non fuerit dignatus*) to people and to confer with them — in order that after receiving teaching from, namely, God he might not be instructed by flesh and blood."[295] Paul's disdain for the apostles casts them in a negative light.

Jerome continues this Porphyrian line of argument with regard to Paul's fight with Peter (Gal 2:11-14):

> In the first volume of his work against us, the Bataneotes and polluted Porphyry in no way understands — he objects that Peter was rebuked by Paul because he was not walking straight (*non recto pede incederet ad evangelizandum*) in the preaching of the gospel. Porphyry wanted to brand the former with the stain of error and the latter with the stain of shamelessness, and in common to accuse them of false teaching because the leaders of the churches disagreed (*discrepent*).[296]

In another text, Jerome notes that Origen and others had responded to the "blasphemous Porphyry who accused Paul of impudence (*procacitatem*) because he dares to rebuke the leader of the apostles and to accuse him to his face and constrain him by reason, because he had done wrong — i. e. he was in error — in which error Paul himself was also, who had accused the other of doing wrong"[297]. Jerome goes on to give his own position: "we have learned that on account of fear of the Jews, Paul and Peter feigned (*finxerint*) to serve the precepts of the law. By what boldness and audacity did Paul rebuke the other for what he himself had done?" Jerome and others had defended the prudence of the apostles in order that:

> ... they might restrain the impudence of the blaspheming Porphyry who said that Peter and Paul had a childish fight; indeed Paul burned with envy at the virtues of Peter and wrote boastfully of things which he had not done, or if he did, he did them impudently — reproving that in another person which he had done himself.[298]

In the next part of the letter Jerome argues against Augustine who appealed to 1 Cor 9:20. Augustine argued that Peter erred in trying to force the gentiles to

---

[294] COOK, Protreptic, 109-10.

[295] HARNACK, Porphyrius, F. 20; Comm. in Gal. 1:16 (PL 26, 351).

[296] HARNACK, Porphyrius, F. 21a; Comm. in Gal. Prologus (PL 26, 334-35).

[297] HARNACK, Porphyrius, F. 21b; Ep. 112.6 (CSEL 55, 372,25-373,5 HILBERG).

[298] HARNACK, Porphyrius, F. 21b; Ep. 112.11 (380,1-11 HILB.).

"Judaize"[299]. Porphyry's technique in this argument is his usual attempt to find a contradiction. In this case the discrepancy is obvious, and even Augustine was forced to admit that one of the apostles was in error — namely, Peter. Porphyry also makes liberal use of the rhetoric of vituperation in finding negative words to describe the actions of Paul and his "childish fight." Augustine's appeal to 1 Cor 9:20 is interesting due to the fact that Macarius' pagan finds that passage thoroughly repugnant and indicating a lack of integrity on Paul's part[300].

Porphyry may have commented on Gal 5:10: "They say that secretly he slanders Peter, about whom he had written above — that he had withstood him to this face because he did not walk straight in preaching the truth of the gospel." Jerome responds that "Neither Paul spoke of the leader of the church with a shameless curse, nor was Peter deserving to be made responsible for a disturbed church."[301] Porphyry, or another pagan opponent, was willing to transfer the argument in Gal 2:11-14 to the situation in Galatia and to make Peter responsible for the disturbance in the church there. Celsus also gleefully noted the disagreements of the Christians as did his successor Porphyry (C. Cels. 3.10, 12, 5.64 [210,14-18; 211,19-25; 67,27-68,2 Koet.]).

2.3.39   F. 37: Paul's Curse in Gal 5:12

Harnack includes an objection to Paul's behavior Gal 5:12 based on Mt 5:44, Rom 12:14 and 1 Cor 6:10. The verses support the objection to Paul's curse in 5:12 against those who had disturbed the church in Galatia[302]. The critic further mentions laws against castration — whether the castration is voluntary or involuntary. Jerome notes that the text is reviled by the "gentiles," but uses it against Marcion and Valentinus. The pagan questions how the following claims of Paul can be true: "Christ lives in me" (Gal 2:20) and "You seek a test of him, the Christ who speaks in me" (2 Cor 13:3). The conclusion points away from Porphyry:

Certainly the voice of the curse cannot be understood to be of him who said, "Learn from me because I am humble and gentle and mild in heart" (Mt 11:29). And it should rather be reckoned that he [Paul] could not control himself because of a Jewish fury (*Judaico furore*) and a certain unbridled insanity — instead of imitating him who like a sheep before the shearer did not open his mouth and did not curse in return those who cursed him (Is 53:7 and Acts 8:32).

---

[299] Jerome, Ep. 112.12 (380,14-381,14 HILB.) = Aug., Ep. 75.11 (I consulted the ET in NPNF 1 in making the above translations).
[300] HARNACK, Porphyrius, F. 27, Apocriticus 3.30 (125,6-26 BLONDEL).
[301] HARNACK, Porphyrius, F. 22; Comm. in Gal. 5:10 (PL 26, 431).
[302] HARNACK, Porphyrius, F. 37; Comm. in Gal. 5:12 (PL 26, 432-33).

160   2. *Porphyry*

Harnack writes that the mention of "Jewish fury" is not Porphyry's style[303]. Although Porphyry attacked the μοχθηρία (wickedness) of the Jewish scriptures, he was not given in the "nominal" fragments to slanders against Judaism[304]. The technique of finding contradictions in scripture is certainly Porphyrian, but the text is probably from another hand.

2.3.40 F. 85: The Son of God

Porphyry also attacked the doctrines and practices of the church in several areas. He appealed to Eccl 4:8 (LXX), for example, to question the existence of a "Son of God." Describing the pagan objector who made use of Porphyry's work, Augustine writes: "After this question, the one who proposed them from Porphyry added: Will you hold me worthy to instruct me if Solomon said truly 'God has no son'?"[305] Augustine denied —apparently unaware of Eccl 4:8 (LXX) — that Solomon said this and affirms that Proverbs 8:25 and 30:3-4 (LXX) speak of Christ as the wisdom of God. Porphyry probably regarded his astute find as a bald contradiction to the Christology of the church. He might also have used the text to undermine the Christian use of the OT to support christological claims. Julian continued this tradition by denying that the OT foresees a divine Son of God or logos[306].

2.3.41 F. 84: The Fragments from Methodius

Although Methodius of Olympus responded to Porphyry with a large book, very little of his work survives. In the material that is left of his work, there are no "nominal" fragments from Porphyry. The MS tradition does include, however, some superscripts that summarize pagan objections to Christianity. One of them reads: "Methodius, bishop, to those who say, 'How did it help us that the Son of God was made flesh on earth (σαρκωθεὶς ἐπὶ γῆς) and became a person? And why did he endure suffering in the form of the cross [or in the manner of the cross, τῷ τοῦ σταυροῦ σχήματι] and not some other punishment? And of what use was the cross?'"[307] Other critics of the NT found Christ's death to be a scandal. Arnobius records a similar objection: "If Christ were god, why did he appear in human shape, why had he to die a

---

[303] HARNACK, Porphyrius, 63. The word *furor* could refer to the frenzy of the Hellenistic prophet as in Cic. De div. 1.31.67.
[304] HARNACK, Porphyrius, F. 39. See § 5.2.30 for Julian's comments on Jewish "rages."
[305] HARNACK, Porphyrius, F. 85; Aug., Ep. 102.28 (569,2-4 GOLD.).
[306] Julian, C.Gal. 290e (163,24-25 MAS.).
[307] HARNACK, Porphyrius, F. 84; C. Porph 1 (GCS Methodius 503, apparatus criticus BONWETSCH). ET in ANF 6.399-400, although the translation above is mine.

human death?"[308] They also asked: "Could not the Supreme King do what he had decided to do on earth without taking on a human shape?"[309]

The phrase "form of the cross" is noteworthy because of the very similar usage *crucis vexillum* (standard of the cross) in one of Pacatus' fragments from Porphyry[310]. Methodius, in his defense of the cross as the way God chose to free people from the power of demons, notes that kings use *vexilla* (standards)[311]. G. Nathanael Bonwetsch refers to other defenses of the imagery of the cross in early Christian apologists[312]. The objection Methodius relates is not so much to the concept of incarnation in itself (as the pagans' objection is in Lact., Div. Inst. 4.22) but to the usefulness of Jesus' life and crucifixion. It is closer to Celsus' position who denied that Jesus' sufferings benefited people (C.Cels. 2.38 [163,1-3 Koet.]) and who found the idea of the Logos (as Son of God) being crucified very distasteful (C.Cels. 2.31 [158,21-25 Koet.]). It may be merely coincidental, but Methodius' fragment and one of the pagan's objections in the *Apocriticus* (3.1 [52,3.8.9 BLONDEL]) share the following words in their discussion of Christ's passion: ἠνέσχετο, τιμωρίαν, and παθεῖν (endure, punishment, to suffer)[313]. The linguistic similarities perhaps indicate the close relationship between Porphyry and Macarius' pagan. Augustine described Porphyry as an individual who rejected Christianity because of the doctrine of the incarnation: "In fact, you regard him with contempt because of the body which he received from a woman (*corpus ex femina acceptum*), and because of the shame of the cross..."[314]. These objections are very close to those alluded to by Methodius.

Another superscript in the MS of Methodius' work against Porphyry has: "From the same Methodius, how was the Son of God, the Christ, in a short and limited time — boundaries (διαστολαῖς) — contained in a body, and how being unaffected by suffering, was he led by suffering (πῶς ὁ τοῦ θεοῦ υἱὸς ὁ Χριστὸς ἐν βραχεῖ τε καὶ περιωρισμένῳ χρόνῳ διαστολαῖς

---

[308] *Sed si deus, inquiunt, fuit Christus, cur forma est in hominis uisus et cur more est interemptus humano* Adv. nat. 1.60 (56,20-22 MARCH.) referred to by COURCELLE, Anti-Christian Arguments, 154.

[309] Arnobius, Adv. nat. 1.61 (57,12-14 MARCH.) *Quid enim, dicit, rex summus ea quae in mundo facienda esse decreuerat sine homine simulato non quibat efficere* ?

[310] HARNACK, Neue Fragmente, 271.

[311] C. Porph. 1 (504,29 BONWETSCH) in Latin transliterated in Greek.

[312] GCS Methodius, xxxix BONWETSCH with reference to Justin, Apol 1.55.1-8 (110,1-111,26 MARC.), Tert., Apol. 16 (115,25-116,39 DEK.) and Ad nation. 1.12.1-16 (30,24-32,12), and Minuc. Felix 29.7 (28,30-32 KYTZLER).

[313] HARNACK, Porphyrius, F. 63.

[314] HARNACK, Porphyrius, Testimony XXI (p. 38) drawn in part from Aug., De civ. D. 10.28 (303,21-23 D./K.). Similar passages may be found in De civ. D. 10.24 (297,12-16 D./K.: Porphyry against the incarnation) and 10.29 (304,6-9 D./K.: incarnation).

σώματι ἐκεχώρητὸ καὶ πῶς ἀπαθὴς ὢν ἤγετο ὑπὸ παθοὺς)?"[315] The syntactic function of διαστολαῖς is unclear[316]. Bonwetsch refers to a text of Methodius in which "the nature of the person is encompassed not only by intervals of the year but also by insight"[317]. The sense may be, "how can it be the case that the Son of God was contained in a body marked by intervals of time...?" This objection to the suffering of the Son of God is quite similar to the previous one. Methodius responds that wisdom (of the Son of God) was invulnerable to pain, even though the body suffered. The suffering was scandalous to the objector. Celsus himself had no trouble saying that Son of God is the Logos, but he also found the idea that the Son of God could suffer to be repellent (C. Cels. 2.31 [158,24-25; 159,4-5 Koet.]) — a pure and holy Logos would not be disgracefully arrested and crucified. The impassability of the gods was a topos in Greco-Roman culture according to de Labriolle[318]. Ambrose preserves an objection of the pagans in which they argue that the son of God could not take up a body. Ambrose responds that the gentiles see their gods in human form[319].

Still another fragment from Methodius' work against Porphyry is headed by "To those who are ashamed of the cross of Christ" and begins: "Some think that God also — whom they liken to the measure of their own disposition — thinks the same things to be praiseworthy and blameworthy as do common people [or "bad people," φαύλοις], using as a rule and measure the opinions of people. And they do not understand because of the ignorance that is in them. For surely every creature falls short of God's beauty."[320] The words of Methodius for praise and blame are the basic concepts used in epideictic rhetoric. The things that Porphyry (and the other pagans) found "praiseworthy" in the NT were few and far between. In fact, the surviving fragments of the C. Chr. contain *no* praise of figures and incidents in the NT. Porphyry, on the other hand, found much to blame. The fact that these objections derive from Methodius' work against Porphyry is strong evidence

---

315 C. Porph. 2 (505, apparatus criticus BONWETSCH); the text is slightly different from HARNACK's F. 84. The ET was done with reference to ANF 6.400.

316 F. SCHEIDWEILER recommends emending the word to διασταλείς. The change makes sense, but the text from Methodius (see the note below) may support the more difficult reading (Zu Porphyrios ΚΑΤΑ ΧΡΙΣΤΙΑΝΩΝ, Ph. 99, 1955, 310).

317 "Zwischenräume" from de Res. 2.30.2, an Armenian text (387,3 BONWETSCH).

318 La réaction, 274 n.3 (commenting on this fragment) with reference to Ovid, Metamorph. 2.621 and Euripides, Hipp. 1396. See also § 3.28 below on impassability in Plotinus etc.

319 Ambrose, Apol. Dauid 2.5.30 (CSEL 32.2, 377,16 SCHENKL). Discussed in COURCELLE, Anti-Christian Arguments, 160.

320 HARNACK, Porphyrius, F. 83; C. Porph. 3 (506,7-10 BONWETSCH).

for their attribution to Porphyry himself, although as Harnack remarks they may not be verbal quotations[321].

2.3.42 A Fragment from Didymus: Christ and Achilles, Satan and Hector

Didymus, in a comment on Eccl 9:10, defends the use of allegorical interpretation. He refers to Porphyry's debate with the Christians about this form of exegesis:

> Now then Porphyry, who wants [to reproach us for doing violence to the literal] meanings by manufacturing figurative references and allegorical meanings, has [himself] allegorized [someplace in Homer] where Achilles and Hector are mentioned, when he spoke in reference to Christ and the Devil. And the things that we are accustomed to say about the Devil, he says about Hector, while what we say about Christ, he says about Achilles. And he employs this sort of expression: "Before the victory of Achilles, Hector used to strut before all his foes, and thought himself more powerful than all. But he did this in order to deceive." Here then he finishes with the anagogic interpretation. Often we in fact do violence to the historical letter, not to explicate the narrative, but rather to lead our hearer to understanding, as "Thorns grow in the hand of a drunkard."
> [Πορφύριος γοῦν θέλων ε . . . [. . . . .]τοις ἀναπλάττοντες ἀναγωγὰς καὶ ἀλλ[η]γ[ορίας . . . . ἔν]θα ὁ Ἀχιλλεὺς καὶ Ἕκτωρ μνημονεύεται, ἠλληγόρησεν φήσας πρὸς τὸν Χ(ριστὸ)ν καὶ τὸν διάβολον· καὶ ἃ ἐλέγομεν ἡμεῖς περὶ τοῦ διαβόλου, αὐτὸς περὶ τοῦ Ἕκτορος, καὶ ἃ περὶ τοῦ Χ(ριστο)ῦ, αὐτὸς περὶ Ἀχιλλέως· καὶ συνεχρᾶτο ταῖς τοιαύταις λέξεσιν ὅτι· "πρὸ τῆς ἐπι[κρ]ατήσεως τοῦ Ἀχιλλέως ἐβρενθύετο κατὰ πάντων ὁ Ἕκτωρ καὶ πάντων δυνατώτερος ἐνομίζετο. ὑπὲρ τοῦ διαβαλεῖν δὲ τοῦτο ἐποίει". ὧδε οὖν τὰ τῆς ἀναγωγῆς πέπαυται. πολλάκις δὲ καὶ ἡμεῖς βιαζόμεθα τὰ τῆς ἱστορίας, οὐχ ἵνα ἱστορίαν δείξωμεν, ἀλλ' ἵνα εἰσ ἔννοιαν ἀγάγωμεν τὸν ἀκούοντα, οἷον· "ἄκανθαι φύονται ἐν χειρὶ τοῦ μεθύσου".][322]

G. Binder refers to Homer, *Il.* 12. 462ff and 9.237-39, to illustrate Hector's strutting[323]. Two scholiasts on *Il.* 11.347 even depict Hector as possessed by a demon in their comments on the verb κυλίνδεται (τὸ δαιμόνιον αὐτῷ συνεργεῖ ... δαιμόνιον αὐτῷ συναίρεται)[324]. The Christian depiction of the struggle between Christ and Satan must have been available to Porphyry[325]. Didymus only summarizes Porphyry's objection to Christian

---

[321] HARNACK, Porphyrius, F. 84.

[322] Comm. in Eccl 9:10; ET by SELLEW, Achilles, 82. Text from ed. M. GRONEWALD, Didymos der Blinde. Kommentar zum Ecclesiastes, pt. 5, PTA 24, Bonn 1979, Codex p. 281. First published by G. BINDER, Eine Polemik, 92.

[323] BINDER, Eine Polemik, 93.

[324] Text given in SELLEW, Achilles, 100 from R. R. SCHLUNK, The Homeric Scholia and the Aeneid, Ann Arbor 1974, 125-26 n. 14.

[325] Didymus and Origen understood the Leviathan and its opponent to be Christ and the devil in Job 3:8 (LXX); BINDER, Eine Polemik, 90-91 refers to Didymus, Comm. in Job 3:8 and Origen, De prin. 4.1.5 (SC 268, 278,40 CROUZEL/SIMONETTI), In Joann. 1.17.96 (GCS Origenes IV, 21,10-12 PREUSCHEN) and Περὶ εὐχῆς 13.4; 16.3 (GCS Origenes II, 329,3-4; 338,3 KOETSCHAU). SELLEW, Achilles, 99 refers to C. Cels. 6.42-44 (110,19-115,29

allegories (ἀναγωγάς). His objection to the allegorical interpretation of the OT by Christians is well known[326]. In this text his meaning is not so clear. Binder claims that Porphyry intends to show the absurd consequences of allegory and to discredit the use of the method on the Bible[327]. Philip Sellew argues that Porphyry's goal is not ridicule of the Christians and sarcasm. Instead he is attempting to find better symbols for "the philosophical and religious truth that is trying to be expressed" (in Homer)[328]. Porphyry did, however, believe Christian allegory of the OT to be "absurd" (τρόπος τῆς ἀτοπίας — as in Eusebius *H.E.* 6.19.5).

Rather than being an argument over the ability to find cryptic references to Christ and the devil (or Achilles and Hector) in texts, Porphyry is attempting to show that Hellenistic culture provides more adequate grounds for understanding texts than Christianity does. In his allegorical interpretation of a text of Homer, Porphyry mentions Christ and the devil — the fundamental opposition used by Christian exegetes. Then Porphyry goes on the show that what the Christians say about Christ can be better said about Achilles. The things Christians say about the devil can be more adequately expressed in reference to Hector. The example Porphyry gives is Hector's strutting and his pretense to be more powerful than all so that he can "deceive" (διαβαλεῖν). Porphyry can use Hellenistic philosophical tradition to find pearls of wisdom in Homer[329]. The truth Christians find in the opposition of Christ and the devil can be better expressed in Hellenistic philosophical terms. The result is that the philosopher can dispense with Christ and the devil.

The trajectory of the argument can be compared with Numenius who was a sort of forerunner of Porphyry in the sense that he was more concerned with Hellenistic philosophical truth than Christian tradition. Numenius had earlier allegorized one of the stories of Jesus without even mentioning Jesus. Probably he found a "deeper meaning" that was philosophical and not an affirmation of Jesus Christ[330]. Much later, in the *Discourse to the Holy Assembly*, the author (Constantine himself?) allegorized Vergil by comparing Achilles with the Savior rushing out to the Trojan war. Troy is the world, and

---

KOET.) for the general conflict between Christ and Satan. GRANT refers to texts in which Origen allegorized the kings of Daniel to be Satan (The Stromateis of Origen, 288-89) with reference to Jerome, In Dan. 3:96 and 4:1 (808,753; 810,792-93 GLORIE) and texts in Origen's own writings.

[326] HARNACK, Porphyrius, F. 39 discussed above in § 2.3.3..

[327] BINDER, Eine Polemik, 94.

[328] SELLEW, Achilles, 99, 100.

[329] As in De antro nympharum and περὶ Στυγός (in SMITH, Porphyrii, 372F, briefly discussed above in § 2.3.3).

[330] Numenius F. 10a (52 DES PLACES) from C. Cels. 4.51 (324,23-25 KOET.). It is possible that Numenius did not actually have Jesus in mind.

the Savior fights the power of evil[331]. Intellectually Porphyry is between Numenius and Constantine. Porphyry defends pagan culture as did Numenius before him. But by Constantine's time, the Achilles narrative has become little more than a sermon illustration.

2.3.43 F. 79: Christian Worship

Porphyry also objected to the Christian critique of pagan worship. Deogratias' pagan friend (who used Porphyry's arguments if not his words) says: "They find fault with the sacred ceremonies, the sacrificial victims, the burning of incense and all the other parts of worship in our temples; and yet the same kind of worship had its origin in antiquity with themselves, or from the God whom they worship, for He is represented by them as having been in need of the first-fruits [Deut. 18:4]."[332] Earlier Celsus' Jew had objected to the Christians' contempt for Jewish worship even though they could name no other origin for their doctrine (C. Cels. 2.4 [130,24-27 Koet.]). Porphyry could be using such an objection, although he generalized it to include Hellenistic worship[333]. Augustine countered with precisely the kind of attack against pagan worship to which Porphyry was objecting[334]. Porphyry himself occasionally argued against elements of Hellenistic religion as in his critique of animal sacrifice in *De abst.* (2.9.1-3 and 2.12.1-3 [79; 81 B./P.]). The original sacrifices were crops (κάρπων) — similar to the first fruits of Jewish tradition to which Porphyry alluded in the above fragment (De abst. 2.27.1 [93 B./P.]). According to Porphyry it is the evil demons who take pleasure in the sacrifices of meat (De abst. 2.42.3 [109 B./P.]), and even if one must offer animal sacrifice one does not have to eat it (2.44.1 [110 B./P.])[335]. Porphyry was obviously responding to a topos in the Christian critique of pagan worship. Arnobius responded to a similar objector who noted the Christian rejection of temple worship, image worship, animal sacrifices, incense and so forth. The ensuing argument showed that Porphyry's objection was current in the debates of late antiquity (Adv. nat. 6.3 [309,9-11 March.])[336]. In another text one of

---

[331] BINDER, Eine Polemik, 93-4 n. 35 with reference to Vergil, Ecl. 4.31-36 in Constantine, Oratio ad coetum sanctorum 20.9 (GCS Eusebius I, 185,18-21 HEIKEL).

[332] HARNACK, Porphyrius, F. 79, Aug, Ep. 102.16 (558,10-14 GOLD.). ET from NPNF 1.418.

[333] Compare LOESCHE, Neuplatonische Polemiker, 269.

[334] Aug, Ep. 102.17-21 (558,15-563,21 GOLD.).

[335] Porphyry's theories on evil demons are in De abst. 2.36.5 and 2.39.1-5 (103; 105; 106 B./P.). J. BOUFFARTIGUE refers to Porphyry's belief that evil demons are nourished by the fumes from the smoke of blood sacrifices (Porphyre. De l'abstinence, II, 219 n. 4).

[336] Compare Tert. Apol. 10.1, 35.1-13 (105,1-2; 144,21=147,67 DEK.); Min. Felix 22, 23; Justin, Apol. 1.13.1-2 (50,1-10 MARC.); and Lactantius, Div. inst. 5.10, 7.6. For Celsus see § 1.7.1 above. Anonymous individuals ask why, if Noah was commanded to sacrifice before the law was given, did Christians not continue to sacrifice after the law in Ps.

Arnobius' anonymous critics claims that Christ deserves hatred because he expelled religions from the world and prohibited the worship of the gods[337].

2.3.44   F. 97: The Role of Women in the Church

The role of women in Christian churches was also objectionable to Porphyry. Jerome writes: "Let us therefore beware, lest we might become tax collectors among the people, lest according to the impious Porphyry, matrons and women be our senate, who rule in churches, and lest the support of women determine the episcopal (or priestly) station" (*Caveamus ergo et nos, ne exactores simus in populo, ne iuxta impium Porphyrium matronae et mulieres sint noster senatus, quae dominantur in ecclesiis, et de sacerdotali gradu fauor iudicat feminarum*)[338]. Whether Porphyry knew of women as deacons or even as elders in churches, he was aware of them as wielders of power[339]. Could he have been aware of women as bishops, presbyters, and prophets in Montanist churches[340]? Jeanne Marie Demarolle refers to a text discussed by Harnack in which a woman (a couturiere) named Paula was excommunicated because of her agitations in Carthage against Cyprian[341]. Whatever roles they had in the

---

Just., Quaest. et resp. ad Orthod. 83, 442a (122 OTTO). See RINALDI, Biblia Gentium, 294. On that text see CPG III, § 6285.

[337] Adv. nat. 2.2 (67,3-7 MARCH.) *At enim odio dignus est, quod ex orbe religiones expulit, quod ad deorum cultum prohibuit acedi. — Ergone ille religionis extinctor et impietatis auctor arguitur, qui ueram in orbe religionem induxit ...?* Compare Adv. nat. 3.2 (160,4-7 MARCH.) where pagans ask Christians why they do not worship gods "with us, why do you not share your rites in common with those of your fellow countrymen." See COURCELLE, Anti-Christian Arguments, 154-55.

[338] HARNACK, Porphyrius, F. 97, Comm. in Jes. 3:12 (CChr.SL 73, 52,14-18 ADRIAEN).

[339] Epitaphs of deacons and elders are included in KRAEMER, Maenads, § 94-100 (deacons), § 93 (a woman as elder). Maenads, § 107 and 109 are regulations for deaconesses (Const. Apost. II.26, 57).

[340] KRAEMER, Maenads, #103 from Epiphanius, Panarion 49; see also #101-106 for the role of women in Montanism. K. J. TORJESEN refers to a text at the church of Sts. Pudentiana and Praxedis (Santa Pudenziana, one of the oldest churches in Rome) in which a woman is identified as "Theodora episcopa" (bishop?) and refers to an Epiktas who is identified as a "presbytis" (elder, presbyter) in an inscription from Thera (When Women Were Priests, San Francisco 1993, 9-10). The entry in LPGL s.v. πρεσβῦτις includes an important reference to CLaod. can. 11 in which the appointment of women as elders is forbidden. This implies some churches endorsed the practice! Such evidence is ignored in R. GRYSON's otherwise important study, The Ministry of Women in the Early Church, trans. J. LAPORTE/M. L. HALL, Collegeville, MN 1976.

[341] J. M. DEMAROLLE, Les femmes chrétiennes vues par Porphyre, JAC 13, 1970, 44 n.21 with reference to A. VON HARNACK, Die Mission und Ausbreitung des Christentums in den ersten drei Jahrhunderten, 2⁴, 1924, 62. See the text in Cypr. ep. 42 (104 BAYARD). One could also consider later texts in which Bishop Chrysostom solicits the support of Olympias (ca 404 CE; KRAEMER, Maenads, § 74-75). Other women were monastic leaders (KRAEMER, Maenads § 71 = Jer. Ep. 108) .

church were scandalous to the culturally conservative Hellenist. Although Celsus did not assert that women were in position of power in the church, he did note the Christians' success in converting women, children and slaves (C. Cels. 3.44, 55 [240,4; 250,20 Koet.]).

2.4 Conclusion

The fury unleashed by Christian leaders against the *Contra Christianos* is an indication how well Porphyry did his work. Of all the works written against the Christians it seems to have aroused the most response — intellectually and politically. There seems to be little chance that a manuscript of his book has survived, although there have been several claims in the modern era that copies of Methodius' and Eusebius' replies to Porphyry existed in monastic libraries[342]. The fragment found in Theophylact is evidence that some part of the book survived into the middle ages[343]. Porphyry seems to have written the most against the Christian scriptures (of all the authors surveyed in this book). That so many of his other writings survived antiquity is also a sign of the veneration in which he was held by some Christian intellectuals (and scribes).

Porphyry's logical skills helped him find contradictions or apparent contradictions in Christian texts. His historical skills enabled him to find problems such as the implausibility of the disciples' immediately following Jesus when he called them or Mark's conflation of Isaiah and Malachi in Mk 1:2-3[344]. His abilities in philosophy enabled him to construct artful dilemmas such as those used against the resurrection of Lazarus and Jesus and against the concept of the logos as applied to Jesus[345]. In addition to the consternation his argumentative skills caused in the Christian community, if Porphyry put his work to use during the Great Persecution one can perhaps partially understand the fury of the book burners who let nothing survive but small fragments of his creation.

---

[342] See COOK, A Possible Fragment, 120-21.
[343] § 2.3.26.
[344] § 2.3.7 and 2.3.12.
[345] § 2.3.26 and 2.3.32.

3. Macarius

The Pagan in Macarius Magnes' Apocriticus

In 1876, using the work of C. Blondel, P. Foucart published an incomplete MS from Athens entitled Μακαρίου Μάγνητος ᾿Αποκριτικὸς ἢ Μονογενὴς πρὸς ῞Ελληνας περὶ τῶν ἀπορουμένων ἐν τῇ Καινῇ Διαθήκῃ ζητημάτων καὶ λύσεων (*Macarius Magnes' Monogenes or Answer-book to the Greeks, An account of the disputed questions and solutions in the New Testament*)[1]. It contains the most extensive comments by a pagan on the NT that have survived from antiquity. It is ostensibly a dialogue between a Christian and a pagan. The pagan asks a number of questions (from six to ten) which are then answered by the Christian apologist. The discussion apparently takes place on five separate days[2]. The lack of actual dialogue between the two figures has convinced most readers that the *Apocriticus* is actually a literary fiction, although the opponents do make occasional comments

---

[1] C. BLONDEL, ΜΑΚΑΡΙΟΥ ΜΑΓΝΗΤΟΣ ΑΠΟΚΡΙΤΙΚΟΣ Η ΜΟΝΟΓΕΝΗΣ Macarii Magnetis quae supersunt ex inedito codice, Paris 1876 — this text will be referred to below as "BLONDEL". The title above is on page 155. The title given on page 49 is Μακαρίου Μάγνητος ᾿Αποκριτικὸς ἢ Μονογενὴς πρὸς ῞Ελληνας περὶ τῶν ἐν τῷ Εὐαγγελίῳ ζητημάτων καὶ λύσεων. The MS was missing books one, five, and part of book two. R. GOULET is preparing an edition and translation of Macarius for the Sources Chrétiennes. His original dissertation was: Makarios Magnès. Monogénès (Apocriticus). Introduction générale, édition, traduction et commentaire du livre IV ainsi que des fragments des livres IV et V, Paris I, 1974. The most extensive ET is by T. W. CRAFER, The Apocriticus of Macarius Magnes, New York/London 1919, xxiv (translation of the title). The fragments of the pagan's objections were published by A. VON HARNACK, Kritik des Neuen Testaments von einem griechischen Philosophen des 3. Jahrhunderts [Die im Apocriticus des Macarius Magnes enthaltene Streitschrift], TU 37.4, Leipzig 1911. An earlier German translation by a scholar who identified the source as Porphyry is J. A. WAGENMANN, Porphyrius und die Fragmente eines Ungenannten in der athenischen Makariushandschrift, JDTh 23, 1878, 267-314. Text critical works on the Apocriticus include: G. SCHALKHAUßER, Zu den Schriften des Makarios von Magnesia, TU 31.4, Leipzig 1907 / J. PALM, Textkritisches zum Apokritikos des Makarios Magnes, SMHVL 4, Lund 1961 / F. SCHEIDWEILER, Zu Porphyrios ΚΑΤΑ ΧΡΙΣΤΙΑΝΩΝ, Ph. 99, 1955, 304-12 / L. DUCHESNE, De Macario Magnete et scriptis eius, Paris 1877, 1-8. GOULET (forthcoming) offers an extensive history of scholarship in his SC edition. See CPG § 6115.

[2] Book 3.proem (55 BLONDEL); 4.proem (157 BLONDEL).

to each other (e.g. 3.14, 3.30)[3]. The fictional dialogue can be compared with another dialogue from the same general period: *The Consultations of Zaccheus the Christian and Apollonius the Philosopher.* In this dialogue a pagan is persuaded by a Christian to become a Christian and a monk[4].

Below I will consider some of the literary-historical issues that the *Apocriticus* raises. It is certainly the most historically obscure text of those surveyed in this book. It is one of the most important, however, not only because of its many attacks on gospel traditions but also because of its critique of the apostle Paul. As in the cases of Celsus and Porphyry, I will order the pagan's comments using the synoptics as a model. Then the traditions of John that the philosopher criticizes will be analyzed. Several of the pagan's texts that critique Acts (with its portrayal of Peter and Paul) have survived and are included below. Then the texts from Paul's letters that the pagan objected to will be examined. The Hellene also attacked two texts in the Apocalypse of Peter, and those objections follow his critique of Paul. Finally the pagan's attack on Christian monotheism and belief in the resurrection are described. A supplement is included of the indexes of some of the lost sections of the *Apocriticus* (from Books I and II). The indexes give an indication of the content of the lost texts.

3.1 Introductory Issues

Richard Goulet argues that the original title of the text probably contained the descriptive word Μονογενής and not Ἀποκριτικὸς ἢ Μονογενής as in the Athens MS of Blondel[5]. The more difficult reading is contained in a MS which includes only the indexes to the first three books of Macarius' text[6].

---

[3] CRAFER was at first convinced that a real dialogue underlies the work given the occasional comments that the pagan and Christian make to each other (Macarius Magnes, A Neglected Apologist, I, JThS 8, 1907, 401-23, (especially 409-11) / Macarius Magnes, A Neglected Apologist, II, JThS 8, 1907, 546-71 / The Work of Porphyry Against the Christians, and its Reconstruction, I, JThS 15, 1914, 360-95 / The Work of Porphyry Against the Christians, and its Reconstruction, II, JThS 15, 1914, 481-512.

[4] Questions d'un Païen à un Chrétien (Consultationes Zacchei christiani et Apollonii philosophi), SC 401, 402, ed. J. L. FEIERTAG/W. STEINMANN, Paris 1994. The editors date the text to the first part of the fifth century (SC 401.16-22). Minucius Felix' *Octavius* can also be compared with the dialogue of Macarius.

[5] The issue is discussed by GOULET in his introduction to the forthcoming SC edition of Macarius' text.

[6] See Vaticanus graecus 1650 which introduces the topics of book I with this title: Τοῦ Μακαρίου Μάγνητος Μονογενὴς πρὸς Ἕλληνας περὶ τῶν ἀπορουμένων ἐν ταῖς ἀρχαῖς ζητημάτων καὶ λύσεων τοῦ εὐαγγελίου. This MS is described by G. MERCATI,

"*Apocriticus*" would have been added to explain the difficult title "Monogenes." The original title would then be Μονογενὴς πρὸς ῞Ελληνας according to Goulet who identifies the following words (περὶ κτλ) as descriptive sub-titles appropriate to each book[7]. Μονογενής can mean "only begotten Son" in Macarius or "unique genre"[8]. The second meaning appears in passages that refer to God's only Son. With reference to Peter's confession of Jesus at Caesarea, for example, Macarius notes: "...he [Peter] has revealed the characteristic of the nature that is of a unique kind (τῆς μονοειδοῦς φύσεως ... τὸ ἰδίωμα). Truly these words are a revelation given by the heavenly Father; truly it is a word unique in its genre (φωνὴ μονογενής) that bears witness to the unique Son" (Μονογενεῖ)[9]. Macarius felt himself to be inspired by the Spirit and by Christ himself[10]. Consequently one can argue (as does Goulet) that the title has a double meaning: "Discourse of a Unique Genre" and "Discourse of the only Son" (who is the real interlocutor of the pagans in the debate) addressed to the Hellenes[11].

Goulet's survey of the manuscript tradition of the Apocriticus in his forthcoming Sources Chrétiennes edition will not be repeated here. What is important to note is that the MS Blondel worked from is now lost, and scholars have not yet succeeded in locating it. Consequently Blondel's transcription is all one has to work from in most cases, although there are brief quotations of the Apocriticus in other writings. One is left with the necessity of a basic trust in Blondel's skill and integrity in the transcription of the MS.

The author may be the Macarius Magnes who appeared at the Synod of the "Oak" (a suburb of Chalcedon) in 403: "The accuser of Heraclides was a bishop of Magnesia named Macarius."[12] He probably lived in Asia Minor

Per L'Apocritico di Macario Magnete. Una Tavole dei Capi dei Libri I, II e III, Nuove note di letteratura biblica e cristiana antica, StT 95, Vatican City 1941, 40-74.

[7] The MSS which contain Macarius' text concerning the Eucharist have titles similar to: Μακαρίου Μάγνητος ἐκ τῶν πρὸς ῞Ελληνας ἀποκρίσεων (see SCHALKHAUßER, Zu den Schriften, 10).

[8] GOULET refers to texts such as Apocrit. 2.8, 3.8 (9,8; 66,1 BLONDEL) for this first meaning and 3.9, 3.27 (71,19; 117,19 BLONDEL) for the second meaning.

[9] Apocr. 3.27 (117.18-20 BLONDEL). This text is discussed by GOULET in his forthcoming edition.

[10] Apocr. 4.10, 4.25 (168,20; 206,6-7 BLONDEL) discussed in GOULET.

[11] GOULET, forthcoming.

[12] Art. Oak, Synod of the, ²ODCC, 987. The text describing the synod is in Photius, Bibliotheca Cod. 59 (CUFr, 52-57 HENRY). Other figures actually make the specific accusations of Origenism against Heraclides. The synod is also discussed in Socrates, H.E. 6.15.14-17 (337,17-338,5 HANSEN) and Sozomen, H.E. 8.17.2-10 (PG 67, 1560 = GCS Sozomenus, 371,19-373,5 BIDEZ/HANSEN). The debate over the identity of the author will be avoided here since it is incidental to this work. CRAFER believed there were two authors: an earlier Macarius; and the bishop of 403. The earlier author was an Origenist who held an actual debate with Hierocles, the excerptor of Porphyry's objections against the Christians (Apocriticus, xix-xxiii). R. WAELKENS notes that the coincidence of two people named

toward the last quarter of the fourth century[13]. The problem of the philosopher's identity is controversial. As we mentioned in the chapter on Porphyry, many scholars have questioned Adolf von Harnack's hypothesis that Porphyry's objections to Christianity were summarized by an anonymous scholar and then used by Macarius to create his "philosopher"[14]. Pierre de Labriolle adopted this position and believed that an excerptor near the beginning of the fourth century created a florilegium from Porphyry's work to popularize his ideas[15]. A chief objection to identifying Porphyry with the pagan is a passage in which Macarius calls his opponent's attention to (3.42) Porphyry's *Philosophy from Oracles* [16].

T. W. Crafer believed Hierocles was responsible using the following arguments (among others): Hierocles and Macarius' pagan share seven "distinctive" words;[17] the treatise Macarius dealt with was in two books as was that of Hierocles (Lact., Div. Inst. 5.2.13); and Hierocles and the pagan both attempt to show inconsistencies in Scripture (Lact. Div. Inst. 5.2.14)[18]. Harnack responded to Crafer's thesis by arguing that Hierocles' reference to Christ leading 900 robbers "absolutely does not match" the pagan's picture of

---

Macarius of Magnesia involved with the Apocriticus is incredible (L'économie, thème apologétique et principe herméneutique dans L'Apocriticos de Macarios Magnès, RTHP 6.4, Louvain 1974, 9-10).

[13] GOULET summarizes the reasons for the geographical and temporal location of the author in his forthcoming SC edition. His arguments will not be repeated here.

[14] HARNACK, Kritik, 141-45. See, for example, BARNES, Porphyry Against the Christians, 428-430. C. EVANGELIOU's perceptive account of many Porphyrian texts is marred by an uncritical acceptance of the fragments from Macarius' pagan as Porphyrian. He does little more than flatly deny BARNES' contention that the two figures cannot be identified (Porphyry's Criticism of Christianity and the Problem of Augustine's Platonism, Dionysius 13, 1985, 67 n. 59).

[15] La réaction, 247.

[16] HARNACK, Kritik, 141.

[17] The major fragment is in Eus., Contra Hieroclem, 2 (486-91 F. C. CONYBEARE, ed. and trans., Philostratus...Treatise of Eusebius, LCL, Cambridge/London 1969). M. FORRAT and É. DES PLACES' edition is used for the text (SC 333). The words in the Hierocles fragment contained in Macarius' Apocriticus in identical or similar forms are: θρυλοῦσι (2.14, 3.7, 15); κουφότητα (4.22); κομπάζω (3.36, 4.7); ἀπαίδευτοι (3.34, 4.6, 3.2), ψεῦσται (3.31); γόητες (3.31); τερατεία (4.6, 3.4, 4.5, 7, 2.15) discussed in CRAFER, Work of Porphyry, 381-82. See also § 4.7.

[18] Other arguments are: Hierocles and the pagan chiefly attacked Peter and Paul (Lact. Div. Inst. 5.2.17); Hierocles disparaged Christ by saying that after his rejection by the Jews he became a robber with 900 followers, and this may have been in Macarius' lost first book (Lact. Div. Inst. 5.3.4); Hierocles and the pagan attempt to discredit the miracles of Jesus, but do not deny them (Lact. Div. Inst. 5.3.7); Hierocles' attempt to show the superiority of Apollonius over Christ included a reference to Apollonius' disappearance from Domitian — Macarius' pagan makes the same reference (Lact. Div. Inst. 5.3.7, 9 and Apocriticus 3.1). CRAFER, Work of Porphyry, 377-79. The edition of Lactantius' *Div. Instit.* used above is SC 204 MONAT.

Christ in Macarius[19]. The indexes to some of the lost portions of the
Apocriticus do not support Crafer's thesis about the 900 followers either. They
are translated in a supplement at the end of this chapter. The pagan stays within
the gospels' portrayal of Christ and does not introduce foreign material. In
addition Hierocles wanted to humanely and kindly counsel the Christians and
so did not write "Against the Christians" but "To the Christians" (Lact. Div.
Inst. 5.2.13). That does not accord with the pagan's attitude in the *Apocriticus*
who writes against the Christians[20]. Crafer, in any case, believed that
Hierocles had used Porphyry's arguments in his *Philalethes logos*, from which
Macarius took the philosopher's positions[21]. Crafer's improbable thesis will
be largely ignored in what follows below.

A consensus position seems to be building that despite the identity of the
Macarius' immediate source, Porphyry is the root of many if not most of the
arguments in the *Apocriticus* [22]. Barnes' skepticism has not shaken the belief
that Macarius probably made use of Porphyry's arguments if not his actual
words: "The epitome of Porphyry can and should be disbelieved. Macarius
may still be supposed to preserve something of the tenor and arguments of
Against the Christians, but only indirectly, from a later writer or later writers
who used Porphyry ... in no case can it be assumed that Macarius preserves
either the words or the precise formulations of Porphyry"[23]. Goulet, in an
extensive comparison of the objections of Celsus, Hierocles, Porphyry and
Julian with those of Macarius' philosopher shows that Porphyry offers by far
the greatest number of parallels to the text of Macarius[24]. The fact that
Macarius points his antagonist to Porphyry's work on oracles is really of little
consequence since the philosopher is fictional to begin with, and Macarius is
concerned to create a debate that is convincing literarily.

---

[19] FRASSINETTI (Sull'autore delle questioni pagane conservate nell'Apocritico di Macario
di Magnesia, NDid 3, 1949, 49 n.2) notes that the indexes to the lost Book I (published by
Card. MERCATI) do not indicate that the pagan discussed either parallels of Apollonius to
Christ or Christ as a Palestinian robber — the two principle arguments of Hierocles.
MERCATI, Per L'Apocritico, 40-74.

[20] HARNACK, Porphyrius, 21.

[21] Work of Porphyry, 510-12.

[22] WAELKENS is perhaps too sanguine about the consensus. He claims, for example,
that FRASSINETTI believes Porphyry is the source of Julian's work, from whom Macarius
took the pagan's objections. FRASSINETTI, however, claims that Julian alone is the source
and thoroughly de-emphasizes Porphyry (L'Économie, 9 with reference to FRASSINETTI,
Sull'autore, 51-54).

[23] BARNES, Porphyry Against the Christians, 430. In Scholarship or Propaganda, 54,
BARNES assumes that Macarius derived most of his knowledge of Porphyry from
Apollinarius.

[24] GOULET, forthcoming introduction.

Some have identified the philosopher with Julian. Paolo Frassinetti believes that Macarius composed a dialogue in which he used Julian's writing *Against the Galilaeans* [25]. He argues that Macarius wrote about 380 (cf. the date in Apocrit. 4.2 read as "330")[26]. In the course of the chapter, some of Frassinetti's parallels between the pagan's objection and those of Julian will be examined. It has been shown in chapter two that there are some very close ties between Macarius' pagan and Porphyry. This argument (consistent with Goulet's similar results) will be continued in this chapter. My position is that the arguments were probably drawn from Porphyry, but that one cannot expect to find verbal excerpts of the *C.C.* in Macarius. The parallels with Porphyry are much stronger than those with Julian that Frassinetti finds.

The date of the work is very obscure — there is a reference to "30 years" that have passed since Paul's letter to the Thessalonians (4.2) and "300 and more years" that have passed since Jesus' death (4.5). The text in 4.2 probably had "300" originally (and not 330)[27]. That would put the date of the ostensible dialogue well into the fourth century. The date of the philosopher's objections is difficult to identify, but a reference he makes in 4.21 to large Christian churches implies the last part of the third century[28]. Since the debate is about

---

[25] FRASSINETTI, Sull'autore, 50-56 (the parallels with Julian). He objects to HARNACK's thesis that the anonymous epitome was in the style of *Quaestiones* by referring to Ps. Justin's *Quaestiones et responsiones ad orthodoxos* and the *Quaestiones graecorum ad christianos*. The excerpts from Macarius' pagan do not have Ps. Justin's "interrogative and synthetic style" (47, attacking HARNACK, Kritik, 143 who hypothesizes that the epitome may have contained 100 questions).

[26] FRASSINETTI, Sull'autore, 41-56 (especially 48). Against a Porphyrian origin are the following arguments: Macarius' pagan (3.15) is not aware of cannibalism among the Scythians, but Porphyry is (De abst. 3.17.3 and 4.21.4 [171 B./P.; 38 P./S./B.]); the pagan's ignorance shows that he has never visited Palestine unlike Porphyry (3.6); unlike Porphyry (Ad Marcellam 33 [sic], De abst. 4.11.1-7 [17-19 P./S./B.]) the pagan is against voluntary poverty (3.5). J. GEFFCKEN originally made the objection about cannibalism (Zwei Griechische Apologeten, Leipzig 1907, 302 n. 1). HARNACK (Kritik, 140) was unwilling to concede this point and claimed that *De abst.* was later than the *C.C.* Despite his objections, GEFFCKEN affirmed that the discourse of the pagan is primarily indebted to Porphyry (idem, 303) and compare Idem, The Last Days of Greco-Roman Paganism, 1st ed. 1920, tr. S. MACCORMACK, Amsterdam et al. 1978, 160, 208 n. 14. In the latter work, GEFFCKEN claims that the excerptor used both Julian (379,11 HERTLEIN = Frag. ep. 89b, 295a [162,16-20 BIDEZ] = II, 312 WRIGHT) and Porphyry (Apocr. 4.21 = F. 76).

[27] See BLONDEL, Macarii, 160. Julian remarks that little more than 300 years have passed since Jesus' time (C.Gal. 191e [136,7-8 MASARACCHIA]). GOULET argues that one should not conjecture "330" here because it would put too much time between Paul and Jesus. In addition Nicephorus has a reading of 300 in a similar context (see GOULET, Introduction to his forthcoming SC edition).

[28] GOULET (forthcoming) refers to Eusebius, H.E. 8.1.5 who describes the large churches built before Diocletian's persecution. Archaeological evidence is lacking for Eusebius' statement (at this time).

images, the fact that the philosopher does not mention Christian cultic use of images implies a pre-Constantinian date[29]. Persecutions are also mentioned (tens of thousands; 2.14, 4.4). The punishment of Christians is not pleasing to God or any intelligent person (2.14) and is inhumane (4.4; ἀπανθρώπως). The pagan's apparent compassion for the martyrs does not cohere with what is known of Hierocles who took part in Diocletian's persecutions[30]. Christians imitate the building of temples by building "large houses" (4.21). Monasticism is not mentioned, nor are the uses of images in Christian churches[31]. That persecutions are mentioned and were apparently still active suggests a third (or early fourth) century date for the anonymous philosopher (or the sources used to create a fictional philosopher).

The possibility remains that the Christian author created a philosopher out of whatever pagan criticisms he could find. Richard Goulet points to many linguistic similarities between the objections and the answers, proving that Macarius has extensively reworked the text of the objections[32]. It is also possible that the author of the objections is an anonymous pagan as Francesco Corsaro argued. If, in Corsaro's belief, the pagan had been well known, Macarius would have had a tremendously difficult time making him anonymous[33]. It is also apparent, according to Corsaro, that older scholars did not know the name of the adversary from the lost parts of the text, because they identified the pagan with Theosthenes, to whom the work is actually dedicated[34]. Sosio Pezzella continues this line of argument by questioning thirty six of Harnack's 95 fragments of Porphyry, and by concluding that the work is a small collection of anti-Christian polemic drawn from Porphyry, Hierocles, and other works[35]. Corsaro is probably incorrect since Macarius'

---

[29] GOULET also notes that Epiphanius fought against images at the end of the fourth century.

[30] Lactantius Inst. 5.2.12 (SC 204, 139 MONAT); De mort. pers. 16.4 (CSEL 27, 189,18-20 BRANDT/LAUBMANN); see art. Hierokles, 13, PRE VIII, 1913, 1477.

[31] HARNACK, Kritik, 108-9. HARNACK mentions that Julian was aware of the Christian use of images (108 n. 2).

[32] Porphyre et Macaire de Magnésie, StPatr XV, ed. E. LIVINGSTONE, TU 128, Berlin 1984, 448-52. GOULET has also done much work on Macarius' theology and argues that Macarius' work was written shortly before the Council of Constantinople (381) in: La théologie de Makarios Magnes, MSR 34, 1977, 45-69, 145-80. See also his forthcoming edition in SC.

[33] F. CORSARO, L'«Apocritico» di Macario di Magnesia e le Sacre Scritture, NDid 7, 1957, 1-24 (especially 23). See also RINALDI, Biblia Gentium, 154.

[34] CORSARO, L'«Apocritico», 23. Theosthenes is mentioned twice in the Apocriticus 3.proem and 4.proem. G. SCHALKHAUßER, Zu den Schriften, 31 n.3, 36 (TURRIANUS' mistake who had seen the complete MS in Venice at least once; TURRIANUS did not make the mistake in his earlier writings!).

[35] S. PEZZELLA, Il Problema del ΚΑΤΑ ΧΡΙΣΤΙΑΝΩΝ di Porfirio, Eos 52, 1962, 87-104 (with the conclusion on 104).

philosopher appears to be a literary fiction. This result is assured by the fact that Porphyry is the ultimate source for many if not most of the objections. The text certainly contains the most extensive pagan critique of the NT that has survived and consequently is of immense value.

In the survey below we will begin with the synoptics, move to John, and then on to the Acts and the Pauline epistles.

3.2 How is it said: Cast thyself down?[36]

The pagan takes exception to Jesus' response in Mt 4:7 par to the tempter's challenge in Mt 4:6 par. Jesus' answer prompts him to say: "...whereby it seems to me that He spoke in fear of the danger from the fall. For if, as you declare, He not only did various other miracles, but even raised up dead men by His word alone, He ought to have shown forthwith that He was capable of hurling Himself down from the height and not receiving any bodily harm thereby."[37] The objector goes on to quote part of Mt 4:6 (from Ps 91:11), "In their hands they shall bear you up lest you dash your foot against a stone," and obscures the text by saying that it is a scripture spoken concerning him (Jesus)[38]. His conclusion is that given that text (from the Psalm), it would have been right to show (δεῖξαι) those in the temple that he was God's son (θεοῦ παῖς)[39] and was "able to deliver from danger both Himself and those who were His." Macarius responds that to accede to the devil's request would be to act in friendliness to him and to accept his counsel[40]. The philosopher demands a demonstration of Christ's identity. His word for proof (δεῖξαι) is the one Aristotle used for rational proofs (or proofs from speech) in rhetoric.

---

[36] The *tituli* used below come from the Athens MS of the Apocriticus published by BLONDEL (49-50, 155; for Books III and IV) and from the Vatican MS (MS Vat. Gr. 1650 = Gregory 623) list of *tituli* for Books I-III published by MERCATI, Per L'Apocritico, 62-63, 66-67, 69-70.

[37] Apocr. 3.18 = HARNACK, Porphyrius F. 48; ET in CRAFER, Apocriticus, 89-90; translations of the pagan's objections may also be found in J. HOFFMANN, Porphyry's Against the Christians, Amherst 1994. HOFFMANN translates only the fragments in Macarius and makes many illuminating comments. CRAFER's translations are more "literal" and will be adopted in this study. Occasionally we will correct CRAFER's work using the translation of R. GOULET (forthcoming in SC). I am grateful to Dr. GOULET for making his fine work on Macarius available to me. One of the many merits of GOULET's translation is that he includes the full text of the Christian's responses.

[38] An anonymous objector in Ambrosiaster questions why Jesus only answered the devil using examples from the Law in Quaestiones de N. Test. 29 (CSEL 50, 438,5-6 SOUTER = RINALDI, Biblia Gentium, F. 547). See Julian's objections to the episode in § 5.2.6.

[39] DE LABRIOLLE comments that this expression was used by Barnabas, Didache, Origen and Athenagoras (La réaction, 269 n. 1).

[40] Apocr. 3.26 (113,4-13 BLONDEL).

They contrast with proofs from *ethos* or the character of the speaker and *pathos* which are designed to rouse the hearers' emotions[41]. By accusing Jesus of fear (the opposite of courage) he employs the rhetoric of vituperation. Courage was a virtue of the soul for the rhetoricians, so one can assume that fear would be a serious defect in their eyes[42].

3.3 What is the meaning of the swine and the demons?

The philosopher found the text in Mt 8:28-34 and Mk 5:1-20 to be extremely objectionable. He noticed a discrepancy between Matthew's two "demons" (meaning "demoniac") that meet Christ and Mark's one demoniac[43]. Macarius makes this clear in his response (3.11 [76 Blondel]) in which he says that Mark refers to the nature (οὐσία) that suffered, and Matthew refers to the number (ὑπόστασις) of persons affected[44]. Mark's story of the 2000 drowned swine prompts the pagan to call the text a myth, humbug, and a big laugh (3.4)[45]. Any sensible person who heard what Christ had done would say: "Alas, what ignorance (ἀπαιδευσίας)! Alas, what foolish knavery, that He should take account of murderous spirits, which were working much harm in the world, and that He should grant them what they wished." He goes on to describe the activities of evil demons in the world and concludes: "So at all events it was not right that, instead of casting these originators of evil, who had treated mankind so ill, into that region of the abyss which they prayed to be delivered from, He should be softened (θηλυνόμενον) by their entreaty and suffer them to work another calamity."[46] The pagan notes that the demons want to make the world a "comic performance" (παίγνιον) and mix earth and sea to create a

---

[41] Aristotle, Rhetoric 1.2.3-5; see LAUSBERG, Handbuch, § 355.

[42] On ἀνδρεία in the rhetoric of praise see LAUSBERG, Handbuch, § 245 where the virtue is an "action of the soul."

[43] Apocr. 3.4 = HARNACK, Porphyrius, F. 49.

[44] Augustine chooses a simpler solution: Mark only spoke of the more famous of the two demoniacs (De cons. ev. 2.24.56 [CSEL 43, 158,11-15 WEIHRICH]). Ambrose records a similar objection concerning the narrative: did Christ meet two people at Gerasa or only one? He does not identify the source of the objection (In Lucam vi.44 [CSEL 32.4, 249,10 SCHENKL] referred to by P. COURCELLE, Anti-Christian Arguments and Christian Platonism: from Arnobius to St. Ambrose, in: The Conflict Between Paganism and Christianity in the Fourth Century, ed. A. MOMIGLIANO, Oxford 1963, 160). The specific reference to Mark indicates that DEMAROLLE's claim that "Porphyry" (Macarius) does not refer specifically to the writings of the evangelists is not quite accurate (J.-M. DEMAROLLE, UN ASPECT DE LA POLEMIQUE PAIENNE A LA FIN DU IIIe SIECLE; LE VOCABULAIRE CHRETIEN DE PORPHYRE, VigChr 26, 1972, 120).

[45] Celsus also found stories such as the serpent in Eden and the six day narrative of creation to be crude or silly (C. Cels. 4.36, 6.60 [306,26-28 KOET.]).

[46] CRAFER, Apocriticus, 62-3.

"sad piece of theater" (πενθικὸν ... θέατρον). Porphyry understood evil demons to be the cause of epidemics, earthquakes, and all kinds of calamities — as does the philosopher[47]. It is also very probable that Porphyry commented on this particular exorcism in the gospels given the evidence from Jerome's work against Vigilantius discussed in the previous chapter[48]. Macarius' philosopher accuses Christ of ignorance, comic error, and of effeminacy in acceding to the demons' demand.

The philosopher also indulges in some higher criticism: "If the incident is really true, and not a fiction (πλάσμα) — as we explain (σαφηνίζομεν) it — it convicts him of much baseness (πολλὴν ... κατηγορεῖ κακίαν)" because Christ sent the demons into the helpless swine and terrified the swineherds and agitated the city. Such an act is not a virtuous action (κατόρθωμα) but an evil deed (κακουργία). If Christ could not send the demons out of the region, but worked a wonder (τερατῶδες), it was also full of the suspicion of evil (φαύλης ὑπονοίας). A good thinker will hear these words and will judge that if Christ cares for some but not others, it is "not safe to flee to him and be saved. For he who is saved spoils the condition of him who is not, while he who is not saved becomes the accuser of him who is. Wherefore, according to my judgment, the record (ἱστορίας) contained in this narrative is a fiction (πλάσμα)."[49] The words used for the literary criticism above (πλάσμα, ἱστορία, σαφηνίζομεν) were also used by Porphyry to discuss various Homeric texts. He "explains" Homer by Homer[50]. In *The Cave of the Nymphs* he discusses *Od.* 13.109-112 (the two entrances of the cave of which one is for mortals and one for the gods) remarking that he will investigate "if Homer's account is factual (ἱστορίαν), or, at any rate, the poet's enigma (αἴνιγμα), if his description (διήγημα) is a fiction (πλάσμα)"[51]. Vituperative and forensic rhetoric are present because of the charges that Christ is responsible for malice (κακίαν) and evil action (κακουργία). The philosopher's careful use of humor is an example of rhetorical *ethos* which is

---

[47] De abst. 2.39.3 and 2.40.1 (105-106 BOUFFARTIGUE/PATILLON). BOUFFARTIGUE refers to a text from Xenocrates in Plut., De def. orac. 14.417d where demons are responsible for epidemics, sterility, wars, and seditions (Porphyre de l'Abstinence, II, 217 n.3).

[48] See § 2.3.11. HARNACK, Porphyrius, F. 49 = Contra Vigilant. 10: *Nisi forte in more gentilium impiorumque Porphyrii et Eunomii has praestigias daemonum esse confingas, et non vere clamare daemones, sed sua simulare tormenta.*

[49] Eusebius uses these terms (πλάσμα, ἱστορίας) in his evaluation of Apollonius' miracle of averting the plague in Ephesus in C.H. 27.15 (156 F./DES P.).

[50] SCHLUNK, Porphyry. The Homeric Questions, Lang Classical Studies 2, New York et al. 1993, 46-7.

[51] De antro nymph. 21 (20,31-22,2 Sem. Cl. 609); ET in Porphyry. The Cave of the Nymphs in the Odyssey, text and trans., Seminar Classics 609, State University of NY at Buffalo, Buffalo 1969, 23. The index of this edition gives many others examples of πλάσμα. Celsus also accused the evangelists of falsity (C. Cels. 2.13 [141,19-22 KOET.]).

designed to create sympathy for the orator and the orator's point of view[52]. Quintilian has an extensive analysis of the orator's use of humor[53]. One of the uses of laughter is to make light of or to deride the arguments of others[54]. Raillery (*vituperatio*) directed at an opponent's "character as revealed in his words and actions" is also an element of humor[55]. The philosopher's raillery directed at Jesus' actions is designed to create sympathy for his position in the audience. The entire critique is oriented toward persuading a person not to join the Christian movement as the philosopher's "hearer" expresses so clearly ("it is not safe to flee to him and be saved"). That is the stuff of deliberative rhetoric with its goal of molding human action.

The philosopher continues by claiming that if the story is not fiction, but has some relation to the truth:

> ... there is really plenty to laugh at for those who like to open their mouths. For come now, here is a point we must carefully inquire into: how was it that so large a herd of swine (χοίρων) was being kept at that time in the land of Judaea, seeing that they were to the Jews from the beginning the most unclean and hated form of beast? And, again, how were all those swine choked, when it was a lake and not a deep sea? It may be left to babes to make a decision about all this.[56]

The ethnographic interest and geographical comments are Porphyrian. Porphyry knew that the Jews did not eat pigs (χοιρίων)[57]. Jerome notes that Porphyry criticized the gospels for calling the Galilee a "sea" and not a "lake"[58]. A scholiast (in the margin of the MS) argues that the Jews raised the pigs and sold the meat to Roman solders and thus broke the law. Consequently the Savior vindicated the law by letting the demons go into the pigs[59]! Thus the scholiast disposes of the philosopher's ethical objections to Jesus' actions. It must be conceded that Macarius has probably influenced the language in the philosopher's objection: some of the philosopher's distinctive vocabulary is also "Macarian"[60]. These results are in accord with those of R. Goulet who has noted this fact about the philosopher's language.

---

[52] LAUSBERG, Handbuch, § 257.2a with reference to rhetorical *delectare*.

[53] Quint. 6.3.1-110 (LCL). The Greeks entitled the topic περὶ γελοίου (6.3.22).

[54] Quint. 6.3.23.

[55] Quint. 6.3.37. Compare Eusebius' use of raillery against the miracles of Apollonius (C.H. 27.25-27 [156 F./DES P.]): "Who, I would ask, after reading this would not laugh heartily at the miracle-mongering of this thaumaturge?" (with reference to Apollonius' exorcism of the Ephesian plague).

[56] CRAFER, Apocriticus, 64.

[57] De abst. 4.11.1 (17 /P./S./B.) with reference to Antiochus Epiphanes.

[58] See § 2.3.15 on HARNACK, Porphyrius, F. 55; Quaest. in Gen 1.10.

[59] Apocr. 3.4 (56 BLONDEL).

[60] For examples from the Christian (Macarius): the verb σεσαφηνίσθαι appears in 2.7 (7,5 BLONDEL); κατόρθωμα is frequently used by Macarius in passages such as 1.6 (3,7

3.4 What is the meaning of: They that are whole need not a physician but they that are sick?

After attacking Mt 11:25 (see below), the pagan introduces Lk 5:31-32: "It is right to examine another matter of a much more reasonable (λογιώτερον) kind — I say this by way of contrast (κατ' ἀντίφρασιν) — 'They that are whole need not a physician, but they that are sick.' Christ unravels these things to the multitude about His own coming (ἐπιδημίας) to earth."[61] He charges Christ with irrationality. The word for Christ's time on earth (ἐπιδημίας) is the same as that used by Porphyry to refer to Asclepius' and other gods' no longer "dwelling" in the city since Christ has been honored[62]. The term for the philosopher's ironic "contrast" is a technical word of the rhetoricians[63]. The irony is a clear accusation of irrationality. The philosopher explains why he believes Christ to have said something thoroughly irrational. "If then it was on account of those who are weak, as He himself says, that He faced sins, were not our forefathers weak, and were not our ancestors diseased with sin?" Porphyry's *C.C.* also attacked Christian dogma because so many people had perished before Christ's coming[64]. The pagan then quotes 1 Tim 1:15 in which Paul identifies himself as a chief sinner. He draws an absurd consequence from the saying in Luke:

> ... if then this is so, and he that has gone astray is called, and he that is diseased is healed, and the unrighteous is called, but the righteous is not, it follows that he who was neither called nor in need of the healing of the Christians would be a righteous man who had not gone astray. For he who has no need of healing is the man who turns away from the word which is among the faithful (πιστοῖς), and the more he turns away from it, the more righteous and whole he is, and the less he goes astray.

In other words, if only the unrighteous and sick are called, then the person who needs no healing rejects (ἀποστραφείς) the word of the faithful and is consequently even more righteous and healthy[65]. Thus Jesus' words would thoroughly contradict themselves. This method is Porphyrian, and is very similar to Porphyry's attack on Lk 14:12-13 preserved by Pacatus (§ 2.3.17 above), although others such as Hierocles also looked for contradictions (Lact.

BLONDEL) and 2.7 (6,4; 7,14 BLONDEL); παίγνιον is also in 2.7 (4,14 BLONDEL). GOULET, *Porphyre et Macaire*, 448-52.

[61] Apocr. 4.10 = HARNACK, *Porphyrius*, F. 87. ET in CRAFER, *Apocriticus*, 136.

[62] HARNACK, *Porphyrius*, F. 80 (= Eus, P.E. 5.1.9-10). See § 2.3.1 above.

[63] LAUSBERG, *Handbuch*, § 885, 904.

[64] HARNACK, *Porphyrius*, F. 81, 82. See § 2.3.29-30 above.

[65] Celsus does not draw the consequence that Christ's teaching would result in people thinking they should become unrighteous, but he was shocked that Christians recruited the unrighteous (C. Cels. 3.59 [254,1 KOET.]).

Div. Inst. 5.2.14). The ultimate goal is apparent and is from deliberative rhetoric: one who turns away from the word of the Christians is righteous and healthy! The interpretation of Jesus' words is thus used against the movement's attempt to recruit. Macarius responded by identifying the "well" and the "righteous" with angels and the "sick" and "sinners" with all humanity[66]. Consequently no one is without need of Christ's call — which took place from Adam onwards. This is similar to Augustine's response to Porphyry's objection about the multitude who perished before Christ[67].

3.5 How did Christ, after being mistreated and crucified, make people believe in him?

The pagan made some kind of attack on the narrative in Mt 9:20-22 par. Only part of Macarius' answer (from the lost Book 1, Chapter 6) is preserved which discusses Berenice, the woman healed of the flow of blood. She was an honored ruler of Edessa and recorded the deed in bronze. Crafer refers to many accounts of a statue of Christ she erected at Paneas. Sozomen claims that Julian took it down and put up his own[68]. The indexes to the other questions of the lost book one mention objections that include the following: the divisions of the Christians and the heresies; the way in which Christ chose his disciples; the temptation of Christ by the devil; and the fact that Christ did not come at the beginning of time[69]. Nicephorus remarks that book one contained remarks about Christ's miracles (περὶ τῶν παρὰ Χριστοῦ τελουμένων θαυμάτων διέξεισιν). The tone of those comments was probably similar to those about the exorcism above[70]. These miracles were apparently used by Macarius to counter the Hellene's question: how could Christ after being crucified have made people believe in him. Stories such as that of the woman healed from the flow of blood must have been used by Macarius to show how Jesus persuaded people. How Macarius used the miracles to explain the methods of persuasion used by the Risen Lord is unclear[71].

---

[66] Apocr. 4.18 (196,11-13; 197,13-16 BLONDEL).

[67] Augustine, Ep. 102.12, 15 discussed in § 2.3.30 above. Augustine does not allegorize the "well" to mean angels.

[68] Apocr. 1.6 (3 BLONDEL = HARNACK, Porphyrius, F. 50). CRAFER, Apocriticus, 31 (referring to Sozomen, H.E. 5.21.1 [228,1-3 B./H.] but contradicted by other church historians such as Malalas' Chronicle 10 [239,8-14 DINDORF]). The text is from Nicephorus' Antirrhetica (published by J. B. PITRA, Spicilegium Solesmense..., I, Paris 1852, 332-33). Nicephorus also excerpted Apocr. 4.26, 27 and 28 in his work against the iconoclasts.

[69] FRASSINETTI, Sull'autore, 52 using MERCATI. See § 3.52 below.

[70] PITRA, Spicilegium 332 and BLONDEL, Macarii 3.

[71] On the use of miracle in ancient Christianity to persuade others to join the movement see COOK, Protreptic Power, 107-10.

3.6 How is it said, I did not come to bring peace to the earth but a sword?

The pagan took exception to Mt 10:34-38. Unfortunately only the *titulus* and Macarius' long and diffuse answer survives[72]. He gives as an example of daughters divided from mothers Thecla and Theocleia from the *Acts of Paul and Thecla* [73]. He interprets the sword to be one that divided without making wounds[74]. Given the philosopher's aversion to the violence practiced against the Christians (2.14, 4.4) and given his objection to the divisions among Christians themselves, it seems likely that he objected to the violence of Jesus' imagery of the sword[75].

3.7 How is it said: Thou hast hid these things from the wise and the prudent and revealed them unto babes?[76]

The philosopher quotes Mt 11:25 par and Dt 29:29 and argues:

...therefore the things that are written for the babes and the ignorant ought to be clearer (σαφέστερα) and not wrapped in riddles (αἰνιγματώδη). For if the mysteries (μυστήρια) have been hidden from the wise, and unreasonably poured out to babes and those that give suck, it is better to be desirous of senselessness (ἀλογίαν) and ignorance, and this is the great achievement (κατόρθωμα) of the wisdom of Him who came to earth (ἐπιδημέσαντος), to hide the rays of knowledge from the wise (σοφῶν), and to reveal them to fools and babes.[77]

The philosopher's conclusion is that it is better to desire irrationality and ignorance, and that this is the achievement of Christ's wisdom — to reveal the light of knowledge to fools and babes. These results are simply absurd in the philosopher's eyes. The text is reminiscent of Celsus' objection to the Christian recruitment of children (C.Cels. 3.55 [250,20 Koet.])[78]. The vocabulary is similar to that of Porphyry. He used a similar word to describe

---

[72] Apocr. 2.7 (4-8 BLONDEL).

[73] 2.7 (6,22 BLONDEL).

[74] 2.7 (7,21-22 BLONDEL).

[75] The objection to Christian heresies is in one of the indexes of the lost book one (FRASSINETTI, Sull'autore, 52). See § 3.52.1.

[76] The first half of this titulus is given below with 4.8 (§ 3.9 of this work) since the MS refers to 4.8 and 4.9 with one index.

[77] Apocr. 4.9 = HARNACK, Porphyrius, F. 52 (ET in CRAFER, Apocriticus, 134).

[78] Celsus also noted Christian recruitment of the stupid (ἀνοήτους) in C. Cels. 3.74 (265,14 KOET.).

Asclepius' sojourn in "the city" (ἐπιδημίας)[79]. Porphyry faults Christians for finding enigmas (αἰνίγματα) and hidden mysteries (κρυφίων μυστερίων) in the writings of Moses that are actually quite clear (φανερῶς ... λεγόμενα)[80]. Porphyry's Homer, on the other hand, speaks about the demons and gods through enigmas (αἰνιγμῶν) and has hidden (ἀπέκρυψε) such things in his poetry. He does not speak directly (προηγουμένως)[81]. The poet also says "unclear things" that must be allegorized by the philosopher (ἀσαφές ... ἀσαφειῶν) and can speak mystically (μυστικῶς)[82]. When Homer speaks allegorically it is evident to the wise and to the amateur (σοφοῖς ... ἰδιώταις)[83]. The philosopher does not find Christian texts to be worthy of the kind of admiration Porphyry felt for Homer.

3.8 How is it said, Behold your mother and your brothers are standing outside desiring to talk with you?

Mt 12:48-49 par posed a problem of some kind for Macarius' pagan. Only the *titulus* of the objection and Macarius' answer are preserved, and it is not easy to reconstruct the objection[84]. Harnack and J. Hoffmann both believe it to have been an attack on Christ's divinity[85]. Macarius has Christ ask questions such as: What mere human (ἄνθρωπος ψιλός) has ever freed leprosy (like scales) from a body[86]? Christ concludes: If no mere human has ever done such deeds, how can you not shrink back from babbling that the only begotten (μονογενῆ) of God is a mere human having brothers. Macarius' pagan evidently believed that a person who had brothers and a mother could only be human and not a god. Anonymous objectors quoted the same text (Mt

---

[79] Eus, P.E. 5.1.9-10 (SC 262, 244 ZINK/DES PLACES) = HARNACK, Porphyrius, F. 80.

[80] Eus., H.E. 6.19.4 = HARNACK, Porphyrius, F. 39. Compare the philosopher's quotation of τὰ φανερὰ ἡμῖν in Dt 29:9.

[81] SMITH, Porphyrii, 372F. Lamberton has a translation of this fragment (Homer 113). Compare the philosopher's reference to ἀπέκρυψας in Mt 11:25 par.

[82] De antro nymph. 3, 4 (5,13.27-31 Sem.Cl. 609). Compare Porphyry's reference to mystical symbols (συμβόλων μυστικῶν) in the ancients' consecrations of sanctuaries in De antro 4 (6,14-15 Sem.Cl. 609).

[83] De antro nymph. 3 (4,1-3 Sem.Cl. 609) with reference to an allegory of Cronius.

[84] Apocr. 2.8 = HARNACK, Porphyrius, F. 53 (paraphrase in CRAFER, Apocriticus, 33-34).

[85] HARNACK, Porphyrius, F. 53, HOFFMANN, Porphyry's, 30 n.3.

[86] Apocr. 2.8 (10,2 BLONDEL). For the expression (mere human) see Socrates, H.E. 7.32.9 (380,28 HANSEN).

12:48,49) along with John 2:4 and accused Jesus of not honoring his mother.[87]

3.9 What is the meaning of the leaven, the mustard seed, and the pearl?...[88]

A teaching even more mythical (μυθωδέστερον) than Is 24:4 in the philosopher's eyes, and like a teaching given in the night, is Jesus' comparisons of the kingdom to a mustard seed (Mt 13:31), leaven (Mt 13:33) and a merchant seeking beautiful pearls (Mt 13:45).

> These imaginings (μυθάρια) do not come from men, nor even from women who dream. For when any one has a message to give concerning great and divine (θείων) matters, he is obliged to make use of common things which pertain to men, in order to make his meaning clear (σαφηνείας), but not such degraded (χυδαίοις) and unintelligible things (ἀσυνέτοις) as these. These sayings, besides being base and unsuitable to such matters, have in themselves no intelligent meaning or clearness. And yet it was fitting that they should be very clear (σαφῆ) indeed, because they were not written for the wise or understanding, but for babes.[89]

The unclarity of the parables contradicts Mt 11:25, because Jesus revealed things to babes and not to the wise. The parables were also problematic to the philosopher because of the crudity of the images used to express great and divine things. Porphyry attacked the parables of Jesus according to Didymus with specific reference to "the one who has ears to hear, let him hear." According to Didymus not all could hear Jesus' hidden words told in parables[90]. Macarius' pagan and Porphyry both seem to agree that the parables are completely obscure. In other contexts Porphyry admired parable-like teaching. Porphyry's Pythagoras taught by discursive reason and symbolically (συμβολικῶς Vita Pyth. 36 [53,3 des Places]). One of his symbolic teachings was "don't put a sword in a fire" — which meant do not speak using sharpened words to a person swollen with rage (Vita Pyth. 42 [55,11-15 des Places]). The philosopher's ideal of "clarity" was shared by grammarians, rhetoricians, philosophers, and scholiasts[91]. A third century rhetorician notes that the

---

[87] Ps. Just., Quaest. et resp. ad Orthod. 136, 485b-c (224-26 OTTO). See RINALDI, Biblia Gentium, 420.

[88] The second half of this *titulus* is given above with Apocr. 4.9 (on Mt 11:25) in § 3.7 of this work.

[89] Apocr. 4.8 = HARNACK, Porphyrius, F. 54 (ET, slightly modified, of CRAFER, Apocriticus, 134).

[90] Didymus' text is discussed in § 2.3.13. The word may not be restored correctly.

[91] A search on the TLG D revealed 996 uses in 112 authors. Eustathius, the scholar of Homer, was responsible for 177.

virtues of narrative are conciseness, clarity, and persuasiveness[92]. Aristotle remarked that examples and parables (παραδείγματα καὶ παραβολὰς) were used for clarity (σαφήνειαν), and should be drawn from things we know (as in Homer)[93]. Porphyry also used the concept in his interpretation of Homer's comparisons (αἱ μὲν παραβολαὶ τριῶν ἕνεκα γίνονται, αὐξήσεως ἐνεργείας σαφηνείας)[94]. Macarius responded to the pagan's critique by noting that philosophers also make comparisons and gave as an example Aratus of Cilicia (the astronomer) who encompassed the heavens in a circle[95].

3.10 How is it said: About the fourth watch of the night he came upon the sea?

Mark 6:48 par is the focus of the philosopher's scorn in *Apocriticus* 3.6: "Come, let us unfold (ἀναπτύξωμεν) for you another saying from the Gospel which is laughably written without any credibility, and has a still more laughable narrative attached to it."[96] The philosopher recounts the story after the meal in which Jesus sends the disciples away and then appears to them (ἐπέστη) in the fourth watch of the night as they are terribly afflicted[97] by the driving rain of the story and are toiling against the violence of the waves. The pagan claims:

> Those who know the truth about places are aware that it is not a sea but a small lake created by a river located under a hill in the country of Galilee, beside the city of Tiberias — that one can cross easily in little one-trunk boats in not more than two hours and which cannot admit waves or a storm. Mark departs far from the truth when he writes the exceedingly laughable story (μύθευμα) that after nine hours Jesus came in the tenth hour (that is, in the fourth watch of the night) and found the disciples sailing in the pond — which he calls a sea and not simply a sea, but a sea storm-tossed and terribly wild and excited by the disturbance of the waves. He does this so that from these things he can bring in Christ as if he had done a great sign (σημεῖον) in calming the huge and extraordinary storm and saving the disciples from the deep and the ocean while they were

---

92 Ἐπειδὴ δὲ τῆς διηγήσεως τὰς ἀρετάς φαμεντήν τε συντομίαν καὶ τὴν σαφήνειαν καὶ τὴν πιθανότητὰ Anonymus Seguerianus, Ars rhetorica (olim sub auctore Cornuto), Section 63.

93 Topica 8.1 (157a).

94 Porphyrius, Quaestionum Homericarum ad Iliadem pertinentium reliquiae, Bk 11.548 (166,13-14 SCHRADER). Porphyry used the word eight times, excluding the two appearances of it in the Apocriticus (e.g. In Aristotelis categorias expositio (60,6 BUSSE); Vita Plotini 26.32 (I, 38 H./S.).

95 Apocr. 4.17 (191,16-18 BLONDEL).

96 HARNACK, Porphyrius, F. 55. ET based on CRAFER, Apocriticus, 73. Although Macarius probably composed these words to tie the narrative together, some of the words from literary criticism appear also in Porphyry (ἀναπτύσσειν SMITH, Porphyrii 372F; διήγημα De antro 21 [22,2 Sem.Cl. 609]).

97 The same word (τετρυχωμένοις) is used by the Christian in 3.24 (109,23 BLONDEL).

in mortal danger. From these childish histories we know that the gospel is a sophisticated theatrical trick (or "theater"; σκηνὴν σεσοφισμένην εἶναι τὸ εὐαγγέλιον).[98] Jerome makes it clear that Porphyry critiques this story by accusing the evangelists of manufacturing a miracle for the ignorant because they called the lake a sea[99]. Frassinetti claims that the author of the text could never have been in Palestine[100]. This claim is simply false because a coastal dweller like Porphyry (in Caesarea) might know very little of the Sea of Galilee. The philosopher conceives of the Galilee as a small lake in which storms cannot happen. Given such an understanding, the critique follows easily. Porphyry had no trouble accepting the accounts of Pythagoras' calming of the waves of rivers and seas so that his disciples could easily cross. Pythagoras crosses rivers and seas himself on the arrow of Apollo[101]. Jerome responds to the philosopher's critique by remarking that the Hebrews called bodies of water "seas." Macarius makes the same response. Goulet notes that the fact that both Macarius and Jerome share the same solution indicates that Jerome is a probable source for Macarius (Apollinarius of Laodicea's treatise against Porphyry may be Macarius' source also)[102]. In a very long answer Macarius also writes that Christ has dominion over the earth to work signs (σημείων) and has the same authority to do wonders (παράδοξα) in the sea[103]. Macarius discusses Peter's walking on the waves and allegorizes the text.

3.11 What is the meaning of: Get thee behind me Satan; and the address to Peter?...[104]

The philosopher attacks Peter by first quoting Mt 16:23 and then 16:18a,b[105]. He introduces his quotation by commenting: "It is only natural that there is much that is unseemly [or "nauseous" ἔχει τὴν ἀηδίαν] in all this long-

---

[98] CRAFER translated σκηνὴν with "curtain," but see LSJ s.v. II.4. HARNACK has "Trugbild." W. DEN BOER traces "Porphyry's" use of stage metaphors to a *Ludus de mysteriis Christianis* dating to the reign of Diocletian; A Pagan Historian and his Enemies: Porphyry Against the Christians, CP 69, 1974, 204. He refers to the *Passio Sancti Genesii ex mimo Martyris*, Acta Martyrum, ed. TH. RUINART, Verona 1731, 236 = Regensburg 1859, 312-13. See BHL § 3315 (Genesius Mimo).

[99] See § 2.3.15 on Quaest. in Genes. 1:10 (F. 55).

[100] Sull'autore, 48.

[101] Vita Pyth. 29 (49,23-26 DES PLACES).

[102] GOULET, Porphyre et Macaire, 452.

[103] Apocr. 3.13 (84-89 and in particular 85,25-27 BLONDEL).

[104] The other half of the titulus (What is the meaning of the seventy times seven?) goes with Apocr. 3.20.

[105] He does not quote 16:18c (the gates of hell...) in Apocriticus 3.19 = HARNACK, Porphyrius, F. 23. ET in CRAFER, Apocriticus, 91-92 (slightly modified).

winded talk thus poured out. The words, one might say, provide a battle of inconsistency against each other (αὐτὰ πρὸς ἑαυτὰ τῆς ἀντιλογίας ἀνακαίει τὴν μάχην)." The word for inconsistency belonged to the rhetorician's vocabulary[106]. It was also used by Porphyry[107]. The "contradiction" seen by the philosopher prompts him to ask: "How would the man on the street (τις ὡς ἐκ τριόδου)[108] explain that Gospel saying...?" After calling Peter "Satan" and cursing him (ἀποσκορακίσαι) as one who committed mortal sin Jesus wants to see him no more and casts him behind him — with the throng of the "outcast and vanished." "How is it right," the pagan asks, "to find this sentence of exclusion (or "negation" τῆς ἀποφάσεως ψῆφον) against the leader and chief (κορυφαίου καὶ πρώτου) of the disciples?" A sober person who ruminates over the verses (in the philosopher's order) will respond as follows:

> ...will he not laugh aloud till he nearly bursts his mouth? Will he not open it wide as he might from his seat (or "orchestra" θυμέλη θεάτρου) in the theater? Will he not speak with a sneer and hiss loudly? Will he not cry aloud to those who are near him? Either when He called Peter "Satan" He was drunk and overcome with wine,[109] and He spoke as though in a fit (or "culpable words" ἐπίληπτα); or else, when He gave this same disciple the keys of the kingdom of heaven, He was painting (ἐζώγραφει)[110] dreams, in the imagination of his sleep. For pray how was Peter able to support the foundation of the Church, seeing that thousands of times he was readily shaken by the recklessness of his judgment? What sort of firm reasoning can be detected in him, or where did he show any unshaken mental power, seeing that, when he heard the word "Jesus," he was terribly frightened because of a sorry maidservant [Mt 26:69], and three times foreswore himself, although no great necessity was laid upon him? We conclude then that, if He was right (εὐλόγως) in taking him up and calling him Satan, as having failed of the very essence of piety, He acted absurdly (ἀτόπως), as though not knowing what He had done, in giving him the authority of leadership.

The somewhat scurrilous rhetoric accuses Jesus of forgetfulness, drunkenness, an epileptic fit (or "culpable words" ἐπίληπτα), and painting dreams[111]. This rhetoric of vituperation is obviously designed to destroy Peter's credibility and that of Jesus. De Labriolle remarks that Peter's importance in early Christianity

---

[106] Aristotle, Rhet. 3.13.3 and 3.17.16 (a speaker contradicting himself while speaking about himself). The word is also used for opposing arguments in the context of chria elaboration (LAUSBERG, Handbuch, § 1119).

[107] In Aristotelis categorias expositio (80,6 BUSSE); De abst. 1.3.3 (44 B./P.) used for "counter-argument" or "opposition."

[108] LSJ s.v. describe this as a place frequented by fortune tellers and loungers.

[109] For a Christian use of this charge in polemic see Eusebius' charge that Philostratus was drunk and consequently told contradictory accounts of Apollonius (Contra Hieroclem 43.34 [194 F./DES P.]).

[110] The Christian uses this expression (painting dreams) in Apocr. 4.30 (224,6-7 BLONDEL) to describe the Hellene's story about the shipwrecked man (Apocr. 4.24).

[111] LSJ s.v. give examples of puns on the meanings of "epilepsy" and "culpable."

was not unknown to the pagans, as this fragment illustrates[112]. The technique is Porphyrian — looking for contradictions. Jesus is inconsistent or irrational and absurd (ἀτόπως ... ἐποίησε). Porphyry accused the Christian exegetes of the OT of being guilty of absurd exegesis (τρόπος τῆς ἀτοπίας)[113].

Macarius responds by noting that if Peter is called "Satan" and has sinned unforgivably then the root of faith has almost been plucked up (τῆς πίστεως μικροῦ δεῖν ἀνέσπασται τὸ ῥίζωμα)[114]. The real speaker of Peter's words in 16:22 is Satan who is rebuked by Christ's "Get thee behind me Satan." Christ then calls Peter an "offense." An onlooker would fail to be persuaded (σφαλλόμενος πείσεσθαι) who sees Peter call Jesus Son of God and then sees Peter persuading Jesus not to complete the economy of his passion[115]. Peter's confession results in his name Peter — since he proclaims the steadfast nature of the immovable rock (πέτρας)[116].

Macarius' response indicates that the philosopher's attack on Peter is also an attack on the persuasiveness of the Christian confession of Jesus as the Christ. The pagan does not actually attack that confession in the text, but by his attack on Peter, the confession also loses credibility. Consequently Macarius affirms Peter's credibility by emphasizing the heavenly source of the confession[117].

3.12 How is it said: Have mercy on my son because he is moonstruck (σεληνιάζεται)?

The verses in Mt 17:15, 17 par were the occasion for one of the philosopher's objections that is missing from the MS of the *Apocriticus*. Only the *titulus* and Macarius' answer (2.10) are preserved. Macarius asks "why is it that with the father kneeling pitiably, Jesus responds to him and the crowds in rebuke."[118] Christ curses (ἀποσκορακίζει) the supplicants' request. Since the philosopher used this word in *Apocr.* 3.19, Macarius may be quoting him here[119]. The philosopher most likely attacked Jesus' apparently unmerciful rebuke. He may also have asserted a contradiction because of the description of the boy as

---

[112] La réaction, 256. He also refers to Contra Celsum 2.55 (178,25-26 KOET.) for a possible reference to Peter.

[113] HARNACK, Porphyrius, F. 39 (Eus., H.E. 6.19.5).

[114] Apocr. 3.27 (115,6.7 BLONDEL). CRAFER, Apocriticus, 93-5 paraphrases the answer.

[115] Apocr. 3.27 (116,24-25 BLONDEL).

[116] 3.27 (117,30-31; see also 115,20-24 BLONDEL). CRAFER's attempt to deny that Macarius identifies Peter with the rock does not seem justified (Apocriticus 93 n.2). Macarius does not separate Peter from his confession.

[117] 3.27 (115,17-20 and 117,23-28 BLONDEL).

[118] 2.10 (15,5-6 BLONDEL). HARNACK, Porphyrius, F. 57.

[119] See HARNACK's comment in Porphyrius, F. 57.

"moonstruck" and "possessed." Macarius explains that the demon attacked the boy at the moon's changes so that people would think he was suffering because of the moon and by implication because of the moon's Creator[120]. Christ calls them "faithless" because of their beliefs about the moon[121].

3.13 What is the meaning of the grain of mustard seed?

The philosopher attacks Mt 17:20 par and includes a phrase (ἄρθητι καὶ βλήθητι) in his text that comes from Mt 21:21 par:

> It is obvious therefore that anyone who is unable to remove a mountain in accordance with his bidding, is not worthy to be reckoned one of the fraternity of the faithful (πιστῶν νομίζεσθαι φατρίας).[122] So you are plainly refuted, for not only are the rest of Christians not reckoned among the faithful, but not even are any of your bishops or priests (ἐπισκόπων ἢ πρεσβυτέρων) worthy of this saying.[123]

The philosopher is aware of bishops, presbyters, and the distinction between catechumens and the "faithful"[124]. In the chapter on Porphyry we noted that Jerome, in his comment on Mt 21:21, described "pagan dogs" who claimed that the apostles had no faith because they could not move mountains. Jerome probably included Porphyry in that group[125]. Didymus also claims that Porphyry and others like him attacked the principle that all things are possible to the believer (Mk 9:23, Mt 17:20)[126]. This topos of attack must have been widespread in Hellenism. The pagans found the idea of moving mountains to be repellent. Macarius' answer is that "this mountain," from which Christ had just come down, refers to the demon that he had exorcized. Consequently Jesus does not speak of a literal mountain (ἁπλῶς ὄρει), but speaks allegorically (ἀλληγορικῶς) of the demon[127].

---

[120] 2.10 (15,15-16,5 BLONDEL).

[121] See CRAFER's paraphrase (Apocriticus, 36-37). 2.10 (16,18-20 BLONDEL).

[122] HARNACK notes that the philosopher (F. 64) also calls Judaism a φρατρία, but that the group of catechumens (whom the philosopher distinguishes from the "faithful") is a "mass" (ἄθροισμα F. 26).

[123] Apocr. 3.17 = HARNACK, Porphyrius, F. 95.

[124] Apocr. 3.22 = HARNACK, Porphyrius, F. 26.

[125] See § 2.3.20 above (Jerome, Comm. in Matth. 21:21).

[126] See § 2.3.21 above.

[127] Apocr. 3.25 (112,8-16 BLONDEL).

3.14 How is it said: No one is good but God alone?

One of Macarius' answers indicates that the philosopher found a contradiction between Mark 10:18 par (No one is good but God alone) and Mt 12:35 par (the good person brings forth good out of the good treasure of the heart)[128]. Macarius argues that Jesus had a divine nature and is God, but denied being "good" because the rich young man addressed him as a mere person (ψιλὸν ... ἄνθρωπον)[129]. To explain the apparent contradiction Macarius argues that God is good by nature (φύσει), but humans are good by designation (θέσει) when they participate in the good by doing something good[130]. The pagan probably found the inconsistency to be between Jesus' use of the word "good" in the verses mentioned above.

3.15 What is the meaning of the saying: It is easier for a camel to go through a needle, than a rich man into the kingdom of God?

The saying "it is easier for a camel to go through a needle than for a rich man to enter the kingdom of heaven" (Mt 19:24 par) was extremely objectionable in the Hellene's eyes[131]. His argument is from consequence[132]. The teaching produces absurd results according to the philosopher:

> If it indeed be the case that any one who is rich is not brought into the so-called kingdom of heaven though they have kept themselves from the sins of life, such as murder, theft, adultery, cheating, impious oaths, body-snatching, and the wickedness of sacrilege, of what use is just dealing to righteous men, if they happen to be rich? And what harm is there for the poor in doing every unholy deed of baseness (ἀνοσιούργημα)?[133] For it is not virtue that takes a person up to heaven, but lack of possessions. For if wealth shuts out the rich person from heaven, by way of contrast (ἐξ ἀντιφάσεως) poverty brings the poor into it. And so it becomes lawful, when someone has learnt this lesson, to pay no regard to virtue, but without let or hindrance to cling to poverty alone, and the things that

---

[128] Apocr. 2.9 (12-14 BLONDEL); paraphrase in CRAFER, Apocriticus, 34-6.

[129] 2.9 (12,6-8; 13,1 BLONDEL).

[130] 2.9 (13,23, 13,11-12 BLONDEL). LSJ s.v. θέσις V.3 give philosophical usage of this distinction.

[131] Apocr. 3.5 = HARNACK, Porphyrius, F. 58. ET in CRAFER, Apocriticus, 69-70. The word "eye" is not included in this tradition.

[132] Aristot., Rhet., 2.23.14 (LCL). On this argument see J. MARTIN, Antike Rhetorik. Technik und Methode, HAW 2.3, Munich 1974, 108.13 and COOK, Protreptic Power, 111-13.

[133] This rare word was used previously by Philo (e.g. De Josepho, 47 and 173). The patristic writers did not adopt it. It is only used twice by Johannes Damascenus (e.g. Passio sancti Artemii [Dub.], PG 96, 1289, line 5) and once by Romanus Melodus (20 occurrences in the TLG-D CD of which 2 are from Macarius' pagan and 11 from Philo).

are most base. This follows from poverty being able to save the poor man, while riches shut out the rich man from the undefiled abode (ἀκηράτου μονῆς).[134]

The philosopher concludes that this is not the teaching of Christ, if he handed down the rule of truth (τὸν τῆς ἀληθείας παρεδίδου κανόνα),[135] but of people who want to take the property of the wealthy. He gives the example, which happened "yesterday," of some people who read Mt 19:21 to some "rich women" who gave away all that they had and were consequently forced to become beggars. His final conclusion is that these are the words of a sick or distressed woman (καμνούσης). The philosopher's somewhat ironic refusal to attack Jesus directly in this fragment has sometimes led interpreters to conclude that Porphyry had some kind of grudging admiration for Jesus which he did not share for the disciples and other Christians. De Labriolle rightly responds that Porphyry (or the philosopher) vilifies the Jesus of the gospels without mercy[136]. It is interesting that the pagan does not mention monasticism, which he may not have known[137]. Julian attacked the similar teaching in Lk 12:33 on similar grounds: society would break down if everyone sold all their possessions[138]. Celsus did not attack Jesus' teaching as nonsensical, but did argue that it was a corruption of a Platonic saying[139]. Celsus was also scandalized by the Christians' recruitment of the uneducated, unwise, and the unrighteous[140]. Porphyry himself was interested in a life free of material attachment. The greatest wealth for Porphyry's "philosophers" was self sufficiency (αὐτάρκειαν). For them it is honorable not to beg (or "need")

---

[134] HARNACK, Porphyrius, F. 58 refers to several uses of ἀκήρατον in Porphyry's writings (Ad Marcellam 13 [18,25 PÖT.] and De imag. 2* BIDEZ). The Christian (Macarius) uses it (3.14 [90,12 BLONDEL]). ἀκηράτου μονῆς is an expression he uses in Apocr. 2.17 (30,5 BLONDEL) and 3.23 (107,5-6 BLONDEL).

[135] Same expression ("rule of truth") in Philo, Leg. Alleg. 3.233. HARNACK calls is a "church expression," but gives no examples (Porphyrius, F. 58). Examples are: Clement, Stromata 4.1.3.2 (GCS Clemens II, 249,11 STÄHLIN); Greg. Naz., Ep. 79.1, (GCS Gregor von Naz. Briefe 69,11 GALLAY). An early philosophical use is in Sext. Emp., Adv. Log. 1.114 (= I, 233,19 DIELS/KRANZ, Fragmente der Vorsokratiker).

[136] La réaction, 279-80 (with reference to HARNACK, Kritik 111, 135, 136 and other scholars). The investigations of this chapter make it abundantly clear that the anonymous philosopher harbored no admiration (hidden or otherwise) for Jesus of Nazareth — at least not for the Jesus depicted in the NT!

[137] HARNACK, Porphyrius, F. 58.

[138] C. Gal. F. 100 (188,2-189,11 MASARACCHIA) discussed in § 5.2.17 below. FRASSINETTI (Sull'autore, 55) uses this parallel to argue for Julian's authorship of the pagan's objections in the Apocriticus. FRASSINETTI's argument that Porphyry was for voluntary poverty as opposed to the philosopher is weak since Porphyry did not believe in begging either (Sull'autore, 47). De abst. 4.11.5 (18 P./S./B.) does not encourage begging, nor does Ad Marc. 33 (36,9-21 PÖT.).

[139] C. Cels. 6.16 (86,15-16 KOET.) and see § 1.2.12 above.

[140] See § 1.6.2, 4 above.

anything from anyone (σεμνὸν τὸ μηδενὸς δεῖσθαι)[141]. However, the impoverished women in the pagan's eyes are driven to dishonorable begging (ἄσεμνον ἀπαίτησιν). As we have noted above, Porphyry accused the apostles of doing signs by magic arts to get wealth from rich women[142]. Macarius responds that it is not wealth but an unseemly course of life that hurts the rich person, and likewise poverty alone does not lead a poor individual to heaven. Virtue is necessary for both individuals[143].

3.16 What is the meaning of: Take heed, for many shall come saying, I am Christ?

The Hellene considers the saying in Mt 24:4, 5 to be doubtful (ἀμφίβολον). His comment is that "three hundred years have passed by, and even more, and no one of the kind has anywhere appeared. Unless indeed you are going to adduce Apollonius of Tyana, a man who was adorned with all philosophy. But you would not find another. Yet it is not concerning one but concerning many that He says that such shall arise."[144] The "300 years and more" is difficult for the hypothesis of Porphyrian authorship, even if one assumed the date of the *C.C.* to be toward the end of the third century. With Porphyry's death around 305, the three hundred years still rules him out. Consequently Harnack assumes that the date is a reference to the time of the composition of the *Apocriticus*, and that Porphyry's text would have read "200 years"[145]. If the three hundred years is not Macarius' chronological change, but belongs to the pagan's text then it would fit the time of Julian better. Julian says that a little more than three hundred years have passed since Jesus' time[146]. It may be the case that Macarius' pagan is compiled from various opponents of the Christian faith and so the chronological datum is only useful for dating the time of Macarius himself. Porphyry was interested in Apollonius and compared him to Christian miracle workers. Hierocles was the first to compare Christ to Apollonius according to Eusebius[147]. In a letter of Marcellinus to Augustine,

---

[141] Ad Marcellam 28 (32,12 PÖT.) Compare 27 and 33 (30,23-26; 36,9-12 PÖT.).

[142] See § 2.3.37 above (F. 4), from Jerome, Tract. de Ps. 81 225.

[143] Apocr. 3.12 (81,12-16 BLONDEL). Paraphrase in CRAFER, Apocriticus, 70-73.

[144] Apocr. 4.5 = HARNACK, Porphyrius, F. 60. ET in CRAFER, Apocriticus, 127-28.

[145] HARNACK, Kritik, 12, 13, 108; Porphyrius, F. 60. On the dating of the C.C. see § 2.3.1. HOFFMANN, (Porphyry's, 70 n. 50) thinks the three hundred years is consistent with an early fourth century date for the C.C. Porphyry's otherwise astute chronological skills (e.g. his comments on Daniel) are not in support of HOFFMANN's position.

[146] C.Gal. 191e (136,7-8 MASARACCHIA). Emphasized by GEFFCKEN, Last Days, 209 n. 14 and FRASSINETTI, Sull'autore, 51.

[147] See § 2.3.37 (Jerome, Tract. de Ps. 81 225 = HARNACK, Porphyrius, F. 4) and § 4.4 with reference to Eus., Contra Hieroclem 1.

pagans regularly referred to the miracles of Apollonius and Apuleius to denigrate Jesus' miracles[148]. Macarius' pagan in this text does not explicitly appeal to Apollonius' miracles, but to his philosophy. But his ironic attempt to see Apollonius as a "false Christ" assumes that Apollonius' wonder working powers are understood. They are explicitly referred to in *Apocriticus* 3.1. The problem with Jesus' saying in the philosopher's mind is that it has been falsified by history. Macarius answers the objection by listing a series of "antichrists" who misused Christ's name such as Manes, Bardesanes, Droserius and Dositheus the Cilician[149]. A fourth or fifth century Christian (Ps. Justin, Theodoret) was willing to concede a pagan's claim that talismans of Apollonius (τελέσματα) were able to prevent floods of the sea, rushing of the wind, and attacks by wild animals. The Christian responds that Apollonius used his knowledge of nature to do such things with physical objects, whereas Christ used his authority in word only to do marvels[150].

3.17 How does he say: The Gospel shall be preached in the world?

The philosopher believes that the words which Matthew says in 24:14 are those of a "millslave": "For lo, every quarter (or "street" ῥύμη) of the inhabited world has experience of the Gospel, and all the bounds and ends of the earth possess it complete, and nowhere is there an end, nor will it ever come. So let this saying only be spoken in a corner!"[151] Here the philosopher finds the prediction to be falsified by history as in the case of Mt 24:4. Porphyry was interested in this section of Matthew as his comment on the figure in Mt 24:15 shows[152]. Macarius responds by mentioning that many nations have not yet heard the gospel including Indians in the south-east, Macrobians from Ethiopia in the south-west, Maurusians (Mauretanians) in the west and Scythians above the river Ister (Danube)[153]. Harnack notes that even though the gospel had come to the borders of these regions, the closer one approaches these peoples, the farther back they move[154]. That such a response was a Christian topos is indicated by Origen's exegesis of Mt 24:14 in which he mentions the *Seras*

---

[148] Aug., Ep. 136.1 (CSEL 44, 94,120-14 GOLDBACHER) and the references in § 2.3.37 above.

[149] Apocr. 4.15 (184,1-26 BLONDEL); summary in CRAFER, Apocriticus, 128-29.

[150] Quaestiones et responsiones ad orthodoxos Quaest. 24, 405a-406a (34-36 OTTO). P. DE LABRIOLLE thinks Theodoret (to whom the text is attributed in one MS) may be the author, and he discusses the text concerning Apollonius (La réaction païenne, 456, 501).

[151] Apocr. 4.3 = HARNACK, Porphyrius, F. 13. ET in CRAFER, Apocriticus, 124.

[152] HARNACK, Porphyrius, F. 44 discussed in § 2.3.22.

[153] Apocr. 4.13 (178-80 BLONDEL); summary in CRAFER, Apocriticus, 124-26.

[154] Kritik, 15 n.1.

(Chinese), *Ariacin* (a Persian province), the Ethiopians "beyond the river," the Britons and the Germans, Dacians, Sarmatians and Scythians[155].

3.18 What is the meaning of the saying: The poor you have with you always, but me you have not always?

Jesus' words, "the poor you have always, but me you do not always have (Mt 26:11 par) were "inconsistent" or "inconsequent" (ἀνακόλουθον) in the philosopher's eyes because they did not cohere with Mt 28:20. He explains that the cause of Jesus' statement (ὑποθέσεως) in Mt 26:10-11 par was a woman who poured a jar of ointment on Jesus' head. The onlookers babbled (θρυλούντων) on about the impropriety (ἀκαιρίαν)[156] of her action and remarked that the price of the ointment could be used to feed the poor. The conclusion is: "Apparently as the result of this inopportune (ἀκαιροφωνίαν) conversation, He uttered this nonsensical (φλυαρῶδες) saying, declaring that He was not always with them, although elsewhere He confidently affirmed and said to them, 'I shall be with you until the end of the world' (Mt 28:20). But when He was disturbed about the ointment, He denied that He was always with them."[157] Some of the words from literary criticism were used by Porphyry in his commentaries on Homer (i.e. ἀνακόλουθον, ὑποθέσεως)[158]. The technique of finding contradictions is also consistent with Porphyry's attack on Christian texts. The contradiction in Matthew is quite obvious to the philosopher. He also indulges in vituperative rhetoric by accusing Jesus of making a foolish statement (φλυαρῶδες) in Mt 26:11. Macarius, however, claims that Mt 26:11 was said before the passion[159]. Before the passion Jesus truly said that he would be bodily (σωματικῶς) separated from the disciples[160].

3.19 How is it said: If it be possible, let the cup pass?

The narrative of Jesus' agony in Gethsemane contains statements that are not worthy of a son of God and that do not cohere with Mt 10:28:

---

[155] In Matt. 24:9 Comment. Ser. 39 (GCS Origenes XI, 76,5-10 KLOSTERMANN).

[156] Macarius also uses this word (3.27 [118,3 BLONDEL]).

[157] Apocr. 3.7 = HARNACK, Porphyrius, F. 61. ET in CRAFER, Apocriticus, 76.

[158] Quaestionum Homericarum ad Odysseam pertinentium reliquiae, Odyssey 1.5,23 (SCHRADER) and SMITH, Porphyrii, 372F. ἀνακόλουθον also appears in Macarius' words, Apocr. 2.17 (31,3 BLONDEL).

[159] 3.14 (90,4-6 BLONDEL).

[160] 3.14 (93,16-18 BLONDEL).

Moreover there is another saying which is full of obscurity (ἀσαφείας)[161] and full of stupidity (ἀπαιδευσίας),[162] which was spoken by Jesus to His disciples. He said, "Fear not them that kill the body," and yet He Himself being in an agony and keeping watch in the expectation of terrible things, besought in prayer that His passion should pass from Him (πάθος αὐτῷ παρελθεῖν), and said to His intimate friends, "Watch and pray, that the temptation may not pass (παρέλθῃ) by you." For these sayings are not worthy of God's child (παιδὸς θεοῦ), nor even of a wise man who despises death.[163]

Celsus also critiqued the Gethsemane episode: how can Jesus be regarded as god when he was caught hiding himself (C. Cels. 2.9 [135,4-8 Koet.]); and what is done of deliberate purpose is not painful to a god, so why did he pray that he might avoid the fear of death, "Father if this cup could pass by me" (C. Cels. 2.23, 24 [152,11-14; 153,7-10 Koet.])[164]? The Hellene's vituperative rhetoric points out Jesus' agony (ἀγωνιῶν) and expectation of fearful things (προσδοκίᾳ τῶν δεινῶν) in the face of his approaching death. These qualities were probably the opposite of a courageous attitude toward death in the philosopher's eyes. Courage was praised by epideictic rhetoricians, and fear is here condemned[165]. Consequently Jesus' words are not worthy of a son of god. Macarius depicts Christ as pretending to be afraid of death as one provokes an animal in a menagerie by using a loud noise[166]. Christ puts the worm (his body) on the hook of divinity in order to catch the dragon (devil)[167].

3.20 What is the meaning of the seventy times seven?[168]

Peter's action of cutting of the ear of the high priest's slave (Mt 26:51 par) is condemned by the Hellene who finds it contrary to Jesus' teaching in Mt 18:22 — particularly since the slave had not sinned:

---

[161] A word used also by Porphyry, De antro 4 (4,27 Sem.Cl. 609) and Macarius (Apocr. 3.9 [69,9 BLONDEL]).

[162] Used by Porphyry (Ad Marcellam 9 [14,23 PÖT.]) and by Hierocles in a similar form in Eus., C. Hierocl. 2.27 (102 F./DES P.; ἀπαίδευτοι).

[163] Apocr. 3.2 = HARNACK, Porphyrius, F. 62. ET in CRAFER, Apocriticus, 57-8.

[164] With reference to the flight to Egypt, Celsus remarks that a god would not fear death (C. Cels. 1.66 [119,6-8 KOET.]).

[165] LAUSBERG, Handbuch, § 245, 558.

[166] Apocr. 3.9 (71,6-9 BLONDEL).

[167] Apocr. 3.9 (72,18-20 BLONDEL). CRAFER, Apocriticus, xix refers to other uses of this imagery in patristic writers. Compare Athanasius, Vita S. Antonii 24.4 (SC 400, 202,22-27 BARTELINK), Gregory of Nyssa, Oratio catechetica (GNO III/4, 62,8-13 MÜHLENBERG) See M. ANASTOS, Porphyry's Attack on the Bible, in: The Classical Tradition: Studies in Honor of Harry Caplan, ed. L. WALLACH, Ithaca 1966, 447 n. 52.

[168] The first part of this titulus is given above in § 3.11 (Apocr. 3.19).

It is also plain that Peter is condemned of many falls (πταίσας κατηγορεῖται), from the statement in that passage where Jesus said to him, "I say not unto thee until seven times, but until seventy times seven that thou forgive the sin of him that does wrong." But though he received this commandment and injunction, he cut off the ear of the high-priest's servant who had done no wrong, and did him harm although he had not sinned at all. For how did he sin, if he went at the command of his master to the attack which was then made on Christ?[169]

It is apparent that one of Peter's "falls" was his sword play — especially since he had been taught to forgive. Macarius concedes this point in his answer to the objection in 3.20[170]. Christ rebuked (or drubbed ἐνέτριψεν) Peter by quickly healing the slave's wound. Christ did not judge Peter by his rash tongue but by the desire of Peter's soul and his mind that clung to love.

3.21 How did Jesus endure to be crucified with insult?

The Hellene finds Christ's actions before the high priest and Pilate to be inferior to those of Apollonius in his trial before Domitian:

Why did not Christ utter anything worthy of one who was wise and divine (σοφοῦ καὶ θείου ἀνδρός), when brought either before the high-priest or before the governor [Mt 26:57-66, 27:1-26]? He might have given instruction to His judge and those who stood by and made them better men. But He endured to be smitten with a reed and spat on and crowned with thorns, unlike Apollonius, who, after speaking boldly (παρρησίας) to the Emperor Domitian, disappeared from the royal court, and after not many hours was plainly seen in the city then called Dicaearchia, but now Puteoli. But even if Christ had to suffer according to God's commands, and was obliged to endure punishment, yet at least He should have endured His Passion with some boldness (παρρησίας), and uttered words of force and wisdom to Pilate His judge, instead of being mocked like any gutter-snipe (ἐκ τριόδου χυδαίων).[171]

Celsus thought Christ should have disappeared from the cross (C. Cels. 2.68 [189,20-21 Koet.]). He also believed that Anaxarchus and Epictetus said inspired things while suffering violence — unlike Jesus[172]. Hierocles was impressed by Apollonius' disappearance before Domitian. In irony Lactantius uses Hierocles' example to show that Apollonius was more skillful than Christ

---

[169] Apocr. 3.20 = HARNACK, Porphyrius, F. 24. ET in CRAFER, Apocriticus, 92.

[170] His answer comprises a few lines of 3.27 (118,3-9 BLONDEL) which is primarily devoted to answering the philosopher's objection in 3.19 concerning Mt 16:23. An anonymous objection to the episode (also referring to Lk 22:36) appears in Ambrosiaster, Quaestiones Vet. et N. Test. 104.1 (227-28 SOUTER; see RINALDI, Biblia Gentium, F. 468).

[171] Apocr. 3.1 = HARNACK, Porphyrius, F. 63. ET in CRAFER, Apocriticus, 52-3. τριόδου is also in 3.19

[172] See § 1.3.2 above (with reference to C. Cels. 7.53 [203,15-23 KOET.]).

who was arrested and nailed to a cross[173]. The fact that both Hierocles and the philosopher compare Apollonius' arrest and disappearance to the passion of Christ is an argument in favor of some kind of dependence (at least in this case) as Crafer argued[174]. The ideal of bold or free speech was widespread in the ancient world[175]. One Roman rhetorician defines it this way: "It is Frankness of Speech (*licentia*) when talking before those to whom we owe reverence or fear, we yet exercise our right to speak out, because we seem justified in reprehending them, or persons dear to them, for some fault."[176] Before Apollonius disappeared from his trial he tried to demonstrate that Domitian was in danger of appearing to have an unjust hatred of philosophy[177]. Jesus gave no such speech as Apollonius and left the philosopher thoroughly unimpressed. Silence at a trial could impress some philosophers in the ancient world such as Maximus of Tyre who devoted an entire oration to the issue of whether or not Socrates did well by not defending himself (Εἰ καλῶς ἐποίησεν Σωκράτης μὴ ἀπολογησάμενος)[178]. Macarius responded that Jesus appeared in humility to fulfill the prophecies of his passion such as Is 53:2[179]. If Christ had disappeared he would have acted like the wizard-philosopher Apollonius. Christ would not have appeared to be God's son, but would have then been like magicians and sophists of this life (περιέργων καὶ σοφιστῶν)[180].

3.22 How is it said, Eliem ele (Ἠλιήμ' ἤλη) lima sabachthanei, Into your hands I commend my spirit?

The Hellene found the narrative of the passion to be utterly discordant: "But he with bitterness, and with very grim look, bent forward and declared to us yet more savagely that the evangelists were inventors (ἐφευρετὰς) and not historians (ἴστορας) of the events concerning Jesus. For each of them wrote

---

[173] Div. inst. 5.3.9 (142 MONAT). Eusebius attempts to devalue Apollonius' words before Domitian in his C. Hierocl. 42 (190 F./DES P.).

[174] CRAFER, Work of Porphyry, 377-79. Jerome also referred to the episode in Adv. Ioh. Hieros. 34 (PL 23, 404c; see HARNACK, Porphyrius, F. 63). HARNACK is apparently unwilling to discuss the parallel with Hierocles.

[175] As in Philodemus' περὶ παρρησίας. See also LAUSBERG, Handbuch, 761 on *licentia*, and H. SCHLIER, Art. παρρησία, TDNT V, 1967, 871-88.

[176] [Cicero] ad c. Herennium 4.36.48.

[177] Philostratus, Vita Apoll. 8.7.1 (Domitian and philosophy), 8.8, 10, 12 (the disappearance).

[178] Diss. 3 (22, app. crit. TR.; a scribe's *titulus*). In 3.7 (27,140-28,153 TR.), for example, Maximus defends Socrates' silence and condemns his judges.

[179] Apocr. 3.8 (64,3-10 BLONDEL), ET in CRAFER, Apocriticus, 53-57.

[180] Apocr. 3.8 (66,19-67,2 BLONDEL). On Macarius' response see FÖGEN, Die Enteignung, 208-209.

an account of the Passion which was not harmonious (σύμφωνον) but as contradictory (ἐτερόφωνον) as could be."[181] De Labriolle notes that the remark distinguishing evangelists and historians is fundamental to the position of Porphyry (or the Hellene in our perspective)[182]. The philosopher then quotes (with some pronounced textual variants) Mk 15:36, Mt 27:33, 34, 46, John 19:29-30, and Lk 23:46. His conclusion from these various accounts of Jesus' passion is:

> From this out-of-date and contradictory record (ἑώλου ἱστορίας καὶ διαφώνου), one can receive it as the statement of the suffering, not of one, but of many. For if one says "Into thy hands I will commend my spirit," and another "It is finished," and another "My God, my God, why hast thou forsaken me?" and another "My God, my God, why didst thou reproach me?" [Mk 15:34] it is plain that this is a discordant invention (ἀσύμφωνος ... μυθοποιία), and either points to many who were crucified, or one who died hard and did not give a clear view of his passion to those who were present. But if these people were not able to tell the manner of his death in a truthful way, and simply repeated it by rote (ἐρραψώδησαν)[183], neither did they leave any clear record concerning the rest.

Celsus argued that the gospels had been altered to cover over difficulties (C. Cels. 2.27 [156,1-5 Koet.]). Porphyry enjoyed investigating gospel accounts by looking for inconsistencies. Lactantius writes that Hierocles finds discrepancies (*contraria*) in Christian texts that contradict (*repugnare*) each other[184]. Unfortunately no examples of his exegetical work are left. Porphyry reminds his readers that ten thousand other more wonderful and divine stories are told about Pythagoras that are in harmony and that agree (ὁμαλῶς καὶ συμφώνως εἴρηται)[185]. These stories are in contrast to the Hellene's judgment on the "inconsistent mythmaking" (ἀσύμφωνος ... μυθοποιία) of the gospel writers. He probably noticed, for example, the difference between a "sponge" of vinegar and a "vessel" of vinegar[186]. Augustine denied that the accounts of the passion contradicted (*repugnare*) each other because one evangelist happened not to mention what another repeats[187]. Macarius also claimed that evangelists said the same things with different words (just as different words can refer to the same object). The terror of the earthquake and darkness did, however, affect the witnesses:

> No man, young or old, no woman, whether aged or virgin, no one of tender age, was possessed of steady reasoning, but all were senseless as though heaven's thunder were

---

[181] Apocr. 2.12 = HARNACK, Porphyrius, F. 15. ET in CRAFER, Apocriticus, 38-9.
[182] La réaction, 251.
[183] This word is used by the Christian (Macarius) in 3.23 (106,2 BLONDEL).
[184] Lact. Div. Inst. 5.2.14 (138 MONAT).
[185] Vita Pyth. 28 (49,12-13 DES PLACES).
[186] SCHALKHAUßER, Zu den Schriften, 38-40. He also refers to PG 10, 1379 where Magnus Crusius comments on Macarius' treatment of discrepancies in the passion narrative.
[187] De cons. 3.18.55 (CSEL 43, 343,21-25 WEIHRICH).

sounding in their ears, and all did different things, losing their wits and not preserving the sequence (ἀκολουθίαν)[188] of things, nor reason, nor habit. Wherefore those who wrote recorded their frenzy and the strange happening that then befell in word and deed, without seemliness, but without a word of falsehood ... And even if some woman or some man said something that was not consistent (ἀνακόλουθον) or was a solecism, all their [the evangelists'] desire was only to set this down.[189]

While not accusing the evangelists of falsehood, (as did Celsus, Porphyry, and Julian), Macarius is willing to admit some confusion in the witnesses' testimony about the events that the evangelists narrate[190].

3.23 How is it said: After rising he did not appear to Pilate?

Although the Hellene had objections to the concept of resurrection itself (see § 3.51 below), he found an argument against it based on the unreliability of the witnesses — an argument drawn from the rhetoric used in the law courts of the Roman empire:

There is also another argument (λόγος) whereby this unsound opinion (σαθράν ... δόξαν) can be refuted. I mean the argument about that Resurrection of His which is such common talk everywhere (θρυλουμένης),[191] as to why Jesus, after His suffering and rising again (according to your story), did not appear to Pilate who punished Him and said He had done nothing worthy of death, or to Herod King of the Jews,[192] or to the High-priest of the Jewish race, or to many men at the same time and to such as were worthy of faith (ἀξιοπίστοις), and more particularly among Romans both in the Senate and among the people. The purpose would be that, by their wonder at the things concerning Him, they might not by a public decree (δόγματι κοινῷ) condemn his faithful ones to death because of impiety (or "those who were persuaded by him" ἀσεβῶν τῶν πειθομένων αὐτῷ). But He appeared to Mary Magdalene, a coarse (χυδαία) woman who came from a wretched little village, and had once been possessed by seven demons, and with her another utterly obscure Mary, who was herself a peasant woman, and a few other people who were not at all well known [Mt 28:9, John 20:16]. Nevertheless according to Matthew, Jesus predicted to the high priest: "Henceforth shall ye see the Son of man sitting on the right hand of power, and coming with the clouds." For if He had shown Himself to men of note, all would believe through them, and no judge would punish them as fabricating

---

[188] The Christian uses this word in 4.26 (212,10 BLONDEL).

[189] Apocr. 2.17 (28-31 BLONDEL); ET in CRAFER, Apocriticus, 39-41.

[190] It is interesting that Hierocles is not included in Jerome's trio (text in HARNACK, Porphyrius, F.2 from Ep. 57.29). Hierocles' attack seems not to have been on the historicity of the Christian texts.

[191] J.-M. DEMAROLLE (La Chrétienté à la fin du IIIe s. et Porphyre, GRBS 12, 1971, 50) comments on this text and refers to other texts in which "Porphyry" (in Macarius) views Christianity as a universal phenomenon.

[192] An anonymous objector also confuses Herod the Great and Herod Antipas in Ambrosiaster, Quaest. de N. Test. 45 (442,22-25 SOUTER = RINALDI, Biblia Gentium, F. 340).

monstrous stories (μύθους ἀλλοκότους ἀναπλάττοντας). For surely it is neither pleasing to God nor to any sensible man that many should be subjected on His account to punishments of the gravest kind.[193]

The pagan's demand for a worthy witness is a protest against witnesses that have no credibility. Celsus also noted that Christ only appeared to a "hysterical female" when he should have appeared to those who condemned him and to all people (C. Cels. 2.55, 63, 70 [178,25; 185,1-2; 193,7-8 Koet.]). If persuasion (πειθώ)[194] is the chief goal of rhetoric, one can consider the persuasion of Christ's followers (τῶν πειθομένων αὐτῷ) to be due to the witness of coarse and insignificant women. In ancient rhetoric one of the issues in a trial was the *stasis* of "conjecture" in which one asked if a person "had committed" (*an fecerit*) a crime. The rhetoricians discussed the evaluation of witnesses in conjectural *stasis*. Hermogenes describes the demand for evidence (ἐλέγχων ἀπαίτησις): one must set "witnesses against witnesses and hold them in balance to determine which of any two is the more trustworthy (δεῖ δὲ καὶ ἀντιτιθέναι τοῖς μάρτυσι τοὺς μάρτυρας, πότεροι μᾶλλον ἀξιοπιστότεροι)"[195]. The Roman Senate would have provided far better credibility — and then the judges would not have put so many to death on account of Christ. The philosopher exhibits some compassion for the martyrs by concluding that it is not pleasing to God or an intelligent person that so many should be punished because of Christ. These persecutions, if they are not a literary fiction of the philosopher, would preclude (at least in this case) the ascription of authorship to Julian. The "common judgment" against the Christians establishes the illegality of the Christian faith, according to de Labriolle, who expresses it in this way: *non licet esse christianos* (it is not legal to be Christian)[196].

Macarius argues that Pilate would not have been a credible witness in the eyes of the Jews. Pilate would have been accused of crucifying a substitute[197]. Christ did not come to important ones (ἀξιολόγοις) in order that he not appear to need human support to confirm the story of the resurrection. Instead he

---

[193] Apocr. 2.14 = HARNACK, Porphyrius, F. 64. ET in CRAFER, Apocriticus, 43-4.

[194] In Cic., Brutus 15.59 the orator creates πειθώ, *suadam*. See other definitions in COOK, Protreptic Power, 105-6.

[195] Hermogenes, On Stases 3 (45,1.13-15 H. RABE, Hermogenis Opera, Rhetores Graeci VI, Leipzig 1913) / ET in R. NADEAU, Hermogenes' On Stases: A Translation with an Introduction and Notes, Speech Monographs 31/4, 1964, 397). Compare the discussion of the *stasis* in Rhet. ad Her. 2.2.3-2.7.11 and in particular the evaluation of testimony in 2.6.9. See also Aristot., Rhet. 1.15.13-20 and Quint. 3.6.73. LAUSBERG summarizes the issue in Handbuch, § 99-103, 150-65. The issue is used with reference to John's Gospel in COOK, Protreptic Power, 108.

[196] DE LABRIOLLE, La réaction, 285 n. 2.

[197] Apocr. 2.19 (33-36 BLONDEL); ET in CRAFER, Apocriticus, 44-46. The reference to Pilate is in 2.19 (33,9-10 BLONDEL).

appeared to women who could not persuade (πεῖσαι) anybody about the resurrection and to obscure disciples[198]. Macarius concludes: "This he did fittingly and well, that the story of the Resurrection might not be heralded by the help of the power of the world's rulers, but that it might be strengthened and confirmed through men who were inferior (εὐτελῶν) and made no show in their life according to the flesh, so that the proclamation might not be a human thing, but a divine."[199]

3.24 How is it said: And if they drink any deadly thing, it shall not hurt them?

Mark 16:18 (reading "deadly poison" θανάσιμον φάρμακον) provides the Hellene with an argument against the faith of any priest or bishop in the church. After quoting it he reasons:

> So the right thing would be for those selected for the priesthood (ἱερωσύνης), and particularly those who lay claim to the episcopate (ἐπίσκοπῆς) or presidency (προεδρίας),[200] to make use of this form of test. The deadly drug should be set before them in order that the man who received no harm from the drinking of it might be given precedence of the rest. And if they are not bold enough to accept this sort of test, they ought to confess that they do not believe in the things Jesus said. For if it is a peculiarity of the faith to overcome the evil of a poison and to remove the pain of a sick man, the believer who does not do these things either has not become a genuine believer (γνησίως οὐ πεπίστευκεν), or else, though his belief is genuine, the thing that he believes in is not potent but feeble.[201]

As in the case of the question in *Apocr.* 3.17 (discussed above in § 3.13), the philosopher does not believe that Christians can demonstrate their faith by fulfilling the demands of the gospel. He obviously found the verse in Mark to have absurd consequences which he expresses in his dilemma at the end of the objection: either people do not have genuine faith, or what they believe in is weak. Porphyry loved such dilemmas[202]. Macarius tries to avoid those consequences by pleading against a "too literal" (σωματικότερον) interpretation of the text which he understands allegorically (τροπικῶς)[203].

---

[198] 2.19 (35,18-21 BLONDEL).

[199] 2.19 (35,21-36,3 BLONDEL).

[200] DEMAROLLE remarks that this term is not attested in the most ancient Christian sources, but only in later ones, e.g. Greg. Naz., Or. 43.26 (SC 384, 186,21 BERNARDI; La Vocabulaire, 125 n. 93). DEMAROLLE has an excellent collection of Christian terms used by the pagan in the Apocriticus although she does not deal with their parallel usage in the Christian's responses.

[201] Apocr. 3.16 = HARNACK, Porphyrius, F. 96. ET in CRAFER, Apocriticus, 85-6.

[202] See § 2.3.26 and 2.3.32.

[203] Apocr. 3.24 (108-110 BLONDEL), ET in CRAFER, Apocriticus, 86-88. Macarius' terms from literary criticism are on 108,1 and 109,10 BLONDEL.

Otherwise the "word of faith" would be contradicted by the fact that unbelievers can drink "deadly drugs" and survive (a question of the drug's "power") and by the fact that unbelievers can also overcome the harm of those suffering from illness (by their knowledge about illness)[204]. Macarius allegorizes "deadly drug" to mean the baptism that frees believers from sin, and he allegorizes "illness" to mean things such as rainless seasons that were "healed" by individuals such as Polycarp[205].

3.25 How is it said: If I bear witness concerning myself, it is not true?

Only the *titulus* and the answer are preserved to the philosopher's objection concerning John 5:31 and 8:12-14[206]. He probably saw a bald contradiction between Jesus' statement in John 5:31, "I do not bear witness concerning myself" and Jesus' statement in John 8:12, 14 in which he does bear witness concerning himself. The Pharisees in 8:13 apparently had the same objection that the philosopher raised. Macarius notes that Jesus was considered a simple human (ἄνθρωπος ... ψιλός) by the Jews[207]. Jesus consequently rejected incorrect judgment concerning himself. Macarius' Christ says: "If (as you hold) I, being human, have witnessed concerning myself, my witness is not true. But if I am not only human but also God, truly I have borne witness saying: I am the light of the world and the truth and the life (John 8:12, 14:6)."[208] The attempt to find such contradictions is Porphyry's method. He, like Celsus before him, was unwilling to see Jesus as a Son of God or divine. Hierocles and Julian also shared the same antipathy toward the church's christology[209].

3.26 How is it said: If you believed Moses, you would believe in me?

The Hellene rejected John 5:46 out of hand:

Again the following saying appears to be full of stupidity (ἀβελτηρίας): "If you believed Moses, you would have believed me, for he spoke concerning me." But all the same nothing which Moses wrote has been preserved. For all his writings are said to have been burnt along with the temple. All that bears the name of Moses was written 1180 years

---

[204] Apocr. 3.24 (108,2-10 BLONDEL).

[205] 3.24 (108,23-24; 109,15-27 BLONDEL).

[206] Apocr. 2.11 (18-19 BLONDEL), ET in CRAFER, Apocriticus, 37-38. The objection is discussed in HARNACK, Porphyrius, F. 67.

[207] Apocr. 2.11 (18,7-8 and compare 19,4-5 BLONDEL).

[208] 2.11 (18,20-19,3 BLONDEL).

[209] See § 4.10 and 5.2.23 on these figures' christology.

afterwards, by Ezra and his entourage. And even if one were to concede that the writing is that of Moses, it cannot be shown that Christ was anywhere called God, or God the Word (θεὸν λόγον), or Creator (δημιουργόν). And pray who has spoken of Christ as crucified?[210]

The philosopher uses vituperative rhetoric in his description of Jesus' teaching as "stupidity"[211]. The reference to the lost writings of Moses is from 4 Esdras 14:21-26. Porphyry believed Moses was prior to the time of the Trojan war[212]. Goulet notes that this objection may come from Porphyry and that Julian may in turn have borrowed much from Porphyry[213]. Julian also objected to the belief that Moses asserted that the Christ would be God[214]. Their predecessor Celsus also did not believe that the prophets predicted someone like Jesus (C.Cels. 2.28, 29 [157,1-3.9-11.13-14 Koet.]). Macarius accepts the philosopher's view about the destroyed writings of Moses, but argues that the same spirit gave them to Moses and to Ezra[215]. Macarius sees the Christ everywhere in the OT: Moses mentions the Christ in Dt 18:15, 18; the burning bush mystically signifies the passion (Ex 3:2); the golden jar containing the manna is like the pure body containing the heavenly Word (Nu 24:17). Macarius finds the divinity of Christ prophesied in Ps 19:7, Is 2:3, and Ps 44:8. Here the argument between the Christian and the Hellene reverts to a question of the exegesis of the OT. It is likely that the pagan would have been unimpressed by the Christian's allegorical treatment of the Torah.

3.27 What is the meaning of: Unless you eat my flesh and drink my blood, you have no life in you?

The pagan believes that Jesus' teaching in John 6:54 is utterly repellent. The Hellene shows an interest in ethnographic description in his attack on Jesus' words:

---

[210] Apocr. 3.3 = HARNACK, Porphyrius, F. 68. ET in CRAFER, Apocriticus, 60.

[211] Porphyry uses ἀβελτέρως in De abst. 3.22.5 (180 B./P.).

[212] Eus., P.E. 10.9.12 = HARNACK, Porphyrius, F. 41. GOULET argues, I believe successfully, that HARNACK's F. 40 (from Eus., Chron. proem) is identical with F. 41 (Porphyre et le datation de Moïse, RHR 4, 1977, 137-164). He refers to Clement of Alexandria's mention of the text from 4 Esdras (Strom. 1.21.124.1-3) and argues that Porphyry (in the fragment in Macarius) could have built his figure of 1180 years by using dates in Clement's Stromata (1.21.141.4-5; Porphyre et le datation, 159-60).

[213] GOULET, Porphyre et le datation, 161. Julian also mentions the tradition of Ezra's role in NEUMANN, Iuliani, F. 14 = F. 34 (130,1-5 MASARACCHIA).

[214] See § 5.2.23.1 below.

[215] Apocr. 3.10 (74-5 BLONDEL), paraphrase in CRAFER, Apocriticus, 61. The remark on Ezra is in 74,9-13 BLONDEL.

That saying of the Teacher is a far-famed one (πολυθρύλητον), which says, "Unless you eat my flesh and drink my blood, you have no life in yourselves." Truly this saying is not merely beast-like and absurd (ἄτοπον), but is more absurd than any absurdity, and more beast-like than any fashion of a beast, that a man should taste human flesh, and drink the blood of members of the same tribe and race, and that by doing this he should have eternal life. For, tell me, if you do this, what excess of savagery do you introduce into life? What kind of evil more under a curse than this defilement (μύσους) could you invent (καινοτομήσετε)? Ears cannot bear it — I do not speak of the deed but also of this new and foreign deed of impiety (ἀνοσιούργημα). The phantoms of the Furies never revealed this to those who lived in strange ways, nor would the Potideans have accepted it unless they had been reduced by a savage hunger.[216]

He gives other examples of figures who became cannibals unintentionally (such as Thyestes and Harpagus). The philosopher further notes that not even in Scythia or among the Macrobian Ethiopians or "through the ocean-girdle round about" (ὠκεάνιου ζώνην ἐν κύκλῳ) do you find people who eat human flesh. He continues his critique:

What does this saying mean? For if it, allegorically understood (ἀλληγορικῶς), has some meaning more mystical (μυστικώτερον) and useful, the odor of the saying going inside through the hearing injures the soul. It disturbs the soul by its odiousness and harms the secret meanings (ἀποκρύφων τὸν λόγον) — makes the entire person dizzy because of the offense.

Not even the nature of irrational creatures (ἀλόγων) eats the flesh of its own. No teacher has ever made up a piece of play acting (τραγῴδημα)[217] as strange as this.

Observe, what has happened to you that you exhort (προτρέπεσθε) people easily convinced in an irrational manner (εὐχερεῖς ἀλόγως) to be won by persuasion (συμπείθεσθαι). Observe what kind of evil has gone careening about not only in the country but also in the cities. Wherefore it seems to me that neither Mark nor Luke nor even Matthew recorded this, because they regarded the saying as not a comely one, but strange and discordant, and far removed from civilized life. Even you yourself could scarcely be pleased at reading it, and far less any person who has had the advantage of liberal education (ἐλευθερίᾳ παιδεύσει).[218]

De Labriolle compares the philosopher's indignation toward the practice of cannibalism with Juvenal's similar expressions of outrage[219]. Much of the language in the text is Porphyrian. He accused the Christians of absurdity

---

[216] Apocr. 3.15 = HARNACK, Porphyrius, F. 69. ET mainly based on CRAFER, Apocriticus, 78-80. PÉPIN comments on the allegory in Porphyre, exégète d'Homère, 235-36. The letter must be acceptable, for Porphyry, before one can allegorize.

[217] Used by the Christian in Apocr. 2.21 (43,14 BLONDEL).

[218] Some of the translation is indebted to HARNACK, Kritik, 45-49 since CRAFER does not translate the entire text.

[219] Sat. 15.78-83 referred to in La réaction, 275.

(Eus. H.E. 6.19.5)[220] and noted their attempts to find hidden mysteries (κρυφίων μυστηρίων, Eus. H.E. 6.19.4). Porphyry was interested in the Barbarian nations around the ocean (*ad Oceanum per circuitum*)[221]. Porphyry argued against Stoic views of animals as ἄλογα, but could use the word in a general sense to describe animals[222]. The Hellene's word for defilement (μύσους) appears in *De abst.* 2.11.2 (80 B./P.) in a passage in which Porphyry notes that Egyptians and Phoenecians would eat human flesh before they would eat the flesh of a cow. It is a "defilement" to eat the flesh of the female (cow). Frassinetti points out that Porphyry was aware that cannibalism existed among the Scythians in *De abst.* 3.17.3 and 4.21.4 (II, 171 B./P.; III, 38 P./S./B.)[223]. Harnack responded that Porphyry had not written his treatise on abstinence when he wrote the *C.C.*[224]. The interest of the Hellene in ethnographic matters concerning food is certainly similar to Porphyry's interest expressed in *De abst.* The Hellene is obviously concerned with the rhetorical effectiveness of Christian discourse that is able to persuade people to accept statements such as the one he is discussing in John[225]. De Labriolle notes that the Hellene (whom he takes to be Porphyry) regarded John as being on a lower level of culture than that of the synoptics[226].

Macarius draws attention to the fact that babies eat milk made from the blood of the mother[227]. He goes on to give a eucharistic interpretation of the text and claims that in the text "this is my body and my blood" the bread and cup are not just symbols (τύπος) of the body and blood[228]. Christ made the earth from which come the bread and the wine. In analogy to the incarnation, Macarius' Christ says: "Therefore I give the bread and the cup, having sealed it as a result of the union wherein I the Holy One was linked with that which is earthly,

---

[220] Compare De abst. 3.5.4 and 3.22.6 (158; 181 B./P.) for uses of ἄτοπον.

[221] HARNACK, Porphyrius, F. 82; from Jerome, Ep. 133 discussed in § 2.3.30.

[222] For views of animals as without reason see De abst. 3.2.2 (153 B./P.). Porphyry uses the word in a general sense in De abst. 1.4.1 and 3.13.1 (I, 44; II, 168 B./P.). It is used by the Christian in Apocr. 2.21 (43,25 BLONDEL) and by the pagan in 3.32.

[223] FRASSINETTI, Sull'autore, 47 and see the originator of this argument (GEFFCKEN, Zwei Griechische Apologeten, 302 n. 1).

[224] HARNACK, Kritik, 140.

[225]On the protreptic branch of deliberative rhetoric see LAUSBERG, Handbuch, § 61.2.a. Aristotle speaks of the one who seeks to convince the audience to act in a certain way as ὁ προτρέπων in Rhet. 1.3.4.

[226] La réaction, 276 n. 1.

[227] Apocr. 3.23 (103,21-22 BLONDEL). ET in CRAFER 80-85. ANASTOS refers to Hippocrates, περὶ ἀδένων 16 (Oeuvres complètes d'Hippocrate 8, 572 Littré) καὶ τὴν τροφήν, ἥν τινα ἕλκουσιν [οἱ μαζοὶ] ἐπὶ σφᾶς, ἀλλοιοῦσιν ἐς τὸ γάλα (Porphyry's Attack, 441 n. 68).

[228] 3.23 (105,33-106,2 BLONDEL).

declaring that this is my flesh and blood."[229] Macarius concludes his response as follows:

> But the bread that is tilled in the blessed land of Christ, being joined with the power of the Holy Spirit, at one taste gives a person immortality. For the mystic bread that has inseparably acquired the Savior's Name, bestowed upon his body and blood, joins the one who eats it to the body of Christ, and makes him/her a member of the Savior....even so the body, that is to say, the bread, and the blood, which is the same as the wine, drawing the immortality of the immaculate Godhead, gives thereof to the one that shares it, and by its means leads him up to the Creator's pure abode itself.[230]

3.28 How is it said, You are of your father the devil?

The Hellene exhibits some sympathy for the slanderer (or "devil" διάβολος) in his attack on John 8:43, 44 ("You cannot hear my word, because you are of your father the devil (slanderer), and you wish to do the desires of your father")[231]. If children act according to the desire of their father, they do so fittingly (πρεπόντως) out of respect. Consequently if the father is evil, that name does not apply to the children. The pagan then attacks the concept of a "slanderer." Whom did he slander, he asks? The name "slanderer" is not original (κύριον) but came from some event. He continues:

> For if it is from a slander (διαβολῆς) that he is called Slanderer (διάβολος), among whom did he appear and work the forbidden action? Even in this, it is he who accepts the slander who will appear credulous (or "reckless" εὐχερής), while he that is slandered is most wronged. And it will be seen that it was not the Slanderer himself who did any wrong (ἠδικηκώς), but he who showed him the excuse for the slander.

A person who places a stake in the road is responsible and not the one who falls. Likewise the person who provided the occasion for the slander is the unrighteous one (ἀδικεῖ), and not the one who takes hold of (κατέχων) the slander or the one who receives it (λαβών). He concludes with a final dilemma: "Is the Slanderer subject to human affections (παθητός) or not (ἀπαθής)? If he is not, he would never have slandered. But if he is subject (ἐμπαθής), he ought to meet with forgiveness; for no one who is troubled by bodily ailments is judged as a wrong doer, but receives pity from all as being sorely tried." The philosopher's apparent view that a divine being (the Slanderer) could not be subject of affections is in accord with Plotinus' views on "The Impassability

---

[229] 106,13-14 BLONDEL.
[230] 106,29-107,6 BLONDEL.
[231] Apocr. 2.16 = HARNACK, Porphyrius, F. 71. ET based on CRAFER, Apocriticus, 48-9.

(ΑΠΑΘΕΙΑΣ) of Things without Body"[232]. The conclusion from this argument is apparently that it is not the devil (slanderer) who is evil, but the one who gave him the opportunity to "slander." The final dilemma, a technique of Porphyry, is also designed to elicit sympathy for the slanderer. If he is subject to human passions (or pain ἐμπαθής), then one should pardon him just as one has mercy on a person troubled by illness. Porphyry edited the writings of Plotinus who was interested in the polar relationship of the concepts ἐμπαθής and ἀπαθής[233]. The philosopher was well aware of Christian beliefs about the tempter or Satan (Apocriticus 3.18 and 3.27). His objection to the concept of an evil slanderer is reminiscent of Porphyry's replacement of the polarity "Christ and Satan" with "Achilles and Hector"[234].

Macarius interprets the phrase in 8:44 as "you belong to the father of the slanderer"[235]. The father of the slanderer is responsible for the slander[236]. The serpent in paradise slandered the human before God and slandered God before the human. An angel (Mac. quotes Job 15:25) dwelt (κατασκηνώσας) in the serpent and sowed the seed of slander in him[237].

3.29 How is it said, The ruler of this world is cast out?

The philosopher introduces John 12:31 ("Now is the judgment of this world, now the ruler of this world shall be cast outside") by claiming that anybody who reads that extremely subtle (τερθρείαν)[238] text will know that it is a tall tale (τερατολογίαν)[239]. He asks what is the judgment that happens then and who is the ruler of the world that is cast out? Anticipating the Christian's answers he argues: "If indeed you intend to say it is the Emperor

---

[232] Plot. Ennead. 3.6 titulus and 3.6.6 (I, 306; 314,1-2 H./S.) where he argues that intelligible realities are without affections.

[233] Plot. 4.7.13 and 5.9.4 (II, 162,2-163,14; 292,12-13 H./S.). ἀπαθής is used in Apocr. 4.21 (HARNACK, Porphyrius, F. 76) and in a probable fragment from Porphyry in Methodius (HARNACK, Porphyrius, F. 84) discussed in § 2.3.41.

[234] See § 2.3.42 above.

[235] Apocr. 2.21 (42-45 BLONDEL). Paraphrase in CRAFER, Apocriticus, 49-50.

[236] Apocr. 2.21 (42,10-14 BLONDEL).

[237] Apocr. 2.21 (44,8-15 BLONDEL).

[238] The Christian uses this word in Apocr. 4.29 (219,8 BLONDEL). Cyril describes the story of Zeus' shield and the Capitoline skull to be τερθρεία ... μειρακιώδη τερετίσματα in C. Jul. 6.194 (PG 76, 797b).

[239] Apocr. 2.15 = HARNACK, Porphyrius, F. 72. ET based on CRAFER, Apocriticus, 46-7.

(αὐτοκράτορα),[240] I answer that there is no sole ruler (for many rule the world), nor was he cast down. But if you mean some one who is intelligible and incorporeal, he cannot be cast outside. For where should he be cast, to whom it fell to be the ruler of the world?" If the Christian responds that there is another world, the philosopher wants to hear a convincing narrative to prove it (πιθανῆς ... ἱστορίας). If there is no other world (and two worlds are an impossibility), where is the ruler cast[241]? If he is cast into a place with spatial dimensions, then it is a world. If he is cast out unwillingly then the wrongdoer is the one who uses force to cast him out. The Hellene ends with another negative remark about women and the unclarity of the Gospels: "All this obscure nonsense (ἀσάφειαν) in the Gospels ought to be offered to silly women, not to men[242]. For if we were prepared to investigate such points more closely, we should discover thousands of obscure stories which do not contain a single word worth finding (treasure trove, ἕρμαιον)."

The text continues the philosopher's sympathy for the devil exhibited in the preceding comments on John 8:43,44. He accuses Jesus of telling tall tales that are obscure nonsense — thus engaging in vituperation of Christ. His apparent unwillingness to use other texts to explain this one shows that the philosopher does not adopt Porphyry's principle of "Homer by Homer" to understand the gospel of John. He also shares Porphyry's unwillingness to find a figurative meaning in Christian texts. The concept of an evil world ruler made no sense to the Hellene. The concept of Satan was also objectionable to Celsus (C. Cels. 6.42 [110,20-113,11 Koet.]).

Macarius remarks that the manuscripts contain the readings "cast out" and "cast down" and adopts the second one[243]. He interprets "world" (κόσμος) to be a synecdoche (whole for the part) in which the world is a metaphor (τροπικῶς ... μεταφορικῶς) for people whom the archdemon rules[244]. Macarius compares a similar use of κόσμος in Gal 6:14[245]. The "casting down" is not spatial (τοπικήν), but means to lose power[246].

---

[240] CRAFER, Apocriticus, 46 n. 1 notes that this may refer to Diocletian's division of the empire into divisions governed by an Augustus and a Caesar of both east and west. Possibly it simply refers to rulers of other nations (such as that of the Parthians).

[241] Plot., Ennead. 2.9.8 (I, 215,26-29 H./S.) is unwilling to contemplate the existence of another cosmos.

[242] Celsus also commented on the attraction of Christianity for women (C. Cels. 3.44, 55 [240,4; 250,20 KOET.]).

[243] Apocr. 2.20 (37-41 BLONDEL). Paraphrase in CRAFER, Apocriticus, 47-8. His discussion of text criticism is in BLONDEL 37,1-4.

[244] 2.20 (37,4-14, and see 38,11-13 BLONDEL). LAUSBERG, Handbuch, § 572-77 examines synecdoche. The Ad Her. 4.33.44 gives a succinct treatment of the figure.

[245] 2.20 (39,21-25 BLONDEL).

[246] 2.20 (41,1 BLONDEL).

3.30 How is it said: Coming to Jesus they did not break his bones?

The narrative about the piercing of Jesus' side (John 19:33-35) was unconvincing to the Hellene who introduces his quotation of John 19:33-34 with "It will be proved from another passage that the accounts of his death were all a matter of guesswork (κατεστοχάσαντα)."[247] He then continues:

> For only John has said this, and none of the others. Wherefore he is desirous of bearing witness to himself when he says: "And he that saw it has borne witness, and his witness is true" [19:35]. This is haply, as it seems to me, the statement of a simpleton (κέπφου). For how is the witness true when its object has no existence (μὴ ὑφεστῶτος)? For a person witnesses to something real (τοῦ ὄντος); but how can witness be spoken of concerning a thing which is not real[248] (μὴ ὄντος)?

The philosopher finds the single attestation of the story by John to indicate its unreliability — the statement of a feather-brain. The narrative must have seemed impossible in the Hellene's eyes because he concludes that the story of blood and water must be unreal. Eusebius records a very similar critique of the gospels in his *Demonstration of the Gospel* when he notes after a discussion of Mark's relationship to Peter that such authors are accused of fabricating things that are not real and freely ascribing things to the teacher that he did not do (ὡς τὰ μὴ ὄντα πλασάμενους, καὶ τῷ οἰκείῳ διδασκάλῳ τὰ μὴ πρὸς αὐτοῦ πραχθέντα κεχαρισμένως ἀναθέντας)[249]. The rhetoric of evaluation of witness is involved in this text. Above we referred to Hermogenes' statement that witnesses must be compared with each other to determine which one is more credible[250]. Plato uses language similar to this to discuss the nature of false statements in his *Sophist* (240e/241a): "And a false statement, I suppose, is to be regarded in the same light, as stating that things that are, are not, and that things that are not, are" (Καὶ λόγος οἶμαι ψευδὴς οὕτω κατὰ ταῦτα νομισθήσεται τά τε ὄντα λέγων μὴ εἶναι καὶ τὰ μὴ ὄντα εἶναι). Aristotle notes that recent witnesses establish whether something is or is not the case (εἰ ἔστιν ἢ μή)[251]. If there are no eye witnesses then the rhetorician must use probability (τὰ εἰκότα) which itself

---

247 Apocr. 2.13 = HARNACK, Porphyrius, F. 16. ET in CRAFER, Apocriticus, 41-2.

248 Instead of "real" and "unreal" GOULET (forthcoming in SC) translates "living" and "unliving." Compare the usage of this concept in Eusebius' Contra Hieroclem 42,9-11 (190 F./DES P.) where he quotes Apollonius' definition of a wizard: "with them the unreal (τὰ γὰρ οὐκ ὄντα) is made real, and the real becomes incredible (τὰ ὄντα ἄπιστα εἶναι)." The text is from Vita Ap. 8.7.3.

249 Eus., D.E. 3.5.96 (GCS Eusebius VI, 128,22-24 HEIKEL).

250 See § 3.23 above concerning Hermogenes, On Stases 3. The critique of the text in John is also discussed in COOK, Protreptic Power, 108.

251 Rhet. 1.15.16.

cannot be accused of bearing false witness (ψευδομαρτυριῶν)[252]. Another rhetorical handbook notes that to attack witnesses one can emphasize that something either could not have happened or did not happen (*fieri non potuisse ... non factum esse*). Another mode of attack is to point out the inconsistency of their evidence (*testimoniorum inconstantiam*)[253]. Celsus earlier attacked the narrative of Jesus' resurrection including the narrative of Thomas (C. Cels. 2.55 [178,23-26 Koet.]) by asking who saw the events. The "hysterical woman" was not a worthy witness in his view. The philosopher attacks the story from John using probability and also using the inconsistency of testimony (because only one witness includes the story).

Macarius is untroubled by the fact that only one evangelist included the story: "... he is naturally to be praised, because in his zeal he called this to mind ... This is true, even though he is the only one who says it, and the other three do not. For another is telling the truth when he tells of the beggar Lazarus and the rich fool, though the other three do not mention them."[254] Macarius also interprets the blood and water soteriologically.

3.31 How did Peter kill Ananias and Sapphira?

The Hellene mounted a sustained attack on the apostles Peter and Paul. In the MS of the *Apocriticus* there is a *titulus* before the question concerning Ananias and Sapphira (3.21): "The Beginning of the Other Subject from the Acts and the Apostle"[255]. This change is reflected in the structure of the *Apocriticus* which tends to discuss Peter and Paul in the rest of the text, even though subjects from the gospels are included in book four. Harnack surmised that it might point to an original division in the Hellene's work used by Macarius to construct his text[256]. Goulet shows by comparing Blondel's MS with Vaticanus 1650 (the *tituli* of Books I-III of the *Apocriticus*) that the *titulus* was (probably) originally a marginal comment and not from Macarius or the pagan[257].

The philosopher's objection is as follows:

This Peter is convicted of doing wrong in other cases also. For in the case of a certain man called Ananias, and his wife Sapphira [Acts 5:1-11], because they did not deposit the

---

[252] Rhet. 1.15.17.

[253] Ad Her. 2.6.9

[254] Apocr. 2.18 (32,1-2, 17-19 BLONDEL). Paraphrase in CRAFER, Apocriticus, 42-3.

[255] 49,19 BLONDEL: Ἑτέρας ὑποθέσεως ἀρχὴ ἐκ τῶν Πράξεων καὶ τοῦ Ἀποστόλου. This is in the list of *tituli* of book III.

[256] HARNACK, Kritik 8-9. CRAFER, Apocriticus, 95 n. 2 argues that it may support his theory of Hierocles' two volume work being used by Macarius.

[257] GOULET, Introduction, forthcoming.

whole price of their land, but kept back a little for their own necessary use, he put them to death, although they had done no wrong. For how did they do wrong, if they did not wish to make a present of all that was their own? But even if he did consider their act to be one of wrongdoing, he ought to have remembered the commands of Jesus, who had taught him to endure (συμπάσχειν) as many as four hundred and ninety sins against him [Mt 18:22]; he would then at least have pardoned (συγγνῶναι) one, if indeed what had occurred could really in any sense be called a sin. And there is another thing which he ought to have borne in mind in dealing with others—namely, how he himself, by swearing that he did not know Jesus, had not only told a lie, but had foresworn himself (ἐπιώρκησε), in contempt of the judgment and resurrection to come [Mt 26:69-75 par].[258]

The problem is one of inconsistency. Instead of forgiving Ananias and Sapphira, Peter kills them. He forgets that he had been guilty of a serious lie and oathbreaking himself when he denied knowing Jesus. The attack is an example of vituperative rhetoric since Peter's virtue is called into question. Rhetoricians praised qualities of the soul (or attacked them), and in Peter's case his injustice is the brunt of the philosopher's attack[259]. Wisdom, justice (*iustitia*), courage, and temperance and their opposites were the topics of epideictic rhetoric when it discussed the attributes of the soul[260]. Porphyry (or another philosopher) also attacked Peter using the narrative concerning Ananias and Sapphira[261].

Macarius notes that Ananias sinned against God and not Peter and so did not receive human forgiveness[262]. By trying to hide his actions Ananias tested the Holy Spirit (Acts 5:9). The Spirit and Ananias' conscience killed him[263]. Once Ananias had given by choice (τῇ προαιρέσει) to Christ, he was no longer in a position (κύριος) to appropriate it for himself[264].

3.32 How did Peter go forth when the prison was shut?

The leader (πρωτοστάτης) of the disciples was taught by God to scorn death, according to the Hellene[265]. The philosopher summarizes the account in Acts 12:3-11, 18, 19 and notes that Peter was the cause of the guards' being "led away" which he interprets to mean "beheaded" (ἀποτμηθῆναι). He argues:

---

[258] Apocr. 3.21 = HARNACK, Porphyrius, F. 25. ET in CRAFER, Apocriticus, 95-6.

[259] For praise of a person as *iustus* see Prisc. praeex. 7 — a description of praise and vituperation — quoted in LAUSBERG, Handbuch, § 376.

[260] Ad Her. 3.6.10-11. Compare the Rhet. ad Alex. 3, 1425b-1426a.

[261] Jer. Ep. 130.14, HARNACK, Porphyrius, F. 25. I. HILBERG notes that earlier editions of the letters had read *Porphyrius* instead of *philosophus* (CSEL 56, 194,16).

[262] Apocr. 3.28 (119-121 BLONDEL). Paraphrase in CRAFER, Apocriticus, 96-7. The passage concerning forgiveness is on 120,22-24 BLONDEL.

[263] 3.28 (121,8-15 BLONDEL).

[264] 3.28 (120,10-11 BLONDEL).

[265] Apocr. 3.22 = HARNACK, Porphyrius, F. 26. ET in CRAFER, Apocriticus, 97-8.

"So it is astonishing how Jesus gave the keys of heaven to Peter, if he were a man such as this; and how to one who was disturbed with such agitation (θορύβῳ) and overcome (καταπεπονημένῳ) by such experiences did He say 'Feed my lambs' [John 21:15]?" He interprets "sheep" (πρόβατα) to mean "the faithful (πιστοί) who have advanced to the mystery of perfection (or "sacrament of initiation" τελειώσεως ... μυστήριον)" and "lambs" to mean "the mass of catechumens (κατηχουμένων ... ἄθροισμα)" who are nourished by the simple milk of teaching. This is one of the few examples in which the philosopher is willing to allegorize a Christian text. He notes that after a few months of feeding sheep, Peter was crucified even though Jesus had said that the "gates of Hades will not overcome him [Mt 16:18]"[266]. He further notes that Paul condemned Peter in the text in Gal 2:12-13a. He concludes:

> In this likewise there is abundant and important condemnation (κατάγνωσις),[267] that a man who had become interpreter of the divine mouth (ὑποφήτην) should live in hypocrisy (ὑποκρίσει),[268] and behave himself with a view to pleasing men. Moreover, the same is true of his taking about a wife, for this is what Paul says: "Have we not power to take about a sister, a wife, as also the rest of the apostles, and Peter?" (1 Cor 9:5). And then he adds (2 Cor 11:13), "For such are false apostles, deceitful workers." If then Peter is related to have been involved in so many base things, is it not enough to make one shudder to imagine that he holds the keys of heaven, and looses and binds (λύειν ... δεσμεῖν), although he is fast bound, so to speak, in countless absurdities (or "offenses" ἀτοπήμασιν).

The rhetoric is that of vituperation. Porphyry had found Gal 2:12-13 to be an excellent basis for an attack against the apostles (see § 2.3.38 above). Peter's lack of courage in facing death shows a lack of virtue in the philosopher's eyes. Cowardice was a topic for vituperative rhetoric. Peter has no courage (*fortitudo*) in the face of death in contrast to Socrates' courageous (ἀνδρωδέστατα) enduring of his sentence of death (Xen, Mem. 4.8.1-2.)[269]. The Hellene finds it amazing (θαυμάσαι) that Jesus would entrust the keys and his lambs to a person so disturbed by such experiences (as the one in Acts 12). Peter's death (after a few months as a pastor) contradicts Jesus' promise in Mt 16:18 according to the philosopher (reading "him" instead of "it"). The

---

[266] The pagan reads αὐτοῦ instead of αὐτῆς. HARNACK finds an identical reading in Tatian (Kritik, 56).

[267] As a legal term it is used in Xen., Mem 4.8.1; compare LSJ s.v.

[268] For an example of this word (ἠθικῆς ὑποκρίσεως) in an ironic expression in which Medea calls the unrighteous Jason "blessed" see LAUSBERG, Handbuch, § 582; Trypho, Trop. 205.2.

[269] Ad Her. 3.6.10-11 includes courage and its opposite as topics of praise and vituperation. LAUSBERG, Handbuch, § 245 includes a text from Doxopater in which ἀνδρεία is a topic of epideictic rhetoric. Compare ἀνδρία in a discussion of praise and blame in Arist., Rhet. 1.9.5. Hermogenes gives a description of encomium and includes being ἀνδρεῖος in a discussion of qualities of the soul (Progymn. 7 [16,8 RABE]).

philosopher constructs another difficulty by quoting 1 Cor 9:5 immediately followed by 2 Cor 11:13 — thus turning Peter into a false apostle. Peter, involved in so many evils, should not have received the keys of heaven.

Macarius denies that Peter fled in fear; instead he knew that he had to preach in Rome (the "royal city") and then be crucified[270]. The death of the soldiers was due to Herod's rage and savagery and was not Peter's responsibility[271]. Peter's desire to save both Jews and Gentiles motivated his behavior in Antioch[272]. Paul was not speaking of Peter when he referred to the "false apostles"[273].

3.33 How did the Lord speak to Paul by a vision, and how did it happen that Peter was crucified?

The Hellene finds a contradiction between the words of the Lord to Paul in Acts 18:9-10, the words of Jesus to Peter in John 21:16, and the fact that both Paul and Peter were martyred:

> Let us look at what was said to Paul, "The Lord spoke to Paul in the night by a vision, Be not afraid, but speak, for I am with you, and no person shall set on you to hurt you" [Acts 18:9-10]. And yet no sooner was he seized in Rome than this fine fellow, who said that we should judge angels [1 Cor 6:3], had his head cut off. And Peter again, who received authority to feed the lambs [John 21:16, 17], was nailed to a cross and impaled on it (ἀνασκολοπίζεται).[274] And countless others, who held opinions like theirs, were either burned, or put to death by receiving some kind of punishment or maltreatment. This is not worthy of the will of God, nor of a pious man (ἀνδρὸς εὐσεβοῦς), that a multitude of people (μύριοι) should be cruelly (ἀπανθρώπως) punished through their relation to his own grace and faith, while the expected resurrection and coming remains unknown.[275]

He seems to show some compassion for the multitudes who have suffered martyrdom. The reference to the "pious man" is probably to Jesus whose resurrection and coming are mentioned in the same sentence. Porphyry (or the oracles of the gods) was willing to call Jesus a "pious" man as his work on oracles makes clear[276]. As in the case of Peter (Apocr. 3.22), the philosopher visualizes Paul being martyred almost immediately after his commission. His

---

[270] Apocr. 3.29 (122-24 BLONDEL). Summary in CRAFER, Apocriticus, 98-9. The text about Peter's reasons for escaping is on 122,13-16 BLONDEL.

[271] 3.29 (122,22-25 BLONDEL).

[272] 3.29 (123,1-14 BLONDEL).

[273] 3.29 (123,32-124,2 BLONDEL).

[274] Lucian uses this work for the crucified Jesus (De morte Peregr. 11, 13).

[275] Apocr. 4.4 = HARNACK, Porphyrius, F. 36. ET based on CRAFER, Apocriticus, 126.

[276] See § 2.2.3 above.

basic technique of finding patent contradictions between different texts in the Christian scriptures is also reminiscent of Porphyry.

Macarius' answer reflects the use of the rhetoric of vituperation by Hellenistic critics of Christian teachers and martyrs[277]. If they had been protected from punishments, the critics would claim that they could not endure, but would deny their faith. And if they overcame tortures [by dying], the critics would charge that they were not pious because they were so judged by providence[278]. Macarius answers that some were protected (like Daniel) and some suffered martyrdom (like Peter and Paul)[279]. Paul and Peter were also accused of doing their acts by magic[280]. This accusation is reminiscent of Porphyry's charge against the apostles[281]. Macarius answers that if Peter and Paul had suffered a common death, then it would not have appeared as special. If they had disappeared from before their tribunals, they would have appeared to have acted by magic[282]. Macarius makes a reference here to the story of Apollonius' disappearance (compare the pagan's use of the example in *Apocr.* 3.8). Consequently Peter and Paul suffered martyrdom. Before that time, for the sake of the proclamation, Christ protected them from the plots of Jews and Gentiles[283].

3.34 How did Paul circumcise Timothy?

In an introductory comment, the Hellene protests that the Christian has not answered the vital points (καίρια) in the questions at hand although he (the Christian) wants other passages to be set out. The philosopher then asks how Paul could say the words in 1 Cor 9:19. He also asks how, given that Paul calls circumcision "mutilation" (Phil 3:2, κατατομήν), could he circumcise Timothy in Lystra (Acts 16:23)[284]. His comment is: "Oh, the downright stupidity (βλακείας)[285] of it all! It is such a stage as this that the scenes in the theater portray, as a means of raising laughter." The philosopher asks how

---

[277] Apocr. 4.14 (181-83 BLONDEL). Summary in CRAFER, Apocriticus, 126-27. The critics' ψόγος is referred to on 183,2 BLONDEL, and they are described with the word ψέγονται on 183,4 BLONDEL. See LAUSBERG, Handbuch, § 61.3.b.

[278] 4.14 (183,3-8 BLONDEL).

[279] 4.14 (183,10-25 BLONDEL).

[280] 4.14 (182,22 BLONDEL). See GOULET's forthcoming translation of this passage (slightly mistranslated by CRAFER, Apocriticus, 127).

[281] Jerome, Tract. de Ps. 81. HARNACK, Porphyrius, F. 4 discussed in § 2.3.37.

[282] 4.14 (182,23-29 BLONDEL).

[283] 4.14 (182,14-16, 29-34 BLONDEL).

[284] Apocr. 3.30 = HARNACK, Porphyrius, F. 27. ET based on CRAFER, Apocriticus, 99-101.

[285] The Christian uses this word in Apocr. 4.14 (183,21 BLONDEL).

Paul, being free, could become slave to all. How can he gain all who yields[286] to all.

> For if he is without law to those who are without law, as he himself says, and he went with the Jews as Jew and with others in like manner [1 Cor 9:19-21], truly he was the slave of manifold baseness, and a stranger to freedom and an alien (ξένον καὶ ἀλλότριον) from it; truly he is a servant and minister (διάκονος) of other people's wrongdoings, and a notable zealot for unseemly things, if he spends his time on each occasion in the baseness of those without law, and appropriates their doings to himself. These things cannot be the teachings of a sound mind, nor the setting forth of reasoning that is free. But the words imply some one who is somewhat feverish[287] in mind, and weak in his reasoning. For if he lives with those who are without law, and also in his writings accepts the Jews' religion gladly [Phil 3:4], having a share in each, he is confused with each, mingling with the falls of those who are not good (ἀστείων), and subscribing himself as their companion. For he who draws a line through circumcision as to curse those who wish to fulfill it [Gal 1:8, 3:10], and then performs circumcision himself, stands as the weightiest of all accusers (κατήγορος) of himself when he says: "If I build again those things which I loosed, I establish myself as a transgressor" [Gal 2:18].

Paul's problem if one of intolerable contradiction — telling some that they will be cursed if they accept circumcision, he circumcises Timothy. Paul at times is like a Jew in his writings and accepts their religion gladly and at other times he lives with lawless people as a servant of unusual evils (ἀλλοτρίων κακῶν ὑπουργός). Such inconsistencies show that Paul's reasoning is not that of a healthy mind. The rhetoric is vituperative, but it is based on what the philosopher sees to be bald contradictions in the written words and behavior of Paul who becomes his own accuser (κατήγορος) — a term from the law courts[288]. Ambrose repeats arguments of pagans or Christians influenced by pagans that are related to those of the Hellene: if circumcision was good in Abraham's time, why is it useless now? Why would the maker of our bodies want such a thing in the first place? Is this part of the body against nature (*praeter naturam*) or is it in accord with nature (*secundum naturae*)? If God wanted many to practice this religion, he would not have discouraged many by the danger or disgrace of circumcision[289]. Ambrosiaster mentions an

---

[286] The codex reads καθηκεύων here and on 122,2 BLONDEL (the Christian speaking). BLONDEL conjectures καθυπείκων or πιθηκεύων (to ape).

[287] ὑποπήρου in the codex. BLONDEL conjectures ὑποπύρου.

[288] LAUSBERG, Handbuch, § 61.1 discusses accusation in judicial rhetoric; compare κατηγοροῦντι in Ari., Rhet. 1.10.6. An anonymous person accuses Paul of hypocrisy because of his words in 1 Cor 9:22 in Ambrosiaster, Quaest. de N. Test. 48 (443,15-17 SOUTER = RINALDI, Biblia Gentium, F. 664).

[289] COURCELLE, Anti-Christian Arguments, 159 with reference to Ambrose, De Abraham 1.4.29 (CSEL 32.1, 524,3 SCHENKL), Epist. ad Constantium 69.1 and 3 (CSEL 82.2, 178,1-11; 179,19-180,2 ZELZER) and in particular Ep. ad Irenaeum 64.1 (149,13-14 ZELZER) where they object that circumcision was formerly believed to be piety or faithfulness (*pietas*) and now is judged to be impiety (*impietas*).

anonymous objection to Paul's circumcision of Timothy given Paul's criticism of Peter's actions in Gal 2:12[290]. Porphyry found the Acts and Galatians to be problematic (see § 2.3.33-39 above), just as Macarius' Hellene and Ambrose's pagans do.

Macarius does not see any real problem in Paul's behavior[291]. Paul does not adopt all the behavior of the "many" (τῶν πολλῶν), but in order to teach Gentiles he does associate with them in fellowship[292]. Paul acts similarly toward the Jews although he does not think in a Jewish manner (ἰουδαϊκῶς). He adopts circumcision so that he can enclose (κατακλείσῃ) the Mosaic law in the Gospel[293]. Like a wise physician who in certain cases uses a normally harmful drug (in combination with others) to cure a person, at a certain time Paul adopts circumcision (that he knows to be hurtful, ἐπιζήμιον) to heal the disease that lurks in the Jews[294]. In this text the philosopher shows far more respect for Judaism than Macarius does. Harnack refers to Porphyry's sympathetic discussion of Judaism in *De abst.* 4.11.1-14.4 (17-23 P./S./B.)[295].

3.35 How does Paul say that he is a Roman, though he was not a Roman?

The Hellene attributes the next problem to Paul's forgetting his own words: he tells the tribune that he is a Roman (Acts 22:25, 27), even though he had earlier said that he was a "Jew (Acts 22:3) from Tarsus of Cilicia, brought up at the feet of Gamaliel and instructed according to the exact teaching of the law of my fathers"[296]. The conclusion the philosopher draws is that Paul is neither a Roman or a Jew although he attaches himself (προσκείμενος) to both. The next remarks show that the philosopher's interests are not confined only to vituperative rhetoric and the finding of logical problems in Christian discourse. He is concerned to show that Christians use language to persuade people to join their movement (an example of deliberative rhetoric which seeks to influence human action):

---

[290] Peter "fears" those who had been circumcised and so does Paul; Quaestiones de N. Test. 60 (453,15-16 SOUTER = RINALDI, Biblia Gentium, F. 683).

[291] Apocr. 3.37 (132-33 BLONDEL). Summary in CRAFER, Apocriticus, 101-102.

[292] 3.37 (133,3-6 BLONDEL).

[293] 3.37 (133,15-21 BLONDEL).

[294] 3.37 (133,24-34 BLONDEL).

[295] HARNACK, Porphyrius, F. 27. Compare Porphyry's remarks on the Hebrews in § 2.2.5 above.

[296] Apocr. 3.31 = HARNACK, Porphyrius, F. 28. ET based on CRAFER, Apocriticus, 102-103. The Hellene omits "in this city."

For he who plays the hypocrite and speaks of what he is not, comports himself according to roles that he has forged in his deceit, and by putting round him a mask of deceit, he cheats the clear issue and steals the truth, laying siege in different ways to the soul's understanding, and enslaving by the magician's art (τέχνη γοητείας) those who are easily influenced (τοὺς εὐχερεῖς[297] δουλούμενος). The man who welcomes in his life such a principle as this, differs not at all from an implacable and bitter foe, who enslaving by his hypocrisy the minds of those beyond his own borders, takes them all captive (αἰχμαλωτίζει) in inhuman fashion.

This concern with the "enslaving" power of discourse such as that of Paul is in line with the Hellenistic attitude toward early Christian language[298].

He sees Paul as pretending at one time or another to be a Jew, a Roman, a person without the law, and a Greek. He continues this line of attack: "... whenever he wishes he is a stranger (ὀθνεῖος) and enemy to each thing, by stealing into each, he has made each useless, stealing the choice ([of life], προαίρεσιν) by his flattery." Paul the liar claims to tell the truth (Rom 9:1), "For the man who has just now taken the form (σχηματιζόμενος) of the law, and today the Gospel, is rightly regarded as a criminal (κακοῦργος) and as deceitful both in private and public life (βίῳ κἀν πολιτείᾳ)." Porphyry uses some of the philosopher's words in his discussion of Origen (ὀθνεῖος, προαίρεσιν) and seems to share the view that Christianity is neither Judaism nor Hellenism[299]. It is as incoherent as Paul's life and teaching.

Macarius apparently concedes the point that Paul could not be a Jew and a Roman citizen[300]. He uses a play on the word ῥώμη (power) to argue that Paul was a Roman who preached in the *power* of the Holy Spirit[301]. Also because of the fact that Paul lived in the Roman empire he is a Roman[302].

3.36 A lost objection concerning faith and works (Romans 4:3)

The pagan may have attacked Christian teachings about faith and works. F. Turrianus (de la Torre)[303] quoted a long Greek passage from one of Macarius'

---

[297] The Christian uses this term for pagan critics in Apocr. 4.14 (183,6 BLONDEL). See also Hierocles in § 4.13.

[298] See COOK, Protreptic Power, 109, 121-25. Compare C. Cels. 2.46 (168,24-26 KOET.) and the remarks of Porphyry about Christian belief in the philosophy drawn from oracles (see § 2.2.3.1 above).

[299] Eus, H.E. 6.19.6-7, see § 2.3.3 and 2.3.4 above (F. 39, F. 1). The Christian also uses προαίρεσιν in Apocr. 3.39 (136,15 BLONDEL.

[300] Apocr. 3.38 (134-35 BLONDEL). Summary in CRAFER, Apocriticus, 103.

[301] 3.38 (134,22-25 BLONDEL).

[302] 3.38 (135,1-3 BLONDEL).

[303] F. TURRIANUS, Dogmaticus de Iustificatione, ad Germanos adversus Luteranos, Rome 1557, f 36b-38a. ET in CRAFER, Apocriticus, 164-66. The Greek text is in CRAFER's article Macarius Magnes, II, 558-59. SCHALKHAUßER, Zu den Schriften, 73-81

responses from the lost fifth book of the *Apocriticus* . The only scriptural text referred to is "Abraham believed God and it was reckoned to him as righteousness" — which could be from Rom 4:3 or James 2:23 (quoting Gen 15:6). Macarius describes Abraham in this way: "By doing these things he caused his faith to shine brighter than the sun. And together with his faith he works what is right, wherefore he is beloved of God and honored. For, knowing that faith is the foundation of virtuous action, he roots it deep, building upon it the multitude of mercies." Macarius continues in this way using examples drawn from architecture, farming and oil lamps. As in the attack on Paul's baptismal teaching (Apoc. 4.19), the Hellene probably saw contradictions in the NT's statements about faith and works — possibly between Paul and James.

3.37 How is it said: The law entered, that the transgression might abound?

Two of Paul's statements that apparently denigrate the law contradict his frequent attempt to persuade people to obey the law, according to the Hellene.

> For see here, look at this clever fellow's narration. After countless utterances which he took from the law in order to get support from it, he made void the judgment of his own words by saying, "For the law entered that the transgression might abound" (Rom 5:20); and before these words, "The goad of death is sin, and the strength of sin is the law" (1 Cor 15:56). He practically sharpens his own tongue like a sword, and cuts the law to pieces (τεμαχίζει) without mercy limb by limb. And this is the man who in many ways encourages (προτρεπόμενος) [others] to obey (πείθεσθαι) the law, and says it is praiseworthy to live according to it. And by taking hold of this ignorant (ἀπαίδευτον)[304] opinion, which he does as though by habit, he has overthrown his own judgments on all other occasions.[305]

He does not specify which of Paul's statements he is thinking of that support obeying the law, although in *Apocriticus* 3.33, he refers to several such verses (Acts 22:3 and Romans 7:12, 14). He uses the language of protreptic rhetoric (προτρεπόμενος) to describe Paul's practice of encouraging people to obey the law[306]. Paul's praise (ἐπαινετόν) of a life guided by the law is reminiscent of the rhetoric of praise (encomium)[307]. Paul's internal inconsistencies are an example of an ignorant or uneducated (ἀπαίδευτον) opinion. Rhetoricians occasionally referred to a person's education in the

---

gives the text and much of the context and discusses the various recensions of the text in TURRIANUS' writings.

[304] τεμαχίζει and ἀπαίδευτον also appear in one of the Christian's responses (Apocr. 3.42 [147,1 BLONDEL]).

[305] Apocr. 3.34 = HARNACK, Porphyrius, F. 31. ET based on CRAFER, Apocriticus, 107-108.

[306] LAUSBERG, Handbuch, § 61.2a and § 433.

[307] LAUSBERG, Handbuch, § 61.3a.

context of encomium or of building an argument based on the characteristics of a person[308]. Not only is the absence of logic in Paul an issue for the Hellene, but his unappealing character (ignorance in this case) is a focus of his critique.

Macarius explains that the law revealed human sin[309]. Sin was a goad of death for the soul which the law wielded (as any goad needs a wielder)[310]. The law is a custodian (παιδαγωγόν), and Paul does not destroy the law any more than one who takes a student from a custodian to a teacher nullifies the work of a custodian — rather Paul leads people to Christ through whom a person destroys sin[311]. The law is like the moon (and the prophets like the stars) when Christ shines as the sun with his crown of the twelve apostles. The law then becomes silent[312].

3.38 What is the meaning of: But you were washed, but you were sanctified?

Christian baptism as interpreted by Paul (1 Cor 6:11) was a shocking doctrine to the Hellene. He introduces his question with laughter by referring to the unstable sentiment (ἀνίδρυτον ... γνώμην) of Hector and quotes Il. 3.83. He opposes Hector's instability to the educated courage of the Greeks who keep silence while Hector speaks. His comparison is between Hector and the Christian:

Even so we now all sit in quietness here; for the interpreter of the Christian doctrines promises us and surely affirms that he will unravel the dark passages of the Scriptures. Tell therefore, friend,[313] to us who are following what you have to say, what the Apostle means when he says, "But such were some of you" (plainly something base), "but you were washed, but you were sanctified, but you were justified in the name of the Lord Jesus Christ, and in the Spirit of our God." For we are surprised and truly perplexed (ἀπορούμεθα) in mind at such things, if a person, when once he is washed from so many defilements and pollutions (μολυσμῶν ... μιασμῶν), shows himself to be pure (καθαρός); if by wiping off the stains of so much stupidity (βλακείας) in his life, fornication, adultery, drunkenness, theft, sodomy, poisoning, and countless base and disgusting things, and simply by being baptized and calling on the name of Christ, he is quite easily (ῥᾷον) freed from them, and puts off the whole of his guilt just as a snake

---

[308] Herm., Progym. 7 (16,3 RABE) has πῶς ἐπαιδεύθη in a discussion of encomium. Aphthonius, Progymn. 8 (36,11 SPENGEL) discussed ἀνατροφήν in a similar context. LAUSBERG, Handbuch, § 376 refers to the use of *educatio* to formulate arguments "from a person." He refers to Quint. 5.10.23.

[309] Apocr. 3.41 (141-44 BLONDEL). Summary in CRAFER, Apocriticus, 108. The function of the law is on 141,26-142,1 BLONDEL.

[310] 3.41 (142,32-35 BLONDEL).

[311] 3.41 (143,7-16 BLONDEL).

[312] 3.41 (143,26-30 BLONDEL).

[313] Cyril also uses this word (τᾶν) in his arguments with Julian in C. Jul. 9.317, PG 76, 988c.

puts off his old skin. Who is there who would not, on the strength of these, venture on evil deeds, some mentionable and others not, and do such things as are neither to be uttered in speech nor endured in deeds, in the knowledge that he will receive remission from so many criminal actions only by believing and being baptized, and in the hope that he will after this receive pardon from Him who is about to judge the living and the dead? These things incline (προτρέπεται) the person who hears them to commit sin, and in each particular they teach the practice of what is unlawful. These things have the power to set aside the training of the law, and cause righteousness itself to be of no avail against the unrighteous. They introduce into the world a form of society which is without law (ἄθεσμον ... πολιτείαν), and teach people to have no fear of ungodliness; when a person sets aside (ἀποτίθεται) a pile of countless wrongdoings simply by being baptized. Such then is the boastful fiction (πλάσμα) of the saying.[314]

The doctrine that baptism could purify a defiled person is simply incredible. The consequences are absurd — such a doctrine will encourage people to commit all kinds of evils and then to believe and be baptized so that God will forgive them. This argument from consequence was a tool in the rhetorician's arsenal[315]. Paul's teaching thus encourages the hearer (προτρέπεται) to commit sin. The philosopher's word for "encourage" is technical term of deliberative rhetoric used to express the rhetor's desire to persuade the audience to adopt a particular course of action[316]. His appeal to the concept of "ease" to ironically describe being freed from sins uses one of the rhetorician's final categories. Those categories served to provide the deliberative rhetorician with arguments for recommending (or discouraging) a particular course of actions[317]. The repetition of words for defilement and guilt amplifies the philosopher's shock that Paul could believe that calling on Christ's name will free a person from so many stains[318]. Some of the philosopher's language for defilement and putting away stains appears in a text in Porphyry in which he relates pollution to human sexuality and diet[319]. The ultimate result of the doctrine of baptism would be a lawless society that does not fear ungodliness (ἀσέβειαν). The philosopher would seem to agree with Plotinus' principle that "It is not lawful for those who have become wicked to demand others to be their saviors (σωτῆρας) and to sacrifice themselves in answer to their

---

[314] Apocr. 4.19 = HARNACK, Porphyrius, F. 88. ET based on CRAFER, Apocriticus, 138-39.

[315] See § 3.15 above on Apocr. 3.5.

[316] Aristotle, Rhet. 1.3.3-4 and see LAUSBERG, Handbuch, § 61.2.a and § 433.

[317] See LAUSBERG, Handbuch, § 375.4.

[318] Such repetition could be called congeries by the rhetoricians, LAUSBERG, Handbuch, § 406 (the use of synonymous words).

[319] De abst. 4.20.1-2 (33-34 P./S./B.; μολυσμόν ... μιασμούς ... ἀποθέσει corresponds with the philosopher's ἀποτίθεται). Porphyry also used the word for "fiction" in his literary criticism (see De antro 4 [4,28; 6,10.16 Sem.Cl. 609] where he uses it three times).

prayers."[320] De Labriolle approvingly follows Geffcken in asking if Porphyry [or the philosopher] would have been so critical with regard to the bloody rites of the taurobolium and criobolium[321].

The Christian responds by describing the mercy and grace of God who can forgive sins[322]. He mentions a "recent" event in which some accused individuals petitioned the king for a pardon. They had bowed before him as he was in procession. The charges were dropped, and they were not punished[323]. The baptismal water, when it is marked (σημειούμενον) by the name of Christ is able to bring purification (κάθαρσιν) and wipe clean the stain of sin[324]. Macarius gives a trinitarian interpretation of 1 Cor 6:11 (τριῶν ὑποστασέων ἐν οὐσίᾳ μιᾷ) because Paul was aware of Mt 28:19[325]. If anyone uses grace as an opportunity to sin, the Giver is not at fault — any more than a host is responsible for his guest's drunkenness[326].

3.39 Concerning how it is said: The form of this world is passing away.

The philosopher finds Paul's assertion that the form of this world is passing away (1 Cor 7:31) to be thoroughly unpersuasive:

What does Paul mean by saying that the form (σχῆμα) of the world passes away? And how is it possible for them that have to be as though they had not, and they that rejoice as though they rejoiced not, and how can the other old-wives' talk[327] be credible? For how is it possible (δυνατόν) for him that has to become as though he had not? And how is it credible (πιθανόν) that he who rejoices should be as though he rejoiced not? Or how can the form of this world pass away? What is it that passes away, and why does it do so?

---

[320] Plotinus, Ennead. 3.2.9 (I, 259,10-12 H./S.; ET ARMSTRONG, Plotinus, LCL, III, 72).

[321] La réaction, 274.

[322] Apocr. 4.25 (206-10 BLONDEL). Summary in CRAFER, Apocriticus, 139-43. The text on God's grace is on 206,19 and 207,7 BLONDEL. ANASTOS (Porphyry's Attack on the Bible, 440 n. 65) draws attention to problems in baptism in early Christianity including postponing baptism until the end of life to avoid the risk of sinning after baptism's purification — with reference to Eus., Vita Constantini 4.61-62 (GCS Eusebius I, 142-43 HEIKEL); Ps. Basil, Homilia exhort. ad sanct. bapt. 13.1ff (PG 31, 425bff), Gregory of Nazianzus, Oratio 40.11-46 (SC 358, 219-311 MORESCHINI/GALLAY), Gregory of Nyssa, Adversus eos qui differunt baptismum (GNO X/2, 357,1-370,27 POLACK).

[323] 4.25 (208,1-5 BLONDEL).

[324] 4.25 (208,31-35 BLONDEL).

[325] 4.25 (209,15-210,3 BLONDEL). CRAFER, wanting to give an ante-Nicene date for the Christian (the first "Macarius") argues that the text is an interpolation (Apocriticus, xviii, xxviii).

[326] 4.25 (210,4-8 BLONDEL).

[327] Celsus calls the narrative of creation in Genesis a myth for old women (C. Cels. 4.36 [306,27-28 KOET.]).

For if the Demiurge (δημιουργός) were to make it pass away He would incur the charge of moving and altering that which was securely founded. Even if He were to change the fashion into something better, in this again He stands condemned, as not having realized at the time of creation a fitting and suitable (ἁρμόζον ... πρέπον) form for the world, but having created it incomplete, and lacking the better arrangement. In any case, how is one to know that it is into what is good that the world would change if it came to an end late in time? And what profit (συμφέρον) is there in the order of phenomena being changed? And if the condition of the visible world is gloomy and a cause for grief, in this, too, the Demiurge is buried to the sound of music (καταψάλλεται), being piped down (καταυλούμενος) by reasonable charges against Him, in that He contrived the parts of the earth in grievous fashion, and in violation of the reasonableness of nature, and afterwards repented, and decided to change the whole. Perchance Paul by this saying teaches him that has, to be minded as though he had not, in the sense that the Creator, having the world, makes the form of it pass away, as though He had it not. And he says that he that rejoices does not rejoice, in the sense that the Creator is not pleased when He looks upon the fair and beautiful thing He has created, but, as being much grieved over it, He formed the plan of transferring and altering it. So then let us pass over this trivial saying with mild laughter.[328]

In this text the Hellene uses vituperative rhetoric against Paul's Creator who is "piped down" or "ridiculed" because of his failure to create the world correctly in the first place[329]. Porphyry's teacher, Plotinus, maintained that the heavens have an everlasting existence[330]. Plotinus vigorously attacked the Gnostics' view that the universe was created as a result of a moral failure[331]. This view is certainly in the background of the Hellene's shock that Christian texts could contemplate the destruction of an everlasting being. Celsus found it incredible that the world could be destroyed[332]. Several of the categories

---

[328] Apocr. 4.1 = HARNACK, Porphyrius, F. 34. ET based on CRAFER, Apocriticus, 118-19.

[329] HOFFMANN, Porphyry's 67 n. 47 refers to the rationality of the created order in Plot., Ennead. 2.9.8 (213,1-214,46 H./S.).

[330] Plot., Ennead. 2.1.2 and 2.1.4 (I, 132,1-133,22; 135,6-11 H./S.). A. H. ARMSTRONG notes that while the Christians may be in Plotinus' mind, he is directing his efforts mainly against Stoics and Stoicizing Platonists (Plotinus, Vol. 2, LCL, Cambridge 1966, 6).

[331] Plot., Ennead. 2.9.4 (I, 207,1-7 H./S.).

[332] C. Cels. 4.79, 6.52 (349,11-14; 123,2-6 KOET.). In middle Platonism there were three competing views: the world is uncreated and indestructible (e.g. the αἰωνίου κόσμου in Alcin., Didask. 14 170,26 [34 WHITTAKER/LOUIS] and compare anon. in Hippolytus 1.19.4 [76,12-13 MARCOVICH]), created and indestructible (Atticus in Eus., P.E. 15.6.4-5 = Fr. 4, ed. É. DES PLACES, Atticus Fragments, CUFr, Paris 1977), or created and destructible (anon. in Hippolytus 1.19.4 [77,16 MARC.]). See ANDRESEN, Logos, 276-283, 295. A. D. NOCK refers to another view: it is created, but by Divine Providence will not perish (Sallustius, lx with reference to Tzetzes, Chil. 10.527ff. (384 KIESSLING). The views are also discussed in Philo, De aeternitate mundi 4.13, Diod. Sic. 1.6.3, Aetius 2.4.2-17 (330,18-332,27 DIELS, Doxogr. Gr.). See also Ps. Sallustius, De diis 7, 13, 17 (12,24; 24,16; 30,6-7 NOCK) who also argues that the universe is uncreated and indestructible

(possible, suitable, profitable) that the philosopher uses to make objections to Paul's view of reality are "final categories" from the rhetorical handbooks (τὸ δυνατόν, τὸ πρέπον, τὸ συμφέρον). They were used to help formulate the arguments of deliberative rhetoric — encouraging people to act in a certain way[333]. It is not profitable that the Demiurge should alter the order of created things. He should have created it suitably in the first place, according to the Hellene. The philosopher is obviously uninterested in apocalyptic literature's view of the end of all things or in Stoic theories of the conflagration of the universe[334].

Macarius does not engage the philosopher with references to Christian apocalyptic hope, but calls his attention to the meaning of σχῆμα and relates it to "illusion" (φαντασία) and shadow[335]. He uses examples such as our transitory life and the changes in the human body, along with the deceitfulness of all things human such as royal power[336]. He refers to the fall of Cyrus, Babylon, and many queens[337]. Nothing created is changeless — all created things love to change[338]. Only the uncreated is without change[339]. Heaven is a created thing as are the earth, sea, and so forth[340]. He chooses to respond on a philosophical and linguistic level.

3.40 How is it said: No one goes to war at his own charge?

Paul's teaching in 1 Cor 9:7-10 is hypocrisy in the interest of securing a large sum of money from those who obey him, according to the philosopher. He introduces 1 Cor 9:7 with this comment: "That he dissembles the Gospel for

---

(ἄφθαρτον ... ἀγένητον). Plotinus, Ennead. 2.1.1-4, 2.9.7 (I, 131,1-136,33; 211,1-212,2 H./S..) argues for the same position. For bibliography on Macarius' text see RINALDI, Biblia Gentium, F. 656 and see the discussion in J. PÉPIN, Théologie cosmique et théologie chrétienne [Ambroise Exam. I. 1, 1-4], Paris 1964, 270-73.

[333] See LAUSBERG, Handbuch, § 61.2 and 375.1-4.

[334] See LSJ s.v. ἐκπύρωσις and CHADWICK's note on C.Cels. 8.72 (288,23 KOET.; Origen, 507 n.2). CHADWICK refers to Dio Chrys. Or. 36.39ff. Celsus seems to be involved in Platonists' arguments about the indestructibility of the world in C.Cels. 4.61 (332,16 KOET.; Origen, 234 n. 1).

[335] Apocr. 4.11 (169-73 BLONDEL). Summary in CRAFER, Apocriticus, 119-20. The linguistic discussion is on 169,12-13 BLONDEL.

[336] 4.11 (169,6-8; 169,15-16 BLONDEL).

[337] 4.11 (170,7-8, 10-15, 20 BLONDEL).

[338] 4.11 (172,21 BLONDEL).

[339] 4.11 (172,25 BLONDEL).

[340] 4.11 (172,26-29 BLONDEL).

the sake of vainglory, and the law for the sake of covetousness, is plain from his words..."[341]. He continues his attack:

And in his desire to get hold of these things, he calls in the law as a supporter (συνήγορον) of his covetousness, saying, "Or does not the law say these things? For in the law of Moses it is written, You shall not muzzle an ox that is treading out the corn" [1 Cor 9:9]. Then he adds a statement which is obscure (ἀσαφῆ) and full of nonsense (φλυαρίας),[342] by way of cutting off the divine forethought (πρόνοιαν) from the brute beasts (ἀλόγων), saying, "Does God take care of the oxen, or does he say it on our account? On our account it was written" [1 Cor 9:10]. It seems to me that in saying this he is mocking the wisdom of the Creator, as if it contained no forethought for the things that had long ago been brought into being. For if God does not take care of oxen, pray, why is it written, "He has subjected all things, sheep and oxen and beasts and birds and the fish" [Ps 8:8-9]? If He takes account of fish, how much more of oxen which plow and labor. Wherefore I am amazed at such an imposter, who pays such solemn respect (σεμνῶς περιέποντα) to the law because he is insatiable, for the sake of getting a sufficient contribution from those who are subject to him.

The text from Ps 8:8-9 (LXX) contradicts Paul's insistence that God is not concerned with animals[343]. Harnack refers to *De abst.* 2.31.1 (98 B./P.) where Porphyry exhibits his sympathy for domestic animals.[344] Porphyry was also concerned with the issue of God's providence[345]. The philosopher uses an argument from the lesser to the greater — "If God takes account of fish, how much more will he take account of oxen who plow and work."[346] Not only does Paul contradict scripture, but with his "unclear and nonsensical" argument about God's lack of concern for oxen, he pretends to admire the law for the sake of personal gain. The vituperative rhetoric used against Paul demonstrates his mishandling of the scriptures and his hypocrisy. Proposing a law (συνηγορία νόμου) was an exercise in deliberative rhetoric[347]. Appealing to a law was a technique of proof that Aristotle classified as "inartificial"[348]. Paul's use of the law is thoroughly objectionable in the eyes

---

[341] Apocr. 3.32 = HARNACK, Porphyrius, F. 29. ET based on CRAFER, Apocriticus, 103-104.
[342] The Christian uses this word in reference to the pagans' critique of the NT in Apocr. 4.14 (183,21 BLONDEL).
[343] Compare the discussion of the use of ἀλόγων for animals in Porphyry in the section § 3.27 above on Apocr. 3.15.
[344] HARNACK, Porphyrius, F. 29.
[345] Compare his use of πρόνοια in Ad Marc. 16 and 22 (22,7; 26,12 PÖT.) and his references to Plotinus' work on the subject in Vita Plot. 6.7 and 24.63 (I, 9; 34 H./S.). Besides the use in HARNACK, Porphyrius, F. 29 it also appears in De phil. ex orac. (178,6 WOLFF) and in nine other usages in Porphyry.
[346] Discussed by Aristotle in his Rhet. 2.23.4-5. See LAUSBERG, Handbuch, § 397.
[347] LAUSBERG, Handbuch, § 1139 with reference to Aphthonius, Progymnasmata 14 (53,25 RABE).
[348] Rhet. 1.15.2-3.

of the Hellene. Porphyry, like the philosopher, also accused the apostles of greed[349].

Macarius responds that the proclaimer of the Gospel loves the work when those who are taught give themselves with zeal to the evangelical laws with love[350]. Paul does not seek gifts for the sake of greed, but wants the Corinthians to be thankful[351]. Both the philosopher and Macarius ignore 1 Cor 9:15 where Paul rejects a salary!

3.41 How is it said: I would not that you should become partners with demons?

The philosopher finds a simple contradiction in Paul's advice to the Corinthians — "do not eat meat offered to idols"; "eating idol meat is a matter of moral indifference." He objects:

> Of course he forbids the eating of meat offered to idols and again he teaches that it is a matter of moral indifference (ἀδιαφορεῖν) saying that they need not be inquisitive (πολυπραγμονεῖν)[352] nor make an examination, but to eat things even though they be sacrificed to idols, provided only that no one speaks to them in warning (1 Cor 10:28). Whereas he is represented as saying, "The things which they sacrifice, they sacrifice to demons, but I would not that you should have fellowship with demons" (1 Cor 10:20). Thus he speaks and writes: and again he writes that such eating is a matter of moral indifference (ἀδιαφόρως), "We know that an idol is nothing in the world, and that there is no other God but one" (1 Cor 8:4), and a little after this, "Meat will not commend us to God, neither if we eat, are we the better, neither, if we eat not, are we the worse" (1 Cor 8:8). Then, after all this prating of extreme subtlety, he ruminated, like a man lying in bed, and said, "Eat all that is sold in the meat market, asking no questions for conscience' sake, for the earth is the Lord's and the fullness thereof" (1 Cor 10:25-26). Oh, what a stage farce (παίγνιον), got from no one! Oh, the monstrous inconsistency (ἀλλόκοτον ... ἀσύμφωνον) of his utterance! A saying which destroys itself with its own sword! Oh, novel kind of archery, which turns against him who drew the bow, and strikes him![353]

Paul's teaching is an arrow that returns to strike the archer. Like the philosopher, Porphyry was concerned with the contradictory or inharmonious nature of Christian teaching. Since idols do not exist according to Paul (1 Cor 8:4) and since Paul counsels the Corinthians to eat what they buy in the meat market (1 Cor 10:25), the philosopher concludes that meat offered to idols is a

---

[349] HARNACK Porphyrius, F. 4, Tract. de Psalmo 81. See § 2.3.37.

[350] Apocr. 3.39 (136-37 BLONDEL). Summary in CRAFER, Apocriticus, 104-5. The response of the hearers is on 136,10-13 BLONDEL).

[351] 3.39 (137,5-7 BLONDEL).

[352] This word is used by Porphyry in Ad Marc. 33 (36,17 PÖT.) and by the Christian in Apocr. 4.29 (218,1-2 BLONDEL).

[353] Apocr. 3.35 = HARNACK, Porphyrius, F. 32. ET based on CRAFER, Apocriticus, 108-10 9.

matter of moral indifference for Paul. An *adiaphoron* was something neither good or evil — especially in Stoic ethics[354]. The Hellene cannot understand how a Christian would eat what is sold in a market and also believe that food offered to idols is forbidden — something he derives form 1 Cor 10:20 and not Acts 15:29.

Macarius responds in the text in which he calls the philosopher's attention to Porphyry's *Philosophy from Oracles*[355]. Macarius begins his response with the use of the word εἰδωλοθύτων (meat sacrificed to idols) instead of the Hellene's ἱεροθύτων (sacrificial meat)[356]. The Christian's word is probably of Christian formulation although it appears in two Jewish texts that may have come under Christian influence. It probably means something like an animal sacrificed in the presence of an idol and eaten in the temple precincts[357]. Macarius summarizes and reformulates traditions in Porphyry's text on oracles in which he (Mac.) notes that people sacrifice things to demons of the air, the earth, and the underworld[358]. Then he remarks that Porphyry reserved this knowledge for his "intimates" (οἰκείοις)[359]. Whereas Macarius uses the word demon, Porphyry (De phil. ex orac.) uses the word "gods" for those who demand sacrifice. By the time Porphyry wrote his *De abst.* he preferred to use the term "demon" for those divinities that demand animal sacrifice[360]. As we remarked in the discussion above concerning the identity of the pagan, Macarius' reference to Porphyry shows that the philosopher cannot be simply identified with Porphyry. Some kind of hypothesis is needed of a fictional philosopher who is a composite of Porphyry's work and perhaps that of others such as Hierocles and even Julian.

Macarius' solution is that Paul forbids Christians to take part in sacrifices to demons[361]. Paul permits them to eat meat sold in the market. The butchers

---

[354] See LSJ s.v. Sextus Empiricus (Pyrr. 3.22.177-78) discusses the concept. He registers his shock that the Stoics held homosexual intercourse to be an ἀδιάφορον (Pyrr. 3.24.200).

[355] Apocr. 3.42 (145-47 BLONDEL). Summary in CRAFER, Apocriticus, 109-113. The reference to Porphyry is on 145,26-146,2 BLONDEL.

[356] 3.42 (145,2 BLONDEL).

[357] B. WITHERINGTON III, Not so Idle Thoughts about EIDOLOTHUTON, TynB 44, 1993, 237-54. The two Jewish texts are 4 Mac 5:2 and Sib. Or. 2:96. WITHERINGTON may be correct about the meaning of the word, even if Jewish scholars coined the word.

[358] Macarius' words are similar but not identical to those of Porphyry. See Eus., P.E. 4.9.2-4.9.3 (SC 262, 128-131 ZINK/DES PLACES) = SMITH, Porphyrii, 314F, 315F.

[359] 3.42 (146,3 BLONDEL); Eus., P.E. 4.7.1-4.8.2 = SMITH, Porphyrii 303F, 304F (WOLFF, Porphyrii, 109ff).

[360] De abst. 2.42.1-3 and compare 2.37.5 (109; 104 B./P.).

[361] 3.42 (145,24 BLONDEL).

work for profit to sustain life and are not in the business for the sake of magic. They consequently do not butcher meat for demons[362].

3.42 How is it said: He is a debtor to do the whole law?

The pagan believes Paul has made his hearers crash against the law and the gospel because of his conflicting teaching about the nature of the law in Galatians and Romans:

> Then he suddenly turns like a man who jumps up from sleep scared by a dream, with the cry, "I Paul bear witness that if anyone do one thing of the law, he/she is a debtor to do the whole law" (Gal 5:3). This is instead of saying simply that it is not right to give heed to those things that are spoken by the law. This fine fellow, sound in mind and understanding, instructed in the accuracy of the law of his fathers (Acts 22:3), who had so often cleverly (δεξιῶς) recalled Moses to mind, appears to be soaked with wine and drunkenness; for he makes an assertion which removes the ordinance of the law, saying to the Galatians, "Who bewitched you that you should not obey the truth," that is, the Gospel (Gal 3:1). Then, using terrifying expressions (δεινοποιῶν), and making it fearful (φρικτόν)[363] for anyone to obey (πείθεσθαι) the law, he says, "As many as rely on works of the law are under a curse" (Gal 3:10).[364] The one who writes to the Romans "The law is spiritual" (7:14), and again, "The law is holy and the commandment holy and just," (7:12) places under a curse those who obey (πειθομένους) that which is holy! Then, completely mixing (φύρων) up the nature of the question, he confounds the whole matter and makes it obscure (ζοφερόν), so that the one who listens to him almost grows dizzy, and dashes against the two things as though in the darkness of the night, stumbling over the law, and knocking against the Gospel in confusion, owing to the ignorance of the one who leads him by the hand.[365]

By omitting the full text of Gal 5:3 (the phrase about circumcision), the Hellene alters Paul's thought and makes the conclusion easier to follow: Paul counsels people to pay no heed to the law. The Hellene apparently prefers to leave the issue of circumcision out of this critique[366]. He finds Paul's assertion in Gal 3:1 to be contradictory to Paul's favorable statements toward the law. He engages in vituperative rhetoric by accusing Paul of drunkenness (as he earlier accused Jesus of drunkenness in *Apocr.* 3.19). He sees Paul using the techniques of rhetorical *pathos* to create fear in his hearers — so that they will

---

[362] 3.42 (147,19-23 BLONDEL).

[363] Used by the Christian in Apocr. 3.40 (138,15 BLONDEL).

[364] An anonymous source in Ambrosiaster questions Paul's curse since he also claims that "in the law no one is justified in the eyes of God" in Quaest. de N. Test. 66 (459,21-27 SOUTER = RINALDI, Biblia Gentium, F. 689).

[365] Apocr. 3.33 = HARNACK, Porphyrius, F. 30. ET based on CRAFER, Apocriticus, 105-106.

[366] But see Apocr. 3.30 for his question about Paul's circumcision of Timothy.

adopt Paul's position toward the law[367]. By creating the fear of a curse in his hearers Paul draws them away from the law. His word for obedience (πείθεσθαι) is the rhetoricians' word for the goal of their discourse — to persuade the audience at any cost[368]. The philosopher probably sees Paul in this unfavorable light. Paul's favorable statements about the law in Romans 7:12 and 14 are in conflict with his attempt to place those who obey the law under a curse (Gal 3:10). In the Hellene's eyes Paul has mixed everything up into a complete and dark mess — leaving hearers dizzy and stumbling in the night against both the law and the gospel!

Macarius is not impressed by the objection and argues that since Christ fulfilled the law, Christians need not be subject to it anymore[369]. He denies that Paul is engaging in vituperative rhetoric (ψέγων) against the law in Gal 5:3[370]. Rather Paul is saying that the law was difficult to carry out and that since Christ fulfilled it he freed a person from much trouble (καμάτου)[371]. Macarius examines some of the minuter points of the law and catalogues them in an attempt to show how difficult it is to fulfill the entire law — e.g. if a mouse touches a vessel the vessel must be destroyed[372].

3.43 How is it said: In the latter times some shall depart from the faith?

Paul's teaching about virginity is confusing to the philosopher — since Paul praises virginity and denounces those who teach against marriage:

> In his epistles we find another saying like these, where he praises virginity, and then turns round and writes, "In the latter times some shall depart from the faith, giving heed to seducing spirits, forbidding to marry and commanding to abstain from meats" (1 Tim 4:1, 3). And in the Epistle to the Corinthians he says, "But concerning virgins I have no commandment of the Lord" (1 Cor 7:25). Therefore the one that remains a virgin (παρθενεύων) does not do well, nor will the one that refrains from marriage persuaded by the guidance of an evil being (ὑφηγήσει πειθόμενος), since they have not a command from Jesus concerning virginity. And how is it that certain women boast

---

[367] The Christian use of arguments from fear is discussed in COOK, Protreptic Power, 118-19. On the use of such arguments in rhetoric see Aristot., Rhet. 2.1.8-9; 2.5.1-15. Compare LAUSBERG, Handbuch, § 257.3 for the rhetoricians' techniques for creating these emotions in the audience. MARTIN, Antike Rhetorik, 161.

[368] Cic., de or. 1.31.138 *primum oratoris officium esse dicere ad persuadendum accomodate* (quoted in LAUSBERG, Handbuch, § 33). See also Plato, Gorgias 453a for Gorgias' definition of rhetoric as "the creator of persuasion" (πειθοῦς δημιουργός).

[369] Apocr. 3.40 (138-40 BLONDEL). Summary in CRAFER, Apocriticus, 106-107. The reference to Christ fulfilling the law is on 140,1-2 BLONDEL .

[370] 3.40 (138,3 and see 140,14 BLONDEL).

[371] 3.40 (138,1-5 BLONDEL).

[372] 3.40 (139,3-33; [the mouse] 139,25-26 BLONDEL).

(κομπάζουσι)[373] of their virginity as if it were some great thing, and say that they are filled with the Holy Spirit similarly to her who was the mother of Jesus (Lk 1:34)? But we will now cease our attack on Paul, knowing what a battle of the giants he arms against him by his language. But if you are possessed of any resources for replying to these questions, answer without delay.[374]

The philosopher does not take any obvious position on the subject of virginity. Harnack notes that Porphyry recommended the single life in his letter of his wife Marcella! He recommended abstention from sex (Ad Marc. 28 [32,4 Pöt.]) and told Marcella that he did not pay attention to her as a woman (Ad Marc. 33 [36,17-18 Pöt.]). All the body brings forth is corrupt to the gods (Ad Marc. 33 [36,21-22 Pöt.])[375]. The Hellene's objection is not to Paul's praise of virginity (1 Cor 7:1, 8?), but to the fact of Paul's change of heart in 1 Tim 4:1, 3 (he of course ascribes that letter to Paul). The fact that Paul admits to have no command from the Lord concerning virgins (1 Cor 7:21) is even more fateful to Paul's praise of virginity according to the philosopher. Those who boast in their virginity have no ground from the Lord. Other pagans responded to the Christian praise of virginity by noting that the Vestal virgins and priestesses of Pallas were in the service of the state[376].

Macarius responds in praise of virginity but notes that Jesus did not command the difficult lifestyle of virginity[377]. He proceeds to catalogue a number of heretical groups that teach against marriage, the eating of meat, and the consumption of wine[378].

---

[373] Compare Hierocles in Eus., C. Hierocl. 2.26 (102 F./DES P.) where κεκομπάκασιν is used for Peter and Paul's boastful tales about Jesus.

[374] Apocr. 3.36 = HARNACK, Porphyrius, F. 33. ET based on CRAFER, Apocriticus, 113.

[375] Porphyry, De abst. 4.11.4 (18 P./S./B.) notes that the Essenes held marriage in contempt. In Sententiae ad intelligibilia ducentes 32, Porphyry claims that the philosophical soul will not participate in food and drink in itself and will not even participate involuntarily in sexual pleasures (ἀφροδισίων δὲ τῶν φυσικῶν οὐδὲ τὸ ἀπροαίρετον) or at least not beyond the uncontrolled fantasy that occurs in sleep (34,8-10 LAMBERZ).

[376] COURCELLE, Anti-Christian Arguments, 161 referring to Ambrose, De virginibus 1.4.14-15 (PL 16, 203B-C). Symmachus, Relatio 11, 14 argues against the decision to remove public support of the vestals (pagan priests also lost their support) in a speech he places on the mouth of Rome herself. Rome claims their virginity is dedicated to the public safety (*saluti publicae dicata uirginitas*; CUFr, Prudence 110-11 LAVARENNE).

[377] Apocr. 3.43 (148-52 BLONDEL). Summary in CRAFER, Apocriticus, 113-116. He praises virginity and ascribes it to προαιρέσεως on 149,21-32 BLONDEL. On the ambivalent attitude toward marriage among Christians in late antiquity see G. CLARK, Women in Late Antiquity. Pagan and Christian Lifestyles, Oxford 1994, 52-3, 73-6.

[378] 3.43 (151,10-152,5 BLONDEL).

3.44 How is it said: We who are alive shall be caught up in the clouds?

Paul's statements in 1 Th 4:15-17 are simply incredible to the philosopher, because even if God could make them come to pass, they are against the coherence of nature. He introduces the verses by saying, "let us consider another sophism of his that is stupid and erroneous" (ἐμβρόντητον καὶ πεπλανημένον)[379]. After Paul's text he continues:

> Here is a thing that indeed rises in the air and shoots up to heaven, an enormous and far-reaching lie.[380] If this is sung in a stage part to irrational creatures, they will bleat and croak with an enormous din when they hear of people in the flesh flying like birds in the air, or carried on a cloud. For this boast (κόμπος) is a mighty piece of quackery, that living things, pressed down by the burden of physical bulk, should receive the nature of winged birds, and cross the wide air like some sea, using the cloud as a chariot. Even if such a thing is possible, it is monstrous (τερατῶδες),[381] and against the sequence [of nature] (ἀκολουθίας ... ἀλλότριον). For nature which created all things from the beginning appointed places befitting the things which were brought into being, and ordained that each should have its proper sphere, the sea for the water creatures, the land for those of the dry ground, the air for winged creatures, and the ether for heavenly bodies. If one of these were moved from its proper abode, it would be annihilated on arrival in a strange condition and abode.

He gives examples such a putting a land creature in water — it will drown. If an astral body is removed from the ether, it will not survive.

> Neither has the divine and active Word of God (ὁ ... τοῦ θείου λόγος) done this, nor ever will do it, although He is able to change the lot of the things that come into being. For He does not do and purpose anything according to His own ability, but according to the sequence [of nature] (ἀκολουθίαν). He preserves things, and keeps the law of good order (εὐταξίας). So, even if He is able to do so, He does not make the earth to be sailed over, nor again does He make the sea to be plowed or tilled; nor does He use His power in making virtue into wickedness nor wickedness into virtue, nor does He adapt a man to become a winged creature, nor does He place the stars below and earth above. Wherefore we may reasonably declare that it is full of twaddle (ἐξηχίας) to say that people will ever be caught up into the air. And Paul's lie becomes very plain when he says, "We which are alive." For it is thirty[382] years since he said this, and no body has anywhere been

---

[379] Apocr. 4.2 = HARNACK, Porphyrius, F. 35. ET based on CRAFER, Apocriticus, 121-22.

[380] Celsus also accused the disciples of lies (C. Cels. 2.13 [140,20-21 KOET.]).

[381] The incongruities of Philostratus' narrative concerning Apollonius' aversion of the Ephesian plague reveal its mythical and miracle-mongering character for Eusebius (μυθῶδές τε καὶ τερατῶδες) in C.H. 36.4 (180 F./DES P.).

[382] HARNACK, Kritik, 74 corrects the text to "three hundred" in accordance with 4.5. He also mentions the possibility that 330 could have been the original reading. GOULET argues for "300" based on a text of Nicephorus (p. 307 PITRA) who speaks of 300 years "since the divine and apostolic preaching" and the fact that "330" would put too many years between Paul and Jesus (Introduction, forthcoming).

caught up, either Paul's or any one else's. So it is time this saying of Paul became silent, for it is driven away in confusion.

The concept of ἀκολουθία (coherence, consistency, suitability) is used against Paul. It was adopted by patristic writers[383]. People flying in the clouds is too bizarre for the philosopher (or his animals) to contemplate. That earthly beings have to remain in their own elements was a topos of Hellenistic philosophy[384]. Porphyry, however, had no trouble with the idea of Abaris the priest (the "ether walker" αἰθροβάτης) flying on the arrow of Apollo. Some suppose Pythagoras to have done the same thing when he spoke to followers in Metapontum and Tauromenium on the same day (Vita Pyth. 29). Porphyry was also concerned — like the philosopher — with the issue of what God could do[385]. Porphyry objected to the statement that "all things are possible to God." People flying in the air is absurd to the philosopher. Even if God could do such a thing, God would not — because it is not suitable and in good order[386]. Celsus also revered the created order and believed that if one thing were changed in the normal course of nature, that all would be destroyed — an argument he used against he incarnation (C. Cels. 4.5 [278,8-9 Koet.]). The philosopher's belief that God does not act according to his ability but according to what is suitable is probably an argument of Macarius that he inserted in the pagan's mouth, according to Richard Goulet[387]. The response of Macarius in

---

[383] See LSJ s.v. (III). DEN BOER, A Pagan Historian, 207, n. 16 describes the word as a conventional term of Christian theology with reference to J. DANIELOU, Akolouthia chez Grégoire de Nysse, RSR 28, 1953, 219-49. It was used by the Stoics (SVF 1.98, and see VON ARNIM's index for five other uses). The term is used to express logical consequence in Alcin., Didask. 36 189,32 ([72 W./L.]; and see WHITTAKER's comment on 154, note 575). Plotinus uses the word in the sense of a "chain of causation" (Ennead. 3.3.2 [I, 274,2 H./S.]).

[384] M. KERTSCH, Traditionelle Rhetorik und Philosophie in Eusebius' Antirrhetikos gegen Hierokles, VigChr 34, 1980, 152, 166 n.30. See Eusebius, Contra Hieroclem 6.12-23 (110-112 F./DES P.). KERTSCH quotes Philo, Quod deterius potiori insidiari soleat 151: "Therefore all creatures die easily if they leave their corresponding elements ..." Patristic writers adopted the topos. In De civ. d. 22.11 (CChr.SL 48, 829,1-830,46 DOMBART/KALB), Augustine describes Platonist philosophers who argue against the heavenly existence of resurrected bodies because the element earth cannot exist in heaven. J. PÉPIN believes that this may be Porphyry's argument (Théologie cosmique, 453 n. 2, 457, and 418-61 for the general topos). The order is: earth, water, air, and heaven (fire). GOULET (Introduction) argues that Macarius may have transformed this argument about the vertical order of elements into an argument about the proper place for living beings.

[385] See § 2.3.21 and compare Apocrit. 4.24.

[386] SCHALKHAUßER, Zu den Schriften, 71-2 refers to TURRIANUS' somewhat confused quotation of this text.

[387] Porphyre et Macaire, 451 with reference to SCHALKHAUßER, Zu den Schriften, 71-72. Only TURRIANUS conserves the answer of Macarius which must be added to BLONDEL's text of Macarius' response in 4.30.

Apocrit. 4.30 (to 4.24) contains a text with a statement that God can do all, but only acts in according with the natural order of things.

The chronological reading (30 years) is probably corrupt. Since the philosopher mentions "three hundred years" in 4.5, one can assume a similar figure here. It is another indication that the philosopher is probably a composite figure created from critics such as Porphyry and others — including perhaps Julian who made specific reference to 300 years having passed since Christ's time[388].

Macarius' answer is that the clouds are angels[389]. He refers to Dan 7:13 and Mt 25:31 to support his interpretation of the clouds[390]. If clouds can draw up water, angels can draw up people[391]. Paul identifies his humanity with all people, and so he uses the term "we" in reference to the return of Christ[392].

3.45 What is the meaning of the judgment in the Apocrypha? How is it said: The heaven shall be rolled together as a scroll, and the stars shall fall as leaves?

This *titulus* (given above) introduces *Apocrit.* 4.6 and 4.7 — texts that the Hellene takes from the Apocalypse of Peter. He argues:

> By way of giving plenty of such sayings, [after *Apocr.* 4.5 which refers to Mt 24:4, 5], let me quote also what was said in the Apocalypse of Peter. He thus introduces the statement that the heaven will be judged together with the earth. "The earth shall present all people to God in the day of judgment, itself too being about to be judged, together with the heaven which contains it." No one is so uneducated or so stupid (ἀπαίδευτος ... ἀναίσθητος) as not to know that the things which have to do with earth are subject to disturbance, and are not naturally such as to preserve their order, but are uneven; whereas the things in heaven have an order which remains perpetually alike, and always goes on in the same way, and never suffers alteration, nor indeed will it ever do so. For it stands as God's most exact piece of work. Wherefore it is impossible that the things should be undone which are worthy of a better fate, as being fixed by a pure divine ordinance (ἀκηράτῳ θεσμῷ). And why will heaven be judged? Will it some day be shown to have committed some sin, though it preserves the order which from the beginning was approved by God, and abides in sameness always? Unless indeed some one will address the Creator, slanderously asserting that heaven is deserving of judgment, as though the judge would endure such marvelous and great things to be spoken against it [heaven or the

---

388 C.Gal. 191E (136,7-8 MASARACCHIA).

389 Apocr. 4.12 (174-77 BLONDEL). Summary in CRAFER, Apocriticus, 121-22. He (174,18-19 BLONDEL) equates clouds and angels.

390 4.12 (174,26-175,4 BLONDEL).

391 4.12 (176,34-177,1 BLONDEL).

392 4.12 (177,5-9 BLONDEL).

judge?] (ὡς τὸν κριτὴν ἀνασχόμενον κατ᾽ αὐτοῦ τινα τερατεύεσθαι οὕτω θαυμαστόν, οὕτω μεγάλα).[393]

The Hellene's NT apparently included the Apocalypse of Peter[394]. His philosophical position is that earth changes whereas the heavens have an order (τάξιν) that never changes and never will change. As in the critique of 1 Cor 7:31 in *Apocrit.* 4.1, the philosopher does not countenance a Stoic conflagration of the universe. The Apocalypse of Peter's insistence that the earth and heaven will be judged (besides all people) is against his view of reality. Since heaven has committed no sin, it does not deserve to be judged — it has preserved the order (τάξιν) given it by the creator.

3.46 How is it said: The heaven shall be rolled together as a scroll, and the stars shall fall as leaves?

The Hellene continues with another quotation that apparently comes from the Apocalypse of Peter which in turn took the text from Is 34:4. He finds the idea that heaven will be dissolved and earth pass away to be utterly preposterous:

> And it makes this statement again, which is full of impiety, saying: "And all the might of heaven shall be dissolved, and the heaven shall be rolled together as a scroll, and all the stars shall fall as leaves from a vine, and as leaves fall from a fig tree" (Apoc. of Peter, Is. 34:4).[395] And another boast (κεκόμπασται) is made in portentous (τερατώδους) falsehood and monstrous quackery (ὑπερφυοῦς ἀλαζονείας):[396] "Heaven and earth shall pass away, but my words shall not pass away" (Mt 24:35). For, pray, how could anyone say that the words of Jesus would stand, if heaven and earth no longer existed: Moreover,

---

[393] Apocr. 4.6 = HARNACK, Porphyrius, F. 89. ET based on CRAFER, Apocriticus, 129-30. My translation of the last phrase reads θαυμαστά as does CRAFER. CRAFER translates the phrase: "as having allowed the judge to speak any portents against it which are so wondrous and so great." HARNACK (Kritik, 79) has: "als ob der Richter sich eine so erstaunliche Kunde von irgend jemandem vorschwindeln ließe." HOFFMANN notes that the text cannot be satisfactorily translated in its present form (Porphyry's, 75).

[394] HOFFMANN, Porphyry's, 74 n. 55 refers to Eusebius (H.E. 6.14.1) who notes that Clement (*Hypotyposeis*) discussed the canonical NT and disputed writings such as Jude, the Catholic Epistles, Barnabas, and the Apocalypse of Peter. HOFFMANN also refers to Plotinus' views on the permanence of the heavenly order (Ennead. 2.1.4 [I, 135,10-11 H./S.]). J. K. ELLIOTT refers Macarius' excerpt to section 4 (Ethiopic) of his edition of the Apocalypse (The Apocryphal New Testament A Collection of Apocryphal Literature in an English Translation, Oxford 1993, 599, 602).

[395] ELLIOTT, Apocryphal New Testament, 599, 602 relates this text to section 5 (Ethiopic) of his English edition. Compare E. HENNECKE/W. SCHNEEMELCHER, New Testament Apocrypha, Vol. 2, Philadelphia 1965, 670-71 (for texts from sections 4 and 5 of the Ethiopic version that correspond to the Macarius fragments).

[396] Celsus also accused Jesus of arrogance and boasting (C. Cels. 2.7, 32 [132,32; 159,6 KOET.]).

if Christ were to do this and bring heaven down, He would be imitating the most impious (ἀσεβεστάτους) of men, even those who destroy their own children. For it is acknowledged by the Son that God is Father of heaven and earth when He says: "Father, Lord of heaven and earth" (Mt 11:25). And John the Baptist magnifies heaven and declares that the divine gifts of grace are sent from it, when he says: "No one can do anything, except it be given him from heaven" (John 3:24). And the prophets say that heaven is the holy habitation of God, in the words: "Look down from the holy habitation, and bless your people Israel" (Dt 26:15). If heaven, which is so great and of such importance in the witness (μαρτυρίαις) borne to it, shall pass away, what shall be the seat thereafter of Him who rules over it? And if the element of earth perishes, what shall be the footstool of Him who sits there, for He says: "The heaven is my throne, and the earth is the footstool of my feet" (Is 66:1).[397]

If the statements from the Apocalypse of Peter and from Mt 24:35 are true, then the other witnesses that the philosopher appeals to create a problem: If heaven is God's dwelling, and if heaven and earth pass away, where will God dwell? And since God is father of heaven and earth, if Christ destroys them he will imitate the most impious of people who destroy their own offspring. Piety was one of the virtues that was the foundation of natural law[398]. In arguments about changing sacrifices, the rhetor could point to the fact that piety (εὐσεβείας) makes the gods rejoice[399]. Plato was horrified by impiety toward the gods (Resp. 615c). Socrates was prosecuted because of his alleged impiety (Euthyphro 5c). Piety as a fundamental value in Greco-Roman culture provides a basis for the philosopher's shock that Christ (or God) could destroy heaven and earth. The philosopher does not mention Plotinus' view that the stars are gods that possess virtue and have an intellect, but such a view might be in the background of his shock at the Apocalypse of Peter[400]. The Hellene's appeal to the testimony of the wise was an accepted form of argument in rhetoric. Theon includes the testimony of famous people such as poets, politicians, and philosophers (ἐπισήμων ἀνδρῶν ποιητῶν τε καὶ πολιτικῶν καὶ φιλοσόφων μαρτυρίας) in the arguments useful for proving a thesis[401]. The witnesses are in apparent conflict with the apocalyptic texts that the philosopher is attacking. Like Macarius' pagan, an anonymous Christian (or pagan) also objected to the concept of the universe passing away based on the assumption that the elements are not corruptible.[402]

Macarius deals with problem of God's dwelling (if heaven and earth pass away) by noting that God had a place to dwell before the creation of heaven

---

[397] Apocr. 4.7 = HARNACK, Porphyrius, F. 90a. ET in CRAFER, Apocriticus, 130-31.
[398] LAUSBERG, Handbuch, with reference to Quint. 7.4.5.
[399] Rhet. ad Alex. 1423b.
[400] Plot., Ennead. 2.9.8 (I, 214,31-38 H./S.).
[401] Theon, Progymnasmata 12 (122,24-25 SPENGEL).
[402] Ps. Just., Quaest. et resp. ad Orthod. 94, 450a (142 OTTO). See RINALDI, Biblia Gentium, 331. The objector quotes Is 34:4 and Mt 24:35.

and earth[403]. God only possesses the quality of eternity (ἀϊδιότητος ... ἀξίωμα)[404]. Macarius relates the destruction of the created order to the fall of humanity. The suffering of creation after the fall was not originally planned[405]. When God again makes the flesh of humanity incorruptible, the creation will receive an even greater beauty[406].

3.47 What is the meaning of the monarchy?

The philosopher continues his attack on Christian teaching after his critique of baptism (Apocr. 4.19). His attack on the Christian concept of "monarchy" (μοναρχία) is designed to prove the polytheistic world view:

> But let us make a thorough investigation concerning the single rule (μοναρχίας) of the only God and the manifold rule (πολυαρχίας) of those who are worshipped as gods. You do not know how to expound the doctrine even of the single rule. For a monarch is not one who is alone in his existence, but who is alone in his rule. Clearly he rules over those who are his fellow-tribesmen, people like himself, just as the Emperor Hadrian was a monarch, not because he existed alone, nor because he ruled over oxen and sheep (over which herdsmen or shepherds rule), but because he ruled over people who shared his race and possessed the same nature. Likewise God would not properly (κυρίως) be called a monarch, unless He ruled over other gods; for this would befit His divine greatness and His heavenly and abundant honor.[407]

The philosopher's linguistic argument is straightforward: if the Christians accept the use of the word "monarchy" to describe the rule of God, then they have to accept the existence of other gods for God to rule. Monarchy does not mean God is alone, but rules alone — just as Hadrian was not alone but ruled other people of like nature to himself (τῶν ὁμογενῶν τὴν αὐτὴν φύσιν ἐχόντων). At this stage the philosopher gives no definition of "gods," but one can assume that he included beings such as "Minerva" (see Apocr. 4.21). Porphyry believed in the divinity of angels (ἄγγελοι θεῖοι) whom he also called "good demons." They watch over human affairs[408]. Those who do not believe the gods exist and that God's providence (προνοίᾳ θεοῦ) does not govern all things will be punished. Porphyry may not be thinking of

---

[403] Apocr. 4.16, (185-90 BLONDEL). Summary in CRAFER, Apocriticus, 131-33.

[404] 4.16 (189,14-18 BLONDEL).

[405] 4.16 (186,16-27 BLONDEL).

[406] 4.16 (187,9-12 BLONDEL).

[407] Apocr. 4.20 = HARNACK, Porphyrius, F. 75. ET in CRAFER, Apocriticus, 143. Nicephorus, Antirrhetica (in PITRA, Spicilegium Solesmense, 309-310) also has the text of 4.20. He includes the first lines of 4.21 in his text of the objection in 4.20 (If you say that angels ... changed or lost by the difference of the names). Those lines give the philosopher's concept of "gods." See the ET of 4.21 (by CRAFER) given below.

[408] Ad Marcellam 21 (26,4-11 PÖT.).

Christians, because his atheists believe the universe is governed by irrational motion (ἀλόγῳ φορᾷ) and they live an "unlawful" life in their efforts to destroy belief in the gods (ἃ μὴ θέμις)[409]. The philosopher's defense of polytheism is reminiscent of that of Celsus and many other Hellenistic thinkers[410].

Macarius responds that only God is eternal and uncreated — the gods are created and so do not share the same nature with God[411]. Hadrian ruled over other humans because of the law of power and tyranny and not by a law in conformity with those beings of like nature [to Hadrian] (θεσμῷ τῆς ἀκολουθίας τῶν ὁμοουσίων ἄρξας). He enslaved those of like nature (ὁμογενεῖς) by force and violence. His human nature, in other words did not make him a ruler[412]. Angels have the name "god" by relation (θέσις) to God and not by nature (φύσις). Consequently one should worship God and not angels[413].

3.48 What is the meaning of the angels having immortality? What is the meaning of the tables being written with the finger of God?

The difference between the words "angels" and "gods" is merely verbal according to the Hellene.

> At any rate, if you say that angels stand before God, who are not subject to feeling and death, and immortal in their nature, whom we ourselves speak of as gods, because they are close to the divinity, why do we dispute about a name? And are we to consider it only a difference of nomenclature? For she who is called by the Greeks Athena is called by the Romans Minerva; and the Egyptians, Syrians, and Thracians address her by some other name. But I suppose nothing in the invocation of the goddess is changed or lost by the difference of the names. The difference therefore is not great, whether a man calls them gods or angels, since their divine nature bears witness to them, as when Matthew writes thus: "And Jesus answered and said, You do err, not knowing the scriptures, nor the power of God; for in the resurrection they neither marry nor are given in marriage, but are as the angels in heaven" (Mt 22:29-30). Since therefore He confesses that the angels have

---

[409] Ad Marcellam 22 (26,11-16 PÖT.). See however Harnack, Porphyrius, F. 1.

[410] See § 1.7.2 and the notes there (e.g. C. Cels. 7.68). Cp., for example, Plotinus, Ennead. 2.9.9 (I, 215,26-217,56 H./S.). Compare Lactantius' response in Div. Inst. 2.16 (believe not in Jupiter and celestial beings but in God and the angels).

[411] Apocr. 4.26 (211-13 BLONDEL). Summary in CRAFER, Apocriticus, 143-44. Nicephorus also quotes the text in the Antirrhetica (in PITRA, Spicilegium Solesmense 311-16). Macarius' remarks on the difference between God and the gods are on 211,19-23; 212,27-29 BLONDEL .

[412] 4.26 (212,9-11 BLONDEL).

[413] 4.26 (211,10-15, 213,1-11 BLONDEL). Angels can turn away from God to darkness (BLONDEL 212,2-4). Macarius is making use of a Stoic distinction (SVF 3.308 from Diog. Laert. 7.128).

a share in the divine nature, those who make a suitable object of reverence (σέβας)[414] for the gods do not think that the god is in the wood or stone or bronze from which the image is manufactured, nor do they consider that, if any part of the statue is cut off, it detracts from the power of the god. For the images of living creatures and the temples were set up by the ancients (παλαιῶν) for the sake of remembrance, in order that those who approach there might come to the knowledge of the god when they go; or, that, as they rest and purify themselves from other things, they may make use of prayers and supplications, asking from them the things of which each has need. For if a man makes an image (εἰκόνα) of a friend, of course he does not think that the friend is in it, or that the limbs of his body are included in the various parts of the representation; but honor is shown towards the friend by means of the image. But in the case of the sacrifices that are brought to the gods, these are not so much a bringing of honor to them as a proof (δεῖγμα) of the inclination (προαιρέσεως) of the worshippers, to show that they are not without a sense of gratitude. It is reasonable that the form of the statues should be the fashion of a human (ἀνθρωποειδῆ), since the human is reckoned to be the fairest of living creatures and an image of God (εἰκὼν θεοῦ). It is possible to confirm this doctrine from another saying, which asserts positively that God has fingers, with which He writes, saying, "And he gave to Moses the two tables which were written by the finger of God" (Ex 31:18). Moreover, the Christians also, imitating the erection of the temples, build very large houses, into which they go together and pray, although there is nothing to prevent them from doing this in their own houses, since the Lord certainly hears from every place.[415]

Here the philosopher gives a clear description of his concept of "gods" — they are without suffering (ἀπαθεῖς), immortal, incorruptible, and are close to divinity (θεότητος). Like the philosopher, Celsus also defended the use of different names for God (C. Cels. 1.24, 5.41 [74,4-10; 44,25-45,4 Koet.])[416]. The philosopher ignores Macarius' claim in 4.26 that God is different from the angels because he is uncreated and eternal. This is one of many such indications that the *Apocriticus* is not a real dialogue even though some of the trappings of a dialogue are present. The antagonists refer to each other, but the debate is one sided. The Christian answers the Hellene's critique, but the Hellene does not get to attack the Christian's answers.

---

[414] The Christian uses this word in Apocr. 4.29 (218,7 BLONDEL).

[415] Apocr. 4.21 = HARNACK, Porphyrius, F. 76. ET in CRAFER, Apocriticus, 145-46. Nicephorus, Antirrhetica (in PITRA, Spicilegium Solesmense, 317-18) also has the text of 4.21, although he puts the first sentences in the text of 4.21 above (the material up to "changed or lost by the difference of the names") at the end of his version of 4.20. For bibliography on the text see RINALDI, Biblia Gentium, F. 392.

[416] See FÉDOU, Christianisme, 232 for a discussion of Hellenistic syncretism with reference to Ps. Aristotle De mundo 7, 401a,1-27 (98-99 LORIMER). Varro argues that names are unimportant and identifies Jupiter with the God of the Jews in Aug., De cons. ev. 1.22.30 (28,16-20 WEIH.).

Porphyry was quite interested in the issue of images of the gods, as Harnack points out[417]. He also, like the Hellene, commented on the inconsistency of the Christian critique of pagan worship, given the fact that Christians themselves (or rather their Jewish predecessors) worshipped in temples[418]. The third century saw the construction of numerous Christian edifices[419]. Porphyry also venerated the traditions of the old ones ("the greatest fruit of piety (εὐσεβείας) is to honor the divine in accord with the traditions of the fathers" [τὰ πάτρια])[420]. Porphyry, however, was willing to devalue the worship of images: "The impious person (ἀσεβής) is not the one who does not treat the statues of the gods with honor (τὰ ἀγάλματα τῶν θεῶν μὴ περιέπων), but the one who adopts the opinions of the many concerning God."[421] Like the philosopher, Celsus defends the worship of images by arguing that only a child would believe they are gods[422].

Macarius describes the blessed heavenly life of the angels — which people may seek[423]. They do not engage in sexual intercourse, and consequently some Christians avoid marriage, in imitation of the angels[424]. Christians wanting this blessed life do not make images of the angels[425]. Linguistic expressions such as "finger of God" are used to aid the human understanding — even though God has no actual feet or hands. Created beings cannot view the uncreated in its "naked" form[426]. The angels that Abraham saw (Gen 18) also appeared in human form even though they were not of human nature. Abraham made no image of them to worship[427].

---

[417] HARNACK, *Porphyrius*, F. 76 with reference to De imag. 2 ἀνθρωποειδεῖς (2* BIDEZ), 6 βρέτας (8* BIDEZ), 8 ἀνθρωποειδές (12* BIDEZ).

[418] HARNACK, *Porphyrius*, F. 79, from Aug., Ep. 102.16, discussed in § 2.3.43.

[419] DE LABRIOLLE, *La réaction*, 283 with reference to Eus., H.E. 7. 13, 8.1.5 and other texts. Where is the archaeological evidence for Eusebius' claims?

[420] Ad Marcell. 18 (22,25 PÖT.), De abst. 2.4.4, 3.1.5, 3.9.5, 3.18.1 (74; 153, 164; 171 B./P.; various usages of παλαιοί).

[421] Ad Marcell. 17 (22,22-23 PÖT.).

[422] C. Cels. 7.62 (212,13-14 KOET.) and see § 1.7.1. GEFFCKEN's article is still of fundamental importance: Der Bilderstreit des heidnischen Altertums, ARW 19, 1916-19, 286-315.

[423] Apocr. 4.27 (214-15 BLONDEL). Summary in CRAFER, *Apocriticus*, 147-48. Nicephorus also quotes the text in the Antirrhetica (in PITRA, Spicilegium Solesmense, 319-28).

[424] 4.27 (214,3-14 BLONDEL).

[425] 4.27 (214,15-16 BLONDEL).

[426] 4.27 (214,25-215,14 BLONDEL).

[427] 4.27 (215,15-34 BLONDEL).

3.49 How was the divine begotten, becoming flesh (σαρκωθέν) in Mary?

The philosopher's last objection related to polytheism and the use of images in worship is an attack on the Christian doctrine of incarnation:

> But even supposing any one of the Greeks were so light-minded (κοῦφος) as to think that the gods dwell within the statues (ἀγάλμασιν), his idea would be a much purer one than that of the person who believes that the Divine (τὸ θεῖον) entered into the womb of the Virgin Mary, and became her fetus (ἔμβρυον), before being born and swaddled in due course, full of blood and gall from a [body] part (χωρίου),[428] and things more unseemly still (ἀτοπωτέρων).[429]

Celsus also objected to the birth story on the grounds that God would not put his spirit into the "foul pollution" (μίασμα) of a woman's body[430]. That some Greeks were "light-minded" enough to think that the gods could dwell in statues is evident from the work of the Neo-Platonist and theurgist named Iamblichus[431]. Some of the pagans' objections to Christian doctrine that Lactantius discusses are similar to Macarius' Hellene. Lactantius describes some of their problems with Christian belief: "'Why then,' they say, 'did He not come as God to teach men? Why did He make Himself so lowly and weak that He could be condemned by men and afflicted with punishment?'"[432] Lactantius devotes a chapter to his answer to the objection against the incarnation[433]. Methodius also includes some probable fragments from Porphyry that express objections to the incarnation[434]. Macarius' response to the Hellene includes the use of several words that Methodius apparently took from Porphyry (ἀπαθής, σεσαρκῶσθαι)[435]. Celsus also had his objections to the incarnation[436]. Augustine described the Platonists' (including Porphyry)

---

[428] The Christian uses this word in Apocr. 4.30 (221,6 BLONDEL) although BLONDEL emends it to χορίου.

[429] Apocr. 4.22 = HARNACK, Porphyrius, F. 77. ET based on CRAFER, Apocriticus, 149. The last phrase is in accord with HARNACK's translation. CRAFER refers the phrase to the womb of Mary ("for it is a place full of blood and gall") and not to the swaddled child.

[430] C. Cels. 6.73 (142,18-23 KOET.). Compare 1.39, 69 (90,12-14; 123,20-21 KOET.).

[431] De myst. 5.23.232-234 (DES PLACES). On Hellenistic critique of statues see COOK, The Logic and Language of Romans 1,20, Biblica 75, 1994, 513-514 n. 49.

[432] Div. inst. 4.22, ET from M. F. MCDONALD, O.P., Lactantius The Divine Institutes Books I-VIII, FC 49, Washington 1964, 302.

[433] Div. inst. 4.24.

[434] HARNACK, Porphyrius, F. 84 discussed in § 2.3.41.

[435] Apocr. 4.28 (216-17 BLONDEL). ET in CRAFER, Apocriticus, 149-51. Nicephorus also quotes the paragraph beginning with the Prometheus example in the Antirrhetica (in PITRA, Spicilegium Solesmense, 329). The words Macarius shares with Methodius are on 216,2.5 BLONDEL.

[436] C. Cels. 2.31, 4.2, 3 (158,21-25; 274,11-14; 275,18-26 KOET.) and compare COOK, Some Hellenistic Responses, 236 and § 1.3.1 above.

objections to the incarnation[437]. The Hellene seems most disgusted that the divine became an embryo or fetus that when born and swaddled was covered with the blood and gall of a "body part." This objection is directed toward the womb (γαστέρα) and birth canal of Mary. Hellenistic writers in late antiquity were interested in the female body[438]. Porphyry himself wrote a treatise on how embryos are ensouled (ad Gaurum πῶς ἐμψυχοῦται τὰ ἔμβρυα). Harnack refers to Augustine's description of Porphyry as an individual who rejected Christianity because of the doctrine of the incarnation: "In fact, you regard him with contempt because of the body which he received from a woman (*corpus ex femina acceptum*), and because of the shame of the cross..."[439]. The result of the birth, the newborn (*parvulum*), was in itself scandalous to some of Ambrose's pagans who thought such a tiny child to be vile (*uilem*)[440]. It is interesting that the Hellene makes no mention of Greek stories of the gods cohabiting with women and begetting children (e.g. Origen's reference to the story of the virgin birth of Plato by Apollo)[441].

Macarius answers the Hellene by discussing the manner in which the logos, undefiled when it became incarnate in human flesh, led the things of the flesh to incorruptibility[442]. He refers to the Greek stories about Prometheus' creation of humans and Zeus' creation of Athena. Greeks do not inquire into the question of hidden parts (μορία, genitalia)[443]. So why, Macarius concludes, should it be shameful for God to create genitals (μορία) and "pass through them for the sake of the dispensation (οἰκονομίας) and the word that brings profit"[444]. After creating humans, God is not ashamed to dwell in one[445].

---

[437] De civ. D. 10.29 (304,6-9 D./K.). See § 2.3.41 above.

[438] CLARK, Women, 70-73.

[439] HARNACK, Porphyrius, F. 77 with reference to his edition of testimony XXI (page 38) drawn in part from Aug., De civ. D. 10.28 (303,21-23 D./K.), and compare 10.29.

[440] In Lucam 2.44 (CSEL 32.4, 66,10 SCH.). Ambrose responds that the magi came all the way from the East to see the newborn.

[441] C. Cels. 6.8 (78,4-6 KOET.; see CHADWICK's note with references to the Hellenistic comments on this tradition in Origen, 321 n. 12) and 1.37 (89,8-21 Koet; where Origen answers Greeks who disbelieve the virgin birth of Jesus). Celsus does not refer to such Greek stories either in his rejection of the virgin birth of Jesus in C. Cels. 1.28, 32 (79,21-22; 83,17-20 KOET.).

[442] Apocr. 4.28 (216,1-8 BLONDEL).

[443] 4.28 (217,3-7 BLONDEL).

[444] 4.28 (217,8-9 BLONDEL).

[445] 4.28 (217,13-14 BLONDEL).

3.50 How is it said: You shall not revile gods?

The philosopher's last objection to the Christian attitude toward polytheism and image worship makes liberal use of the Hebrew Scriptures:

I could also give proof to you of that much seen (πολύοπτον) name of "gods" from the law, when it cries out and admonishes the hearer with much reverence (αἰδοῦς), "You shall not revile gods, and you shall not speak evil of the ruler of your people" (Ex 22:28). For it does not speak to us here of gods other than those which we reckon to be so, from the things which we know in the words, "You shall not go after other gods" (Jer 7:6); and again, "If you go and worship other gods" (Dt 12:28). It is not people, but the gods who are held in honor (δοξαζομένους) by us, that are meant, not only by Moses, but by his successor Joshua. For he says to the people, "And now fear him and serve him alone, and put away the gods whom your fathers served" (Josh 24:14). And it is not concerning people, but incorporeal beings that Paul says, "For though there be those that are called gods, whether on earth or in heaven, yet to us there is but one God and Father, of whom are all things" (1 Cor 8:5). Therefore you make a great mistake in thinking that God is angry if any other is called a god, and obtains the same title (προσηγορίας) as Himself. For even rulers do not object to having the same name (ὁμωνυμίας) as their subjects, nor do masters [object to having the same name as] slaves. And it is not right (θεμιτόν) to think that God is more petty-minded (μικροψυχότερον) than people. Enough then about the fact that gods exist, and ought to receive honor (τιμᾶσθαι).[446]

The conclusion of the Hellene's argument is clear: It is enough that the gods exist and that they should be honored. His argument rests on the OT's explicit declarations that other gods exist besides the God of Israel. Celsus also argued that God would not object to the worship of the subordinate divinities (C. Cels. 7.68, 8.2 [217,3-11; 222,12-20 Koet.]) since they keep his law[447]. The philosopher makes no reference to Macarius' answer in *Apocr.* 4.26 in which the Christian concedes the existence of "gods," but differentiates them from God who is uncreated and eternal. They are "gods" relatively (θέσις) and not by nature (φύσις). In that response (4.26), Macarius refers to 1 Cor 8:5 (211,13-15 Blondel). The philosopher also quoted 1 Cor 8:5 in the text above — it is quite obvious that Macarius does not allow his fictional opponent to respond to the Christian's responses. The Hellene's appeal to "Moses" also shows that his earlier reference to Ezra's being the actual author of the OT texts is not very important in his understanding and use of the OT scriptures (Apocr. 3.3). Possibly (as he mentioned in 3.3) he is conceding that Moses is the "actual" author. He apparently believed that the statement in Ex 22:28 implies that the gods should be honored. An unstated corollary of that conclusion is that statues of the gods should be honored.

---

[446] Apocr. 4.23 = HARNACK, Porphyrius, F. 78. ET based on CRAFER, Apocriticus, 151-52.
[447] See § 1.7.2 above.

Macarius quotes John 10:34-35 in his response[448]. He denies that we should call elements or stars "gods." Neither should statues be called "gods" even if they should be able (or appear to able) to speak[449]. Macarius is probably referring to theurgic practices or to narratives such as those of Lucian in which statues move or even speak oracles[450]. Moses does not call such statues "gods" — but those to whom the word of God has come (in accord with John 10:34-35). In *Apocr.* 4.26 Macarius shows that he understands angelic beings to receive the name of "gods" occasionally in the scriptures. He refers to 1 Cor 8:5-6[451].

3.51 What is the meaning of the resurrection of the flesh?

The philosopher was scandalized by the Christian belief in the resurrection of the dead. He delivers an extensive critique of the Christian teaching:

Let us once again discuss the question of the resurrection of the dead. For what is the reason that God should act thus, and rashly (προχείρως) upset the succession of events (διαδοχήν) that has held good until now, whereby He ordained that races should be preserved and not come to an end, though from the beginning He has laid down these laws and framed things thus? The things which have once been determined by God, and preserved through such long ages, ought to be everlasting, and ought not to be condemned by Him who wrought them, and destroyed as if they had been made by some mere human, and arranged as mortal things by one who is a mortal. Wherefore it is irrational (ἄλογον) if, when the whole is destroyed, the resurrection shall follow, and if He shall raise — shall we say? — one who died three years before the resurrection, and along with him Priam and Nestor who died a thousand years before, and others who lived before them from the creation (γενέσεως) of the human race. And if anyone is prepared to grasp even this, he/she will find that the question of the resurrection is one full of silliness (ἀβελτηρίας).[452] For many have often perished in the sea, and their bodies have been consumed by fish, while many have been eaten by wild beasts and birds. How then is it possible for their bodies to rise up? Come then, and let us examine this statement in detail. Let us take an example. A man was shipwrecked, the mullets devoured his body, next these were caught and eaten by some fisher folk, who were killed and devoured by dogs; when the dogs died ravens and vultures feasted (ἐθοινήσαντο)[453] on them and

---

[448] Apocr. 4.29 (218-19 BLONDEL). Summary in CRAFER, Apocriticus, 152-53. Nicephorus also quotes the response (and not the question in 4.23) in his Antirrhetica (in PITRA, Spicilegium Solesmense, 330-31). The reference to John 10:34-35 is on 218,10-11 BLONDEL.

[449] 4.29 (218,4.5.7 BLONDEL).

[450] Syr. D. 10, 35, 36 and see COOK, Logic and Language, 513-14 n. 49. Macarius knows that pagans seek oracles from statues (218,14 BLONDEL).

[451] 4.26 (BLONDEL 211,10-15; 212,28).

[452] HARNACK, Porphyrius, F. 94 notes that Porphyry used this word in De abst. 3.22.5 (180 B./P.) and Celsus used it in C. Cels. 3.55 (251,2 KOET.). See also § 3.26 above.

[453] Porphyry used this word in De abst. 2.2.2 (72 B./P.).

entirely consumed them. How then will the body of the shipwrecked person be brought together, seeing that it was absorbed by so many creatures? Again, suppose another body to have been consumed by fire, and another to have come in the end to the worms, how is it possible for it to return to the essence (ὑπόστασιν) which was there from the beginning?

You will tell me that this is possible with God, but this is not true. For all things are not possible with Him (οὐ γὰρ πάντα δύναται);[454] He simply cannot bring it about that Homer should not have become a poet, or that Troy should not be taken. Nor indeed can He make twice two, which make the number four, to be reckoned as a hundred, even though this may seem good to Him. Nor can God ever become evil, even though He wishes; nor would He be able to sin, as being good by nature (ὢν τὴν φύσιν). If then He is unable to sin or to become evil, this does not befall Him through His weakness. In the case of those who have by nature a disposition and fitness (παρασκευὴν καὶ ἐπιτηδειότητα)[455] for a certain thing, and then are prevented from doing it, it is clear that it is by their weakness that they are prevented. But God is by nature good, and is not prevented from being evil; nevertheless, even though He is not prevented, he cannot become bad.

And pray consider a further point. How unreasonable it is if the Creator shall stand by and see the heaven melting, though no one ever conceived anything more wonderful than its beauty, and the stars falling, and the earth perishing;[456] and yet He will raise up the rotten and corrupt bodies of people, some of them it is true, belonging to admirable people, but others without charm or symmetry before they died, and affording a most unpleasant sight. Again, even if He could easily make them rise in a comely form, it would be impossible (ἀδύνατον) for the earth to hold all those who had died from the beginning of the world, if they were to rise again.[457]

The Hellene's objection is similar to his problem with Christian apocalyptic hope (Apocrit. 4.6, 7). It disturbs the order of creation which should remain everlasting (αἰώνια). To him it was absurd that a person who died three years before the resurrection should rise together with the Homeric figures such as Priam and Nestor who died a "thousand years before." Apparently the dating of the Trojan war in the philosopher's mind was about 700 BCE given his claim that 300 years have passed since the letter of Paul to the Thessalonians (Apocr. 4.2). His attack is based on the concept of impossibility — one of the rhetoricians' final categories in deliberative arguments[458]. The philosopher clearly regards his statement that the resurrection is impossible to be a powerful

---

[454] Compare Porphyry in § 2.3.21.

[455] In the fragment from Didymus mentioned above, he denies that God has "passive powers" — αἱ κατ᾽ ἐπιτηδειότητα δυνάμεις.

[456] Compare Plotinus' remarks about the beauty of the universe in Ennead. 6.6.1 (III, 153-54 H./S.).

[457] Apocr. 4.24 = HARNACK, Porphyrius, F. 94. ET based on CRAFER, Apocriticus, 153-54.

[458] LAUSBERG, Handbuch, § 375. See Aristot. Rhet. 1.6.18, 27 and 2.19.1-27. Athenagoras preserves a similar objection in which unnamed pagans claim that the resurrection is impossible (De resur. mort. 2.3 [90-92 SCHOEDEL]) or that it is against the divine will.

argument, although he wavers from that commitment when he concedes that even if the resurrection were possible, the earth could not hold everyone! The Christian response that God can do everything is false since God cannot do what is logically impossible (such as making 2 x 2 = 100), nor can God do evil — according to the Hellene[459]. In his eyes the story about the dead person who is eaten by fish and then by other people is a *reductio ad absurdum* of the Christian belief in the resurrection. One can assume that the philosopher shares Plotinus' views on the immortality of the soul[460]. The resurrection would be an absurd addition in his eyes to the Platonist's assurance in the immortality of his or her soul. He may have been more attracted to Plotinus' vision of an ultimate union with the Good — a vision of ultimate reality without the hindrance of a body[461].

Geffcken notes that it was customary for pagans to object to the resurrection by denying its possibility and by using counter-examples such as that of a corpse burned to ashes[462]. Due to the difference between Porphyry's objection

---

[459] CHADWICK notes that it was a Christian topos to appeal to divine omnipotence in their defence of the resurrection of the body: Clement of Rome 27.2, Justin, Apol. 1.19.4-8 (60,10-61,29 MARC.), Athenagoras, De resur. 9.2 (108-110 SCHOEDEL), Irenaeus, Adv. haer. 5.3.2-3 (SC 153, 44,30-54,91 ROUSSEAU et al.), Tertullian, De resur. 57.1-13 (1004,1-1005,60 BORLEFFS) and Apocalypse of Peter (Ethiopic version) ("Origen" 84). Celsus also criticized the Christians' use of the principle to defend the doctrine of resurrection (C. Cels. 5.14 [15,13-14 KOET.]). In the same text Celsus denies that God could desire evil.

[460] Ennead. 4.7.10 (II, 159,13-16 H./S.).

[461] Ennead. 6.9.9-11 (III, 285,1-290,51 H./S.).

[462] Zwei Griechische Apologeten, 302 n. 1 and 245 n. 1 with reference to, among others, Tert., Apol. 48.5 (166,40 DEKKERS) and Minucius Felix 34.10 (33,4-9 KYT.). Cp. Tert. De resur., 13.3 (936,10-13 BOR.) for his use of the analogy of the Phoenix and the resurrection ("a bodily substance may be recovered even from the fires"). The counter-example that used the narrative of the person eaten by animals also appears in Athenagoras, De resur. 4.1-4 (96-98 SCHOEDEL) and Ps. Just., Quaest. gentil. ad Christ. 15, 200c-e (330 OTTO; which HARNACK, Porphyrius prints as fragment 93). Ps. Just. has an objection in which Christians are asked how burned and cut up seeds will rise, with reference to 1 Cor 15 in Quaest. et resp. ad Orthod. 111, 465c-d (180 OTTO). CHADWICK, in his discussion of this section of the Apocriticus, also refers to Contra Celsum 5.14 (15,1-25 KOET.; and compare 8.49 [263,28-264,15 KOET.]), Tertullian, De resur. 4.1-7 (925,1-926,30 BOR.) and Tatian, Oratio ad Gr. 6 (PTS 43, 15,1-16,21 MARCOVICH) for pagan objections to the traditional doctrine of the resurrection (Origen, Celsus, and the Resurrection of the Body, HThR 41, 1948, 89). CHADWICK traces the roots of the debate to the Academy's critique of the Epicurean notion that the gods had physical bodies (Origen, 91-94). ANASTOS refers to passages in Ps.-Athanasius, Quaestiones ad Antiochum ducem 114 (bodies eaten by fish which are then eaten by people who are themselves then eaten by lions; PG 28, 668dff), Gregory of Nyssa, De anima et resurrectione (PG 46, 72c-76b; 80a; 108a; 108c-109a; 156c-157b; 160abc; will appear as GNO III/3, ed. A. SPIRA), Gregory of Nyssa, De hominis opificio 26 (bodies eaten by fish), 25 and 27 (PG 44, 224f; 213-29; will appear as GNO IV/2, ed. H. HÖRNER), Anastasius Sinaita, Interrogationes et responsiones, Quaestio 92 (PG 89,

to the resurrection (based on the analogy between Lazarus and Jesus' resurrections) and those of Macarius' Hellene, Geffcken asserts that the Hellene cannot be identified *in toto* with Porphyry[463]. On the other hand there is a lost objection from the *Apocriticus* whose *titulus* was "How is Lazarus raised from the dead on the fourth day?" (See § 3.52.2) Consequently Macarius' pagan may have used Porphyry's argument. Eusebius preserves an account of the martyrs of Lyon during the reign of Marcus Aurelius in which the pagans reduced the corpses of the martyrs to ashes so that the martyrs could not be resurrected[464]. Lactantius refers to another kind of objection in which pagans claim the resurrection is impossible because of the injustice in the world (Div. Inst. 7.22). He responds in a chapter which includes a quotation from Chrysippus (Div. Inst. 7.23), in which the Stoic claims: "Since this is so, it is clear that nothing is impossible, even that we, after our death, when a certain space of time has gone by, are to be restored into the same state in which we seem to be now."[465] Other figures in Roman culture were apparently open to the possibility of some kind of earthly life after death. In popular legend the witch Erichtho was able to force the gods to resuscitate a dead corpse which then proceeded to prophesy the outcome of a battle[466]. In Porphyry's work on statues he mentions a plant Asclepius knew of that was reputed to have the ability to raise the dead (καὶ μυθεύεται τῆς ἀναβιώσεως εἰδέναι τινὰ βοτάνην)[467].

Macarius does not include the philosopher's alternative to belief in resurrection — if indeed the philosopher had such an alternative. Augustine does however show the larger context in which such debates between pagans and Christians were probably carried out:

> But of all these, the most difficult question is, into whose body that flesh shall return which has been eaten and assimilated by another person constrained by hunger to use it so; ... For the sake, then, of ridiculing the resurrection, they ask, Shall this return to the person whose flesh it first was, or to the one whose flesh it afterwards became? And thus, too, they seek to give promise to the human soul of alternations of true misery and false happiness, in accordance with Plato's theory; or, in accordance with Porphyry's, that, after many transmigrations into different bodies, it ends its miseries, and never more returns to

---

725b) (Porphyry's Attack, 444 n. 75). For bibliography see RINALDI, Biblia Gentium 556-57.

[463] Zwei Griechische Apologeten, 302 n. 1. See the section above on authorship. GEFFCKEN thinks the Hellene might have been a Roman given the Roman references in Apocrit. 3.1 (52,7 BLONDEL; Potioli) and Apocrit. 4.21 (200,4 BLONDEL; Minerva, Porphyry used Greek names for the gods).

[464] Eus., H.E. 5.62-63.

[465] ET in MCDONALD, Lactantius 529.

[466] Lucan, Pharsalia 6.588-830. Line 6.660 describes the state as "new life" (*nova ... vita*).

[467] De imag. 8. from Eus., P.E. 3.11.26 (SC 228, 222,7-8 DES PLACES). See BOWERSOCK, Fiction as History, 99-119 for a survey of "resurrection" in Greek romance.

them, not, however, by obtaining an immortal body, but by escaping from every kind of body.[468]

Augustine understands Plato's doctrine to be one of reincarnation, although Porphyry provides the possibility of eventual release from the cycle[469]. Ambrose also records the pagans' incredulity with regard to the resurrection: "You wonder in what way putrefied remains can become sound, how dispersed members can come together, how destroyed parts can be renewed ... It disturbs the gentiles much, how it can come to pass, that the earth can restore those whom the sea has absorbed, those whom wild beasts have torn apart, and those whom beasts have devoured[470]. Philosophical critics of Christianity apparently found the doctrine of immortality to be more attractive than that of resurrection. Augustine's reference to the attempt to throw scorn on the resurrection is an indication that the argument about the fate of a human body at the hands of animals was designed to discourage people from believing Christian teaching.

Macarius has an extended and somewhat rambling answer to the philosopher's objections to the belief in the resurrection of the dead. Some of the passages are of great beauty and power[471]. Macarius begins with a request that the philosopher not trouble him or anyone of the others sitting at the debate[472]. He mentions that certain people are disgusted at the Christian belief in resurrection[473]. Consequently the Christian must offer persuasion and credible and obvious images (σὺν τῇ πειθοῖ καὶ ἀξιοπίστους εἰκόνας ... ἐπιφανεῖς)[474]. His reference to persuasion is a use of the word that expressed one of the fundamental purposes of rhetoric — the change of the hearer's mind. The Hellene uses the word "credible" (ἀξιοπίστους) in *Apocr.* 2.14 (see § 3.23), and as we remarked in that section, it was a word rhetoricians could use to describe reliable witnesses. In a discussion of God's power to create from nothing Macarius gives this image of creation: "For our present life is like a womb containing a babe, for it holds down the whole being of things in obscurity, in the forgetfulness of ignorance, where the light does not penetrate.

---

[468] Aug., De civ. D. 22.12 (832,51-833,64 D./K.); ET in NPNF (First Series) 2, 494.

[469] See § 2.2.1.3 on Porphyry; and compare Plato, Resp. 619d. In Phaedrus 249a a wise soul can, after 3000 years of reincarnation, return to the place from which it came (heaven).

[470] Ambrose, De excessu fratris 2.55.1 (CSEL 73, 278 FALLER), 2.58.1 (280 FALLER) referred to by COURCELLE, Anti-Christian Arguments, 161.

[471] Apocr. 4.30 (220-27 BLONDEL). Summary and extensive translation in CRAFER, Apocriticus, 155-63.

[472] 4.30 (220,2-3 BLONDEL).

[473] 4.30 (220,3-4 BLONDEL).

[474] 4.30 (220,7-8 BLONDEL). See the references to the rhetoricians' use of these categories in § 3.23 above.

The whole of what is growing must rise from the present age as from the membrane which holds it in the womb, and must receive a second mode of life in the light of the abiding place which is inviolable (ἀκηράτου μονῆς)."[475] Macarius then describes the suffering of the present age and accuses the philosopher of wanting that corruption to be without end[476]. Priam and Nestor and the person who dies three days before the resurrection will be judged in accord with the lives they have lived and will receive praise or blame (ψέγων ...ἐπαινῶν) in consequence of those lives[477]. The words for praise or blame are the key terms of epideictic rhetoric[478]. To answer the problem of the shipwrecked person, Macarius draws an analogy with the ability to fire to burn soil to separate out the silver and gold— just as the rational treasure (κειμήλιον λογικόν) of human beings is contained in various kinds of matter. God can keep that treasure safe even after it has been eaten by wild animals and turned into fine dust[479]. Macarius has a very interesting text on logic in which he treats the issue of God's ability to do all. If God could make what has already been made to be not made, then all kinds of incoherence results — e.g. everything is uncreated or nothing is created. Macarius thus concedes that God cannot create a logical contradiction[480].

3.52 The Indexes to the Lost Sections of Books I and II of the Apocriticus

Cardinal Giovanni Mercati has published some indexes from MS Vat. Gr. 1650 from circa 1036 C.E.[481]. Besides sections of Paul's epistles and Acts, the MS contains τίτλοι (indexes) for the Hellene's questions in Books I-III of the *Apocriticus*. Blondel's MS begins with the answer in *Apocr.* 2.7 and does not contain any questions from the Hellene until 2.12. The MS of Blondel only contains indexes from Books III and IV. Consequently Mercati's find is quite valuable, because only it gives any indication of the content of the ten lost questions of the Hellene in Book I and the first six questions in Book II. The indexes in Book III in Blondel's MS closely correspond to those of Mercati's MS. Below is a translation of the indexes that are not found in Blondel's MS:

3.52.1 Book I

1. What is the saying concerning the va[rious ...] heresies?

---

[475] 4.30 (221,4-7 BLONDEL). ET in CRAFER, Apocriticus, 155-56.
[476] 4.30 (221,8-222,23 BLONDEL).
[477] 4.30 (223,14-32 BLONDEL).
[478] LAUSBERG, Handbuch, 61.3.
[479] 4.30 (223,32-224,25 BLONDEL).
[480] 4.30 (225,4-6 BLONDEL).
[481] MERCATI, Per L'Apocritico, 52 with bibliography. Its GREGORY number is 623 in the minuscule series.

Celsus also noticed the Christian "heretics" (C. Cels. 3.12, 5.63 [211,20; 66,8-10 Koet.]) as did Julian (C. Gal. 206a [142,5-7 MASARACCHIA]).

2. How did the Lord choose the disciples and with them the betrayer?

One of Ambrose's pagans objected to the choice of Judas as an Apostle and argued that it shows Jesus' lack of foresight (or imprudence *inprudentiam*). They consequently denigrated the divine power of Jesus[482]. See also C. Cels. 2.12 (140,17-12 Koet.; discussed in § 1.2.14).

3. What is the saying: "Follow me and I will make you fishers of people?"

See Porphyry's objection to this story discussed in § 2.3.12 (F. 6).

4. How was it said, "Jesus was tempted in the wilderness by the devil?"

See Julian's treatment of the temptation discussed in § 5.2.6 (F. 94).

5. For what reason did Christ not come (ἐπεδήμησεν) in the beginning but in the end of time?

Compare C. Cels. 4.7 (279,11 Koet.; discussed in § 1.3.1), Porphyry in § 2.3.30 (F. 82), and § 3.4 above.

6. How did Christ, after being mistreated (ὑβρισθείς) and crucified, make people believe in him?

7. How was it said, "There were five thousand men in the wilderness not including women and children?"

Compare Julian's discussion in § 5.2.15 (F. 105).

8. What is the saying to the apostles to teach the entire world, and how did he heal the ringleader Peter from his denial?

9. Why is it said concerning[483] the fig tree, "Let not one ever again eat fruit from you"?

10. How did Pilate go out from the Praetorium saying to the Jews, "Take him yourselves and judge him according to you law"?[484]

3.52.2 Book II

1. How is it said, "Heaven was closed up [for three years] and six months," in the gospel?

2. How is it said by Jesus, "The little girl is not dead but sleeping"?

3. How is Lazarus raised from the dead on the fourth day?

Porphyry had objections to the resurrection of Lazarus compared to that of Jesus (§ 2.3.32 [F. 92]).

4. [Corrupt text]

5. [Corrupt text]

---

[482] De paradiso 8.38 (CSEL 32.1, 294,9 SCHENKL) discussed in COURCELLE, Anti-Christian Arguments, 160. The pagan makes a similar objection to God's foresight in giving Adam a command he knew (or did not know) would be broken.

[483] Instead of ὑπό (by), one should probably read ὑπέρ (concerning). MERCATI (Per L'Apocritico, 65) conjectures κατά to be the original reading.

[484] MERCATI, Per L'Apocritico, 62-3.

6. How is it said, "If any one comes after me and does not hate his father he is not worthy of me"?

7. How is it said, "I did not come to bring peace to the earth but a sword"?

8. How is it said, "Behold your mother and your brothers are standing outside desiring to talk with you"?

9. How is it said, "No one is good but the one God"?

10. How is it said, "Have mercy on my son because he is moonstruck" (σεληνιάζεται)?

11. How is it said, "If I bear witness concerning myself it is not true"?

12. How is it said, "Eliem ele ('Ηλιήμ' ἤλη) lima sabachthanei   Into your hands I commend my spirit"?

13. How is it said "Coming to Jesus they did not break his bones"?

14. How is it said, "After rising he did not appear to Pilate"?

15. How is it said, "The ruler of this world will be cast out"?

16. How is it said, "You are of your father the devil"?[485]

3.52.3 Book III

The titles correspond almost exactly to those found in Blondel's MS[486]. They are included in the relevant sections above.

3.53 Conclusion

Although the dialogue of the Christian and the pagan is fictional it is of unique importance because it has so much pagan exegesis of the NT that cannot be found elsewhere. This chapter and the one on Porphyry argue that Porphyry is probably the source for many of the objections Macarius attributes to his anonymous philosopher. Macarius may have used one or more of the refutations of Porphyry written by people like Apollinarius or Methodius. There is also the likelihood that Macarius may have used some objections from other pagans such as Julian or Hierocles. The result is that the philosopher is a fictional construct — but one based on actual objections by people such as Porphyry.

One finds the most quotations of the OT and NT in the anonymous philosopher when compared with the other authors surveyed in this book. He shows the finest eye for exegetical details — likely a trait of Porphyry. The existing nominal fragments of Porphyry are not extensive enough to tell for sure how much scripture Porphyry quoted. Like Porphyry the philosopher

---

[485] MERCATI, Per L'Apocritico, 66-67.

[486] BLONDEL, Macarii, 49, 50 compared to MERCATI, Per L'Apocritico, 69-70. MERCATI's MS breaks off at question 15 "No one serves at his own expense." The five following questions are contained in BLONDEL's list of τίτλοι.

enjoys constructing dilemmas and searches out contradictions[487]. His philosophical interests including defending polytheism and image worship, and the concept of resurrection was incoherent in his eyes. He was troubled by the powers of persuasion exercised by Christians who use texts such as John 6:54 (§ 3.27) and by the persuasive power of Paul's discourse (§ 3.35). The philosopher delights in drawing absurd consequences from Christian texts. Luke 5:32-32 (§ 3.4) implies, for example, that the ones who turn away from Christians' words have no need of healing and are righteous. Mt 11:25 (§ 3.7) implies that it is better to desire ignorance and senselessness. He does not shrink from accusing Jesus of drunkenness (§ 3.11) because he called Peter "Satan" and made him the foundation of the Church. One gets the impression that he found that his philosophical training and education rendered the NT an easy mark for his critical powers.

---

[487] See § 3.24 and 3.28 for dilemmas.

4. Hierocles

Hierocles, the Lover of Truth

Sossianus Hierocles wrote a two-volume work addressed to the Christians around the time of the Great Persecution in February 303. He entitled the work "The Lover of Truth" (Φιλαλήθης) or "The Truth-Loving Discourse" (Φιλαλήθης λόγος)[1]. In this work he carried out a sustained comparison of Apollonius of Tyana[2] and Jesus. Below I will first discuss Hierocles' career of public service and then treat his literary work directed to the Christians. His career is of interest because Hierocles was an active persecutor of the church. He was willing to use law and reason to overthrow the Christian faith. The legal role Hierocles played illustrates the cultural context for his work that was

---

[1] The edition used is Eusèbe de Césarée Contre Hiéroclès, SC 333, intro. and trans. M. FORRAT, ed. É. DES PLACES, Paris 1986. The ET is mine done with reference to those of F. C. CONYBEARE, ed. and trans., Philostratus...Treatise of Eusebius, LCL, Cambridge/London 1969 and M. FORRAT. On the title see T. HÄGG, Hierocles the Lover of Truth and Eusebius the Sophist, SO 67, 1992, 140-143. The longer form of the title is probably in C.H. 1.19 and 2.33 (100, 104 F./DES P.). Hierocles' comments from Lactantius are in Lactance. Institutions divines, livre V, Vols. 1-2, ed. P. MONAT, SC 204/205, Paris 1973. The second volume is MONAT's commentary and will be cited below as MONAT, SC 205. Eusebius' treatise will be referred to as *Contra Hieroclem* (C.H.).

[2] On Apollonius see, among much literature: K. GROSS, Art. Apollonius von Tyana, RAC I, 1950, 529-533 / G. PETZKE, Die Traditionen über Apollonius von Tyana und das Neue Testament, SCHNT 1, Leiden 1970 / W. SPEYER, Zum Bild des Apollonios von Tyana bei Heiden und Christen, JAC 17, 1974, 47-63 / E. L. BOWIE, Apollonius of Tyana. Tradition and Reality, ANRW II.16.2, 1978, 1652-1699 / G. FOWDEN, The Pagan Holy Man in Late Antique Society, JHS 102, 1982, 36-37 / BETZ, Gottmensch, 249-51 / FORRAT/DES PLACES, Eusèbe, 26-43 with bibliography on 91-95. For a brief but excellent portrayal of Eusebius' method in C.H. see P. COX, Biography in Late Antiquity. A Quest for the Holy Man, Berkeley et al. 1983, 73-76. She discusses techniques of portrayal of holy men (including Apollonius) in her chapter on "Biography and Paradigms of the Divine Sage" (17-44). On general background of the divine man see G. PATERSON CORRINGTON, "The Divine Man" His Origin and Function in Hellenistic Popular Religion, American University Studies VII.17, New York et al. 1986.

designed to bring Christians to their senses. The same kind of context[3] (the Great Persecution) could explain the genesis of Porphyry's *Contra Christianos*.

After a summary of Hierocles' public life, I will discuss some of the literary issues surrounding his work including the identity of the Christian author, "Eusebius," who responded to Hierocles. Lactantius' important comparison of Hierocles (whom he leaves unnamed) to an anonymous high priest of philosophy will then be developed. That philosopher wrote to the Christians to help them find their way away from the faith and so avoid brutal persecution. Then I will survey Hierocles' attack on the character of the scriptures, the disciples, and the Christian understanding of Jesus' identity. Hierocles made frequent use of the life of Apollonius of Tyana to carry out his critique. He found Christians to be credulous people and completed his work with an encomium of the supreme God — apparently pushing Christians in the right direction.

4.1 Hierocles' Career

Hierocles' political career is known through several scattered references, some of which describe his active role in the persecutions of Diocletian and Maximin Daia[4]. He first surfaces as a governor of the equestrian class of Syria Phoenice in several inscriptions. He helped in the construction of a permanent military installation in Palmyra in an inscription that appears on the lintel of the Temple of the Standards during the era of Diocletian's tetrarchy (293-305):

> The Repairers of their world and propagators of the human race, our Lords Diocletianus and Maximianus, the most unconquered Imperatores, and Constantius and Maximianus [i.e., Galerius], the most noble Caesares, have successfully founded the camp (*castra*), under the care of Sossianus Hierocles, *vir perfectissimus*, governor (*praeses*) of the province, devoted to their *numen* and *maiestas*.[5]

---

[3] See § 2.3.1.

[4] Sossianus Hierocles 4, PLRE 432 / FORRAT/DES PLACES, Eusèbe, 11-19 / T. D. BARNES, Sossianus Hierocles and the Antecedents of the 'Great Persecution', HSCP 80, 1976, 243-45 / W. SPEYER, Art. Hierokles I (Sossianus Hierocles), RAC XV, 1991, 103-104 / R. HANSLIK, Art. Hierokles 3, KP II, 1967, 1132-33. HANSLIK does not explain why he dates Hierocles to 297 in Palmyra. O. SEECK, Art. Hierokles, 13, PRE VIII, 1913, 1477.

[5] CIL III.6661 = 133. ET by F. MILLAR, The Roman Near East 31 BC - AD 337, Cambridge, MA/London 1993, 182. On the issue of the province in which Palmyra lay see MILLAR 122, 192, 204 and T. D. BARNES, The New Empire of Diocletian and Constantine, Cambridge, MA/London 1982, 223-24 who argues that despite the appearance of an *Augusta Libanensis* on the Verona list (205ff), *Phoenice* was probably not divided at the time of Ammianus Marcellinus (14.8.9) and the Nicene Council. MILLAR refers to Eus. H.E. 9.5.2 and 9.6.1 that locate Damascus and Emesa in *Phoenice*.

Hierocles was also credited with helping build the baths of Diocletian in Palmyra[6].

He then served as *vicarius* (in charge of judicial functions) of one of Diocletian's dioceses — perhaps Pontica[7]. Lactantius describes Hierocles as governor (of Bithynia) after his vicariate (*ex vicario praesidem*)[8]. In the *Contra Hieroclem* (*Against Hierocles*) Eusebius describes the vicariate of Hierocles with these expressions: "who has taken possession of the highest and general courts"; and "Hierocles, who has been entrusted with the highest and most general courts" (τὰ ἀνωτάτω καὶ καθόλου δικαστήρια πεπιστευμένῳ)[9]. Although his next move to governor of Bithynia was technically a demotion, it gave him the opportunity to actively participate in the persecutions[10]. When he was governor he seems to have given a public recitation of his work in the court of Nicomedia — that Lactantius was obliged to hear[11]. Hierocles participated in the planning of the Great Persecution (*auctor et consiliarius ad faciendam persecutionem*) and tortured Lactantius' friend Donatus[12]. In 310 Hierocles was prefect of Egypt (ὃς τὴν Αἴγυπτον ἐξουσίᾳ τῇ ἑαυτοῦ πᾶσαν διεῖπεν) where a Christian named Aedesius became outraged because the prefect was delivering Christian virgins to brothel keepers. Aedesius

---

6 SEG 7, 1934, #152.

7 *Oriens* is another possibility. See BARNES, Scholarship, 60 n. 35 On the institution of the *vicarius* (deputy) see BARNES, New Empire 224 with reference to Lactantius, De mort. pers. 7.4, 48.9 (ed. and trans. J. L. CREED, Lactantius de mortibus persecutorum, OECT, Oxford 1984, 12, 73). BARNES, Sossianus Hierocles, 245 refers to Acta Marcelli. In that text the centurion Marcellus is referred to the deputy (*vicarius*) by the governor for trial (A. Marc. 4 [MUSURILLO]). FORRAT (FORRAT/DES PLACES, Eusèbe, 13 n. 1 with reference to F. DE MARTINO, Storia della costituzione romana, Naples 1967, 269-275) remarks that deputies received reports from governors and transmitted them to the central administration and were the first judges of appeal. Even though deputies were equestrians, they were in a sense the superior of the governors of senatorial rank.

8 De mort. pers. 16.4 (24 CREED).

9 C.H. 4.39-40, 20.1-2 (SC 333. 108, 144). BARNES, Sossianus Hierocles, 245 notes that using "province" to translate the texts does not do justice to the judicial functions of the vicariate.

10 BARNES, Sossianus Hierocles, 243-44; FORRAT/DES PLACES, Eusèbe, 13-14.

11 Lactantius, Div. inst. 5.2.12, 5.4.1 (138, 146 MON.). These events happened while Lactantius was teaching rhetoric in Bithynia (5.2.2 [134 MON.]). Hierocles is anonymous in this text, but few doubt that the figure is Hierocles. GEFFCKEN, Zwei Griechische Apologeten, 291 n.1 argues that Lactantius' anonymous figure and Hierocles are not identical because Eus. C.H. 2 (100-104 F./DES P.) pictures Jesus as a wise "Gottesmann." That argument is weak since Hierocles in C.H. 2 makes no mention that Jesus was wise or divine. Lactantius' reference to the anonymous figure as the author of the φιλαληθεῖς clinches his identity as Hierocles (Div. inst. 5.3.22 [144 MON.]).

12 Lact., De mort. pers. 16.4

slapped Hierocles and threw him on the ground according to Eusebius' account[13]. Aedesius' martyrdom probably took place in 310 given the evidence from the papyri about the date of Hierocles' administration[14].

4.2 Date and Title of Hierocles' Work

The date and precise title of Hierocles' writing to the Christians are contested. Lactantius' states that he first persecuted the Christians and then added to his evil by writing his book:

> He was then of the number of governors (*iudicum*) and was among the first to be responsible for the beginning of the persecution. Not content with this crime, he pursued with his writings those whom he persecuted. He composed two volumes[15] not *Against the Christians* but *To the Christians* lest he appear to rail at them in an unfriendly way — so that he might be judged to humanely and kindly counsel them (*quo scelere non contentus, etiam scriptis eos quos afflixerat insecutus est, composit enim libellos duos, non contra Christianos, ne inimice videretur, sed ad Christianos, ut humane ac benigne consulere putaretur*).[16]

It is possible that he composed the book, gave it out to be read privately, participated in the persecutions as governor of Bithynia, and then gave public recitations of it in Nicomedia[17]. The reason for contesting Lactantius' statement that the persecution came first is that there is no mention of Hierocles' role as persecutor in the reply to his work by Eusebius. Tomas Hägg undermines his critique of Lactantius' order somewhat by claiming that the *C.H.* did not have to be written before 303 even though the author of the *C.H.* is only aware of Hierocles' role as *vicarius Orientis*[18]. He could have written the *C.H.* after the spring of 303 and have simply been unaware of Hierocles'

---

[13] De mart. pal. 5.3, Long recension (SC 55, 137-38 BARDY). See also Epiphanius, Panarion 68.1.4 (GCS Epiphanius III, 141,8-9 H./D., ἔπαρχος, Hierocles, prefect in Alexandria).

[14] Sammelbuch 9186 = P. Cairo Isid. 69 (year 18 of Galerius, 6 of Maximinus). Hierocles was governor in April 310 (P. Oxy. XLIII.3120). See BARNES, Sossianus Hierocles, 245 n. 25, and his New Empire, 150, and P. Berol. inv. 21654 (H. MAEHLER, Zur Amtszeit des Präfekten Sossianus Hierocles, in: Collectanea Papyrologica. Texts Published in Honor of H. C. Youtie, Vol. 2., ed. A. E. HANSON, PTA 20, Bonn 1976, 527-33). MAEHLER shows that Hierocles was prefect in 310 and in the first half of 311.

[15] HÄGG, Hierocles, 142 refers to OLD, *liber* 2b where the word can mean "volume." See also LEWIS AND SHORT, A Latin Dictionary, Oxford 1879, 4.*liber* II.C.1.

[16] Lact. Div. inst. 5.2.12-13 (138 MON.). ET modified of Sister M. F. MCDONALD, O.P. Lactantius The Divine Institutes, FC 49, Washington 1964, 332. Note that Eusebius describes Hierocles' work as καθ' ἡμῶν in C.H. 1.4 (98 F./DES P.).

[17] Div. inst. 5.4.1 (146 MON.). Reconstructions of events in HÄGG, Hierocles, 142.

[18] HÄGG, Hierocles, 145 (he assumes the diocese was *Oriens*).

later activities, according to Hägg. If this is true, then one could still accept Lactantius' statement that the book was written after the persecution began. Whether the book was written shortly before or after the Great Persecution began, the important fact is that Hierocles was active in theory and in practice.

The title of Hierocles' work may have been *Truth Loving Discourse* since Eusebius refers to the book as Φιλαλήθους τουτουὶ λόγου and Φιλαλήθη λόγον[19]. The adjective "loving truth" would seem to apply better to a book than to a doctrine as in the usage of Origen, *Contra Celsum* 6.16 where he describes the scriptures as "truth loving" (φιλαλήθεις ... γραφαί)[20]. Eusebius refers to Origen's refutation of Celsus whose arguments Hierocles had shamelessly plagiarized (*C.H.* 1.3-13). Even more pretentious than Hierocles' "Lover of Truth," writes Eusebius, is Celsus' title for his work, "True Discourse" ('Αληθῆ λόγον). The closeness of the comparison may indicate that Hierocles used a similar title (Φιλαλήθης λόγος)[21]. Lactantius uses the plural to describe the work ("Truth Loving" or "Truth Lovers" φιλαληθεῖς)[22]. This also may indicate that the title of the work did not refer to the narrator as the "truth lover," but to the discourse itself as "truth loving." Despite these considerations, it is still possible that Marguerite Forrat and others are correct in entitling the book *The Lover of Truth*. Eusebius delights in ironic comments and apostrophes to Hierocles as the "lover of truth" who gullibly accepts the stories of Apollonius as credible[23]. Lactantius' statement quoted above that Hierocles wrote not against the Christians but to them prompts Hägg to conclude that the full title of the work was Φιλαλήθης λόγος πρὸς Χριστιανούς (Truth Loving Discourse to the Christians)[24]. The parallel with Celsus' title and Lactantius' plural support including "Discourse" in the title.

---

[19] C.H. 1.19 and 2.33 (100, 104 F./DES P.). Compare 1.4-5 and 1.12-13 where the adjectives appear in proximity to the noun even though they are not in the same grammatical case (HÄGG, Hierocles, 143).

[20] Origenes II, 86,23-24 KOETSCHAU. In the same section Origen denies that the word describes Celsus (87,2 KOET.). HÄGG, Hierocles 140. E. SCHWARTZ also believed the book was entitled Φιλαλήθης λόγος (Art. Eusebios 24, PRE VI ,1909, 1394).

[21] HÄGG, Hierocles, 140-41.

[22] Div. inst. 5.3.22 (144 MON.).

[23] Eusèbe 18, 19. C.H. 4.2, 4.39, 14.2, 17.6, 25.6, 34.6, 43.54 (104, 108, 132, 138, 150, 176, 196 F./DES P.). See BARNES, Sossianus Hierocles, 242 n. 15. BARNES opts for translating expressions such as Φιλαλήθη λόγον "the book entitled 'Lover of Truth.'"

[24] HÄGG, Hierocles, 141.

4.3 Eusebius' Reply and Identity

The title of Eusebius' reply, according to the MSS, is ΕΥΣΕΒΙΟΥ ΤΟΥ ΠΑΜΦΙΛΟΥ ΠΡΟΣ ΤΑ ΥΠΟ ΦΙΛΟΣΤΡΑΤΟΥ ΕΙΣ ΑΠΟΛΛΩΝΙΟΝ ΔΙΑ ΤΗΝ ΙΕΡΟΚΛΕΙ ΠΑΡΑΛΗΦΘΕΙΣΑΝ ΑΥΤΟΥ ΤΕ ΚΑΙ ΤΟΥ ΧΡΙΣΤΟΥ ΣΥΓΚΡΙΣΙΝ (*Of Eusebius Son of Pamphilus Against the Writings of Philostratus Concerning Apollonius*[25] *Occasioned by the Parallel Established by Hierocles Between Him and Christ*)[26]. It is possible that πρός should be translated "in reply to" instead of "against"[27]. Eric Junod argues that the work should be referred to not as *Against Hierocles* but with the title as it appears in the manuscripts or something such as *Against the Writings of Philostratus in favor of Apollonius* [28]. Junod's point is that the book is not primarily against Hierocles but against the menace created by Philostratus' Apollonius. Of course Hierocles is the one who was able to exploit the menace so well.

Recently Hägg has questioned the long standing belief that Eusebius of Caesarea composed the reply. Photius and *Paris gr.* 451 (copied in 914 for Arethas) bear witness to Eusebius' authorship[29]. Hägg bases his attack on the traditional authorship on several grounds. Eusebius is silent about the work in his other writings. Eusebius knows that Hierocles was a persecutor of the church in his treatise on the martyrs of Palestine, but does not mention this fact in the *C.H.* The author of the *C.H.* states that Hierocles was alone in making the comparison of Jesus and Apollonius. The fact that Eusebius of Caesarea wrote 25 books against Porphyry makes it unlikely that he would have been unaware of Porphyry's mention of Apollonius in his attack on the Christians. The author of the *C.H.* does not quote the Bible one time, and the style of the work is that of the second sophistic — in contrast to the other works of Eusebius[30].

The fact that Eusebius knows of Hierocles as persecutor (in contrast to the author of the *C.H.*) is certainly mystifying. Forrat argues that Eusebius chose only to exalt martyrs in his work on the Palestinian martyrs (*De mart. Pal.*) and

---

[25] Or "in favor of Apollonius". But "in favor of" is unnecessary. See LSJ, εἰς IV.b.

[26] C.H. inscriptio (98 F./des P).

[27] LSJ, s.v. C.I.4. HÄGG, Hierocles, 139 n.7.

[28] E. JUNOD, Polemique chrétienne contre Apollonius de Tyane, RThPh 120, 1988, 482.

[29] Photius, Bibl. 39 (CUFr, 23,26-8 HENRY): Εὐσεβίου τοῦ Παμφίλου ἀνασκευαστικὸν βιβλιδάριον πρὸς τοὺς ὑπὲρ 'Απολλωνίου τοῦ Τυανέως 'Ιεροκλέους λόγους. HÄGG, Hierocles, 150 n. 36.

[30] HÄGG, Hierocles,145-48. How often does Eusebius refer to his own work *Contra Porphyrium*? HARNACK, Porphyrius, Test. VIII (30) finds *no* references in Eusebius to his own work against Porphyry. On the survival of this work into the modern era see COOK, A Possible Fragment, 120-21.

chose to stay on an ideological level in the *C.H.* [31]. Barnes' response to this problem seems more plausible: "If Eusebius knew that Hierocles had already condemned, tortured, and executed Christians, he would surely not have failed to allude to the fact."[32] Such arguments prompt Barnes to date the *C.H.* to the period before the persecution in 303. There is a problem with Hägg's argument concerning Porphyry. In the fragment that explicitly names Porphyry, Jerome only mentions that Porphyry compared Apollonius to the miracle working of the apostles[33]. The other two fragments Hägg mentions are from Macarius' *Apocriticus* which cannot be used without further argument to reconstruct Porphyry's thought. One of them compares Apollonius' miraculous disappearance at his trial before Domitian with Jesus' unimpressive behavior at his own trial[34]. One can only assert that Porphyry may have compared Jesus and Apollonius. There is no explicit proof of this in the existing fragments. At the least Hägg has succeeded in showing that one need not fit the *C.H.* into Eusebius' body of work since it may have been written by Eusebius the sophist. In a recent essay Barnes notes that "Thomas Hägg has now rendered it probable that the Eusebius who wrote against Hierocles is not the ecclesiastical historian Eusebius of Caesarea at all, but an otherwise unknown accidental homonym, who was probably a Christian sophist in Asia Minor." Further work on style and vocabulary using the *Thesaurus Linguae Graecae* may strengthen Hägg's case[35].

To date the *C.H.* the triumphalistic tone concerning the triumph of Christianity needs to be taken into account. Eusebius assumes Christianity will overwhelm the world:

> ... by his own divinity and virtue he [Christ] saved the entire inhabited world and now still draws tens of thousands of multitudes from everywhere to his divine teaching; ... [he] is the only one who ever after being fought against during so many years by — one may almost say — all people, both those who govern and those who are governed, has been proved to be stronger and much more powerful due to his divine and indescribable power than those unbelievers who bitterly persecuted him.[36]

The Christian herald of truth in the final chapter has an assured tone that also prompts Forrat to deny that the *C.H.* predated Diocletian's persecution[37].

---

[31] FORRAT/DES PLACES, Eusèbe, 22-3.

[32] Sossianus Hierocles, 242.

[33] HARNACK, Porphyrius, F.4. See § 2.3.37.

[34] HARNACK, Porphyrius, F. 60 and 63 from Apocriticus 4.5 and 3.1 (163,5; 52,5 BLONDEL). See § 3.16 and § 3.21 in this work.

[35] BARNES, Scholarship, 60 n. 35. The author's search on the TLG CD-ROM revealed no quotations in Eusebius' corpus that use Hierocles' name except the De mart. Pal. 5.3 already discussed above.

[36] C.H. 4.14-23 (106 F./DES P.).

[37] C.H. 48.1-25 (210-212 F./DES P.). FORRAT/DES PLACES, Eusèbe, 20-26.

However, the persecutors that Eusebius mentions may be Decius and Valerian, and (even though later proved to be incorrect) a Christian writing before 303 may have believed that the cause of Christ was going to be victorious[38].

Forrat also uses a text-external argument for a later dating of the *C.H.* given Maximin Daia's attempt at counter-propaganda. *The Acts of Pilate and Our Savior* were fabricated for such a purpose with Maximin's approval according to Eusebius. Those *Acts* — full of blasphemies against Christ — were publicly displayed, and elementary school teachers used them[39]. Consequently Forrat argues that Eusebius could have discussed Hierocles' work after Galerius' death (311) and before the end of Maximin's persecution in 312 (Eus. H.E. 9.10.6ff). However in (ca.) 303 another pamphleteer also wrote a three-volume work against the Christians (Lact. Div. inst. 5.2.2-4). So in 303 an atmosphere of "counter-propaganda" also existed and Forrat's text-external argument is inconclusive.

A date before or after the Great Persecution for the *C.H.* would seem to be possible. Although the author only knows of Hierocles as a *vicarius* he may have written after 303 and simply have been unaware of Hierocles' later role in the persecution[40]. Friedhelm Winkelmann has doubts about the later dating of the *C.H.* because of the strong differences in style between it and Eusebius' other works[41]. Although Édouard des Places[42] does not question Eusebius' authorship he does find in it many traces of the second sophistic (epithets, indignant exclamations, apostrophes, and picturesque traits and phrases from Philostratus). Eusebius practices the diatribe in this work as he may have in his lost treatise against Porphyry[43]. These remarks on the style of the *C.H.*,

---

[38] BARNES, Sossianus Hierocles, 242, HÄGG, Hierocles,145.

[39] H.E. 9.5.1 and 9.7.1. FORRAT/DES PLACES, Eusèbe, 24-26. FORRAT's theory (using Lact., Div. inst. 5.3.22 φιλαληθεῖς) that Hierocles published his work first in two volumes and later in one for the sake of greater persuasiveness is unnecessary as is BARNES' (Sossianus Hierocles, 242-43) theory that Lactantius only knew a later enlarged edition (HÄGG, Hierocles, 141 n. 16). The two *libellos* or *libros* are volumes of Hierocles' work (Lact. Div. inst. 5.2.13, 5.3.22 [138, 144 MON.]) and not two editions.

[40] HÄGG, Hierocles, 145 versus BARNES, Sossianus Hierocles, 242.

[41] F. WINKELMANN, Review of SC 333 in ThLZ 113, 1988, 680-81.

[42] É. DES PLACES, La second sophistique au service de l'apologétique chrétienne: Le Contre Hiéroclès d'Eusèbe de Césarée, CRAI 1985, 423-27. Compare P.-M. HOMBERT on Eusebius' mordant irony (review of SC 333) in MSR 45, 1988, 111-12.

[43] É. DES PLACES, Le Contre Hiéroclès d'Eusèbe de Césarée à la lumière d'une édition récente, in: StPatr XIX, ed. E. A. LIVINGSTONE, Leuven 1989, 40, 41.

gathered by Hägg, contrast with the judgment Karl Mras (editor of the *P.E.*) made in reference to Eusebius' *P.E.*: "So sehr er [Eusebius] gedanklich und sachlich von Clemens abhängig ist, in seinem Stil ist er von diesem (der mit der zweiten Sophistik kokettiert) ganz unbeeinflußt."[44] These remarks of Mras were reflected in Eduard Schwartz's (editor of the *H.E.*) earlier impression of the *C.H.*: "Die Form des Werkchens ist von einer bei E. ungewöhnlichen Affektation, wozu ihn vielleicht die Lektüre Philostrats verführt hat."[45] In the history of scholarship the *C.H.* has consequently been placed before 303 or after 311 (April/May — the death of Galerius)[46]. Until the necessary stylistic studies are carried out to determine if the *C.H.* is sufficiently different from the rest of Eusebius' corpus to warrant denial of his authorship, it seems premature to decide on a date before 303 or after 311. As Hägg himself notes, he has not "proved" that Eusebius of Caesarea did not write the *C.H.*[47]. There are strong reasons for doubting Eusebius' authorship, and those doubts leave a date before 303 or after 311 (i.e. not during the Great Persecution itself) as viable possibilities for the treatise's composition.

4.4 The Character of Eusebius' Reply

Eusebius (the Sophist) wrote his treatise for an unnamed friend who was aware of the life of Apollonius (*Vita Apollonii*) by Philostratus and who knew it well enough not to need references to the text[48]. Eusebius attacks Hierocles (from the beginning) and Philostratus (from chapter 7), and it is not always easy to decide which author he is referring to in the treatise. He may have directed his work in part to cultured pagans and in part to Christians who had not completely separated themselves from pagan beliefs[49]. The Bible is never quoted[50]. Whether Eusebius directs his work to cultivated pagans with an interest in Christianity or cultivated Christians still attracted to paganism, he

---

[44] GCS VIII/1, IX (Vorwort).

[45] Eusebios 24, 1394.

[46] BARNES has an excellent survey of the question in Sossianus Hierocles, 240. Compare for example HARNACK, Porphyrius, 29 (before 303, a work of Eusebius' youth; Hierocles wrote in Palmyra) and SCHWARTZ, Eusebios 24, 1394 (after the death of Galerius which he finds alluded to in the triumphalistic text from C.H. 4 quoted above).

[47] HÄGG, Hierocles, 149.

[48] FORRAT/DES PLACES, Eusèbe, 70 makes this point.

[49] FORRAT/DES PLACES, Eusèbe, 70-72.

[50] HÄGG, Hierocles, 147 notes that P. MARAVAL takes this fact to be an indication that the author addressed cultivated pagans (Review of SC 333 in RHPhR 68, 1988, 360-61). However, according to HÄGG, the book's "ironic and condescending tone throughout towards pagan beliefs makes it evident that CH was intended for internal use." Eusebius' friend (real or fictional) to whom he dedicated the book was also a Christian.

makes no use of arguments overtly drawn from biblical materials. His confident explanation of Apollonius' miracles as the work of a demon probably indicates that at least some of his readers were Christians. The friend has been attracted to the comparison between Jesus and Apollonius. Eusebius says that he will not attack the rest of Hierocles' work since Hierocles plagiarized the rest of his material from other authors: the contents of the "Lover of Truth" are "not his own, but have been shamelessly stolen from others, not only the thoughts themselves, but also the words and syllables"[51]. The matter of a discourse and the words used to express that matter is a basic distinction used by the rhetoricians[52]. These borrowed objections have already been refuted by Origen in his work against Celsus.

The author also makes the somewhat curious claim that "... of all those who have ever written against us he [Hierocles] alone has made the unique parallel and comparison (παράθεσίς τε καὶ σύγκρισις) between our savior and this man [Apollonius]."[53] Forrat attempts to weaken the force of Eusebius' statement by translating: "seul parmi tous les écrivains qui nous ont jamais attaqués, Hiéroclès a récemment mis au premier plan le parallèle et la comparaison entre cet homme et notre Sauveur"[54]. The ἐξαίρετος ... παράθεσις τε καὶ σύγκρισις (unique parallel and comparison) is clear: alone of all writers Hierocles has made this comparison and has not just made it of paramount interest (in relation to others who have made similar comparisons before)[55]. The author may not have been aware of Porphyry or may have thought that Porphyry's statement (F. 4, Harnack) was unimportant since it was only a comparison between Apollonius and the apostles.

4.5 Hierocles and the High Priest of Philosophy

Lactantius gives a general characterization of Hierocles' work (whom he does not mention by name) by stating that "Another one [Hierocles] , of a stinging manner (*mordacius*), wrote the same kind of material."[56] The person who

---

[51] C.H. 1.6-8 (98 F./DES P.).

[52] Quintilian 3.5.1: *rebus et verbis*. Compare Cicero, De orat. II.14.63: matter or story and diction created by the historian (*rebus et verbis*) are based on the fundamentals (*fundamenta*) supplied by annals and so forth.

[53] Comparison was one of the exercises young rhetoricians practiced in learning epideictic rhetoric. See Theon, Progymnasmata, 9: Περὶ Συγκρίσεως (112 SPENGEL). Further references in LAUSBERG, Handbuch, § 1130.

[54] C.H. 1.22-25 (100-101 F./DES P.).

[55] HÄGG, Hierocles, 146 n. 23. See also 2.3.37 for pagans who compared Jesus to Apollonius.

[56] Div. inst. 5.2.12 (138 MON.; ET here and in what follows slightly modified from MCDONALD's translation in FC 49, 331-32).

wrote the similar material was a self-professed high priest of philosophy who is also anonymous[57]. He was a wealthy landowner in or near Bithynia who taught parsimony and poverty but was avaricious and lustful. His table at home was richer than that of the palace. He used his political connections with the governors (*iudicum*) to prevent his neighbors from recovering their homes and fields that he had taken[58]. The importance of the comparison is the identical context of persecution and counter-propaganda:

> And at the very same time in which a just people were being harassed (*lacerabatur*), he vomited three books against the Christian religion and name. He professed that "before all things the duty of a philosopher was to undermine the errors of men and to recall them to the true way, that is, to the worship of the gods by whose power and majesty (*numine ac maiestate*)[59] the world is governed, and not to allow unskilled (*imperitos*)[60] people to be ensnared by the deceits of certain others, lest their simplicity (*simplicitas*) be a prize and fodder of clever people. So he had undertaken this duty worthy of philosophy, to hold forth the light of wisdom to those not seeing it, not only that they might grow healthy again (*resanescant*)[61] by undertaking the worship of the gods, but also that they might renounce their pertinacious obstinacy (*pertinaci obstinatione deposita*)[62] to avoid the fixed tortures of the body and not to want to endure the severe lacerations of their members in vain."[63] But in order that it might be clear that he had put forth that work for this reason, he was effusive in the praises of princes whose piety and providence, as, indeed, he himself used to say, "has shone forth brightly both in other respects and especially in defending the religions of the gods, and finally it was for the good of human interests that

---

[57] The attempted identification of this philosopher with Porphyry is probably incorrect (see MONAT, SC 205, 37).

[58] Div. inst. 5.2.3 (134 MON.).

[59] This pair of words appears (abbreviated) in the inscription from Diocletian's tetrarchy as a description of the rulers. The inscription also mentions Hierocles (CIL III.133 = 6661).

[60] Porphyry charged that the Christians abused the *simplicitate et imperitia* of the audience (HARNACK, Porphyrius, F. 5). Compare F. 6 and 14 for descriptions of their ignorance (*imperitia*) (see § 2.3.36, 2.3.12, and 2.3.23 of this work).

[61] On the description of Christianity as a disease by the cities petitioning Maximin (Arykanda inscription) and by Julian see § 5.2.23.3. Maximin also described Christianity in this way in Eus. H.E. 9.7.11 (rescript to Tyre).

[62] Compare Pliny's statement that Christians should be punished for their *pertinaciam certe et inflexibilem obstinationem* (Ep. 10.96.3).

[63] Eusebius describes the mutilation of feet and eyes and castration of Christians destined for the mines in De mart. Pal. 7.4, 8.1 (SC 55, 142; 144 BARDY). These events took place during Maximin's persecution.

all people, laying aside and restraining impious and old-womanish superstition,[64] should be free for legitimate practices (*legitimis sacris uacarent*)[65] and should experience the propitiousness of the gods toward them."[66]

Although some have identified this figure with Porphyry, the libertine's lifestyle argues against such a thesis[67]. Lactantius' comparison of Hierocles with this figure is important, however, because it shows the political relevance of both philosophers' activities in their writings to the Christians. The well-fed philosopher is a sycophant and opportunist (*philosophum adulatorem ac tempori seruientem*) according to Lactantius' vituperative judgment[68]. Such a context also describes Hierocles' intellectual activity and role as one of the counselors in the Diocletian's court. Hierocles' desire to humanely and kindly counsel Christians is similar to the other philosopher's desire to free Christians from error and help them avoid the laceration of their bodies[69]. Even Maximin desired that Christians be freed from error, folly and illness[70]. This desire to change peoples' lives is one of the concerns of deliberative rhetoric and is obviously one of Hierocles' chief goals.

4.6 Character of the Scriptures

Besides being among the first to instigate the persecution, in order to "humanely counsel" Christians, Hierocles wrote his volumes to them and not against them[71]. Presumably his counsel (*consulere*) was similar to that of the wealthy philosopher — the counselor for the interests of others (*consultor utilitatis alienae*) — to convince Christian people to see the light of wisdom, undertake the worship of the gods (*cultus deorum*), and avoid physical

---

[64] Tacitus describes Christianity as a superstition in Ann. 15.44 (*exitiabilis superstitio*) as does Suetonius, Nero 16.3 (*superstitionis novae et maleficae*). On the proverbial nature of the expression see MONAT, SC 205, 42.

[65] Compare the similar phrase in the Arykanda inscription (ILCV 1b = CIL III.12132.23): the cities petition that the practice of the atheists (Christians) be forbidden that all have the opportunity to worship the gods your (Maximin and Licinius') kin (τῶν ὁμογενῶν ὑμῶν θεῶν θρησκείᾳ σχολά[ζειν]). On the familiar charge that Christians are responsible for the ungraciousness shown by the gods toward humans see MONAT, SC 205, 42 and § 2.3.1 above.

[66] Div. inst. 5.2.4-7 (134-36 MON.).

[67] See BARNES' discussion in Scholarship, 58-59. One of those who considers such an identification as a possibility is H. CHADWICK, The Sentences of Sextus, TaS 5, Cambridge 1959, 142-43.

[68] Div. inst. 5.2.10 (138 MON.).

[69] Div. inst. 5.2.13 (138 MON.): *humane ac benigne consulere*.

[70] Eus. H.E. 9.7.11-12 commented on in DROGE, Homer, 179.

[71] Div. inst. 5.2.12-13.

torture[72]. To the best of Lactantius' knowledge (even though he may have been wrong about the order of events), Hierocles persecuted and then tried to convince Christians to change their actions so that they could avoid the very persecutions Hierocles helped create. His concern to change their behavior is an element of deliberative rhetoric. To that end he attacked the character of the Christian scriptures in his two volumes:

> In these he tried so to reveal falsity in Sacred Scripture (*falsitatem scripturae sacrae*) that it seems as though it were entirely contrary to itself (*tota contraria*). For certain passages (*capita*)[73] which seemed to contradict themselves (*repugnare sibi uidebantur*), he exposed (*exposuit*), enumerating so many and such intimate points of detail that, at times, he seems to have been of the same training (*disciplina*).[74]

The intimate knowledge of the scriptures that Hierocles possessed made him appear like one trained in Christianity (much as Porphyry appeared to certain later Christian writers)[75]. In that case, Lactantius charges, Hierocles is a betrayer of the faith and sacrament (*sacramenti*)[76]. Lactantius concedes that the scriptures may have fallen into the hands of Hierocles. In that case he attempted to destroy (or "explain" *dissoluere*) that which had never been interpreted to him[77]. His method of looking for contradictions in scripture is similar to that of Porphyry[78]. These characteristics of Hierocles' work are largely passed over by Eusebius who traces the source of most of Hierocles' arguments to Celsus. But Celsus, as we know from Origen, was not very interested in the kinds of philological details that Porphyry was so concerned with. Hierocles must have shared some of Porphyry's interest in looking for

---

[72] Div. inst. 5.2.6, 8 (136 MON.).

[73] MCDONALD translates "chapters or topics" FC 49, 332. For a similar phrase compare Cicero's *capita exposita nec explicata* in Brutus 44.164.

[74] Div. inst. 5.2.13-14.

[75] See § 2.1 above.

[76] Instead of "sacrament" one could translate "revelation" in accord with the use in 1.1.19. See V. FÀBREGA, Die chiliastische Lehre des Laktanz. Methodische und theologische Voraussetzungen und religionsgeschichtlicher Hintergrund, JAC 17, 1974, 126.

[77] Div. inst. 5.2.15-16 (138 MON.). MONAT (SC 205, 47) refers to another meaning of the verb *dissoluere* in Cic. De orat. 2.38.158 *ea quae iam not possint ipsi dissoluere* where the verb means "to resolve" or explain.

[78] See § 2.3.6, 17, 25, and 40 in this work. In § 2.3.25 (F. 91 HARNACK) Augustine uses the word *contrarie* to describe one of Porphyry's comments on Jesus' teachings. Pacatus also uses the word to describe the technique of the antagonist (who is probably Porphyry; see § 2.3.6).

contradictions. This search was in the cause of "counseling" Christian people to find a better way of life.

4.7 Paul, Peter, and the Disciples

To discredit the scriptures Hierocles attacked the sources: "He especially lacerated[79] Paul and Peter and other disciples as though they were 'sowers of falsehood' (*fallaciae seminatores*), and he charged that they were 'rude and unlearned (*rudes et indoctos*) because certain ones of them had made a living from fishing,' just as though he took it hard that some Aristophanes or Aristarchus did not comment on that subject (*illam rem*)."[80] Apparently Hierocles traced some of the gospel traditions (Mark?) to Peter[81]. He surely knew that Paul proclaimed Jesus' cross and resurrection (to the exclusion of other gospel traditions). Consequently Hierocles may have attacked the resurrection as did Porphyry and the anonymous philosopher of Macarius[82]. His comments about "sowers of lies" indicate that he attacked the veracity of at least some of the traditions about Jesus[83]. The charge that the disciples were crude and ignorant was a topos in the pagan critique of Christianity[84]. Celsus envisioned Christians in general as unlearned and uneducated[85]. A person's education was a topic in the rhetoric of praise and blame according to Quintilian[86]. Hierocles' scorn for the disciples' vocation is also present in Celsus' scorn for the abominable tax collectors and sailors that Jesus gathered around himself[87]. Some Romans had a scorn for most types of manual labor,

---

[79] Lactantius' anonymous philosopher refers to the laceration of Christian bodies (Div. inst. 5.2.6 [136 MON.]). Lactantius describes the time as one in which the Christian religion was being "lacerated" (5.2.4).

[80] Div. inst. 5.2.17 (138 MON.). MONAT notes that this reference is probably to the literary critics Aristarchus and his teacher Aristophanes of Byzantium (SC 205, 48).

[81] As in Eus. H.E. 3.39.14-15.

[82] § 2.3.32 (F. 92) and § 3.51 (Apocr. 4.24).

[83] Compare Lactantius' description of the attack on the "falsity of scripture" in Div. inst. 5.2.13 (138 MON.). Arnobius refers to this charge of the pagans in 1.57.

[84] Compare Caecilius' charges in Min. Felix 5.4 (*studiorum rudes, litterarum profanos*) and Arnobius 1.58 (*sed ab indoctis hominibus et rudibus scripta sunt*). See MONAT in SC 205, 47.

[85] Contra Cels. 3.44 (239,27-29 KOET.) and see § 1.6.2 and 1.6.4 above.

[86] On education (*disciplina*) see Quint. 3.7.15. Enthymemic arguments were also drawn from a person's education and training (*educatio et disciplina*) 5.10.25.

[87] Contra Cels. 1.62, 2.46 (113,7-10; 168,13-14 KOET.).

and Hierocles joined them in the denigration of such a way of making a living[88].

Eusebius has a parallel to Lactantius' version of Hierocles' charges about the disciples. Hierocles continues that attack in Eusebius' version by arguing for the reliability of the sources of Apollonius' life:

> This point is worth being considered, namely that Peter and Paul and others like them have boasted (κεκομπάκασιν) about the deeds of Jesus — people who are liars and without education and magicians (ψεῦσται καὶ ἀπαίδευτοι καὶ γόητες), — but in respect to the deeds of Apollonius, Maximus of Aegae,[89] and Damis the philosopher[90] who was always with him, and Philostratus of Athens, people who had advanced furthest in education (παιδεύσεως μὲν ἐπὶ πλεῖστον ἥκοντες), and who honored the truth, for the sake of their love of humanity did not want the acts of a noble man and friend of the gods to be forgotten.[91]

A number of words in this fragment also were used by Macarius' anonymous philosopher — a fact that probably only shows their usefulness in pagan polemic against Christianity since the words occur in many different contexts[92]. Hierocles' charges against the disciples in Eusebius' version (that they are liars and ignorant) are present in Lactantius' version, but the charge that the disciples are magicians (γόητες) is not. Hierocles must also have been aware of the traditions of apostolic miracles in works such as the Acts of the Apostles. Porphyry's statement about apostolic miracles is relevant enough to be quoted here: "Rustic and poor people, since they had nothing, did certain signs (*signa*) by magic arts. To do signs, however, is nothing great, because

---

[88] Dio Chrysostom Or. 7.2-3 has a positive depiction of fishermen and in 7.114-116 he describes those who scorn humble occupations such as those of the schoolmaster, wet-nurse, and grape picker. See R. MACMULLEN, Roman Social Relations. 50 B.C. to A.D. 284, New Haven 1974, 138-41 for a "lexicon of snobbery" in which contempt is expressed for many occupations such as those of the τελώνης and κάπηλος. Romans could be proud of their trades as the inscriptions show (MACMULLEN 202 n. 105). The higher classes (Cicero, Juvenal, Tacitus and so forth) had contempt for the lower occupations (MACMULLEN 114). The vocation of gentleman farmer was an exception. Cicero describes occupations including fishermen as in *sordida arte ... Minimeque artes ... piscatores* (De officiis 1.42.150).

[89] On this source see F. GRAF, Maximos v. Aigai, JAC 27/28, 1984/85, 65-73 and Art. Maximus (36), PRE XIV/2, 1930, 2555.

[90] On Damis and the contemporary view that the documents of Damis are not historical or are a forgery see FORRAT/DES PLACES (Eusèbe, 36-37).

[91] C.H. 2.24-32 (102-04 F./DES P.).

[92] κομπάζω (Apocriticus 3.36, 4.7 [131,8; 165,5 BLONDEL]); ἀπαίδευτοι (3.34, 4.6, 3.2 [129,8; 164,4; 53,1 BLONDEL]), ψεῦσται (3.31 [126,15 BLONDEL]), γόητες (3.31 [126,9 BLONDEL]). Some of the words in Macarius are of a slightly different grammatical form. For a different conclusion (discussed in § 3.1) see T. W. CRAFER, Work of Porphyry, 381-82.

the magicians also did signs in Egypt against Moses. Apollonius also did signs as did Apuleius, and they did innumerable signs."[93] Porphyry's comment is quoted by Jerome in the midst of his own discussion of Peter and Paul. It seems possible that Hierocles was aware of Porphyry's work. Macarius Magnes also notes the accusation of magic made against Peter and Paul in his response to one of the philosopher's objections[94]. Later in his text, Eusebius takes up Hierocles' charge against Peter and Paul and applies it to Damis and Philostratus who contradict themselves (ἐναντιολογοῦντας) in their boasting (κομπάζοντάς τε ἀληθῶς) about Apollonius. Their inconsistencies (τοῖς μαχομένοις) show them to be liars, people without education and charlatans (ψεύστας ... ἀπαιδεύτοις καὶ γόητας)[95]. The word "wizard" is probably used here in a metaphorical sense[96]. However "wizard" is probably a better translation for Hierocles' claim about Peter and Paul given his views on Jesus as magician and that attitude towards the apostles held by one of his probable sources — Porphyry.

4.8 Jesus' Miracles

To create a polemical context for his comparison of Jesus with Apollonius, Hierocles described some of Jesus' miracles as follows: "They go up and down glorifying (σεμνύνοντες) Jesus and babbling (θρυλοῦσιν)[97] that he made the blind to see and did some other similar wonders."[98] He chooses not to question the veracity of the accounts of Jesus' miracles of healing. He did describe the authors or sources of the traditions about Jesus as liars, however, so it is possible that he questioned the historicity of certain gospel narratives in the lost sections of his work. Eusebius does not refer to Hierocles' evaluation of Jesus as a magician. Eusebius does comment that Hierocles did not attribute Apollonius' miracles to magic (γοητείας), but attributed them to his "divine and unutterable wisdom" (θείᾳ τινὶ καὶ ἀρρήτῳ σοφίᾳ)[99]. This issue (the source of Apollonius' ability to work wonders) became a major topic in

---

[93] HARNACK, Porphyrius, F. 4, Jerome, Tract. de psalmo 81. See § 2.3.37 in the present work.

[94] Apocriticus 4.14 (182,22 BLONDEL). See § 3.33 in this work.

[95] C.H. 43.58-60 (196 F./DES P.).

[96] FORRAT/DES PLACES, Eusèbe, 223 (F. also translates the word as charlatan in 2.27).

[97] Macarius' philosopher uses this word to describe the resurrection which is "babbled" about everywhere (Apocrit. 2.14 [23,2 BLONDEL], and see 3.7, 15 [62,5; 94,6 BLONDEL] for other usages).

[98] C.H. 2.5-7 (100 F./DES P.).

[99] C.H. 2.1-2 (100 F./DES P.).

Eusebius' polemic against Apollonius[100]. Lactantius, however, does preserve Hierocles' understanding of Jesus' miracles as the work of a magician: "...Christ was a magician 'because he did miracles' (*quia mirabilia fecit*)"[101]. Although the statement that "Christ was a magician" may not be a direct quote from Hierocles (in Eusebius' texts he refers to him as "Jesus" and not "Christ"), Lactantius makes it clear that Hierocles shared this judgment of Christ with certain Jewish authors: "'He did miracles.' We would have judged (*putassent*) him [Christ] to be a magician, as you judge him now and as the Jews judged him then, if all the prophets had not by the one Spirit predicted that he would do miracles."[102] Celsus' evaluation of Jesus as a magician was probably Hierocles' source for this statement[103].

4.9 Apollonius and Jesus

While conceding that Jesus worked miracles, Hierocles finds a more impressive wonder-worker:

"Let us, however, examine how much better and more intelligently we understand such deeds and what view we have concerning men who possess miraculous powers" (ἐναρέτων ἀνδρῶν). And then after passing by Aristeas the Proconnesian[104] and Pythagoras[105] as too ancient he continues saying: "But in the time of our ancestors during the reign of Nero, Apollonius of Tyana reached his prime, who from the time he was a very young boy and since he became a priest in Aegae of Cilicia of Asclepius, the

---

[100] Lactantius also evaluates Apollonius and Apuleius as magicians in Div. inst. 5.3.21 (144 MON.).

[101] Div. inst. 5.3.9 (142 MON.).

[102] Div. inst. 5.3.19 (144 MON.). On the argument from prophecy see COOK, Protreptic Power, 113-15.

[103] See § 1.2.5 (C. Cels. 1.28, 38, 71) and 1.2.8 (C. Cels. 1.68, 2.49) in this work. Certain Talmudic evaluations of Jesus as a magician are also discussed in those sections. See also Aug., Sermo 71.3 (PL 38.447a: *Christum magicis artis fecisse miracula*) and Arnobius 1.43. For other references see MONAT (SC 205, 53)

[104] See § 1.4.5 and 1.5 in this work for Celsus' use of Aristeas and his denial that Aristeas was a god even though one oracle thought he was (C. Cels. 3.26, 29 [222,10-15; 226,20.24 KOET.]). See also ANDRESEN, Logos und Nomos, 47.

[105] Many wonders of Pythagoras are recounted in the respective *Vitae Pyth.* of Porphyry and Iamblichus. In Porphyry's *Vita Pyth.* 28 (49,5-7 DES PLACES) Pythagoras is taken to be the Hyperborean Apollo. His disciples also counted him among the gods (Vita Pyth. 20 [45,11-12 DES PLACES]). On the usefulness of texts such as these and the *Vita Ap.* in gospel studies see J. Z. SMITH, Good News is no News: Aretalogy and Gospel, in: Christianity, Judaism and Other Greco-Roman Cults. Studies for Morton Smith at Sixty, Part One, New Testament, SJLA 12.1, ed. J. NEUSNER, Leiden 1975, 21-38.

lover of humankind, accomplished many wonders (θαυμαστά), of which I will omit most and only mention a few." Then he enumerates his marvels (τὰ παράδοξα) starting with the first ...[106]

Lactantius' parallel to this passage is brief: "He also, when he was weakening his [Christ's] miracles (*mirabilia destrueret*) but not indeed denying them, wanted to show 'that Apollonius did either equal or greater deeds' (*uel paria uel maiora*)." Lactantius then adds: "It is astonishing that he omitted Apuleius whose many and marvelous acts (*multa et mira*) people usually remember."[107] To build his argument against the Christian understanding of Jesus, Hierocles established the fact that Apollonius worked as many miracles as Jesus. Hierocles viewed Apollonius as a remarkable person or a person endowed with mysterious virtues (ἐναρέτης). This understanding of "virtues" is similar to the use of the noun in Strabo, *Geog.* 17.1.17 where Strabo speaks of temple texts describing the ἀρεταί (divine acts) of Serapis at his temple at Canopus[108]. Hierocles' choice was inspired since Apollonius' influence lasted well into late antiquity — although it was a "magical" influence. An inscription that may be from Aegae itself (now in the museum in Adana) attests to his continuing influence[109]. Roman aristocrats created medallions that featured Apollonius[110]. A fourth or fifth century Christian was willing to concede that talismans of Apollonius could prevent certain evils[111]. The author (whoever it was)[112] of the *SHA* describes a scene in which Aurelian was considering the

---

[106] C.H. 2.8-18 (100-02 F./DES P.).

[107] Div. inst. 5.3.7 (142 MON.). MONAT (SC 205, 52) notes that Apuleius and Apollonius were habitually paired (Aug. Ep. 136.1, 138.18)

[108] LSJ, ἀρετή refer also to SIG 1172, IG 14.966, and 1 Peter 2:9. On aretalogies see K. BERGER, Hellenistische Gattungen im Neuen Testament, ANRW II.25.2, 1984, (1034-1379) 1219, 1220 and COOK, Structure and Persuasive Power, 77-79.

[109] PETZKE, Die Traditionen, 19-36 gives much archaeological and literary evidence. FORRAT/DES PLACES, Eusèbe, 215-19 conveniently print the various reconstructions of the inscription.

[110] A. ALFÖLDI/E. ALFÖLDI, Die Kontorniat-Medaillons, Deutsches Archäologisches Institut Antike Münzen und Geschnittene Steine 6.1, 2, Berlin/New York 1990, 6.1: Table 38,1-4; 6.2: Table 215.1-2 and see the discussion in 6.2: 53-55, 103-104.

[111] Ps. Just., Quaestiones et responsiones ad orthodoxos 24, 405a-406a (34-36 OTTO); briefly discussed in § 3.16 in the present work. For other evidence see FORRAT/DES PLACES, Eusèbe, 33 with particular reference to W. L. DULIÈRE, Protection permanente contra des animaux nuisibles assurée par Apollonios de Tyane dans Byzance et Antioche. Évolution de son mythe, ByZ 63, 1970, 247-277.

[112] The putative author of Aurelian's biography, Vopiscus, may be imaginary. See Flavius Vopiscus, PLRE 981. A. RÖSGER describes Vopiscus this way, "the author, whatever his name was and whenever he may have lived," in Vopiscus und das Authentizitätsproblem (Car. 4,1-5,3), Bonner Historia-Augusta-Colloquium 1986/1989, ed. K. ROSEN, Antiquitas 4. BHAF 21, Bonn 1991, (179-82) 182. R. SYME describes the author of the SHA as "the imposter who passed himself off as six biographers writing in the

destruction of Tyana: "...but Apollonius of Tyana, a sage of the greatest renown and authority, a philosopher of former days, the true friend of the gods, and himself even to be regarded as a supernatural being (*pro numine frequentandum*) as Aurelian was withdrawing to his tent, suddenly appeared to him in the form in which he is usually portrayed, and spoke to him as follows ..."[113]. If this text was written in the fourth century, it is fine evidence that some pagan was willing to conceive of the possibility of Apollonius' continuing graceful activity. Apollonius has even graced a French magician of the nineteenth century, Eliphas Lévi, with an appearance in a mirror[114].

4.10 Versus Christian Belief in Jesus as a God

After establishing the miracles done by Apollonius, Hierocles concludes that Christians are foolish to believe Jesus is a god on the basis of lesser miracles:

> Why have I remembered these things? In order that it might be possible to compare our precise and certain judgment on each point (τὴν ἡμετέραν ἀκριβῆ καὶ βεβαίαν ἐφ' ἑκάστῳ κρίσιν) with the lightheadedness (κουφότητα) of the Christians. For on the one hand we think that the one who did such things is not a god but a man favored by the gods (θεοῖς κεχαρισμένον ἄνδρα), but they proclaim Jesus god on the basis of a few prodigies (τερατείας).[115]

Lactantius presents a similar argument of Hierocles that may be from the same context in Hierocles' work:

> I do not claim, he says, that because Apollonius was not taken to be a god that he would have refused it, but in order that it would appear that we are wiser (*sapientiores*) than you, because after all his miracles (*mirabilibus factis*) we did not immediately add faith in his divinity, while you in consideration of a few prodigies (*exigua portenta*) believed him god.[116]

---

age of Diocletian and Constantine" (Ignotus, the Good Biographer, in: Bonner Historia-Augusta-Colloquium 1966/1967, ed. A. ALFÖLDI, Antiquitas 4. BHAF 4, Bonn 1968, (131-53) 132.

[113]SHA 24.2-9 (LCL). On this text see J. SCHWARTZ, A propos du Vocabulaire religieux de l'Histoire Auguste, in: Bonner Historia-Augusta-Colloquium 1975/1976, ed. A. ALFÖLDI, Antiquitas 4. BHAF 13, Bonn 1978,187-93.

[114] E. LÉVI, Transcendental Magic, trans. A. E. WAITE, London, n.d., 154-57 noted by J. Z. SMITH, Good News is no News, 22.

[115] C.H. 2.18-23 (102 F./DES P.)

[116] Div. inst. 5.3.16 (144 MON.).

Celsus used a similar argument against considering Jesus to be a god: Christians "regarded him as Son of God for this reason, because he healed the lame and the blind"[117]. Lactantius replied that Christians believe Jesus to be God not because of the miracles but because he fulfilled prophecies. The cross is also central: "We believe him to be God less because of his miracles than because of the cross which was also prophesied."[118] Origen's response to Celsus' objection was also similar in that he appealed to Isaiah 35:5-6: "Because he healed the lame and the blind, we therefore regard him as Christ and Son of God; it is clear to us from what has been written in the prophecies: 'Then shall the eyes of the blind be opened, and the ears of the deaf shall hear. Then shall the lame man leap like a deer.'"[119] Hierocles' comments on Christian credulity will be discussed below. He obviously viewed the argument from miracle to be seriously flawed. Apparently he did not attack the Christian use of Hebrew prophecy as Celsus did, since Lactantius so confidently responds with an argument from prophecy[120].

Hierocles concedes that Apollonius was honored as a god by some, although it is clear that he does not so evaluate the wonder-worker: "he was adored by some as god, and his statue was raised in Ephesus under the name of Hercules 'the Averter of evil' (*Alexicaci*)[121] and is still honored even now"[122]. Lactantius argues that Apollonius would not have denied the title "god" if he could have obtained it. Celsus also notes that Apollo commanded the Metapontines to view Aristeas as a god — although Celsus himself does not view Aristeas as divine[123].

4.11 Jesus as a Robber

Lactantius refers to several traditions of the life of Jesus that are not found in Eusebius. A tradition apparently unique to Hierocles claimed Jesus became a robber captain: "Christ himself, he affirmed, put to flight by the Jews, assembled a band of 900 men and committed robberies."[124] In a tradition in

---

[117] C. Celsum 2.48 (169,16-18 KOET.).

[118] Div. inst. 5.3.19-20 (144 MON.). On the patristic argument from prophecy see COOK, Protreptic Power, 113-15.

[119] C. Celsum 2.48 (169,19-23 KOET.). See further § 1.2.8 above.

[120] See § 1.4.2 above.

[121] Compare LEWIS and SHORT s.v. *alexipharmacon* — an antidote to poison (found in Plinius 21.20.84 § 146). MONAT (SC 205, 54-55) refers to the temple of Heracles ἀποτρόπαιος that Apollonius had built in Ephesus (Vita Ap. 8.7.31) and to the veneration of Heracles as ἀλεξίκακος in Athens (Dict. antiquités III.111).

[122] Lact, Div. inst. 5.3.14 (142 MON.).

[123] Contra Celsum 3.26 (222,13-15 KOET.).

[124] Lact, Div. inst. 5.3.4 (140 MON.).

the Slavonic translation of Josephus' *Jewish War*, 150 servants assemble around Jesus and a large number of other people. When they see his power [healings by word], they ask him to enter Jerusalem and to massacre the Roman troops and Pilate and to reign over them. Jesus refuses, and Pilate is later bribed by the doctors of the law. Pilate then gives them licence to execute Jesus[125]. Celsus uses robbers several times to make adverse comparison with Jesus: Jesus did not inspire the loyalty in his disciples that robber-captains do (Contra Celsum 2.12 [140,20-23 Koet.]); and any robber or murderer could claim to have foreseen his miserable death and so lay claim to being a god (Contra Celsum 2.44 [166,24-27 Koet.]). Celsus, however, does not identify Jesus as a robber. Lactantius asks how one would contradict such a great authority (as Hierocles). He mocks Hierocles and remarks "Perhaps Apollo told him in a dream."[126] Lactantius was aware (as was Porphyry) that Apollo's oracles occasionally commented on Jesus[127]. He adds that robbers die daily and that Hierocles himself has condemned many and concludes with this question: which of them, after being crucified was called, I shall not say, "god" but "man"[128]. Hierocles' claim is certainly an example of vituperative rhetoric. He may have used it to explain the crucifixion of Jesus — an exercise in forensic rhetoric.

---

[125] Text and French trans. in V. ISTRIN, La prise de Jérusalem de Josèphe le Juif, Paris 1934, II.9.3 pp. 148-51. See also LODS, Les sources juives de Celse, 18-19. In LODS' version Jesus attempts to storm Jerusalem and is imprisoned. ISTRIN's text is different from the tradition LODS mentions.

[126] Compare Vergil Ecl. 3.104 *Et eris mihi magnus Apollo* (used in mockery of those who pretend to know more than others). See MONAT's commentary on the passage in Lactantius (SC 205, 50).

[127] See § 2.2.2 in this work for an oracle from Didyma concerning Christ (from Div. inst. 4.13.11). On Didyma's role in the great persecution see Lact, De mort. pers. 11.7 (18 CREED; In response to an envoy from Diocletian, "Apollo replied as one would expect of an enemy of the religion of God"). Compare Eus. Vita Const. 2.50 (GCS Eusebius I, 62,16-17 HEIKEL) where Apollo states that "the righteous on earth were an obstacle to his telling the truth." On the oracle at Daphne's role in that persecution see BARNES, Sossianus Hierocles, 251-52.

[128] Div. inst. 5.3.5 (140 MON.).

4.12 Jesus' Trial

Jesus' conduct at his trial was also objectionable to Hierocles, according to Lactantius version: "If Christ is a magician 'because he did miracles,' 'Apollonius' is certainly more skillful [*peritior*] (because as you describe 'when Domitian wanted to punish him suddenly [*repente*] he was no longer present [*comparuit*] in the tribunal') than he who was arrested and fastened to the cross."[129] Macarius' philosopher was also impressed by Apollonius' behavior at his trial[130]. The philosopher also noted Apollonius' bold speech which he contrasted with Jesus' behavior before Pilate.

Lactantius apparently summarizes Hierocles' conclusion next: "But perhaps from this he wanted to prove the arrogance (*insolentiam*) of Christ who appointed (*constituerit*) himself god, so that he appears more modest (*uerecundius*) who when he [Apollonius] accomplished greater things, as this one [Hierocles] judges, did not nevertheless arrogate to himself the title."[131] Lactantius refuses to compare their deeds because he states that he has already dealt with works of magic and fraud in another context[132]. Obviously both thinkers are at an impasse: Lactantius attributed Apollonius' works to magic as Hierocles attributed Jesus' work to magic. There is a close parallel in Lactantius' treatment of the oracle of Apollo at Didyma. Apollo called Jesus a wise man who was crucified, but then claimed that Jesus accomplished miracles not by supernatural power but by magic (*miranda uerum non diuina uirtute, sed magica*)[133]. The charge of magic was obviously a double-edged sword.

4.13 Christian Credulity

Hierocles contrasts "our own accurate and well-established judgment (ἀκριβῆ καὶ βεβαίαν ἐφ' ἑκάστῳ κρίσιν) on each point" with the "easy credulity" or "light-headedness" (κουφότητα) of the Christians. He criticizes Christians for

---

[129] Div. inst. 5.3.9 (142 MON.). See Vita Ap. 8.5 and Jerome, Adv. Ioh. Hieros. 34 (PL 23, 404c): *Apollonius Tyaneus scribitur, cum ante Domitianum staret in consistorio, repente non comparuisse.* Lactantius' quote from Hierocles is: *cum Domitianus eum punire uellet, repente in iudicio non comparuit.* MONAT (SC 205, 53), who gives the reference to Jerome, also notes that Lactantius uses the identical expression for Nero's disappearance from the earth in De mort. pers. 2.7 (6 CREED)..

[130] Apocriticus 3.1 (52,4-7 BLONDEL). See the discussion in § 3.21.

[131] Div. inst. 5.3.10 (142 MON.).

[132] Div. inst. 5.3.11 and see Div. inst. 2.16 (SC 337, 194-207 MONAT) passim (on magic and demons).

[133] Div. inst. 4.13.11,16 (SC 377, 116,46-51; 118,73-74 MONAT).

their credulity since they claim Jesus to be a god because of a few miracles, while the Hellenes only claim Apollonius to be a man graced by the gods[134]. This accusation cut "Eusebius" to the quick because he repeats it in four other contexts[135]. In those contexts Eusebius adds εὐχέρειαν (ease, recklessness) to κουφότητα (credulity, légèreté) when referring to Hierocles' charges. His response to Hierocles' critique is to question the credibility of the sorts of miracles that Philostratus ascribes to Apollonius. In *C.H.* 18, for example, Eusebius attacks various marvels that come to pass when Apollonius meets the Brahmans. The Brahmans have two jars of which one contains rain and one winds[136]. In *C.H.* 20 after repeating Hierocles' charge or recklessness and credulity Eusebius again quotes Hierocles' phrase: "Let us, however, examine how much better and more intelligently we understand such deeds and what view we have concerning men who possess miraculous powers (ἐναρέτων ἀνδρῶν)." Eusebius then lists more of Philostratus' tales of the Brahmans including a marvelous drinking bowl that fills itself with wine and self-moving tripods — the last story Eusebius describes as mythology[137].

Hierocles' charge was a topos in the Hellenistic critique of Christianity. Galen charges that Christians (and others) could not follow demonstrative arguments, but needed parables (such as tales of future judgment.)[138]. Celsus noted that Christians were like gullible people who did not want their faith examined and did not want to offer reasons for it.[139] Porphyry described the Christian faith as unexamined and irrational and noted the recklessness (εὐχερείας) of abandoning one's native traditions for such a faith[140]. With regard to John 6:54, which he found utterly repugnant, Macarius' philosopher describes Christian people as those who are easily convinced in an irrational manner (εὐχερεῖς ἀλλόγως)[141].

Hierocles compares the credulity and recklessness of Christian belief with his own careful and firm judgment (κρίσιν). Marcus Aurelius used the same term (judgment) to contrast the Stoic's readiness to die with the Christians "bare (or unreasoned) obstinacy" in the face of death:

---

[134] C.H. 2.21-23 (102 F./DES P.).

[135] C.H. 4.2, 4.44, 17.7, 20.3 (104, 108, 138, 144 F./DES P.).

[136] See Vita Ap. 3.14.

[137] C.H. 21.15-18 (146 F./DES P.; from Vita Ap. 3.32) and C.H. 24.3-7 (150 F./DES P.; Vita Ap. 3.27).

[138] The text is from Abulfeda's Universal Chronicle 3.3 of the section of pre-Islamic history and is translated and edited by R. WALZER, Galen on Jews and Christians, London: 1949, 15-16, 90. See COOK, Some Hellenistic Responses, 239.

[139] See § 1.6.1 above and C. Cels. 1.9 (61,17-19 KOET.).

[140] Eus. P.E. 1.2.4 (SC 206, 106 SIRINELLI/DES PLACES) = HARNACK, Porphyrius, F. 1 (§ 2.3.4 above).

[141] Apocriticus 3.15 (95,9 BLONDEL) = HARNACK, Porphyrius, F. 69

A soul that is ready is of this kind: if it must be separated from the body it is ready either to be extinguished (σβεσθῆναι), or to be scattered or to continue (συμμεῖναι). This readiness arises from one's own judgment (ἰδικῆς κρίσεως) and not from bare obstinacy (κατὰ ψιλὴν παράταξιν)[142] — as in the case of the Christians — but reasonably and reverently (λελογισμένως καὶ σεμνῶς) in order to persuade (πεῖσαι) another without tragic display (ἀτραγῳδως).[143]

In the Stoics' discussion of the criterion for truth κρίσις could be used to describe the critical faculty[144]. Marcus has little respect for the rationality of the Christians and denies them the critical faculty of judgment itself. They are not rational or reverent in his depiction of their willingness to die. He surely must have been aware of their endurance to the death in Lyon[145]. In a rescript, Marcus exiled to an island anyone "who does anything whereby people's light minds are frightened by superstitious awe" (*Si quis aliquid fecerit, quo leues hominum animi superstitione numinis terrentur*)[146]. He and Hierocles probably shared similar views about Christians' "light minds." Hierocles apparently assumed some rationality on the part of the people he was trying to persuade to abandon the Christian faith.

His word for Christian recklessness (εὐχέρεια) is defined by Hesychius to mean κουφότης — which often means "lightness." Consequently Forrat's translation for the two words is "insouciance" (carelessness) and "légèreté" (facility)[147]. Macarius' philosopher has a use of the adjective κοῦφος (light, airy) to describe hypothetical Greeks who are so foolish as to believe that the gods live in statues[148]. Gregory of Nazianzus uses "lightness" in an invective against the Jews who were going to help Julian in his plan to restore the temple[149]. Gregory also applied the category to Julian himself in reference to an episode that is probably legendary. A Persian envoy to Julian pretends to be a traitor to Persia. His words persuaded Julian (ἔπεισεν) to burn his fleet.

---

[142] See LSJ, ψιλός IV.1 for a connotation of "unargued" or "unproven" for this word. Aristotle, Rhet. ad Alex. 1438b uses it for the "bare facts" presented in the narratio of a speech.

[143] In semet ipsum 11.3.2 (SCHENKL) in W. den Boer, Scriptorum paganorum I-IV saec. de christianis testimonia, Textus Minores II, Leiden 1948. For another use of "tragic display" see 1.16.3.

[144] SVF 1.107 = Sext. Emp., Adv. math. 7.35.

[145] Eus. H.E. 5.5.3 describes the persecution in Lyon.

[146] Justinian, Digesta 48.19.30 (852 MOMMSEN/KRUEGER/WATSON).

[147] Eusèbe, 145.

[148] Apocriticus 4.22 (202,1-2 BLONDEL).

[149] Or. 5.3 (SC 309, 298,15 BERNARDI).

Julian's credulity (κουφότης) was easily persuaded (εὔπιστον) by the envoy's words[150]. To the intellectual weakness of the Christians, Hierocles opposed his own careful judgment and to the Christians' foolish belief in Christ he apparently opposed the Hellenic belief in a supreme God.

4.14 Hierocles' God

Lactantius completes his account of Hierocles' work with a remark that Hierocles ended his own "truth loving discourse" with an encomium of God. Lactantius himself is unwilling to admit the intellectual coherence of Hierocles' polytheism. Expressions of his polytheism are explicitly found in Celsus and Macarius' philosopher[151]. In that philosophy the Hellenes assert the existence of a supreme deity with a host of subordinate deities. Such a position Lactantius finds untenable: "What truth have you at last brought us — if not that as the defender of the gods you ultimately betrayed them (*assertor deorum eos ipsos ad ultimum prodidisti*)?"[152] Hierocles' fault was to have written an encomium on the supreme God:

> For pursuing the praises of the "Supreme God" (*summi dei laudes*) whom you admitted to be "the King, the Greatest, the Maker of things, the Source of good, the Parent of all, the Maker and Sustainer of all the living," you took the kingdom from your Jupiter, and when he was thus removed from supreme power (*summa potestate*),[153] you reduced him into the number of ministers (*ministrorum numerum*). So your epilogue convicts you of folly and vanity and error. For you affirm that there are gods, and yet you subject them and put them in bondage to the God whose religion you are attempting to overthrow (*dei cuius religionem conaris euertere*).[154]

Lactantius locates Hierocles' exercise in epideictic rhetoric in the epilogue of the *Truth Loving Discourse*. Such examples of praise of the gods considered their power, gifts, acts, antiquity, and virtue[155]. For praise of Jupiter, Quintilian

---

[150] Or. 5.12 (314,2 BERNARDI). Compare his use of the word in 5.20 (332,19 BERN.) where Julian's deceit (ἀπάτης) preys on the credulity (κουφότητος) of his friends that he persuades to come to court.

[151] See § 1.7.2 (e.g. C. Cels. 7.68, 8.2), § 3.47 (Apocr. 4.20) above.

[152] Lact, Div. inst. 5.3.24 (146 MON.).

[153] MONAT (SC 205, 58) refers to Plato, Phaedrus 246e where Zeus is a powerful chief whom the other gods follow. Tert. Apol. 24.3 (134,16-18 DEKKERS) describes Plato's view thus: *Plato Iouem magnum in caelo comitatum exercitu describit, deorum pariter et daemonum.*

[154] ET from MACDONALD, Lactantius 336-37.

[155] LAUSBERG, Handbuch, § 243. On praise of the gods see Quint. 3.7.6-9. On the progymnastic exercise of praising people and cities see Hermogenes, Progymn. 7. It is understandable that Quintilian provides no corresponding method for denunciation (*vituperatio*) of the gods in 3.7.19.

writes: "For example, in the case of Jupiter, we shall extol his power as manifested in the governance of all things (*Vis ostenditur ... regendorum omnium*)."[156] Hierocles' titles for God are commonplaces. Alcinous, for example, called God the "creator (ποιητής) of all" who prevents the dissolution of the universe[157]. God is the father of all things and the demiurge of the universe (πατρὶ πάντων ... ὁ τῶν ὅλων δημιουργός)[158]. He is the cause of all good[159]. Maximus of Tyre calls God the father and demiurge of all[160]. He is a great king with many gods who are his subjects[161]. Zeus is the father and provider (χορηγός) of human goods[162]. Hierocles' concentration on the benefits that God bestows probably implies that returning to Hellenism would assure the continuation of such benefits for the wayward Christians[163]. The epilogue helps show the foundation of Hierocles' faith in the Hellenes' supreme God. Perhaps it explains his willingness to both use the sword against the Christians and to use the power of his intellect to save Hellenism as the Christians' benevolent and humane counselor[164].

4.15 Conclusion

One of the most interesting aspects of Hierocles' text is the close relationship between the cultural context (the Great Persecution) and the counter propaganda of the *Truth Loving Discourse*. One senses that paganism felt the power of Christian persuasion and needed to find ways to defuse the threat. Hierocles' attempt to save Christians from their easy credulity has to be seen in light of the violence he was willing to practice against Christian people. Surely he attained some modest success in his attempt to convince some intelligent people that belief in Christ as god was not a rational position — if one can attribute to

---

[156] Quint. 3.7.8.

[157] Didask. 15 171,21-23 (35 W./L.)

[158] Didask. 16 172,5-7 (37 W./L.). On God as the father and cause of all things see also Didask. 9 163,13-14; 10 164,40 (20; 23 W./L.).

[159] Didask. 10 164,37 (23 W./L.).

[160] Diss. 2.10, 11.12 (20,183; 99,274 TRAPP). Cp. Plato, Tim. 41a.

[161] Diss. 11.12 (100,289 TRAPP) and see Ps. Arist., De mundo 6 discussed in § 1.7.2. God is "king and father of all" in Diss. 11.5 (91,78 TRAPP) and "father and begetter (γεννητήν) of all" in 11.9 (96,200 TRAPP).

[162] Diss. 41.2 (330,32 TRAPP). See M. B. TRAPP's comment on this text in his translation, Maximus of Tyre. The Philosophical Orations, Oxford 1997, 324 n.8 with reference to many philosophical texts.

[163] See Porphyry's similar view in § 2.3.1 (F. 80) above and the note related to pagan charges that Christians were responsible for disasters sent by the gods because of their apostasy from Hellenism.

[164] Lact, Div. inst. 5.2.12-13 (138 MON.).

Hierocles' text some of the force of Porphyry's *Contra Christianos*. The people most vulnerable to Hierocles' argumentation may have been intellectuals (such as the friend Eusebius writes the *Contra Hieroclem* for) who were attracted to paganism and Christianity. For the obstinate Hierocles had an easy solution — death or torture.

There are some mysteries of a literary-historical nature that remain especially with regard to the identity of "Eusebius." If he was not Eusebius of Caesarea, then it is easier to understand why he makes no mention of Hierocles as a persecutor in the *C.H.* If the Christian author is correct, then Hierocles has the distinction of being the first to carry out a systematic comparison between Jesus and Apollonius. But the rest of his material apparently came from authors such as Celsus. The charge of magic (used by pagans and Christians against each other's holy figures) had become an argumentative tool — that was almost neutral in itself because either side could use it with equal force. Lactantius' comments about the High Priest of philosophy's attempt to defend Roman religion and Hierocles' encomium of the supreme God show that both were defending Hellenistic culture. Could they feel the pillars of Olympus tottering?

5. Julian

Julian Against the Galilaeans

The emperor Julian in his brief life (331/32-363) mounted the last attack on the Christians to be considered in this volume. While not having the historical and philological skill of Porphyry, Julian's literary gifts were formidable. His conversion form Christianity to paganism and his criticism of the "Galilaeans" have earned him a sort of immortality as Julian the "Apostate."

Since his own conversion helps illuminate the passion of his attack on Christendom I will devote the first part of the chapter to that event in Julian's life. Some fascinating accounts of the experiences that may have led up to the conversion remain. They illustrate the personal and cultural issues that underlie the pagans' attempt to refute the NT. Then the relevant sections of the *Contra Galilaeos* (*Against the Galilaeans*) will be reviewed. Again I will adopt the NT as a template to structure Julian's comments — although he certainly did not attempt to write a commentary on the NT. After considering Julian's work on synoptic traditions, his critique of John's christology will be presented along with his critique of Acts and Paul. Then some general issues in Julian's work will be examined including his views on the following: the consequences of Christian belief, his law against Christian teachers, his views of contemporary Christian practices, his defense of polytheism, and his admiration of Asclepius. Julian represents the last great attempt to stem the tide.

5.1 Julian's Conversion

Julian dated his conversion to a period in his life when he was twenty (351/52)[1]. Robert Wilken notes that at this time Julian was getting interested in

---

[1] Ep. 111, 434d (I/2, 191,1-3 BIDEZ = III, 148 WRIGHT). Below the C. Gal. will be cited using the edition of E. MASARACCHIA, Giuliano Imperator Contra Galilaeos, Testi e Commenti 9, Roma 1990. The ET of the C. Gal. and other texts from Julian below is by W. CAVE WRIGHT, The Works of the Emperor Julian, Vols. I-III, LCL, London/New York, 1913-23. J. BIDEZ and G. ROCHEFORT's edition will also be cited below: L'Empereur Julien. Oeuvres complètes, Vol. I/1, I/2, II/1, II/2, CUFr, Paris 1932-1972.

the practices of theurgy guided by the philosopher Maximus of Ephesus[2]. This Maximus, whom Valentinian later executed for magic, came to Nicomedia after Constantius had sent Julian there. Socrates wrote that "after Julian tasted the words of the philosophers with Maximus he began to imitate the religion of his teacher, who gave him the desire for the empire"[3]. In Nicomedia where Libanius had gone from Constantinople, Julian privately procured the rhetor's orations. Julian had been forbidden to study with him because of Libanius' paganism. Constantius' provision, according to Socrates, was that Julian "should have no pagan masters lest he should be seduced to the pagan superstitions"[4]. Julian later went to Ionia to pursue his philosophical studies. Eunapius tells the story of Julian's studies under several philosophers in Pergamum. A teacher named Eusebius told Julian a story of Maximus in which Maximus made a statue of Hecate laugh and kindled her torches. Julian found Maximus in Ephesus and became interested in "this kind of lore"[5].

Gregory of Nazianzus has an account of an initiation of Julian and probably refers to Maximus as mystagogue although Maximus is not mentioned by name:

> Julian descended into one of the fearful sanctuaries (ἀδύτων) not to be trodden (ἀβάτων) by ordinary people ... having with him one worthy of many sanctuaries, who was wise concerning such things, or rather a sophist. This is a sort of divination for them — to consult darkness and underworldly demons concerning things that are going to happen ... Fearful things approached the noble man as he went forward, and became more numerous and more terrifying. They said that there were strange sounds and nauseating odors, and fiery appearances, and I don't know what other nonsense and humbug. Struck by this unexpected scene, being late to learn such things, he sought refuge in the cross, the old medicine (φάρμακον), and with this he signed himself against the fearful things, and made the persecuted one his helper. And the things that followed were even more terrifying. The seal was powerful, the demons were overcome, the fears dissipated. Then what? He breathed the evil again and again took courage, there was an immediate rush, and the same fearful things, and again the seal, and the demons were quiet. The initiate (μύστης) was in wonder and the mystagogue, nearby, was misinterpreting the truth: "We are loathsome," he said, "we have not frightened them. The evil has won." He said these things, and speaking he persuaded (πείθει), and persuading he led the disciple into the abyss of perdition ... What he then said or did, or what he was deceived by before he was

---

[2] The material on Julian's conversion is dependent on my article: Some Hellenistic Responses, 251-54. See also WILKEN, Christians, 169.

[3] Socrates, Hist. Eccl. 3.1.18 (PG 67, 372 = GCS Sokrates 188,25-27 HANSEN): Παρὰ τούτῳ δὴ φιλοσόφων λόγων γευσάμενος, εὐθὺς ἐμιμεῖτο καὶ τὴν θρησκείαν τοῦ παιδευτοῦ. Libanius and Eunapius date Julian's encounter with Maximus to his stay in Ionia (see the texts below). There are also several letters (two of which are spurious) from Julian to the philosopher (Ep. 26, 414a; 190, 383a; 191, 383c [I/2, 52,5; 246,3; 247,2 BIDEZ]).

[4] Socrates, H.E. 3.1.11 (188,8-9 HANS.).

[5] Eunapius, Vita 475 (LCL, Philostratus and Eunapius, 434 WRIGHT).

sent up — those who have been initiated in such things (or those who initiate) would know. He went up under the power of a demon both in his soul and in his deeds, and in the madness of his eyes he showed the ones whom he served. In any case from that day he was filled with demons — from the day in which he committed such evils.[6]

Neither Sozomen nor Theodoret, who also tell similar stories, identify the mystagogue[7]. It is probably Maximus, though certainty is impossible. The allusions to Hades and to Maximus, according to Rowland Smith, indicate that it was a sanctuary of Hecate[8]. Bidez is content to identify the ritual as "Neo-Platonic theurgy"[9]. What is decisive, if it is true, is that the episode figured in Julian's conversion. Sozomen attests to Julian's interest in divination (H.E. 5.2) as does Ammianus Marcellinus (22.12.7, 23.5.10-14).

Of this time Libanius later wrote to Julian: "Upon your arrival in Ionia you beheld a man wise both in repute and in reality [Maximus], heard of the gods who fashioned and maintain this whole universe, gazed upon the beauty of philosophy and tasted of its sweetest springs. Then you quickly cast off your error and, lionlike, burst your bonds, released yourself from darkness, and grasped truth instead of ignorance, the real instead of the false, our old gods instead of this recent intruder and his baneful rites."[10] The recent intruder and

---

[6] Greg. Naz. Or. 4.55-6 (PG 35, 577, 580 = SC 309, 158-60 BERNARDI). Translation done with reference to that of J. BIDEZ, La vie de l'empereur Julien, Paris 1965, 79-80.

[7] Sozomen, H.E. 5.2.5-6 (GCS Sozomenus 191,3-14 BIDEZ/HANSEN), Theodoret, H.E. 3.1 (GCS Theodoret 178,5-18 PARMENTIER/SCHEIDWEILER)

[8] R. SMITH, Julian's Gods. Religion and Philosophy in the Thought and Action of Julian the Apostate, London/New York 1995, 130. The text in Eunapius (Vita 475 [434 WRIGHT]) supports the identification. P. ATHANASSIADI-FOWDEN (Julian and Hellenism. An Intellectual Biography, Oxford 1981, 38) also assumed that Julian was initiated into Mithraism around 351. DE LABRIOLLE, La réaction, 383 also believes the initiation in Gregory (4.55) was Mithraic. Unfortunately there is no clear evidence. Gregory (Or. 4.52 [PG 35, 576 = SC 309, 154-56 BERNARDI]) may be a reference to a taurobolium, but that is a rite of Metroac mysteries according to SMITH, Julian's Gods 262 n. 74. W. BURKERT, Ancient Mystery Cults, Cambridge 1987, 91-94, describes several experiences of initiation in which terrors (*deimata*) play a role including Plutarch, Frag. 178 (107,1-16 SANDBACH = Stobaeus 4.52.49). Unlike Gregory's account however, Plutarch's end with a vision of light: "And then some wonderful light comes to meet you, pure regions and meadows are there to greet you, with sounds and dances and solemn, sacred words and holy views; and there the initiate, perfect by now, set free and loose from all bondage, walks about crowned with a wreath, celebrating the festival together the other sacred and pure people..."

[9] La Vie de l'Empereur 80. G. RICCIOTTI (Julian the Apostate, trans. J. COSTELLOE, S.J., Milwaukee 1960, 41) calls the episode an initiation into "the theurgic mysteries."

[10] Lib., Or. 13.12 (Libanius. Selected Works, ed. and trans. A. F. NORMAN, Vol. 1, LCL, Cambridge/London 1987). Text quoted in WILKEN, Christians, 169. See also G. BARDY, La conversion au christianisme durant les premiers siècles, Theol(P) 15, Paris 1949, 339-48 on the "apostasy" of Julian. SMITH also discussed the conversion in Julian's Gods 180-89. J.-C. FOUSSARD summarizes Julian's philosophy in Julien Philosophe, in:

his baneful rites was of course Jesus. René Braun argues that Julian's devotion to Christianity was at best weak during the time before his conversion[11]. Ammianus Marcellinus supports this position: "Although Julian from the earliest days of his childhood had been more inclined toward the worship of the pagan gods (*numinum cultum*), and as he gradually grew up burned with longing to practice it, yet because of his many reasons for anxiety he observed certain of its rites with the greatest possible secrecy."[12] Pierre de Labriolle concludes that "Nothing proves a solid faith in the adolescent Julian, and nothing proves that he ever touched the depth of the Christian spirit."[13] Julian's reported childhood longing for the rays of Helios and his mystical experiences of the beauties of the heavens supports Ammianus' views[14].
Libanius also describes Julian's conversion in another passage:

> Finally, he met with people who were steeped with the learning of Plato, and he learned of gods and spirits and the real creators and saviours of this whole universe: He gained knowledge of the nature of the soul, its origin and its destination, the causes of its glory and elevation, and of its ruin and debasement: he discovered its bondage and its freedom, and the means to avoid the one and attain the other, and he washed a sour story clean with sweet discourse, casting out all that earlier nonsense and in its place introducing into his soul the beauty of truth, no less than if he had brought into some mighty temple statues of gods that had been in times past befouled and besmirched.[15]

Julian's conversion was to Neo-Platonism, but Gregory shows that theurgy was probably involved in the conversion.

Julian found his Christian upbringing unpersuasive, although he did retain an interest in the texts of the Christians as his desire to acquire the library of the deceased Bishop George shows[16]. In his letter to the Alexandrians, Julian reproaches the Alexandrians for believing in an unseen Jesus as God the word (θεὸν λόγον). Julian attempts to persuade them to worship Helios and writes: "For you will not stray from the right road if you heed one who till his twentieth year walked in that road of yours, but for twelve years now has walked in this road I speak of, with the gods" (σὺν θεοῖς)[17]. He describes

---

L'Empereur Julien. De l'histoire à la légende, ed. R. BRAUN/J. RICHER, Paris: 1978, 189-212.

[11] R. BRAUN, Julien et le christianisme, in: L'Empereur Julien. De l'histoire à la légende, ed. R. BRAUN/J. RICHER; Paris 1978, (57-87) 163.

[12] Res gestae 22.5.1.

[13] DE LABRIOLLE, La réaction, 378.

[14] Or. 11.1, 130c,d (II/2, 100 ROCHE.)

[15] Libanius, Or. 18.18 (I, 290 NORMAN).

[16] Jul., Ep. 107, 377d-378c and 106, 411c,d (I/2, 185,3-186,3; 184,10-20 BIDEZ). Julian does wish that the Galilaean books might be annihilated, but does not want the wish carried out. The library contained works on philosophy and rhetoric also.

[17] Jul., Ep. 111, 434c,d (I/2, 191,1-3 BIDEZ = III, 148 WR.). FOUSSARD (Julien, 204-205) places Julian's thought about Helios in a metaphysical triad: the Good (source of the

his time as a Christian as "darkness" and asks that it be buried in oblivion (λήθη δὲ ἔστω τοῦ σκότους ἐκείνου)[18]. He thanked the Mother of the gods: "she did not disregard me when I wandered as it were in darkness"[19]. How Julian explained his conversion is hard to tell. Of Christians he writes: "... we suffer in sympathy with those who are afflicted by an ill, but rejoice with those who are being released and set free by the aid of the gods (τοῖς δὲ ἀπολυομένοις καὶ ἀφιεμένοις ὑπὸ τῶν θεῶν συνηδόμεθα)"[20]. Julian doesn't use fate in this passage, as Porphyry's oracles did, to explain Christian belief, but he does compare it to illness[21]. And he does see supernatural intervention as playing a role in the cure of Christians who return to the gods.

In his seventh *Oration* to the Cynic Heracleios (*How it is Proper to Behave and Whether a Cynic Ought to Compose Myths*) Julian gives a myth[22] of his own religious experience. He first describes the legacy of Constantine and his sons:

> The sons demolished the ancestral temples which their father before them had despised and had stripped of the votive offerings that had been dedicated by many worshippers, but not least by his own ancestors. And besides demolishing the temples they erected sepulchres (μνήματα) both on new sites and on the old sites of the temples, as though impelled by fate or by an unconscious presentiment that they would ere long need many such sepulchres, seeing that they so neglected the gods.[23]

Julian was repelled by Christian worship around sepulchres[24] and devoted part of his life to purifying Greek places of worship. G. W. Bowersock describes this activity: "He had had removed the corpses buried near the Castalian spring at Delphi, he had had the corpses of martyrs near the temple of Didyma burned, he had eulogized the people of Emesa for burning Christian tombs, and at Daphne near Antioch he had had the remains of the martyr Babylas removed to revive the oracle of Apollo."[25] Philostorgius relates an account that may be a

---

intelligible gods); Helios (source of the intellectual gods); Sun (region of the visible gods). See his Hymn to King Helios (Or. 11.5-7, 132d-133d [II/2, 103-105 ROCHE.).

[18] Jul., Or.11.1, 131a (II/2, 101 ROCHE.).

[19] Or. 8.14, 174c (II/1, 123 ROCHE. = I, 486-87 WR.).

[20] Jul., Ep. 114, 438c (I/2, 195,23-24 BIDEZ = III, 134 WR.).

[21] Compare Jul., Ep. 98, 401c, 61c, 424b and Or. 7, 229c (I/2, 183,4; 75,23 BIDEZ; II/1, 77 ROCHE).

[22] Julian becomes a mythmaker [μυθοποιόν] in Or. 7.21, 227b (II/1, 74 ROCHE.) to show the cynic how it should be done.

[23] Or. 7.22, 228b,c (II/1, 76 ROCHE. = II, 132-34 WR.)

[24] C. Gal. 335b-d (175,4-18 MAS.) and see § 4.2.30.3 below.

[25] G. W. BOWERSOCK, Julian the Apostate, Cambridge 1978, 93. Amm. Marc. 22.12.8 (Delphi); Sozomen 5.20.7 (227,18-23 B./H.; Didyma); Julian, Misop. 12.28, 357c (II/2, 182 ROCHE.; Emesa); Sozomen 5.19.4-19 (223,24-226,10 B./H.; Babylas and Antioch). According to Sozomen 5.19.10-11 (225,2-6 B./H.) the Castalian spring in question was at Daphne (and not Delphi) which Hadrian had closed in order that no one gain knowledge about the future. On Julian's program of restoration of paganism and his program

genuine oracle from Delphi during Julian's time. In the story Julian sent the physician and quaestor Oribasius to revive the temple of Apollo at Delphi. The oracle responded: "Tell the king: the glorious dwelling (δαίδαλος αὐλά) has fallen to earth. Phoebos no longer has a chamber (καλύβαν) nor the prophetic bay leaf (μάντιδα δάφνην)[26] nor the spring that speaks; the speaking water has been quenched."[27] Hellenistic cities appreciated such efforts of Julian and one inscription entitled him the "restorer of liberty and of the Roman religion"[28].

Julian sees his conversion as a result of divine grace and describes his experience of Christianity as "darkness" as did Libanius in the letter quoted above:

> Next Zeus thus addressed Helios: "Thou seest yonder thine own child [Julian]." (Now this was a certain kinsman of those brothers who had been cast aside and was despised though he was that rich man's nephew and the cousin of his heirs.) "This child," said Zeus, "is thine own offspring. Swear then by my sceptre and thine that thou wilt care especially for him and cure him of this malady (θεραπεύσειν τῆς νόσου). For thou seest how he is as it were infected with smoke and filth and darkness and there is danger that the spark of fire which thou didst implant in him will be quenched, unless thou clothe thyself with might. Take care of him therefore and rear him. For I and the Fates yield thee this task."[29]

If Julian the mythmaker can be trusted, then he conceived of his experience as a cure wrought by Zeus and the fates. Julian's images of light and darkness and health and illness can be compared to those of Lucretius who uses them similarly to describe the positive results of his teaching on people suffering

---

against the Christians see BRAUN, Julien et le christianisme, 166-75 / SMITH, Julian's Gods, 207-18 / DE LABRIOLLE, La réaction, 370-76, 384-90 / BIDEZ, Vie de l'Empereur Julien, 225-35 / GEFFCKEN, The Last Days, 140-150.

[26] On the prophetic bay leaves (Apollo's plant) at Parnassus and Delphi see the entries δάφνη and γύαλος in LSJ. FONTENROSE, The Delphic Oracle, 56, 353 questions the authenticity of this oracle.

[27] Philostorgius, H.E. 7.1 (GCS Philostorgius, 77 BIDEZ); parallel text in Cedrenus I.532 (quoted by BIDEZ). SMITH notes that there is a question about the date of the oracle, but argues that it may well be Julianic (Julian's Gods, 224 and 285 n. 31).

[28] ILS 752 (*restitutori libertatis et R[omanae] religionis*) See SMITH, Julian's Gods, 280-281 n. 133 / BIDEZ, Vie de l'Empereur Julien, 393 n. 12 / and A. D. NOCK, Sallustius Concerning the Gods and the Universe, Hildesheim 1966 (rep. of 1926 ed.), ciii n. 19. A milestone proclaims him to be born for the good of the republic (*bono r[ei] p[ublicae] nato*) in CIL 5.8024. The same phrase appears on a milestone in ILS 8946 with the addition of the phrase *dele[t]a vitia temporum preteri[torum*. The reference to the crimes of past times that have been erased could be a reference to Christianity (as claimed in the edition in CIL III.10648b). ILS 750 describes Julian as the restorer of public liberty (*restitutori p. libertatis*). A similar text praises him as liberator of the Roman world and restorer of temples (*R[o]mani orbis liberat[or]i, templorum [re]stauratori*) in AE 1969/70.631.

[29] Jul., Or. 7.22, 229c,d (II/1, 77 ROCHE. = II, 136 WR.).

from religion[30]. Perhaps one can also describe the doctrine of conversion (from Christianity to Hellenism) as a Hellenistic theory of predestination[31].

Julian saw his life's goal as a divinely given vocation. In the same myth in which he describes his conversion, Julian writes that Helios sent him back to earth with the following mission: "For return thou must, and cleanse away all impiety (ἀσεβήματα) and invoke me to aid thee, and Athene and the other gods."[32] Julian adopted the category "impious" for Christians[33]. In his satirical address to the citizens of Antioch who had neglected their own sacred rites, Julian described his displeasure at their neglect of the shrine of Daphne: "Your city possessed ten thousand lots of land privately owned, and yet when the annual festival in honor of the god of her forefathers is to be celebrated for the first time since the gods dispelled the cloud of atheism, she does not produce in her own behalf a single bird..."[34]. By "atheism" Julian referred to Christian theology (and its Jewish ancestry)[35]. This goal (the conversion of the "atheists" to Hellenism) provides a clear context for Julian's work *Against the Galilaeans.*

Julian's views on his own conversion illuminate his attitude toward the conversion of Christians to Hellenism. He did not believe in violent conversions: "It is by reason that we ought to persuade (πείθεσθαι) and instruct people, not by blows, or insults or bodily violence."[36] Hellenes who owned Christian slaves were to attempt to convert them: "It follows, does it not, that if one of us who call ourselves servants of the gods has a favorite slave who abominates the gods and turns from their worship, we must in justice either convert (πείθειν) him and keep him, or dismiss him from the house and sell him, in case some one does not find it easy to dispense with owning a slave?"[37] The word for "conversion" is the rhetoricians' word for the goal of their art[38]. Julian's goal is to reclaim the world for Hellenism. As for Christian schoolboys Julian has clear goals: "...nor indeed would it be reasonable to shut out from the best way boys who are still too ignorant to know which way to turn, and to overawe them into being led against their will

---

[30] Lucretius, De rerum natura 1.931-50. I thank Prof. J. FINAMORE for this reference.

[31] Compare Hecate's and Porphyry's approach above § 2.2.9 where Christian belief is explained by "fate."

[32] Or. 7.22, 231d (II/1, 80 ROCHE. = II, 142-43 Wr).

[33] δυσσεβῶν, C. Gal. 333b (173,5 MAS.). See also Ep. 79, Ep. 84, 430d (I/2, 86,13-14; 145,18 BIDEZ).

[34] Misopogon 12.35, 362c (II/2, 188 ROCHE. = II, 488-89 WR.).

[35] C. Gal. 43b (89,11 MAS.) and Ep. 84, 429d (I/2, 144,13 BIDEZ). Compare Lucian, Alexander 25 (atheists, Christians, and Epicureans forbidden to see the mysteries of Glycon). On the charge of Christians as atheists see SCHÄFKE, Frühchristlicher Widerstand, 627-30.

[36] Ep. 114, 438b (I/2, 195,13-15 BIDEZ = III, 134-35 WR.).

[37] Ep. 86 (I/2, 149,2-6 BIDEZ = III, 112-13 WR.).

[38] See the introduction for a brief discussion.

to the beliefs of their ancestors (τὰ πάτρια). Though indeed it might be proper to cure these, even against their will, as one cures the insane, except that we concede indulgence for this sort of disease. For we ought, I think, to teach, but not punish, the demented (τοὺς ἀνοήτους)."[39]

5.2 The Contra Galilaeos

The *Contra Galilaeos* of Julian did not provoke the extreme response (burning) that Porphyry's *Contra Christianos* did[40]. Christians such as Cyril felt compelled to refute it, and the fragments found in Cyril's work are the primary source for our knowledge of Julian's attack. Wolfram Kinzig points out that Cyril's attack reflects an ongoing debate between Christians and non-Christians in the fifth century.[41] Fragments of the *C. Gal.* in Theodore of Mopsuestia survive that may come from a work against Julian[42]. Cyril's work survives in ten books with various fragments (up to book 19) existing in scattered

---

[39] Ep. 61c, 424a,b (I/2, 75,18-24 BIDEZ = III, 122-23 WR.).

[40] Julian made a law demanding that Christians be called Galilaeans according to Greg. Naz., Or. 4.76 (SC 309, 194-96 BERNARDI) = J. BIDEZ/F. CUMONT, Iuliani Imperatoris epistulae leges poemata fragmenta, Paris 1922, 151 (Γαλιλαίους ἀντὶ Χριστιανῶν ὀνομάσας τε καὶ καλεῖσθαι νομοθετήσας). See also Greg., Or. 4.74 (190 BERNARDI). Epictetus, Diss. 4.7.6 used Γαλιλαῖοι to describe Christians.

[41] Zur Notwendigkeit einer Neuedition von Kyrill von Alexandrien, *Contra Iulianum*, in: StPatr XXIX, ed. E. A. LIVINGSTONE, Leuven 1997, 488-89.

[42] See the fragments in MASARACCHIA's edition, Giuliano Imperator, 180-191 and see her comments on 22. See also A. GUIDA, FRAMMENTI INEDITI DEL 'CONTRA I GALILEI' DI GIULIANO E DELLA REPLICA DI TEODORO DI MOPSUESTIA, Prometheus 9, 1983, 139-63 and Teodoro di Mopsuestia, Replica a Giuliano Imperatore. Adversus criminationes in Christianos Iuliani Imperatoris. In appendice Testimonianze sulla polemica antigiulianea in altre opere di Teodoro, con nuovi frammenti del «Contro i Galilei» di Giuliano, ed. A. GUIDA, Biblioteca Patristica, Florence 1994. There were also works of Philip of Side (composed ca 400) and Alexander of Hierapolis (the age of Cyril) against Julian. On Alexander see C. J. NEUMANN, Iuliani Imperatoris librorum contra Christianos quae supersunt, Leipzig 1880, 87 and on Philip see NEUMANN, Iuliani, 35-36 quoting Socrates, H.E. 7.27.2 (376,7-8 HANSEN). Apollinarius of Laodicea attacked Julian's opinions about God in a work entitled The Truth (without using Scripture; Sozomen, H.E. 5.18.6 [223,2-5 B./H.]), but apparently did not write specifically against the C. Gal. (NEUMANN 10-12). Ephraem Syrus' work against Julian also does not appear to have been specifically against the C. Gal. (NEUMANN 13). NEUMANN argues that an alleged excerpt from Chrysostom's work against Julian probably comes from that of Cyril (13-14). On the response to Julian's work see P. ALLARD, Julien l'Apostat, Vol. III, Studia Historica 102, Rome 1972, 122-29 and Cyrille d'Alexandrie, Contre Julien, ed. P. BURGIÈRE/ P. ÉVIEUX, SC 322, Paris 1985, 52-58. Below I will use W. C. WRIGHT's translation with occasional modifications.

sources[43]. Julian was concerned with the persuasive abilities of the Christian message and used his literary skill to argue that Christianity was neither Hellenistic nor Jewish and that Christianity was in fundamental conflict with its Hebrew roots. It was written in the winter nights of 362-363 preceding Julian's campaign against Persia. It seems to have originally comprised three books[44]. Cyril wrote that Julian composed three books against the holy Gospels and against the revered religion of the Christians[45]. In his dedication to Theodosius II (in the 430s)[46], Cyril continues by charging that Julian's writing "shook up many people, and he did no little damage. Light-minded and credulous people fell easily into his way of thinking and became a sweet prey for demons."[47] Chrysostom had a different point of view and argued that no wise or unwise person nor even a small child was persuaded (μεταπεῖσαι ἴσχυσαν) by the writings against the Christians. These works against the Christians often perished as soon as they were born, and the ones that survived were in Christian libraries[48]. A law of Justinian (between 529 and 534) consigns the works of Porphyry and those like him to the flames[49]. Copies of Julian's work may have perished in those flames.

Libanius described the genesis of the work in this way:

---

[43] NEUMANN, Iuliani. See also the edition of MASARACCHIA, Giuliano Imperator. NEUMANN, Iuliani, F. 46, p. 86 is an excerpt from Book 19 of Cyril's work. MASARACCHIA, Giuliano, 20-39 has an extensive discussion of the MS tradition of Cyril's work. The first two books of Cyril's work have appeared in SC 322. The other books can be found in PG 76. MIGNE's section numbers are used below since the SC edition is unfinished.

[44] Jerome mentions seven, but that may be the number of books in one of the Christian refutations of Julian (Ep. 70 ad magnum and Comm in Osee 2.1; See MASARACCHIA, Giuliano, 12). Jerome may simply be in error (BURGIÈRE/ÉVIEUX in SC 322, 26-27).

[45] C. Jul. 3 (PG 76, 508b). Julian mentions another book in C. Gal. 218a and 261e (145,3; 159,6 MAS.). MASARACCHIA, Giuliano, 12 refers to other manuscript evidence.

[46] SMITH, Julian's Gods, 190. DE LABRIOLLE, La réaction, 396 dates it between 431 and 441. NEUMANN, Iuliani, 36-37 dates the work (at least the first ten books) between 429 and 441 due to the mention of Bishop John of Antioch in Ep. 83 (SCHULZ) of Theodoret (to whom Cyril had sent a copy of his work). BURGIÈRE and ÉVIEUX date the text between 434-37 or 439-441 in SC 322, 10-15.

[47] C. Iul. 3 (PG 76, 508c).

[48] Chrysostom, De Babylo contra Julianum et gentiles 11,26-30 (SC 362, 106 SCHATKIN/BLANC/GRILLET).

[49] Codex Iust. 1.1.3 quoted in NEUMANN, Iuliani, 8: θεσπίζομεν πάντα ὅσα Πορφύριος ὑπὸ τῆς ἑαυτοῦ μανίας ἐλαυνόμενος ἢ ἕτερός τις κατὰ τῆς εὐσεβοῦς τῶν Χριστιανῶν θρησκείας συνέγραψε πυρὶ παραδίδοσθαι. This version of the law differs slightly from that of Theodosius II and Valentinian in Acta Conciliorum Oecumenicurum I.1.4 (66,3-4.8-12 SCHWARTZ) from Feb. 17, 448 (= SMITH, Porphyrii, 40T). The earlier form of the law specifically consigns only the work of Porphyry to the flames.

As winter lengthened the nights, besides many other fine compositions, he attacked the book in which that fellow from Palestine is claimed to be a god and child of god (θεοῦ παῖδα). In a long polemic and by dint of forceful argument, he proved such claims to be stupid, idle chatter. On the same subject he showed himself wiser than the old sage from Tyre: and right pleased and happy may this Tyrian be to accept this statement, beaten as it were by his son.[50]

The Tyrian is Porphyry. The burning of Apollo's temple at Daphne in October of 362 may also have occasioned Julian's decision to write against the Christians[51]. Julian himself describes his intentions in his letter to the Christian heretic Photinus. With reference to the Christian priest named Diodorus, Julian wrote: "But if only the gods and goddesses and all the Muses and Fortune will lend me their aid, I hope to show that he [Diodorus] is feeble and a corrupter of laws and customs, of pagan Mysteries and Mysteries of the gods of the underworld, and that the new-fangled Galilaean god of his, whom he by a false myth styled eternal, has been stripped by his humiliating death and burial of the divinity falsely ascribed to him by Diodorus."[52] Johannes Geffcken argued that the work offers little that is new based on his comparisons of Julian with Celsus and Porphyry[53]. Julian's emphasis on the continued validity of the Jewish law is, however, a characteristic of his thought that does not play a large role in the surviving fragments of his predecessors. Porphyry's careful analysis of biblical texts using philological and historical methods is different from the critique that one finds in Julian and Celsus[54].

5.2.1 Christian Writings as Fiction

Julian attacked the Christian message as a fiction[55]. He was also concerned to show that the fictions helped persuade the audience.

> It is, I think, expedient to set forth to all people the reasons by which I was convinced that the fabrication (σκευωρία)[56] of the Galilaeans is a fiction (πλάσμα) of people

---

[50] Lib., Oration 18.178 (I, 396 NORMAN).

[51] See Norman in Libanius, I, 397. The burning is mentioned by Libanius, Or. 17.30 and Or. 60 (Monody on the Daphnaean Temple). Amm. Marc. 22.13.1-3 (the date and the comment that Julian, furious, suspected the Christians; others, on slight evidence, expected an accident caused by a philosopher named Asclepiades), Julian, Misop. 361b. Zonaras 13.12 (213,17-18 DINDORF) claims a thunderbolt destroyed the temple.

[52] Ep. 90 (I/2, 174,18-23 BIDEZ = III, 186-89 WR.).

[53] Zwei Griechische Apologeten, 304-306. DE LABRIOLLE has a similar judgment concerning Julian's relations to Celsus and Porphyry (La réaction, 421).

[54] SMITH, Julian's Gods, 206.

[55] C. Gal. 39a (87,1-6 MAS. = III, 318-19 WR.). I am indebted to E. MASARACCHIA's superb notes on Julian in many of the comments below (MASARACCHIA, Giuliano, 195-243).

[56] Julian also describes the "miracle-working and the fabrication of the gospels" [εὐαγγελίων τερατουργίας καὶ σκευωρίας] in C. Gal. 218a (145,4 MAS. = III, 380-381

composed by wickedness. Though it has nothing in it divine, by making full use of that part of the soul which loves fable (φιλομύθῳ) and is childish and foolish, it has induced people to believe (εἰς πίστιν ἤγαγεν) that the monstrous tale (τερατολογίαν) is truth.

Christian "myths" were repellent to Julian, but he had a far more tolerant view of Hellenistic "myths"[57]. Paradox helps the interpreter detect "fiction" (πλάσμα): "Now I think ordinary people (ἰδιώταις) derive benefit enough from the irrational myth which instructs them through symbols alone. But those who are more highly endowed with wisdom will find the truth about the gods helpful; though only on condition that such a person examine and discover and comprehend it under the leadership of the gods..."[58]. In another oration Julian argues that "Whenever myths (μῦθοι) on sacred subjects are incongruous in thought (κατὰ μὲν τὴν διάνοιαν ἀπεμφαίνοντες), by that very fact they cry aloud, as it were, and summon us not to believe them literally but to study and track down their hidden meaning."[59] Julian notes that the danger with straightforward or serious (σεμνοῦ) language about the gods is that people may think of them as great but nevertheless as human beings, while with incongruous language "...there is some hope that people will neglect the more obvious sense of the words, and that pure intelligence may rise to the comprehension of the distinctive nature of the gods that transcends all existing things"[60]. Julian apparently saw no need for such interpretation of the Christian narratives.

In his *Letter to a Priest* Julian counsels priests not to read "...the sort of thing our poets in the first place have brought themselves into disrepute by writing, and in the second place such tales as the prophets of the Jews take pains to invent, and are admired for so doing by those miserable people who have attached themselves to the Galilaeans. But for us it will be appropriate to read such narratives as have been composed about deeds that have actually been done; but we must avoid all fictions (πλάσματα) in the form of narrative (ἐν ἱστορίας εἴδει) ..."[61]. Julian's word for fiction (πλάσμα) was a literary

---

WR.). Celsus also accused the evangelists of deception (C. Cels. 2.13, 15 [141,20-21; 144,15-16 KOET.]).

[57] On Julian's view of myths see J. PÉPIN, Mythe, 466-69.

[58] Or. 8.10, 170a,b (II/1, 118 ROCHE. = I, 474-75 WR.).

[59] Or. 7.17, 222c (II/1, 68 ROCHE. = II, 119 WR.). Ps. Sallustius has a similar approach in De diis 3 (4,17.18 NOCK). "Strangeness" (ἀτοπία) encourages philosophically minded people to seek hidden meaning.

[60] Or. 7.17, 222d (II/1, 68 ROCHE. = II, 119 WR.). Compare his statement to his friend Ps. Sallustius who had written on the allegorical interpretation of Hellenistic myths (De diis): "for they [the Greeks] sought after truth, as its nature requires, by the aid of reason and did not suffer us to pay heed to incredible fables [ἀπίστοις μύθοις] or impossible miracles [παραδόξῳ τερατείᾳ] like most of the barbarians (Or. 4.8, 252b [I/1, 205,17-19 BIDEZ = II, 194-95 WR.]). See FOUSSARD, Julien, 197.

[61] Frag. Ep. 89b, 301a,b (I/2, 169,1-9 BIDEZ = II, 326-27 WR.).

critical term used by Celsus and Macarius' anonymous philosopher[62]. Some of Eusebius' anonymous pagans (identified by Harnack as Porphyry) also accused the gospel writers of pure invention[63]. Celsus and Porphyry also complained about the irrationality of the Christian faith[64]. Anonymous pagans in Eusebius argued that the Christians do not offer proof for what they believe[65]. Galen also attacked Christianity from this perspective[66]. Macarius' philosopher noted that Christ's teaching was not for the wise but for babes and the unintelligent[67]. Julian's charge that Christians told monstrous tales is similar to charges made by Macarius' philosopher and others[68]. The Milesian Apollo has a similar word for Christ's deeds, but his point of view is different. He described Christ as a wise man with wonderful works (σοφὸς· τερατώδεσιν ἔργοις)[69].

Cyril, responding to Julian, makes a distinction between two Galilees: one in Judea and the other the "Galilee of the Gentiles" (Is 9:1)[70]. By this dubious argument he claims that Julian's condemnation of "Galilaean" literature also applies to Greek literature[71]. He remembers that Plato criticizes the things said by Homer about the gods and goddesses — in particular their lusts, their addiction to human greed, and their lamentations over the death of kin[72]. Consequently Cyril concludes that Julian's term μυθῶδες (fabulous/mythical) applies to Greek literature[73].

Julian attacked the historicity of the NT documents after mentioning Jesus and Paul's ability to delude maidservants and slaves, and individuals such as Cornelius (Acts 10) and Sergius (Acts 13:6-12). He charges: "But if you can show me that one of these people is mentioned by the well-known writers of

[62] C. Cels. 2.26 (155,21-22 KOET.) and compare Origen's comments in 1.46, 2.15, 3.43 [96,15; 144,15; 239,21 KOET.]; Macarius, Apocrit. 3.4 (57,12 BLONDEL and see § 3.3 above). For comparative material see MASARACCHIA, Giuliano, 195.

[63] HARNACK, Porphyrius, F. 7. Eus. Dem. E. 3.5.96 (ὡς τὰ μὴ ὄντα πλασαμένους).

[64] C. Cels. 1.9 ([61,15-17 KOET.] and see § 1.6.1 above); HARNACK, Porphyrius, F. 1 (ἀλόγῳ δὲ καὶ ἀνεξετάστῳ πίστει).

[65] Dem. E. 1.1.12 (identified by HARNACK as Porphyrius F. 73).

[66] Galen in Cook, Some Hellenistic Responses, 1993, 239-40.

[67] Apocrit. 4.9 (167,1-11 BLONDEL).

[68] Apocrit. 3.4 (57,5 BLONDEL; τερατῶδες) with reference to Christ sending the demons into the pigs, 4.2 (159,14 BLONDEL; τερατῶδες) with reference to the believers caught up in the clouds in 1 Th 4:15-17.

[69] SMITH, Porphyrii, note to 343F from Lactantius, Div. inst. 4.13.11.

[70] C. Jul. 2.39 (PG 76, 560d = SC 322, 212 B./É.).

[71] C. Jul. 2.39, 40 (PG 76, 561a = 214 B./É.).

[72] C. Jul. 2.40 (PG 76, 561b = 214-16 B./É.).

[73] C. Jul. 2.40 (PG 76, 561c = 216 B./É.). Julian uses the word in C. Gal. 75b (102,12 MAS.) to apply to the story of Eden. In C. Gal. 134d and 135b (116,5.23 MAS.) he uses it to apply to the story of Babel and its parallel in Homer's narrative of the Aloadae.

the time, (ὧν εἶς ἐὰν φανῇ τῶν τηνικαῦτα γνωριζομένων ἐπιμνηθείς) — these events happened in the reign of Tiberius or Claudius, — then you may consider that I speak falsely about all matters."[74] Although Julian is not arguing here explicitly that the NT authors wrote falsehoods, he is aware that the events of the NT were not described by Greco-Roman historians. Julian's point is that the events and people were not important enough for such attention[75].

5.2.2 The Genealogies

Julian's attacks on gospel traditions indicate a close knowledge of the texts. He quotes Gen 49:10 and denies that it is a prophecy of Jesus. The genealogies (Mt 1:1-17, Lk 3:23-38) were contradictory in his reading: "But it is very clear that not one of these sayings relates to Jesus; for he is not even from Judah. How could he be when according to you he was not born of Joseph but of the Holy Spirit? For though in your genealogies you trace Joseph back to Judah, you could not invent (πλάσαι) even this plausibly. For Matthew and Luke are refuted (ἐλέγχονται) by the fact that they disagree (διαφωνοῦντες) concerning his genealogy."[76] Jerome preserves a similar tradition from Julian. With reference to "Jacob begot Joseph" Jerome writes: "Julian objected here against the discordance (dissonantiae) of the gospels — why Matthew [1:16] said that Joseph was the son of Jacob and Luke [3:23] called him the son of Heli — not understanding the custom of the scriptures since one is the father according to nature and one according to law."[77] Jerome thus uses the concept of Levirate marriage to explain the discrepancy. Porphyry also attacked the

---

[74] C. Gal. 206a,b (142,10-14 MAS. = III, 376-77 WR.). DE LABRIOLLE, La réaction, 413 translates "if ... they succeeded in convincing one distinguished person" — an interesting translation, but not close enough to the text.

[75] Compare C. Gal. 191e (136,8-9 MAS.) where Julian asserts that Jesus did nothing worth mentioning.

[76] C. Gal. 253e (157,27-158,32 MAS. = III, 394-97 WR.).

[77] F. 90 (184 MAS.) = F. 1 (234 NEUMANN), from Jerome, Comm in Matth. 1.3 (CChr.SL 77, 9,46 HURST/ADRIAEN). For bibliography see RINALDI, Biblia Gentium, F. 319. Isho'dad of Merv (Comm. in Mt 1:15 [I, 12 GIBSON; in GUIDA, Teodoro di Mopsuestia, 200]) has: "But Julianus the Apostate, that is to say, the liar in his promise, and Porphyry, the reprobates, contradict the Evangelists, that Luke, forsooth, is not speaking of a legal descent: and if he were, why does he not mention the legal father of Obed, whom Boaz raises as seed to one of the sons of Naomi, but recalls his natural one?" Ambrosiaster preserves an almost identical objection in Quaestiones Vet. et N. Test. 56 (CSEL 50, 101 SOUTER; DE LABRIOLLE, La réaction 497; and see RINALDI, Biblia Gentium, F. 320). There are similar objections in Ps. Just., Quaest. et resp. ad Orthod. 133, 483 a,b; 131, 481b,c (220, 216 OTTO) in which Christians are asked how Matthew and Luke knew the names of the ancestors after the Babylonian exile (since they are not in scripture) and in which the problem of the different numbers of generations in the gospels is pointed out. See also RINALDI, Biblia Gentium, 424, 429.

genealogies because of their disagreements[78]. Cyril does not respond to Julian's attack on the genealogies except to quote Num 36:6ff. to prove that Mary was of the tribe of Joseph, and that consequently Jesus was of the tribe of Judah even though Joseph was not his natural father[79]. The fact that Julian wrote that he would deal with the genealogies at more length in his second volume suggests that Cyril might have responded in one of the lost books of the *Contra Julianum* [80].

5.2.3 The Star

Julian seems to have attacked the tradition of the star at Jesus' birth (Mt 2:2). In one of the Syriac fragments of Cyril's work, Cyril writes: "What is novel, friend, if by the will of God a star against its usual custom rises, in the time in which the word of God was incarnate. Because often on account of great matters on the earth wandering stars have appeared which are called comets ... others are called meteors. That star however was not of the group of those ordinary ones, nor was it a morning star (כוכבא נוגהא, *lucifer*) as he [Julian] called it."[81] Celsus also attacked the narrative of the star at Jesus' birth — although his objection is not recorded by Origen (C. Cels. 1.34 [85,30-32 Koet.]). Ambrosiaster mentions an anonymous objection to the narrative: "How was it that the wise men from the East understood by the appearance of the star that Christ was born king of the Jews, when usually it is a temporal king who is designated by the sign of a star?"[82] De Labriolle holds that Julian seems to have argued that the star was simply not miraculous[83].

5.2.4 Against Mt 2:15 and its Use of the OT

Julian is thoroughly unpersuaded by Matthew's use of OT prophecies to interpret the life of Jesus. While commenting on Hosea 11:1, Jerome quotes Julian: "The words that were written concerning Israel, Matthew the Evangelist (2:15) transferred to Christ, that he might mock the simplicity (*simplicitati*) of those of the Gentiles who believed."[84] Porphyry made a similar charge about

---

[78] See § 2.3.8 and 2.3.9 above.

[79] C. Jul. 8.261 (PG 76, 900c). Cyril's answer to this part of the C. Gal. takes up columns 888-900 of Migne and is concerned with Christological issues (e.g. did Jesus fulfill prophecies of Moses).

[80] C. Gal. 261e (159,6 MAS.).

[81] F. 91, (185 MAS.) = F. 3 (52 [Syriac], 64-65 [Latin] NEUMANN).

[82] Ambrosiaster, Quaestiones Vet. et N. Test. 63 (111,14-17 SOUTER; RINALDI, Biblia Gentium, F. 333).

[83] La réaction, 412.

[84] C. Gal. F. 101 (189 MAS. = III, 432-33 WR.) = F. 15 (237 NEUMANN) from Jerome's Comm. in Osee lib. III cap. XI.

the apostles' use of the Hebrew scriptures[85]. Julian's concern for the persuasiveness of Christian language is apparent here. In his view, Matthew misuses the text from Hosea. His charges that the Christians are "simple" is also reminiscent of Celsus' attack on the stupidity of Christian believers[86].

5.2.5 Jesus' Fast

Jesus' fast (Mt 4:2 par) does not impress Julian in a fragment from Theodore of Mopsuestia: "Moses after fasting forty days received the law [Ex 31:18], and Elijah, after fasting for the same period, was granted to see God face to face [1Kings 19:9]. But what did Jesus receive, after a fast of the same length?"[87] As with many other events in Jesus' life, Julian finds the story to be insignificant. Theodore responded to Julian: "Is not receiving the gospel and proclaiming the kingdom of God equal to receiving the law and being considered worthy of a vision of God?"[88]

5.2.6 The Temptation

Julian also finds unconvincing several details in the narrative of Jesus' temptation according to another fragment in Theodore of Mopsuestia. Theodore asks Julian: Why do you marvel that although there is no high mountain in the wilderness the devil is said to lead him up to a very high mountain?" Theodore responds that "It says in a moment of time [Lk 4:5, cf. Mt 4:8], clearly showing that the devil made a vision of the mountain and was also able to do the same thing with regard to the vision of the kingdoms of the world." He also records an objection of Julian to the presence of Jesus on the pinnacle of the Temple: "And how, he [Julian] says, could he lead Jesus to the pinnacle of the Temple when Jesus was in the wilderness?" Theodore takes the same approach to the pinnacle — Jesus never left the desert! The geographical changes probably indicate the absurdity of the story for Julian. Unfortunately the fragment is too small to leave a larger impression of Julian's view of the account[89].

---

[85] HARNACK, Porphyrius, F. 5, Jerome Comm in Joel 2:28 discussed in § 2.3.38 above.

[86] § 1.6.4 above (e.g. C. Cels. 3.44).

[87] C. Gal. F. 93 (185 MAS. = III, 428-29 WR. = GUIDA, Teodoro di Mopsuestia, 80). Ambrosiaster has an anonymous objection to the fact that Jesus apparently was not hungry during the fast in Quaestiones de N. Test. 17 (434,1-3 SOUTER; RINALDI, Biblia Gentium, F. 343).

[88] C. Gal. F. 93 (185,6-7 MAS.).

[89] C. Gal. F. 94 (186 MAS. = III, 428-29 WR. = GUIDA, Teodoro di Mopsuestia, 82-84). Ambrosiaster has an objection to the tempter's questioning Jesus' identity as Son of God since he was called that after his birth in Quaestiones de N. Test. 28, (437,15-18 SOUTER; RINALDI, Biblia Gentium, F. 344).

5.2.7 Jesus' Consumption of Food

Julian apparently found it absurd that Jesus ate and drank. In one of the Syriac fragments of his work, Cyril does not identify the specific text that Julian used. The *titulus* of Cyril's text reads: "From Cyril's fifteenth book against Julian, when Julian interpreted with derision the fact that Jesus ate and drank."[90] Julian may have attacked Jesus' consumption of vinegar or found a contradiction between Mt 27:34 and Mk 15:23[91]. Celsus also found it scandalous that Jesus ate food and drank (C. Cels. 1.70, 2.37, 7.13 [124,5; 162,18-19; 165,1-2 Koet.]).

5.2.8 The Disciples' Quick Response

Julian was not impressed by the disciples who followed Jesus so quickly (Mt. 9:9 par.). Jerome wrote: "Porphyry and Julian Augustus argued concerning this text for either the ignorance (*imperitiam*) of a lying historian or for the stupidity of those who immediately followed the savior — as if they would have irrationally followed any person who called them."[92] Jerome defends the apostles by pointing to the signs and miracles that had preceded the call — and that there is no doubt that they had seen before they believed. In his letter to Photinus, Julian refers to the disciples to whom the priest Diodorus was devoted as "base and ignorant creed-making fishermen" (*degenerum et inperitorum eius theologorum piscatorum*)[93]. Julian generally understood the Galilaeans to be ignorant and uneducated[94].

5.2.9 Jesus on the Law

Cyril writes that Julian made reference to Mt 5:17-19 to prove that Jesus did not come to destroy the Jewish Law. Julian apparently used this argument in context of his critique of the Christian refusal to practice circumcision (to be discussed below). After quoting Genesis 17:11, Cyril notes that Julian refers to Mt 5:17 and 19. His conclusion shows that Julian believed that Christ taught that the law should be kept: "Therefore when He has undoubtedly taught that it is proper to observe the law, and threatened with punishment those who transgress one commandment, what manner of defending yourselves will you devise, you who have transgressed them all without exception?"[95] Julian seems to be referring to a text such as Mt 5:19 in which Jesus warns against

---

[90] C. Gal. F. 97 (187 MAS.) = F. 9 (55 [Syriac], 236 [Latin] NEUMANN).

[91] C. Jul. Text 14 (69 NEUMANN) from a Catena that quotes the two verses and notes that the text is from Cyril's 13th book against Julian. Julian's objection is unclear.

[92] C. Gal. F. 102 (189 MAS.) = F. 16 (238 NEUMANN) = HARNACK, Porphyrius, F. 6 (see § 2.3.12 above).

[93] Ep. 90 (I/2, 175,4-5 BIDEZ = III, 188 WR.) in Facundus' Latin translation.

[94] See Or. 7.18, 224b (II/1, 70 ROCHE.; Christians as ἀνοήτων).

[95] C. Gal. 351c (180,19-23 MAS. = III, 420-23 WR. = 229,10-19 NEUMANN).

loosing one of the commandments. Like Julian, Celsus also emphasized the contradictions between the Old Testament and Christian practice and teaching[96]. Julian's attitude to the Jewish law is clear: Christians are at fault for abandoning it[97]. That position is a part of Julian's more encompassing view that Christians are neither Hellenes nor Jews[98]. Celsus also looked on Christians as apostates from Judaism[99]. For Julian, Christians combine bad elements of both Judaism and Hellenism: "from both religions they have gathered what has been engrafted like powers of evil, as it were, on these nations — atheism from the Jewish levity, and a sordid and slovenly way of living from our indolence and vulgarity (χυδαιότητος); and they desire that this should be called the noblest worship of the gods"[100]. Celsus also commented on the miscellaneous ideas that Christians put together to persuade people (C. Cels. 3.16 [214,22-23 Koet.]). Porphyry claimed that the Christians were atheists who had abandoned their ancestral traditions (πατρίων)[101].

5.2.10 Versus Jesus' Teaching in Mt 5:17-19

In one of the Syriac fragments of Cyril, Julian attacked Jesus' statements in Mt 5:17, 19. The text (and its *titulus*) reads:

> From Cyril's sixteenth book against Julian the Apostate: When he derided Christ who said that he came to fulfill the law and that whoever loosed one of the least of the commandments and so taught people would be called "least." Julian: He loosed the sabbath because he said [Mt 12:8], the Son of Man is lord of the sabbath and "[Mt 15:11] not what enters into the mouth defiles a person," but the law defiles foods.[102]

Cyril responded by claiming that Christ was not against the law, but rather changed what was the image of truth (the law) into incorruptible truth. He goes on to argue that circumcision and sacrificial action were permitted on the sabbath. Ambrosiaster records an anonymous objection to Lk 16:16 based on Mt 5:17 ("If from now on, with the preaching of John, or the Savior, the law

---

[96] Compare C. Cels. 7.18 and 6.29 (169,10-27; 99,3-18) with C. Gal. 253b, 291a, 320a and 351a,b (156,6-14; 163,26-33; 169,15-20; 179,5-180,14 MAS.). See also LOESCHE, Neuplatonische Polemiker, 292.

[97] See ROKEAH, Jews, 119-21 and MEREDITH, Porphyry and Julian, 1145.

[98] C. Gal. 43a (88,4-5 MAS.). Compare F. 1 of Porphyry (HARNACK) in § 2.3.4 above.

[99] C. Cels. 2.1 (126,13 KOET.).

[100] C. Gal. 43a,b (89,10-14 MAS. = III, 320 WR.)

[101] HARNACK, Porphyrius, F. 1.

[102] C. Gal. F. 98 (187 MAS. = F. 10 (56 [Syriac], 75 [Latin] NEUMANN). Ambrosiaster has an anonymous objection to Mt 12:1-8 par in Quaestiones Vet. et N. Test. 61 (109 SOUTER; RINALDI, Biblia Gentium, F. 451).

has ceased the function, why does the Savior say "I have not come the destroy the law or the prophets, but to fulfill them...")[103].

5.2.11 Julian on Christian Practices around Tombs (Mt 23:27 and 8:21-22)

Julian quoted Mt 23:27 and concludes: "If, then, Jesus said that sepulchres are full of uncleanness, how can you invoke God at them?"[104] Cyril remarks that Julian then quotes Mt 8:21-22[105]. Julian's conclusion from Mt 8:21-22 is: "Therefore, since this is so, why do you grovel (προσκαλινδεῖσθε) among tombs?"[106] The reason Julian finds is that Christians seek visions (ἐνύπνια) among the tombs of the dead. Julian also apparently used Mt 8 to show that Christians should not venerate the relics of martyrs[107].

Cyril argues that in Mt 23:27 Jesus is not speaking of actual tombs, but of the hypocrisy of the Pharisees[108]. He continues by enumerating Jesus' contacts with the dead such as the miracles in John 11:43, Mark 5:41 and Luke 7:14[109]. Cyril then denies that Christians seek visions among the tombs and uses Is 65:3-4 to argue that the practice was pagan[110]. He quotes Porphyry's *Life of Pythagoras* to show that divination from dreams was a pagan practice[111]. Cyril also appeals to Porphyry's work to show that the Greeks sought oracles and worshipped at sanctuaries where tombs existed (e.g. the tomb of Apollo at Delphi and the tomb of Zeus in the Idaean cave in Crete)[112]. He then quotes Clement's *Protrepticus* 3 to show that Greek temples are tombs (e.g. the daughters of Celeus buried in the Eleusinium below the Acropolis in Athens)[113].

5.2.12 Apocalyptic Signs

The signs mentioned in passages such as Mt 24:3-14 were absurd to Julian: "Such things have often happened and still happen, and how can these be signs of the end of the world (συντελείας σημεῖα)?"[114] Although the fragment is

---

[103] Ambrosiaster, Quaestiones Vet. et N. Test. 69 (118 SOUTER; RINALDI, Biblia Gentium, F. 348).

[104] C. Gal. 335c (175,13-14 MAS. = III, 414-17 WR.).

[105] C. Gal. 335c,d (176,14-17 MAS.).

[106] C. Gal. 339e (176,2-3 MAS. = III, 416-17 WR.).

[107] See C. Gal. 339e (176,3-5 MAS. = III, 417 WR.). See also Misopogon 12.10, 344a (165 ROCHE.). Eunapius is also repelled by the worship of martyrs (Vita 472 [424 WR.]).

[108] C. Jul. 10.337 (PG 76, 1020a, b).

[109] C. Jul. 10.337 (PG 76, 1020b,c).

[110] C. Jul. 10.341 (PG 76, 1026c,d).

[111] C. Jul. 10.340-41 (PG 76, 1026a) quoting Vita Pyth. 11 (41,6-11 DES PLACES).

[112] C. Jul. 10.342 (PG 76, 1028a,b) quoting Vita Pyth. 16-17 (43,3-12.16-22 DES PLACES).

[113] C. Jul. 10.342-43 (PG 76, 1028c,d).

[114] C. Gal. F. 92 (185 MAS. = III, 428-29 WR.).

small, it is clear that the signs mentioned in the synoptic apocalypse had no "eschatological" nature in Julian's eyes. Celsus also attacked apocalyptic tradition by arguing that floods and conflagrations are part of the normal course of history (C. Cels. 4.11, 79 [281,17-23; 349,11-14 Koet.]) and do not signify that God will come down and "bring fire like a torturer."

5.2.13 Versus Mt 28:19

Julian found a contradiction between Deut 6:13 (..."him only shall you serve") and Mt 28:19. After quoting the text in Deuteronomy, Julian asks: "How then has it been handed down in the Gospels that Jesus commanded: 'Go therefore and teach all nations, baptizing them in the name of the Father, and of the Son, and of the Holy Spirit,' if they were not intended to serve him also? And your beliefs also are in harmony with these commands, when along with the Father you pay divine honors to the son (θεολογεῖτε τὸν υἱόν)."[115] The Christian divinization of Jesus contradicts the Hebrew scriptures in Julian's interpretation. In response Cyril claims that Moses and the prophets believed in the consubstantial Trinity[116]! Jacob wrestles with the Word (Cyril's reading of the LXX's Εἶδος θεοῦ), for example, in Gen 32:22-30[117].

5.2.14 Luke 2:2

Julian makes several remarks on the Gospel of Luke: "Even Jesus, who was proclaimed among you, was one of Caesar's subjects (ὑπηκόων). And if you do not believe me I will prove it a little later, or rather let me simply assert it now. However, you admit that with his father and mother he registered his name in the governorship of Cyrenius (Lk 2:2)."[118] Julian uses this passage to illustrate his general point of view that the Jews have been enslaved to various empires during their history. Jesus is no different from his kinsfolk with regard to their subjection to foreign rulers.

5.2.15 The Feeding of the 5000

A fragment from Theodore of Mopsuestia contains a critical remark of Julian about the feeding of the 5000 (Lk 9:14-15 par): "The Apostate accuses the evangelists of a contradiction (διαφωνίαν) since one has 'by hundreds and by fifties [Mk 6:40],' and another has only 'by fifties' [Lk 9:14]."[119] This technique of looking for contradictions in scripture is Porphyrian[120].

---

[115] C. Gal. 291a (163,26-33 MAS. = III, 402-403 WR.).

[116] C. Jul. 9.294 (PG 76, 952d).

[117] C. Jul. 9.295 (PG 76, 953b).

[118] C. Gal. 213a (144,3-6 MAS. = III, 378 WR.).

[119] C. Gal. F. 105 (190 MAS.) = GUIDA, Teodoro di Mopsuestia, 86-88 with comment on 147-54 in regard to contradictions in scripture.

[120] See § 2.3.10, 2.3.18, 2.3.24, 2.3.25 above.

5.2.16 The Transfiguration

Julian, in another fragment from Theodore, also attacked a detail in the transfiguration narrative (Lk 9:28-36 par). He asks: "How did they know it was Moses and Elijah — not knowing them or having their writings?" Theodore replied that Jesus explained it to them either immediately or later[121]! Tertullian had earlier argued that Peter knew "in the spirit" who Moses and Elijah were since the people had no statues of them[122].

5.2.17 Jesus on Possessions

Jesus' teaching about possessions in Luke is also a subject for Julian's scorn since it would result in the breakdown of society.

> Listen to a fine statesmanlike (πολιτικοῦ) piece of advice: "Sell your possessions and give to the poor; provide yourselves with bags which do not grow old" (Lk 12:33). Can anyone quote a more statesmanlike ordinance than this? For if all were to obey you, who would there be to buy? Can anyone praise this teaching when, if it be carried out, no city, no nation, not a single family will hold together? For, if everything has been sold, how can any house or family be of any value? Moreover the fact that if everything in the city were being sold at once there would be no one to trade is obvious, without being mentioned.[123]

Julian's critique is a version of the argument from consequence: the results of people obeying Jesus' teaching would be absurd, therefore the teaching itself is absurd[124]. Macarius' philosopher also critiqued Jesus' teaching concerning possessions because it would turn wealthy people into beggars (Apocrit. 3.5 [58,15-19,6 Blondel). He asserts that he has witnessed such people become impoverished due to Christian teaching. An anonymous pagan objected that Jesus' teaching in Luke 14:33 contradicted his acceptance of Zaccheus and Joseph of Arimathea as disciples[125].

Julian considers other consequences of Jesus' teaching on possessions on several occasions. He is aware of Christian monks (ἀποτακτίτας) who have given away everything, but he is unimpressed: "They are for the most part people who by making small sacrifices gain much or rather everything from all sources, and in addition secure honors, escort soldiers, and services."[126] He compares their behavior with that of the cynic Heracleios, to whom the oration

---

[121] C. Gal. F. 106 (190 MAS.) = GUIDA, Teodoro di Mopsuestia, 90 with comment on 158-60.

[122] Tert., Adv. Marc. 4.22.5 (601,5-602,9 KROYMANN).

[123] C. Gal. F. 100 (188-89 MAS. = III, 430-31 WR.). Compare the tradition of Julian in Arethas, Scripta Minora 14 (168,2 WESTERINK) quoted in Masaracchia, Giuliano, 242.

[124] On Aristotle's argument from consequence see § 5.2.26 below.

[125] See § 3.15 above for Macarius' text. Quaestiones de N. Test. 69 (463,1-11 SOUTER; RINALDI, Biblia Gentium, F. 458).

[126] Or. 7.18, 224b (II/1, 70 ROCHE. = II, 122-23 WR.).

is written. Julian also notes "And perhaps too there is this difference that you [Heracleios] have no excuse for levying tribute on specious pretexts as they do; which they call 'alms' (ἐλεημοσύνην)."[127] In another text Julian writes Hecebolius, an official of Edessa, and directs him to deal with the unruly Arians in that city: "Therefore, since by their [the Arians] most admirable law they are bidden to sell all they have and give to the poor so that they may attain more easily to the kingdom of the skies, in order to aid those persons in that effort, I have ordered that all their funds, namely, that belong to the church of the people of Edessa, are to be taken over that they may be given to the soldiers, and that its property be confiscated to my private purse."[128] Julian's contempt for the teaching about possessions is obvious, but he is willing to use it to curb the violence of the Arians whom he accused of attacking the Valentinians.

5.2.18 The Rich Man

One of the Syriac fragments of Cyril's work seems to show that Julian attacked the narrative of the rich man in Lk 18:25 par[129]. Cyril mentions the eye of the needle and camel and claims that it is not an animal as the impious and foolish Julian believes but a thick rope used in ships. Celsus also attacked the same text (C. Cels. 6.16 [86,12-18 Koet.]).

5.2.19 Gethsemane

The episode in Gethsemane is pitiful in Julian's eyes. He chooses to attack Luke's version in particular:

> Furthermore, Jesus prays in such language as would be used by a pitiful (ἄθλιος) wretch who cannot bear misfortune with serenity (εὐκόλως), and though he is a god is reassured by an angel. And who told you, Luke, the story of the angel (Lk 22:43), if indeed this ever happened? For those who were there when he prayed could not see the angel; for they were asleep. Therefore when Jesus came from his prayer he found them fallen asleep from their grief and he said: "Why do you sleep? Arise and pray," and so forth. And then, "And while he was yet speaking, behold a multitude and Judas (Lk 22:46-47)." That is why John did not write about the angel, for neither did he see it.[130]

Aristotle's use of εὐκόλως ("serenely," "with good grace") perhaps shows the context of Julian's critique of Jesus' pain: "Still, nobility shines through even in such circumstances, when a man bears many great misfortunes with good grace not because he is insensitive to pain but because he is noble and high

---

[127] Or. 7.18, 224b,c (II/1, 70 ROCHE.).

[128] Ep. 115, 424c,d (I/2, 196,10-16 BIDEZ = III, 126-27 WR.).

[129] C. Jul. Text 29 (56 [Syriac], 75 [Latin] NEUMANN).

[130] C. Gal. F. 95 (186 MAS. = III, 430-31 WR.).

minded."[131] Julian's attack is twofold. First, Christ does not exhibit proper equanimity in the face of misfortune. Second, the narrative of the angel is inherently doubtful since none of the disciples could have seen it. Julian argues that John's silence with regard to the angel supports his critique. Celsus also found the episode objectionable because of Jesus' cries of lamentation (C. Cels. 2.24 [153,7-10 Koet.]). He asked questions about Jesus' baptism (who saw the dove?) similar to those Julian asked about Gethsemane (C. Cels. 1.41 [92,3-5 Koet.]).

5.2.20 The Trial before Herod

A fragment from Theodore of Mopsuestia apparently contains an objection against the narrative of Jesus' trial before Herod Antipas (Lk 23:8) that is similar to one in the anonymous philosopher: "When Jesus was led before Herod he did no sign (σημεῖον), even though he wanted to see or hear him saying something."[132] Theodore remarks that Jesus knew that "it would produce no good result. Jesus did not do miracles to be admired but so that people will be saved." The anonymous philosopher asked why Jesus did no miracles in his trial as Apollonius did before Domitian (see the discussion in § 3.21).

5.2.21 Jesus' Miracles

Julian attacks the synoptic tradition of Jesus' miracles with several different arguments: "Yet Jesus, who won over the least worthy of you, has been known by name for but little more than three hundred years[133]; and during his lifetime he accomplished nothing worth hearing of, unless anyone thinks that to heal crooked and blind men and to exorcize those who were possessed by evil demons in the villages of Bethsaida and Bethany can be classed as a mighty achievement (μεγίστων ἔργων)."[134] Celsus also asked what amazing (θαυμάσιον) thing Jesus had done in deed or in word[135]. In one of the

---

[131] E.N. 1100b 31; ET from M. OSWALD's translation in Aristotle, Nicomachean Ethics, New York 1962, 23-24. Compare the usage in Xenophon, Mem. 4.8.2.

[132] C. Gal. F. 104 (195 MAS.= PG 66.725c = GUIDA, Teodoro di Mopsuestia, 100 with comment on 186-92). Julian is mentioned as the source of the previous objection to the Gethsemane story, but is not mentioned by name in this text. GUIDA notes that Vat. Pal. gr. 20 f. 208ᵛ identifies the text as from Ἐκ τῶν πρὸς Ἰουλιανόν (FRAMMENTI INEDITI, 146).

[133] Arnobius 2.71 (149,20 MARCHESI) has a pagan who says "your religion did not exist 300 years ago" (the MS has "400"). For a similar comment about 300 years see Macarius' pagan in Apocr. 4.5 (163,4 BLONDEL; discussed in § 3.16).

[134] C. Gal. 191e (136,6-11 MAS. = III, 376-77 WR.). On Julian's argument concerning miracles see MEREDITH, Porphyry and Julian, 1146. Celsus also comments on Jesus' "recent" appearance (C. Cels. 1.26, 2.4, 6.10, 8.12 [77,28; 130,22; 80,29; 229,13 KOET.]).

[135] C. Cels. 1.67 (121,10 KOET.).

fragments, Porphyry asks how the son of God "helped us when he became flesh"[136]? Julian's evaluation of the miracles as small works or achievements coheres with his evaluation of those persuaded by Jesus: they were the "least worthy of you" (τὸ χείριστον τῶν παρ᾽ ὑμῖν)[137]. His devaluation of Jesus' followers and deeds is an example of the rhetoric of vituperation. Interestingly enough he does not deny the reality of the miracles. He was apparently willing to recognize the reality of Hellenistic miracles (and surely those recounted by Porphyry and Iamblichus in their lives of Pythagoras). In his oration to Heracleios, he wrote that it is "...my belief that he himself walked on the sea as though it were dry land. For what was impossible to Heracles"[138]? Julian also accepts a story concerning Clauda, priestess of Cybele, who made a ship move that contained a statue of the goddess[139]. Julian's views on the social status of Christian converts will be treated below — they are fully in accord with those of Celsus (see § 1.6.2, 4 above). Cyril responds by claiming that Julian calls the number of those netted by Christ to be small and believes that the dwellers of the earth can be easily numbered[140]. Cyril asks if after the incarnation Julian would have liked to see some kind of miracle concerning the sun and the moon. He goes on to the enumerate the ways in which Christ freed people from the quackeries of demons. Miracles draw people to faith, according to Cyril, and he summarizes the miracles of Christ and concludes: What is more magnificent[141]?

To support his argument that the Jews are in miserable circumstances Julian summarizes their history of subjection to various empires of the world. He then supports this argument by claiming that Jesus conferred no benefit on his people. He notes that Jesus' miracles were unable to convince the Jews:

> But what benefit did he confer on his own kinsfolk? Nay, the Galilaeans answer, they refused to hearken unto Jesus. What? How was it then that this hardhearted [Ezek 3:7] and stubborn-necked people hearkened unto Moses; but Jesus, who commanded the spirits [Mk 1:27 par] and walked on the sea [Mk 6:49 par] and drove out demons, ... could not this Jesus change (μεταστῆσαι) the dispositions (προαιρέσεις) of his own friends and kinsfolk to the end that he might save them?[142]

---

[136] HARNACK, Porphyrius, F. 84. See § 2.3.41 above.

[137] Compare Celsus' similar view (C. Cels. 2.46 [168,14-15 KOET.]).

[138] Or. 7.14, 219d (II/1, 63 ROCHE. = II, 110 WR.) On the tradition see Seneca, Her. Fur. 324. Orion is given the power to walk on water in Apollodorus 1.4.3 and Eratosthenes, Cataster. 32.

[139] Or. 8.2, 160a-d (II/1, 104-105 ROCHE.).

[140] C. Jul. 6.192 (PG 76, 793a).

[141] C. Jul. 6.192 (PG 76, 793b-d).

[142] C. Gal. 213b,c (144,6-145,15 MAS. = III, 380-81 WR.). I have slightly altered WRIGHT's translation since it is unnecessary to insert ἄνθρωπος in the first line of the ET ("when he became human what..."). See MASARACCHIA, Giuliano, 66 who points out that the comparison is between the time before Jesus' birth and after.

Celsus asked a similar question: "What fine action did Jesus do like a god?"[143] Celsus also emphasized the fact that Jesus did not persuade anyone but ten disciples[144]. One of Arnobius' pagans argued like Julian: "... if God is powerful, merciful, willing to save us, let Him change our dispositions, and compel us to trust in His promises"[145]. Julian does not question the reality of the miracles, but asserts that they were ineffective in changing his audience. In addition Jesus gave his people nothing good. Julian's statement about the "Miracle working and fabrication of the gospels" (εὐαγγελίων τερατουργίας καὶ σκευωρίας) indicates that he could question the veracity of the gospel narratives, but in general he does not seem to question the belief that Jesus performed miracles[146]. Cyril's response stresses the spiritual benefits of Christ's coming and the fact that God does not force faith. We partake in the divine nature due to the incarnation[147]. If Christ came to earth with irresistible authority he would have commanded faith in himself and faith would no longer be the fruit of conviction[148].

5.2.22 The Resurrection Narratives

The synoptic accounts of the resurrection contained a contradiction in Julian's view because of the indications of the time of the events. In one of the Syriac fragments of Cyril's work against Julian the text has:

> He wrote that the holy evangelists contradict themselves (דלוקבל חדדא) when they say: Mary Magdalene and the other Mary (following Matthew [Mt 28:1]), late on the sabbath when the first of the week began to dawn, came to the tomb; according to Mark, [16:2] however, after it began to be daylight and the sun had risen. And according to Matthew they saw an angel [28:2]; according to Mark a young man [16:5]; and according to Matthew they left and told the disciples about the resurrection of Christ [28:8] — according to Mark they were silent and told no one anything [16:8]. By means of these things he brings censure on the holy scriptures and says that they contradict each other.[149]

Julian thus found the resurrection narratives to be riddled with contradictions. This approach is slightly different from those of Celsus, Porphyry and the

---

[143] C. Cels 2.33 (159,26 KOET.).

[144] C. Cels 2.39, 43, 46, 70 (163,26; 166,5; 168,14-15 192,18 KOET.).

[145] Adv. nat. 2.65 (141,2-22 MARCH.). See ROKEAH, Jews, 143.

[146] C. Gal. 218a (145,4 MAS.).

[147] C. Jul. 6.214 (PG 76, 828c).

[148] C. Jul. 6.215 (PG 76, 829b).

[149] C. Gal. F. 96 (187 MAS.) = C. Jul., Text 18 (54 [Syriac], 70 [Latin] NEUMANN who numbers it as F. 8 of the C. Gal.). For similar texts (with reference to anonymous objectors) from Theodore of Mopsuestia see GUIDA, Teodoro di Mopsuestia, 206-25. Cp. the text of Ish'odad in § 2.3.32.

anonymous philosopher[150]. Cyril responded to Julian by claiming that different journeys to the tomb were narrated[151]. Though Cyril does not record Julian's argument, in another text, he notes that "the enemy of the truth laughs at all the other things as though it is not possible to God who can do all things and also things greater than death ..." The "other things" include the doctrine of the resurrection from the dead in Christ as Cyril makes clear in his introduction to Julian's point of view[152]. This point of view is close to that of the other pagans mentioned above[153].

5.2.23 The Christology of John

The Gospel of John was a focus of Julian's criticism because of its high christology. One of his main arguments is that John's christology is not found in the OT. He also argues that the christology of John cannot be found in other NT authors.

5.2.23.1 John 1:1, 3 and the Prophets

After quoting texts that emphasize Israel's belief in one God (Deut 4:35, 39, 6:4, 32:39) Julian concludes:

> These then are the words of Moses when he insists that there is only one God. But perhaps the Galilaeans will reply: "But we do not assert that there are two gods or three." But I will show that they do assert this also, and I call John to witness, who says: "In the beginning was the Word, and the Word was with God and the Word was God [John 1:1]." Now whether this is he who was born of Mary or someone else, — that I may answer Photinus at the same time, — this now makes no difference; indeed I leave the dispute to you; but it is enough to bring forward the evidence that he says "with God," and "in the beginning." How then does this agree with the teachings of Moses?"[154]

Photinus, who denied the divinity of Jesus, is more congenial to Julian's way of thinking[155]. In his letter to him Julian approved of his teaching. In another context Julian recognizes that the Word is identical with the Son[156]. But any belief in a "Logos" (orthodox or not) is contrary to Moses' monotheism according to Julian, who thereby disagrees with any branch of Christian theology.

---

[150] C. Cels. 5.14 (15,1-25 KOET. discussed in § 1.2.23). HARNACK, Porphyrius, F. 92 (§ 2.3.32). Macarius, Apocrit. 4.24 (204,1-205,9 BLONDEL; see § 3.51).

[151] C. Jul. Text 18 (70 NEUMANN).

[152] C. Gal. F. 61 (156 MAS. = F. 17 NEUMANN), from Cyril, C. Jul. 7.250b.

[153] C. Cels. 5.14 (15,13-14 KOET.). See in particular the anonymous pagans in Ps. Justin, Quaest. gentil. ad Christ. 15, 200c-e (330 OTTO).

[154] C. Gal. 262b-c (160,21-31 MAS. = III, 396-99 WR.)

[155] See Julian's letter to him, Ep. 90 (I/2, 174,10-175,14 BIDEZ). Sozomen discusses his work in H.E. 4.6.1-3 (143,13-24 B./H.) and see Socrates, H.E. 2.29.1-5; 7.32.9 (140,9-141,5; 380,28 HANSEN).

[156] C. Gal. 333d (174,18-20 MAS.). See SMITH, Julian's Gods, 202

John 1:3, "All things were made by him, and without him was not anything made," cannot be true if Gen 49:10 is a genuine prophecy of the Messiah — the "ruler from Judah." Julian writes: "But granted that he really is 'a ruler from Judah,' then he is not 'God born of God,' as you are in the habit of saying, nor is it true that 'All things were made by him; and without him was not any thing made.'"[157] Presumably Julian interprets the figure in Gen 49:10 to be fully human and not divine. Julian concludes from the same argument that Jesus is not "God born of God" (θεὸς ἐκ θεοῦ)[158]. In another text Julian again attacks John 1:3 by asking "can anyone point this out among the utterances of the prophets"[159]? He then quotes texts from the prophets such as Is 26:13 and 37:16 — strong affirmations of monotheism that leave no place for a second god in Julian's approach.

Julian also points out that nowhere does Isaiah mention the "only begotten son of God" (John 1:18). The figure prophesied in Is 7:14 is not called a god. Here Julian also questions why Christians call Mary the "mother of God" (θεοτόκον)[160]. Julian again asks a similar question about the virgin: "But if, as you believe, the Word (λόγος) is God born of God and proceeded from the substance of the Father, why do you say that the virgin is mother of God? For how could she bear a god since she is, according to you, a human being? And moreover, when God declares plainly 'I am he, and there is none that can deliver beside me,' do you dare to call her son Savior?"[161]   Julian's fundamental approach in these arguments is that the Hebrew Scriptures do not prophesy the Messiah to be God. Celsus, on the other hand, simply argued that thousands of other people could fulfill the prophecies (C. Cels. 2.28 [157,1-3 Koet.], see § 1.4.2). A passage in Iamblichus may help explain why Julian was reluctant to see a god born of a human mother. Iamblichus did not believe that the Intellect of the gods descended to earth and rejected the belief in Pythagoras as a son of god:

> We must reject here the view of Epimenides, Eudoxus, and Xenocrates, who assumed that Apollo had intercourse with Parthenis [the mother of Pythagoras] at that time, and when she was not pregnant, made her so, and announced it through his prophetess. This view deserves no acceptance. Nevertheless, no one would dispute, judging from his very birth and the all around wisdom of his life, that Pythagoras' soul was sent down under Apollo's

---

[157] C. Gal. 261e (159,7-9 MAS. = III, 396-97 WR.).

[158] This formulation appears to be from the Nicene creed (symbol. Nic. 54 [30,3 DENZINGER]).

[159] C. Gal. 262d,e (160,37-43 MAS. = III, 398-99 WR.).

[160] MASARACCHIA, Giuliano, 234 refers to Greg. Naz., Ep. 1 (ad. Cleod.): εἴ τις οὐ θεοτόκον τὴν ἁγίαν Μαρίαν ὑπολαμβάνει, χωρίς ἐστι τῆς θεότητος.

[161] C. Gal. 276e (161,1-6 MAS. = III, 400-401 WR.). The scripture quotation is similar to Deut 32:39.

leadership, either as a follower in his train, or united with this god in a still more intimate way.[162]

Julian was not even willing to see Christ as a "pure human soul"[163].

Cyril responds at length to this section of Julian's work with two main arguments[164]. The first is that the doctrine of the three persons of the Trinity is present in OT texts. The second is that Greek philosophers have a doctrine similar to that of the Christian Trinity. For Cyril God is unattainable except through the Son[165]. The "we" of Gen 1:26 includes the Son and Holy Spirit according to Cyril[166]. Cyril makes similar exegetical moves with Gen 11:7, 18:3, 19:24[167]. From Hellenistic thought Cyril quotes Plutarch and Plato on the unity of God[168]. He then chooses texts from Porphyry, Plato, Numenius and Plotinus that assert some type of divine triad[169]. In a text from Numenius, for example, the philosopher argues for the existence of a First God that is indivisible. Associated with this God are a second and third God who are one[170]. From Porphyry, Cyril quoted his statement about the Platonic Good, Demiurge, and World soul — the three hypostases of God[171].

5.2.23.2 Against Jesus as Creator

Julian also finds an inconsistency in the fact that only John claims that Jesus created the world: "...and as you yourselves assert made the heavens and the earth, — for no one of his disciples ventured to say this concerning him, save only John, and he did not say it clearly or distinctly; still let us at any rate admit

---

[162] Iamblichus On the Pythagorean Way of Life: Text, Translation, and Notes, ed. J. M. DILLON/J. HERSHBELL, Atlanta 1991, 7-8. JOHN FINAMORE quotes this text in an unpublished paper, Julian and the Descent of Asclepius, to help explain Julian's possible views on the nature of Asclepius as a pure human soul and not a god descended to earth.

[163] On descent by such souls see Iamblichus, De Anima (I.379, 380 Stobaeus, WACHSMUTH) and Julian, Or. 58.6, 166d (II/1 113 ROCHE.).

[164] C. Jul. 8.263-276 (PG 76, 901-924).

[165] C. Jul. 8.265 (PG 76, 906c).

[166] C. Jul. 8.267 (PG 76, 909c).

[167] C. Jul. 8.268 (PG 76, 912a).

[168] C. Jul. 8.266 (PG 76, 908b-d). The quotation from Plato includes Tim. 31a and ends with ποτε εἴη. The next section of text which Migne prints in italics is not from Plato (according to a TLG search). Consequently the crucial phrase, Λόγος δέ ἐστιν εἰς ἕνα θεὸν ..., in Cyril's argument is not Platonic! One of the allegedly Platonic phrases, (ὑπερτάτῃ φύσει), occurs not in Plato but elsewhere in Cyril's work (C. Jul. 10.328 [PG 76, 1004c]), and this is an indication that the passage may be his own composition. Cyril quotes Plutarch's De E apud Delphos 392a, 393a,b more accurately.

[169] C. Jul. 8.270-76 (PG 76, 913-24).

[170] C. Jul. 8.272 (PG 76, 918c) quoting part of Numenius, F. 11 (DES PLACES).

[171] C. Jul. 8.271 (PG 76, 916b) printed in NAUCK's edition of Porphyry's Hist. Philos. as F. 16 (14,1-7 N.).

that he said it ..."[172]. The fact that only John (of Jesus' disciples) claims that Jesus created the universe is just another reason to find John's christology doubtful. Macarius' philosopher asked a similar question with regard to John 5:46-47: "And even if one were to concede that the writing is that of Moses, it cannot be shown that Christ was anywhere called God, or God the Word, or Creator."[173] In his critique of the incident of the piercing Christ's side, the same philosopher notes that "...only John has said this, and none of the others"[174]. Both Julian and the anonymous philosopher have a strong aversion to Johannine thought.

5.2.23.3 The Synoptics versus John

The synoptic gospels also disagree with John, according to Julian. Here his technique is very similar to that of Porphyry. He charges:

> But you are so misguided that you have not even remained faithful to the teachings that were handed down to you by the apostles. And these also have been altered, so as to be worse and more impious, by those who came after. At any rate neither Paul nor Matthew nor Luke nor Mark ventured to call Jesus God. But the worthy John, since he perceived that a great number of people in many of the towns of Greece and Italy had already been infected by this disease,[175] and because he heard, I suppose, that even the tombs of Peter and Paul were being worshipped — secretly, it is true, but still he did hear this, — he, I say, was the first to venture to call Jesus God.[176]

Julian finds this contrast in christology to be fatal to John's point of view. Cyril denies Julian's claim and argues that all four writers (Paul and the

---

[172] C. Gal. 213 b,c (144,10-13 MAS. = III, 380-81, WR.).

[173] Apocrit. 3.3 (54,6-8 BLONDEL) discussed in § 3.26 above.

[174] Apocrit. 2.13 (22,5 BLONDEL) discussed in § 3.30 above.

[175] Julian calls Christianity a "disease" (νόσος) in Or. 7.22, 229c and Ep. 98, 401c (II/1, 77 ROCHE.; I/2 183/4 BIDEZ). See also Ep. 89a, 454b and 61c, 424b (I/2, 155,9; 75,23 BIDEZ). GEFFCKEN (Zwei Griechische Apologeten, 306) compares Julian's word for Christianity to Porphyry's claim that "disease" has not left the city since the gods have left and since Christ has been honored (F. 80, HARNACK). See also ILCV 1b (= CIL III.12132, lines 9-27) in which Maximin Daia is petitioned by the cities of Lycia and Pamphylia who request that "the Christians, long suffering from madness (?) and even now maintaining the same disease (νόσον), should at length be made to cease and not give offense by some ill-omened new cult to the worship due to the gods" (in DROGE, Homer, 178 quoting R. M. GRANT, The Religion of Maximin Daia, in: Christianity, Judaism and Other Greco-Roman Cults: Studies for Morton Smith at Sixty, Vol. 4, ed. J. NEUSNER, Leiden 1975, 143-166). Maximin, in a rescript, responds to the citizens of Colbasa (in Lycia and Pamphylia): "And may those, who after being freed from those blind and wandering (?) by-ways, have returned to a right and goodly frame of mind, rejoice most of all, and, as though preserved from a sudden tempest or snatched from a grave illness (morbo), let them henceforward feel a more pleasant enjoyment of life" in S. MITCHELL, Maximinus and the Christians in A.D. 312: A New Latin Inscription, JRS 78, 1988, (105-24) 108.

[176] C. Gal. 327a,b (172,5-13 MAS. = III, 412-413 WR.).

synoptics) depict Jesus with titles and characteristics of divinity[177]. In Romans 9:5, for example, Cyril believes that Paul spoke of Jesus as God[178]. The description of Jesus in Mt 1:21 and Jesus' ability to forgive sins in that gospel are indications of divinity for Cyril[179]. The title in Mark 1:1 is another indication[180]. The Christological title in Luke 1:32 is also a sign of divinity and Cyril sees a reference to Jesus in the word "Highest" in Luke 1:76-77[181]. It seems likely that Julian would have been unconvinced by Cyril's arguments.

5.2.23.4 Versus John 1:14, 18

Julian also quotes John 1:14, "The word was made flesh and dwelt among us" and notes:

> But how, he does not say, because he was ashamed. Nowhere, however, does he call him either Jesus or Christ, so long as he calls him God and the Word, but as it were insensibly and secretly he steals away our ears, and says that John the Baptist bore this witness on behalf of Jesus Christ, that in very truth he it is whom we must believe to be God the Word.[182]

Julian is aware that some Christians deny that Jesus Christ is the Word:

> But that John says this ["the Word was made flesh"] concerning Jesus Christ, I for my part do not deny. And yet certain of the impious think that Jesus Christ is quite distinct from the Word that was proclaimed by John.[183] That however is not the case. For he whom John himself calls God the Word, this is he who, says he, was recognized by John the Baptist to be Jesus Christ.[184] Observe accordingly how cautiously, how quietly and insensibly he introduces into the drama the crowning word of his impiety; and he is so rascally and deceitful that he rears his head once more to add, "No one has seen God at any time; the only begotten Son which is in the bosom of the Father, he has declared him (John 1:18)." Then is this only begotten Son which is in the bosom of the Father the God who is the Word and became flesh? And if, as I think, it is indeed he, you also have

---

[177] C. Jul. 10.327-333 (PG 76, 1004-12).

[178] C. Jul. 10.328 (PG 76, 1004d).

[179] C. Jul. 10.329 (PG 76, 1006d-1008a).

[180] C. Jul. 10.330 (PG 76, 1008b).

[181] C. Jul. 10.331 (PG 76, 1010b).

[182] C. Gal. 327b,c (172,15-173,20 MAS. = III, 412-13, WR.).

[183] MASARACCHIA, Giuliano, 238 quotes the ἔκθεσις μακρόστιχος 5 (M. SIMONETTI, Il Cristo II. Testi teologici e spirituali in lingua greco dal IV al VII secolo, Milano 1986, 146,8) for a condemnation of Christians who believe that the Word is different from Christ. See also Alexander Alexandrinus, Ep. ad omnes episc. 6. (SIMONETTI, Il Cristo, 84,5) for a statement by individuals such as Arius who believe that Christ is a created thing and οὔτε ἀληθινὸς καὶ φύσει τοῦ πατρὸς λόγος ἐστίν.

[184] There is an anonymous objection to the tension between John 1:31, 33 and Mt 3:14 (John knowing Jesus' status) in Ambrosiaster, Quaestiones Vet. et N. Test. 58 (104,9-13 SOUTER; RINALDI, Biblia Gentium, F. 3). Compare Quaest. de N. T. 55 (448,19-20 SOUTER; RINALDI, Biblia Gentium, F. 363) which finds a tension between John 1:32 and Mt 11:3.

certainly beheld God. For "He dwelt among you, and you beheld his glory (John 1:14)."
Why then do you add to this that "No one has seen God at any time"? For you have
indeed seen, if not God the Father, still God who is the Word. But if the only begotten
Son is one person and the God who is the Word another, as I have heard from certain of
your sect, then it appears that not even John made that rash statement.[185]

Julian finds John 1:18 and 1:14 to be a clear contradiction[186]. Here Julian's
line of attack is internal consistency and not the fact that John's christological
formulations are alien to the OT. Julian's critique of the worship of Jesus as
the word is also present in his letter to the Alexandrians whom Julian berates
for abandoning the worship of the Hellenistic gods in favor of a god that they
have never seen — Jesus[187]. Julian is not really concerned to determine
whether Jesus can be "seen" or not. His point in the *Contra Gal.* is that John
contradicts himself. While writing to the Alexandrians he contrasts Jesus with
the God Helios — whose image can at least be seen. Cyril resolves the
contrasting statements by arguing that with regard to his divine nature the Son
is invisible, but with regard to the glory appropriate to God he was visible
(John 1:14)[188]. Cyril uses this approach to interpret Jesus' statement to Philip
in John: "The one who has seen me has seen the father (14:9)"[189].

5.2.23.5 John 1:29

Julian also attacks John's concept of redemption:

First of all how did the Word of God take away sin [John 1:29], when it caused many to
commit the sin of killing their fathers, and many their children [Mt 10:21]? And people
are compelled either to uphold the ancestral (τοῖς πατρίοις) customs and to cling to the
pious traditions (εὐσεβείας) that they have inherited from the ages or to accept this
innovation (καινοτομίαν)... Why do you not consider him [Moses] able to take away sin
[ἀναιρέτην ... τῆς ἁμαρτίας]? ... Jesus came to take away sin [as you say] and is
discovered to have multiplied it (ἀναιρέτης ... ἐλθών Ἰησοῦς ἁμαρτίας
πλειστηριάσας ταύτην κατείληπται). [190]

The patricide and killing of one's own children occasioned by the preaching of
the gospel is inconsistent with the claim that Christ takes away sin according to
Julian. Those who do not accept the Christian gospel also do not apparently
have their sins taken away either — because they remain Hellenes. For Julian
as for other Hellenes it was self-evident that one should uphold one's ancestral

---

[185] C. Gal. 333b, c, d (173,3-174,20 MAS. = III, 412-415, WR.).

[186] An anonymous objector finds a contradiction between Isaiah 6:5 and John 1:18 in
Ambrosiaster, Quaest. Vet. et N. Test. 71 (122 SOUTER; RINALDI, Biblia Gentium, F. 223).

[187] Ep. 111, 434c (I/2, 190,15-20 BIDEZ).

[188] C. Jul. 10.334 (PG 76, 1016a).

[189] C. Jul. 10.334 (PG 76, 1013c,d).

[190] C. Gal. F. 107 (191 MAS.). The ET in the LCL is from NEUMANN's reconstruction
(III, 423-33 WR.) and is slightly altered above in favor of MASARACCHIA's quotation of the
text in Aretas, Scripta minora 24 (I, 221 WESTERINK).

traditions: "For I hold that we ought to observe the laws that we have inherited from our forefathers, since it is evident that the gods gave them to us."[191]

5.2.24 Acts

5.2.24.1 Acts 3:22, Cornelius, and Sergius

Julian made a few scattered comments about the book of Acts in the fragments that survive. He attacks Peter's use of Deut 18:18 in Acts 3:22 ("A prophet shall the Lord your God raise up unto you of your brethren, like unto me; to him shall ye hearken") by noting that the words "were certainly not said of the son of Mary. And even though to please you, one should concede that they were said of him, Moses says that the prophet will be like him and not like God, a prophet like himself and born of people, not of a god."[192] He was aware of Cornelius (Acts 10) and Sergius (13:6-12) who were convinced by the apostles to become Christians. Jesus and Paul "were content if they could delude (ἐξαπατήσουσι) maidservants and slaves, and through them the women, and men like Cornelius and Sergius"[193]. Julian obviously regards them as exceptional since he views the majority of early Christians as slaves. He may also refer to prominent women "deluded" by Paul such as Lydia (Acts 16:11-15). Julian was aware that prominent women were being recruited to the Christian movement. With regard to Athanasius, Julian wrote: "He has had the audacity to baptize Greek women of rank (τῶν ἐπισήμων) during my reign! Let him be driven forth!"[194] Julian's view of the apostles is similar to Porphyry's who claimed that the apostles did miracles by magic arts in order to get money from wealthy women whom they persuaded[195].

5.2.24.2 Acts 10:15, The Christians' Diet

The diet of the Christians was objectionable to Julian because of their abandonment of their Jewish ancestral traditions: "Why in your diet are you not as pure as the Jews, and why do you say that we ought to eat everything 'even as the green herb,'[196] putting your faith in Peter, because as the Galilaeans say, he declared, 'What God has cleansed, do not call common'

---

[191] Ep. 89a, 453b (I/2, 153,19-21 BIDEZ = III, 58-59 WR.).

[192] C. Gal. 253c, d (157,18-22 MAS. = III, 394-395 WR.). Compare Celsus' approach in C. Cels. 2.28 (156,21-24 KOET.).

[193] C. Gal. 206a,b (142,10-11 MAS. = III, 376-77 WR.).

[194] Ep. 112, 376c (I/2, 192,19-20 BIDEZ = III, 142-43 WR.).

[195] HARNACK, Porphyrius, F. 4. See the section below on Julian's views concerning the social status of Christians (§ 5.2.29).

[196] Gen 1:29 and 9:3. In Or. 9.12, 192d (II/1, 160 ROCHE.), Julian calls Christians παμφάγων (eaters of all things) and also refers to Gen 9:3. See also C. Gal. 238d (153,23 MAS.). On Julian's interpretation of the law see ROKEAH, Jews, 120.

[Acts 10:15]."[197] Julian's point is that the Christians have no roots in Jewish tradition. Julian cannot accept that what God once considered "abominable" (μιαρά) he would now make "pure" (καθαρά). He goes on to discuss Mosaic legislation about "clean" animals and those that part the hoof and chew the cud (Lev 11:3):

> Now if, after the vision (φαντασίας) of Peter, the pig has now taken to chewing the cud, then let us obey Peter; for it is in very truth a miracle if, after the vision of Peter, it has taken to that habit. But if he spoke falsely when he said that he saw this revelation, — to use your own way to speaking, — in the house of the tanner, why are we so ready to believe him in such important matters?[198]

Peter's contradiction with Mosaic legislation invalidates the Christian diet in Julian's interpretation of the texts. Julian then considers the Christians' defense that God appointed a second law after the first. He finds it incredible that the Mosaic law could be limited by space and time and refers to such passages as Ex 12:14-15 that mention all generations bound by the law[199].

Cyril uses allegory to respond to Julian's arguments about food[200]. The law is "shadows and types" (Heb 10:1) appointed until the "time of reformation" (Heb 9:10)[201]. Cyril argues that the vision of Peter in Acts indicates that the time has arrived for the transformation of the shadows to the truth[202]. Those who are strong enough intellectually to understand the hidden meanings of the law will know, for example, that vultures were forbidden because they are symbols of greed, robbery, and so forth[203]. Because all things were created good (Gen 1:31), Cyril concludes that the pig can be eaten[204]. In another text Julian claims that Christians have abandoned the teaching of the Jews for the sake of the prophets and eat everything. In response, Cyril again takes up the issue of diet [205]. He notes that Christians adopt the moral teachings of the law, but eat freely[206]. He uses texts such as 1 Cor 8:8, 1 Tim 4:4, and Mt 15:11, 19 to make his point that Christian need reject no food[207].

---

[197] C. Gal. 314c (168,2-5 MAS. = III, 406-07 WR.). See Christian (or pagan?) concern over similar issues of diet in Ps. Justin, Quaest. et Resp. ad Orthod. 47 (53,11-25 PAPADOPOULOS-KERAMEUS).
[198] C. Gal. 314d (168,9-14 MAS. = III, 408-09 WR.)
[199] C. Gal. 319d,e (169,2-13 MAS. = III, 408-09 WR.).
[200] C. Jul. 9.315-19 (PG 76, 984-92).
[201] C. Jul. 9.319 (PG 76, 992b).
[202] C. Jul. 9.319 (PG 76, 992a).
[203] C. Jul. 9.317 and 318 (PG 76, 988b, 989c).
[204] C. Jul. 9.319 (PG 76, 992a,b).
[205] C. Gal. 238b-d (152,3-153,23 MAS.), C. Jul. 7.241-43 (PG 76, 868c-872c.).
[206] C. Jul. 7.241 (PG 76, 868d).
[207] C. Jul. 7.242-43 (PG 76, 869c-872a).

5.2.24.3 Acts 15:28-29: The Apostolic Decree

In the same context Cyril notes that Julian discussed the apostolic decree in Acts 15:28-29 which forbade the eating of strangled things and meat offered to idols. Julian apparently argued that the Holy Spirit did not find it necessary to disable that law of Moses (τὸν Μωσέως χρῆναι παραλύεσθαι νόμον), and that it is necessary to keep the Mosaic law[208]. Such an attitude toward the law is characteristic of Julian. Porphyry had some sort of objection to the similar verse in Acts 15:20, although he may have focused his objection on the golden rule[209].

5.2.24.4 Apostolic Visions

Although Julian does not identify any specific visions in Acts, he attacks apostolic visions in general. He accused the apostles of the practice of spending the night among tombs in order to obtain dream-visions or oracles. It is part of Julian's critique of the Christian veneration of the martyrs and their "groveling" (worship) among the martyrs' tombs. Julian finds the reason for the "groveling" in the prophet Isaiah (65:4):

> "They lodge among tombs and in caves for the sake of dream visions" (ἐνύπνια). You observe, then, how ancient among the Jews was this work of witchcraft (μαγγανείας), namely, sleeping among tombs for the sake of dream visions. And indeed it is likely that your apostles, after their teacher's death, practiced this and handed it down to you from the beginning, I mean to those who first adopted your faith, and that they themselves performed their spells (μαγγανεῦσαι) more skilfully than you do, and displayed openly to those who came after them the places in which they performed this witchcraft and abomination.[210]

This practice is horrifying in Julian's eyes — although he seems to have harbored no similar qualms towards his teacher Maximus' practice of theurgy. Probably Julian could not accept religious rituals being carried out near corpses[211]. Maximus was reputed, for example, to have made the image of Hecate smile, seem to laugh aloud, and her torches burst into flame[212]. Eunapius tells no accounts of Maximus practicing incubation, however, and Julian may have found certain theurgical acts more acceptable than any magic

---

[208] C. Gal. 324e, 325a (171,1-7 MAS.).

[209] HARNACK, Porphyrius, F. 8.

[210] C. Gal. 339e-340a (176,2-11 MAS. = III, 416-17 WR.).

[211] The Athenians once purified the island of Delos (426, 25 B.C.E.) by taking all the sepulchres away. Earlier the part of the island that could be seen from the temple had been purified (Thucydides 3.104 discussed by W. BURKERT, Greek Religion. Archaic and Classical, trans. J. RAFFAN, 1st ed. 1977, Cambridge 1985, 87).

[212] See Socrates, H.E. 3.1.16-18 (188,21-27 HANSEN) on Maximus. The narrative is in Eunapius, Vita 475 (432-35 WR.).

performed around tombs[213]. Prophecy was acceptable to Julian who had received that function from the god at Didyma[214]. Cyril simply denied that Christians practiced such forms of divination[215].

5.2.25 Paul

Julian sporadically attacked Paul. He accused Paul of being a magician: "Now I will only point out that Moses himself and the prophets who came after him and Jesus the Nazarene, and Paul also, who surpassed all the magicians and charlatans of every place and every time, assert that he is the God of Israel alone and of Judaea, and that the Jews are his chosen people"[216]. Celsus also made liberal use of the accusation of magic against Jews and Christians[217]. Julian's distaste for Paul is similar to that of Macarius' philosopher who mainly attacked Paul's teachings (as in 1 Cor 9:20): "... truly he is a servant and minister of other people's wrong doings, and a notable zealot for unseemly things, if he spends his time on each occasion in the baseness of those without law, and appropriates their doings to himself"[218]. Macarius later notes that Paul was accused of doing his acts by magic[219].

5.2.25.1 Paul on the Jews: Romans 3:29

Like Porphyry Julian is concerned with the fate of the generations before Christ (§ 2.3.30). He uses a different line of attack, however, because he is interested in the critique of the belief that only the Jews were God's portion:

> But that from the beginning God cared only for the Jews and that He chose them out as his portion, has been clearly asserted not only by Moses and Jesus but by Paul as well, though in Paul's case this is strange. For according to circumstances he keeps changing his views about God, as the polypus changes its colors to match the rocks, and now he insists that the Jews alone are God's portion (κληρονομίαν), and then again, when he is trying to persuade (ἀναπείθων) the Hellenes to take sides with him, he says: "Do not think that he is the God of Jews only, but also of Gentiles; yea of Gentiles also [Rom 3:29]." Therefore, it is fair to ask of Paul why God, if he was not the God of the Jews only but also of the Gentiles, sent the blessed gift of prophecy to the Jews in abundance and gave them Moses and the oil of anointing, and the prophets and law and the incredible and monstrous elements in their myths? For you hear them crying aloud: "Humans did

---

[213] On Julian's attitude toward theurgy see Letter to a Priest, Ep. 89b, 292b (I/2, 159,21-22 BIDEZ) and Or. 8.20, 180b (II/1, 130-31 ROCHE.): "make me perfect in theurgy." See SMITH, Julian's Gods 91.

[214] Ep. 88, 451b (I/2, 151,6-7 BIDEZ). Cf. J. FONTENROSE, Didyma. Apollo's Oracle, Cult, and Companions, Berkeley, Los Angeles, London 1988, 25.

[215] See § 5.2.11 above.

[216] C. Gal. 100a (109,20-110,24 MAS. = III, 340-41 WR.).

[217] C. Cels. 1.26 (77,13 KOET.) and § 1.2.9 in this work. Julian also speaks of other magical Christian rites in C. Gal. 340a (176,10 MAS.).

[218] Apocrit. 3.30 (125,16-18 BLONDEL).

[219] See the discussion in § 3.33 above.

eat angels' food" [Ps 78:25]. And finally God sent unto them Jesus also, but unto us no prophet, no oil of anointing, no teacher, no herald to announce his love for people which should one day, though late, reach even us also.[220]

Julian concludes God is only one of the crowd of deities since he was only concerned with a small part of the world — namely Palestine, while for thousands of years people in their ignorance served "idols." Celsus shared this point of view: "...if God ... woke up out of his long slumber and wanted to deliver the human race from evils, why on earth did he sent this spirit that you mention into one corner"[221]? It is difficult to decide which text of Paul Julian is referring to when he claims that Paul believed only Israel was God's "portion." Perhaps he intends Rom 3:2 with its reference to the prophecies entrusted to Israel. In any case he finds Rom 3:29 to be contradictory to the view that only the Jews are God's chosen people. Macarius' Hellene also found Paul to be thoroughly contradictory as in the case of his circumcision of Timothy (Acts 16:3) and his denigration of the ritual in Phil 3:2 and the law itself in Gal 1:8, 3:10[222]. Porphyry is worried about the salvation of those generations before Christ, while Julian wants to show that the God of the Hebrews showed no concern for the Gentiles by not sending a prophet or herald to announce God's love for people. Celsus posed this question: "Is it only now after such a long age that God has remembered to judge the life of people? Did he not care before?"[223] Porphyry wondered why a merciful God would allow so many nations to perish in ignorance of the law and commandments before Christ came[224]. If Christ is the way of salvation, the grace, and the truth, Porphyry asked, what happened to all the generations of people before Christ who were without the Christian law (and the Jewish law too for that matter).[225] Macarius' philosopher also had a similar question[226].

Cyril believes that God is God of the nations (Rom 3:29) because they are aware of a natural law (Rom 2:14-15)[227]. He also believes that there was no polytheism from Adam until Noah[228]. Abraham was called from the error of polytheism and is the first fruit of the call to the Gentiles by Christ[229]. Cyril

---

[220] C. Gal. 106a-d (111,2-112,17 MAS. = III, 342-43, WR.). See ROKEAH, Jews, 79, 163.
[221] C. Cels. 6.78 (149,23-26 KOET.). Compare Porphyry's reference to the narrow region of Syria in which the Jewish law flourished (HARNACK, Porphyrius, F. 81).
[222] Apocrit. 3.30 (125,8-26 BLONDEL) and see § 3.34 above.
[223] C. Cels. 4.7 (279, 11-12 KOET.).
[224] HARNACK, Porphyrius, F. 82.
[225] HARNACK, Porphyrius, F. 81. Compare the anonymous pagan in Arnobius who asks similar questions (2.63 [139,11-14 MARCH.]).
[226] See the index to the lost objection in § 3.52.1. See also § 3.4 (Apocr. 4.10).
[227] C. Jul. 3.110 (PG 76, 668d).
[228] C. Jul. 3.107-108 (PG 76, 665a).
[229] C. Jul. 3.110-111 (PG 76, 670b-d).

finds prophecies of this call of the nations in Zech 2:10-11, 14:9 and Haggai 2:6-7[230]. He also quotes 1 Tim 2:4 "God wants all people to be saved and come to the knowledge of the truth."[231]

Julian develops this charge in another text in which he argues that it is demonstrably false to assert that God cared for the Hebrews alone: "Furthermore observe from what follows that God did not take thought for the Hebrews alone, but though he cared for all nations, he bestowed on the Hebrews nothing considerable or of great value, whereas on us he bestowed gifts far surpassing theirs."[232] Examples Julian gives are the wise men of the ancient world such as Hermes of the Egyptians, Hellenic science, philosophical study and astronomy[233]. Celsus has a similar argument against God's preference for the Jews: "Nor is it likely that they are in favor with God and are loved any more than other folk, and that angels are sent to them alone, as though indeed they had been assigned some land of the blessed. For we see both the sort of people they are and what sort of a land it was of which they were thought worthy."[234]

5.2.25.2 Paul on Circumcision

It is natural that Julian also found Paul's attitude toward circumcision to be highly objectionable:

> Now I must take up this other point and ask them, Why, pray, do you not practice circumcision? Paul, one says, said that circumcision of the heart but not of the flesh was granted, and this given to Abraham [Rom 2:29 and 4:11-12 may be the reference]. He [Paul] said that one should no longer believe in the things of the flesh — i. e. in the impious words that were proclaimed by him [Paul] and by Peter.[235]

Here Julian recasts Christian thought with some biting irony as he subtly modifies the Christian position and identifies it as impiety. Julian quotes Gen 17:10-11 and Mt 5:17-19 to show that the law of circumcision should be kept[236]. Julian concludes: "For either Jesus will be found to speak falsely, or rather you will be found in all respects and in every way to have failed to

---

[230] C. Jul. 3.111-12 (PG 76, 672a,b).

[231] C. Jul. 3.112 (PG 76, 672d).

[232] C. Gal. 176a,b (132,4-7 MAS. = III, 366-67 WR.).

[233] C. Gal. 176b,c; 178a-c (132,7-13; 133,3-15 MAS.).

[234] C. Cels. 5.50 (54,11-14 KOET.).

[235] C. Gal. 351a (179,5-180,9 MAS. = III, 420-21 WR.). The translation is according to the text of MASARACCHIA which does not adopt NEUMANN's emendations including οὐκ ἀσέβεσιν for οὐκ εὐσεβέσιν in the final line above (180,9). See MASARACCHIA, Giuliano, 69-71 where she discusses impersonal uses of "one says" in Julian (e.g. Misopogon 12.28, 357a [II/2, 181 ROCHE.] who accepts the emendation to φασίν). With his emendations, NEUMANN translates: "He speaks not of fleshly circumcision and one must believe the pious words that he and Peter proclaim" (Giuliano, 70 n. 164).

[236] C. Gal. 351b,c (180,9-19 MAS.).

preserve the law."[237] Celsus also accused Jesus (or Moses) of lying, but he found Jesus' teaching to be contradictory to that of Moses[238]. Julian notes that Moses demands circumcision of the flesh, and the Galilaeans practice circumcision of the heart. He finds their practice to be a violation of Mosaic law and seems to have no use for Paul's arguments. Others questioned why circumcision was used in the past (the law) and not in the present by Christians. They also asked why God would make a superfluous part in the body that needed to be cut off.[239]

Cyril responds by repeating Paul's text in Rom 2:28-29 about the circumcision of the heart[240]. He uses texts such as Jer 4:4 and 9:26 to give a metaphorical interpretation of circumcision. Cyril finds the original justification for physical circumcision to have been typological: it was a symbol for the removal of lawless desires and pleasures. The Holy Spirit has that effect on people. That is the circumcision most loved by God[241]. Julian would have found these arguments unsatisfactory!

5.2.25.3 Christ the End of the Law? Romans 10:4

Julian also attacked Paul's claim that "Christ is the end of the law" in Romans 10:4[242]. This argument is in a larger context in which Julian rejected Peter's claim (Acts 10:15) that God had cleansed all foods[243]. In the same context Julian criticizes Christians who assert that the Mosaic law is circumscribed by time and place[244]. His argument against Romans 10 is: "But do you point out to me where there is any statement by Moses of what was later on rashly uttered by Paul, I mean that 'Christ is the end of the law.' Where does God announce to the Hebrews a second law besides that which was established? Nowhere does it occur, not even a revision of the established law." Julian goes on to quote texts such at Deut 4:2 and 27:26 that support a continuous obedience to the Mosaic law[245].

---

[237] C. Gal. 351c (180,22-23 MAS. = III, 422-23 WR.).

[238] C. Cels. 7.18 (169,10-27 KOET.).

[239] Ps. Just., Quaest. et resp. ad Orthod. 102, 457c (160 OTTO). See RINALDI, Biblia Gentium, 249 for bibliography on this issue. See also § 3.34 above for the objection of Macarius' pagan.

[240] C. Jul. 10.351 (PG 76, 1042d).

[241] C. Jul. 10.353 (PG 76, 1044c,d).

[242] C. Gal. 320b (169,15-20 MAS. = III, 410-411 WR.).

[243] C. Gal. 314c (168,2-5 MAS. = III, 406-407 WR.). On the text see ROKEAH, Jews, 121.

[244] C. Gal. 319d (169,2-5 MAS. = III, 408-409 WR.).

[245] C. Gal. 320b,c (169,17-170,24 MAS. = III, 410-411 WR.).

5.2.25.4 1 Cor 6:9-11 and Baptism

Julian, like the anonymous pagan, felt that Baptism was a useless rite. He uses Paul's words in 1 Corinthians to prove his point:

> But the following are the very words that Paul wrote concerning those who had heard his teaching, and were addressed to the people themselves: "Be not deceived: neither idolaters, nor adulterers, nor effeminate, nor abusers of themselves with men, nor thieves, nor covetous, nor drunkards, nor revilers, nor extortioners, shall inherit the kingdom of God. And of this you are not ignorant, brethren, that such were you also; but you washed yourselves, but you were sanctified in the name of Jesus Christ." Do you see that he says that these people too had been of such sort, but that they "had been sanctified" and "had been washed," water being able to cleanse and winning power to purify when it shall go down into the soul? And baptism does not take away his leprosy from the leper, or scabs, or pimples, or warts, or gout, or dysentery, or dropsy, or a whitlow, in fact no disorder of the body, great or small, then shall it do away with adultery and theft and in short all the transgressions of the soul?[246]

In his *Caesars* Julian develops a critique of Constantine and a similar argument against baptism in a scene in which the rulers choose their gods. Constantine chooses Pleasure (ἡ Τρυφή) who embraces him tenderly:

> There too he [Constantine] found Jesus, who had taken up his abode with her and cried aloud to all comers: "he that is a seducer, he that is a murderer, he that is sacrilegious and infamous, let him approach without fear! For with this water will I wash him and straightway make him clean. And though he should be guilty of those same sins a second time, let him but smite his breast and beat his head and I will make him clean (καθαρόν) again."[247]

Macarius' anonymous philosopher expressed the same revulsion at the Christian understanding of baptism and also attacked Paul's text in 1 Cor 6:11[248]. Celsus was also put off by the Christian invitation to sinners[249]. René Braun points out that Julian was concerned with the concept of purity (ἁγνεία) and found Christians to be polluted and immoral[250]. The oracles in Porphyry's *Philosophy from Oracles* also believed that Christians were "polluted"[251]. For Julian baptism is a mockery of ethical purity.

5.2.25.5 Sacrificial Meat: 1 Cor 8:7-13

Julian makes a brief reference to Paul's belief that the eating of sacrificial meat does no harm unless the conscience of one who observes it is harmed:

---

[246] C. Gal. 245b-d (154,10-155,23 MAS. = III, 392-93 WR.).
[247] Caesars (Symposion) 10.38, 336a,b (II/2, 70-71 ROCHE. = II, 412-13 WR.).
[248] See § 3.38 above (Apocr. 4.19).
[249] See § 1.6.3 above (e.g. C. Cels. 3.59).
[250] Julien et le Christianisme, 183. He refers to C. Gal. 69c (99,15 MAS.) and other texts. See also DE LABRIOLLE, La réaction, 419 and BIDEZ, Lettres, 129-130.
[251] See § 2.2.3 above (e.g. SMITH, Porphyrii, 343F).

If the reading of your own scriptures is sufficient (αὐτάρκης) for you, why do you nibble at the learning of the Hellenes? And yet it were better to keep people away from that learning than from the eating of sacrificial meats (ἱεροθύτων). For by that, as even Paul says [1 Cor 8.7-13], he who eats thereof is not harmed, but the conscience of the brother who sees him might be offended (σκανδαλισθείη) according to you, O most wise and arrogant ones! But the learning of ours has caused every noble being that nature has produced among you to abandon atheism (ἀθεότητος). Accordingly everyone who possessed even a small fraction of innate virtue has speedily abandoned your atheism. It were therefore better for you to keep people from learning rather than from sacrificial meats.252

Julian goes on to argue that the education in Hellenistic literature produces thinkers, founders of constitutions, great military leaders, and travelers. His comment about Paul's view on sacrificial meat is merely a cog in his argument that Christians should stay away from Hellenistic literature. Macarius' Hellene argued that Paul's views on the eating of sacrificial meat were contradictory, but Julian is not interested in pursuing that point253. His argument presupposes that there were Christians who converted to Hellenism due to the influence of Hellenistic literature on their noble spirits. Julian's law against Christian teachers using Hellenistic literature (unless they will argue that those writers did not commit errors concerning the gods) is related to this argument254. But his concern with Christian teachers who used Hellenistic literature for their own purpose indicates that perhaps Julian was not as convinced as he appears to be by his argument that the study of Hellenistic literature will result in conversion to Hellenism. Perhaps he believed that only in the hands of the right (i.e. Hellenistic) teachers will Hellenistic literature produce the desired effects. Cyril responds that it is sweet to know all things and consequently Christians study Hellenistic literature. He continues by pointing out the errors about the gods in that literature255. He stresses the benefits of the study of the Scriptures and quotes Eupolemus in support of the argument that the Greeks took their alphabet from the Hebrews via the Phoenecians256. Christians (who are not weak) can eat sacrificial meat in good conscience (1 Cor 8:4, 10:30), and there is no reason to forbid the study of Hellenistic texts257.

5.2.25.6 Peter and Paul at Antioch (Gal 2:11-14)

Julian scoffs at the encounter between Peter and Paul in Antioch. He wrote that "the select one of the apostles is a hypocrite and was refuted (ἐληλέγχθαι) by

---

252 C. Gal. 229c,d (149,2-12 MAS. = III, 384-85 WR.).
253 Apocrit. 3.35 (130,1-14 BLONDEL). See § 3.41 above.
254 Jul., Ep. 61c, 423a-d (I/2, 74,17-75,11 BIDEZ).
255 C. Jul. 7.230-231 (PG 76, 852b-d).
256 C. Jul. 7.231 (PG 76, 854).
257 C. Jul. 7.233 (PG 76, 856b-d).

Paul because at one time he lived according to Hellenic customs (ἔθεσι) and at another time according to Jewish customs"[258]. Cyril defends Peter by charging that Julian did not recognize Peter's most skillful arrangement (τὴν ἔν γε τούτοις εὐτεχνεστάτην οἰκονομίαν) in these actions. Porphyry also found this episode objectionable as did Macarius' Hellenic philosopher[259].

5.2.25.7 Colossians 1:15

Julian briefly attacked the letter to the Colossians by charging that the title "first born of all creation" does not appear in Isaiah[260]. This argument is in the midst of Julian's attack on Johannine christology — whose main premise is that John's christological formulations do not appear in the Hebrew prophets.

5.2.25.8 Julian on Omnipotence?

A mysterious fragment from Suidas' entry on "madness" (ἀπόνοια) contains an attack on the understanding of the "possible" that may be an attack on the Christian belief that "all things are possible to God" — similar to attacks in Celsus, Porphyry, and the anonymous philosopher[261]. The entry reads: "And, in turn, Julian: A sign of extreme madness[262] is being unable to foresee what is possible and impossible in events (τὸ μὴ προϊδέσθαι τό τε δυνατὸν καὶ τὸ ἀδύνατον ἐν πράγμασι)."[263] Neumann refers to 1 Th 4:13ff in his edition of the fragment and apparently believes that the attack is similar to one in the anonymous philosopher who critiqued Paul's claim that some would meet Jesus in the clouds[264].

5.2.26 The Consequences of Christian Belief

Julian noticed that the Christians were able to use persuasion to gain converts. At the end of a discussion of the Christians' rejection of the Jewish law, Julian scoffs: "But you have thought it a slight thing to diminish and to add to the things which were written in the law; and to transgress it completely you have thought to be in every way more manly and more high-spirited, because you do not look to the truth, but to that which will persuade all people (εἰς τὸ πᾶσι

---

258 C. Gal. 325c (171 MAS.).

259 HARNACK, Porphyrius, F. 21 and Macarius, Apocrit. 3.22 (102,13-18 BLONDEL) discussed in § 2.3.38 and § 3.32 above.

260 C. Gal. 262d (160,34-37 MAS. = III, 398-99 WR.).

261 C. Cels. 5.14 (15,13-14 KOET. in § 1.2.23 above); Apocrit. 4.24 (204,21-205,9 BLONDEL; § 3.51); and Didymus' fragment of Porphyry discussed in § 2.3.21.

262 Julian uses the same word ("madness of the Galilaeans") in Ep. 46, 404c (I/2, 66,1-2 BIDEZ).

263 C. Gal. F. 103 (189 MAS.) = F. 18 NEUMANN.

264 NEUMANN, Iuliani, 137, 238; Macarius, Apocrit. 4.2 (159,1-160,8 BLONDEL).

πιθανὸν βλέποντες)."[265] He is aware of the effectiveness of the Christian use of persuasion. In another argument he poses this question to them: "Why were you so ungrateful to our gods so as to desert them for the Jews?"[266] In his answer he compares Roman freedom with Jewish slavery and their domination by Assyrians, Medes, Persians, and finally by the Romans themselves. Celsus also argued that the Jews had done nothing of significance[267]. Julian then questions Jesus' ministry from this point of view: "But what benefits (τίνων ἀγαθῶν αἴτιος) did he confer on his own kinsfolk: Nay, the Galilaeans answer, they refused to hearken unto Jesus." Julian then recounts some of Jesus' miracles (see above § 5.2.21) and concludes: "...could not this Jesus change (μεταστῆσαι) the dispositions (προαιρέσεις) of his own friends and kinsfolk to the end that he might save them?"[268] Here Julian's critique is twofold: like Celsus (C. Cels. 2.39, 43 [163,26; 166,5 Koet.]) he charges that Jesus was unable to persuade many people to change; and Jesus conferred few good things on his people. This last charge is an argument from consequence: the consequences of Jesus' ministry among his people were unimpressive — they are still dominated by the nations[269].

Julian continues this line of attack by comparing the wonderful achievements of the Hellenes (law, city administration, liberal arts, medicine, great generals)[270]. He then crafts an argument from consequence to compare the different effects of Hellenic and Christian writings on people:

> But you yourselves know, it seems to me, the very different effect on the intelligence of your writings as compared with ours; and that from studying yours no man could attain to excellence (γενναῖος ἀνήρ) or even to ordinary goodness (ἐπιεικής), whereas from studying ours everyone would become better than before, even though he were altogether without natural fitness (ἀφυής). But when a person is well endowed, and moreover receives the education (παιδείας) of our literature, he becomes actually a gift of the gods to humankind, either by kindling the light of knowledge, or by founding some kind of political constitution, or by routing numbers of his country's foes, or even by traveling far over the earth and far by sea, and thus proving himself a person of heroic mold...

Isocrates also emphasized how useful education could be for those with "natural fitness" (ἐν τοῖς εὐφυέσιν)[271].

Julian then devises an experiment to test his hypothesis:

---

[265] C. Gal. 320b, c (170,24-27 MAS. = III, 410-11, WR.).

[266] C. Gal. 209d (143,3-4 MAS. = III, 378-79, WR.).

[267] C. Cels. 4.31, 5.41 (301,1-3; 45,4-9 KOET.; their laws are similar to those of other cultures). On this motif see ROKEAH, Jews, 198.

[268] C. Gal. 213b (144,6-145,15 MAS. = III, 380-81 WR.). See ROKEAH, Jews, 82.

[269] C. Gal. 210a, 213a (143,15-144,19; 144,3 MAS.); 218a,b (145,3-8 MAS.).

[270] C. Gal. 218b-224c (145,9-147,6 MAS.).

[271] Isocrates, C. soph. 13.14 ff. quoted in MASARACCHIA, Giuliano, 229.

Now this would be a clear proof (τεκμήριον ... σαφές): Choose out children from among you all and train and educate them in your scriptures, and if when they come to manhood they prove to have nobler qualities than slaves, then you may believe that I am talking nonsense and am suffering from spleen. Yet you are so misguided and foolish that you regard those chronicles of yours as divinely inspired, though by their help no one could ever become wiser or braver or better than he was before; while, on the other hand, writings by whose aid people can acquire courage, wisdom and justice, these you ascribe to Satan and to those who serve Satan?[272]

The word for "proof" (τεκμήριον) is itself a technical term of the rhetoricians[273]. Julian's argument from consequence against educating children in Christian scriptures is similar to his argument concerning the consequences of Jesus' ministry: in neither case does the Christian faith have good consequences in peoples' lives. The argument (the consequences of the different types of education will establish what kind of religion one should adhere to — Hellenism or Christianity) is an example of deliberative rhetoric. Aristotle remarks that the argument from the consequences of an action can function to exhort or dissuade[274]. Jesus' audience (the Jews) received no appreciable benefits, and those who study Christian writings become like slaves. They do not become wiser or braver or more just. This argument parallels the one he used to compare Greek and Hebrew culture. The Hebrews (and Christians) did not produce brilliant generals, physicians, or wise people such as Phocylides and Isocrates. Cyril simply denies Julian's picture of the consequences of studying Christian literature, but does not deny that Christians should study Hellenistic texts. Their study is "sweet"[275].

5.2.27 Julian's Law Concerning Christian Teachers

Julian's famous law on Christian teachers forbids them to teach Homer, Hesiod, Demosthenes, Herodotus, Thucydides, Isocrates, and Lysias unless they will argue that those writers (who received their learning from the gods) did not commit errors concerning the gods[276]. Instead the Christian

---

[272] C. Gal. 229d-230a (150,22-29 MAS. = III, 384-87, WR.). On the text see ROKEAH, Jews, 196-97.

[273] LAUSBERG, Handbuch, § 361. Aristotle uses the word for a necessary sign [σημεῖον...ἀναγκαῖον] such as the sign "fever" which shows that a man is ill (Rhet 1.2.16-18).

[274] Aristot., Rhet. 2.23.14.

[275] See the references in § 5.2.25.5.

[276] Jul., Ep. 61c, 423a-d (I/2, 74,10-75,11 BIDEZ). Cf. B. C. HARDY, Kaiser Julian und sein Schulgesetz, in: Julian Apostata, ed. R. KLEIN, Wege der Forschung 509, Darmstadt 1978, 387-408 (original ET in ChH 37, 1968, 131-43). HARDY argues that the law was part of Julian's conservative political program and can be compared to the ancient practice of banning certain philosophers and rhetoricians who opposed the thinking of the majority in Rome (394). H. RAEDER notes that Ammianus Marcellinus called the law

rhetoricians (with Christian grammarians and sophists) should exegete Matthew and Luke. Christian teachers pretend to praise Hellenistic authors but actually are "...cheating and enticing by their praises those to whom they desire to transfer their worthless wares" (ἐξαπατῶντες καὶ δελεάζοντες τοῖς ἐπαίνοις εἰς οὓς μετατιθέναι τὰ σφέτερα ἐθέλουσιν, οἶμαι, κακά)[277]. They are like hucksters (or shopkeepers - καπήλων). The version of the law in the *Codex Theodosianus* (June 17, 362) expresses the issue in moral terms:

> It is proper that teachers of school (*magistros studiorum*) and professors (*doctores*) should excel in morals first and then in eloquence. But as I cannot be present in person in each city, I judge that anyone who wills to teach should not leap suddenly and casually into this employment,[278] and that after being approved by the judgement of the order of curials he should obtain a resolution with the unanimous consent of the best ones. Then this decree should be submitted to my examination in order that those who enter the school of the cities obtain higher honor because of our judgment.[279]

Prohaeresius and Marius Victorinus were two teachers who were removed from their office[280]. Eunapius writes: "In the reign of the Emperor Julian, Prohaeresius was shut out of the field of education because he was reputed to be a Christian." The texts of the law that survive do not explicitly forbid education to Christian students. In fact Julian states that "any youth who wishes to attend the schools is not excluded; nor indeed would it be reasonable to shut out from the best way boys who are still too ignorant to know which way to turn, and to overawe them into being led against their will to the beliefs of their ancestors. Though indeed it might be proper to cure these, even against their will, as one cures the insane, except that we conceded indulgence to all for this sort of disease (νόσου). For we ought, I think, to teach, but not punish, the demented."[281] Theodoret, however, argued that at first Julian forbade the children of the Galilaeans to take part in the study of poetry, rhetoric, and philosophy. He quotes a statement of Julian that does not appear in our texts: "In effect, he says, we are struck, as in the proverb, by our own arrows because they draw from our literature that with which they can arm themselves in order to engage in war against us."[282] Sozomen has: "He forbade the

---

"unfair" (*inclemens*; 22.10.7, 25.4.19). See idem, Kaiser Julian als Philosoph, in: KLEIN, Julian Apostata, (206-21) 214 (originally published in CM 6, 1944, 179-193).

[277] Jul., Ep. 61c, 422b,c (I/2, 73,13-15 BIDEZ = III, 116-23 WR.).

[278] The Scholia Vaticana interprets this to mean that they should not enter teaching immediately after leaving school (*statim exeuntes ex auditoriis*). Text included with Ep. 61b (I/2, 72,21-24 BIDEZ).

[279] Cod. Theodos. 13.3.5 (included as Ep. 61b [I/2, 72,10-19 BIDEZ]).

[280] MEREDITH, Porphyry, 1138. Prohaeresius (Eunapius, Vit. Sophist 493 [513 WR.]) and Victorinus (Aug., Conf. 8.5).

[281] Ep. 61c, 424a,b (I/2, 75,17-24 BIDEZ = III, 120-23 WR.).

[282] Theodoret, Hist. Eccl. 3.8.1-2 (185,6-15 P./S.) quoted in BIDEZ, L'Empereur Julien ... Lettres, 47. Socrates, H.E. 3.12.7 (207,3-6 HANSEN) and Zonaras 13.12.21 have a

children of Christians from frequenting the public schools and from being instructed in the writings of the Greek poets and authors. ... His sole motive for excluding the children of Christian parents from instruction in the learning of the Greeks, was because he considered such studies conducive to the acquisition of persuasive power (τὸ πεῖθον). Apollinarius, therefore, employed his great learning and ingenuity in the production of a heroic epic on the antiquities of the Hebrews ..."[283]. Probably Julian did not forbid Christian children to attend the schools, but due to the renewed Hellenism of those institutions Christian children would have been forbidden *de facto* from attending[284]. Sozomen's statement about "argumentative and persuasive power" is important because it indicates that persuasion and argument were at the focus of the entire issue. Julian is concerned with conversion to Christianity and conversion to Hellenism.

5.2.28 Julian on Grace

One of the fragments of Cyril notes that Julian criticized the Christian willingness to show mercy to sinners. Cyril wrote: "He rebukes those who beseech God concerning those who are in [guilty of] unrighteous deeds. He thought that it lacks rationality (ἀφαμαρτάνειν τοῦ εἰκότος), and he calls those who have compassion on evil workers 'evil'."[285] Julian's objections to Christian ideas of grace are very similar to those of Celsus and the anonymous philosopher of Macarius[286].

5.2.29 Social Status of Converts

Julian was unimpressed with the kinds of people who had been persuaded to become Christian. His description of the converts of Jesus and Paul includes a social dimension: "... for they were content if they could delude maidservants and slaves, and through them the women, and men like Cornelius and Sergius"[287]. The main element in the community is slaves according to Julian — with a few from the aristocracy such as Sergius and Cornelius. The "women" may be influential people such as Lydia, but the reference of that category is not particularly clear. His attitude is similar to that of Celsus (C. Cels. 3.44, 3.55 [240,4; 250,20 Koet.]) and Porphyry (F. 97, Harnack) who

---

similar statement, but are not so clear about students. Gregory of Nazianzus also comments (Or. 4.102 [250 BERNARDI]) as does Philostorgius, H.E. 7.4 (81 BIDEZ).

283 Sozomen, H.E. 5.18.1-3 (222,2-4.8-13 B./H.; ET from NPNF 2, 340). Augustine, De civ. Dei 18.52 states that Julian forbade Christians to give or receive a liberal education.

284 See BIDEZ, L'Empereur Julien ... Lettres, 45.

285 C. Gal. F. 99 (188 MAS.) = F. 11 NEUMANN.

286 See C. Cels. 3.59 (253,30-254,3 KOET.) in § 1.2.12 above and the pagan's attack on baptism in § 3.38.

287 C. Gal. 206a (142,10-11 MAS. = III, 376-77, WR.). See Acts 10, 13:6-12.

complains that women were the "senate" of the Christians[288]. Plotinus also complained that the Gnostics call the lowest of people "brothers"[289]. Julian probably refers to Christian women who have a strong effect on children in his address to the citizens of Antioch: "Then what effect have the women on the children? They induce them to reverence the same things as they do (τὰ σφέτερα σεβάσματα) by means of pleasure, which is, it seems, the most blessed thing and the most highly honored, not only by people but by beasts also... first you begin by refusing slavery to the gods..." He continues by noting of the Antiochians that they claim the Chi (Christ) "never harmed the city in any way"[290]. Porphyry also charged that the apostles persuaded rich women to get their hands on their wealth[291]. Macarius' philosopher charged that Paul enslaved those who are easily influenced by means of sorcery (τέχνῃ γοητείας τοὺς εὐχερεῖς δουλούμενος)[292]. Other Christians, according to the philosopher, were able to persuade wealthy women to become paupers[293]. It is interesting that Celsus does not mention recruits such as Cornelius and Sergius. Julian was willing to admit their existence, although it was the exception to the rule in his view.

In another passage Julian continues the same theme in an enumeration of the occupations of the Galilaeans. They have seized "the blasphemy of the gods" from the Hebrews and the vulgarity (χυδαιότητα) of the Hellenistic tradition: "But to tell the truth, you have taken pride in outdoing our vulgarity, (this, I think is a thing that happens to all nations, and very naturally) and you thought that you must adapt your ways to the lives of other people,[294] shopkeepers (καπήλων), tax-gatherers, and dancers ready for any change (ἑτεροτρόπων)."[295] He supports this argument by quoting 1 Cor 6:9-11. He also describes Christians as shopkeepers or hucksters in his rescript against Christian teachers[296]. He does this because Christian teachers praise the things they believe to be worthless (i.e. Hellenistic literature) and thereby entice those

---

[288] On Julian's comments see MASARACCHIA's commentary, Giuliano, 226.

[289] Plotinus, Ennead. 2.9.18 (I, 231,17-18 H./S.).

[290] Misopogon 12.27-28, 356c,d, 357a (II/2, 181 ROCHE. = II, 472-73 WR.). DE LABRIOLLE refers to a passage in Libanius (Or. 16.45 [II, 178 FÖRSTER]): "When (you Christians), one speaks to you about a Plato or a Pythagoras, you speak of your mother, your wife, your servant ..." (La réaction, 418 n.4).

[291] HARNACK, Porphyrius, F. 4.

[292] Apocrit. 3.31 (126,9-10 BLONDEL). "Sorcery" is probably Paul's skill with words in this context.

[293] Apocrit. 3.5 (58,17-59,4 BLONDEL).

[294] MASARACCHIA adopts the reading of the MSS, ἑτέρων, and not the conjecture εὐτελῶν (153,25-26 MAS.).

[295] NEUMANN conjectures ἑταιροτρόφων (208,18 NEUMANN). C. Gal. 238d,e (153,23-27 MAS. = III, 390-91 WR.). Compare 191d (136,6-7 MAS.).

[296] Ep. 61c, 422c (I/2, 73,12 BIDEZ).

whom they wish to recruit to the Christian movement. They deceive those to whom they wish to sell their worthless goods. Celsus' opinions of people in shops recruited to the Christian faith was equally low (C. Cels. 3.55 [251,7 Koet.]). He also despised the tax collectors whom Jesus gathered around himself (C. Cels. 1.62, 2.46 [113,8; 168,14 Koet.]).

With regard to Julian's dim view of the social status of Christians, Cyril claims that he does not understand the freedom of the Christian religion and its careful discipline in moral actions[297]. Cyril contrasts this discipline with events of his own time in the temple of Cronos where well raised women have been forced into sexual immorality — at the behest of the god[298]. Julian's comment about the women "deluded" by Christian teaching prompts Cyril to respond that women believed and slaves were called, and that Julian does not understand the Savior's clemency[299]. A person in a humble station in life can be wise, according to Cyril, and a poor person can exercise a righteous life. Julian complains in vain about those who are "netted (τῷ θείῳ κηρύγματι σεσαγηνευμένους) by the divine proclamation" for a true and unblemished contemplation of God[300]. From the Hellenic world of the philosophers Cyril draws a number of similar examples. Socrates' mother was a nurse and his father a stone mason (λιθουργός) or maker of statues (ἑρμογλύφος)[301]. Plato went from wrestling to philosophy[302]. Cyril concludes there is nothing demeaning about manual labor and exertion and such activities do not prevent people from becoming wise. Zamolxis was Pythagoras' servant, according to Cyril, and became a learned person. With regard to women helped by Christian teaching, Cyril notes that Plato called the wife of Dionysus to philosophy. Porphyry likewise admires Marcella's gifts in philosophy, and Pythagoras gathered a group of Crotonian women and lectured to them[303]. Cyril concludes that Christ called all without distinction, women and men both illustrious and in humble station, rich and poor, and slaves to learn who is the God of all[304].

5.2.30 Julian on the Practices of Christians

Julian found the destruction of temples and altars by Christians to be highly offensive. In an attack on the relationship of Christianity to Judaism he writes:

---

[297] C. Jul. 7.242 (PG 76, 869c).
[298] C. Jul. 7.244 (PG 76, 873b-c).
[299] C. Jul. 6.207 (PG 76, 816d).
[300] C. Jul. 6.207 (PG 76, 817a).
[301] Cyril quotes Porphyry's Hist. Phil. 3, F. 11 (10,1.11 NAUCK).
[302] C. Jul. 6.208 (PG 76, 817d-820a).
[303] See Porphyry, Ad Marc. 3 (8,5-6 PÖT.); Vita Pyth. 18 (44,12 DES PLACES).
[304] C. Jul. 6.208-209 (PG 76, 820a-c).

...but you emulate the rages and bitterness of the Jews, overturning temples and altars, and you slaughtered not only those of us who remained true to the teachings of their fathers (τοῖς πατρῴοις), but also those who were as much astray as yourselves, heretics, because they did not wail over the corpse (τὸν νεκρόν) in the same fashion as you yourselves."[305]

Not only do Christians destroy pagan shrines, but Julian charges them with the death of loyal pagans and Christian heretics[306]. Julian and Celsus both attack Christian thought about Jesus by identifying him as a corpse[307]. De Labriolle believes Julian may take this identification from Celsus. He also asks this intriguing question: could Julian's position be a response to the attack Christians made on statues inhabited by the dead[308]? It is certainly a rejection of the Christian belief in resurrection.

5.2.30.1 Altars and Circumcision

The Christian refusal to sacrifice at altars disturbed Julian also: "For you do not imitate Abraham by erecting altars to him [God], or building altars of sacrifice and worshipping him as Abraham did, with sacrificial offerings. For Abraham used to sacrifice even as we Hellenes do, always and continually."[309] Julian's love of sacrifice and pagan ritual is well known, and he found a common ground with Judaism with regard to sacrifice[310]. He was aware that Jews could no longer sacrifice given the destruction of the temple and planned to rebuild it[311]. In conjunction with his critique of the Christian refusal to offer

---

[305] C. Gal. 205e-206a (142,3-7 MAS. = III, 376-77 WR.). Compare Misopogon 12.33, 361b,c (II/2, 187 ROCHE.) and see also 12.15, 346b (168 ROCHE.). See GEFFCKEN, Last Days 141. In Ep. 80 (I/2, 88,15-18 BIDEZ), for example, Julian directs the repair of the temple at Daphne where the Christians had removed some columns. He also comments on the destruction in Ep. 98, 400b (181,7 BIDEZ). See Zonaras 13.12 (212,12-18 DINDORF) where Julian forces Christians to restore some columns of Asclepius' temple in Aegae that they had removed. In Ep. 60, 379a (70,1-3 BIDEZ), Julian describes a Christian prefect (Artemius) who stripped a shrine of its statues and offerings. On Julian's restorations see BIDEZ/CUMONT, ELF, Text 42.

[306] He also describes Christian (Constantius') slaughter of heretics in Ep. 114, 436a (I/2, 193,7 BIDEZ).

[307] See C. Cels. 7.68 (217,1 KOET.). On Celsus' thinking about Jesus as a man (and not God) see 2.79 and 7.36 (201,8-9; 186,25-26 KOET.).

[308] La réaction, 415 n. 2.

[309] C. Gal. 354b-c, 356c (181,13-15/ 182,1-2 MAS. = III, 422-23, WR.). Julian commented on Christian refusal to worship at temples [ἱερείων] in Ep. 61c, 423d (I/2, 75,12 BIDEZ.).

[310] An example is his shock at the laxity of the sacrifice not prepared for the shrine of Apollo at Daphne, Misopogon 12.34, 361d, 362a (II/2, 187-88 ROCHE.).

[311] C. Gal. 306a (167,11-12 MAS.); (a doubtful letter) Ep. 204, 398a (ELF, 281,18-282,2 BIDEZ/CUMONT.); and Ep. 134 (I/2, 197,10-11 BIDEZ, from Lydus, de mens. 4 [110,4 WÜNSCH]) "I will raise with all zeal the temple of the Highest God." Lydus notes that Julian wrote the letter when he was fighting the Persians. Compare Ammianus Marcellinus 23.1.1-

sacrifice he wrote that they say: "'We cannot observe the rule of unleavened bread or keep the Passover; for on our behalf Christ was sacrificed once and for all [ἅπαξ, cf. Heb 9:28].' Then did he forbid you to eat unleavened bread?"[312] The Galilaeans' refusal to sacrifice and participate in Jewish feasts such as the Passover is typical of their rejection of the law — in Julian's eyes — even though Jesus himself taught that the law should be preserved[313]. He also disapproved of the Christians' refusal to practice circumcision: "'The circumcision shall be of the flesh' says Moses [Gen 17:13]. But the Galilaeans do not heed him, and they say: 'We circumcise our hearts.' By all means. For there is among you no evildoer, no sinner, so thoroughly do you circumcise your hearts."[314] Julian goes on to argue that Chaldeans such as Abraham and Jacob learned circumcision from the Egyptians[315]. Celsus also charged that the Jews got circumcision from the Egyptians[316]. Julian's comment about the moral uprightness of Christian converts is clearly ironic.

5.2.30.2 Worship of a "Corpse"

What Christians do choose to worship is repellent to Julian. He describes the worship of Jesus as the worship of a "corpse"[317]. This designation shows Julian's contempt for the Christian claim concerning Jesus' resurrection. After describing the shield of Zeus that fell from heaven, Julian compares the correct worship of this admirable object to the Christians' disgusting adoration of the cross:

And yet, you misguided people, though there is preserved among us that weapon which flew down from heaven, which mighty Zeus or father Ares sent down to give us a warrant, not in word but in deed, that he will forever hold his shield before our city, you have ceased to adore (προσκυνεῖν) and reverence (σέβεσθαι) it, but you adore the wood of the cross and draw its likeness on your foreheads and engrave it on your housefronts.... they have abandoned the everliving gods and have gone over to the corpse of the Jew... For I say nothing about the Mysteries of the Mother of the Gods, and I admire Marius.[318]

---

3 on the "fireballs" that prevented the reconstruction. See also Theodoret 3.20 (198,15-200,5 P./S.), Sozomen, H.E. 5.22.4-8 (230,4-231,6 B./H.) and Socrates, H.E. 3.20.1-15 (215,3-216,12 HANSEN). See M. ADLER, Kaiser Julian und die Juden, (48-111) 71-72 in: KLEIN, Julian Apostata (original ET in JQR 5, 1893, 591-651).
312 C. Gal. 354a (181,6-7 MAS. = III, 422-23, WR.).
313 C. Gal. 351b,c (180,15-19 MAS.).
314 C. Gal. 354a (181,2-5 MAS. = III, 422-23, WR.).
315 C. Gal. 354b (181,9-11 MAS.).
316 C. Cels. 1.22, 5.41 (72,24-25; 45,5-6 KOET.).
317 C. Gal. 206a; 194d; 335b (142,7; 138,16; 175,5 MAS.). For Christian worship of the "dead" (Christ and the martyrs) see Ep. 114, 438c (I/2, 195,21 BIDEZ). Compare Celsus in C. Cels. 7.36, 68 (186,26; 217,1 KOET.) who describes Christian worshippers as νεκρὸν σέβοντες.
318 C. Gal. 194c,d, 197c (138,7-16; 138,3-4 MAS. = III, 370-73 WR.).

Julian finds the shield of Zeus to have superior value to that of the cross. In one of his letters Julian complains that Christians make the sign of the "impious one on their forehead." He summarizes their actions in this way: "For these two things are the quintessence of their theology, to hiss at demons and make the sign of the cross on their foreheads."[319] Pagans were put off by the worship of a man who died on a cross according to the apologists.[320] Justin, for example, states that the pagans "proclaim our madness to consist in this, that we give to a crucified person a place second to the unchangeable and eternal God, the Creator of all"[321]. Arnobius' pagan claims: "the deities are not inimical to you, because you worship the omnipotent God; but because you both allege that one born as humans are, and put to death on the cross (*hominem ... crucis supplicio interemptum*), which is a disgraceful punishment even for worthless men, was God, and because you believe that He still lives, and because you worship Him in daily supplications"[322]. Julian's view that the Christ of the Christian faith is a "corpse" explains his view of the adoration of the cross as an absurdity.

Cyril calls the narrative of Zeus' shield and the skull found on the Capitoline hill "hair splitting" and "childish wonder tales" (τερθρεία ... μειρακιώδη τερετίσματα)[323]. He defends the Christian use of the sign of the cross as a remembrance (ἀνάμνησιν) of the work of Christ (freeing people from the snares of death, the power of sin, and their adoption as children of God, and so forth)[324]. Cyril asks Julian if he would like to have paintings put in households to reinforce the moral teachings of instructors so that youth avoid licentious behavior and women avoid disgraceful lives. Cyril then proposes such Hellenistic themes as Zeus' lovers Ganymede and Alcmene or Aphrodite and her lovers. Would Julian rather Christians give up their symbol (the cross) that leads people to virtue or would he wish them to use Hellenistic pictures of the lewd gods and goddesses[325]? Cyril objects to Julian's term "corpse" for Christ arguing that he does not understand the mystery of the incarnation. Christ tasted death that he might destroy death and become the "firstborn of the dead"[326]. After his response to Julian's conception of Christ as a "corpse" Cyril includes Julian's comment quoted above concerning the mother of the gods and his admiration of Marius. Cyril makes a remark about the mania of

---

[319] Ep. 79 (I/2, 86,13-17 BIDEZ = III, 52-53 WR.).

[320] Arnobius, Adv. nat. 1.36, 41 (30,1-6; MARCH.). Tert., Apol. 21.3 (123,10-13 DEKKERS). See MASARACCHIA's commentary, Giuliano, 223.

[321] Apol. 1.13.4 (51,15-19 MARC.), ET in ANF 1.167.

[322] 1.36 (30,1-5 MARCHESI); ET in ANF 6.422.

[323] C. Jul. 6.194 (PG 76, 797b).

[324] C. Jul. 6.195 (PG 76, 797b-d).

[325] C. Jul. 6.195-96 (PG 76, 797d-800c).

[326] C. Jul. 6.197 (PG 76, 800d-802a).

the Corybants and the licentious mysteries in the Idaean caves. He then claims
that Marius sacrificed a child to the gods and encouraged the Romans to do the
same[327].

5.2.30.3 Martyrs and Graves

The Christian veneration for martyrs and their graves was equally repulsive to
Julian. He may have been unaware of Plato's statement that Hellenes will
worship the tombs of divine people[328]. He asserted that John "... since he
perceived that a great number of people in many of the towns of Greece and
Italy had already been infected by this disease, and because he heard, I
suppose, that even the tombs of Peter and Paul were being worshipped —
secretly, it is true, but still he did hear this, — he, I say, was the first to venture
to say [that Jesus is God]"[329]. The explanation for John's christological
affirmation, Julian finds, may lie in his awareness of the number of Christians
and of the worship of martyrs. After a prolonged critique of Johannine
christology (see above), Julian concludes:

> However this evil doctrine did originate with John; but who could detest as they deserve
> all those doctrines that you have invented as a sequel, while you keep adding many corpses
> newly dead to the corpse of long ago? You have filled the whole world with tombs and
> sepulchres, and yet in your scriptures it is nowhere said that you must grovel
> (προσκαλινδεῖσθε) among tombs and pay them honor.[330]

Julian concludes with a quotation of Mt 23:27 with which he argues that Jesus
would have disapproved of such veneration of martyrs and their tombs[331].
Cyril argued that the Greeks themselves worshipped in temples that were
tombs[332].

Julian also obliquely refers to the veneration of martyrs in his argument that
if Christians were faithful to the teachings of the Hebrews they would not
worship Christ and the others: "If you had at any rate paid heed to their
teachings, you would not have fared altogether ill, and though worse than you
did before, when you were with us, still your condition would have been
bearable and supportable. For you would be worshipping (ἐσέβεσθε) one

---

327 C. Jul. 6.197-98 (PG 802a-d). For another Christian view of Marius' cruelty see
Augustine, De civ. Dei 2.23.
328 Resp. 469a.
329 C. Gal. 327b (172,9-13 MAS. = III, 412-13, WR.).
330 C. Gal. 335b (174,3-175,7 MAS. = III, 414-16 WR.). See also Misopogon 12.10,
344a (II/2, 165 ROCHE.) and Ep. 79 (I/2, 86,5-6 BIDEZ). On worship among tombs compare
Eunapius, Vita 472 (424 WR.).
331 See above on Julian's use of Mt 8:21,22 to support his point of view.
332 See § 5.2.11 above.

god, instead of many, not a person (ἄνθρωπον), or rather many wretched people."[333]

5.2.30.4 Benevolence

Julian was concerned with Christian benevolence because of its promotion of "atheism." In his displeasure at the carelessness of the citizens of Antioch for Hellenistic festivals Julian wrote: "But as it is, every one of you allows his wife to carry everything out of his house to the Galilaeans, and when your wives feed the poor at your expense they inspire a great admiration for atheism (ἀθεότητος) in those who are in need of such bounty..."[334]. He wrote the high priest Arsacius using a similar argument: "... why do we not observe that it is their benevolence to strangers (ἡ περὶ τοὺς ξένους φιλανθρωπία), their care for the graves of the dead and the pretended holiness of their lives that have done most to increase atheism? ... For it is disgraceful that, when no Jew ever has to beg, and the impious Galilaeans support not only their own poor but ours as well, all men see that our people lack aid from us."[335] Julian's pastoral advice is that Hellenes should do the same thing. In his *Letter to a Priest* Julian argues in a similar vein: "For when it came about that the poor were neglected and overlooked by the priests, then I think the impious Galilaeans observed this fact and devoted themselves to philanthropy. And they have gained ascendancy in the worst of their deeds through the credit that they win for such practices." Julian then compares this form of Christian recruitment to slavers who entice children with a cake and then sell them into slavery: "...by the same method, I say, the Galilaeans also begin with their so-called love-feast, or hospitality (ὑποδοχῆς), or service of tables, — for they have many ways of carrying it out and hence call it by many names, — and the result is that they have led very many into atheism..."[336]. Julian's practical response is that candidates for the Hellenic priesthood should show love for God by inducing others to reverence of the gods and love for people by giving willingly to those in need[337]. It is apparent that Julian's concern with Christian benevolence was in its recruiting value. The Christians' willingness to share possessions resulted in converts to "atheism." This indicates that Julian is interested in deliberative rhetoric. Persuading others not to convert to "atheism" was a fundamental concern of his reforms.

---

[333] C. Gal. 201e (141,4-8 MAS. = III, 374-75, WR.).

[334] Misopogon 12.35, 363a (II/2, 189 ROCHE. = II, 490-91 WR.).

[335] Ep. 84, 429d, 430a, 430d (I/2, 144,13-16; 145,17-20 BIDEZ = III, 68-71 WR.).

[336] Fragm. ep. 89b, 305c,d (I/2, 174,3--7 BIDEZ = II, 336-339 WR.).

[337] Fragm. ep. 89b, 305b (I/2, 173,14-20 BIDEZ). Julian discusses his own philanthropy in Ep. 89b, 290d (158,7-9 BIDEZ).

5.2.31 The Defense of Polytheism

Julian's negative views on Christian understanding of Jesus are related to his spirited defense of polytheism. He defends polytheism — as do Celsus and Macarius' philosopher[338] — as an integral part of his critique of the Christian worship of Jesus as Son of God. His argument has two prongs. One of his starting points is the Hellenistic belief in God and the many viceroys who serve God. The other prong is the statements in the OT in which "Moses" recognizes the existence of "sons of God" or "angels." Julian also uses the OT prohibitions against serving other gods to oppose the Christian worship of Jesus. Both forms of Julian's argument (Hellenistic theology and the OT) are intended to question the rationality of worshipping Jesus Christ as God's son.

Julian adopts the common cultural premise of Hellenism to argue for polytheism. This cultural premise was also adopted by Celsus and by Macarius' philosopher in their critique of Christianity.

> If the immediate creator (δημιουργός) of the universe be he who is proclaimed by Moses, then we hold nobler beliefs concerning him, inasmuch as we consider him to be the master (δεσπότην) of all things in general, but that there are besides national gods who are subordinate to him and are like viceroys (ὕπαρχοι) of a king, each administering separately his own province; and, moreover, we do not make him the sectional rival of the gods whose station is subordinate to his.[339]

Julian concludes that Moses pays heed to a sectional god (the god of Israel). In other contexts Julian appears to be willing to ascribe more transcendence to the god of Israel: "But these Jews are in part god-fearing, seeing that they revere a god who is truly most powerful and most good and governs this world of sense, and, as I will know, is worshipped by us also under other names."[340] Smith cautions, however, that Julian does not identify the god of Israel with Helios[341]. Julian's synthesis of Hellenistic thought concerning the supreme God and the subordinate deities is similar to that of Ps. Aristotle, Celsus and

---

[338] C. Cels. 5.25 (26,1-12 KOET.; defense of polytheism), 8.12 (229,11-15 KOET.; inconsistency of Christian monotheism with the worship of Jesus). See § 3.47 above for the philosopher's defense (Apocr. 4.20).

[339] C. Gal. 148b,c (124,2-8 MAS. = III, 358-59, WR.). On Julian's defense of polytheism see ROKEAH, Jews, 161, 164-66. Compare the discussion of Celsus' defense of polytheism in § 1.7.2 of this work.

[340] Ep. 89a, 453d-454a (I/2, 154,14-155,3 BIDEZ = III, 60-61 WR.). See also Or. 7.22, 231a (II/1, 79 ROCHE.). FOUSSARD refers to Ps. Aristot. De mundo 7, 401a,12 (98 LORIMER) εἷς δὲ ὢν πολυώνυμός ἐστι for the Stoic counterpart to Julian's views. FOUSSARD notes that Julian seems to recognize that the individual divinities have their own (even if derived) reality (Julien, 205).

[341] Julian's Gods, 201.

Maximus of Tyre[342]. Celsus also shared Julian's belief that Hellenes had nobler beliefs[343]. Julian also uses the statements in the OT to establish polytheism:

> And that Moses calls the angels gods you may hear from his own words, "The sons of God saw the daughters of people were fair; and they took for themselves wives of all which they chose [Gen 6:2]." ... Again, when Moses speaks of many sons of God and calls them not people but angels, would he not then have revealed to humankind, if he had known thereof, God the "Only begotten Word," or a son of God or however you call him? But is it because he did not think this of great importance that he says concerning Israel, "Israel my firstborn son [Ex 4:22]?" Why did not Moses say this about Jesus also? He taught that there was only one God, but that he had many sons who divided the nations among themselves.[344]

Thus Julian shows a contradiction between the teaching of Moses and Christian monotheism. Julian is of course aware that Moses did not believe other gods should be worshipped[345]. Macarius' philosopher also defended polytheism using statements in the OT[346]. Cyril uses Paul's statement in 1 Cor 8:5 to argue that there are gods by name (and not by nature). They are not gods by nature, but by grace (ἐν χάριτος μοίρᾳ) who are part of the "intellectual creation" (τὴν λογικὴν κτίσιν). Ps 81:6 indicates that Christians also can be called "gods" because they are being transformed into the image of God's Son. The angels are also images of God's Son. Because Christ is spoken of as the image of God in Paul, the reference to "image" in Gen 1:27 is to the Son[347].

Julian uses both these arguments (Hellenistic principle of polytheism with a supreme God and Moses' belief in the existence of angelic sons of God) to argue that Christians should not worship Christ. With reference to Exodus 20:5 he criticizes the statement "for I the Lord am a jealous God." Julian creates the following dilemma: "For if he is indeed jealous, then against his will are all other gods worshipped, and against his will do all the remaining nations worship their gods."[348] Julian argues that God is either unable to prevent the worship of other gods, or God does not wish to prevent other gods

---

[342] Ps. Aristotle, *De mundo* 6, 398a,1-398b,10 (82-85 LORIMER), Maximus, *Diss.* 11.12 (100,289-97 TR.), *C. Cels.* 8.35 (250,16-24 KOET.). Compare Ps. Sallustius' discussion of the First Cause and subordinate gods in *De diis* 5 (10,5-27 NOCK).

[343] *C. Cels.* 6.1, 5.65; and especially his preference for Plato in 7.42 (70,4-7; 68,24-25; 192,25-193.3 KOET.). Julian clearly prefers Plato's account of creation (*C. Gal.* 49a [91,3-10 MAS.]; 57c,d; 57e-58e, 65b-66,a [94,1-9; 95,4-96,34; 97,4-98,34 MAS.]).

[344] *C. Gal.* 290b-e (162,5-163,23 MAS. = III, 400-402, WR.).

[345] *C. Gal.* 291a (163,27-28 MAS.) alluding to a text such as Deut 6:13.

[346] *Apocrit.* 4.21, 23 (200,1-201,8; 203,1-16 BLONDEL) and see § 3.47 and 3.48 in this work.

[347] *C. Jul.* 9.291-92 (PG 76, 948b-d).

[348] *C. Gal.* 155c,d (126,2-127,16 MAS. = III, 360-363, WR.). Celsus attacks the concept of God's jealousy in *C. Cels.* 8.21 (238,13-15 KOET.).

from being worshipped. He concludes: "For if it is God's will that none other should be worshipped, why do you worship this illegitimate son (νόθον υἱόν)[349] of his whom he has never yet recognized or considered as his own? This I shall easily prove. You, however, I know not why, foist on him a counterfeit son (ὑπόβλητον)."[350] The anonymous philosopher also argued that God is not angry if another has the same title, just as rulers do not object if people have the same title[351]. Julian makes a subtle use of the OT — both to show that Moses recognizes the existence of other gods and that Moses' prohibition against the worship of other gods precludes the legitimacy of Christian worship of Jesus. Julian's claim that God did not recognize Jesus is similar to Celsus' belief that God showed no special care for Jesus who was punished so cruelly[352]. Julian's reference to Jesus as "illegitimate" is also an obvious rejection of the narrative of the virgin birth[353]. While expounding "Moses," Julian also attacks the concept of God's jealousy.

Smith notes that the Trinity was a departure from Judaism and Hellenism according to Julian[354]. Cyril summarizes an argument of Julian's in which he notes that Jewish practices agree with Hellenic practices in most matters except the worship of one God. Jews serve one God. Hellenes say there are many. Christians err in that they do not believe (προσίεσθαι) in many gods nor the one according to the law but confess three. Cyril notes that Julian believed the consubstantial (ὁμοούσιον) Trinity (with one divine nature) was divided into three gods[355]. Trinitarian theology obviously left Julian cold.

Julian expresses pity for the misery of Christianity: "Would not anyone be justified in detesting the more intelligent among you, or pitying the more foolish, who, by following you, have sunk to such depths of ruin that they have abandoned the ever living gods and have gone over to the corpse of the Jew."[356] Abandoning polytheism goes against both Hellenistic culture, and in Julian's interpretation, the statements of "Moses."

---

[349] Compare Ps. Julian's usage of the word in Ep. 191, 383d (247,11 BIDEZ).

[350] C. Gal. 159e (127,13-16 MAS. = III, 362-363, WR.).

[351] Apocrit. 4.23 (203,12-14 BLONDEL).

[352] C. Cels. 8.41 and compare 1.54 (255,11-14; 105,4-5 KOET.).

[353] Compare the Letter to Photinus, Ep. 90 (I,2 174,12-14 BIDEZ = III, 186-191 WR.) which mentions Photinus who "does well to believe that he whom one holds to be a god can by no means be brought into the womb." Celsus also rejected the virgin birth (C. Cels. 1.28, 6.73 [79,23-28; 142,18-23 KOET.]). See § 1.2.3 above and for Macarius' philosopher's objection see § 3.49.

[354] Julian's Gods, 202.

[355] C. Jul. 9.314 (PG 76, 984a,b).

[356] C. Gal. 194d (138,13-16 MAS. = III, 372-73 WR.).

5.2.32 Christians and Others under Demonic Influence

Julian was probably referring to Christians (monks and martyrs in particular) in his *Letter to a Priest* in which he describes the pitiful fate of atheists — one of his favored terms for Christians[357]:

> And the tribe of evil demons (πονηρῶν δαιμόνων) is appointed to punish those who do not worship the gods, and stung to madness by them many atheists are induced to court death in the belief that they will fly up to heaven when they have brought their lives to a violent end. Some there are also who, though a person is naturally a social and civilized being, seek out desert places instead of cities, since they have been given over to evil demons and are led by them into this hatred of their kind (μισανθρωπίαν). And many of them have even devised fetters and stocks to wear; to such a degree does the evil demon to whom they have of their own accord given themselves abet them in all their ways, after they have rebelled against the everlasting and saving gods.[358]

The misanthropy Julian accuses the anchorites of is reminiscent of Tacitus' charge against the Christians ("hatred of the human race" *odio humani generis*)[359]. On the other hand Julian was well aware of Christian philanthropy and complains about it in the same letter[360]. Julian's charge is somewhat ironic given the fact that he must have been aware that Christians made the identical charge: pagans are under domination of demonic powers. The text from Gregory of Nazianzus quoted above about Julian's own experience of theurgy is an illustration (§ 5.1). One of Porphyry's oracles also accused the Christians of being devoted to demonic powers. The oracle claimed that ungodly natures who had rejected the living gods reverenced forbidden demons[361]. Julian probably refers to the martyrs when he mentions those who were driven by the demons to seek a violent end. In his treatise against the Galilaeans he again mentions demonic influence on Christians: "But you concern yourselves with incomplete and partial powers, which if anyone call demonic he does not err. For in them are pride and vanity, but in the gods there is nothing of the sort."[362] Braun refers to the topos in Christian apologetics which identified the gods with demons. Julian, Braun writes, practices retort[363]. Rejection of polytheism entails demonic influence according to Julian.

---

[357] For Julian's use of "atheism" to describe Christians see C. Gal. 43b (89,11 MAS.) and Ep. 84, 429d (I/2, 144,13 BIDEZ).

[358] Frag. Ep. 89b, 288b (I/2, 155,12-156,4 BIDEZ = II, 296 WR.). DE LABRIOLLE sees the reference in the text to be monks and martyrs (La réaction 419). Compare BRAUN, Julien et le Christianisme, 186.

[359] Annales 15.44.5.

[360] See Frag. ep. 89b, 305c (I/2, 173,22 BIDEZ) discussed in § 5.2.30.4.

[361] See the text in § 2.2.3.4 above.

[362] C. Gal. 224e (148,18-21 MAS. = III, 384-85 WR.).

[363] Julien et le Christianisme, 186.

5.2.33 Julian's Devotion to Asclepius

Although Julian does not make a specific comparison of Christ and Asclepius, he does enumerate the great blessings of Hellenism in contrast to the meager things God has given the Hebrews[364]. Porphyry had earlier blamed the existence of a plague in the "city" on the fact that Asclepius and the other gods no longer were present since Jesus has been worshipped[365]. In the context of the argument Julian remembers Asclepius:

> I had almost forgotten the greatest of the gifts of Helios and Zeus ... I mean to say that Zeus engendered Asclepius from himself among the intelligible gods (τοῖς νοητοῖς), and through the life of generative Helios he revealed him to the earth. Asclepius, having made his visitation to earth from the sky, appeared at Epidaurus singly, in the shape of a human (ἀνθρώπου μορφῇ); but afterwards he multiplied himself, and by his visitations stretched out over the whole earth his saving right hand. He came to Pergamon, to Ionia, to Tarentum afterwards; and later he came to Rome. And he travelled to Cos and thence to Aeae. Next he is present everywhere on land and sea. He visits no one of us separately, and yet he raises up souls that are sinful and bodies that are sick.[366]

After his comparison of the consequences of studying Hellenic and Christian writings (C. Gal. 229e, 230a in § 5.2.26 above), Julian notes that "Asclepius heals our bodies"[367]. He lists many other benefits given by the gods and claims the Hellenes to be superior to Christians in arts, wisdom and intelligence. This superiority includes "the art of healing derived from Asclepius whose oracles are found everywhere on earth, and the god grants to us a share in them perpetually." He vouches for the effectiveness of Asclepius: "At any rate, when I have been sick, Asclepius has often cured me by prescribing remedies; and of this Zeus is witness. Therefore, if we who have not given ourselves over to the spirit of apostasy, fare better than you in soul and body and external affairs, why do you abandon these teachings of ours and go over to those of others?"[368] It is not clear exactly how Julian conceived Asclepius (pure human soul, demon) given Iamblichus' belief that the gods could not descend to earth. John Finamore argues that Julian probably viewed

---

[364] C. Gal. 176a,b (132,4-13 MAS.). Celsus also admires Asclepius (C. Cels. 3.3, 3.22, 24, 42 [205,8; 218,11-15; 220,13-17; 238,9 KOET.]). See LOESCHE's note on paganism's use of Asclepius in response to Christianity in Neuplatonische Polemiker, 295 n. 1 and see ROKEAH, Jews, 196-97 and SMITH, Julian's Gods, 203.

[365] HARNACK, Porphyrius, F. 80. See § 2.3.1 above.

[366] C. Gal. 200a, b (140,2-15 MAS. = III, 374-75 WR.). Compare Or. 11.22, 144b; 11.39, 153b Asclepius the "savior of the world" (II/2, 119; 131 ROCHE.).

[367] C. Gal. 235b (151,2 MAS. = III, 386-87 WR.).

[368] C. Gal. 235c,d (151,2-16 MAS. = III, 388-39 WR.).

Asclepius as a pure human soul descending to earth from the intelligible realm[369].

Cyril notes that some gods are healers and some teach that it is necessary to commit murder. Still others are inventors of vulgar handicrafts[370]. Hellenistic artisans create gods that are not really gods but impure demons. Julian forgets that Asclepius himself was struck by fire and thunderbolt. Julian also thinks that no Christians are experts in medicine or in other areas such as eloquence and military tactics. If each human activity needs a god, then a multitude of gods will be necessary. Christians on the other hand claim that benefits such as knowledge, wisdom, and technical arts are a gift of God[371].

5.3 Conclusion

Julian's own conversion and his *Contra Galilaeos* are an important example of the cultural context of works written against the Christian scriptures. While earlier Celsus, Porphyry, and Hierocles had written during the time of persecutions of Christianity, Julian wrote when (at least in his own eyes) there was still a chance to reverse the progress of post-Constantinian Christianity. He was living proof that people could be freed from the darkness of error and return to the light of paganism. Julian was well aware of the persuasive force of Christian texts and proclamation and makes frequent reference to it in his writings[372]. Cyril concedes that Julian's own work was effective in drawing back to paganism "light minded and credulous people"[373].

Julian knew that to stop the progress of Christianity he would have to attack the sources, and he argued that the gospels were fictions composed by wickedness[374]. Libanius' summary of Julian's work makes it clear that Julian's attack was on the book in which "the fellow from Palestine is claimed

---

[369] Unpublished paper, "Julian and the Descent of Asclepius". FINAMORE notes that Julian believed Helios generated Asclepius as the "savior of the universe" (Or 11.39, 153b [II/2, 131 ROCHE.]). Iamblichus, De myst. 1.12 (DES PLACES) claimed that theurgists could not draw the intellect of the gods down to themselves. Compare De myst. 3.16 (in divination the intellect of the gods is not dragged down) and 1.8-9 (gods do not have bodies). This explains Iamblichus' rejection of the belief that Pythagoras is son of Apollo (On the Pythagorean Way of Life [7-8 DILLON/HERSHBELL]). Pythagoras' soul, rather, was sent down from Apollo. For Julian, Heracles was a pure soul descended to earth (Or. 8.6, 166d [II/1, 113 ROCHE.]).

[370] C. Jul. 7.235 (PG 76, 860c).

[371] C. Jul. 7.236-37 (PG 76, 862b-d).

[372] § 5.2.1, 5.2.21, 5.2.24.1, 5.2.26.

[373] See § 5.2 first paragraph.

[374] § 5.2.1.

to be god and son of god"[375]. The christology as described by Libanius (the identity of Jesus as God's son) was the primary focus of Julian's attack. His methods were varied. He argued that the OT did not support christological claims. He (like Porphyry) occasionally found contradictions in NT texts — and in particular made the claim that John's christology cannot be found elsewhere in the NT[376]. He also used an argument from consequence. Christian belief does not make better people whereas Hellenistic texts do[377]. One wonders how successful Julian would have been if he had had more time to carry out his program of counter propaganda including the reconstruction of the temple of Jerusalem.

---

[375] See § 5.2.
[376] § 5.2.23.1.
[377] § 5.2.26.

Conclusion

The pagans who read the NT were not favorably impressed. One searches the above authors in vain for positive comments. None of them expressed the admiration for the NT that is found in the fragment of Amelius (Plotinus' student) in which he showed approval for the prologue of John[1]. Occasionally one finds a comment (as in one of Porphyry's oracles) that Jesus was "most devout" or one of the "wise men," but those comments are embedded in the midst of massive attacks on Christian error[2]. The many references to the shock and derisive laughter of Macarius' pagan philosopher may be rhetorical flourishes of the Christian author. On the other hand they may be real indicators of the kind of effects the NT had on its cultured despisers.

The political context for the works written against the NT illustrates the importance of the argument between Hellenism and Christianity. Hierocles is particularly important in understanding the close relationships between the argument and the persecution of ancient Christians. Hierocles apparently conceived of his work as a form of humane counsel to help the Christians abandon the error of their ways. But he was quite prepared to persecute those who refused to be convinced[3]. Such a context is also likely for Porphyry's work against the Christians — especially if it was written in service of the Great Persecution[4]. The other authors surveyed in this book also mentioned the fact of persecution, and Celsus explicitly justifies the persecutions[5]. The authors did not write in a cultural vacuum. They were (consciously or not) arming the magistrates who chose to put Christians to death.

The fact that some pagan philosophers devoted so much time to the refutation of the NT was consequently not merely an intellectual exercise. They do not all articulate the following position in the same way, but it is lurking in the background of at least most of the works surveyed above: the NT (and consequent Christian proclamation) is dangerous because of its ability to recruit people to the Christian movement. Arnobius' anonymous pagans, for

---

[1] Eus., Praep. Ev., 11.18.26-11.19.1 (540a-c, GCS 43/2, 44-45 MRAS) quoted in part in § 2.3.26. See COOK, Some Hellenistic Responses, 244.

[2] § 2.2.4 and § 2.2.5.

[3] § 4.1 and 4.5.

[4] § 2.3.1.

[5] § 1.6.5. Compare § 3.23, 33 (Macarius' pagan) and § 5.2.32 (Julian) for recognitions of persecution.

example, believed that the Senate should abolish Christian writings because by means of them "the Christian religion is confirmed and the authority of ancient times is overthrown"[6]. Celsus, while believing that Jesus himself convinced few people, was very concerned about the Christians' ability to persuade simpletons to join them[7]. Toward the end of the *Contra Celsum* (8.71), Celsus makes the horrified comment that "... this proposal of yours is not tolerable: If those who rule over us after being persuaded by you are captured, you will persuade those who rule afterward ..." Did he foresee someone like Constantine? One can sense the shiver down his spine. Porphyry believed that the apostles were able to abuse the simplicity of their hearers[8]. Porphyry also complains that the apostles were able to persuade rich women by the means of miracle (which he attributed to magic)[9]. Augustine in turn complains that the oracles described in Porphyry's work on oracles were designed to keep people from becoming Christians[10]. Porphyry's work *Against the Christians* drew many people away from the faith, according to Severian. The violent reaction in Christian circles to Porphyry's work illustrates the persuasive power of Porphyry himself in his attack on Christian scriptures[11]. He knew that Christian "propaganda" needed an equally powerful piece of "counter-propaganda." Macarius' pagan believed that Christians could persuade credulous people, and he gives a text from John and a quotation from Paul as examples. He accuses Paul of using wizardry to enslave the gullible[12]. Hierocles charges the Christians with credulity and is consequently aware of the ability of Christian language to persuade "credulous" people. Julian charged Christians with abandoning truth in favor of what will "persuade all." He was aware how captivating Christian texts were and even devised an experiment to see whether Christian texts or Hellenistic texts would produce better people — he obviously believed he knew the answer[13]! The pagan authors are clearly aware that to stop the Christian movement the NT needed to be shown to be false.

They were genuinely concerned with what is true. For that reason they argued that the gospels were fictions. Celsus claims he could do better than the fictional narratives of Jesus[14]. Jerome summarized the position of Celsus,

---

[6] Arn., Adv. nat. 3.7 (165,6-9 MARCH.) discussed in the introduction.
[7] § 1.6.1
[8] See § 2.3.36.
[9] § 2.3.37.
[10] § 2.2.9.
[11] See § 2.3.2.
[12] John 6:54 (§ 3.27), Paul (§ 3.35).
[13] § 5.2.26.
[14] See the first paragraph of § 1.2.

Porphyry, and Julian who he says all accused the evangelists of "falsehood"[15]. Macarius' pagan argued that the gospel authors are inventors (of fiction) and not historians[16]. Hierocles attempted to reveal the falsity of Christian texts about Jesus by showing them to be entirely self-contradictory[17]. They share a concern for historical truth and do not find it in the gospels.

This attack on the narrative truth of the gospel texts needs to be seen in light of the pagans' awareness of the persuasive power of Christian proclamation. They seem to assume that one needs to show the falsity of the sources (e.g. the biblical literature) of the Christians' message before one can stop the religion. They knew the stubbornness of Christian belief and were probably realistic about their chances of winning their argument on an intellectual level[18]. This may explain the willingness of people like Hierocles to take part in actual persecutions.

The response of the philosophers to the Christian message can be briefly summarized using an outline based on the Apostles Creed[19].

I believe in one God, the Father Almighty, Creator of heaven and earth.

The pagans accepted the existence of God, but rejected Christian monotheism in favor of a belief in God and many subordinate divinities. Celsus affirmed that the universe was eternal and indestructible, so he had problems with doctrines of creation that he was aware of[20]. He also believed that God did not make bodies (other immortal beings made them)[21].

I believe in Jesus Christ, his only Son, our Lord.

They denied that Jesus was God's Son and devoted much space to their rejection of the Christian understanding of Jesus — whether as God's Son or as the word of God[22]. Celsus could call Jesus a magician, demon, or angel[23].

---

[15] § 2.3.5.

[16] § 3.22.

[17] § 4.6.

[18] See, for example, Porphyry on the stubbornness of a Christian woman's belief (§ 2.2.7). Julian attributed Christian "madness" (willingness to die for the faith) to evil demons (§ 5.2.32). Hierocles described Christians as "credulous" (§ 4.9). Lactantius compares Hierocles' work with that of the High Priest of philosophy who sought to free Christians from their pertinacious obstinacy (see § 4.5).

[19] There is no claim here about the date of the creed's origin. It is used here merely as a template to organize some of the most important objections.

[20] C. Cels. 4.79 (see § 1.7.3). See also § 3.39 for Macarius' philosopher who cannot believe that the world could pass away.

[21] § 1.3.1 with reference to C. Cels. 4.52.

[22] § 1.2.18, 1.3.1 § 2.3.26, § 4.10, § 5.2.23.

[23] § 1.3.3.

Porphyry's oracles could call him a "wise man" or a "god who died in delusions"[24]. Julian simply called him a "corpse"[25].

He was conceived by the power of the Holy Spirit and born of the Virgin Mary.

The virgin birth was incredible to Celsus and Macarius' pagan[26]. Julian doubted aspects of the birth narratives and probably rejected the entire story[27].

He suffered under Pontius Pilate, was crucified, dead and buried.

The philosophers do not reject the historicity of the crucifixion, but none of them admire Jesus' passion or are willing to attribute any significance to it. Celsus is unimpressed that Jesus did not save himself from the cross, while Macarius' pagan and Hierocles are unimpressed by Jesus' behavior at his trial[28]. Julian expected Jesus to do or say something more impressive at the trial before Herod[29]. Porphyry asked the purpose of the cross[30]. Celsus denied that God's Son would have been crucified[31].

He descended to the dead.

Celsus simply found the claim that Jesus went to Hades and preached to be incredible[32].

On the third day he rose again.

They attacked the resurrection on conceptual and historical grounds. The conceptual attack (resurrection is not possible in the first place) was probably informed by Hellenistic belief in the immortality of the soul[33]. The historical grounds were based on inconsistencies in the resurrection narratives and on the character of the witnesses to the resurrection[34].

---

[24] § 2.2.2.

[25] § 5.2.30.2.

[26] § 1.2.3, § 3.49.

[27] § 5.2.3, 5.2.4 and 5.2.31. Julian calls Jesus an "illegitimate son" in C. Gal. 159e (127,13-16 MAS. = III, 362-363, WR.).

[28] § 1.2.17 with reference to C. Cels. 2.35. See also § 3.21 and § 4.12.

[29] § 5.2.20.

[30] § 2.3.41.

[31] § 1.2.18.

[32] § 1.2.20.

[33] For Celsus see § 1.2.23 and compare his belief in reincarnation and eternal life discussed in § 1.7.4. For Porphyry see § 2.3.32 and for Macarius' pagan see § 3.51.

[34] § 1.2.21, § 3.23, § 5.2.22.

He ascended into heaven and is seated at the right hand of the Father.

The philosophers' attacks on the witnesses to the resurrection would have probably inclined them to doubt the narrative of the ascension although they do not mention it specifically[35].

He will come again to judge the living and the dead.

Macarius' pagan doubts the promise of the end of the world. The gospel has been preached to all nations, and there has been no end yet (vs. Mt 24:14)[36]. He (and Celsus) also deny that God will destroy the universe at a universal last judgment[37]. Porphyry found the idea of an everlasting hell to be irrational, and Celsus criticizes the Christians' use of hell in recruitment[38].

I believe in the Holy Spirit, the holy catholic church, the communion of saints, the forgiveness of sins, the resurrection of the body, and the life everlasting.

That these authors did not attack the Christians' conception of the Holy Spirit is interesting. They apparently found christology far more objectionable than pneumatology[39]. They did not find the church to be a "holy" place and rejected the Christian understanding of baptism and forgiveness. Macarius' pagan found the idea incredible, for example, that baptism could bring forgiveness for criminal offenses[40]. Julian shared the same revulsion[41]. Celsus claimed that Jesus taught forgiveness without the necessity of repentance[42]. He was also repelled by the Christians' predilection for inviting sinners to the faith[43]. None of the authors admired the idea bodily resurrection, although they were open to the idea of eternal life (as a soul)[44].

This book helps answer the question how the NT would appear to a philosophically-minded pagan. They used literary criticism (e.g. finding contradictions), historical methodologies (e.g. Galilee is not a sea), rhetoric (especially vituperation and protreptic), Hellenistic philosophical presuppositions (e.g. the eternity of the universe), and ethics (e.g. Jesus

---

[35] § 1.2.21 (Celsus) § 3.23 (Macarius).
[36] § 3.17. See § 3.33 for scepticism with regard to the resurrection and return of Christ.
[37] § 3.39 and § 1.7.3.
[38] § 2.3.25 and 1.7.3.
[39] Celsus did object to the concept of God's spirit entering the womb of a woman (§ 1.2.3). For a different problem see § 1.2.23.
[40] § 3.38.
[41] § 5.2.25.4
[42] § 1.2.12 with reference to C. Cels. 2.71.
[43] § 1.6.3.
[44] For example, Celsus believed in eternal life but rejected resurrection (§ 1.2.23 and 1.7.3).

should not have killed the herd of pigs) to attack the NT. It is apparent that they used the arsenal of Hellenistic literary criticism, rhetoric, historical criticism, and philosophy to overthrow the NT. That they were unsuccessful ultimately is less a comment on their skill as philosophers than it is on the extraordinary persuasive power of ancient Christian texts and proclamation.

Bibliography

Ancient Sources

Editions from which I have taken translations and notes are included below. Some of the other texts are also included. Normally the Loeb Classical Library, Oxford Classical Texts, or Teubner editions were used for classical authors. The Corpus scriptorum ecclesiasticorum latinorum (CSEL), Corpus christianorum series latina (CChr.SL), Sources chrétiennes (SC), Die griechischen christlichen Schrifsteller der ersten Jahrhunderte (GCS), and Migne Patrologia Graeca and Patrologia Latina (PG and PL) series were used for patristic sources. Abbreviations are from S. Schwertner, Internationales Abkürzungsverzeichnis für Theologie und Grenzgebiete, Berlin/New York ²1993 supplemented by the Journal of Biblical Literature guidelines, the Oxford Classical Dictionary, and Liddell Scott Jones (LSJ).

Acta martyrum, Acts of the Christian Martyrs, ed. H. Musurillo, Oxford 1972.

Albinus, Didaskalikos = Alcinoos, Enseignement des Doctrines de Platon, ed. John Whittaker/Pierre Louis, CUFr, Paris 1990.

Ambrosiaster, Pseudo-Augustini quaestiones veteris et novi testamenti CXXVII, ed. A. Souter, CSEL 50, Vienna 1908.

Aphthonius, Progymnasmata, in: Rhetores graeci Vol. 2, ed. L. Spengel, Leipzig 1854. ET in Ray Nadeau, The Progymnasmata of Aphthonius, Speech Monographs 19, 1952, 264-285.

Aristobulus, Fragments from Hellenistic Jewish Authors. Volume III. Aristobulus, ed. Carl R. Holladay, SBLTT 39, Pseudepigrapha Series 13, Atlanta 1995.

Aristotle, Aristotle XXII. The "Art" of Rhetoric, ed. and trans. J. H. Freese, LCL, Cambridge/London 1982.

____, Aristotle, The Poetics, ed. and trans.W. H. Fyfe, LCL, Cambridge/London 1965.

____, The Complete Works of Aristotle, ed. Jonathan Barnes, Bollingen Series 71.2, Princeton 1984.

Ps. Aristotle, Aristotelis qui fertur libellus de mundo, ed. W. L. Lorimer with a translation of the Syriac fragments by E. König, CUFr, Paris 1933.

Arnobius, Adversus nationes, ed. C. Marchesi, Corpus Paravianum, Turin 1953.

Asclepius Texts, Asclepius. A Collection and Interpretation of the Testimonies, ed. and trans. Emma J. Edelstein/Ludwig Edelstein, Vol. 1-2, New York 1975 (rep. of 1945 ed).

Athanasius, Athanasius Werke: Urkunden zur Geschichte des arianischen Streites 318-328, ed. H. G. Opitz, Vol. 3.1, Berlin 1935.

Athenagoras, Legatio and De Resurrectione, ed. William R. Schoedel, Oxford, 1972.

Atticus, Atticus Fragments, ed. Édouard des Places, CUFr, Paris,1977.

Augustine, Sancti Aurelii Augustini de civitate Dei, ed. B. Dombart/A. Kalb, CChr.SL 47-48, Turnholt 1950-55.

Barhebraeus, Gregorii Barhebraei chronicon ecclesiasticum, ed. and trans. into Latin Jean Baptiste Abbeloos/Thomas J. Lamy, Vol. 1, Louvain 1872.

Biblia Gentium, Biblia Gentium: primo contributo per un indice delle citazioni, dei riferimenti e delle allusioni alla bibbia negli autori pagani, greci e latini, di eta imperiale, ed. Giancarlo Rinaldi, Rome 1989.

Celsus, Der ΑΛΗΘΗΣ ΛΟΓΟΣ des Kelsos, ed. Robert Bader, TBAW 33, Stuttgart/Berlin 1940.

_____, ET by R. Joseph Hoffmann, Celsus. On the True Doctrine. A Discourse Against the Christians, New York/Oxford 1987.

[Cicero], [Cicero] ad C. Herennium..., ed. and trans. Harry Caplan, LCL, Cambridge 1989.

Consultations of Zaccheus and Apollonius, Questions d'un Païen à un Chrétien (Consultationes Zacchei christiani et Apollonii philosophi), ed. Jean Louis Feiertag/W. Steinmann, SC 401, 402, Paris 1994.

Cyril of Alexandria, Cyrille d'Alexandrie, Contre Julien, ed. Paul Burgière/Pierre Évieux, SC 322, Paris 1985.

Didymus, Didymus der Blinde, Psalmenkommentar, Ed.M. Gronewald, Pt. 5, PTA 12, Bonn 1970.

_____, Didymus der Blinde, Kommentar zu Hiob, ed. U. Hagedorn/D. Hagedorn/K. Koenen, Pt. 3, PTA 3, Bonn 1968.

Eunapius, Vita Sophistarum, Philostratus and Eunapius, The Lives of the Sophists, ed. and trans. W. C. Wright, LCL, London 1922.

Eusebius, Eusebius. Ecclesiastical History, ed. and trans. Kirsopp Lake/J. E. L. Oulton, 2 vols., LCL, Cambridge 1980.

_____, Eusèbe de Césarée Histoire Ecclésiastique, ed. Gustave Bardy, Livres V-VII, SC 41, Paris 1955.

_____, Praeparatio evangelica, ed. Karl Mras, GCS 43.1 (Eusebius 8), Berlin 1954.

_____, Eusèbe de Césarée. La Préparation Évangélique, ed. Jean Sirinelli/Édouard des Places, s.j. SC 206, 228, 262, 266, 369, Paris 1974-91.

_____, Contra Hieroclem, Philostratus...Treatise of Eusebius, ed. and trans. F. C. Conybeare, LCL, Cambridge/London 1969.

_____, Eusèbe de Césarée. Contre Hiéroclès, Intro. and trans. Marguerite Forrat and ed. Édouard des Places, SC 333, Paris 1986.

Heraclitus, Héraclite. Allégories d'Homère, ed. Félix Buffière, CUFr, Paris 1989.

Epicurus, Epicurea, ed. H. Usener, Rome 1963 (reprint of 1887 ed.).

Hermogenes, Hermogenis opera, ed. H. Rabe, Rhetores Graeci 6, Leipzig 1913, ET in R. Nadeau, Hermogenes' On Stases: A Translation with an Introduction and Notes, Speech Monographs 31/4, 1964, 361-424.

Iamblichus, Jamblique, Les Mystères d'Égypte, ed. and trans. É. des Places, CUFr, Paris 1966.

____, Iamblichus. On the Pythagorean Way of Life: Text, Translation, and Notes, ed. J. M. Dillon/J. Hershbell, Atlanta 1991.

Irenaeus (Pacatus fragments), Sancti Irenaei Lugdunensis ..., ed. Franciscus Feuardentius, Paris 1639 (1st ed. 1596).

Isho'dad of Merv, The Commentaries of Isho'dad of Merv bishop of Hadatha (c. 850 A.D.), ed. and tr. by M. D. Gibson, Horae Semiticae 5, 6, 7, 10, 11, Cambridge 1911-1916.

Jerome, Hieronymus, Liber de optimo genere interpretandi (epistula 57), ed. G. J. M. Bartelink, Leiden 1980.

____, Comm. in Danielem, CChr.SL 75a, ed. F. Glorie, Turnholt 1964, with ET by Gleason L. Archer, Jerome's Commentary on Daniel, Grand Rapids 1958.

Josephus (Slavonic), La prise de Jérusalem de Josèphe le Juif, ed. and trans. V. Istrin, Paris 1934.

Julian, The Works of the Emperor Julian, ed. and trans. W. C. Wright, Vols. 1-3, LCL, Cambridge, MA/London 1923.

____, L'Empereur Julien. Oeuvres complètes, Vol. I/1, I/2, II/1, II/2, ed. J. Bidez/G. Rochefort, CUFr, Paris 1932-1972.

____, Iuliani imperatoris epistulae leges poematia fragmenta, ed. J. Bidez/F. Cumont, Paris 1922.

____, Iuliani imperatoris librorum contra Christianos quae supersunt, ed. Carl J. Neumann, Leipzig 1880.

____, Giuliano imperator contra Galilaeos, ed. Emanuela Masaracchia, Testi e Commenti 9, Roma 1990.

____, Guida, Augusto, FRAMMENTI INEDITI DEL 'CONTRA I GALILEI' DI GIULIANO E DELLA REPLICA DI TEODORO DI MOPSUESTIA, Prometheus 9, 1983, 136-163.

____, Teodoro di Mopsuestia, Replica a Giuliano Imperatore. Adversus criminationes in Christianos Iuliani Imperatoris. In appendice Testimonianze sulla polemica antigiulianea in altre opere di Teodoro, con nuovi frammenti del «Contro i Galilei» di Giuliano, ed. A. Guida, Biblioteca Patristica, Florence 1994.

Justin, Justini Martyris apologiae pro Christianis, ed. Miroslav Marcovich, PTS 38, Berlin/New York 1994.

____, Justini Martyris dialogus cum Tryphone, ed. Miroslav Marcovich, PTS 47, Berlin/New York 1997.

____, Iustini Philosophi et Martyris Opera, Corpus Apologetarum Christianorum V, ed. J. C. T. Otto, Wiesbaden 1969 (Ps. Justin, Quaest. et Resp. ad Orth.; rep. of 1881 ed.).

____, ΘΕΟΔΩΡΗΤΟΥ ΕΠΙΣΚΟΠΟΥ ΠΟΛΕΩΣ ΚΥΡΡΟΥ ΠΡΟΣ ΤΑΣ ΕΠΕΝΕΞΘΕΙΣΑΣ ΑΥΤΩΙ ΕΠΕΡΩΤΗΣΕΙΣ ΠΑΡΑ ΤΙΝΟΣ ΤΩΝ ΕΞ ΑΙΓΥΠΤΟΥ ΕΠΙΣΚΟΠΩΝ ΑΠΟΚΡΙΣΕΙΣ, ed. A. Papadopoulos-Kerameus, Zapiski Istoriko-filologicheskago fakulteta Imperatorskago s.-peterburgskago universiteta 36, St. Petersburg 1895 (the above text of Ps. Justin with 15 additional questions; rep. Leipzig 1975, ed. G. Hansen).

Lactantius, Lactance. Institutions divines, livre V, ed. Pierre Monat, Vols. 1-2, SC 204/205, Paris 1973.

____, Lactantius. The Divine Institutes Books I-VII, Trans. Mary F. McDonald, O.P., FC 49, Washington 1964.

____, Lactantius de mortibus persecutorum, ed. and trans. J.L. Creed, Oxford Early Christian Texts, Oxford 1984.

Libanius, Libanius. Selected Works, ed. and trans. A. F. Norman, Vol. 1, LCL, Cambridge/London 1987.

Lucian, Lukian von Samosata. Alexandros oder der Lügenprophet, ed., trans, and comm. Ulrich Victor, Religions in the Graeco-Roman World 132, Leiden/New York/Köln 1997.

Macarius Magnes, ΜΑΚΑΡΙΟΥ ΜΑΓΝΗΤΟΣ ΑΠΟΚΡΙΤΙΚΟΣ Η ΜΟΝΟΓΕΝΗΣ Macarii Magnetis quae supersunt ex inedito codice, ed. C. Blondel, Paris 1876.

____, Kritik des Neuen Testaments von einem griechischen Philosophen des 3. Jahrhunderts [Die im Apocriticus des Macarius Magnes enthaltene Streitschrift], ed. Adolf von Harnack,TU 37.4, Leipzig 1911.

____, Richard Goulet's dissertation was: Makarios Magnès. Monogénès (Apocriticus). Introduction générale, édition, traduction et commentaire du livre IV ainsi que des fragments des livres IV et V, Paris I, 1974, (His SC edition of Macarius is forthcoming).

____, The indexes to some of the lost texts of the Apocriticus can be found in: Giovanni Mercati, Per L'Apocritico di Macario Magnete. Una Tavole dei Capi dei Libri I, II e III, in: Nuove note di letteratura biblica e cristiana antica, StT 95, Vatican City 1941, 40-74.

____, Until Goulet's work appears the most extensive translation is T. W. Crafer, The Apocriticus of Macarius Magnes, New York/London 1919.

____, The pagan's material (and not the nominal Porphyrian texts) only is translated in: Joseph Hoffmann, Porphyry's Against the Christians, Amherst 1994.

____, A German translation is: J. A. Wagenmann, Porphyrius und die Fragmente eines Ungenannten in der athenischen Makariushandschrift, JDTh 23, 1878, 267-314.

Maximus of Tyre, Dissertationes, ed. Michael B. Trapp, BiTeu, Stuttgart/Leipzig, 1994.

____, Maximus of Tyre. The Philosophical Orations, trans. with notes M. B. Trapp, Oxford 1997.

Methodius, Methodius, ed. G. Nathanael Bonwetsch, GCS 27, Leipzig 1917.

New Testament Apocrypha, The Apocryphal New Testament. A Collection of Apocryphal Literature in an English Translation, ed. J. K. Elliott, Oxford 1993.

Numenius, Numénius. Fragments, ed. Édouard des Places, CUF, Paris 1973.

Origen, Origen: Contra Celsum. Translated with an Introduction & Notes, ed. and trans. Henry Chadwick, Cambridge 1953.

____, Origenes Werke I, II, ed. Paul Koetschau, GCS 2, 3, Leipzig 1899.

____, Origène Contre Celse. Introduction, Texte Critique, Traduction et Notes, ed. Marcel Borret, s.j. Vols. 1-5, SC 132, 136, 147, 150, 227, Paris 1967-1976.

Panegyric, Panégyriques Latins, ed. E. Galletier,Vol. 3, CUF, Paris 1955.

Photius, Bibliotheca, ed. R. Henry, CBy, Paris 1959.

Plato, Platonis opera, ed. J. Burnet, Vols. 1-5, OCT, Oxford 1900-1907.

____, The Collected Dialogues of Plato, ed. Edith Hamilton/Huntington Cairnes, Bollingen Series 71, Princeton 1961.

Plotinus, Plotini Opera, Vols. 1-3, OCT, Oxford 1954-1982.

Porphyry, Porphyrii philosophi platonici opuscula selecta, ed. Augustus Nauck, Bibliotheca Teubneriana, Leipzig 1886.

____, Porphyrii de philosophia ex oraculis haurienda librorum reliquiae, ed. G. Wolff, Hildesheim 1962 (1st ed. 1856).

____, Porphyrius "Gegen die Christen," 15 Bücher. Zeugnisse, Fragmente und Referate, ed. Adolf von Harnack, APAW.PH 1, Berlin 1916.

____, A. von Harnack, Neue Fragmente des Werks des Porphyrius gegen die Christen. Die Pseudo-Polycarpiana und die Schrift des Rhetors Pacatus gegen Porphyrius, SDAW.PH, 1921, 266-284 / Nachträge zur Abhandlung "Neue Fragmente des Werks des Porphyrius gegen die Christen," ibid., 834-5.

____, M. Stern, Greek and Latin Authors on Jews and Judaism. From Tacitus to Simplicius, Vol. 2, Jerusalem 1980, 423-83 (many texts of Porphyry concerning the Jews).

____, Various (some are disputed) fragments of the C.C. may be found in:

G. Binder, Eine Polemik des Porphyrios gegen die allegorische Auslegung des alten Testaments durch die Christen, ZPE 3, 1968, 81-95.

M. Gronewald, Porphyrios Kritik an den Gleichnissen des Evangeliums, ZPE 3, 1968, 96.

Franz Altheim and Ruth Stiehl, Neue Bruchstücke aus Porphyrios' κατὰ Χριστιανούς [sic], in: Gedenkschrift für Georg Rohde, ΑΠΑΡΧΑΙ: Untersuchungen zur klassischen Philologie und Geschichte des Altertums 4, 1961, 23-38.

Dieter Hagedorn and Reinhold Merkelbach, Ein neues Fragment aus Porphyrios Gegen die Christen, VigChr 20, 1966, 86-90.

P. Nautin, Trois autres fragments du livre de Porphyre «Contre les Chretiens», RB 57, 1950, 409-416.

John G. Cook, A Possible Fragment of Porphyry's Contra Christianos from Michael the Syrian, ZAC 2, 1998, 113-22.

____, Robert M. Berchman has also made a translation of many of the fragments of the Contra Christianos in Porphyry Against the Christians. Introduction, Fragments, Translation, Notes, [forthcoming for U. of Pennsylvania Press].

____, Porphyry, Sententiae ad intelligibilia ducentes, ed. E. Lamberz, BiTeu, Leipzig 1975.

____, Porphyre. La vie de Plotin, ed. Luc Brisson/Marie-Odile Goulet-Cazé/Richard Goulet/Denis O'Brien et al., Vols. 1-2, Histoire des doctrines de l'antiquité classique 6, Paris 1982/1992.

____, Porphyre. De l'abstinence, ed., trans., with notes by J. Bouffartigue/M. Patillon/A. Segonds/L. Brisson Vols. I-III, CUF, Paris 1977-1995.

____, Porphyry, The Homeric Questions, ed. and trans. Robin R. Schlunk, Lang Classical Studies 2, New York et al. 1993.

____, Porphyry, The Cave of the Nymphs in the Odyssey, (text and trans.) Seminar Classics 609, State University of NY at Buffalo, Buffalo 1969.

____, Porphyrii philosophi fragmenta, ed. Andrew Smith, BiTeu, Stuttgart/Leipzig 1993.

_____, Porphyre. Vie de Pythagore. Lettre a Marcella, ed. Édouard des Places, s.j. CUF, Paris 1982.

_____, Porphyrios ΠΡΟΣ ΜΑΡΚΕΛΛΑΝ, ed., trans., and comm. Walter Pötscher, Philosophia Antiqua 15, Leiden 1969.

Pre-Socratic Fragments, Die Fragmente der Vorsokratiker, ed. Hermann Diels/Walther Kranz, Vol. 1, Berlin 1954.

Prosopographies:

Prosopographia imperii romani ... Pars II, ed. E. Groag/A. Stein, Berlin 1936.

The Prosopography of the Later Roman Empire, ed. A. H. M. Jones/J. R. Martindale/J. Morris, Vol. 1, Cambridge 1971 (PLRE).

Ps. Sallustius, De diis, Sallustius Concerning the Gods and the Universe, ed. A. D. Nock, Hildesheim 1966 (rep. of 1926 ed.).

Sentences of Sextus, The Sentences of Sextus, ed. Henry Chadwick, TaS 5, Cambridge 1959.

Stoic Fragments, Stoicorum veterum fragmenta I-IV, ed. Johannes von Arnim, Leipzig 1903 (SVF).

Symmachus, Relatio, in: Prudence, ed. M. Lavarenne, CUF, Paris 1963, 85-113.

Tertullian,Tertulliani Opera, CChr.SL 1-2, ed. E. Dekkers et al., Turnholt 1954.

Theodore of Mopsuestia, see Julian.

Thesaurus Linguae Graecae (TLG), Thesaurus Linguae Graecae CD ROM #D, U. Cal. Irvine 1992. The authors on the disk are listed by: Berkowitz, Luci/ Karl A.Squitier, Thesaurus Linguae Graecae. Canon of Greek Authors and Works, 3rd ed., New York/Oxford 1990.

Scholarship

Alföldi, Andreas, Studien zur Geschichte der Weltkrise des 3. Jahrhunderts nach Christus, Darmstadt 1967, 342-74 = CAH XII.165-231.

Allard, Paul, Julien l'apostat, Vol. 3, Studia Historica 102, Rome 1972.

Amandry, P., La mantique apollinienne à Delphes, Paris 1950.

Anastos, Milton V., Porphyry's Attack on the Bible, The Classical Tradition: Studies in Honor of Harry Caplan, ed. L. Wallach, Ithaca 1966, 421-450.

Andresen, Carl, Logos and Nomos. Die Polemik des Kelsos wider das Christentum, AKG 30, Berlin 1955.

Athanassiadi-Fowden, Polymia, Julian and Hellenism. An Intellectual Biography, Oxford 1981.

Bardy, Gustave, La conversion au christianisme durant les premiers siècles, Theol(P) 15, Paris 1949.

Baehrens, W. A., Pacatus, Hermes 56, 1921, 443-45.

Barnes, Timothy D., Porphyry Against the Christians: Date and the Attribution of Fragments, JThS 24, 1973, 424-442.

_____, The Chronology of Plotinus' Life, GRBS 17, 1976, 65-70.

_____, Sossianus Hierocles and the Antecedents of the 'Great Persecution,' HSCP 80, 1976, 239-52.

_____, The New Empire of Diocletian and Constantine, Cambridge, MA/London 1982.

_____, Scholarship or Propaganda? Porphyry Against the Christians and its Historical Setting, BICS 39, 1994, 53-65.

_____, Statistics and the Conversion of the Roman Aristocracy, JRS 85, 1995, 135-147.

_____, Constantine and Eusebius, Cambridge 1981.

Bauer, W., Das Leben Jesu bei den jüdischen und heidnischen Gegnern des Christentums, in: Das Leben Jesu im Zeitalter der neutestamentlichen Apokryphen, Tübingen 1909, 452-486.

Beatrice, Pier Franco, Towards a New Edition of Porphyry's Fragments Against the Christians, in: ΣΟΦΙΗΣ ΜΑΙΗΤΟΡΕΣ «Chercheurs de sagesse» Hommage à Jean Pépin, ed. Marie-Odile Goulet-Cazé/Goulven Madec/Denis O'Brien, Collection des Études Augustiniennes 131, Paris 1992, 347-55.

_____, LE TRAITÉ DE PORPHYRE CONTRE LES CHRÉTIENS. L'ÉTAT DE LA QUESTION, Kronos 4, 1991, 119-138.

Benko, Stephen, Pagan Criticism of Christianity During the First Two Centuries A.D., ANRW II.23.2, 1980, 1055-1118.

_____, Pagan Rome and the Early Christians, Bloomington/Indianapolis 1986.

Benoit, André, Le «Contra Christianos» de Porphyre: Où en est la collecte des fragments?, in: Paganisme, Judaïsme, Christianisme, Mélanges offerts à Marcel Simon. Influences et affrontements dans le monde antique, Paris 1978, 262-275.

Berchman. Robert M., In the Shadow of Origen: Porphyry and the Patristic Origins of New Testament Criticism, in: Origeniana Sexta. Origène et la Bible / Origen and the Bible, ed. Gilles Dorival/Alain le Boulluec et al., BEThL 118, Leuven 1995, 657-673.

Bernard, Wolfgang, Spätantike Dichtungstheorien. Untersuchungen zu Proklos, Herakleitos und Plutarch, Beiträge zur Altertumskunde 3, Stuttgart 1990.

Betz, Hans-Dieter, Gottmensch II (Griechisch-römische Antike und Urchristentum), RAC XII, 1982, 234-311.

Berger, Klaus, Hellenistische Gattungen im Neuen Testament, ANRW II.25.2, 1984, 1034-1379.

Beutler, Rudolf, Porphyrios 2, PRE XXII, 1954, 275-313.

Bidez, J., Vie de Porphyre, le philosophe néo-platonicien, Hildesheim 1964 (1st ed. 1913).

_____, La vie de l'empereur Julien, Paris 1965.

Blumenthal , H. J./R. A. Markus, ed., Neoplatonism and Early Christian Thought. Essays in Honour of A. H. Armstrong, London 1981.

Blois, Lukas De, The Policy of the Emperor Gallienus, Studies of the Dutch Archaeological and Historical Society 7, Leiden 1976.

Boer, W. den, Scriptorum paganorum I-IV saec. de christianis testimonia, Textus Minores II, Leiden 1948.

_____, A Pagan Historian and his Enemies: Porphyry Against the Christians, CP 69, 1974, 198-208.

Bowersock, G. W., Julian the Apostate, Cambridge 1978.

_____, Fiction as History. Nero to Julian, Sather Classical Lectures 58, Berkeley et al. 1994.

Bowie, E. L., Apollonius of Tyana. Tradition and Reality, ANRW II.16.2, 1978, 1652-1699.

Braun, René, Julien et le christianisme, L'Empereur Julien. De l'histoire à la légende, ed. René Braun/Jean Richer, Paris 1978, 157-87.

Buffière, Félix. Les mythes d'Homère et la pensée grecque, Paris 1956.

Burkert, Walter, Greek Religion. Archaic and Classical, Trans. John Raffan, Cambridge 1985 (1st ed. 1977).

____, Ancient Mystery Cults, Cambridge 1987.

Cataudella, Quintino, Celso e l'Epicureismo, ASNSP 12, 1943, 1-23.

____, Celso e gli Apologeti Cristiani, NDid 1, 1947, 28-34.

Cameron, Alan, The Date of Porphyry's ΚΑΤΑ ΧΡΙΣΤΙΑΝΩΝ, CQ 17, 1967, 382-384.

Casey, P. M., Porphyry and the Origin of the Book of Daniel, JThS 27, 1976, 15-33.

Chadwick, Henry, See also under Origen in Ancient Sources

____, Origen, Celsus, and the Stoa, JThS 48, 1947, 34-49.

____, Origen, Celsus, and the Resurrection of the Body, HThR 41, 1948, 83-102.

____, Early Christian Thought and the Classical Tradition, Oxford 1984 (1st edition 1966).

Clark, Gillian, Women in Late Antiquity. Pagan and Christian Lifestyles, Oxford 1994.

Cook, John G., Some Hellenistic Responses to the Gospels and Gospel Traditions, ZNW 84, 1993, 233-54.

____, The Protreptic Power of Early Christian Language: From John to Augustine, VigChr 48, 1994, 105-134.

____, The Logic and Language of Romans 1,20, Bib. 75, 1994, 494-517.

____, The Structure and Persuasive Power of Mark, Semeia Studies, Atlanta 1995.

____, In Defense of Ambiguity: Is There a Hidden Demon in Mark 1.29–31? NTS 43, 1997, 184-208.

Corrington, Gail Paterson, "The Divine Man" His Origin and Function in Hellenistic Popular Religion, American University Studies VII.17, New York et al. 1986.

Corsaro, Francesco, L'«Apocritico» di Macario di Magnesia e le Sacre Scritture, NDid 7, 1957, 1-24.

Courcelle, Pierre, Anti-Christian Arguments and Christian Platonism: from Arnobius to St. Ambrose, in: The Conflict Between Paganism and Christianity in the Fourth Century, ed. Arnaldo Momigliano, Oxford 1963, 151-92.

Cox, Patricia, Biography in Late Antiquity. A Quest for the Holy Man, Berkeley et al. 1983.

T.W. Crafer, Macarius Magnes, A Neglected Apologist, I, JThS 8, 1907, 401-23.

____, Macarius Magnes, A Neglected Apologist, II, JThS 8, 1907, 546-71.

____, The Work of Porphyry Against the Christians, and its Reconstruction, I, JThS 15, 1914, 360-95.

____, The Work of Porphyry Against the Christians, and its Reconstruction, II, JThS 15, 1914, 481-512.

Croke, Brian, The Era of Porphyry's Anti-Christian Polemic, JRH 14, 1983, 1-14.

____, Porphyry's Anti-Christian Chronology, JThS 34, 1983, 168-185.

Culdaut, Francine, Un oracle d'Hécate dans la Cité de Dieu de Saint Augustin: «Les dieux ont proclamé que le Christ fut un homme très pieux» (XIX, 23, 2), REAug 39, 1992, 271-289.

Daniélou, J., Review of Andresen, RSR 44, 1956, 580-85.

Decharme, Paul, La critique des traditions religieuses chez les Grecs, Paris 1904.

Demarolle, Jeanne-Marie, Les femmes chrétiennes vues par Porphyre, JAC 13, 1970, 42-47.

_____, La Chrétienté à la fin du IIIe s. et Porphyre, GRBS 12, 1971, 49-57.

_____, UN ASPECT DE LA POLEMIQUE PAIENNE A LA FIN DU IIIe SIECLE; LE VOCABULAIRE CHRETIEN DE PORPHYRE, VigChr 26, 1972, 117-129.

Dowd, Sharyn, Prayer, Power, and the Problem of Suffering: Mark 11:22-25 in the Context of Markan Theology, SBLDS 105, Atlanta 1988.

Droge, Arthur, Homer or Moses? Early Christian Interpretations of the History of Culture, HUTh 26, Tübingen 1989.

Duchesne, L., De Macario Magnete et scriptis eius, Paris 1877.

Dulière, W. L., Protection permanente contra des animaux nuisibles assurée par Apollonios de Tyane dans Byzance et Antioche. Évolution de son mythe, ByZ 63, 1970, 247-277.

Ensslin W., The Senate and the Army, CAH XII, 1939, 57-95.

Evangeliou, Christos, Porphyry's Criticism of Christianity and the Problem of Augustine's Platonism, Dionysius 13, 1985, 51-70.

Fàbrega, Valentin, Die chiliastische Lehre des Laktanz. Methodische und theologische Voraussetzungen und religionsgeschichtlicher Hintergrund, JAC 17, 1974, 126-146.

Fascher, Erich, Προφήτης Eine sprach- u. religionsgeschichtliche Untersuchung, Giessen 1927.

Fédou, Michel, Christianisme et religions païennes dans le Contre Celse d'Origène, ThH 81, Paris 1988.

Feldman, Louis, Jew and Gentile in the Ancient World, Attitudes and Interactions from Alexander to Justinian, Princeton 1993.

Ferch, Arthur J., Porphyry: An Heir to Christian Exegesis?, ZNW 73, 1983, 141-47.

Fögen, Marie Theres, Die Enteignung der Wahrsager. Studien zum kaiserlichen Wissensmonopol in der Spätantike, Frankfurt am Main 1993.

Foussard, Claude, Julien Philosophe, L'Empereur Julien. De l'histoire à la légende, ed. René Braun/Jean Richer, Paris 1978, 189-212.

Fox, Robin Lane, Pagans and Christians, Cambridge et al. 1988.

Frassinetti, Paolo, Sull'autore delle questioni pagane conservate nell'Apocritico di Macario di Magnesia, NDid 3, 1949, 41-56.

Frede, Michael, Celsus Philosophus Platonicus, ANRW II.36.7, 1994, 5183-5213.

_____, Celsus' Attack on the Christians, in: Philosophia Togata II. Plato and Aristotle at Rome, ed. Jonathan Barnes/Miriam Griffin, Oxford 1997, 218-40.

Frend, W. H. C., Martyrdom and Persecution in the Early Church, New York 1967.

Fowden, Garth, The Pagan Holy Man in Late Antique Society, JHS 102, 1982, 33-59.

Friedländer, M., Geschichte der jüdischen Apologetik als Vorgeschichte des Christenthums, Zurich 1903.

Gallagher, Eugene V., Divine Man or Magician? Celsus and Origen on Jesus, SBLDS 64, Chico, Calif. 1982.

Gantz, Timothy, Early Greek Myth. A Guide to Literary and Artistic Sources, Baltimore/London 1993.

Geffcken, Johannes, Zwei Griechische Apologeten, Leipzig 1907.

_____, Der Bilderstreit des heidnischen Altertums, ARW 19, 1916-19, 286-315.

_____, The Last Days of Greco-Roman Paganism, Tr. Sabine MacCormack, Amsterdam et al. 1978 (1st ed. 1920).

Girgenti, Giuseppe, Porfirio negli ultimi cinquant'anni. Bibliografia sistematica e ragionata della letteratura primaria e secondaria riguardante il pensiero porfiriano e i suoi influssi storici, Centro di Ricerche di Metafisica. Temi metafisici e problemi del pensiero antico. Studi e testi 35, Milano 1994.

Goulet-Cazé, Marie-Odile, L'école de Plotin, in : Brisson et al., Porphyre La Vie de Plotin, I.231- 57 (see Porphyry under Ancient Sources).

Goulet, Richard, Porphyre et la datation de Moïse, RHR 4, 1977, 137-164.

_____, La théologie de Makarios Magnes, MSR 34, 1977, 45-69, 145-80.

_____, Porphyre, Ammonius, les deux Origène et les autres, RHPhR 57, 1977, 471-96.

_____, Le système chronologique de la Vie de Plotin, in : Brisson et al., Porphyre. La vie de Plotin, 1.189-227 (see Porphyry under Ancient Sources).

_____, Porphyre et Macaire de Magnésie, StPatr XV, ed. Elizabeth Livingstone, TU 128, Berlin 1984, 448-52.

Graf, F., Maximos v. Aigai, JAC 27/28, 1984/85, 65-73.

Grant, Robert M., The Earliest Lives of Jesus, New York 1961.

_____, The Stromateis of Origen, in: Epektasis. Mélanges patristiques offerts au Cardinal Jean Daniélou, ed. Jacques Fontaine/Charles Kannengiesser, Paris 1972, 285-92.

_____, Porphyry among the Early Christians, in: Romanitas et Christianitas. Studia J. H. Waszinck, ed. W. den Boer et al., Amsterdam/London 1973, 181-87.

_____, The Religion of Maximin Daia, in: Christianity, Judaism and Other Greco-Roman Cults: Studies for Morton Smith at Sixty, ed. J. Neusner, Vol. 4, Leiden 1975, 143-166.

_____, Greek Apologists of the Second Century, Philadelphia 1988.

Gross, K., Apollonius von Tyana, RAC I, 1950, 529-533.

Gryson, Roger,The Ministry of Women in the Early Church, Trans. Jean Laporte and Mary Louise Hall, Collegeville, MN 1976.

Hägg, Tomas, Hierocles the Lover of Truth and Eusebius the Sophist, SO 67, 1992, 138-150.

Hahn, Johannes, Der Philosoph und die Gesellschaft: Selbstverständnis, öffentliches Auftreten und populäre Erwartungen in der hohen Kaiserzeit, Heidelberger althistorische Beiträge und epigraphische Studien 7, Stuttgart 1989.

Hanslik, R., Hierokles 3, KP II, 1967, 1132-33.

Harnack, A. von, Die Mission und Ausbreitung des Christentums in den ersten drei Jahrhunderten,Vols. 1-2, Leipzig 1924 (4th ed.).

_____, Über den privaten Gebrauch der heiligen Schriften in der alten Kirche, Beiträge zur Einleitung in das Neue Testament, Leipzig 1912.

Hengel, Martin, Judaism and Hellenism. Studies in Their Encounter in Palestine in the Hellenistic Period, Vols. 1-2, Philadelphia 1974 (German ed. 1973).

Herford, R. Travers, Christianity in Talmud & Midrash, New York 1975 (rep. of 1903 ed.).

Hombert, Pierre-Marie, Review of Eusèbe (SC 333), MSR 45, 1988, 111-12.

Hulen, Amos B., Porphyry's Work Against the Christians. An Interpretation, YSR 1, Scottdale 1933.

Johnson, Sarah I., HEKATE SOTEIRA A study of Hekate's Roles in the Chaldean Oracles and Related Literature, Atlanta 1990.

Junod, Eric, Polemique chrétienne contre Apollonius de Tyane, RThPh 120, 1988, 475-82.

Keresztes, Paul, Rome and the Christian Church I. From Nero to the Severi, ANRW, II.23.1, 1979, 247-315.

____, Rome and the Christian Church II. From Gallienus to the Great Persecution, ANRW II.23.1, 1979, 380-84

Kertsch, Manfred, Traditionelle Rhetorik und Philosophie in Eusebius' Antirrhetikos gegen Hierokles, VigChr 34, 1980, 145-171.

Kinzig, Wolfram, War der Neuplatoniker Porphyrios ursprünglich Christ?, in: Mousopolos Stephanos. Festschrift für Herwig Görgemanns, ed. Manuel Baumbach/Helga Köhler/Adolf Martin Ritter, Bibliothek der Klassischen Altertumswissenschaften. Reihe 2. Neue Folge 102, Heidelberg 1998, 320-32.

____, Zur Notwendigkeit einer Neuedition von Kyrill von Alexandrien, *Contra Iulianum*, in: StPatr XXIX, ed. E. A. LIVINGSTONE, Leuven 1997, 484-94.

Klauck, H.-J., Allegorie und Allegorese in synoptischen Gleichnistexten, NTA 13, München [2]1986.

Klein, Richard, ed., Julian Apostata, Wege der Forschung 509, Darmstadt, 1978.

Knox, W. L., Hellenistic Elements in Primitive Christianity, London 1944.

Kraemer, Ross S., Maenads, Martyrs, Matrons, Monastics. A Sourcebook on Women's Religions in the Greco-Roman World, Philadelphia 1988.

de Labriolle, Pierre, La réaction païenne. Étude sur la polémique antichrétienne du Ier au VIe Siècle, Paris 1948.

Lamberton, Robert, Homer the Theologian: Neoplatonist Allegorical Reading and the Growth of the Epic Tradition, Berkeley et al. 1989.

Lardner, Nathaniel The Works of Nathaniel Lardner ... The Credibility of the Gospel History..., Vol. 7.2, London 1837 (1st ed. 1788).

Lausberg, Heinrich, Handbuch der literarischen Rhetorik. Eine Grundlegung der Literaturwissenschaft, Stuttgart [3]1990.

Lauterbach, Jacob Z., Jesus in the Talmud, Rabbinic Essays, Cincinnati 1951, 473-570.

Lefkowitz, Mary R., and Maureen B. Fant, Women's Life in Greece & Rome, Baltimore 1992.

Lewy, H., Chaldaean Oracles and Theurgy. Mysticism, Magic and Platonism in the Later Roman Empire, Reedited by Michel Tardieu, Paris 1978.

Lietzmann, H., The Church in the West, CAH XII, 1939, 515-43.

Lods, Marc, Étude sur les sources juives de la polémique de Celse contre les chrétiens, RHPhR 21, 1941, 1-33.

Loesche, G., Haben die späteren Neuplatonischen Polemiker gegen das Christenthum das Werk des Celsus benutzt? ZWTh 27, 1884, 257-302.

Long, A. A., Stoic Readings of Homer, in: Homer's Ancient Readers. The Hermeneutics of Greek Epic's Earliest Exegetes, ed. Robert Lamberton/John J. Keaney, Princeton 1992, 41-66.

MacMullen, Ramsey, Roman Social Relations. 50 B.C. to A.D. 284, New Haven 1974.

―――, Two Types of Conversion to Early Christianity, Vig Chr 34, 1983, 174-192.

―――, Christianizing the Roman Empire (A.D. 100―400), New Haven 1984.

Maehler, Herwig, Zur Amtszeit des Präfekten Sossianus Hierocles, in: Collectanea Papyrologica. Texts Published in Honor of H. C. Youtie, ed. Ann E. Hanson, Vol. 2, PTA 20, Bonn 1976, 527-33.

Maraval, P., Review of Eusèbe (SC 333), RHPhR 68, 1988, 360-61.

Martin, Josef, Antike Rhetorik. Technik und Methode, HAW 2.3, Munich 1974.

Martino, Francesco de, Storia della costituzione romana, Naples 1967.

May, G. Kelsos und Origenes über die ewigen Strafen, in: Mousopolos Stephanos. Festschrift für Herwig Görgemanns, ed. M. Baumbach/H. Köhler/A. M. Ritter, Bibliothek der Klassischen Altertumswissenschaften. Reihe 2. Neue Folge 102, Heidelberg 1998, 346-51

Meredith, Anthony, Porphyry and Julian Against the Christians, ANRW II. 23.2, 1980, 1114-49.

Michel, Otto, τελώνης, TDNT VIII, 88-105.

Millar, Fergus, The Roman Near East 31 BC - AD 337, Cambridge, MA/London 1993.

―――, Porphyry: Ethnicity, Language, and Alien Wisdom, in: Philosophia Togata II. Plato and Aristotle at Rome, ed. Jonathan Barnes/Miriam Griffin, Oxford 1997, 241-262.

Miller, S. N., The Army and the Imperial House, CAH XII, 1939, 1-56.

Momigliano, Arnaldo, The Disadvantages of Monotheism for a Universal State, in: On Pagans, Jews, and Christians, Hanover, NH 1987, 142-58.

Nautin, P., Sanchuniathon chez Philon de Byblos et chez Porphyre, RB 56, 1949, 259-73.

Neugebauer, O., A History of Ancient Mathematical Astronomy, Vol. 2, Berlin 1975.

B. Neuschäfer, Origenes als Philologe, Schweizerische Beiträge zur Altertumswissenschaft 18/1, 2 Vols., Basel 1987.

Nock, A. Darby, Review of Andresen, JThS 7, 1956, 314-317.

O'Meara, John J., Porphyry's Philosophy from Oracles in Augustine, Paris 1959.

Pagels, Elaine, The Gnostic Paul. Gnostic Exegesis of the Pauline Letters, Philadelphia 1975.

―――, The Gnostic Gospels, New York 1979.

―――, The Origin of Satan, New York 1995.

Palm, Jonas, Textkritisches zum Apokritikos des Makarios Magnes, SMHVL 4, Lund 1961.

Pelagaud, É., Un conservateur au second siècle. Étude sur Celse et la première escarmouche entre la philosophie et le christianisme naissant, Lyon, et al. 1878.

Pépin, Jean, Mythe et Allégorie. Les Origines Grecques et les Contestations Judéo-Chrétiennes, Aubier 1958.

―――, Théologie cosmique et théologie chrétienne (Ambroise Exam. I. 1, 1-4), Paris 1964.

―――, Porphyre, exégète d'Homère, in: Porphyre, Entretiens sur l'Antiquité Classique 12, Vandoeuvres-Geneva 1965, 231-72.

Petzke, Gerd, Die Traditionen über Apollonius von Tyana und das Neue Testament, SCHNT 1, Leiden 1970.

Pezzella, Sosio, Il Problema del ΚΑΤΑ ΧΡΙΣΤΙΑΝΩΝ di Porfirio, Eos 52, 1962, 87-104.

Pirioni, Patrizia, Il soggiorno siciliano di Porfirio e la composizione del Κατὰ Χριστιανῶν, RSCI 39, 1985, 502-508.

Pitra, J. B., Spicilegium Solesmense...,Vol. 1; Paris 1852.

Pfeiffer, Rudolf, History of Classical Scholarship. From the Beginnings to the End of the Hellenistic Age, Oxford 1968.

Pichler, Karl, Streit um das Christentum. Der Angriff des Kelsos und die Antwort des Origenes, Regensburger Studien zur Theologie 23, Frankfurt am Main/Bern 1980.

Places, Édouard des, La second sophistique au service de l'apologétique chrétienne: Le Contre Hiérocles d'Eusèbe de Césarée, CRAI 1985, 423-27.

____, Le Contre Hiérocles d'Eusèbe de Césarée à la lumière d'une édition récente, StPatr XIX, ed. Elizabeth A. Livingstone, Leuven 1989, 37-42.

Ricciotti, Giuseppe, Julian the Apostate, Trans. J. Costelloe, s.j. Milwaukee 1960.

Rinaldi, Giancarlo, See the Ancient Sources section at Biblia Gentium.

Rokeah, David, Jews, Pagans and Christians in Conflict, StPB 33, Jerusalem-Leiden 1982.

____, Ben Stara is Ben Pantera — Towards the Clarification of a Philological-Historical Problem, Tarb. 39, 1969, 9-18 (Hebrew).

Rosenbaum, H.-U., Zur Datierung von Celsus' ΑΛΗΘΗΣ ΛΟΓΟΣ, VigChr 26, 1972, 102-11.

Rostovtzeff, Michael, Rome, ed. Elias Bickermann, London et al. 1960.

Schäfke, Werner, Frühchristlicher Widerstand, ANRW II.23.1, 1979, 460-723.

Schalkhaußer, Georg, Zu den Schriften des Makarios von Magnesia, TU 31.4, Leipzig 1907.

Scheidweiler, Felix, Zu Porphyrios ΚΑΤΑ ΧΡΙΣΤΙΑΝΩΝ, Ph. 99, 1955, 304-12.

Schlunk, Robin R., The Homeric Scholia and the Aeneid, Ann Arbor 1974.

Schmidt, Kurt, De Celsi libro qui inscribitur Alethes Logos, quaestiones ad philosophiam pertinentes, Diss. Göttingen 1921.

Schwartz, Eduard, Eusebios 24, PRE VI, 1909, 1370-1439.

Schwartz, J., Celsus Redivivus, RHPhR 53, 1973, 399-405.

____, Du Testament de Lévi au Discours véritable de Celse, RHPhR 40, 1960, 126-45.

Seeck, O., Art. Hierokles, 13, PRE VIII, 1913, 1477.

Sellew, Philip, Achilles or Christ. Porphyry and Didymus in Debate Over Allegorical Interpretation, HThR 82, 1989, 79-100.

M. Simonetti, Il Cristo II. Testi teologici e spirituali in lingua greco dal IV al VII secolo, Milano 1986.

Simmons, M. B., The Function of Oracles in the Pagan-Christian Conflict during the Age of Diocletian: The Case of Arnobius and Porphyry, StPatr XXXI, ed. E. A. Livingstone, Leuven 1997, 349-56.

Smith, Jonathan Z., Good News is no News: Aretalogy and Gospel, in: Christianity, Judaism and Other Greco-Roman Cults. Studies for Morton Smith at Sixty. Part One. New Testament, ed. J. Neusner, SJLA 12.1, Leiden 1975, 21-38.

Smith, Morton, Jesus the Magician, New York 1978.

Smith, Rowland, Julian's Gods. Religion and Philosophy in the Thought and Action of
    Julian the Apostate, London/New York 1995.

Speyer, W., Zum Bild des Apollonios von Tyana bei Heiden und Christen, JAC 17, 1974,
    47-63.

_____, Art. Hierokles I (Sossianus Hierocles), RAC XV, 1991, 103-109.

Vermander, J.-M., Celse, source et adversaire de Minucius Felix, REAug 17, 1971,13-25.

Voss, Bernd Reiner, Der Dialog in der frühchristlichen Literatur, Studia et testimonia antiqua
    9, München 1970.

von Wilamowitz-Moellendorff, U., Ein Bruchstück aus der Schrift des Porphyrius gegen die
    Christen, ZNW 1, 1900, 101-5.

Waelkens, Robert, L'économie, thème apologétique et principe herméneutique dans
    L'Apocriticos de Macarios Magnès, RTHP 6.4, Louvain 1974.

Walzer, R., Galen on Jews and Christians, London 1949.

Waszink, J. H., Review of Andresen, VigChr 12, 1958, 166-77.

Wifstrand, A., Die wahre Lehre des Kelsos, Bulletin de la Société royale des Lettres de Lund
    1941-42, 5, 1942, 391-431.

Wilken, Robert, The Christians as the Romans Saw Them, New Haven/London 1984.

Winkelmann, Friedhelm, Review of Eusèbe (SC 333), ThLZ 113, 1988, 680-81.

Witherington, Ben, Not so Idle Thoughts about EIDOLOTHUTON, TynB 44, 1993, 237-54.

Sources

Greek and Latin Literature

ILS		261e	290, 302
752	282	262b,c	202, 301
		262d	302, 316
Isocrates		262e	302
C. soph.		276e	302
13.14ff	317	290b-e	329
		290d,e	156
Julian		290e	160
Contra Galilaeos		291a	293, 295, 329
(Masaracchia)		306a	323
39a	286-87	314c	308, 313
43a,b	293	314d	308
43b	283, 331	319d	308, 313
49a	329	319e	308
57c,d	329	320a	293
57e-58e	329	320b	313, 317
65b-66a	329	320c	313, 317
69c	314	324e	309
100a	310	325a	309
106a-d	311	325c	316
148b,c	328	327a	304
155c,d	329	327b	304, 305, 326
159e	330	327c	305
176a,b	312, 332	333b	283, 306
176c	312	333c	306
178a-c	312	333d	301
191e	191, 231, 289, 298	335,b-d	281
194c	324	335b	324, 326
194d	324, 330	335c	294
197c	324	335d	294
200a,b	332	339e	294, 309
201e	327	340a	309, 310
205e	323	351a	293, 312
206a	139, 247, 320, 323, 324	351b	293, 312, 324
206a,b	8, 289, 307	351c	292, 312, 313, 324
209d	317	354a	324
210a	317	354b	323, 324
213a	295, 317	356c	323
213b	299, 304, 317	F. 34	202
213c	299, 304	F. 61	301
218a	286, 300	F. 90	289
218b-224c	317	F. 91	290
224e	331	F. 92	294
229c,d	315	F. 93	291
229d-230a	318	F. 94	247, 291
235b	332	F. 95	297
235c,d	332	F. 96	300
238b-d	308	F. 97	292
238d	307, 321	F. 98	293
238e	321	F. 99	320
245b-d	314	F. 100	190, 296
253b	293	F. 101	290
253c,d	156, 307	F. 102	292
253e	289	F. 103	316

Old Testament

New Testament

8:7-13	314-15	3:4	214
8:8	224, 308	3:8	25
9:5	211, 212		
9:7-10	222	*Colossians*	
9:7	222	1:15	93, 316
9:9	223	2:18	25
9:10	223		
9:15	224	*1 Thessalonians*	
9:19-21	214	4:13ff	316
9:19	213	4:15	59
9:20	158, 159, 310	4:15-17	229
10:20	25, 96, 118, 224		
10:25-26	224	*2 Thessalonians*	
10:28	224	2:1-12	38
10:30	315	2:10	38
15:35-38	60		
15:56	217	*1 Timothy*	
		1:15	179
2 Corinthians		2:4	312
11:13	211, 212	4:1, 3	227-28
13:3	159	4:4	308
Galatians		*2 Timothy*	
1:8	214, 311	2:12	145
2:11-14	158, 159, 315-16		
2:12-13	211	*Hebrews*	
2:18	214	6:18	145
2:20	159	9:10	308
3:1	226	9:28	324
3:10	214, 226-27, 311	10:1	308
5:3	226-27	11:37-38	42
5:10	159		
5:12	159	*James*	
6:14	207	2:23	217
Philippians		*1 Peter*	
2:5-9	64	3:39	54
3:2	213, 311	4:6	54

Ancient Jewish Literature

Aristobulus		Josephus	
F. 2	3-4	*Contra Apionem*	
F. 3	4	2.66	5
F. 4	4	2.68-70	5
		2.73-75	4
Demetrius		2.80-81	4
F. 2	2, 3	2.91-96	4
F. 3	3	2.125-26	5
F. 5	3	2.135	81
		2.148	5

2.168	4
2.242-49	4
2.255-57	4, 129
2.255	71
2.256	4
2.257	4
2.281	4

Philo
de agric.

51	54

de conf. ling.

146	54

Slavonic Josephus
Bellum

II.9.3	270

Talmud
b Gittin

56b, 57a	40

b. Sanhedrin

67a	32
107b	32

b. Shabb.

104b	32

Ancient Christian Literature

Acta Pauli et Theclae 181

Acta Scilit. martyr.

14	114

Ambrose
Apol. Dauid

2.5.30	162

De Abraham

1.4.29	214

De excessu fratris

2.55.1	245
2.58.1	245

De paradiso

8.38	247

De virginibus

1.4.14-15	228

Epist. ad Constantium

69.1, 3	214

Epist. ad Irenaeum

64.1	214

In Lucam

2.44	239
3.17	136

Ambrosiaster
Quaest. de N.T.

17	291
28	291
29	175
45	198
55	305
57	136
60	215
66	226
69	296

Quaest. de Vet. Test.

47	42

Quaest. Vet. et N. Test.

56	289
58	305
61	293
63	290
65	147
69	294
71	306
74	150
83	151
86	28
104.1	195

Anastasius Sinaita
Inter. et resp.

Quaestio 92	244

Hodegos

13	154

Apocalypse of Peter	
(Elliott)	
4	231-32
5	232-33
Aristides	
Apologia	
8.2	5
13.7	5, 51
17.2	5
Aristo of Pella	
Altercatio Iasonis et	
Papisci	64
Arnobius	
Adv. nat.	
1.3	124
1.36	108, 325
1.41	325
1.42	62
1.43	108
1.45	108
1.60	161
2.14	98
2.63	152, 311
2.65	300
2.71	298
2.76	89
3.7	15
4.36	15
5.32	129
5.38-45	129
6.3	165
Athanasius	
De decret. Nic.	
synod.	
39.1-2	125
Ps. Athanasius	
Quaest. ad	
Antiochum ducem	
114	243
Athenagoras	
De res.	
4.1-4	8, 243
9	60
9.2	8, 243
Legatio	
3.1-2	8
4.1-2	8

13.1-4	8
18.1	8
20.3	8
22.1-12	8
31.1	8
Augustine	
De civ. Dei	
10.11	118
10.28	161, 239
10.29	239
10.32	123, 125
19.23	116, 117
22.11	154
22.12	245
De cons. ev.	
1.7.10	15
1.7.11	118
1.9.14	32
1.11.17	32
1.15.23	118
1.16.24	118
1.22.30	236
1.34.52	118
2.1.2-3	28
2.3.5-2.4.10	137
2.5.17	138
2.11.24	138
2.24.56	176
3.13.40-50	147
3.18.55	197
Ep.	
31.8	140
75.11	159
102.1	147
102.8	148
102.12	152, 180
102.15	152, 180
102.22	148
102.23-27	148
102.28	148
136.1	157, 192
137.13	157
138.18	157
Bar Hebraeus	
Chron. Eccl.	
1.15.11	128

2.60	21, 56	3.71	87
2.61	56	3.72	87
2.62	56	3.73	84
2.63	26, 56, 199	3.74	87
2.67	57	3.75	20, 87, 88
2.68	53, 195	3.76	87
2.70	26, 49, 57, 199, 300	3.77	87
2.71	44, 86	3.78	87, 88
2.72	26, 34	3.80	18
2.73	57	4.2	62, 238
2.74	84	4.3	66, 238
2.75	63, 84	4.4	21
2.76	40, 84	4.5	7, 63, 230
2.77	74, 84	4.6	66
2.78	84	4.7	7, 66, 151, 247, 311
2.79	69, 323	4.8	66
3.3	58, 69, 332	4.9	66
3.5	89, 132	4.10	88, 98, 99, 148
3.10	159	4.11	6, 98, 295
3.12	159, 247	4.12	98, 231
3.14	89, 132	4.14	64
3.15	22, 124	4.15	64
3.16	24, 84, 97, 99, 148, 293	4.18	64
3.18	83, 88	4.21	71, 129
3.19	68, 71	4.22	51
3.22	18, 26, 58, 63, 70, 332	4.23	67
3.23	58	4.28	67
3.24	7, 38, 58, 59, 63, 64, 69, 332	4.30	230-31
		4.31	317
3.25	59, 79	4.36	18, 81, 176
3.26	58, 64, 69, 81, 269	4.38	71, 81
3.29	69, 81	4.47	24, 71
3.31	69	4.48	71
3.32	69	4.49	71
3.33	58, 69	4.50	71
3.34	68	4.51	71, 129
3.35	18, 21	4.52	26, 64
3.36	68	4.54	18, 22
3.37	69, 93	4.62	65, 98
3.39	83	4.65	65, 66
3.41	63	4.67	60, 98
3.42	58, 69, 332	4.68	98
3.43	54, 288	4.73	40, 53, 101
3.44	84, 88, 167, 263, 291, 320	4.74	21
		4.75	21
3.49	18, 88	4.79	6, 221, 295
3.55	85, 87, 167, 181, 320, 322	4.86	21
		4.99	101
3.59	44, 86, 88, 179, 320	5.2	62, 63
3.62	86	5.3	18, 21, 22
3.63	86	5.14	6, 7, 8, 59, 98, 243, 301, 316
3.64	86		
3.65	84, 86	5.15	60
3.70	87	5.16	60

Ancient Individuals

Modern Authors

Subjects